TAKING SIDES

Clashing Views in

United States History, Volume 1, The Colonial Period to Reconstruction

FOURTEENTH EDITION

TAKING SIDES

Clashing Views in

United States History, Volume 1, The Colonial Period to Reconstruction

FOURTEENTH EDITION

Selected, Edited, and with Introductions by

Larry Madaras
Howard Community College

and

James M. SoRelle
Baylor University

McGraw Hill

Connect
Learn
Succeed™

TAKING SIDES: CLASHING VIEWS IN UNITED STATES HISTORY, VOLUME 1:
THE COLONIAL PERIOD TO RECONSTRUCTION, FOURTEENTH EDITION

Published by McGraw-Hill, a business unit of The McGraw-Hill Companies, Inc., 1221 Avenue
of the Americas, New York, NY 10020. Copyright © 2011 by The McGraw-Hill Companies, Inc.
All rights reserved. Previous edition(s) 2009, 2007, and 2005. No part of this publication may
be reproduced or distributed in any form or by any means, or stored in a database or retrieval
system, without the prior written consent of The McGraw-Hill Companies, Inc., including, but not
limited to, in any network or other electronic storage or transmission, or broadcast for distance
learning.

Some ancillaries, including electronic and print components, may not be available to customers
outside the United States.

Taking Sides® is a registered trademark of the McGraw-Hill Companies, Inc.
Taking Sides is published by the **Contemporary Learning Series** group within the McGraw-Hill
Higher Education division.

1 2 3 4 5 6 7 8 9 0 DOC/DOC 1 0 9 8 7 6 5 4 3 2 1 0

MHID: 0-07-804996-2
ISBN: 978-0-07-804996-5
ISSN: 1091-8833

Managing Editor: *Larry Loeppke*
Director, Specialized Production: *Faye Schilling*
Senior Developmental Editor: *Jill Meloy*
Editorial Coordinator: *Mary Foust*
Production Service Assistant: *Rita Hingtgen*
Permissions Coordinator: *Shirley Lanners*
Editorial Assistant: *Cindy Hedley*
Senior Marketing Manager: *Julie Keck*
Senior Marketing Communications Specialist: *Mary Klein*
Marketing Coordinator: *Alice Link*
Project Manager: *Erin Melloy*
Design Specialist: *Brenda A. Rolwes*
Cover Graphics: *Rick D. Noel*

Compositor: MPS Limited, A Macmillan Company
Cover Image: Library of Congress, Prints and Photographs Division

Library of Congress Cataloging-in-Publication Data

Main entry under title:
 Taking sides: clashing views in United States history, volume 1, the colonial period to
 reconstruction/selected, edited, and with introductions by Larry Madaras and
 James M. SoRelle.—14th ed.

Includes bibliographical references.
 1. United States—History. I. Madaras, Larry, *comp*. SoRelle, James M. *comp*.
 973

www.mhhe.com

Editors/Academic Advisory Board

Members of the Academic Advisory Board are instrumental in the final selection of articles for each edition of TAKING SIDES. Their review of articles for content, level, and appropriateness provides critical direction to the editors and staff. We think that you will find their careful consideration well reflected in this volume.

TAKING SIDES: Clashing Views in UNITED STATES HISTORY, VOLUME 1, THE COLONIAL PERIOD TO RECONSTRUCTION

Fourteenth Edition

EDITORS

Larry Madaras
Howard Community College

and

James M. SoRelle
Baylor University

Preface

The success of the past 13 editions of *Taking Sides: Clashing Views in United States History* has encouraged us to remain faithful to its original objectives, methods, and format. Our aim has been to create an effective instrument to enhance classroom learning and to foster critical thinking. Historical facts presented in a vacuum are of little value to the educational process. For students, whose search for historical truth often concentrates on *when* something happened rather than on *why,* and on specific events rather than on the *significance* of those events, *Taking Sides* is designed to offer an interesting and valuable departure. The understanding that the reader arrives at based on the evidence that emerges from the clash of views encourages the reader to view history as an *interpretive* discipline, not one of rote memorization.

As in previous editions, the 17 issues and 34 essays that follow are arranged in chronological order and can be incorporated easily into any American history survey course. Each issue has an *Introduction,* which sets the stage for the debate that follows in the pro and con selections and provides historical and methodological background to the problem that the issue examines. Each issue concludes with a *Postscript,* which ties the readings together, briefly mentions alternative interpretations, and supplies detailed *suggestions for further reading* for the student who wishes to pursue the topics raised in the issue. Also, Internet site addresses (URLs), which should prove useful as starting points for further research, have been provided on the *Internet References* page that accompanies each unit opener. At the back of the book is a listing of all the *contributors to this volume* with a brief biographical sketch of each of the authors whose views are debated here.

Changes to this edition In this edition, we have continued our efforts to maintain a balance between traditional political, diplomatic, and cultural issues and the new social history, which depicts a society that benefited from the presence of Native Americans, African Americans, women, and workers of various racial and ethnic backgrounds. With this in mind, we present seven new issues: Did the Chinese Discover America? (Issue 2); Was There a Great Awakening in Mid-Eighteenth Century America? (Issue 5); Was the American Revolution Largely a Product of Market-Driven Consumer Forces? (Issue 6); Did Andrew Jackson's Removal Policy Benefit Native Americans? (Issue 9); Was Antebellum Temperance Reform Motivated Primarily by Religious Moralism? (Issue 11); Is Robert E. Lee Overrated as a General? (Issue 15); and Was Abraham Lincoln America's Greatest President? (Issue 16).

A word to the instructor An *Instructor's Resource Guide with Test Questions* (multiple-choice and essay) is available through the publisher for the instructor using *Taking Sides* in the classroom. A general guidebook, *Using Taking Sides* *in the Classroom,* which discusses methods and techniques for integrating the procon approach into any classroom setting, is also available. An online version of *Using Taking Sides in the Classroom* and a correspondence service for *Taking Sides* adopters can be found at www.mhhe.com/cls.

Acknowledgments Many individuals have contributed to the successful completion of this edition. We appreciate the evaluations submitted to McGraw-Hill Contemporary Learning Series by those who have used *Taking Sides* in the classroom. Special thanks to those who responded with specific suggestions for past editions.

We are particularly indebted to Maggie Cullen, Cindy SoRelle, the late Barry Crouch, Kimberly Kellison, Virginia Kirk, Joseph and Helen Mitchell, Jean Soto, and Julie Anne Sweet, who shared their ideas for changes, pointed us toward potentially useful historical works, and provided significant editorial assistance. Lynn Wilder performed indispensable typing duties connected with this project. Ela Ciborowski, James Johnson, and Sharon Glover in the library at Howard Community College provided essential help in acquiring books and articles on interlibrary loan. Finally, we are sincerely grateful for the commitment encouragement, advice and patience provided in recent years by Jill Meloy, senior development editor for the *Taking Sides* series, and the entire staff of McGraw-Hill Contemporary Learning Series.

Larry Madaras
Emeritus, Howard Community College

James M. SoRelle
Baylor University

Contents In Brief

Contents

UNIT 1   COLONIAL SOCIETY   1

Issue 1.   Is History True?   2

Oscar Handlin insists that historical truth is absolute and knowable by historians who adopt the scientific method of research to discover factual evidence that provides both a chronology and context for their findings. William McNeill argues that historical truth is general and evolutionary and is discerned by different groups at different times and in different places in a subjective manner that has little to do with a scientifically absolute methodology.

Issue 2.   Did the Chinese Discover America?   25

Gavin Menzies surmises that between 1421 and 1423 a Chinese fleet spent four months exploring the Pacific coastline of North America and leaving behind substantial evidence to support his contention that the Chinese discovered America long before the arrival of European explorers. Robert Finlay accuses Menzies of ignoring the basic rules of historical study and logic to concoct an implausible interpretation of Chinese discovery based upon a misreading of Chinese imperial policy, misrepresentation of sources, and conjecture that has no evidentiary base.

Issue 3.   Was Disease the Key Factor in the Depopulation of Native Americans in the Americas?   46

Colin Calloway says that while Native Americans confronted numerous diseases in the Americas, traditional Indian healing practices failed to

Professor T. H. Breen maintains that "the colonists shared experiences as consumers provided them with the cultural resources needed to develop a bold new form of political protest"—the non-importation agreements which provided link to the break with England. Professor Carl N. Degler argues that the American Revolution was a political rebellion led by a group of reluctant revolutionaries who opposed Parliament's attempt to impose taxes without the consent of the colonists.

Robert V. Remini insists that President Andrew Jackson demonstrated a genuine concern for the welfare of Native Americans by proposing a voluntary program that would remove the Five Civilized Tribes west of the Mississippi River, where they could avoid dangerous conflict with white settlers and preserve their heritage and culture. Alfred A. Cave accuses Andrew Jackson of abusing his power as president by failing to adhere to the letter of the Indian Removal Act by transforming a voluntary program into a coercive one and by ignoring the provisions in his own removal treaties that promised protection to the various southern tribes.

According to Nancy F. Cott, when merchant capitalism reached its mature phase in the 1830s, the roles of the middle-class family became more clearly defined, and new economic opportunities opened for women within a limited sphere outside the home. According to Gerda Lerner, while Jacksonian democracy provided political and economic opportunities for men, both the "lady" and the "mill girl" were equally disenfranchised and isolated from vital centers of economic opportunity.

UNIT 3   ANTEBELLUM AMERICA   239

Mark Edward Lender and James Kirby Martin argue that the impetus for the temperance movement in the first half of the nineteenth century was grounded deeply in Protestant denominations whose clergy and lay leaders supported reforms that would create a social-moral order that was best for the public welfare. John J. Rumbarger concludes that nineteenth-century temperance reform was the product of a pro-capitalist market economy whose entrepreneurial elite led the way toward abstinence and prohibition campaigns in order to guarantee the availability of a more productive work force.

Professor Walter Nugent argues that President James K. Polk was a narrow-minded, ignorant but not stupid individual with one big idea: Use the power of the presidency to force Mexico to cede California and the current Southwest to the United States. Professor of diplomatic history Norman A. Graebner argues that President James Polk pursued an aggressive policy that he believed would force Mexico to sell New Mexico and California to the United States and to recognize the annexation of Texas without starting a war.

James N. Gilbert says that John Brown's actions conform to a modern definition of terrorist behavior in that Brown considered the United States incapable of reforming itself by abolishing slavery, believed that only violence would accomplish that goal, and justified his actions by proclaiming adherence to a "higher" power. Scott John Hammond insists that John Brown's commitment to higher moral and political goals conformed to the basic principles of human freedom and political and legal quality that formed the heart of the creed articulated by the founders of the American nation.

UNIT 4   CONFLICT AND RESOLUTION   309

Charles B. Dew uses the speeches and public letters of 41 white southerners who, as commissioners in 1860 and 1861, attempted to secure support for secession by appealing to their audiences' commitment to the preservation of slavery and of white supremacy. Marc Egnal argues that the decision of Lower South states to secede from the Union was determined by an economically based struggle between residents with strong ties to the North and Upper South who embraced an entrepreneurial outlook, on one hand, and those who were largely isolated from the North and who opposed the implementation of a diversified economy, on the other hand.

Attorney Alan T. Nolan argues that General Robert E. Lee was a flawed grand strategist whose offensive operations produced heavy casualties in an unnecessarily prolonged war that the South could not win. According to professor of American history Gary W. Gallagher, General Lee was the most revered and unifying figure in the Confederacy, and he "formulated a national strategy predicated on the probability of success in Virginia and the value of battlefield victories."

Phillip Shaw Paludan contends that Abraham Lincoln's greatness exceeds that of all other American presidents because Lincoln, in the face of unparalleled challenges associated with the Civil War, succeeded in preserving the Union and freeing the slaves. M. E. Bradford characterizes Lincoln as a cynical politician whose abuse of authority as president and commander-in-chief during the Civil War marked a serious departure from the republican goals of the Founding Fathers and established the prototype for the "imperial presidency" of the twentieth century.

George M. Fredrickson concludes that racism, in the form of the doctrine of white supremacy, colored the thinking not only of southern whites but of most white northerners as well and produced only half-hearted efforts by the Radical Republicans in the postwar period to sustain a commitment to black equality. Heather Cox Richardson argues that the failure of Radical Reconstruction was primarily a consequence of a national commitment to a free-labor ideology that opposed an expanding central government that legislated rights to African Americans that other citizens had acquired through hard work.

Correlation Guide

The *Taking Sides* series presents current issues in a debate-style format designed to stimulate student interest and develop critical thinking skills. Each issue is thoughtfully framed with an issue summary, an issue introduction, and a postscript. The pro and con essays—selected for their liveliness and substance—represent the arguments of leading scholars and commentators in their fields.

Taking Sides: Clashing Views in United States History, Volume 1: The Colonial Period to Reconstruction, 14/e is an easy-to-use reader that presents issues on important topics such as *colonial society, the revolution,* and *conflicts and resolutions.* For more information on *Taking Sides* and other *McGraw-Hill Contemporary Learning Series* titles, visit www.mhhe.com/cls.

This convenient guide matches the issues in **Taking Sides: United States History, Vol. 1, 14/e** with the corresponding chapters in two of our best-selling McGraw-Hill history textbooks by Brinkley and Davidson et. al.

Taking Sides: United States History, Volume I: The Colonial Period to Reconstruction, 14/e	American History, Vol 1, 13/e by Brinkley	U.S. Narrative History Vol 1: to 1877 by Davidson et. al.
Issue 1: Is History True?	**Chapter 1:** The Collision of Cultures	
Issue 2: Did the Chinese Discover America?	**Chapter 13:** The Impending Crisis	**Chapter 2:** Old Worlds and New Worlds (1400–1600) **Chapter 14:** Western Expansion and the Rise of the Slavery Issue (1820–1850)
Issue 3: Was Disease the Key Factor in the Depopulation of Native Americans?	**Chapter 1:** The Collision of Cultures **Chapter 2:** Transplantations and Borderlands	**Chapter 1:** The First Civilizations of North America **Chapter 11:** The Rise of Democracy (1824–1840)
Issue 4: Was the Salem Witchcraft Hysteria Caused by a Fear of Women?	**Chapter 3:** Society and Culture in Provincial America	**Chapter 4:** Colonization and Conflict in the North (1600–1700)
Issue 5: Was There a Great Awakening in Mid-Eighteenth Century America?	**Chapter 3:** Society and Culture in Provincial America	**Chapter 5:** The Mosaic of Eighteenth Century America (1689–1771) **Chapter 9:** The Early Republic (1789–1824)
Issue 6: Was the American Revolution Largely a Product of Market-Driven Consumer Forces?	**Chapter 5:** The American Revolution	**Chapter 6:** Toward the War for American Independence (1754–1776) **Chapter 7:** The American People and the American Revolution (1775–1783) **Chapter 10:** The Opening of America (1815–1850)

(Continued)

Taking Sides: United States History, Volume I: The Colonial Period to Reconstruction, 14/e	American History, Vol 1, 13/e by Brinkley	U.S. Narrative History Vol 1: to 1877 by Davidson et. al.
Issue 7: Were the Founding Fathers Democratic Reformers?	**Chapter 8:** Varieties of American Nationalism **Chapter 9:** Jacksonian America	**Chapter 8:** Crisis and Constitution (1776–1789)
Issue 8: Was Alexander Hamilton an Economic Genius?	**Chapter 5:** The American Revolution **Chapter 6:** The Constitution and the New Republic	**Chapter 9:** The Early Republic (1789–1824)
Issue 9: Did Andrew Jackson's Removal Policy Benefit Native Americans?	**Chapter 9:** Jacksonian America **Chapter 12:** Antebellum Culture and Reform	**Chapter 1:** The First Civilizations of North America **Chapter 11:** The Rise of Democracy (1824–1840)
Issue 10: Did the Industrial Revolution Provide More Opportunities for Women in the 1830s?	**Chapter 10:** America's Economic Revolution	**Chapter 10:** The Opening of America (1815–1850) **Chapter 12:** The Fires of Perfection (1820–1850)
Issue 11: Was Antebellum Temperance Reform Motivated Primarily by Evangelical Fervor?	**Chapter 3:** Society and Culture in Provincial America **Chapter 12:** Antebellum Culture and Reform	**Chapter 12:** The Fires of Perfection (1820–1850)
Issue 12: Was the Mexican War an Exercise in American Imperialism?	**Chapter 13:** The Impending Crisis	**Chapter 14:** Western Expansion and the Rise of Slavery (1820–1850)
Issue 13: Was John Brown an Irrational Terrorist?	**Chapter 13:** The Impending Crisis	**Chapter 15:** The Union Broken (1850–1861)
Issue 14: Was Slavery the Key Issue in the Sectional Conflict Leading to the Civil War?	**Chapter 11:** Cotton, Slavery, and the Old South **Chapter 14:** The Civil War	**Chapter 8:** Crisis and Constitution (1776–1789)
Issue 15: Is Robert E. Lee Overrated as a General?	**Chapter 14:** The Civil War	**Chapter 16:** Total War and the Republic (1861–1865)
Issue 16: Was Abraham Lincoln America's Greatest President?	**Chapter 13:** The Impending Crisis **Chapter 15:** Reconstruction and the New South	**Chapter 15:** The Union Broken (1850–1861) **Chapter 16:** Total War and the Republic (1861–1865) **Chapter 17:** Reconstructing the Union (1865–1877)
Issue 17: Did Reconstruction Fail as a Result of Racism?	**Chapter 3:** Society and Culture in Provincial America **Chapter 13:** The Impending Crisis **Chapter 15:** Reconstruction and the New South	**Chapter 3:** Colonization and Conflict in the South (1600–1750) **Chapter 11:** The Rise of Democracy (1824–1840) **Chapter 17:** Reconstructing the Union (1865–1877)

Introduction

The Study of History

Larry Madaras
James M. SoRelle

In a pluralistic society such as ours, the study of history is bound to be a complex process. How an event is interpreted depends not only on the existing evidence but also on the perspective of the interpreter. Consequently, understanding history presupposes the evaluation of information, a task that often leads to conflicting conclusions. An understanding of history, then, requires the acceptance of the idea of historical relativism. Relativism means that redefinition of our past is always possible and desirable. History shifts, changes, and grows with new and different evidence and interpretations. As is the case with the law and even with medicine, beliefs that were unquestioned 100 or 200 years ago have been discredited or discarded since.

Relativism, then, encourages revisionism. There is a maxim that "the past must remain useful to the present." Historian Carl Becker argued that every generation should examine history for itself, thus ensuring constant scrutiny of our collective experience through new perspectives. History, consequently, does not remain static, in part because historians cannot avoid being influenced by the times in which they live. Almost all historians commit themselves to revising the views of other historians, synthesizing theories into macro-interpretations, or revising the revisionists.

Schools of Thought

Three predominant schools of thought have emerged in American history since the first graduate seminars in history were given at The Johns Hopkins University in Baltimore in the 1870s. The *progressive* school dominated the professional field in the first half of the twentieth century. Influenced by the reform currents of Populism, progressivism, and the New Deal, these historians explored the social and economic forces that energized America. The progressive scholars tended to view the past in terms of conflicts between groups, and they sympathized with the underdog.

The post–World War II period witnessed the emergence of a new group of historians who viewed the conflict thesis as overly simplistic. Writing against the backdrop of the Cold War, these *neoconservative*, or *consensus*, historians argued that Americans possess a shared set of values and that the areas of agreement within our nation's basic democratic and capitalistic framework are more important than the areas of disagreement.

In the 1960s, however, the civil rights movement, women's liberation, and the student rebellion (with its condemnation of the war in Vietnam) fragmented the consensus of values upon which historians and social scientists of the 1950s had centered their interpretations. This turmoil set the stage for the emergence of another group of scholars. *New Left* historians began to reinterpret the past once again. They emphasized the significance of conflict in American history, and they resurrected interest in those groups ignored by the consensus school. In addition, New Left historians critiqued the expansionist policies of the United States and emphasized the difficulties confronted by Native Americans, African Americans, women, and urban workers in gaining full citizenship status.

Progressive, consensus, and New Left history is still being written. The most recent generation of scholars, however, focuses upon social history. Their primary concern is to discover what the lives of "ordinary Americans" were really like. These new social historians employ previously overlooked court and church documents, house deeds and tax records, letters and diaries, photographs, and census data to reconstruct the everyday lives of average Americans. Some employ new methodologies, such as quantification (enhanced by advancing computer technology) and oral history, whereas others borrow from the disciplines of political science, economics, sociology, anthropology, and psychology for their historical investigations.

The proliferation of historical approaches, which are reflected in the issues debated in this book, has had mixed results. On the one hand, historians have become so specialized in their respective time periods and methodological styles that it is difficult to synthesize the recent scholarship into a comprehensive text for the general reader. On the other hand, historians know more about the American past than at any other time in history. They dare to ask new questions or ones that previously were considered to be germane only to scholars in other social sciences. Although there is little agreement about the answers to these questions, the methods employed and issues explored make the "new history" a very exciting field to study.

Issue 1 discusses the key element of historical truth and the extent to which historians, applying the technique of empirical research, can determine exactly what happened in the past. Oscar Handlin insists that the truth of past events is absolute and knowable if pursued by historians employing the scientific method of research. William McNeill, however, argues that the absolute truth about human behavior is unattainable because historians do not have all the facts at their disposal and because they tend to organize their evidence and make intellectual choices based on subjective judgments. Consequently, historians' interpretations may be challenged by others who approach the evidence from a different point of view.

The topics that follow represent a variety of perspectives and approaches. Each of these controversial issues can be studied for its individual importance to our nation's history. Taken as a group, they interact with one another to illustrate larger historical themes. When grouped thematically, the issues reveal continuing motifs in the development of American history.

The New Social History

Some of the most innovative historical research over the last 40 years reflects the interests of the new social historians. The work of several representatives of this group who treat the issues of race, gender, and class appears in this volume. For example, in Issue 3, Colin Calloway and David Jones discuss the impact of the encounters between Europeans and Native Americans. Calloway says that although Native Americans confronted numerous diseases in the Americas, traditional Indian healing practices failed to offer much protection from the diseases introduced by Europeans beginning in the late-fifteenth century, which decimated the indigenous peoples. Jones recognizes the disastrous impact of European diseases on Native Americans, but he insists that Indian depopulation also was a consequence of the forces of poverty, malnutrition, environmental stress, dislocation, and social disparity.

Issue 9 blends social history with politics in Jacksonian America by examining the motivation behind the Indian Removal Act of 1830. Robert V. Remini insists that President Andrew Jackson demonstrated a genuine concern for the welfare of Native Americans by proposing a voluntary program that would remove the Five Civilized Tribes west of the Mississippi River, where they could avoid dangerous conflict with white settlers and preserve their heritage and culture. Alfred A. Cave accuses Jackson of abusing his power as president by failing to adhere to the letter of the Indian Removal Act by transforming a voluntary program into a coercive one and by ignoring the provisions in his own removal treaties that promised protection to the various southern tribes.

Two issues explore the field of women's history. Study of the Salem witch trials has produced several quite imaginative scholarly explanations for this episode in New England's history. In Issue 4, Carol F. Karlsen analyzes the relationship between the Salem witchcraft hysteria of 1692 and Puritan attitudes toward women. The belief that women were inherently evil, Karlsen concludes, operated at the core of Puritan culture. Such attitudes made it easy to blame women for disruptions in New England society. Laurie Winn Carlson takes the matter of witchcraft hysteria in an entirely different direction. She concludes that what happened in Salem in 1692 was the product of people's responses to physical and neurological behaviors resulting from an undiagnosed epidemic of encephalitis.

Issue 10 addresses the economic opportunities available to women in the 1830s. According to Nancy F. Cott, when merchant capitalism reached its mature phase in the 1830s, the roles of the middle-class family became more clearly defined, and new economic opportunities opened for women within a limited sphere outside the home. Gerda Lerner counters this more optimistic view of women's status by concluding that most women in Jacksonian America were disfranchised and isolated from vital centers of economic opportunity.

Revolution, Religion, and Reform in the New Nation

Issue 6 provides a discussion of the factors contributing to the American colonists' decision to seek independence through a war with England. T. H. Breen maintains that the American Revolution was the product of a larger "market revolution" that led the colonists, who shared experiences as consumers, to break with England. Carl N. Degler argues that the American Revolution was a political rebellion led by a group of reluctant revolutionaries who opposed Parliament's attempt to impose taxes without the consent of the colonists.

Religion has played a significant role in the development of American society from the earliest colonial beginnings. In Issue 5, Thomas S. Kidd and Jon Butler debate whether it is appropriate to identify revival activity in the mid-eighteenth century as "The Great Awakening." Kidd insists that preachers such as George Whitefield engineered a powerful series of revivals in the mid-eighteenth century that influenced all of the British North American colonies and gave birth to a spirit of evangelicalism that initiated a major alteration of global Christian history. Jon Butler claims that to describe the religious revival activities of the eighteenth century as the "Great Awakening" is to seriously exaggerate their extent, nature, and impact on pre-revolutionary American society and politics.

Issue 11 also concerns the influence of religious impulses. Mark Edward Lender and James Kirby Martin argue that the impetus for the temperance movement in the first half of the nineteenth century was grounded deeply in Protestant denominations whose clergy and lay leaders supported reforms that would create a social-moral order that was best for the public welfare. John J. Rumbarger, however, concludes that nineteenth-century temperance reform was the product of a pro-capitalist market economy whose entrepreneurial elite led the way toward abstinence and prohibition campaigns in order to guarantee the availability of a more productive work force.

The major and most controversial reform effort in the pre–Civil War period was the movement to abolish slavery. Issue 13 examines the terrorist activities carried out by John Brown and his followers. James N. Gilbert says that John Brown's actions conform to a modern definition of terrorist behavior in that Brown considered the United States incapable of reforming itself by abolishing slavery, believed that only violence would accomplish that goal, and justified his actions by proclaiming adherence to a "higher" power. Scott John Hammond insists that Brown's commitment to higher moral and political goals conformed to the basic principles of human freedom and political and legal equality that formed the heart of the creed articulated by the founders of the American nation.

War, Leadership, and Resolution

As a nation committed to peace, the United States has faced some of its sternest tests in times of war. Such conflicts inevitably have challenged the leadership abilities of the commanders-in-chief, the commitment of the nation to involve itself in war, and the ideals of the republic founded on democratic principles. Several issues in this volume address the response to war and its aftermath. In Issue 12, Walter Nugent and Norman Graebner debate the rationale behind the war between the United States and Mexico in 1846. Walter Nugent argues that President James K. Polk was an imperialist motivated to use the power of the presidency to force Mexico to cede California and the current

Southwest to the United States. Graebner contends that President Polk pursued an aggressive (but not imperialistic) policy that would force Mexico to recognize the U.S. annexation of Texas and to sell New Mexico and California to its northern neighbor without starting a war.

Two issues cover topics relating to the Civil War and its consequences. In Issue 14, Charles B. Dew and Marc Egnal debate the causes of the Civil War. Dew employs the words of white southerners whose job it was to promote the cause of secession following Abraham Lincoln's election by appealing to their audiences' commitment to the preservation of slavery and the doctrine of white supremacy. Egnal argues that the decision of Lower South states to secede from the Union was determined by an economically based struggle between residents with strong ties to the North and Upper South who embraced an entrepreneurial outlook, on one hand, and those who were largely isolated from the North and who opposed the implementation of a diversified economy, on the other hand.

Issue 15 offers an assessment of the military leadership of General Robert E. Lee. Alan T. Nolan characterizes Lee as a flawed grand strategist whose offensive operations produced heavy casualties in an unnecessarily prolonged war that the South could not win. For Nolan, then, Lee's reputation as a military leader has been vastly overrated. According to Gary W. Gallagher, however, General Lee was the most revered and unifying figure in the Confederacy, and he "formulated a national strategy predicated on the probability of success in Virginia and the value of battlefield victories."

With the end of slavery, one of the most controversial questions confronting those responsible for reconstructing the nation following the war involved the future of African Americans. Perhaps no other period of American history has been subjected to more myths than has this postwar era. Even though most scholars today recognize that Reconstruction did not achieve its most enlightened economic and social goals, they differ in their explanations about the source of this failure. In Issue 17, George M. Fredrickson concludes that racism, in the form of the doctrine of white supremacy, colored the thinking not only of southern whites but of most white northerners as well and produced only halfhearted efforts by the Radical Republicans in the postwar period to sustain a commitment to black equality. Heather Cox Richardson, on the other hand, argues that the failure of Radical Reconstruction was primarily a consequence of a national commitment to a free-labor ideology that opposed an expanding central government that legislated rights to African Americans that other citizens had acquired through hard work.

Politics in America

The American people gave legitimacy to their revolution through the establishment of a republican form of government. The United States has operated under two constitutions: the first established the short-lived confederation from 1781 to 1789; the second was written in 1787 and remains in effect over two hundred years later. In Issue 7, John P. Roche contends that the drafters of the Constitution of the United States were democratic reformers. Howard Zinn describes the founders as members of an economic elite who desired a stronger central government to protect their property rights.

Alexander Hamilton was one of the most significant leaders of the early national period. Issue 8 explores Hamilton's skills as the primary architect of the nation's economic policies. John Steele Gordon views Hamilton as the person most responsible for the powerful national economy we enjoy today. Carey Roberts, however, argues that Hamilton's economic policies diminished people's confidence in the Federalist Party and its leadership.

No discussion of American politics is complete without examining some of the individuals who have served as president of the United States. Andrew Jackson's leadership already has been discussed above in connection with his policy toward the removal of Native Americans from the southeastern United States (Issue 9). In Issue 16, Philip Shaw Paludan and M. E. Bradford debate Abraham Lincoln's presidential legacy. Paludan contends that Lincoln deserves to be recognized as the nation's greatest president for facing the unparalleled challenges associated with the Civil War, preserving the Union, and freeing the slaves. M. E. Bradford characterizes Lincoln as a cynical politician whose abuse of authority as president and commander-in-chief during the Civil War marked a serious departure from the republican goals of the Founding Fathers and established the prototype for the "imperial presidency" of the twentieth century.

Comparative History: America in a Global Perspective

The role of American history within the larger framework of world history is central to the discussion presented in Issue 2 of this volume. In sharp contrast to our traditional understanding of the "discovery" of the New World, Gavin Menzies surmises that between 1421 and 1423 a Chinese fleet spent four months exploring the Pacific coastline of North America and leaving behind substantial evidence that supports his contention that the Chinese discovered America long before the arrival of European explorers. Robert Finlay accuses Menzies of ignoring the basic rules of historical study and logic to concoct an implausible interpretation of Chinese discovery based upon a misreading of Chinese imperial policy, misrepresentation of sources, and conjecture that has no evidentiary base. In so doing, he carries us back to the questions raised in the first issue of this volume concerning the nature of historical truth.

Conclusion

The process of historical study should rely more on thinking than on memorizing data. Once the basics of who, what, when, and where are determined, historical thinking shifts to a higher gear. Analysis, comparison and contrast, evaluation, and explanation take command. These skills not only increase our knowledge of the past but also provide general tools for the comprehension of all the topics about which human beings think.

The diversity of a pluralistic society, however, creates some obstacles to comprehending the past. The spectrum of differing opinions on any particular subject eliminates the possibility of quick and easy answers. In the final analysis, conclusions often are built through a synthesis of several different interpretations, but, even then, they may be partial and tentative.

The study of history in a pluralistic society allows each citizen the opportunity to reach independent conclusions about the past. Since most, if not all, historical issues affect the present and future, understanding the past becomes essential to social progress. Many of today's problems have a direct connection with the past. Additionally, other contemporary issues may lack obvious direct antecedents, but historical investigation can provide illuminating analogies. At first, it may appear confusing to read and to think about opposing historical views, but the survival of our democratic society depends on such critical thinking by acute and discerning minds.

Internet References . . .

The Columbus Navigation Homepage

This noted site by Keith A. Pickering examines the history, navigation, and landfall of Christopher Columbus. Click on "Links to other sites about Columbus and his times" to find dozens of sites on Columbus, including scholarly papers on Columbus's treatment of the American Indians.

http://www.columbusnavigation.com/

Virginia's Indians, Past and Present

Drawn from collections at James Madison University, under the Internet School Library Media Center, this site provides links to historical information, lesson plans, and bibliographies as well as links to tribal home pages.

http://www.lva.virginia.gov/public/guides/IndianVirginians.pdf

Salem Witch Trials Documentary Archive

This collection at the University of Virginia provides access to documents and links to archives relating to the Salem witchcraft trials.

http://etext.virginia.edu/salem/witchcraft/

The First Great Awakening

This site is maintained by the National Endowment for the Humanities and includes teacher lesson plans and links to important primary resources related to this event.

http://edsitement.neh.gov/view_lesson_plan.asp?id=698

Colonial Society

*C*olonial settlement in British North America took place in the context of regional conditions that varied in time and place. The ethnic identity of the European colonists affected their relations with Native Americans and Africans, as well as with each other. Many of the attitudes, ideals, and institutions that emerged from the colonial experience served the early settlers well and are still emulated today.

- Is History True?
- Did the Chinese Discover America?
- Was Disease the Key Factor in the Depopulation of Native Americans in the Americas?
- Was the Salem Witchcraft Hysteria Caused by a Fear of Women?
- Was There a Great Awakening in Mid-Eighteenth Century America?

ISSUE 1

Is History True?

YES: Oscar Handlin, from *Truth in History* (The Belknap Press of Harvard University Press, 1979)

NO: William H. McNeill, from "Mythistory, or Truth, Myth, History, and Historians," *The American Historical Review* (February 1986)

ISSUE SUMMARY

YES: Oscar Handlin insists that historical truth is absolute and knowable by historians who adopt the scientific method of research to discover factual evidence that provides both a chronology and context for their findings.

NO: William McNeill argues that historical truth is general and evolutionary and is discerned by different groups at different times and in different places in a subjective manner that has little to do with a scientifically absolute methodology.

The basic premise of this volume of readings is that the study of history is a complex process that combines historical facts and the historian's interpretation of those facts. Underlying this premise is the assumption that the historian is committed to employing evidence that advances an accurate, truthful picture of the past. Unfortunately, the historical profession in the last several years has been held up to close public scrutiny as a result of charges that a few scholars, some quite prominent, have been careless in their research methods, have cited sources that do not exist, and have reached conclusions that were not borne out by the facts. The result has been soiled or ruined reputations and the revocation of degrees, book awards, and tenure. Certainly, this is not the end to which most historians aspire, and the failures of a few should not cast a net of suspicion on the manner in which the vast majority of historians practice their craft.

In reflecting upon her role as a historian, the late Barbara Tuchman commented, "To write history so as to enthrall the reader and make the subject as captivating and exciting to him as it is to me has been my goal. . . . A prerequisite . . . is to be enthralled one's self and to feel a compulsion to communicate the magic." For Tuchman, it was the historian's responsibility to the

2

reader to conduct thorough research on a particular topic, sort through the mass of facts to determine what was essential and what was not, and to formulate what remained into a dramatic narrative. Tuchman and most practicing historians also agree with the nineteenth-century German historian Leopold von Ranke that the task of the historian is to discover what really happened. In most instances, however, historians write about events at which they were not present. According to Tuchman, "We can never be certain that we have recaptured [the past] as it really was. But the least we can do is to stay within the evidence."

David Hackett Fischer has written about the difficulties confronting historians as they attempt to report a truthful past, and he is particularly critical of what he terms the "absurd and pernicious doctrine" of historical relativism as it developed in the United States in the 1930s under the direction of Charles Beard and Carl Becker. Becker's suggestion that each historian will write a history based upon his or her own values or the climate of opinion in a particular generation strikes Fischer as a slippery slope leading to the loss of historical accuracy. In conclusion, Fischer writes, "The factual errors which academic historians make today are rarely deliberate. The real danger is not that a scholar will delude his readers, but that he will delude himself."

The selections that follow explore the topic of historical truth. In the late 1970s, Oscar Handlin, like Fischer, became extremely concerned about the impact of the historical and cultural relativism of postmodern and deconstructionist approaches to the study of history. For Handlin, historical truth is absolute and knowable if pursued by the historian adopting the scientific method of research. The value of history, he believes, lies in the capacity to advance toward the truth by locating discrete events, phenomena, and expressions in the historical record.

In contrast, William McNeill recognizes a very thin line between fact and fiction. He claims that historians distinguish between the truth of their conclusions and the myth of those conclusions they reject. The result is what he terms "mythistory." Moreover, the arrangement of historical facts involves subjective judgments and intellectual choices that have little to do with the scientific method. Historical truth, McNeill proposes, is evolutionary, not absolute.

YES ↵

Oscar Handlin

The Uses of History

Why resist the temptation to be relevant? The question nags historians in 1978 as it does other scholars. The world is turning; it needs knowledge; and possession of learning carries an obligation to attempt to shape events. Every crisis lends weight to the plea: transform the library from an ivory tower into a fortress armed to make peace (or war), to end (or extend) social inequality, to alter (or preserve) the existing economic system. The thought boosts the ego, as it has ever since Francis Bacon's suggestion that knowledge is power. Perhaps authority really does lie in command of the contents of books!

In the 1960s the plea became an order, sometimes earnest, sometimes surly, always insistent. Tell us what we need to know—straight answers. Thus, students to teachers, readers to authors. The penalties for refusal ranged from mere unpopularity to organized boycotts and angry confrontations—in a few cases even to burning manuscripts and research notes. Fear added to the inducements for pleasing the audience, whether in the classroom or on the printed page.

To aim to please is a blunder, however. Sincere as the supplicants generally are, it is not knowledge they wish. Having already reached their conclusions, they seek only reassuring confirmation as they prepare to act. They already know that a unilateral act of will could stop wars, that the United States is racist, and that capitalism condemns the masses to poverty. The history of American foreign policy, of the failure of post-Civil War Reconstruction, and of industrial development would only clutter the mind with disturbing ambiguities and complexities.

At best, the usable past demanded of history consists of the data to flesh out a formula. We must do something about the war, the cities, pollution, poverty, and population. Our moral sense, group interest, and political affiliation define the goals; let the historian join the other social scientists in telling us how to reach them. At worst, the demand made of the past is for a credible myth that will identify the forces of good and evil and inspire those who fight with slogans or fire on one side of the barricades or the other.

The effort to meet either demand will frustrate the historian true to his or her craft. Those nimble enough to catch the swings of the market in the classroom or in print necessarily leave behind interior standards of what is important and drop by the wayside the burden of scrupulous investigation and rigorous judgment. Demands for relevance distort the story of ethnicity as they corrupt the historical novel.

Whoever yields, forgoes the opportunity to do what scholars are best qualified to do. Those who chase from one disaster to another lose sight of the long-term trend; busy with the bandaids, they have no time to treat the patient's illness. The family did not originate yesterday, or the city, or addiction to narcotics; a student might well pick up some thoughts on those subjects by shifting his sights from the 1970s to Hellenistic society.

Above all, obsession with the events of the moment prevents the historian from exercising the faculty of empathy, the faculty of describing how people, like us, but different, felt and behaved as they did in times and places similar to, but different, from our own. The writer or teacher interested only in passing judgment on the good guys and the bad will never know what it meant to be an Irish peasant during a famine, or the landlord; an Alabama slave in the 1850s, or the master; a soldier at Antietam, or a general.

The uses of history arise neither from its relevance nor from its help in preparing for careers—nor from its availability as a subject which teachers pass on to students who become teachers and in turn teach others to teach.

Nevertheless, again and again former pupils who come back for reunions after twenty-five years or more spontaneously testify to the utility of what they had learned at college in the various pursuits to which life's journey had taken them. Probing usually reveals not bits of information, not a general interpretation, but a vague sense that those old transactions of classroom and library had somehow expanded their knowledge of self. The discipline of history had located them in time and space and had thereby helped them know themselves, not as physicians or attorneys or bureaucrats or executives, but as persons.

These reassuring comments leave in suspense the question of why study of the past should thus help the individuals understand himself or herself. How do those who learn this subject catch a glimpse of the process of which they are part, discover places in it?

Not by relevance, in the competition for which the other, more pliable, social sciences can always outbid history. Nor by the power of myth, in the peddling of which the advantage lies with novelists. To turn accurate knowledge to those ends is, as C. S. Peirce noted, "like running a steam engine by burning diamonds."

The use of history lies in its capacity for advancing the approach to truth.

The historian's vocation depends on this minimal operational article of faith: Truth is absolute; it is as absolute as the world is real. It does not exist because individuals wish it to anymore than the world exists for their convenience. Although observers have more or less partial views of the truth, its actuality is unrelated to the desires or the particular angles of vision of the viewers. Truth is knowable and will win out if earnestly pursued; and science is the procedure or set of procedures for approximating it.

What is truth? Mighty above all things, it resides in the small pieces which together form the record.

History is not the past, any more than biology is life, or physics, matter. History is the distillation of evidence surviving from the past. Where there is no evidence, there is no history. Much of the past is not knowable in this way, and about those areas the historian must learn to confess ignorance.

No one can relive the past; but everyone can seek truth in the record. Simple, durable discoveries await the explorer. So chronology—the sequential order of events reaching back beyond time's horizon—informs the viewer of the long distance traversed and of the immutable course of occurrences: no reversal of a step taken; no after ever before. The historian cannot soar with the anthropologists, who swoop across all time and space. Give or take a thousand years, it is all one to them in pronouncements about whether irrigation systems succeeded or followed despotisms, or in linking technology, population, food, and climatic changes. In the end they pick what they need to prop up theory. The discipline of dates rails off the historian and guards against such perilous plunges. No abstraction, no general interpretation, no wish or preference can challenge chronology's dominion, unless among those peoples who, lacking a sense of time, lack also a sense of history. And whoever learns to know the tyranny of the passing hours, the irrecoverable nature of days passed, learns also the vanity of all aspirations to halt the clock or slow its speed, of all irridentisms, all efforts to recapture, turn back, redeem the moments gone by.

Another use of history is in teaching about vocabulary, the basic component of human communication. Words, singularly elusive, sometimes flutter out of reach, hide in mists of ambiguity, or lodge themselves among inaccessible logical structures, yet form the very stuff of evidence. The historian captures the little syllabic clusters only by knowing who inscribed or spoke them—a feat made possible by understanding the minds and hearts and hands of the men and women for whom they once had meaning. Words released by comprehension wing their messages across the centuries. A use of history is to instruct in the reading of a word, in the comprehension of speakers, writers different from the listener, viewer.

And context. Every survival bespeaks a context. Who graved or wrote or built did so for the eyes of others. Each line or shape denotes a relation to people, things, or concepts—knowable. The identities of sender and recipient explain the content of the letter; the mode of transmission explains the developing idea, the passions of employers and laborers, the organization of the factory. A use of history is its aid in locating discrete events, phenomena, and expressions in their universes.

The limits of those universes were often subjects of dispute. Early in the nineteenth century Henry Thomas Buckle complained, in terms still applicable decades thereafter, of "the singular spectacle of one historian being ignorant of political economy; another knowing nothing of law; another nothing of ecclesiastical affairs and changes of opinion; another neglecting the philosophy of statistics, another physical science," so that those important pursuits, being cultivated, "some by one man, and some by another, have been isolated rather than united," with no disposition to concentrate them upon history. He thus echoed Gibbon's earlier injunction to value all facts. A Montesquieu, "from the meanest of them, will draw conclusions unknown to ordinary men" and arrive at "philosophical history."

On the other hand, a distinguished scholar fifty years later pooh-poohed the very idea that there might be a relation among the Gothic style, feudalism, and scholasticism, or a link between the Baroque and Jesuitism. Nevertheless, the dominant thrust of twentieth-century historians has been toward recognition of the broader contexts; in a variety of fashions they have searched for a totality denominated civilization, culture, or spirit of an epoch, and which they have hoped would permit examination of enlightening linkages and reciprocal relations. Even those who deny that history is a single discipline and assert that it is only "congeries of related disciplines" would, no doubt, expect each branch to look beyond its own borders.

In the final analysis, all the uses of history depend upon the integrity of the record, without which there could be no counting of time, no reading of words, no perception of the context, no utility of the subject. No concern could be deeper than assaults upon the record, upon the very idea of a record.

⋘◉⋙

Although history is an ancient discipline, it rests upon foundations laid in the seventeenth century, when a century of blood shed in religious and dynastic warfare persuaded those who wrote and read history to accept a vital difference in tolerance between facts and interpretation. The text of a charter or statute was subject to proof of authenticity and validity, whatever the meanings lawyers or theologians imparted to its terms. The correct date, the precise phrasing, the seal were facts which might present difficulties of verification, but which, nevertheless, admitted of answers that were right or wrong. On the other hand, discussion of opinions and meanings often called for tolerance among diverse points of view, tolerance possible so long as disputants distinguished interpretation from the fact, from the thing in itself. Scholars could disagree on large matters of interpretation; they had a common interest in agreeing on the small ones of fact which provided them grounds of peaceful discourse.

From that seminal insight developed the scientific mechanisms that enabled historians to separate fact from opinion. From that basis came the Enlightenment achievements which recognized the worth of objectivity and asserted the possibility of reconstructing the whole record of the human past.

True, historians as well as philosophers often thereafter worried about the problems of bias and perspective; and some despaired of attaining the ideal of ultimate objectivity. None were ever totally free of bias, not even those like Ranke who most specifically insisted on the integrity of the fact which he struggled to make the foundation of a truly universal body of knowledge. But, however fallible the individual scholar, the historian's task, Wilhelm von

Humboldt explained, was "to present what actually happened." It may have been a dream to imagine that history would become a science meaningful to all people, everywhere. If so, it was a noble dream.

By contrast, historians in the 1970s and increasingly other scientists regarded the fact itself as malleable. As the distinction between fact and interpretation faded, all became faction—a combination of fact and fiction. The passive acceptance of that illegitimate genre—whatever mixes with fiction ceases to be fact—revealed the erosion of scholarly commitment. More and more often, the factual elements in an account were instrumental to the purpose the author-manipulator wished them to serve. It followed that different writers addressing different readers for different purposes could arrange matters as convenient. In the end, the primacy of the fact vanished and only the authority of the author, the receptivity of the audience, and the purpose intended remained.

Whence came this desertion, this rejection of allegiance to the fact?

Chroniclers of the past always suffered from external pressure to make their findings relevant, that is, to demonstrate or deny the wisdom, correctness, or appropriateness of current policies. They resisted out of dedication to maintaining the integrity of the record; and long succeeded in doing so. In the 1970s, however, the pressures toward falsification became more compelling than ever before.

Although the full fruits of the change appeared only in that decade, its origins reached back a half-century. It was one of Stalin's most impressive achievements to have converted Marxism from its nineteenth-century scientific base to an instrument of state purpose, and it was not by coincidence that history was the first discipline to suffer in the process. The Soviet Union did more than impose an official party line on interpretations of Trotsky's role in the revolution of 1917; it actually expunged the name Trotsky from the record, so that the fact of the commissar's existence disappeared. What started in the domain of history led in time to Lysenko's invasion of the natural sciences. The Nazis, once in power, burned the nonconforming books; and after 1945 the assault spread to all countries subject to totalitarian control. Those developments were neither surprising nor difficult to comprehend; they followed from the nature of the regimes which fostered them.

More surprising, more difficult to comprehend, was the acquiescence by the scholars of free societies in the attack on history, first, insofar as it affected colleagues less fortunately situated, then as it insinuated itself in their own ranks. External and internal circumstances were responsible.

In a sensate society the commercial standards of the media governed the dissemination of information. Since whatever sold was news, the salient consideration was one of attracting attention; factual accuracy receded to the remote background. An affluent and indulgent society also mistook flaccid permissiveness for tolerance. Everything went because nothing was worth defending, and the legitimate right to err became the disastrous obliteration of the difference between error and truth.

Difficult critical issues tempted the weak-minded to tailor fact to convenience. In the United States, but also in other parts of the world, the spread of a kind of tribalism demanded a history unique to and written for the specifications of particular groups. Since knowledge was relative to the knowers, it was subject to manipulation to suit their convenience. The process by which blacks, white ethnics, and women alone were conceded the capability of understanding and writing their own histories wiped out the line between truth and myth.

That much was comprehensible; these forces operated outside the academy walls and were not subject to very much control. More important, more susceptible to control, and less explicable was the betrayal by the intellectuals of their own group interests and the subsequent loss of the will to resist. A variety of elements contributed to this most recent *trahison des clercs*. Exaggerated concern with the problems of bias and objectivity drove some earnest scholars to despair. Perhaps they reacted against the excessive claims of the nineteenth century, perhaps against the inability of historians, any more than other scholars, to withstand the pressures of nationalism in the early decades of the twentieth century. In any case, not a few followed the deceptive path from acknowledgment that no person was entirely free of prejudice or capable of attaining a totally objective view of the past to the conclusion that all efforts to do so were vain and that, in the end, the past was entirely a recreation emanating from the mind of the historian. Support from this point of view came from the philosophers Benedetto Croce in Italy and, later, R. G. Collingwood in England. Support also came from a misreading of anthropological relativism, which drew from the undeniable circumstances that different cultures evolved differently, the erroneous conclusion that judgments among them were impossible.

Perhaps playfully, perhaps seriously, Carl L. Becker suggested that the historical fact was in someone's mind or it was nowhere, because it was "not the past event," only a symbol which enabled later writers to recreate it imaginatively. His charmingly put illustrations deceived many a reader unaware that serious thinkers since Bayle and Hume had wrestled with the problem. "No one could ever object to the factual truth that Caesar defeated Pompey; and whatever the principles one wishes to use in dispute, one will find nothing less questionable than this proposition—Caesar and Pompey existed and were not just simple modification of the minds of those who wrote their lives"—thus Bayle.

The starting point in Becker's wandering toward relativism, as for others among his contemporaries, was the desire to be useful in solving "the everlasting riddle of human experience." Less subtle successors attacked neutrality "toward the main issues of life" and demanded that society organize all its forces in support of its ideals. "Total war, whether it be hot or cold, enlists everyone and calls upon everyone to assume his part. The historian is no freer from this obligation than the physicists." Those too timid to go the whole way suggested that there might be two kinds of history, variously defined: one, for instance, to treat the positive side of slavery to nurture black pride; another, the negative, to support claims for compensation.

Historians who caved in to pressure and ordered the past to please the present neglected the future, the needs of which would certainly change and in unpredictable ways. Scholarship could no more provide the future than the present with faith, justification, self-confidence, or sense of purpose unless it first preserved the record, intact and inviolable.

History does not recreate the past. The historian does not recapture the bygone event. No amount of imagination will enable the scholar to describe exactly what happened to Caesar in the Senate or to decide whether Mrs. Williams actually lost two hundred pounds by an act of faith. History deals only with evidence from the past, with the residues of bygone events. But it can pass judgment upon documentation and upon observers' reports of what they thought they saw.

Disregarding these constraints, Becker concluded that, since objectivity was a dream, everyman could be his own historian and contrive his own view of the past, valid for himself, if for no one else. He thus breached the line between interpretation, which was subjective and pliable, and fact, which was not.

Internal specialization allowed historians to slip farther in the same direction. The knowledge explosion after 1900 made specialization an essential, unavoidable circumstance of every form of scholarly endeavor. No individual could presume to competence in more than a sector of the whole field; and the scope of the manageable sector steadily shrank. One result was the dissolution of common standards; each area created its own criteria and claimed immunity from the criticism of outsiders. The occupants of each little island fortress sustained the illusion that the dangers to one would not apply to others. Lines of communication, even within a single faculty or department, broke down so that, increasingly, specialists in one area depended upon the common mass media for knowledge about what transpired in another.

The dangers inherent in these trends became critical as scholarship lost its autonomy. Increasingly reliance on support from external sources—whether governments or foundations—circumscribed the freedom of researchers and writers to choose their own subjects and to arrive at their own conclusions. More generally, the loss of autonomy involved a state of mind which regarded the fruits of scholarship as dependent and instrumental—that is, not as worthy of pursuit for their own sake, not for the extent to which they brought the inquirer closer to the truth, but for other, extrinsic reasons. Ever more often, scholars justified their activity by its external results—peace, training for citizenship, economic development, cure of illness, and the like—in other words, by its usefulness. The choice of topics revealed the extent to which emphasis had shifted from the subject and its relation to the truth to its instrumental utility measured by reference to some external standard.

The plea from utility was dangerous. In the 1930s it blinded well-intentioned social scientists and historians to the excesses of totalitarianism. It was inevitable in creating the omelette of a great social experiment that the shells of a few eggs of truth would be broken, so the argument ran. So, too, in the avid desire for peace, in the praiseworthy wish to avoid a second world war, Charles A. Beard abandoned all effort at factual accuracy. Yet the errors to which the plea for utility led in the past have not prevented others from proceeding along the same treacherous path in pursuit of no less worthy, but equally deceptive utilitarian goals.

Finally, the reluctance to insist upon the worth of truth for its own sake stemmed from a decline of faith by intellectuals in their own role as intellectuals. Not many have, in any conscious or deliberate sense, foresworn their allegiance to the pursuit of truth and the life of the spirit. But power tempted them as it tempts other men and women. The twentieth-century intellectual had unparalleled access to those who actually wielded political or military influence. And few could resist the temptation of being listened to by presidents and ministers, of seeing ideas translated into action. Moreover, a more subtle, more insidious temptation nested in the possibility that possession of knowledge may itself become a significant source of power. The idea that a name on the letterhead of an activist organization or in the endorsement of a political advertisement might advance some worthy cause gives a heady feeling of sudden consequence to the no-longer-humble professor. Most important of all is the consciousness that knowledge can indeed do good, that it is a usable commodity, not only capable of bringing fame to its possessor but actually capable of causing beneficent changes in the external world.

All too few scholars are conscious that in reducing truth to an instrument, even an instrument for doing good, they necessarily blunt its edge and expose themselves to the danger of its misuse. For, when truth ceases to be an end in itself and becomes but a means toward an end, it also becomes malleable and manageable and is in danger of losing its character—not necessarily, not inevitably, but seriously. There may be ways of avoiding the extreme choices of the ivory tower and the marketplace, but they are far from easy and call for extreme caution.

In 1679 Jacques Bossuet wrote for his pupil the Dauphin, heir apparent to the throne of France, a discourse on universal history. Here certainly was an opportunity to influence the mind of the future monarch of Europe's most powerful kingdom. Bossuet understood that the greatest service he could render was to tell, not what would be pleasant to hear, but the truth about the past, detached and whole, so that in later years his pupil could make what use he wished of it.

Therein Bossuet reverted to an ancient tradition. The first law for the historian, Cicero had written, "is never to dare utter an untruth and the second, never to suppress anything true." And, earlier still, Polybius had noted that no one was exempt from mistakes made out of ignorance. But "deliberate misstatements in the interest of country or of friends or for favour" reduced the scholar to the level of those who gained "their living by their pens" and weighed "everything by the standard of profit."

In sum, the use of history is to learn from the study of it and not to carry preconceived notions or external objectives into it.

The times, it may be, will remain hostile to the enterprise of truth. There have been such periods in the past. Historians would do well to regard the example of those clerks in the Dark Ages who knew the worth of the task. By retiring from an alien world to a hidden monastic refuge, now and again one of them at least was able to maintain a true record, a chronicle that survived the destructive passage of armies and the erosion of doctrinal disputes and informed the future of what had transpired in their day. That task is ever worthy. Scholars should ponder its significance.

Mythistory, or Truth, Myth, History, and Historians

Myth and history are close kin inasmuch as both explain how things got to be the way they are by telling some sort of story. But our common parlance reckons myth to be false while history is, or aspires to be, true. Accordingly, a historian who rejects someone else's conclusions calls them mythical, while claiming that his own views are true. But what seems true to one historian will seem false to another, so one historian's truth becomes another's myth, even at the moment of utterance.

A century and more ago, when history was first established as an academic discipline, our predecessors recognized this dilemma and believed they had a remedy. Scientific source criticism would get the facts straight, whereupon a conscientious and careful historian needed only to arrange the facts into a readable narrative to produce genuinely scientific history. And science, of course, like the stars above, was true and eternal, as Newton and Laplace had demonstrated to the satisfaction of all reasonable persons everywhere.

Yet, in practice, revisionism continued to prevail within the newly constituted historical profession, as it had since the time of Herodotus. For a generation or two, this continued volatility could be attributed to scholarly success in discovering new facts by diligent work in the archives; but early in this century thoughtful historians began to realize that the arrangement of facts to make a history involved subjective judgments and intellectual choices that had little or nothing to do with source criticism, scientific or otherwise.

In reacting against an almost mechanical vision of scientific method, it is easy to underestimate actual achievements. For the ideal of scientific history did allow our predecessors to put some forms of bias behind them. In particular, academic historians of the nineteenth century came close to transcending older religious controversies. Protestant and Catholic histories of post-Reformation Europe ceased to be separate and distinct traditions of learning—a transformation nicely illustrated in the Anglo-American world by the career of Lord Acton, a Roman Catholic who became Regius Professor of History at Cambridge and editor of the first *Cambridge Modern History*. This was a great accomplishment. So was the accumulation of an enormous fund of exact and reliable data through painstaking source criticism that allowed the

As seen in *The American Historical Review,* vol. 91, no. 1, February 1986, pp. 1–10; adapted from *Mythistory and other Essays* (University of Chicago Press, 1986). Copyright © 1986 by William H. McNeill. Reprinted by permission of the author.

writing of history in the western world to assume a new depth, scope, range, and precision as compared to anything possible in earlier times. No heir of that scholarly tradition should scoff at the faith of our predecessors, which inspired so much toiling in archives.

Yet the limits of scientific history were far more constricting than its devotees believed. Facts that could be established beyond all reasonable doubt remained trivial in the sense that they did not, in and of themselves, give meaning or intelligibility to the record of the past. A catalogue of undoubted and indubitable information, even if arranged chronologically, remains a catalogue. To become a history, facts have to be put together into a pattern that is understandable and credible; and when that has been achieved, the resulting portrait of the past may become useful as well—a font of practical wisdom upon which people may draw when making decisions and taking action.

Pattern recognition of the sort historians engage in is the chef d'oeuvre of human intelligence. It is achieved by paying selective attention to the total input of stimuli that perpetually swarm in upon our consciousness. Only by leaving things out, that is, relegating them to the status of background noise deserving only to be disregarded, can what matters most in a given situation become recognizable. Suitable action follows. Here is the great secret of human power over nature and over ourselves as well. Pattern recognition is what natural scientists are up to; it is what historians have always done, whether they knew it or not.

Only some facts matter for any given pattern. Otherwise, useless clutter will obscure what we are after: perceptible relationships among important facts. That and that alone constitutes an intelligible pattern, giving meaning to the world, whether it be the world of physics and chemistry or the world of interacting human groups through time, which historians take as their special domain. Natural scientists are ruthless in selecting aspects of available sensory inputs to pay attention to, disregarding all else. They call their patterns theories and inherit most of them from predecessors. But, as we now know, even Newton's truths needed adjustment. Natural science is neither eternal nor universal; it is instead historical and evolutionary, because scientists accept a new theory only when the new embraces a wider range of phenomena or achieves a more elegant explanation of (selectively observed) facts than its predecessor was able to do.

No comparably firm consensus prevails among historians. Yet we need not despair. The great and obvious difference between natural scientists and historians is the greater complexity of the behavior historians seek to understand. The principal source of historical complexity lies in the fact that human beings react both to the natural world and to one another chiefly through the mediation of symbols. This means, among other things, that any theory about human life, if widely believed, will alter actual behavior, usually by inducing people to act as if the theory were true. Ideas and ideals thus become self-validating within remarkably elastic limits. An extraordinary behavioral motility results. Resort to symbols, in effect, loosened up the connection between external reality and human responses, freeing us from instinct by setting us adrift on a sea of uncertainty. Human beings thereby acquired a new capacity to err, but also to change, adapt, and learn new ways of doing things. Innumerable errors, corrected by experience, eventually made us lords of creation as no other species on earth has ever been before.

The price of this achievement is the elastic, inexact character of truth, and especially of truths about human conduct. What a particular group of persons understands, believes, and acts upon, even if quite absurd to outsiders, may nonetheless cement social relations and allow the members of the group to act together and accomplish feats otherwise impossible. Moreover, membership in such a group and participation in its sufferings and triumphs give meaning and value to individual human lives. Any other sort of life is not worth living, for we are social creatures. As such we need to share truths with one another, and not just truths about atoms, stars, and molecules but about human relations and the people around us.

Shared truths that provide a sanction for common effort have obvious survival value. Without such social cement no group can long preserve itself. Yet to outsiders, truths of this kind are likely to seem myths, save in those (relatively rare) cases when the outsider is susceptible to conversion and finds a welcome within the particular group in question.

The historic record available to us consists of an unending appearance and dissolution of human groups, each united by its own beliefs, ideals, and traditions. Sects, religions, tribes, and states, from ancient Sumer and Pharaonic Egypt to modern times, have based their cohesion upon shared truths—truths that differed from time to time and place to place with a rich and reckless variety. Today the human community remains divided among an enormous number of different groups, each espousing its own version of truth about itself and about those excluded from its fellowship. Everything suggests that this sort of social and ideological fragmentation will continue indefinitely.

Where, in such a maelstrom of conflicting opinions, can we hope to locate historical truth? Where indeed?

Before modern communications thrust familiarity with the variety of human idea-systems upon our consciousness, this question was not particularly acute. Individuals nearly always grew up in relatively isolated communities to a more or less homogeneous world view. Important questions had been settled long ago by prophets and sages, so there was little reason to challenge or modify traditional wisdom. Indeed there were strong positive restraints upon any would-be innovator who threatened to upset the inherited consensus.

To be sure, climates of opinion fluctuated, but changes came surreptitiously, usually disguised as commentary upon old texts and purporting merely to explicate the original meanings. Flexibility was considerable, as the modern practice of the U.S. Supreme Court should convince us; but in this traditional ordering of intellect, all the same, outsiders who did not share the prevailing orthodoxy were shunned and disregarded when they could not be converted. Our predecessors' faith in a scientific method that would make written history absolutely and universally true was no more than a recent example of such a belief system. Those who embraced it felt no need to pay attention to ignoramuses who had not accepted the truths of "modern science." Like other true believers, they were therefore spared the task of taking others' viewpoints seriously or wondering about the limits of their own vision of historical truth.

But we are denied the luxury of such parochialism. We must reckon with multiplex, competing faiths—secular as well as transcendental, revolutionary as well as traditional—that resound amongst us. In addition, partially autonomous professional idea-systems have proliferated in the past century or so. Those most important to historians are the so-called social sciences—anthropology, sociology, political science, psychology, and economics—together with the newer disciplines of ecology and semeiology. But law, theology, and philosophy also pervade the field of knowledge with which historians may be expected to deal. On top of all this, innumerable individual authors, each with his own assortment of ideas and assumptions, compete for attention. Choice is everywhere; dissent turns into cacaphonous confusion; my truth dissolves into your myth even before I can put words on paper.

The liberal faith, of course, holds that in a free marketplace of ideas, Truth will eventually prevail. I am not ready to abandon that faith, however dismaying our present confusion may be. The liberal experiment, after all, is only about two hundred and fifty years old, and on the appropriate world-historical time scale that is too soon to be sure. Still, confusion is undoubted. Whether the resulting uncertainty will be bearable for large numbers of people in difficult times ahead is a question worth asking. Iranian Muslims, Russian communists, and American sectarians (religious and otherwise) all exhibit symptoms of acute distress in face of moral uncertainties, generated by exposure to competing truths. Clearly, the will to believe is as strong today as at any time in the past; and true believers nearly always wish to create a community of the faithful, so as to be able to live more comfortably, insulated from troublesome dissent.

The prevailing response to an increasingly cosmopolitan confusion has been intensified personal attachment, first to national and then to subnational groups, each with its own distinct ideals and practices. As one would expect, the historical profession faithfully reflected and helped to forward these shifts of sentiment. Thus, the founding fathers of the American Historical Association and their immediate successors were intent on facilitating the consolidation of a new American nation by writing national history in a WASPish mold, while also claiming affiliation with a tradition of Western civilization that ran back through modern and medieval Europe to the ancient Greeks and Hebrews. This version of our past was very widely repudiated in the 1960s, but iconoclastic revisionists felt no need to replace what they attacked with any architectonic vision of their own. Instead, scholarly energy concentrated on discovering the history of various segments of the population that had been left out or ill-treated by older historians: most notably women, blacks, and other ethnic minorities within the United States and the ex-colonial peoples of the world beyond the national borders.

Such activity conformed to our traditional professional role of helping to define collective identities in ambiguous situations. Consciousness of a common past, after all, is a powerful supplement to other ways of defining who "we" are. An oral tradition, sometimes almost undifferentiated from the practical wisdom embodied in language itself, is all people need in a stable social universe where in-group boundaries are self-evident. But with civilization, ambiguities multipled, and formal written history became useful in defining "us" versus "them." At first, the central ambiguity ran between rulers and ruled. Alien conquerors who lived on taxes collected from their subjects were at best a necessary evil when looked at from the bottom of civilized society. Yet in some situations, especially when confronting natural disaster or external attack, a case could be made for commonality, even between taxpayers and tax consumers. At any rate, histories began as king lists, royal genealogies, and boasts of divine favor—obvious ways of consolidating rulers' morale and asserting their legitimacy vis-à-vis their subjects. . . .

All human groups like to be flattered. Historians are therefore under perpetual temptation to conform to expectation by portraying the people they write about as they wish to be. A mingling of truth and falsehood, blending history with ideology, results. Historians are likely to select facts to show that we—whoever "we" may be—conform to our cherished principles: that we are free with Herodotus, or saved with Augustine, or oppressed with Marx, as the case may be. Grubby details indicating that the group fell short of its ideals can be skated over or omitted entirely. The result is mythical: the past as we want it to be, safely simplified into a contest between good guys and bad guys, "us" and "them." Most national history and most group history is of this kind, though the intensity of chiaroscuro varies greatly, and sometimes an historian turns traitor to the group he studies by setting out to unmask its pretensions. Groups struggling toward self-consciousness and groups whose accustomed status seems threatened are likely to demand (and get) vivid, simplified portraits of their admirable virtues and undeserved sufferings. Groups accustomed to power and surer of their internal cohesion can afford to accept more subtly modulated portraits of their successes and failures in bringing practice into conformity with principles.

Historians respond to this sort of market by expressing varying degrees of commitment to, and detachment from, the causes they chronicle and by infusing varying degrees of emotional intensity into their pages through particular choices of words. Truth, persuasiveness, intelligibility rest far more on this level of the historians' art than on source criticism. But, as I said at the beginning, one person's truth is another's myth, and the fact that a group of people accepts a given version of the past does not make that version any truer for outsiders.

Yet we cannot afford to reject collective self-flattery as silly, contemptible error. Myths are, after all, often self-validating. A nation or any other human group that knows how to behave in crisis situations because it has inherited a heroic historiographical tradition that tells how ancestors resisted their enemies successfully is more likely to act together effectively than a group lacking such a tradition. Great Britain's conduct in 1940 shows how world politics can be redirected by such a heritage. Flattering historiography does more than assist a given group to survive by affecting the balance of power among warring peoples, for an appropriately idealized version of the past may also allow a group of human beings to come closer to living up to its noblest ideals. What is can move toward what ought to be, given collective commitment to a flattering self-image. The American civil rights movement of the fifties and sixties illustrates this phenomenon amongst us.

These collective manifestations are of very great importance. Belief in the virtue and righteousness of one's cause is a necessary sort of self-delusion for human beings, singly and collectively. A corrosive version of history that emphasizes all the recurrent discrepancies between ideal and reality in a given group's behavior makes it harder for members of the group in question to act cohesively and in good conscience. That sort of history is very costly indeed. No group can afford it for long.

On the other hand, myths may mislead disastrously. A portrait of the past that denigrates others and praises the ideals and practice of a given group naively and without restraint can distort a people's image of outsiders so that foreign relations begin to consist of nothing but nasty surprises. Confidence in one's own high principles and good intentions may simply provoke others to resist duly accredited missionaries of the true faith, whatever that faith may be. Both the United States and the Soviet Union have encountered their share of this sort of surprise and disappointment ever since 1917, when Wilson and Lenin proclaimed their respective recipes for curing the world's ills. In more extreme cases, mythical, self-flattering versions of the past may push a people toward suicidal behavior, as Hitler's last days may remind us.

More generally, it is obvious that mythical, self-flattering versions of rival groups' pasts simply serve to intensify their capacity for conflict. With the recent quantum jump in the destructive power of weaponry, hardening of group cohesion at the sovereign state level clearly threatens the survival of humanity; while, within national borders, the civic order experiences new strains when sub-national groups acquire a historiography replete with oppressors living next door and, perchance, still enjoying the fruits of past injustices.

The great historians have always responded to these difficulties by expanding their sympathies beyond narrow in-group boundaries. Herodotus set out to award a due meed of glory both to Hellenes and to the barbarians; Ranke inquired into what really happened to Protestant and Catholic, Latin and German nations alike. And other pioneers of our profession have likewise expanded the range of their sympathies and sensibilities beyond previously recognized limits without ever entirely escaping, or even wishing to escape, from the sort of partisanship involved in accepting the general assumptions and beliefs of a particular time and place.

Where to fix one's loyalties is the supreme question of human life and is especially acute in a cosmopolitan age like ours when choices abound. Belonging to a tightly knit group makes life worth living by giving individuals something beyond the self to serve and to rely on for personal guidance, companionship, and aid. But the stronger such bonds, the sharper the break with the rest of humanity. Group solidarity is always maintained, at least partly, by exporting psychic frictions across the frontiers, projecting animosities onto an outside foe in order to enhance collective cohesion within the group itself. Indeed, something to fear, hate, and attack is probably necessary for the full expression of human emotions; and ever since animal predators ceased to threaten, human beings have feared, hated, and fought one another.

Historians, by helping to define "us" and "them," play a considerable part in focusing love and hate, the two principal cements of collective behavior known to humanity. But myth making for rival groups has become a dangerous game in the atomic age, and we may well ask whether there is any alternative open to us.

In principle the answer is obvious. Humanity entire possesses a commonality which historians may hope to understand just as firmly as they can comprehend what unites any lesser group. Instead of enhancing conflicts, as parochial historiography inevitably does, an intelligible world history might be expected to diminish the lethality of group encounters by cultivating a sense of individual identification with the triumphs and tribulations of humanity as a whole. This, indeed, strikes me as the moral duty of the historical profession in our time. We need to develop an ecumenical history, with plenty of room for human diversity in all its complexity.

Yet a wise historian will not denigrate intense attachment to small groups. That is essential to personal happiness. In all civilized societies, a tangle of overlapping social groupings lays claim to human loyalties. Any one person may therefore be expected to have multiple commitments and plural public identities, up to and including membership in the human race and the wider DNA community of life on planet Earth. What we need to do as historians and as human beings is to recognize this complexity and balance our loyalties so that no one group will be able to command total commitment. Only so can we hope to make the world safer for all the different human groups that now exist and may come into existence.

The historical profession has, however, shied away from an ecumenical view of the human adventure. Professional career patterns reward specialization; and in all the well-trodden fields, where pervasive consensus on important matters has already been achieved, research and innovation necessarily concentrate upon minutiae. Residual faith that truth somehow resides in original documents confirms this direction of our energies. An easy and commonly unexamined corollary is the assumption that world history is too vague and too general to be true, that is, accurate to the sources. Truth, according to this view, is only attainable on a tiny scale when the diligent historian succeeds in exhausting the relevant documents before they exhaust the historian. But as my previous remarks have made clear, this does not strike me as a valid view of historical method. On the contrary, I call it naive and erroneous.

All truths are general. All truths abstract from the available assortment of data simply by using words, which in their very nature generalize so as to bring order to the incessantly fluctuating flow of messages in and messages out that constitutes human consciousness. Total reproduction of experience is impossible and undesirable. It would merely perpetuate the confusion we seek to escape. Historiography that aspires to get closer and closer to the documents—all the documents and nothing but the documents—is merely moving closer and closer to incoherence, chaos, and meaninglessness. That is a dead end for sure. No society will long support a profession that produces arcane trivia and calls it truth.

Fortunately for the profession, historians' practice has been better than their epistemology. Instead of replicating confusion by paraphrasing the totality of relevant and available documents, we have used our sources to discern, support, and reinforce group identities at national, transnational, and subnational levels and, once in a while, to attack or pick apart a group identity to which a school of revisionists has taken a scunner.

If we can now realize that our practice already shows how truths may be discerned at different levels of generality with equal precision simply because different patterns emerge on different time-space scales, then, perhaps, repugnance for world history might diminish and a juster proportion between parochial and ecumenical historiography might begin to emerge. It is our professional duty to move toward ecumenicity, however real the risks may seem to timid and unenterprising minds.

With a more rigorous and reflective epistemology, we might also attain a better historiographical balance between Truth, truths, and myth. Eternal and universal Truth about human behavior is an unattainable goal, however delectable as an ideal. Truths are what historians achieve when they bend their minds as critically and carefully as they can to the task of making their account of public affairs credible as well as intelligible to an audience that shares enough of their particular outlook and assumptions to accept what they say. The result might best be called mythistory perhaps (though I do not expect the term to catch on in professional circles), for the same words that constitute truth for some are, and always will be, myth for others, who inherit or embrace different assumptions and organizing concepts about the world.

This does not mean that there is no difference between one mythistory and another. Some clearly are more adequate to the facts than others. Some embrace more time and space and make sense of a wider variety of human behavior than others. And some, undoubtedly, offer a less treacherous basis for collective action than others. I actually believe that historians' truths, like those of scientists, evolve across the generations, so that versions of the past acceptable today are superior in scope, range, and accuracy to versions available in earlier times. But such evolution is slow, and observable only on an extended time scale, owing to the self-validating character of myth. Effective common action can rest on quite fantastic beliefs. *Credo quia absurdum* may even become a criterion for group membership, requiring initiates to surrender their critical faculties as a sign of full commitment to the common cause. Many sects have prospered on this principle and have served their members well for many generations while doing so.

But faiths, absurd or not, also face a long-run test of survival in a world where not everyone accepts anyone set of beliefs and where human beings must interact with external objects and nonhuman forms of life, as well as with one another. Such "foreign relations" impose limits on what any group of people can safely believe and act on, since actions that fail to secure expected and desired results are always costly and often disastrous. Beliefs that mislead action are likely to be amended; too stubborn an adherence to a faith that encourages or demands hurtful behavior is likely to lead to the disintegration and disappearance of any group that refuses to learn from experience.

Thus one may, as an act of faith, believe that our historiographical myth making and myth breaking is bound to cumulate across time, propagating mythistories that fit experience better and allow human survival more often, sustaining in-groups in ways that are less destructive to themselves and to their neighbors than was once the case or is the case today. If so, ever-evolving mythistories will indeed become truer and more adequate to public life, emphasizing the really important aspects of human encounters and omitting irrelevant background noise more efficiently so that men and women will know how to act more wisely than is possible for us today.

This is not a groundless hope. Future historians are unlikely to leave out blacks and women from any future mythistory of the United States, and we are unlikely to exclude Asians, Africans, and Amerindians from any future mythistory of the world. One hundred years ago this was not so. The scope and range of historiography has widened, and that change looks as irreversible to me as the widening of physics that occurred when Einstein's equations proved capable of explaining phenomena that Newton's could not.

It is far less clear whether in widening the range of our sensibilities and taking a broader range of phenomena into account we also see deeper into the reality we seek to understand. But we may. Anyone who reads historians of the sixteenth and seventeenth centuries and those of our own time will notice a new awareness of social process that we have attained. As one who shares that awareness, I find it impossible not to believe that it represents an advance on older notions that focused attention exclusively, or almost exclusively, on human intentions and individual actions, subject only to God or to a no less inscrutable Fortune, while leaving out the social and material context within which individual actions took place simply because that context was assumed to be uniform and unchanging.

Still, what seems wise and true to me seems irrelevant obfuscation to others. Only time can settle the issue, presumably by outmoding my ideas and my critics' as well. Unalterable and eternal Truth remains like the Kingdom of Heaven, an eschatological hope. Mythistory is what we actually have—a useful instrument for piloting human groups in their encounters with one another and with the natural environment.

To be a truth-seeking mythographer is therefore a high and serious calling, for what a group of people knows and believes about the past channels expectations and affects the decisions on which their lives, their fortunes, and their sacred honor all depend. Formal written histories are not the only shapers of a people's notions about the past; but they are sporadically powerful, since even the most abstract and academic historiographical ideas do trickle down to the level of the commonplace, if they fit both what a people want to hear and what a people need to know well enough to be useful.

As members of society and sharers in the historical process, historians can only expect to be heard if they say what the people around them want to hear—in some degree. They can only be useful if they also tell the people some things they are reluctant to hear—in some degree. Piloting between this Scylla and Charybdis is the art of the serious historian, helping the group he or she addresses and celebrates to survive and prosper in a treacherous and changing world by knowing more about itself and others.

Academic historians have pursued that art with extraordinary energy and considerable success during the past century. May our heirs and successors persevere and do even better!

POSTSCRIPT

Is History True?

Closely associated to the question of historical truth is the matter of historical objectivity. Frequently, we hear people begin statements with the phrase "History tells us . . ." or "History shows that . . . ," followed by a conclusion that reflects the speaker or writer's point of view. In fact, history does not directly tell or show us anything. That is the job of historians, and as William McNeill argues, much of what historians tell us, despite their best intentions, often represents a blending of historical evidence and myth.

Is there such a thing as a truly objective history? Historian Paul Conkin agrees with McNeill that objectivity is possible only if the meaning of that term is sharply restricted and is not used as a synonym for certain truth. History, Conkin writes, "is a story about the past; it is not the past itself. . . . Whether one draws a history from the guidance of memory or of monuments, it cannot exactly mirror some directly experienced past nor the feelings and perceptions of people in the past." He concludes, "In this sense, much of history is a stab into partial darkness, a matter of informed but inconclusive conjecture. . . . Obviously, in such areas of interpretation, there is no one demonstrably correct 'explanation,' but very often competing, equally unfalsifiable, theories. Here, on issues that endlessly fascinate the historian, the controversies rage, and no one expects, short of a great wealth of unexpected evidence, to find a conclusive answer. An undesired, abstractive precision of the subject might so narrow it as to permit more conclusive evidence. But this would spoil all the fun." For more discussion on this and other topics related to the study of history, see Paul K. Conkin and Roland N. Stromberg, *The Heritage and Challenge of History* (Dodd, Mead & Company, 1971).

The most thorough discussion of historical objectivity in the United States is Peter Novick, *That Noble Dream: The 'Objectivity Question' and the American Historical Profession* (Cambridge University Press, 1988), which draws its title from Charles A. Beard's article in the *American Historical Review* (October 1935) in which Beard reinforced the views expressed in his 1933 presidential address to the American Historical Association. (See "Written History as an Act of Faith," *American Historical Review* [January 1934].) Novick's thorough analysis generated a great deal of attention, the results of which can be followed in James T. Kloppenberg, "Objectivity and Historicism: A Century of American Historical Writing," *American Historical Review* (October 1989); Thomas L. Haskell, "Objectivity Is Not Neutrality: Rhetoric vs. Practice in Peter Novick's *That Noble Dream*," *History & Theory* (1990); and the scholarly forum "Peter Novick's *That Noble Dream*: The Objectivity Question and the Future of the Historical Profession," *American Historical Review* (June 1991). A critique of recent historical writing that closely follows the concerns expressed by

Handlin can be found in Keith Windschuttle, *The Killing of History: How Literary Critics and Social Theorists Are Murdering Our Past* (The Free Press, 1996).

Readers interested in this subject will also find the analyses in Barbara W. Tuchman, *Practicing History: Selected Essays* (Alfred A. Knopf, 1981); and David Hackett Fischer, *Historians' Fallacies: Toward a Logic of Historical Thought* (Harper & Row, 1970) to be quite stimulating. Earlier, though equally rewarding, volumes include Harvey Wish, *The American Historian: A Social-Intellectual History of the Writing of the American Past* (Oxford University Press, 1960); John Higham, with Leonard Krieger and Felix Gilbert, *History: The Development of Historical Studies in the United States* (Prentice-Hall, 1965); and Marcus Cunliffe and Robin Winks, eds., *Pastmasters: Some Essays on American Historians* (Harper & Row, 1969).

ISSUE 2

Did the Chinese Discover America?

YES: Gavin Menzies, from *1421: The Year China Discovered America* (William Morrow, 2003)

NO: Robert Finlay, from "How Not to (Re)Write World History: Gavin Menzies and the Chinese Discovery of America," *Journal of World History* (June 2004)

ISSUE SUMMARY

YES: Gavin Menzies surmises that between 1421 and 1423 a Chinese fleet spent four months exploring the Pacific coastline of North America and leaving behind substantial evidence to support his contention that the Chinese discovered America long before the arrival of European explorers.

NO: Robert Finlay accuses Menzies of ignoring the basic rules of historical study and logic to concoct an implausible interpretation of Chinese discovery based upon a misreading of Chinese imperial policy, misrepresentation of sources, and conjecture that has no evidentiary base.

"**I**n fourteen hundred ninety-two/Columbus sailed the ocean blue." For generations of school children in the United States in the twentieth century, these two lines marked their introduction to American history. What followed from their teachers was a recounting of a story that the vast majority of Americans still accept as true. We do know that on October 12, 1492, Christopher Columbus (Cristobal Colon; Cristoforo Colombo), a Genoese mariner sailing under the flag and patronage of the Spanish monarchy, made landfall on a tropical Caribbean island, which he subsequently named San Salvador. This action established for Columbus the fame of having discovered the New World and, by extension, America. Of course, this "discovery" was ironic because Columbus and his crew members were not looking for a new world but, instead, a very old one—the much-fabled Orient. By sailing westward instead of eastward, Columbus was certain that he would find a shorter route to China. He did not anticipate that the land mass of the Americas would prevent him from reaching this goal or that his "failure" would guarantee his fame for centuries thereafter.

Over the course of the five centuries that have followed, there have been efforts to revise the historical record pertaining to Columbus's voyages (there were four that took place between 1492 and 1504) as a means of calling into question this traditional portrait of discovery. First, none of Columbus's expeditions explored the coastlines of the region that would become the United States. That particular credit went to Amerigo Vespucci, although modern scholars question whether he, in fact, explored the coasts of Central America, the Gulf of Mexico, and the South Atlantic shoreline of North America in the late 1490s. True or not, it was Vespucci's name that was attached to this landmass in 1507 by cartographer Martin Waldseemüller. Second, even earlier, the Norsemen had visited the eastern coasts of present-day Canada and perhaps even New England during a series of voyages from the eleventh to the fourteenth centuries. Third, Columbus's encounter with indigenous peoples whom he named "Indians" (*los indios*) raises obvious questions about the validity of the traditional Eurocentric model of discovery. The presence of significant numbers of these Indians (or Native Americans) provides very strong evidence that Europeans had not discovered America.

Anthropological studies tell us that these "Indians" were descendants of the first people who migrated from Asia at least 30,000 years earlier and fanned out in a southeasterly direction until they had populated much of North and South America. By the time of Columbus, Native Americans numbered approximately 40 million, 3 million of whom resided in the continental region north of Mexico.

None of this, however, should dilute the significance of Columbus's explorations, which were representative of a wave of Atlantic voyages emanating from Europe in the fifteenth, sixteenth, and seventeenth centuries. Spawned by the intellectual ferment of the Renaissance in combination with the rise of the European nation-state, these voyages of exploration were made possible by advances in shipbuilding, improved navigational instruments and cartography, the desirability of long-distance commerce, support from ruling monarchs, and, to be sure, the courage and ambition of the explorers themselves.

The consequences of Columbus's expeditions attracted a significant amount of scholarly and media attention in 1992 in connection with the quincentennial celebration of Columbus's first voyage. More recently, however, the story of American discovery has taken a dramatically different turn with the fanfare surrounding the argument that it is the Chinese, not the Europeans, who deserve recognition as the discoverers of America.

Gavin Menzies, a retired British submarine officer, contends that in 1421, seven decades before Columbus set sail from Spain, the Chinese armada, comprised of four fleets of ships, set sail for a voyage around the world that would take two and a half years. During this voyage, Menzies argues, one of the fleets under the direction of Admiral Zhou Man spent four months exploring the Pacific coastline of North America, including present-day California, and left behind evidence of Chinese colonization in the form of Chinese plants, animals, and ceramics.

Menzies's interpretation is challenged directly by Robert Finlay in a rejoinder that is at times humorous and at others blistering. Finlay assails Menzies for ignoring the most basic precepts of scholarly research, and in a point-by-point critique, concludes that the voyages described by Menzies are not supported by surviving documentation but rather are the product of baseless conjecture.

YES

Gavin Menzies

1421: The Year China Discovered America

The Emperor's Grand Plan

On 2 February 1421, China dwarfed every nation on earth. On that Chinese New Year's Day, kings and envoys from the length and breadth of Asia, Arabia, Africa and the Indian Ocean assembled amid the splendours of Beijing to pay homage to the Emperor Zhu Di, the Son of Heaven. A fleet of leviathan ships, navigating the oceans with pinpoint accuracy, had brought the rulers and their envoys to pay tribute to the emperor and bear witness to the inauguration of his majestic and mysterious walled capital, the Forbidden City. No fewer than twenty-eight heads of state were present, but the Holy Roman Emperor, the Emperor of Byzantium, the Doge of Venice and the kings of England, France, Spain and Portugal were not among them. They had not been invited, for such backward states, lacking trade goods or any worthwhile scientific knowledge, ranked low on the Chinese emperor's scale of priorities. . . .

This array of foreign heads of state kow-towing before the emperor was the culmination of fifteen years' assiduous diplomacy. Chinese foreign policy was quite different from that of the Europeans who followed them to the Indian Ocean many years later. The Chinese preferred to pursue their aims by trade, influence and bribery rather than by open conflict and direct colonization. Zhu Di's policy was to despatch huge armadas every few years throughout the known world, bearing gifts and trade goods; the massive treasure ships carrying a huge array of guns and a travelling army of soldiers were also a potent reminder of his imperial might: China alone had the necessary firepower to protect friendly countries from invasion and quash insurrections against their rulers. The treasure ships returned to China with all manner of exotic items: 'dragon saliva [ambergris], incense and golden amber' and 'lions, gold spotted leopards and camel-birds [ostriches] which are six or seven feet tall' from Africa; gold cloth from Calicut in south-west India, studded with pearls and precious stones; elephants, parrots, sandalwood, peacocks, hardwood, incense, tin and cardamom from Siam (modern Thailand). . . .

For a further month after the inauguration of the Forbidden City, the rulers and envoys in Beijing were provided with lavish imperial hospitality— the finest foods and wines, the most splendid entertainments and the most

From *1421: The Year China Discovered America* by Gavin Menzies (William Morrow, 2003), pp. 19, 33, 37–38, 42–43, 199–200, 201–204, 206–210 (excerpts). Copyright © 2003 by Gavin Menzies. Reprinted by permission of HarperCollins Publishers.

beautiful concubines, skilled in the arts of love. Finally, on 3 March 1421, a great ceremony was mounted to commemorate the departure of the envoys for their native lands. . . . The emperor appeared, striding through the smoke to present the departing ambassadors with their farewell gifts—crates of blue and white porcelain, rolls of silk, bundles of cotton cloth and bamboo cases of jade. His great fleets stood ready to carry them back to Hormuz, Aden, La'Sa and Dhofar in Arabia; to Mogadishu, Brava, Malindi and Mombasa in Africa; to Sri Lanka, Calicut, Cochin and Cambay in India; to Japan, Vietnam, Java, Sumatra, Malacca and Borneo in south-east Asia, and elsewhere.

Admiral Zheng He, dressed in his formal uniform, a long red robe, presented the emperor with his compliments and reported that an armada comprising four of the emperor's great fleets was ready to set sail; the fifth, commanded by Grand Eunuch Yang Qing, had put to sea the previous month. The return of the envoys to their homelands was only the first part of this armada's overall mission. It was then to 'proceed all the way to the end of the earth to collect tribute from the barbarians beyond the seas . . . to attract all under heaven to be civilised in Confucian harmony'. Zheng He's reward for his lifelong, devoted service to his emperor had been the command of five previous treasure fleets tasked with promoting Chinese trade and influence in Asia, India, Africa and the Middle East. Now he was to lead one of the largest armadas the world had ever seen. Zhu Di had also rewarded other eunuchs for their part in helping him to liberate China. Many of the army commanders in the war against the Mongols were now admirals and captains of his treasure fleets. Zheng He had become a master of delegation. By the fourth voyage fleets were sailing separately. On this great sixth voyage loyal eunuchs would command separate fleets. Zheng He would lead them to the Indian Ocean then return home confident that they would handle their fleets as he had taught them. . . .

As the admirals and envoys embarked, and the armada was readied for sea, the water around the great ships was still black with smaller craft shuttling from ship to shore. For days the port had been in turmoil as cartloads of vegetables and dried fish and hundreds of tons of water were hauled aboard to provision this armada of thirty thousand men for their voyage. Even at this late hour, barges were still bringing final supplies of fresh water and rice. The great armada's ships could remain at sea for over three months and cover at least 4,500 miles without making landfall to replenish food or water, for separate grain ships and water tankers sailed with them. The grain ships also carried an array of flora the Chinese intended to plant in foreign lands, some as further benefits of the tribute system and others to provide food for the Chinese colonies that would be created in new lands. Dogs were also taken aboard as pets, others to be bred for food and to hunt rats, and there were coops of Asiatic chickens as valuable presents for foreign dignitaries. Separate horse-ships carried the mounts for the cavalry.

The staggering size of the individual ships, not to mention the armada itself, can only be understood in comparison with other navies of the same era. In 1421, the next most powerful fleet afloat was that of Venice. The Venetians possessed around three hundred galleys—fast, light, thin-skinned ships built with softwood planking, rowed by oarsmen and only suitable for island-hopping in the calm of a Mediterranean summer. The biggest Venetian galleys were some 150 feet long and 20 feet wide and carried at best 50 tons of cargo. In comparison, Zhu Di's treasure ships were ocean-going monsters built of teak. The rudder of one of these great ships stood 36 feet high—almost as long as the whole of the flagship the *Niña* in which Columbus was later to set sail for the New World. Each treasure ship could carry more than two thousand tons of cargo and reach Malacca in five weeks, Hormuz in the Persian Gulf in twelve. They were capable of sailing the wildest oceans of the world, in voyages lasting years at a time. That so many ships were lost on the Chinese voyages of discovery testifies not to any lack of strength in their construction but rather to the perilous, uncharted waters they explored, from rocky coasts and razor-sharp coral reefs to the ice-strewn oceans of the far north and far south. Venetian galleys were protected by archers; Chinese ships were armed with gunpowder weapons, brass and iron cannon, mortars, flaming arrows and exploding shells that sprayed excrement over their adversaries. In every single respect—construction, cargo capacity, damage control, armament, range, communications, the ability to navigate in the trackless ocean and to repair and maintain their ships at sea for months on end—the Chinese were centuries ahead of Europe. Admiral Zheng He would have had no difficulty in destroying any fleet that crossed his path. A battle between this Chinese armada and the other navies of the world combined would have resembled one between a pack of sharks and a shoal of sprats.

By the end of the middle watch—four in the morning—the last provisions had been lashed down and the armada weighed anchor. A prayer was said to Shao Lin, Taoist goddess of the sea, and then, as their red silk sails slowly filled, the ships, resembling great houses, gathered way before the winds of the north-east monsoon. As they sailed out across the Yellow Sea, the last flickering lights of Tanggu faded into the darkness while the sailors clustered at the rails, straining for a last sight of their homeland. In the long months they would spend travelling the oceans, their only remaining links to the land would be memories, keepsakes and the scented roses many brought with them, growing them in pots and even sharing their water rations with them. The majority of those seamen at the rails would never see China again. Many would die, many others would be shipwrecked or left behind to set up colonies on foreign shores. . . .

The First Colony in the Americas

. . . I knew that Zhou Man had arrived in Nanjing on 8 October 1423, carrying no foreign envoys. What had he been doing and where had he sailed in the four months he had been in the Pacific?

The north Pacific is a vast circulatory system, with winds constantly blowing in a clockwise oval direction. In June, the prevailing wind off Leyte is to the north. As Admiral Zhou Man's fleet entered the Pacific, the Kuroshio or Japanese current would also have carried them northwards before starting a clockwise sweep towards the coast of North America. In fact, had Zhou Man simply unfurled his sails off Leyte, the winds and currents would have carried him to the Pacific coast of modern Canada. The California current would then have taken over, sweeping the fleet southwards down the western seaboard of the United States to Panama. From there, the north equatorial current would carry a square-rigged ship back across the Pacific towards the Philippines. The whole round trip, before the wind and current all the way, would have been about sixteen thousand nautical miles. At an average of 4.8 knots, the voyage would have taken some four months, matching the date of Zhou Man's return to Nanjing in October. My surmise . . . was that squadrons of ships from the main fleet were detached to establish colonies along the Pacific coast from California down to Ecuador.

I began the search for corroboration that Zhou Man's fleet had indeed reached the Pacific coast of North America. The first European to explore that coast was Hernando de Alarcón in 1540. Having sought fame and fortune in New Spain, he left Acapulco on 9 May of that year in command of a fleet supporting the conquistador Coronado's expedition to New Mexico. Alarcón first charted the peninsula of Bahía California, and then California itself. I knew that he was the first European to chart it, for neither Columbus nor any of the other early explorers reached any part of the west coast of North America, so any map of the Pacific coast pre-dating Alarcón's voyage would be powerful evidence that he was not the first to reach it.

Such evidence does exist in the form of the Waldseemüller world map, a beautifully coloured large map published in 1507 and the first to chart latitude and longitude with precision. Originally owned by Johannes Schöner (1477–1547), a Nuremberg astronomer and geographer, it had long been thought lost and was only rediscovered in 1901 in the castle of Wolfegg in southern Germany. It remained there in relative obscurity until 2001, when in a blaze of publicity the US Library of Congress acquired it from Prince Johannes Waldburg-Wolfegg for ten million dollars. The man who drew the map, Martin Waldseemüller (c. 1470–1518), was German-born and one of the foremost cosmographers—combining the study of geography and astronomy—of his era. . . .

The Pacific coast of America is strikingly drawn on the Waldseemüller chart and the latitudes correspond to those of Vancouver Island in Canada right down to Ecuador in the south. This is completely consistent with a cartographer aboard a ship sailing down the Pacific coast, but not charting the coast in great detail. Oregon is clearly identifiable, and several very old wrecks have been discovered there on the beach at Neahkahnie. One was of teak with a pulley for hoisting sails made of caeophyllum, a wood unique to south-east Asia. The wood has yet to be carbon-dated, but if it proves to be from the early fifteenth century it will provide strong circumstantial evidence that one of Zhou Man's junks was wrecked in Neahkahnie Bay. Some examiners of the wreckage there claim to have found paraffin wax, which was used by Zheng He's fleet to desalinate sea-water for the horses.

Even without finds from wrecked junks, the Pacific coasts of Central and South America are full of evidence of Chinese voyages. The Asiatic chickens found from Chile to California . . . and many other flora and fauna were carried across the globe by the Chinese fleets. On my first visit to California many years ago, I remember coming across a bank of beautiful camellia roses (*Rosa laevigata*). It was a still summer's evening and their lovely fragrance filled the air around me. In 1803, European settlers found a beautiful fragrant rose growing wild; they named it the Cherokee Rose. Yet it was indigenous to south-east China and had been illustrated in a twelfth-century Chinese pharmacopoeia. 'When and by what means it reached America is one of the unsolved problems of plant introductions,' but it was a common practice for sailors aboard Zheng He's junks to keep pots of roses, their scent an enduring reminder of home. The Chinese also took plants and seeds home with them. Amaranth, a native North American grain with a high protein content, was brought from America to Asia in the early fifteenth century, as of course was maize—brought to the Philippines and seen there by Magellan. Coconuts, native to the South Pacific, were found by the first Europeans on the Pacific coasts of Costa Rica, Panama and Ecuador and on Cocos Island west of Costa Rica. The carriers of grain from the Americas to Asia, of roses and chickens from China to the Americas, and coconuts from the South Pacific to Ecuador can only have been the Chinese.

San Francisco and Los Angeles are clearly depicted at the correct latitudes on the Waldseemüller chart, and I was certain that Zhou Man must have sailed down that coast. Crossing such an enormous expanse of ocean after two years at sea must have left some of his junks in bad condition and in urgent need of repair. Even the best-built ships could not remain at sea for such long periods without suffering at least some damage from storms and the pounding of the waves. At the very least they would have required running repairs and careening—scraping the barnacles from their hulls—and the most badly damaged might well have been cannibalized to repair the others. If so, the remains of these wrecked ships should have been found off the coast of California, just as other wrecks had been in Australia and other parts of the globe.

My enquiries into strange wrecks on the coast of California drew a blank, but I did discover that museums there held substantial quantities of Ming blue and white ceramics. The accepted wisdom is that these items were brought to California in the holds of Spanish galleons, but a number of medieval Chinese anchors have been found off the California coast, and these are unlikely to have been brought by Spanish ships. I began to question seriously the provenance of the Ming porcelain; had it really been brought by the Spanish? Medieval Chinese porcelain can be dated by its cobalt content: the greater the amount of iron in the cobalt, the deeper blue the glaze. The dark cobalt of the Mongol era came from Persia, also ruled by the Mongols, but Zhu Di's father sealed the Chinese borders after he drove out the Mongols in 1368 and Persian cobalt was no longer available. However, Zhu Di reopened the frontiers and restored trade along the Silk Road through Asia allowing Persian cobalt to be imported once more. The period when Chinese pale blue porcelain was produced and used in Ming China is thus limited, and the colour of the porcelain held by Californian museums would indicate whether or not it was made during this period in China's history.

I was certain that a great treasure fleet had discovered the Pacific coasts of North and South America, but my researches failed to uncover conclusive evidence such as the wreck of a Chinese junk. In the hope that others might have found traces I had missed, I decided to 'go public' on the issue in a lecture at the Royal Geographical Society in London in March 2002. It was broadcast around the world; within forty-eight hours reports began to come in from California, drawing my attention to the wreck of a medieval Chinese junk buried under a sandbank in the Sacramento River off the north-east corner of San Francisco Bay. My first reaction was to discount the reports—the site was more than a hundred miles from open sea and the discovery seemed too good to be true—but over the next few days more e-mails describing the same junk continued to arrive. As soon as I had carried out some preliminary research, I discovered that the prevailing north-easterly winds on this coast could have blown a junk straight across the bay and into the Sacramento River. Six centuries ago the river was broader and deeper than today, for deforestation has reduced rain- and snowfall in the area causing the water level to fall. It was indeed possible, if not probable, that a junk entering San Francisco Bay would have been driven by the winds into the Sacramento River.

Dr John Furry of the Natural History Museum of Northern California first became aware of the junk twenty years ago when he read an account of the strange armour that once had been found in its hold (the wreck was then evidently less deeply buried in sand and silt than it is now). The armour was of an unusual metal (native Americans did not know how to forge metal) and curiously silver-grey in colour. It was shown to a local expert who is said to have identified it as of medieval Chinese origin. Dr Furry's attempts to pursue the story met a brick wall—the expert had died in the intervening years, and the armour had been lent to a local school and was now lost—but he was sufficiently intrigued to begin investigating the wreck-site.

The site was covered with a 40-foot layer of the accumulated sand and silt of centuries, so Dr Furry began by taking magnetometer readings of the area. These showed a strong magnetic anomaly outlining a buried object 85 feet long and 30 feet wide, very similar in size and shape to the trading junks that accompanied Zheng He's fleets. Core samples were then extracted from the site. The fragments of wood brought up were carbon-dated to 1410, indicating that the junk was built in that year, 'a period that included a maritime highpoint for the ancient Chinese', as local newspapers laconically reported.

The evidence from the carbon-dating encouraged Dr Furry to drill again with more sophisticated equipment. This yielded much larger samples including further pieces of wood and a compacted 80lb mass of millions of black seeds. He sent fragments of the wood and the seeds to China for analysis, and according to Dr Furry, the Chinese Academy of Forestry have provisionally identified the wood as Keteleria, a conifer native to south-east China but not to North America. In the Middle Ages, the Chinese cultivated Keteleria for ship-building. Dr Furry also told me that Dr Zhang Wenxu, a former professor at the Chinese Agricultural University in Beijing and the leading Chinese expert on ancient seeds, had provisionally identified four different types of seeds in the black mass brought up from the wreck-site. Three were native to both China and North America, but the other was found only in China. Most interesting of all, however, was Dr Furry's further discovery of rice grains and the body of a beetle among the material raised. Rice, indigenous to Africa and China, was unknown in the Americas in the fifteenth century. Further analysis of the rice and the beetle is being carried out as I write, but to date no written reports on the analysis of the wood or the seeds have been received from China.

I now had little doubt that the site contained the wreck of a Chinese junk; it was exactly the evidence I had been looking for. It seemed highly improbable that the crew would have drowned when the junk grounded on the sandbank in the Sacramento River. It was far more likely that they had come ashore onto the lush, fertile lands of the valley. Their first task would have been to rescue as much rice as possible from the holds of the ship. Much would have been needed to meet their short-term food requirements, but they would also have set some aside as seed and planted it in a suitable location— the floodplain of the Sacramento River.

It has long been claimed that rice was introduced to West Africa by Europeans and then to the Americas by the Spanish, but Professor Judith A. Carney of the University of California has argued that this thesis is fundamentally flawed. It is widely accepted that the Chinese made a major contribution to developing agriculture in the rich soils of California, particularly the cultivation of rice in the swamplands of the lower Sacramento. By the 1870s, 75 percent of the farmers in California were of Chinese origin. 'The Chinese actually taught the American farmer how to plant, cultivate and harvest.' But were these Chinese working in the fields and plantations of the Sacramento Valley all part of the great nineteenth-century waves of immigration into the United States, or could some have been descendants of settlers left on the banks of the Sacramento by Zhou Man in 1423? I found a clue to this mystery in an unlikely source.

In 1874, Stephen Powers, an official inspector appointed by the government of California who had spent years collecting data on the languages of the tribes of California, published an article claiming that he had found linguistic evidence of a Chinese colony on the Russian River in California, some seventy miles north-west of the Sacramento junk. Powers also claimed that diseases brought by European settlers had decimated this Chinese colony as well as the other Indian people of California, '[the] remittent fever which desolated the Sacramento valleys in 1833 and reduced these great plains from a condition of remarkable populousness to one of almost utter silence and solitude . . . there was scarcely a human being left alive'. Powers' report was badly received by his government employers, and although he courteously and bravely attempted to maintain his position, his official report, published in 1877, is a watered-down version of his claims. Nonetheless, it makes for fascinating reading.

Quite apart from his claim of a Chinese colony based on linguistic evidence, Powers described Chinese settlers as having intermarried with local Indians over centuries. Their descendants were paler than the people of the coast, and, unlike other Indian tribes, the older generation had magnificent beards while the women 'are as proud of their black hair as the Chinese'. Rather than skins, women wore 'a single garment in the shape of a wool sack, sleeveless and gathered at the neck, more or less white once'. They were 'simple, friendly, peaceable and inoffensive'. After death, 'they generally desire like the Chinese to be buried in the ancestral soil of their tribe'. Again like the Chinese, but unlike other hunter-gatherer tribes of North America, the peoples around the Sacramento and Russian Rivers were sedentary: 'at least four fifths of their diet was derived from the vegetable kingdom . . . They knew the qualities of all herbs, shrubs, leaves, having a command of much greater catalogue of [botanical] names than nine tenths of Americans.' Their ancestors' legacy could also be seen in pottery beautifully formed in classic Chinese shapes, whereas the '[modern] Indian merely picks up a boulder of trap [a dark, igneous rock] or greenstone and beats out a hollow leaving the outside rough'. The ancestors of the Sacramento and Russian River tribes also used 'long, heavy knives of obsidian or jasper' their descendants, Powers found, no longer knew how to make. And while the ancestors had fashioned elegant tobacco pipes from serpentine, their descendants made use of simple wooden ones. They had also 'developed a Chinese inventiveness' in devising methods of snaring wildfowl using decoy ducks—a Chinese custom, but one not found among the Indians. Like the Chinese, they ate snails, slugs, lizards and snakes, and built large middens of clam shells.

On the eastern side of San Francisco Bay, some seventy miles south of the site of the Sacramento junk, there is a small, stone-built village with low walls. In 1904, Dr John Fryer, Professor of Oriental Languages at University College, Berkeley, California, stated, 'This is undoubtedly the work of Mongolians . . . The Chinese would naturally wall themselves in, as they do in all their towns in China.' This accords with Powers's succinct description of Chinese people who had created a colony and then intermarried with native Americans.

It certainly seems that Zhou Man's fleet left a settlement in California. Were they the first to cultivate rice in the Americas? And was the wealth of blue and white Ming porcelain found in California really brought by Spanish galleons, as conventional wisdom has it, or was it carried in the holds of the junks of Zhou Man's fleet? . . .

After emerging from the bay, Zhou Man's fleet would have been carried southwards by the wind and current to New Mexico. The Waldseemüller map shows the coast with reasonable accuracy, charted just as one would expect from a ship passing by, but there is a gap at the latitude of the Gulf of Tehuantepec in Guatemala, as if the Pacific and Atlantic Oceans met there, which of course is not the case. This is consistent with the Chinese having sailed into the Gulf, but finding it too shallow to proceed, turning back and then drawing what they could see from the entrance: water stretching away for miles in front of them, marking an apparent opening between North and South America.

I made the assumption that they had sailed beyond the isthmus of Panama, clearly shown on the Waldseemüller, and then been driven back across the Pacific towards China by the winds and current, as one would expect with a square-rigged sailing ship. But on their way down that coast they would have been swept across the Gulf of California and could have made a landfall on the Mexican coast somewhere near Manzanillo in the modern province of Colima. Here a spectacular volcano, the Colima, some 12,700 feet high and clearly visible for miles out to sea, would have attracted them.

I decided to make a search for another wreck between Manzanillo and Acapulco, a stretch of coastline only around three hundred miles long and again clearly shown on the Waldseemüller map. I started my search with the accounts of the first Spaniards to reach that coast in the 1520s, Fra Bernardino de Sahagún and Bernal Diaz del Castillo, both of whom described the exotic Mayan civilization, still surviving in 1421 but in decline when they arrived. Many of the things de Sahagún and del Castillo described—chickens, lacquer boxes, dye-stuffs, metalwork and jewellery—seemed to have the imprint of China all over them.

As in California, when they arrived in Mexico the conquistadors found Asiatic chickens quite different from the European fowl they had left behind. The Mayan names for the birds, *Kek* or *Ki,* were identical to those used by the Chinese; like the Chinese but unlike the Europeans, Mexicans used chickens only for ceremonial purposes such as divination, not for eggs or meat. These were such remarkable similarities that for these reasons alone I felt a visit to that small strip of the Mexican coast was justified.

Before departing, I also investigated whether plants originating in China grew in New Mexico or western Mexico. The Chinese Rose did, but that could have been propagated southwards from California. Other than the rose, I found no plants growing in Mexico that had originated in China, but I did find the opposite; plants indigenous to Central America had found their way across the world before the European voyages of discovery. Sweet potatoes, tomatoes and papayas were found in Easter Island, sweet potatoes in Hawaii, and maize in China and the Philippines. Maize could have come from South or North America, but the other plants had come from a much narrower area, from what we now call Mexico, Guatemala and Nicaragua. . . .

How Not to (Re)Write World History: Gavin Menzies and the Chinese Discovery of America

In *1421: The Year China Discovered America* (2002), Gavin Menzies aspires to rewrite world history on a grand scale. He maintains that four Chinese fleets, comprising twenty-five to thirty ships and at least 7,000 persons each, visited every part of the world except Europe between 1421 and 1423. Trained by Zheng He, the famous eunuch-admiral, Chinese captains carried out the orders of Zhu Di (r. 1402–1424), the third Ming emperor, to map coastlines, settle new territories, and establish a global maritime empire. According to Menzies, proof of the passage of the Ming fleets to the Americas, Australia, New Zealand, and Polynesia is overwhelming and indisputable. His "index of supporting evidence" includes thousands of items from the fields of archaeology, cartography, astronomy, and anthropology; his footnotes and bibliography include publications in Chinese, French, Portuguese, Spanish, Italian, German, Arabic, and Hebrew.

Menzies claims that Chinese mariners explored the islands of Cape Verde, the Azores, the Bahamas, and the Falklands; they established colonies in Australia, New Zealand, British Columbia, California, Mexico, Puerto Rico, and Rhode Island; they introduced horses to the Americas, rice to California, chickens to South America, coffee to Puerto Rico, South American sloths to Australia, sea otters to New Zealand, and maize to the Philippines. In addition, Chinese seamen toured the temples and palaces of the Maya center of Palenque in Mexico, hunted walruses and smelted copper in Greenland, mined for lead and saltpeter in northern Australia, and established trading posts for diamonds along the Amazon and its tributaries.

Inasmuch as Menzies believes that he has collected a veritable mountain of evidence, he is not disheartened by skepticism about some of his astonishing assertions. As he told *People Magazine* (24 February 2003) after *1421* hit the New York Times bestseller list, "[t]here's not one chance in a hundred million that I'm wrong!" He regards his investigation as an ongoing project: a website (www.1421.tv) provides yet more evidence, . . ., and a team of researchers currently is assisting him in combing medieval Spanish and Portuguese documents for added proof of his contentions. . . .

Menzies is contemptuous of professional historians who ignore evidence of Chinese influence in the Americas, "presumably because it contradicts the

From *Journal of World History* by Robert Finlay, vol. 15, no. 2, June 2004, pp. 229–42 (refs. omitted). Copyright © 2004 by University of Hawaii Press. Reprinted by permission.

accepted wisdom on which not a few careers have been based." He explains that he has uncovered information that has eluded many eminent historians of China, even though it was right before their eyes, "only because I knew how to interpret the extraordinary maps and charts that reveal the course and the extent of the voyages of the great Chinese fleets between 1421 and 1423." A former submarine commander in the British Royal Navy, he has sailed in the wake of Christopher Columbus, Ferdinand Magellan, and James Cook, hence he recognizes that those mariners, who navigated with copies of Chinese maps in hand, were themselves merely sailing in the backwash of Zheng He's fleets.

Menzies intends his work for the general reader, and his style is vigorous, clear, and informal. Most strikingly, he makes his own search for evidence of the Ming fleets the narrative framework for recounting their achievements. He describes his frustrations and triumphs as he travels everywhere following "an elusive trail of evidence," sometimes discouraged but never defeated. He also brings his narrative to life by recounting his own experiences in places visited by the fleets of Zheng He, including savoring rum toddies and roast lobster on Guadeloupe beaches, braving the dangers of the Great Barrier Reef of Australia, and rounding the Cape of Good Hope into the South Atlantic. The underlying message of these frequent vignettes is that the author's astonishing conclusions are validated by the unique personal experience he brings to his research as well as by his transparent account of how he struggled toward those conclusions. This approach makes for a lively, engaging work that surely will attract many readers who otherwise would never open a 500-page tome on Chinese maritime enterprise and European exploration.

The good news conveyed by *1421* is that there are big bucks in world history: Menzies received an advance of £500,000 ($825,000) from his British publisher, whose initial printing runs to 100,000 copies. The bad news is that reaping such largesse evidently requires producing a book as outrageous as *1421*. Menzies flouts the basic rules of both historical study and elementary logic. He misrepresents the scholarship of others, and he frequently fails to cite those from whom he borrows. He misconstrues Chinese imperial policy, especially as seen in the expeditions of Zheng He, and his extensive discussion of Western cartography reads like a parody of scholarship. His allegations regarding Nicolò di Conti (c. 1385–1469), the only figure in *1421* who links the Ming voyages with European events, are the stuff of historical fiction, the product of an obstinate misrepresentation of sources. The author's misunderstanding of the technology of Zheng He's ships impels him to depict voyages no captain would attempt and no mariner could survive, including a 4,000-mile excursion along the Arctic circle and circumnavigation of the Pacific after having already sailed more than 42,000 miles from China to West Africa, South America, Australia, New Zealand, and the Philippines.

Portraying himself as an innocent abroad, forthrightly seeking truths the academic establishment has disregarded or suppressed, Menzies in fact is less an "unlettered Ishmael" than a Captain Ahab, gripped by a mania to bend everything to his purposes. His White Whale is Eurocentric historiography, which celebrates Columbus . . . and Vasco da Gama . . . without realizing they merely aped the epic deeds of the Chinese. More generally, Menzies, in an unacknowledged echo of Joseph Needham, laments that China did not become "mistress of the world," with Confucian harmony and Buddhist benevolence uniting humankind. Instead, the cruel, barbaric West, secretly and fraudulently capitalizing on Chinese achievements, imposed its dominion around the globe.

The wounded leviathan of Eurocentricism no doubt deserves another harpoon, but *1421* is too leaky a vessel to deliver it. Examination of the book's central claims reveals they are uniformly without substance: first, that the 1421–1423 voyages Menzies describes could not have taken place; second, that Conti played no role in transmitting knowledge of Chinese exploration to European cartographers; and third, that all Menzies's evidence for the presence of the Chinese fleets abroad is baseless.

1421 concentrates on what Menzies terms "the missing years" of the sixth voyage of Zheng He, that is, the two and a half years between March 1421 and October 1423, during which the fleets of Zheng He supposedly roamed the globe. Menzies is not interested in the well-known, much-studied voyages of Zheng He, and he ignores the extensive literature on them. He dispenses with six of the seven expeditions (between 1405 and 1433) in one page. He singles out the sixth voyage because it was the only one in which Zheng He returned to China early, leaving his subordinate eunuch-captains to carry out their mission of returning tribute envoys to their kingdoms. This circumstance offers Menzies a window of opportunity to imagine that the armada left the Indian Ocean to seek new lands in the Atlantic and Pacific. Since he claims that the mariners sailed about 40,000 miles in their world-girdling odysseys, two and a half years is just barely enough time for them to journey such a vast distance while also charting coasts, mining ore, meeting alien peoples, and founding colonies.

In addition, Menzies feels free to speculate about "missing years" because of a presumed dearth of sources. He casually dismisses the principal source of information on Zheng He's voyages, Ma Huan's *Ying-Yai Sheng-Lan* [The overall survey of the ocean's shores], by declaring that its author, an official translator on the staff of Zheng He in 1421, "left the treasure fleets at Calicut" (a port on the Malabar coast in southwestern India), hence he did not take part in the global exploration. Menzies provides no evidence for his assertion, which, in any case, mistakes the nature of Ma's account. The author sailed on three of the Ming expeditions, and his book is a protoethnographic survey of the places visited by the fleets over several decades, not "diaries" of his participation in a specific voyage. He incorporated information on countries he did not visit, and he apparently continued making revisions to his book until it was published about thirty years after the last expedition. Menzies does not address the awkward question of why Ma, a stickler for detail and an aficionado of novelties, never mentions the wondrous excursion of his comrades to the Americas and Australia.

Throughout *1421*, Menzies places great emphasis on imperial officials in 1477 destroying many of the documents regarding the Ming expeditions in order to prevent a renewal of the project. In a manner of speaking, the author sails the ships of Zheng He through that supposed evidentiary void.

There are plentiful surviving documents on the expeditions, however, that prove there were no "missing years." The sources indicate that an imperial order for the sixth voyage was issued in March 1421, although the flotilla did not leave China until the turn of the year. It reached Sumatra around July 1422, after many stops in Southeast Asia; Zheng He returned home to Nanjing by September 1422, leaving his subordinates to sail on to thirty-six ports in Ceylon, India (both Bengal and the Malabar coast), the Persian Gulf, and East Africa. The last of the squadrons returned to China on 8 October 1423, having completed their journey of some 11,000 miles in the expected time, about one year and three months after departing Sumatra. Thus there are no "missing years" for the Ming fleets, no time for even a portion of the extraordinary exploits narrated in *1421*.

Even taking Menzies's account at face value, however, it is far-fetched. The author asserts that Zheng He arrived home in November 1421 and that his captains completed their errands in the Indian Ocean in July of the same year, a mere three months after departing Sumatra. After rendezvousing at Sofala (across from Mozambique on the East African coast), they doubled the Cape of Good Hope in August and headed north to the Cape Verde Islands, reaching them in late September; a month later, they made landfall off the Orinoco River in Brazil, and by November they were approaching Cape Horn in the South Atlantic. In other words, Menzies proposes that Zheng He's captains completed a voyage of some 17,000 miles in mainly unknown seas in seven months, including dozens of stops in the Indian Ocean, while Zheng He took the same amount of time to journey about 3,500 miles from Sumatra to Nanjing.

By this account, then, Zheng He sailed sluggishly but his captains made spectacularly rapid progress. Menzies claims that the average speed of Zheng He's vessels over their seven voyages in the Indian Ocean was 4.8 knots (or 132 miles per day). Menzies has no basis for this estimate since an average speed can be calculated only for the 1431–1433 expedition, for which a detailed itinerary survives. Naturally, speeds differed considerably, depending on the time of year and the passage being traversed. In the seventh voyage, distances covered varied from a high of 106 miles per day (3.8 knots) to a low of 37.5 miles per day (1.4 knots), with an average of 69 miles per day (or 2.5 knots). Menzies assumes, however, that his undocumented estimate of 4.8 knots for the Indian Ocean voyages holds as well for the global cruises of the Ming fleets. His calculation helps him narrowly fit the agenda of the fleets into the alleged "missing years": having doubled the time the junks actually were away from China (from fifteen months to thirty), he also hurries the ships along by granting them an average speed 52 percent higher than what they generally achieved in the steady, familiar monsoon winds of the southern seas. On its own terms, then, Menzies's scenario is highly implausible. Taking into account the surviving evidence for the timetable of the sixth expedition, it is impossible.

Menzies's evidence for the role of Conti in transmitting Chinese geographical knowledge to European cartographers is even flimsier than his argument for "missing years." A native of Venice, Conti lived in Asia for some thirty-five years, and when he returned to Europe around 1441, he sought absolution from Pope Eugenius IV (r. 1431–1447) for having converted to Islam. As instructed by the pope, Conti told the story of his travels to the humanist Poggio Bracciolini (1380–1459), who incorporated it into his *De Varietate Fortunae,* completed in 1448. His account was widely read, for Conti provided the best source of information on the East, especially India and Southeast Asia, that Europe had received since Marco Polo's *Travels* (c. 1298).

Conti is essential to Menzies's argument since he represents the sole vehicle by which Chinese geographical knowledge reached the West. Much of *1421* is devoted to interpreting European maps in the light of that knowledge, and without Conti as "the crucial link" in the chain of evidence, the central thesis of the book collapses.

To establish the relevance of Conti, Menzies splices into one quotation a passage from Poggio and another from Pero Tafur (c. 1410–c. 1484), a Spaniard who met Conti at Mt. Sinai (Egypt) in 1437, when the Venetian was planning to return home. Poggio refers to large Indian ships, with five sails, many masts, and hull compartments. Since only Chinese ships possessed the latter, it is generally assumed that Conti actually described Chinese vessels, evidently without knowing their origins. Tafur writes of ships "like very large houses" [*como casas muy grandes*], with ten or more sails and large cisterns of water inside, that delivered cargo to Mecca. Neither Poggio nor Tafur refer to Calicut in connection with the large ships, to Chinese vessels visiting India, or to the fleet of Zheng He; neither chronicler provides a date for Conti's stay in Calicut. Still, Menzies takes for granted that Conti was in Calicut in 1421 when the Ming armada anchored there, and since both Conti and Ma Huan describe similar scenes in Calicut, Menzies surmises that Conti must have met the Chinese chronicler in that port.

Based on these presumptions, Menzies creates an incredible scenario: he declares that Conti boarded Zheng He's junks for their voyages to the Cape Verde Islands, Brazil, Patagonia, Australia, New Zealand, North America, and Mexico. Moreover, after the fleet returned to Southeast Asia and China in late 1423, Conti dashed home to Venice, where in 1424 he was "debriefed" by the Infante Dom Pedro of Portugal (d. 1449), older brother of Prince Henry (1394–1460), the so-called "Navigator," and where Conti handed over copies of Chinese charts produced during the great voyage. Those charts, Menzies asserts, formed the basis for all subsequent European maps that showed lands across the Atlantic, including, inter alia, the Pizzigano map (1424), the (disputed) Vinland map (1420–1440?), the Cantino planisphere (1502), and the Waldseemuller maps (1507, 1513). Furthermore, Conti's information prompted Prince Henry to secretly dispatch settlers to Puerto Rico in 1431, where (Menzies suggests) they perhaps found evidence of a previous Chinese colony. European copies of Ming charts also explain Columbus's ambition to voyage across the Ocean Sea, Magellan's conviction that he could sail around South America, and Cook's alleged "discovery" of Australia.

Even though "The Travels of Nicolò di Conti" is silent about the global journey of the Venetian—one wonders why he kept that thrilling news from Poggio—Menzies repeatedly claims the document proves that Conti "sailed with the Chinese fleet from India to Australia and China." Thus with no more warrant than a passing mention by Poggio and Tafur of large ships in the Indian Ocean, Menzies concocts a scenario in which Conti tours the world on Zheng He's junks, collecting information that transforms European cartography and inspires European overseas expansion. In a book bloated with extravagant arguments, Menzies's assertions regarding Poggio's well-known text stand out for their obdurate distortion of evidence.

Menzies's claims regarding the fleet's "missing years" and Conti's global cruise clearly cannot be sustained. The author's proof for the presence of the Ming argosy in new lands also lacks substance. In his first two chapters, he lays the groundwork for his claims when describing Zheng He's fleet before its departure from Nanjing. Although the portrait lacks any documentation, it provides the foundation for virtually all the evidence Menzies later cites for Chinese exploration. His depiction, then, does not represent mere scene setting aimed at engaging the reader—a rhetorical tactic that perhaps does not call for footnotes—but assumptions read back into the narrative itself. In effect, the author stocks the ships on their exodus from China with the very items that will confirm that the mariners reached their far-flung destinations.

Thus while no evidence survives of the garb worn by Zheng He's sailors, Menzies describes them as wearing long white robes because legends and folklore from Australia and the New World speak of visits from white-robed aliens. Although sources are silent on the presence of women in the fleet, Menzies assumes that many prostitutes were aboard because the colonies supposedly founded during the voyages required Chinese mates for the men. In like fashion, he infers that many coops of Asiatic chickens were loaded on the junks (as "valuable presents for foreign dignitaries,") because the presence of chickens in the New World is a central part of his proof of the passage of the Ming fleets. Since Central American natives used chicken entrails for divination, Menzies presumes they were "indoctrinated" in the practice by the fowl-bearing colonists of Zheng He.

There is no evidence for masons and stone carvers in Zheng He's flotilla, but Menzies believes they were aboard because no one else could have carved the numerous stone markers supposedly left behind by the fleets in the Cape Verde Islands and other landing spots, and they must have built the "pyramids" and astronomical "observation platforms" found just about everywhere else. The latter, Menzies claims, were needed by Chinese astronomers, indispensable passengers in the fleet since they had to carry out the (undocumented) imperial command to detect "guiding stars" in order to "correctly locate the new territories." Teak was not used in building Zheng He's fleets, as sources supposedly consulted by Menzies make clear, yet he regards any appearance of teak in marine excavations as marking the presence of the Ming vessels. It is highly unlikely that the Chinese junks (or any ships at any time) carried specially carved stones for ballast, as Menzies imagines, yet he elaborately describes how the mariners built a slipway to refloat grounded junks at Bimini in the Bahamas, the evidence for which is "tongued and grooved" rectangular rocks found underwater there—ballast, the author declares, from the Ming ships.

Zheng He's armada almost certainly included some horses used by the admiral and other high commanders. Menzies claims, however, that thousands of horses were transported, many being used to stock the Americas and to explore the interior of Australia. At sea for months at a time, the mariners allegedly nourished the horses with boiled, mashed rice and with water distilled from seawater, "using paraffin wax or seal blubber for fuel." Although Needham states that there is no evidence that the Chinese knew how to desalinate seawater, Menzies asserts that a ship wrecked off the Oregon coast is reported to have carried paraffin wax, hence he regards the rumor as implicit verification of his contentions about both desalination and hordes of junk-journeying steeds.

The seamen, prostitutes, and eunuchs were kept in fresh fish at sea by "trained otters, working in pairs to herd shoals into the nets . . ." These marvelous creatures, alas, remain unheralded in any document, but since some wild ones "have been seen swimming in the fjords of South Island" (New Zealand), Menzies infers that their forbears must have jumped Zheng He's ships there. Chinese shar-peis must have sailed with the Ming flotilla because an animal resembling the dog appears in a Mexican painting discovered in the nineteenth century. One audacious shar-pei, Menzies proposes, absconded from the junks in the Falklands and mated with an indigenous fox, giving birth to a now-extinct animal called a warrah—DNA results, the author promises, will be posted on the website.

Menzies also goes beyond his portrait of Zheng He's armada in Nanjing to point to evidence deriving from its global adventures. He suggests that the Chinese captured a few giant South American sloths (or mylodons) in Patagonia. This deduction arises from the author's notion that a "dog-headed man" depicted on the Piri Reis map of 1513—which, of course, Menzies regards as based upon a copy of a Chinese map from Conti's collection—is in fact a mylodon, an animal (he assumes) that Zheng He's captains desired for the emperor's zoo. He further supposes that one of the sloths aroused itself enough to escape Chinese incarceration in Australia because a stone carving near Brisbane (he thinks) looks something like the Patagonian beast.

It is impossible to keep track of how many self-confirming assumptions are at work in such citations of alleged evidence. Piling supposition upon supposition, Menzies never considers a question that he does not beg: every argument in *1421* springs from the fallacy of petitio principii. The author's "trail of evidence" is actually a feedback loop that makes no distinction between premise and proof, conjecture and confirmation, bizarre guess and proven fact.

Thus just as Menzies describes the junks as supplied with all the paraphernalia that will prove they sailed where he contends, he also reconstructs the routes of the voyages by treating European maps, supposedly based on Conti's cache, as the by-product of those very voyages. This inevitably leads to some curious conclusions. Since the Waldseemüller map of 1507 seems to show an open sea passage between the Arctic Circle and Eurasia from the Barents Sea to the Bering Straits, a distance of more than 4,000 miles, Menzies concludes that the route was surveyed by a Ming fleet taking a shortcut home after its exploration of Greenland, boldly going where no eunuch had gone before.

The author, however, does not discuss this epic voyage except to observe that the Waldseemüller map proves it took place.

Similarly, since Menzies believes that the Chinese first navigated around South America and that the Piri Reis map is proof of that achievement, he declares that the map does not show a landlocked Atlantic, with an eastward extension of the Americas linking up with the peninsula of Southeast Asia, but, rather, "what appears to be ice connecting the tip of South America to Antartica." Rivaling his mistreatment of Poggio's "Travels," Menzies makes this claim even though his own reproductions of the Piri Reis chart patently contradict it. Not only that, Piri Reis himself states the contrary, for he noted on his map that Spanish and Portuguese explorers "have found out that coasts encircle this sea [that is, the Atlantic], which has thus taken the form of a lake. . . ." Menzies does not think it necessary to inform his readers of this evidence.

Unfortunately, this reckless manner of dealing with evidence is typical of *1421*, vitiating all its extraordinary claims: the voyages it describes never took place, Chinese information never reached Prince Henry and Columbus, and there is no evidence of the Ming fleets in newly discovered lands. The fundamental assumption of the book—that Zhu Di dispatched the Ming fleets because he had a "grand plan," a vision of charting the world and creating a maritime empire spanning the oceans—is simply asserted by Menzies without a shred of proof. It represents the author's own grandiosity projected back onto the emperor, providing the latter with an ambition commensurate with the global events that Menzies presumes *1421* uniquely has revealed, an account that provides evidence "to overturn the long-accepted history of the Western world." It is clear, however, that textbooks on that history need not be rewritten. The reasoning of *1421* is inexorably circular, its evidence spurious, its research derisory, its borrowings unacknowledged, its citations slipshod, and its assertions preposterous.

Still, it may have some pedagogical value in world history courses. Assigning selections from the book to high-schoolers and undergraduates, it might serve as an outstanding example of how not to (re)write world history. . . .

POSTSCRIPT

Did the Chinese Discover America?

The foregoing debate speaks to some of the same questions addressed in Issue 1, as well as in the introduction to this volume. What are the key elements of historical research? Is some evidence better than others? Why is corroboration of sources so important? What should it tell us that researchers can interpret the same factual evidence in widely different ways without destroying historical truth? If, as Robert Finlay suggests, Gavin Menzies's book amounts to little more than a historical hoax, it would not be the first such publication. Menzies, however, appears undeterred by the fact that no academic specialist in fifteenth-century Chinese history subscribes to his conclusions. He argues, instead, that these scholars are embarrassed that he has discovered evidence that was right under their noses, or that he has the skill that others do not to read the navigational maps upon which his study is based. Moreover, Menzies maintains a Web site connected to this research project, and a paperback edition of his book was published in 2008. Nor is he without his defenders. See, for example, Anatole Andro, *The 1421 Heresy: An Investigation into the Ming Chinese Maritime Survey of the World* (AuthorHouse, 2005), which supports some but not all of Menzies's contentions, and Paul Chiasson, *The Island of Seven Cities: Where the Chinese Settled When They Discovered America* (St. Martin's Griffin, 2007), which claims to identify an ancient Chinese colony on Cape Breton Island. The most respected scholarly work on Chinese maritime history is Louise Levathes, *When China Ruled the Seas: The Treasure Fleet of the Dragon Throne, 1405–1433* (Simon & Schuster, 1994).

There are a number of other studies that make cases for pre-Columbian contacts in the Americas from Europeans and non-Europeans alike. These include Alexander von Wuthenau, *Unexpected Faces in Ancient America, 1500 BC–AD1500: The Historical Testimony of Pre-Columbian Artists* (Outlet, 1975); Barry Fell, *America BC: Ancient Settlers in the New World,* rev. ed. (Artisan Publishers, 2008), which suggests Celtic influences in the eleventh century; and Charles C. Mann, *1491: New Revelations of the Americas Before Columbus* (Alfred A. Knopf, 2005). Ivan Van Sertima, *They Came Before Columbus: The African Presence in Ancient America* (Random House, 1976) provides an Afrocentric perspective that is perhaps as controversial as the speculations of Menzies.

The era of European exploration during the fifteenth, sixteenth, and seventeenth centuries is covered in J. H. Parry, *The Age of Reconnaissance: Discovery, Exploration, and Settlement, 1450 to 1650* (Praeger, 1963), and Boies Penrose, *Travel and Discovery in the Renaissance, 1420–1620* (Harvard University Press, 1952). Samuel Eliot Morison, *The European Discovery of America: The Northern Voyages* (Oxford University Press, 1971); David Beers Quinn, *England and the Discovery of America, 1481–1620* (Harper & Row, 1974); Wallace Notestein,

The English People on the Eve of Colonization, 1603–1630 (Harper & Brothers, 1954); Charles Gibson, *Spain in America* (Harper & Row, 1966); and W. J. Eccles, *France in America* (Harper & Row, 1972), all discuss European contacts in North America. Howard Mumford Jones, *O Strange New World* (1964), describes the impact of North American images on the European mind.

Perhaps the best biographical treatment of Columbus remains Samuel Eliot Morison's generally sympathetic *Admiral of the Ocean Sea: A Life of Christopher Columbus,* 2 vols. (Little, Brown, 1942). For a more recent objective and scholarly study, see Felipe Fernandez-Armesto, *Columbus* (Oxford University Press, 1991).

ISSUE 3

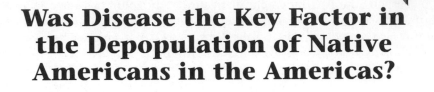

Was Disease the Key Factor in the Depopulation of Native Americans in the Americas?

YES: Colin G. Calloway, from *New Worlds for All: Indians, Europeans, and the Remaking of Early America* (The Johns Hopkins University Press, 1997)

NO: David S. Jones, from "Virgin Soils Revisited," *William & Mary Quarterly* (October 2003)

ISSUE SUMMARY

YES: Colin Calloway says that while Native Americans confronted numerous diseases in the Americas, traditional Indian healing practices failed to offer much protection from the diseases that were introduced by Europeans beginning in the late-fifteenth century and which decimated the indigenous peoples.

NO: David Jones recognizes the disastrous impact of European diseases on Native Americans, but he insists that Indian depopulation was also a consequence of the forces of poverty, malnutrition, environmental.

Relations between Native Americans and Europeans were marred by the difficulties that arose from people of very different cultures encountering each other for the first time. These encounters led to inaccurate perceptions, misunderstandings, and failed expectations. While at first the American Indians deified the explorers, experience soon taught them to do otherwise. European opinion ran the gamut from admiration to contempt; for example, some European poets and painters expressed admiration for the Noble Savage, while other Europeans accepted as a rationalization for military aggression the sentiment that "the only good savage is a dead one."

Spanish, French, and English treatments of Native Americans differed and were based to a considerable extent on each nation's hopes about the New World and how it could be subordinated to the Old. The Spanish exploited the Indians most directly, taking their gold and silver, transforming their government, religion, and society, and even occasionally enslaving them. The French posed a lesser threat than did the others because there were fewer of them and because many French immigrants were itinerant trappers and priests rather than settlers. In the long run, emigration from England was the most threatening of all. Entire families came from England, and they were determined to establish a permanent home in the wilderness.

The juxtaposition of Native Americans and English from the Atlantic to the Appalachians resulted sometimes in coexistence, other times in enmity. Large-scale violence erupted in Virginia in the 1620s, the 1640s, and the 1670s. In the latter decade, frontiersmen in the Virginia piedmont led by Nathaniel Bacon attacked tribes living in the Appalachian foothills. In New England, from the 1630s through the 1670s, Pequots, Wampanoags, Narragansetts, Mohegans, Podunks, and Nipmunks united to stop the encroachments into their woodlands and hunting grounds. King Philip's War erupted in June 1675 and lasted until September 1676, with isolated raids stretching on until 1678. Casualties rose into the hundreds, and Anglo-Indian relations deteriorated.

William Bradford's account of the Pilgrims' arrival at Cape Cod describes the insecurity the new migrants felt as they disembarked on American soil. "[T]hey had now no friends to welcome them nor inns to entertain or refresh their weatherbeaten bodies; no houses or much less towns to repair to, to seek for succor. . . . Besides, what could they see but a hideous and deserted wilderness, full of wild beasts and wild men. . . . If they looked behind them there was the mighty ocean which they had passed and was not a main bar and gulf to separate them from all the civil parts of the world." Historical hindsight, however, suggests that if anyone should have expressed fears about the unfolding encounter in the Western Hemisphere, it should have been the Native Americans because their numbers declined by as much as 95 percent in the first century following Columbus's arrival. Although some of this decline can be attributed to violent encounters with Europeans, there seems to have been a more hostile (and far less visible) force at work. As historian William McNeill has suggested, the main weapon that overwhelmed indigenous peoples in the Americas was the Europeans' breath!

The following essays explore the role played by disease in the depopulation of Native Americans in the Western Hemisphere. Colin G. Calloway makes clear that Indian doctors possessed a sophisticated knowledge of the healing power of plants that they shared with Europeans, but these curatives were insufficient in providing protection against the variety of new diseases introduced into the Americas by European explorers and settlers. The "Columbian exchange" included epidemics that decimated indigenous tribes.

Physician David S. Jones recognizes the consequences of the introduction of European diseases among Native Americans, but he contends that there were other factors at work that explain the drastic loss of life among American Indians. For example, poverty, malnutrition, environmental stress, dislocation, and social disparity exacerbated the conditions within which infectious diseases could spread in such dramatic proportions.

YES ↩

Colin G. Calloway

New Worlds for All: Indians, Europeans, and the Remaking of Early America

Healing and Disease

North American Indians did not inhabit a disease-free paradise prior to European invasion. The great epidemic diseases and crowd infections that ravaged Europe and Asia—smallpox, diphtheria, measles, bubonic and pneumonic plague, cholera, influenza, typhus, dysentery, yellow fever—were unknown in America. Indian peoples faced other, less devastating, problems. Bioarchaeological studies reveal evidence of malnutrition and anemia resulting from dietary stress, high levels of fetal and neonatal death and infant mortality, parasitic intestinal infections, dental problems, respiratory infections, spina bifida, osteomyelitis, nonpulmonary tuberculosis, and syphilis. Indian people also suffered their share of aches and pains, breaks and bruises, digestive upsets, arthritis, wounds, and snakebites. To deal with these things, Indian doctors employed a rich knowledge of the healing properties of plants and what today we would call therapeutic medicine. They combined knowledge of anatomy and medicinal botany with curative rituals and ceremonies.

Traditional Native American and contemporary Western ways of healing are not necessarily in conflict, and are often complementary, as evidenced when Navajo medicine men and Navajo oral traditions helped investigators from the Indian Health Service and the Centers for Disease Control identify deer mice as the source of the "mystery illness" that struck the Southwest in 1993. So too in early America, European and Indian cures could work together. Contrary to the popular modern stereotype that all Indians were and are attuned to plant life, all Europeans totally out of touch with nature, many early explorers and colonists possessed an extensive knowledge of plants and their properties, knowledge that modern urban Americans have lost. Europeans in the seventeenth century generally believed that for every sickness there were natural plant remedies, if one only knew where to find them. Indian healers, many of them women, knew where to find them, and Europeans were receptive to the cures they could provide. . . .

Unfortunately, traditional Indian cures offered little protection against the new diseases that swept the land after Europeans arrived in North America. Separated from the Old World for thousands of years, the peoples of America escaped great epidemics like the Black Death, which killed perhaps a third of the population in fourteenth-century Europe. But they were living on borrowed time. Lack of exposure to bubonic plague, smallpox, and measles allowed Indian peoples no opportunity to build up immunological resistance to such diseases. From the moment Europeans set foot in America, hundreds of thousands of Indian people were doomed to die in one of the greatest bio logical catastrophes in human history.

Imported diseases accompanied Spanish conquistadors into Central and South America at the beginning of the sixteenth century, wreaking havoc among the great civilizations of Mexico, Peru, and Yucatán, and facilitating their conquest by the invaders. It was not long before the unseen killers were at work among the Indian populations of North America.

Established and well-traveled trade routes helped spread disease. Indians who came into contact with Europeans and their germs often contaminated peoples farther inland who had not yet seen a European; they in turn passed the disease on to more distant neighbors. It is likely that most Indian people who were struck down by European diseases like smallpox died without ever laying eyes on a European. In tracing the course of imported plagues among Indian populations in colonial America, many scholars describe them not as epidemics but as pandemics, meaning that the same disease occurred virtually everywhere.

As many as 350,000 people lived in Florida when the Spaniards first arrived, but the populations of the Calusa, Timucua, and other tribes plummeted after contact. Calusas who canoed to Cuba to trade may have brought smallpox back to the Florida mainland as early as the 1520s. When Hernando de Soto invaded the Southeast in 1539, the Spaniards found that disease had preceded them. In the Carolina upcountry, they found large towns abandoned and overgrown with grass where, said the Indians, "there had been a pest in the land two years before." In 1585, Sir Francis Drake's English crew, returning from plundering Spanish ships in the Cape Verde Islands, brought a disease that was probably typhus to the Caribbean and Florida. Indians around St. Augustine died in great numbers, "and said amongste themselves, it was the Inglisshe God that made them die so faste." The population collapse continued in the seventeenth century. Governor Diego de Rebolledo reported in 1657 that the Guale and Timucua Indians were few "because they have been wiped out with the sickness of the plague and smallpox which have overtaken them in past years." Two years later the new governor of Florida said 10,000 Indians had died in a measles epidemic. According to one scholar, the Timucuans numbered as many as 150,000 people before contact; by the end of the seventeenth century, their population had been cut by 98 percent. The Apalachee Indians of northern Florida numbered 25,000–30,000 in the early seventeenth century; by the end of the century, less than 8,000 survived. Two and a half centuries after contact with the Spaniards, all of Florida's original Indian people were gone.

The pattern repeated itself elsewhere. In 1585, the English established a colony at Roanoke Island in Virginia. Almost immediately, local Indians began to fall ill and die. "The disease was so strange to them," wrote Thomas Hariot, "that they neither knew what it was, nor how to cure it." Across the continent, Pueblo Indians in New Mexico may have suffered from a huge smallpox epidemic that spread as far south as Chile and across much of North America in 1519–24. When they first encountered Europeans in 1539, the Pueblos numbered at least 130,000 and inhabited between 110 and 150 pueblos. By 1706, New Mexico's Pueblo population had dropped to 6,440 people in 18 pueblos. When de Soto's Spaniards passed through the area now known as Arkansas in 1541–43, the region was densely populated. Thousands of people lived in large towns, cultivating extensive cornfields along rich river valleys. One hundred thirty years later, these thriving communities were gone, victims of disease and possibly drought. When French explorers arrived in the mid-seventeenth century, they found Caddoes, Osages, and Quapaws living on the peripheries of the region, but central Arkansas was empty. Epidemic diseases continued their devastation. In 1698, Frenchmen found less than one hundred men in the Quapaw villages after a recent smallpox epidemic killed most of the people. "In the village are nothing but graves," the French chronicler reported.

Indian peoples in eastern Canada who had been in contact with French fur traders and fishermen since early in the sixteenth century experienced the deadly repercussions of such commerce. Jesuit Father Pierre Biard, working among the Micmacs and Maliseets of Nova Scotia in 1616, heard the Indians "complain that since the French mingle and carry on trade with them they are dying fast, and the population is thinning out. For they assert that before this association and intercourse all their countries were very populous and they tell how one by one different coasts, according as they traffic with us, have been reduced more by disease."

Deadly pestilence swept the coast of New England in 1616–17. Indians "died in heapes," and the Massachusett Indians around Plymouth Bay were virtually exterminated. As reported by Governor William Bradford, the Pilgrims found cleared fields and good soil, but few people, the Indians "being dead & abundantly wasted in the late great mortalitiy which fell in all these parts about three years over before the coming of the English, wherin thousands of them dyed, they not being able to burie one another; their sculs and bones were found in many places lying still above ground, where their houses & dwellings had been; a very sad spectacle to behold."

Smallpox was a fact of life—or death—for most of human history. An airborne disease, normally communicated by droplets or dust particles, it enters through the respiratory tract. People can become infected simply by breathing. Not surprisingly, it spread like wildfire through Indian populations. However, because early chroniclers sometimes confused smallpox with other diseases and because the contagions came so quickly, it is difficult to discern which disease was doing the killing at any particular time. By the seventeenth century, smallpox in Europe was a childhood disease: most adults, having been infected as children, had acquired lifelong immunity and were not contagious. The long transatlantic crossings further reduced the chances that European crews could transmit the disease to America. Not until children crossed the Atlantic did smallpox, and the other lethal childhood diseases that plagued Europe, take hold on Native American populations. The Spanish brought children to the Caribbean early, but not until the beginning of the seventeenth century did Dutch and English colonists bring their families to New York and New England. The arrival of sick European children sentenced thousands of Indian people to death.

Smallpox struck New England in 1633, devastating Indian communities on the Merrimack and Connecticut Rivers. Bradford reported how "it pleased God to visit these Indeans with a great sickness, and such a mortalitie that of a 1000 above 900, and a halfe of them dyed, and many of them did rott above ground for want of buriall." The epidemic reduced the Pequots in southern Connecticut from perhaps as many as thirteen thousand people to only three thousand, setting the stage for their defeat by the English in 1637, and it may have reduced the Mohawks in eastern New York from almost eight thousand to less than three thousand. Such mortality rates were not unusual when virulent new diseases cut through previously unexposed populations. Indians from the Hudson River told Adriaen Van der Donck in 1656 "that before the smallpox broke out amongst them, they were ten times as numerous as they are now." John Lawson estimated that in 1701 there was "not the sixth Savage living within two hundred Miles of all our Settlements, as there were fifty Years ago." A recent smallpox epidemic in the Carolina upcountry had "destroy'd whole towns."

At the beginning of the seventeenth century, the Huron Indians numbered as many as 30,000–40,000 people, living in perhaps twenty-eight villages on the northern shores of the Great Lakes in southern Ontario. The French identified them as crucial to their plans for North American empire. The Hurons were the key to extensive trade networks reaching far beyond the Great Lakes, and their villages could also serve as "jumping-off points" for Jesuit missionary enterprises among more distant tribes. French traders and missionaries arrived in Huronia, and it was not long before the new diseases were reaping a grim harvest among the Hurons. Their longhouses were transformed into death traps. The smallpox epidemic that ravaged New England in 1633 reached Huronia in 1634. Smallpox or measles was thinning Huron numbers in 1635–36. A Huron elder, blaming the epidemic on the Jesuits, said, "The plague has entered every lodge in the village, and has so reduced my family that today there are but two of us left, and who can say whether we two will survive." Influenza struck in 1636–37. Smallpox returned in 1639. Huron population was scythed in half between 1634 and 1640. In 1648–49, famine and the attacks of the Iroquois completed the deadly work the diseases had begun. The Hurons scattered, most of the survivors being absorbed by other tribes.

Smallpox continued throughout the eighteenth century. It killed half the Cherokees in 1738 and returned in 1760; the Catawbas of South Carolina lost half their number to the epidemic of 1759. In 1763, the British doled out blankets from the smallpox hospital at Fort Pitt to visiting Indians; smallpox erupted among the tribes of the Ohio Valley soon thereafter. Outbreaks of smallpox were reported among Indian populations in New Mexico in 1719,

1733, 1738, 1747, and 1749; in Texas recurrently between 1674 and 1802; and in California, where Indian neophytes congregated in Spanish mission villages made easy targets for new crowd-killing diseases.

The massive smallpox epidemic that ravaged western North America between 1779 and 1783 illustrates the speed with which the disease could spread its tentacles throughout Indian country. The epidemic seems to have broken out in Mexico, and it afflicted Indian peoples in Peru and Guatemala. Spreading north to Spanish settlements like San Antonio and Santa Fe, it was picked up by Indians who visited the area to trade for horses. It was then quickly transmitted north and west, through the Rockies and across the plains, slaughtering as it went. It spread into the Canadian forests, killed as many as 90 percent of the Chipewyans in the central subarctic, and by 1783 was killing Cree Indians around Hudson Bay.

Abundant sources of fish and other marine resources supported dense populations on the Northwest Coast before European maritime traders and explorers brought smallpox in the late eighteenth century. When English explorer George Vancouver sailed into Puget Sound in 1793, he met Indian people with pockmarked faces and found human skulls and bones scattered along the beach, a grim reminder of the ravages of an earlier epidemic. These northwestern populations declined dramatically over the next century.

Smallpox was probably the number-one killer of Indian people, but it was by no means the only fatal disease. Epidemics of measles, influenza, bubonic plague, diphtheria, typhus, scarlet fever, yellow fever, and other un-identified diseases also took their toll. Alcoholism added to the list of killer diseases imported from Europe. "A person who resides among them may easily observe the frightful decrease of their numbers from one period of ten years to another," said John Heckewelder, lamenting the impact of alcohol. "Our vices have destroyed them more than our swords."

Recurring epidemics allowed Indian populations no opportunity to bounce back from earlier losses. They cut down economic productivity, generating hunger and famine, which rendered those who survived one disease more vulnerable to affliction by the next. New diseases combined with falling birth rates, escalating warfare, alcoholism, and general social upheaval to turn Indian America into a graveyard. Decreased fecundity hindered population recovery. Nantucket, off the coast of Massachusetts, was once described as "an island full of Indians" and is estimated to have had a population of about 3,000 in the mid-seventeenth century. By 1763, there were 348 people. An epidemic of yellow fever that year left only twenty survivors. Some 3,000 Indians inhabited Martha's Vineyard in 1642; 313 survived in 1764. Mohawk population continued to decline to little more than 600 by the time of the Revolution. At the western door of the Iroquois confederacy, Seneca population remained stable, but this was largely because they adopted captives and immigrants from other communities ravaged by war and disease. The Illinois Indians of the Great Lakes region numbered more than ten thousand people in 1670; by 1800, no more than five hundred survived. On the banks of the Missouri in present-day Nebraska, the Omaha Indians numbered more than three thousand in the late 1700s; cholera and smallpox cut their population to less than three hundred by 1802. In years when Indian peoples needed all their resources to deal with Europeans and to cope with a world that was changing around them, their numbers were being steadily eroded by disease.

Survivors, many of them disfigured by pockmarks, faced the future bereft of loved ones and without the wisdom of elders to guide them. Societies woven together by ties of kinship and clan were torn apart. After disease struck Martha's Vineyard in 1645–46, one survivor lamented that all the elders who had taught and guided the people were dead, "and their wisdom is buried with them." In 1710, Indians near Charleston, South Carolina, told a settler they had forgotten most of their traditions because "their Old Men are dead." In some cases, power struggles followed the deaths of traditional leaders. Old certainties no longer applied, and long-established patterns of behavior must sometimes have seemed irrelevant. The impact of such losses on Indian minds and souls is incalculable.

Traditional healing practices proved powerless against the onslaught. Fasting, taking a sweat bath, and plunging into an icy river—a common Indian remedy for many ailments—aggravated rather than alleviated the effects of smallpox. Just as some Europeans looked to Indian skills and practices to deal with snakebites and ailments native to North America, so some Indian people looked to Europeans to provide relief from European sicknesses. Some believed that European witchcraft caused the new diseases; so it made sense to combat them with European power and medicine. Others, with their loved ones dying around them, were willing to try anything. Many Hurons accepted baptism from Jesuit priests, regarding it as a curative ritual and hoping it could save their children.

Despite instances of genocide and germ warfare against Indian populations, Europeans frequently provided what help and comfort they could. Dead Indians were of no value to European missionaries seeking converts, European merchants seeking customers, or European ministers seeking allies. Hearing that Massasoit "their friend was sick and near unto death," Governor William Bradford and the Plymouth colonists "sente him such comfortable things as gave him great contente, and was a means of his recovery." French nuns ministered to sick Indians in seventeenth-century Quebec. Most Spanish missions in eighteenth-century California had dispensaries, medical supplies, and medical books, and some padres displayed genuine concern for the health of their mission populations. The state of medical knowledge was still rudimentary in the eighteenth century, but Europeans, motivated by self-interest as much as humanitarian concern, shared with Indians what medical advances there were. British Indian superintendent Sir William Johnson had the Mohawks inoculated against smallpox, and some Indians were vaccinated after Edward Jenner developed the cowpox vaccine in 1796. Many Indian people overcame their suspicion of the white man's medicine to accept the protection it could offer against the white man's diseases.

Nevertheless, the protection was too little and too late to stop demographic disaster. Not all Indian populations suffered 75 percent or 90 percent mortality rates—indeed, in some areas of the country Indian populations were on the rise in the eighteenth century—but the result was a world newly emptied of Indian inhabitants. Europeans arriving in Indian country in the wake of one or more epidemics made inaccurate estimates of precontact Indian population size on the basis of head counts of survivors. Seeing remnant populations, they gained a distorted impression of the size and sophistication of the societies that had once existed—and that distorted impression entered the history books. America, many believed, was an "empty wilderness," a "virgin land." If the country was empty, that was a recent development; it was depopulated rather than unpopulated. The new world of opportunity, which "free lands" opened for Europeans in North America, was in itself a by-product of European invasion.

Historians working to revise the old view of the European settlement of America as a story of progress and triumph have rightly stressed the biological cataclysm that followed European "discovery." But epidemic diseases also plagued European societies and shattered European families. France suffered epidemics and famine with appalling regularity throughout the seventeenth and eighteenth centuries. Recurrent outbreaks of plague devastated overcrowded London in the seventeenth century, sometimes, as in 1625, killing 25 percent of the population. In 1665, London experienced the horror of the Great Plague, which did not end until the Fire of London destroyed much of the city the following year. European immigrants to America did not entirely escape Old World diseases, and they succumbed to some new ones. Malaria wreaked havoc among Spanish expeditions in the sixteenth century. Early settlers at Jamestown, Virginia, suffered high death rates in unfamiliar environments. In 1740, Ephraim and Elizabeth Hartwell of Concord, Massachusetts, watched helplessly as all five of their young children died of the "throat distemper" that ravaged New England. Boston suffered recurrent outbreaks of smallpox in the seventeenth and eighteenth centuries. Yellow fever, imported from the Tropics, killed one out of every ten people in Philadelphia, then the capital of the United States, in 1793. But with less crowded communities, more sanitary conditions, improved diet, and greater economic opportunities, most colonists enjoyed a healthier life and longer life expectancy in their new world than did their contemporaries in Europe.

Though scholars disagree widely in their estimates, it is likely that in what is today the United States, Indian population stood at somewhere between 5 million and 10 million in 1492. By 1800, the figure had fallen to around 600,000. By contrast, the European population of the English colonies in America doubled every twenty-five years in the late eighteenth century. The first U.S. census in 1790 counted a total population of 3.9 million people. By 1800, North America had just under 5 million whites and about 1 million blacks. As James Axtell points out, the Indian people who survived in the eastern United States were being engulfed in a sea of white and black faces. The demographic complexion of the new world created by the interaction of Europeans, Indians, and Africans was very different in 1800 from what it had been three centuries before.

Nevertheless, the American population of 1800 combined Indian and European healing practices. Indians and Europeans alike employed "folk remedies" as well as doctors to cure diseases and injuries. The British lagged behind the Spaniards in establishing hospitals in the New World: Cortez built the first hospital in Mexico City for Indian and Spanish poor in 1521, and by the end of the seventeenth century, there were more than one hundred fifty hospitals in New Spain. In contrast, the first general hospital to care for the sick poor in the British colonies was established in Philadelphia in 1752; Massachusetts General Hospital, not until 1811. The first medical school was established at the University of Pennsylvania in 1765; Harvard Medical School, not until 1783. For most of the eighteenth century, American physicians who wanted a medical education had to go to Europe. With few trained physicians and few medical facilities available, people in rural and small-town communities turned in times of sickness to family, neighbors, clergymen, skilled women, and local healers. In many areas of the country, itinerant Indian physicians remained common well into the twentieth century, providing health care for America's poor, whether Indian, white, or black. Many Indian people preserved their belief in the efficacy of traditional medicine—both herbal and spiritual— even as they benefited from European medicine as practiced by white doctors. False Face societies and curing rituals continued among the Iroquois long after many Iroquois had embraced Christianity. Medicine was power, and Indian people needed to draw on all the power available to them as they struggled to survive in the disease-ridden land that was their new world.

Virgin Soils Revisited

T he decimation of American Indian populations that followed European arrival in the Americas was one of the most shocking demographic events of the last millennium. Indian populations declined by as much as 95 percent in the first century after the arrival of Christopher Columbus, prompting one historian to conclude that "early America was a catastrophe—a horror story, not an epic." This collapse established the foundation for the subsequent social and political developments of American history. Since the earliest encounters of colonization, colonists and their descendants have struggled to explain how and why depopulation occurred. They have debated the role of race, politics, and even genocide. All have concluded that infectious diseases, introduced by Europeans and Africans, played a decisive role. American Indians suffered terrible mortality from smallpox, measles, tuberculosis, and many other diseases. Their susceptibility led to American Indian decline even as European populations thrived.

Discussions of the epidemiological vulnerability of American Indians rose to prominence with the work of William McNeill and Alfred W. Crosby in the 1970s. Both argued that the depopulation of the Americas was the inevitable result of contact between disease-experienced Old World populations and the "virgin" populations of the Americas. As Crosby defined them in 1976, "Virgin soil epidemics are those in which the populations at risk have had no previous contact with the diseases that strike them and are therefore immunologically almost defenseless." His theory provided a powerful explanation for the outcomes of encounter between Europeans and indigenous groups, not just in the Americas but throughout the world. Since Crosby's analysis of virgin soil epidemics appeared in the *William and Mary Quarterly*, countless writers have cited his definition and attributed the devastation of American Indian populations to their immunologic inadequacy. As argued in Jared Diamond's Pulitzer Prize-winning *Guns, Germs, and Steel*, "The main killers were Old World germs to which Indians had never been exposed, and against which they therefore had neither immune nor genetic resistance." Such assertions, which apply the intuitive appeal of natural selection to the demographic history of the Americas, dominate academic and popular discussions of depopulation.

From *William & Mary Quarterly*, October 2003, pp. 703–705, 734–742. Copyright © 2003 by Omohundro Institute of Early American History & Culture. Reprinted by permission.

Even as Crosby's model of virgin soil epidemics remains a central theme of the historiography of the Americas, it has been misunderstood and misrepresented. Crosby actually downplayed the "genetic weakness hypothesis" and instead emphasized the many environmental factors that might have contributed to American Indian susceptibility to Old World diseases, including lack of childhood exposure, malnutrition, and the social chaos generated by European colonization. Subsequent historians, however, have often reduced the complexity of Crosby's model to vague claims that American Indians had "no immunity" to the new epidemics. These claims obscure crucial distinctions between different mechanisms that might have left American Indians vulnerable. Did American Indians lack specific genes that made Europeans and Africans, after generations of natural selection, more resistant to smallpox and tuberculosis? Did they lack antibodies that their Eurasian counterparts acquired during childhood exposure to endemic infections? Were their immune systems compromised by the malnutrition, exhaustion, and stress created by European colonization? These different explanations, blurred within simple claims of no immunity, have very different implications for our understanding of what was responsible for this demographic catastrophe.

It is now possible to revisit the theory of virgin soil epidemics and reassess the many possible causes of American Indian susceptibility to European pathogens. The confusion can be untangled by surveying and resynthesizing diverse research about Indian depopulation. A review of the literature of colonization shows the prevalence of simplistic assertions of no immunity and their possible ideological appeals. It also demonstrates the importance of defining the specific claims contained within the theory of virgin soil epidemics and evaluating each of them separately. Recent immunological research has clarified the different mechanisms that can compromise human immunity. Parallel work by biological anthropologists, archaeologists, and historians has elucidated the details of the mortality of specific Indian populations. Taken together, this work suggests that although Indians' lack of prior exposure might have left them vulnerable to European pathogens, the specific contribution of such genetic or developmental factors is probably unknowable. In contrast, the analyses clearly show that the fates of individual populations depended on contingent factors of their physical, economic, social, and political environments. It could well be that the epidemics among American Indians, despite their unusual severity, were caused by the same forces of poverty, social stress, and environmental vulnerability that cause epidemics in all other times and places. These new understandings of the mechanisms of depopulation require historians to be extremely careful in their writing about American Indian epidemics. If they attribute depopulation to irresistible genetic and microbial forces, they risk being interpreted as supporting racial theories of historical development. Instead, they must acknowledge the ways in which multiple factors, especially social forces and human agency, shaped the epidemics of encounter and colonization. . . .

Taken as a whole, recent immunological research offers many clues about the state of Indian immunity. American Indians could certainly mount immune responses to European pathogens. Perhaps their "naïveté" left them without protective genes, making them incrementally susceptible. Perhaps their homogeneity left them vulnerable to adaptable pathogens. Research about these questions continues on the cutting edge of immunology. It is possible that definitive evidence of demographically significant resistance genes will emerge. The historical experiment, however, has run its course. European and American populations mixed for over five hundred years before scientists could study them adequately. The opportunity for further research on first contact populations remains remote. As a result, the state of virgin immunity will forever remain contested. This leaves the literature on genetics and immunity promising, but unsatisfying. Genetic arguments of population-wide vulnerability must therefore be made with great caution. Other immunological mechanisms remain plausible, but problematic. Initial lack of adaptive immunity likely left American Indian societies vulnerable to certain pathogens, but certainly not to all of them, and adaptive immunity does not seem to have been relevant for the dominant causes of mortality in developing societies.

Furthermore, the mechanisms of adaptive immunity, along with the impact of simultaneous and successive synergistic infections, emphasize the importance of the disease environment, and not only the population itself, in shaping a population's susceptibility to infection. Other features of the environment, defined broadly, also have profound effects on immunity. A population's physical, social, economic, and political environments all interact to create patterns of vulnerability, regardless of its genetic substrate.

Such vulnerabilities have long been recognized. Even as observers began asserting racial arguments of disease susceptibility in the nineteenth century, they saw that a wide range of social factors created susceptibility to epidemic disease. After studying an outbreak of measles among the indigenous populations of Fiji in 1875, W. Squire concluded, "We need invoke no special susceptibility of race or peculiarity of constitution to explain the great mortality." He blamed social conditions, especially "want of nourishment and care." In 1909, anthropologist Aleš Hrdlička reached a similar conclusion about American Indians: "Doubtless much of what now appears to be greater racial susceptibility is a result of other conditions." Sherburne Cook came to believe that disease amongst indigenous populations worldwide "acted essentially as the outlet through which many other factors found expression."

Malnutrition provides the most obvious, and prevalent, demonstration of the links between social conditions, environmental conditions, and disease. In addition to causing deficiency diseases, such as rickets and pellagra, malnutrition increases susceptibility to infection. Some vitamin deficiencies cause skin breakdown, eroding the first barrier of defense against infection. Protein deficiencies impair both cellular and humoral responses. Malnutrition during infancy and childhood has particularly devastating effects on subsequent immune function. Certain diseases have more specific connections to nutrition. Malnutrition, especially vitamin A deficiency, increases mortality from measles. Malnourished children are more likely to die from chicken pox. Such interactions create "a vicious circle. Each episode of infection increases the need for calories and protein and at the same time causes anorexia; both of these aggravate the nutritional deficiency, making the patient even more susceptible to infection." Understanding these relationships, scientists have realized that malnutrition "is the most common cause of secondary immuno-deficiency in the world."

Historians have thoroughly documented the impact of malnutrition on disease susceptibility. Such connections have clear importance for American Indians, who faced both disease and social disorder following European colo-nization. As Cronon describes, villages disrupted by disease and social break-down "often missed key phases in their annual subsistence cycles—the corn planting, say, or the fall hunt and so were weakened when the next infection arrived." This would have been particularly damaging for the many popu-lations that eked out only a precarious subsistence before European arrival. Although some writers have described American Indians living in bountiful harmony with their environment, archaeologists and physical anthropolo-gists have shown that many groups were terribly malnourished. The accom-plishments of the Mayan civilization might have been undone by climate change, crop failures, and famine. Disease, malnutrition, and violence made Mesoamerican cities as unhealthful as their medieval European counterparts, with life expectancies of 21 to 26 years. The Arikaras had life expectancies as low as 13.2 years. Careful study of skeletal remains has found widespread evidence of nutritional deficiencies, with health conditions worsening in the years before contact with Europeans. Baseline malnutrition, especially in the large agricultural societies in Mexico and the Andes, left American Indians vulnerable—at the outset—to European diseases. When the conditions of colo-nization disrupted subsistence, the situation only grew worse.

Malnutrition may be the most obvious factor, but it was only one of many. Environmental historians have shown how physical environments can leave populations susceptible to disease. Lowland Ecuadorians, weak-ened by endemic parasites and intestinal diseases, were more vulnerable to European infections than their highland compatriots. After Spanish arrival in Mexico, a "plague of sheep" destroyed Mexican agricultural lands and left Mexicans susceptible to famine and disease. Colonization introduced a host of damaging changes in New England. Deforestation led to wider tempera-ture swings and more severe flooding. Livestock overran Indian crops and required pastures and fences, leading to frequent conflict and widespread seizure of Indian land. Europeans also introduced pests, including blights, insects, and rats. All of these changes fueled rapid soil erosion and under-mined the subsistence of surviving Indian populations. More dramatic envi-ronmental events also wreaked havoc. Drought, earthquakes, and volcanic eruptions undermined resistance to disease in Ecuador in the 1690s. A devas-tating hurricane struck Fiji in 1875, exacerbating the measles outbreak there. As one observer commented, "Certainly for the last 16 years there has been experienced no such weather, and nothing could be more fatal to a diseased Fijian than exposure to it."

Historians and anthropologists have also documented many cases in which the varied outcomes of specific populations depended on specific social environments. The Lamanai Mayas, heavily colonized by the Spanish regime, had higher mortality than the more isolated Tipu Mayas. While much of Peru suffered severely, the region of Huamanga lost only 20 percent of its population between 1532 and 1570, the result of "a high birth rate, the relative immunity of remote high-altitude areas to disease, shrewd politics, and good luck." The Pueblos suffered when "the endemic problems of drought and famine were superimposed upon the economic disruption caused by the Spanish drain on food and labor." Severe outbreaks of smallpox and erysipelas in Peru from 1800 to 1805 reflected a combination of drought, crop failures, famines, mining failures, and economic collapse. The introduction of specific epidemics reflected specific historical events. Dauril Alden and Joseph Miller traced outbreaks of smallpox from West African droughts, through the middle passage of the slave trade, to Brazil. Measles raced down the political hierarchy in Fiji in 1875 as a series of conferences carried news of a treaty with the British empire, along with the virus, from the royal family to regional and local leaders throughout the island. Local variability and contingency led Linda Newson to conclude that "levels of decline and demographic trends were influenced by the size, distribution, and character of populations, especially their settlement patterns, social organization, and levels of subsistence." Even in the late twentieth century, specific social factors left isolated indigenous populations vulnerable to European pathogens. Magdalena Hurtado, who has witnessed first-contact epidemics in South America, emphasizes the adverse consequences of "sedentism, poverty, and poor access to health care."

Studies of North American tribes in the nineteenth and twentieth centuries have found similar local variability. Geographer Jody Decker shows how a single epidemic among the northern Plains tribes had disparate effects, "even for contiguous Native groups," depending on "population densities, transmission rates, immunity, subsistence patterns, seasonality and geographic location." Drought and famine left the Hopis particularly susceptible to an epidemic in 1780. The Mandans suffered severely from smallpox in 1837: famine since the previous winter had left them malnourished, and cold, rainy weather confined them to their crowded lodges. When smallpox struck, they had both high levels of exposure and low levels of resistance. As Clyde Dollar concludes, "It is no wonder the death rate reached such tragically high levels." Once North American tribes came under the care of the federal governments in the United States and Canada, they often suffered from malnutrition and poor sanitation. Mary-Ellen Kelm, who has studied the fates of the Indians of British Columbia, concludes that "poor Aboriginal health was not inevitable"; instead, it was the product of specific government policies.

Comparative studies have particular power for demonstrating the local specificity of depopulation. Stephen Kunitz has shown that Hawaiians suffered more severely than Samoans, a consequence of different patterns of land seizure by colonizing Europeans. The Navajo did better than the neighboring Hopi because their pastoral lifestyle adapted more easily to the challenges imposed by American settlers. In these cases similar indigenous populations encountered similar colonizers, with very different outcomes: "The kind of colonial contact that occurred was of enormous importance." Kunitz's cases demonstrate that "diseases rarely act as independent forces but instead are shaped by the different contexts in which they occur."

Paralleling this work, some historians have begun to provide integrated analyses of the many factors that shaped demographic outcomes. Any factor that causes mental or physical stress—displacement, warfare, drought, destruction of crops, soil depletion, overwork, slavery, malnutrition, social and economic chaos—can increase susceptibility to disease. These same social and environmental factors also decrease fertility, preventing a population from replacing its losses. The magnitude of mortality depended on characteristics of precontact American Indian populations (size, density, social structure, nutritional status) and on the patterns of European colonization (frequency and magnitude of contact, invasiveness of the European colonial regime). As anthropologist Clark Spencer Larsen argues, scholars must "move away from monocausal explanations of population change to reach a broad-based understanding of decline and extinction of Native American groups after 1492."

The final evidence of the influence of social and physical environments on disease susceptibility comes from their ability to generate remarkable mortality among even the supposedly disease-experienced Old World populations. Karen Kupperman has documented the synergy of malnutrition, deficiency diseases, and despair at Jamestown, where 80 percent of the colonists died between 1607 and 1625. Smallpox mortality, nearly 40 percent among Union soldiers during the Civil War, reflected living conditions and not inherent lack of innate or adaptive immunity. Mortality among soldiers infected with measles, which exceeded 20 percent during the United States Civil War, reached 40 percent during the siege of Paris in the Franco-Prussian War. Poverty and social disruption continue to shape the distribution of disease, generating enormous global disparities with tuberculosis, HIV, and all other diseases.

Is it possible to quantify the variability, to delineate the relative contribution of potential genetic, developmental, environmental, and social variables? Detailed studies have documented "considerable regional variability" in American Indian responses to European arrival. Many American Indian groups declined for a century and then began to recover. Some, such as the natives of the Bahamas, declined to extinction. Others, such as the Navajo, experienced steady population growth after European arrival. More precise data exist for select groups. Newson, for instance, has compiled data about die-off ratios, the proportion of those who died to those who survived. While die-off ratios were as high as 58:1 along the Peruvian coast, they were lower (3.4:1) in the Peruvian highlands. In Mexico they varied between 47.8:1 and 6.6:1, again depending on elevation. They ranged from 5.1:1 in Chiapas to 24:1 in Honduras and 40:1 in Nicaragua. Mortality rates from European diseases among South Pacific islanders ranged between 3 percent and 25 percent for measles, and 2.5 percent to 25 percent for influenza. Such variability among relatively homogeneous populations, with die-off ratios differing by an order of magnitude, most likely reflects the contingency of social variables. But most of these numbers are, admittedly, enormous: a 4:1 die-off ratio indicates that 75 percent died. Why did so many populations suffer such high baseline mortality? Does this reflect a shared genetic vulnerability, whose final intensity was shaped by social variables? Or does it reflect a shared social experience, of pre-existing nutritional stress exacerbated by the widespread chaos of encounter and colonization? Both positions are defensible.

The variability of outcomes reflected in the different fates of different Indian populations provides powerful evidence against the inevitability of mortality. It undermines popular claims, made most influentially by Henry Dobyns, that American Indians suffered universal mortality from infectious diseases. Noble David Cook, for instance, argues that the vulnerability was so general that Indians died equally whatever the colonial context, "no matter which European territory was involved, regardless of the location of the region. It seemed to make no difference what type of colonial regime was created." Such assertions, which reduce the depopulation of the Americas to an inevitable encounter between powerful diseases and vulnerable peoples, do not match the contingency of the archaeological and historical records. These, instead, tell a story of populations made vulnerable.

One could argue that the differences in American and European disease environments, the nutritional status of precontact Americans, and the disruptions of colonization created conditions in which disease could only thrive. Only a time traveler equipped with a supply of vaccines could have altered the demographic outcomes. But it is also possible that outcomes might have been different. Suppose Chinese explorers, if they did reach the Americas, had introduced Eurasian diseases in the 1420s, leaving American populations two generations to recover before facing European colonization. Suppose smallpox struck Tenochtitlan after Cortés's initial retreat and not during his subsequent siege of the city. An epidemic then might have been better tolerated than during the siege. Or suppose that the epidemics of 1616–1617 and 1633–1634 struck New England tribes during the nutritionally bountiful summers and not during the starving times of winter (or perhaps it was because of those starving times that the epidemics tended to appear in winters). The historic record of epidemic after epidemic suggests that high mortality must have been a likely consequence of encounter. But it does not mean that mortality was the inevitable result of inherent immunological vulnerability.

Consider an analogous case, the global distribution of HIV/AIDS. From the earliest years of the epidemic, HIV has exhibited striking disparities in morbidity and mortality. Its prevalence varies between sub-Saharan Africa and developed countries and between different populations within developed countries. Few scientists or historians would argue that these disparities between African and Europeans or between urban minorities and suburban whites exist because the afflicted populations have no immunity to HIV. Instead, the social contingency of HIV on a local and global scale has long been recognized. We should be just as cautious before asserting that no immunity led to the devastation of the American Indians.

Historians and medical scientists need to reassess their casual deployment of deterministic models of depopulation. The historic record demonstrates that we cannot understand the impact of European diseases on the Americas merely by focusing on Indians' lack of immunity. It is certainly true that epidemics devastated American Indian populations. It is also likely that genetic mechanisms of disease susceptibility exist: they influence the susceptibility of American Indians—and everyone else—to infectious disease. What remains in doubt is the relative contributions of social, cultural, environmental, and genetic forces. Even when immunologists demonstrate that a wide variety of genes contribute to susceptibility to infectious disease, it will likely remain unknown how these factors played out among American Indians in past centuries. Demographic data, meanwhile, provide convincing evidence of the strong impact of social contingency on human disease. This uncertainty leaves the door open for the debates to be shaped by ideology.

Although unprecedented in their widespread severity, virgin soil epidemics may have arisen from nothing more unique than the familiar forces of poverty, malnutrition, environmental stress, dislocation, and social disparity that cause epidemics among all other populations. Whenever historians describe the depopulation of the Americas that followed European arrival, they should acknowledge the complexity, the subtlety, and the contingency of the process. They need to replace homogeneous and ambiguous claims of no immunity with heterogeneous analyses that situate the mortality of the epidemics in specific social and environmental contexts. Only then can they overcome the widespread public and academic appeal of immunologic determinism and do justice to the crucial events of the encounter between Europeans and Americans.

POSTSCRIPT

Was Disease the Key Factor in the Depopulation of Native Americans in the Americas?

The so-called "Columbian Exchange" involved a reciprocal trade in plants and animals, human beings, and ideas, as well as diseases. With regard to the exchange of diseases, this was not a one-way street. For example, the introduction of destructive microorganisms produced epidemic diseases (smallpox, tuberculosis, measles, typhoid, and syphilis) that decimated human populations on both sides of the Atlantic. On a more positive note, Europeans brought food stuffs such as wheat and potatoes to the New World and carried home maize, beans, and manioc. Native Americans benefited from horses and other farm animals introduced from Europe, but these were offset by the efforts of the Europeans to enslave and kill the indigenous peoples whom they encountered. The best study of these various by-products of European exploration is Alfred W. Crosby, *The Columbian Exchange: Biological and Cultural Consequences of 1492* (Greenwood Press, 1973). Crosby's conclusions are largely shared by William H. McNeill, *Plagues and Peoples* (Doubleday, 1977), and Jared Diamond, *Guns, Germs, and Steel: The Fates of Human Societies* (W. W. Norton, 1997).

The effects of the encounters between Europeans and Native Americans is explored in Gary B. Nash, *Red, White & Black: The Peoples of Early North America*, 3d ed. (Prentice Hall, 1992) and three works by James Axtell: *The European and the Indian: Essays in the Ethnohistory of Colonial North America* (Oxford University Press, 1981), *The Invasion Within: The Contest of Cultures in Colonial North America* (Oxford University Press, 1985), and *Beyond 1492: Encounters in Colonial North America* (Oxford University Press, 1992). Francis Jennings, *The Invasion of America: Indians, Colonialism, and the Cant of Conquest* (University of North Carolina Press, 1975), and David E. Stannard, *American Holocaust: Columbus and the Conquest of the New World* (Oxford University Press, 1992), which accuses Europeans and white Americans of conducting a full-blown campaign of genocide against native peoples in the Americas, offer two of the harshest critiques of European dealings with American Indians. The relationship between disease and environmental conditions is explored in William Cronon, *Changes in the Land: Indians, Colonists, and the Ecology of New England* (Hill & Wang, 1983); Karen Ordahl Kupperman, *Indians and English: Facing Off in Early America* (Cornell University Press, 2000); and Russell Thornton, *American Indian Holocaust and Survival: A Population History Since 1492* (University of Oklahoma Press, 1987). Alvin M. Josephy Jr. examines the pre-Columbian Native Americans in *America in 1492: The World of the Indian Peoples Before the Arrival of Columbus* (Alfred A. Knopf, 1992).

The era of European exploration during the fifteenth, sixteenth, and seventeenth centuries is covered in J. H. Parry, *The Age of Reconnaissance: Discovery, Exploration, and Settlement, 1450 to 1650* (Praeger, 1963). Samuel Eliot Morison, *The European Discovery of America: The Northern Voyages* (Oxford University Press, 1971); David Beers Quinn, *England and the Discovery of America, 1481–1620* (Harper & Row, 1974); Wallace Notestein, *The English People on the Eve of Colonization, 1603–1630* (Harper & Brothers, 1954); Charles Gibson, *Spain in America* (Harper & Row, 1966); and W. J. Eccles, *France in America* (Harper & Row, 1972), all discuss European contacts in North America.

ISSUE 4

Was the Salem Witchcraft Hysteria Caused by a Fear of Women?

YES: Carol F. Karlsen, from *The Devil in the Shape of a Woman: Witchcraft in Colonial New England* (W. W. Norton, 1987)

NO: Laurie Winn Carlson, from *A Fever in Salem* (Ivan R. Dee, 1999)

ISSUE SUMMARY

YES: Carol Karlsen contends that the belief that woman was evil existed implicitly at the core of Puritan culture and explains why alleged witches, as threats to the desired order of society, were generally seen as women.

NO: Laurie Winn Carlson believes that the witchcraft hysteria in Salem was the product of people's responses to physical and neurological behaviors resulting from an unrecognized epidemic of encephalitis.

Although an interest in the occult, including witchcraft and devil worship, exists in modern society, for most of us the images of witches are confined to our television and movie screens or perhaps to the theatrical stage where a Shakespearean tragedy is being performed. We can watch the annual presentation of *The Wizard of Oz* and reruns of *Bewitched* or hear the cries of "Bubble, bubble, toil and trouble" in a scene from *Macbeth,* with as little concern for the safety of our souls as we exhibit when black-garbed, broomstick-toting children appear on our doorsteps at Halloween. But such was not always the case.

Prehistoric paintings on the walls of caves throughout Europe, from Spain to Russia, reveal that witchcraft was of immediate and serious concern to many of our ancestors. The most intense eruptions in the long history of witchcraft, however, appeared during the sixteenth and seventeenth centuries. In the British North American colonies, there were over 100 witchcraft trials in seventeenth-century New England alone, and 40 percent of those accused were executed. For most Americans the events that began in the kitchen of the Reverend Samuel Parris in Salem, Massachusetts, in 1692 are the most notorious.

A group of young girls, with the assistance of Parris's West Indian slave, Tituba, were attempting to see into the future by "reading" messages in the white of a raw egg they had suspended in a glass. The tragic results of this seemingly innocent diversion scandalized the Salem community and reverberated all the way to Boston. One of the participants insisted she saw the specter of a coffin in the egg white, and soon after, the girls began to display the hysterical symptoms of the possessed. Following intense interrogation by adults, Tituba, Sarah Good, and Sarah Osborne were accused of practicing magic and were arrested. Subsequently, Tituba confessed her guilt and acknowledged the existence of other witches but refused to name them. Accusations spread as paranoia enveloped the community. Between May and September 1692, hundreds of people were arrested. Nineteen were convicted and hanged (not burned at the stake, as is often assumed), and another, a man who refused to admit either guilt or innocence, was pressed to death under heavy weights. Finally, Sir William Phips, the new royal governor of the colony, halted court proceedings against the accused (which included his wife), and in May 1693, he ordered the release of those who were still in jail.

Throughout history, witchcraft accusations have tended to follow certain patterns, most of which were duplicated in Salem. Usually, they occurred during periods of political turmoil, economic dislocation, or social stress. In Salem, a political impasse between English authorities and the Massachusetts Bay Colony, economic tensions between commercial and agricultural interests, and disagreements between Salem Town and Salem Village all formed the backdrop to the legal drama of 1692. In addition, the events in Salem fit the traditional pattern that those accused were almost always women. To what extent did sexism play the central role in the Salem witchcraft hysteria of 1692? Are there other equally valid explanations that place little or no weight on the gender of the accused?

In the selections that follow, Carol F. Karlsen and Mary Beth Norton offer two varying interpretations that seek to explain the events in Salem over 300 years ago. For Karlsen, gender is the key factor. Negative views of women as the embodiment of evil were deeply imbedded in the Puritan (and European) world view. But through most of the seventeenth century, according to Karlsen, New Englanders avoided explicit connections between women and witchcraft. Nevertheless, the attitudes that depicted witches as women remained self-evident truths and sprang to the surface in 1692. Laurie Winn Carlson, on the other hand, insists that previous explanations for the events in Salem fail to take into account the physical and neurological symptoms exhibited by many of the residents of the town. Those symptoms, she argues, correspond very closely to behaviors described during the pandemic of encephalitis lethargica that struck the United States in the early twentieth century, and they provide a reasonable explanation for many of the unanswered questions about the events in Salem.

YES

Carol F. Karlsen

The Devil in the Shape of a Woman: Witchcraft in Colonial New England

Handmaidens of the Lord

There is a curious paradox that students of New England witchcraft encounter. The characteristics of the New England witch—demographic, economic, religious, and sexual—emerge from *patterns* found in accusations and in the life histories of the accused; they are not visible in the content of individual accusations or in the ministerial literature. No colonist ever explicitly said why he or she saw witches as women, or particularly as older women. No one explained why some older women were suspect while others were not, why certain sins were signs of witchcraft when committed by women but not when committed by men, or why specific behaviors associated with women aroused witchcraft fears while specific behaviors associated with men did not. Indeed, New Englanders did not openly discuss most of their widely shared assumptions about women-as-witches.

This cultural silence becomes even more puzzling when we consider that many of these assumptions had once been quite openly talked about in the European witchcraft tradition. In the late fifteenth and early sixteenth centuries especially, defenders of the Christian faith spelled out in elaborate detail why they believed women rather than men were likely to join Satan's forces. The reasons they gave are not very different from those evident in the patterns the New England sources reveal. This presses upon us a question of some consequence: Why had once-explicit beliefs about women's proclivity to witchcraft become implicit in their New England setting?

We can probe this question by following the lead of the anthropologist Mary Douglas and other scholars who have explored the social construction of knowledge. In Douglas's analysis, human societies relegate certain information to the category of self-evident truths. Ideas that are treated as self-evident, "as too true to warrant discussion," constitute a society's implicit knowledge. At one time explicit, implicit ideas have not simply been forgotten, but have been "actively thrust out of the way" because they conflict with ideas deemed more suitable to the social order. But the conflict is more apparent than real. In the "elusive exchange" between implicit and explicit knowledge, the implicit is "obliquely affirmed" and the society is shielded from challenges to its world view. The implicit resides in a society's symbols, rituals, and myths, which simultaneously describe, reflect, and mask that world view. To understand these processes, implicit and explicit knowledge must be examined together and in the context of their social environment.

In colonial New England, the many connections between "women" and "witchcraft" were implicitly understood. In Europe, several generations before, the connections had still been explicit. Over time, these established "truths" about women's sinfulness had increasingly come into conflict with other ideas about women—ideas latent in Christian thought but brought to the fore by the Reformation and the political, economic, and social transformations that accompanied it. For the Puritans who emigrated to New England in the early seventeenth century, once-explicit assumptions about why witches were women were already self-evident.

The swiftly changing conditions of early settlement left it uncertain at first whether, or how, witchcraft would serve the goals of New England society. Though men in positions of authority believed that certain women were working against the new colonies' interests, others did not see these women as witches. By the late 1640s, however, New Englanders embraced a witchcraft belief system as integral to their social order. Over the course of the seventeenth century, Puritan rituals, symbols, and myths perpetuated the belief that women posed ever-present dangers to human society, but the newer, post-Reformation ideas about women forced colonists to shrink from explicitly justifying this belief. They therefore continued to assume the complex of ideas about women-as-witches as self-evident truths. . . .

Seventeenth-century Puritan writings on women and family life reveal that the sexual hierarchy was at stake for them also, but with this difference: knowledge that detailed, explained, and justified the denigration of women had come into conflict with newer views of women. Though still vital, the old truths had been thrust from sight by the new.

The fundamental tenet of European witchcraft—that women were innately more evil than men—did not fit with other ideas Puritans brought with them to their new world. This tenet was still as necessary to Puritans as it had been for their Catholic predecessors, but it was incompatible with the emphasis Puritanism placed on the priesthood of all believers, on the importance of marriage and family relations, and on the status of women within those relations.

Puritanism took shape in late sixteenth- and early seventeenth-century England amidst a heated controversy over the nature of women, the value of marriage, and the propriety of women's social roles. The dominant attitude toward women in the popular press and on stage did not differ very much from the views of Catholic witch-hunters except that overall it was less virulent, delivered as often in the form of mockery as invective. According to this opinion, women were evil, whorish, deceitful, extravagant, angry, vengeful, and, of course, insubordinate and proud. Women "are altogether a lumpe of pride," one author maintained in 1609—"a masse of pride, even altogether made of pride, and nothing else but pride, pride." Considering the nature of women, marriage was at best man's folly; at worst, it was the cause of his destruction.

The problem, as some writers of this school had it, was women's increasing independence, impudence, "masculine" dress, and "masculine" ways. The presence of women in the streets and shops of the new commercial centers was merely symptomatic of their newly found "forwardness" and desire for "liberties." But more than likely it was not so much women's increasing independence in the wake of commercial development that troubled these commentators; rather it was the increasing visibility of women within their traditional but increasingly commercialized occupations. Solutions to the problem, when offered, echoed a 1547 London proclamation that enjoined husbands to "keep their wives in their houses."

Other writers argued that women were equal if not superior to men, called for recognition of the abuse women suffered under men's tyranny, and intimated that society would be better served if economic power resided in women's hands—but their voices were few and barely heard. More often, defenders of women simply took exception to the worst of the misogynists' charges and recounted the contributions women made to the welfare of their families and their society. The most serious challenge to prevailing opinion, however, came from a group of men who shared some of the concerns and goals of women's most avid detractors. Most of these men were Protestant ministers, and they entered the debate indirectly, through their sermons and publications on domestic relations. Though not primarily interested in bettering women's position in society, they found certain transformations in attitudes toward women essential to their own social vision. Among them, it was the Puritan divines—in both old and New England—who mounted the most cogent, most sustained, and most enduring attack on the contemporary wisdom concerning women's inherent evil.

From the publication of Robert Cleaver's *A Godly Form of Householde Governement* in 1598 until at least the appearance of John Cotton's *A Meet Help* in 1699, a number of Puritan ministers did battle with "Misogynists, such as cry out against all women." If they were not unanimous on every point, most of them agreed with John Cotton that women were not "a necessary Evil," but "a necessary good." For justification of this belief, they turned to the Scriptures, to the story of the Creation. God in his infinite wisdom, John Robinson contended, had created woman from man and for man, when he "could find none fit and good enough for the man . . . amongst all the good creatures which he had made." He had made woman *from* man's rib, Samuel Willard noted, "Partly that all might derive Originally from One; Partly that she might be the more Dear and Precious to him, and Beloved by him as a piece of himself." He had made her *for* "man's conveniency and comfort," Cotton said, to be a helpmeet in all his spiritual and secular endeavors and "a most sweet and intimate companion." It followed from both the means and purposes of God's Creation that women and men were "joynt Heirs of salvation," that marriage was an honorable, even ideal state, and that women who fulfilled the purposes of their creation deserved to be praised, not vilified by godly men. In 1598,

Cleaver called men foolish who detested women and marriage. For Cotton, a century later, such men were "a sort of Blasphemers."

What had happened? Why did Puritans (along with their reforming brethren) insist on a shift in attitude that would by the nineteenth century result in a full reversal of a number of sixteenth-century notions about the "innate" qualities of men and women? We can begin to answer this question by considering a few elements critical in bringing about the transformation.

The Puritan challenge to the authority of church and state covered many issues, but one point not in dispute was the necessity of authority itself. Puritans were as disturbed by the lack of order in their society as were their enemies and were as fully committed to the principle of hierarchy. Though Puritanism developed during the period of upheavel that followed the breakup of the feudal order, Puritans were nevertheless determined to smother the sources of upheaval. Like other propertied Englishmen, Puritan men worried especially about masterlessness—insubordination in women, children, servants, vagabonds, beggars, and even in themselves.

Where they differed with other men of property was in their belief that existing authority was both ineffective and misplaced. "Faced with the ineffectuality of authorities in everyday life," one historian has argued, "the Puritans dramatically and emphatically denied the chain of authority in the church and enthroned conscience in its place. . . . The radical solution to social deterioration was not the strengthening of external authority. It was, rather, the internalization of authority itself." Foremost among the lessons Puritans taught was God's insistence on complete submission to divine will as expressed in the Bible and interpreted by ministers and magistrates. Outward compliance was not enough. Individuals who were fully committed to following the laws of God were *self*-controlled, needing only the Scriptures and an educated ministry to guide them on the path of right behavior. Submission to God's will had to be not only complete but voluntary. External discipline was still necessary to control the ungodly, but even they could be taught a measure of self-discipline.

The internal commitment to God's laws was to be inculcated primarily within the family, under the guidance and watchful eye of the head of the household, who conducted family prayer and instilled moral values in his dependents. It was not easy for family heads to ensure willing submission in their dependents, Puritans readily admitted. Minister John Robinson was talking specifically about children when he said that the "stubbornness, and stoutness of mind arising from natural pride . . . must . . . be broken and beaten down, . . . [the] root of actual rebellion both against God and man . . . destroyed," but his remarks reflect the larger Puritan belief in the difficulty of curbing human willfulness. For subordinates to accept their places in the hierarchical order, they must first be disciplined to accept the *sin* in their very tendency to rebel. From there, it was possible to develop enlightened consciences.

The family was also crucial as a symbol of a hierarchical society. Functioning as both "a little Church" and "a little Commonwealth," it served as a model of relationships between God and his creatures and as a model for all social relations. As husband, father, and master to wife, children, and servants, the head of the household stood in the same relationship to them as the minister did to his congregants and as the magistrate did to his subjects. Also, his relationship to them mirrored God's to him. Indeed, the authority of God was vested in him as household head, and his relationship to God was immediate: he served God directly. There was therefore no need for a priesthood to mediate between God and family heads. Other household members had immortal souls and could pray to God directly, but they served God indirectly by serving their superiors within the domestic frame. This model enhanced the position of all male heads of household and made any challenge to their authority a challenge to God's authority. It thereby more firmly tied other family members into positions of subordination.

The relationship of household heads to other family members fit within a larger Puritan world view. God had created the world, Puritans maintained, in the form of a great "Chain of Being" in which man was both above other creatures and subordinate to the Deity. God had ordained that human relationships were to be similarly patterned, with husbands superior to wives, parents to children, masters to servants, ministers to congregants, and magistrates to subjects. All, however, were subordinate to God. In each of these relations, inferiors served God by serving their superiors. While Puritans viewed the parent-child relation as a natural one, all other unequal relationships were described as voluntary, based on a covenant between the individuals concerned. God also required that family heads enter into another contractual relationship, called a "family covenant." Under this agreement, men promised to ensure obedience in all their dependents, in return for God's promise of prosperity.

Finally, the family also guided children in the right selection of their "particular callings." For the English divine William Perkins, particular callings were of two types. The first was God's call to individuals to enter into one or more of the several kinds of unequal social relations (husband/wife, parent/child, master/servant, and so on), relations that were "the essence and foundation of any society, without which the society cannot be." The second was God's call to specific kinds of employment by which individuals earned their livelihoods. In each case, God did the calling, but children had to endeavor to know what God had in mind for them, and parents were responsible to see that their charges made appropriate choices. Once chosen, callings were to be attended to conscientiously, not for honor or material reward but in the service of God. What Perkins did not say was that for Puritans the second sort of calling did not apply to females. Woman was called for only one employment, the work of a wife. . . .

As the old idea of woman as a necessary evil was gradually transformed into the idea of woman as a necessary good, the fear and hostility that men felt toward women remained. The old view of woman was suppressed, but it made its presence known in the many faults and tensions that riddled Puritan formulations on woman. Though largely unspoken, the old assumptions modified the seemingly more enlightened knowledge Puritans imparted. The new discourse, "first uttered out of the pulpit," was in fact dedicated to affirming the beliefs of the old, but in ways that would better serve male interests in a society that was itself being transformed.

The belief that woman was evil continued to reside in the myth at the core of Puritan culture—the biblical tale of human origins. Really two myths in one, it is the story of Creation in the Garden of Eden and the story of Adam and Eve's fall from grace. Our concern is mostly with the latter, but the two tales are nonetheless interdependent—the joys of Paradise making comprehensible the agonies of Paradise lost.

In their version of human origins, the Puritan clergy were more ambiguous than usual about when they were discussing "man, male and female," and when they were discussing men only. Despite its many contradictions, this creation myth allowed the Puritans to establish their two most cherished truths: hierarchy and order. Even before the Fall, they maintained, God had designated woman as both inferior to and destined to serve man—though her original inferiority was based "in innocency" and without "grief." Woman's initial identity was not—like man's—as a separate individual, but as a wife in relation to a husband. The very purpose of her creation allowed Puritans to extend the idea of her subordination *as wife* to her subordination *as woman*, in much the same manner as Anglican minister Matthew Griffiths did when he observed: "No sooner was she a Woman, but presently a Wife; so that Woman and Wife are of the same standing." So interchangeable were these terms in the minds of the clergy that they could barely conceive of woman's relationship to God except through a husband.

Woman's position in the Puritan version of Eden was analogous to that of the angels and the animals. Angels were formed before Creation as morally perfect spiritual beings. Though angels were clearly above man in the hierarchy of Creation, and though man was not to have dominion over them, God would require the angels to "minister for man." Animals were even closer to the position of woman since they too were created specifically to serve man.

The Puritan account of the Fall follows the standard Christian version in its general outlines. Discontented with their position in the hierarchical order, Adam and Eve succumbed to the Devil's temptation to eat the forbidden fruit, thus challenging God's supremacy over them and rebelling against the order of Creation. Guilty of pride, both were punished, but Eve doubly because she gave in to the temptation first, thereby causing man's downfall.

Puritan elaborations on this tale are revealing. According to Samuel Willard, Adam and Eve were both principal causes of man's fall, but there were also three instrumental causes: the serpent, the Devil, and the woman. Exonerating the serpent as a creature lacking the ability to reason, he went on to discuss the two "blamable Causes," the Devil and Eve. The events of the Fall originated with the Devil, he said, explaining that the word "Devil" was a collective term for a group of apostate angels. Filled with pride in their positions as the most noble of God's creations, discontented that they were assigned to serve "such a peasant as man," envious of what they saw as a "greater honour conferred upon him," and consumed with malice against God and man, the apostate angels sought revenge by plotting man's downfall. What motivated them was not their displeasure at their place in the hierarchical order, Willard claimed, for only God was above them. Rather it was their "supreme contempt for their employment." United by their evil intentions, they are called "Satan" in the Scriptures as a sign that they had traded their natural subjection to God for a diabolical subjection to the "Prince of Evil." In the process of accomplishing their ends, they were the first to speak falsehoods in Eden, becoming in the process blasphemers against God and murderers of the bodies and souls of men. "They seduced them . . . and thus in procuring of man's fall, they compleated their own; in making of him miserable, they made themselves Devils."

Eve's story—and her motivations—were more complex. Entering the body of the serpent, the Devil addressed himself to Eve, Willard said, suggesting to her that if she ate the fruit he offered, she would become godlike. Her senses suddenly deluded, she gave in to her lusts: "the lusts of the flesh, in giving way to carnal appetite, good for food; the lust of the eye, in entertaining the desirable aspect of the forbidden fruit, pleasant to the eyes; [and] the lusts of pride, in aspiring after more wisdom than God saw meet to endow a creature withal, to make one wise." Easily seduced, she in turn seduced Adam, thereby implicating him in her guilt. She commended the fruit, "makes offers to him, insinuates herself into him, backs all that the Serpent had said, and attracts him to joint consent with her in the great Transgression." Eve was moved not only by her sensuality but, like Satan, by pride. Her action bespoke the pride of a desire for knowledge, and by extension for God's position, rather than the resentment of her obligation to serve man.

Adam and Eve were both punished for the sin of pride, for rebelling against the order of Creation, but Eve rebelled both as part of man and as man's "other." For this reason, Willard called her both a principal and an instrumental cause of man's fall. According to Willard, when God commanded man not to eat the fruit of the tree of knowledge, "though their prohibition be expresst as given to Adam in the singular [necessarily so, as Eve had yet to be created in the chapter Willard was citing]. . . yet Eve understood it as comprehending them both." Thus she shared with Adam responsibility as a principal in the matter. "Yet, looking upon her as made for the man, and by the Creators law owing a subordination to him, so she may also be looked upon as instrumental." Elaborating on this point, Willard argued that having been created as his helpmeet, she ought to have encouraged and fortified him in that obedience which God had required of them both. Instead she became a mischief, "an occasion, yea a blamable cause of his ruin." For this, the Lord placed his "special curse" upon the female sex: "Unto the woman he said, I will greatly multiply thy sorrow and thy conception: in sorrow shalt thou bring forth children: and thy desire shall be to thy husband, and he shall rule over thee."

Part of woman's sin, then, was the seduction of man; another part was her failure to serve man. Though Willard never explicitly charged woman with having the same sinister motives as Satan, he did strengthen the association between these two instruments of man's fall by defining her as the Devil's willing agent: she acted "upon deliberation," he said, "and was voluntary in what she did."

In contrast, Adam (as distinguished from "man") lacked any motive for his sin. His role in the Fall was essentially passive. When God confronted the pair about their sin Adam defended himself by pointing the accusatory finger at his mate: "the woman which thou gavest to be with me, she gave me of the tree, and I did eat." Willard exonerated Adam by supporting his disclaimer and by describing him as an unwitting victim of his temptress wife: "Adam was not deceived, but the woman being deceived, was in the transgression." The burden of Adam's guilt was thereby lifted, and the blame placed on Eve. If "man's" sin in the Garden of Eden was pride, it was woman subsumed in man who committed it. Her male counterpart deserved a share of the punishment, but merely for allowing himself to be made "a servant of servants." Willard reinforced this point in his description of the sins that made human beings like devils. It is by now a familiar list: pride, discontent, envy, malice, lying, blasphemy, seduction, and murder. Some were explicitly Eve's, others implicitly hers; none were attributed to Adam.

⚜

Eve was the main symbol of woman-as-evil in Puritan culture. She was, in many ways, the archetypal witch. Whatever the new beliefs affirmed about women's potential goodness, the persistence of Eve as a figure in the Puritan cosmology signals the endurance of older if more covert beliefs. Women could be taught to internalize the authority of men, Puritans thought—but they knew that the sweeping denial of self they demanded of women was "too bitter a pill to be well digested," that it had to "be sweetened" before it could "be swallowed." The story of the Fall taught the lesson that female submission would not come easily—not, certainly, through a theological reformulation alone. Their continuing references to the Fall bespeak Puritan belief that the subjection of the daughters of Eve, whether religious, economic, or sexual, would have to be coerced. That was the message of Eve's punishment.

Ever fearful that women's conversion to virtuous womanhood was incomplete, ministers sometimes resorted to more vivid images of physical and psychological coercion. They warned the Puritan husband that he should not "bee satisfied that hee hath robed his wife of her virginitie, but in that hee hath possession and use of her will." Women tempted to abandon their chastity, and therefore their God, were told to resolve "that if ever these Other Lords do after this Obtain any thing from you, it shall be by the Violence of a Rape." For women who had yet to learn the necessity of subjection came the ever-present threat of additional punishment: "Christ will sorely revenge the rebellion of evill wives." Though the clergy protested again and again that the position of wives was different from that of servants, when they tried to picture what husbands' position would be like if the power relations within marriage were reversed, they envisioned men kept as vassals or enchained as slaves.

Ministers described this reversal of the sexual order as a complete perversion of the laws of God and the laws of nature. The most frequently employed symbols of female usurpers were perversions of those other beings destined to serve man: angels and animals. For woman to be "a man-kinde woman or a masterly wife" conjured up images of fallen angels, demons, and monsters, distortions of nature in every respect.

The tensions within the new ideology suggest that Puritans could no more resolve the ambivalence in their feelings than they could the contradictions in their thought. There was a deep and fundamental split in the Puritan psyche where women were concerned: their two conflicting sets of beliefs about women coexisted, albeit precariously, one on a conscious level, the other layers beneath. If woman was good—if she was chaste, submissive, deferential—then who was this creature whose image so frequently, if so fleetingly, passed through the mind and who so regularly controlled the night? Who was this female figure who was so clearly what woman was not? The ministers were not the only ones who lived with this tension, of course. The dual view of women affected everyone, male and female alike. Still, as the primary arbiters of culture in an age when God still reigned supreme, the clergy played the crucial role not only in creating the virtuous wife but in perpetuating belief in her malevolent predecessor.

In colonial New England, the intensity of this psychic tension is best seen in the writings of Cotton Mather—perhaps simply because he wrote so much, perhaps because his own ambivalence was so extreme.

In 1692, Mather published his lengthiest treatise on womanhood, *Ornaments for the Daughters of Zion.* His purpose, as he stated in his preface, was "to advocate virtue among those who can not forget their Ornaments and to promote a fear of God in the female sex." He was concerned both with women's behavior and with their relationship to God. He devoted much of his attention to the celebration of individual women, mostly biblical figures, whose lives were distinguished by quiet piety and godly ways. He presented them as models for New England women to emulate.

That same year, Mather completed *Wonders of the Invisible World,* his major justification for the Salem witchcraft trials and executions. Mather's focus here was on the behavior of witches and their relationships with the Devil—particularly women's complicity in Satan's attempts to overthrow the churches of New England. The book featured the witchcraft testimony presented against five of the accused at Salem, four of whom were women.

The nearly simultaneous publication of these two mirror-image works was not, it would seem, merely coincidental. Though Mather's witchcraft book does not explicitly address the reason why most of his subjects are women, his witches are nonetheless embodiments of peculiarly female forms of evil. Proud, discontented, envious, and malicious, they stood in direct contrast to the embodiments of female good in *Ornaments,* all of whom fully accepted the place God had chosen for them and regarded a willing and joyous submission to his will as the ultimate expression of their faith. Unable to ignore the profound uneasiness these two diametrically opposed views generated, Mather, like other New Englanders, relegated the still-powerful belief in women's evil to witches, on whom his fear and hatred could be unleashed. He was thereby freed to lavish praise on virtuous women—women who repressed the "witch" in themselves. Though his resolution allowed him to preserve man's superior position in the universe, Mather's heavy reliance in *Ornaments* on figures of Eve reveals how very delicate the balance was.

Mather's resolution was also his culture's. In the late sixteenth and seventeenth centuries, Puritans and other like-minded Protestants were engaged in the task of transforming an ideology, formulating beliefs that would better serve them in a world in which many of the old hierarchies and truths were no longer useful or plausible. They devised a new conception of man which, though drawn from the old, increasingly conceived him as an individual in relation to his God and his neighbors. It was a formulation that better fit the new economic order. The new man required a new woman: not an individual like himself, but a being who made possible his mobility, his accumulation of property, his sense of self-importance, and his subjection to new masters. By defining women as capable and worthy of the helpmeet role, the Puritan authorities offered a powerful inducement for women to embrace it. But they also recognized that the task they had set for themselves was a difficult one. If women were to repress their own needs, their own goals, their own interests—and identify with the needs, goals, and interests of the men in their families—then the impulse to speak and act on their own behalf had to be stifled.

As the witchcraft trials and executions show, only force could ensure such a sweeping denial of self. New England witches were women who resisted the new truths, either symbolically or in fact. In doing so, they were visible—and profoundly disturbing—reminders of the potential resistance in all women.

Puritans' witchcraft beliefs are finally inseparable from their ideas about women and from their larger religious world view. The witch was both the negative model by which the virtuous woman was defined and the focus for Puritan explanations of the problem of evil. In both respects, Puritan culture resembles other cultures with witchcraft beliefs: the witch image sets off in stark relief the most cherished values of these societies. A central element in these cosmologies, witches explain the presence of not only illness, death, and personal misfortune, but of attitudes and behavior antithetical to the culture's moral universe.

For Puritans, hierarchy and order were the most cherished values. People who did not accept their place in the social order were the very embodiments of evil. Disorderly women posed a greater threat than disorderly men because the male/female relation provided the very model of and for all hierarchical relations, and because Puritans hoped that the subordination of women to men would ensure men's stake in maintaining those relations. Many years ago the anthropologist Monica Hunter Wilson said that witchcraft beliefs were "the standardized nightmare of a group, and . . . the comparative analysis of such nightmares . . . one of the keys to the understanding of society." New England's nightmare was what the historian Natalie Zemon Davis has called "women on top": women as the willing agents of the Prince of Evil in his effort to topple the whole hierarchical system.

Laurie Winn Carlson ➜ **NO**

A Fever in Salem: A New Interpretation of the New England Witch Trials

During the latter part of the seventeenth century, residents of a northeastern Massachusetts colony experienced a succession of witchcraft accusations resulting in hearings, trials, imprisonments, and executions. Between 1689 and 1700 the citizens complained of symptoms that included fits (convulsions), spectral visions (hallucinations), mental "distraction" (psychosis), "pinching, pin pricking and bites" on their skin (clonus), lethargy, and even death. They "barked like dogs," were unable to walk, and had their arms and legs "nearly twisted out of joint."

In late winter and early spring of 1692, residents of Salem Village, Massachusetts, a thinly settled town of six hundred, began to suffer from a strange physical and mental malady. Fits, hallucinations, temporary paralysis, and "distracted" rampages were suddenly occurring sporadically in the community. The livestock, too, seemed to suffer from the unexplainable illness. The randomness of the victims and the unusual symptoms that were seldom exactly the same, led the residents to suspect an otherworldly menace. With the limited scientific and medical knowledge of the time, physicians who were consulted could only offer witchcraft as an explanation.

These New Englanders were Puritans, people who had come to North America to establish a utopian vision of community based upon religious ideals. But, as the historian Daniel Boorstin points out, their religious beliefs were countered by their reliance on English common law. The Puritans did not create a society out of their religious dogma but maintained the rule of law brought from their homeland. They were pragmatic, attempting to adapt practices brought from England rather than reinventing their own as it suited them. When problems arose that were within the realm of the legal system, the community acted appropriately, seeking redress for wrongs within the courts.

Thus when purported witchcraft appeared, church leaders, physicians, and a panicked citizenry turned the problem over to the civil authorities. Witchcraft was a capital crime in all the colonies, and whoever was to blame for it had to be ferreted out and made to stop. Because no one could halt the outbreak of illness, for ten months the community wrestled with sickness, sin, and the criminal act of witchcraft. By September 1692, nineteen convicted witches had been hanged and more than a hundred people sat in prison awaiting sentencing when the trials at last faded. The next year all were released and the court closed. The craze ended as abruptly as it began.

Or did it? There had been similar sporadic physical complaints blamed on witchcraft going back several decades in New England, to the 1640s when the first executions for the crime of witchcraft were ordered in the colonies. Evidence indicates that people (and domestic animals) had suffered similar physical symptoms and ailments in Europe in still earlier years. After the witch trials ended in Salem, there continued to be complaints of the "Salem symptoms" in Connecticut and New Hampshire, as well as in Boston, into the early eighteenth century. But there were no more hangings. The epidemic and witchcraft had parted ways.

By examining the primary records left by those who suffered from the unexplainable and supposedly diabolical ailments in 1692, we get a clear picture of exactly what they were experiencing. *The Salem Witchcraft Papers,* a three-volume set compiled from the original documents and preserved as typescripts by the Works Progress Administration in the 1930s, has been edited for today's reader by Paul Boyer and Stephen Nissenbaum. It is invaluable for reading the complete and detailed problems people were dealing with. Like sitting in the physician's office with them, we read where the pain started, how it disappeared or progressed, how long they endured it.

A similar epidemic with nearly exact symptoms swept the world from 1916 to 1930. This world-wide pandemic, sleeping sickness, or encephalitis lethargica, eventually claimed more than five million victims. Its cause has never been fully identified. There is no cure. Victims of the twentieth-century epidemic continue under hospitalization to the present day. An excellent source for better understanding encephalitis lethargica is Oliver Sacks's book *Awakenings,* which is now in its sixth edition and has become a cult classic. A movie of the same title, based on the book, presents a very credible look at the physical behaviors patients exhibited during the epidemic. While encephalitis lethargica, in the epidemic form in which it appeared in the early twentieth century, is not active today, outbreaks of insect-borne encephalitis do appear infrequently throughout the country; recent outbreaks of mosquito-borne encephalitis have nearly brought Walt Disney World in Florida to a halt, have caused entire towns to abandon evening football games, and have made horse owners anxious throughout the San Joaquin Valley in California.

Using the legal documents from the Salem witch trials of 1692, as well as contemporary accounts of earlier incidents in the surrounding area, we can identify the "afflictions" that the colonists experienced and that led to the accusations of witchcraft. By comparing the symptoms reported by seventeenth-century colonists with those of patients affected by the encephalitis lethargica epidemic of the early twentieth century, a pattern of symptoms emerges. This pattern supports the hypothesis that the witch-hunts of New England were a response to unexplained physical and neurological behaviors resulting from an epidemic of encephalitis. This was some form of the same encephalitis epidemic that became pandemic in the 1920s. In fact it is difficult to find anything in the record at Salem that *doesn't* support the idea that the symptoms were caused by that very disease. . . .

What Happened at Salem?

. . . Historical explanations of witchcraft dwell on what Thomas Szasz calls the "scapegoat theory of witchcraft," which explores who was accused and why in the context of larger societal issues. Inevitably they fail to examine the accusers or the "afflicted," who themselves were often tried for witchcraft.

Sociologists have pointed to community-based socioeconomic problems as the causative agent in the events at Salem. They propose that there were really two Salems: Salem Town (a prosperous sector on the well-developed east side of town) and Salem Village (a less-developed, very swampy and rocky area on the west side). Likening Salem Village to a troubled backwater, the accusations and afflictions emanated from the west side, where the residents directed their animosity toward their wealthier, more powerful eastern counterparts by accusing individuals on the east side of witchcraft. Examining the struggles, failures, broken dreams, and lost hopes of the Salem Village residents, sociologists began to view the village as "an inner city on a hill." Social conflict, in this case between prosperous merchants and struggling subsistence farmers, was examined. In the case of the Salem witch hunts, the theory may better explain who was accused and convicted of witchcraft than why individuals were afflicted. Division along class and religious lines has been well documented in determining criminal accusations.

Other investigators have blamed the situation on village factionalism, claiming that Salem Village was rife with suspicious, disgruntled, jealous settlers whose frustrations had festered for years before exploding in the court record with witchcraft accusations and trials. But that does not explain why twenty-two *other* towns in New England were eventually connected to the proceedings in some way; villagers throughout Maine, New Hampshire, Connecticut, Massachusetts, and Rhode Island were brought into the trial records. Victims, accused witches, and witnesses came from other locales as far away as the Maine frontier. Other locations, such as Connecticut, conducted witch trials that preceded or coincided with those at Salem. Choosing to view the problems as power struggles or personality differences within a small village strikes one as too parochial. Many of the possessed claimants barely knew the people they named as their tormenters, in fact several had never even met the persons they accused of fostering their problems—hardly enough tension to support the idea that the entire uproar was based on long-standing animosities. Socioeconomic divisions did engender problems in the region, and while they ultimately may be used to explain who was accused and why, they do not explain the many physical symptoms or who experienced them.

Carol Karlsen has viewed what happened at Salem in her book *The Devil in the Shape of a Woman,* which relates the events to women's oppressed status within Puritan society. She considers New Englanders' "possession" to have been a cultural performance—a ritual—performed by girls, interpreted by ministers, and observed by an audience as a dramatic event. Karlsen claims the possessed individuals exhibited learned behavior patterns and that words and actions varied only slightly among them. The affected women experienced an inner conflict which was explained by ministers as a struggle between good and evil: God versus Satan. The outcome revolved around whether or not the young women would later lead virtuous lives or fall into sin. Karlsen suggests that a woman's possession was the result of her indecision or ambivalence about choosing the sort of woman she wanted to be. She views the possession as a "collective phenomenon" among women in Connecticut between 1662 and 1663, and in Massachusetts from 1692 to 1693. It was a "ritual expression of Puritan belief and New England's gender arrangements," and a challenge to society. It was ultimately a simple power struggle between women and their oppressors.

As to the physical symptoms: the fits, trances, and paralyzed limbs, among others, Karlsen attributes them to the afflicted girls' actual fear of witches as well as the idea that once they fell into an afflicted state they were free to express unacceptable feelings without reprisal. The swollen throats, extended tongues, and eyes frozen in peripheral stares were manifestations of the inner rage they felt toward society; they were so upset they literally *couldn't* speak. Their paralysis was based on anger over having to work; their inability to walk meant they could not perform their expected labor—in other words, a passive-aggressive response to a situation that incensed them. Karlsen views witchcraft possession in New England as a rebellion against gender and class powers: a psychopathology rooted in female anger.

Misogyny may well explain who was accused of witchcraft, but it lacks an explanation for the wide-ranging symptoms, the ages of the afflicted, and the patterns of symptoms that occurred across time and distance in seventeenth-century New England. Scholars who take this route, however, conveniently ignore the fact that men too were accused, tried, and hanged for witchcraft, both in the colonies and in Europe. In fact, Robin Briggs states that though "every serious historical account recognizes that large numbers of men were accused and executed on similar charges, this fact has never really penetrated to become part of the general knowledge on the subject." His research shows that a misogynistic view of witch-hunts lacks complete credibility.

Many researchers have proposed that mass hysteria affected the young women of Salem. The term *hysteria*, essentially a female complaint, has recently been dropped from use by the psychiatric profession in favor of "conversion symptom," which describes the manner in which neurotic patients suffer emotional stress brought on by an unconscious source. This stress or tension can undergo "conversion" and reveal itself in a variety of physical ailments. Conversion, a very pliable disorder, can be explained by almost any societal pressure in any particular culture. It is a psychological catchall for unexplained neurological or emotional problems. But its victims are always the same, according to analysts: unstable females.

Jean-Martin Charcot, a French physician, worked extensively with epileptic and hysteric female patients at the Salpêtrière Hospital in Paris between 1862 and 1870. He laid the groundwork for hysteria theory, calling it hystero-epilepsy.

He accused his patients of being deceitful, clever actresses who delighted in fooling the male physician. Charcot's medical students claimed to be able to transfer diseases from hysterics with the use of magnets, something they called the "metal cure." Eventually his professional standing as a neurologist diminished and faded, and he turned to faith healing. Sigmund Freud, one of his students, began his work under Charcot's direction.

A more modern version of the hysteria complex is called Mass Psychogenic Illness, or MPI, which is defined as the contagious spread of behavior within a group of individuals where one person serves as the catalyst or "starter" and the others imitate the behavior. Used to describe situations where mass illness breaks out in the school or workplace, it is usually connected to a toxic agent—real or imagined—in a less than satisfactory institutional or factory setting. MPI is the sufferer's response to overwhelming life and work stress. It relies on the individual's identification with the index case (the first one to get sick, in effect the "leader") and willingness to succumb to the same illness. A classical outbreak of MPI involves a group of segregated young females in a noisy, crowded, high-intensity setting. It is most common in Southeast Asian factories crowded with young female workers; adults are not usually affected. Symptoms appear, spread, and subside rapidly (usually over one day). Physical manifestations usually include fainting, malaise, convulsions with hyperventilation, and excitement. Transmission is by sight or sound brought about by a triggering factor which affects members of the group, who share some degree of unconscious fantasies. A phenomenon more related to the industrial world of the nineteenth and twentieth centuries than to pastoral village life in colonial New England, MPI does not address the question of why men and young children, who would not have identified emotionally and psychologically with a group of young girls, suffered. The New England colonists scarcely fit the pattern for this illness theory that demands large groups of people of similar age, sex, and personality assembled in one confined location.

Salem's witches cannot, of course, escape Freudian critique. Beyond the hysteria hypothesis, John Demos, in *Entertaining Satan,* looked at the evidence from the perspective of modern psychoanalysis. He pointed out that witchcraft explained and excused people's mistakes or incompetence—a failure or mistake blamed on witches allowed a cathartic cleansing of personal responsibility. Witches served a purpose; deviant people served as models to the rest of society to exemplify socially unacceptable behavior. But Demos's explanation that witch-hunts were an integral part of social experience, something that bound the community together—sort of a public works project—does not address the physical symptoms of the sufferers.

For the most part, examinations of the afflicted individuals at Salem have focused on the young women, essentially placing the blame on them instead of exploring an organic cause for their behaviors. Freudian explanations for the goings-on have attributed the activities of the possessed girls to a quest for attention. Their physical manifestations of illness have been explained as being conversion symptoms due to intrapsychic conflict. Their physical expression of psychological conflict is a compromise between unacceptable impulses and the mind's attempt to ignore them. Demos uses the example of Elizabeth

Knapp, whose fits became increasingly severe while strangers gathered to view her behavior. Instead of considering that she was beset by an uncontrollable series of convulsions which were likely worsened by the excited witnesses who refused to leave her alone, he attributes her worsening condition to her exhibitionist tendencies, motivated by strong dependency needs. Elizabeth's writhing on the floor in a fetal position is seen as an oral dependency left over from childhood, causing her regression to infancy.

But "inner conflict" simply does not explain the events at Salem. Neither does the idea that the young afflicted girls were motivated by an erotic attraction to church ministers who were called in to determine whether Satan was involved. The girls' repressed adolescent sexual wishes (one girl was only eleven years old) and their seeking a replacement for absent father figures scarcely explains the toll the disease was taking on victims of both sexes and all ages. No Freudian stone has been left unturned by scholars; even the "genetic reconstruction" of Elizabeth Knapp's past points out that her childhood was filled with unmet needs, her mother's frustration because of an inability to bear additional children, and her father's reputation as a suspected adulterer. "Narcissistic depletion," "psychological transference," "a tendency to fragment which was temporarily neutralized"—the psycho-lingo just about stumbles over itself in attempts to explain the afflicted girls at Salem. But unanswered questions remain: Why the sharp pains in extremities? The hallucinations? The hyperactivity? The periods of calm between sessions of convulsions? Why did other residents swear in court that they had seen marks appear on the arms of the afflicted?

The opinion that the victims were creating their own fits as challenges to authority and quests for fame has shaped most interpretations of what happened in 1692. But would the colonists have strived for public notice and attention? If the afflicted individuals were behaving unusually to garner public notice, why? Did women and men of that era really crave public attention, or would it have put them in awkward, critical, and socially unacceptable situations? How socially redeeming would writhing on the ground "like a hog" and emitting strange noises, "barking like a dog," or "bleating like a calf" be for a destitute young servant girl who hoped to marry above her station? It is difficult to accept that these spectacles, which horrified viewers as well as the participants themselves, were actually a positive experience for the young women. That sort of suspicious activity usually met with social stigma, shunning, or, at the least, brutal whipping from father or master.

Puberty, a time of inner turmoil, is thought to have contributed to the victims acting out through fits, convulsions, and erratic behavior. The victims' inability to eat is explained away as a disorder related to the youthful struggle for individuality: anorexia nervosa. What about the young men who reported symptoms? Freudian interpretation attributes their behavior to rebellion against controlling fathers. How have psycho-social interpretations explained the reason witch trials ended after 1692 in Salem? As communities grew into larger urban units, people no longer knew their neighbors, grudges receded in importance as a factor in social control, and witches were no longer valuable to society. John Demos observes that witchcraft never appeared in cities, and that it lasted longest in villages far removed from urban influence. That linkage between witchcraft outbreaks and agricultural villages is important when establishing a connection with outbreaks of encephalitis lethargica, which appeared largely in small towns and rural areas in the early twentieth century. Rather than accepting the idea that witchcraft receded because it was no longer useful in a community context, one must examine why epidemics occurred in waves and how particular diseases affected isolated population groups.

The situation in seventeenth-century New England fails psycho-social explanation because too many questions remain unanswered. Not only can we not make a strong case that infantilism, sexual repression, and a struggle for individuality caused the turmoil in Salem, but a psycho-social explanation does not answer why the symptoms, which were so *obviously physical,* appeared with such force and then, in the autumn of 1692, largely disappeared from Salem.

Because the complexity of psychological and social factors connected with interpreting witchcraft is so absorbing, the existence of a physical pathology behind the events at Salem has long been overlooked. Linnda Caporeal, a graduate student in psychology, proposed that ergot, a fungus that appears on rye crops, caused the hallucinogenic poisoning in Salem. Her article appeared in 1976 in *Science* while Americans were trying to understand the LSD drug phenomenon. Hers is one of the few attempts made to link the puzzling occurrences at Salem with biological evidence.

Ergot was identified by a French scientist in 1676, in an explanation of the relation between ergotized rye and bread poisoning. It is a fungus that contains several potent pharmacologic agents, the ergot alkaloids. One of these alkaloids is lysergic acid amide, which has ten percent of the activity of LSD (lysergic acid diethylamide). This sort of substance causes convulsions or gangrenous deterioration of the extremities. Caporeal proposed that an ergot infestation in the Salem area might explain the convulsions attributed to witchcraft. If grain crops had been infected with ergot fungus during the 1692 rainy season and later stored away, the fungus might have grown in the storage area and spread to the entire crop. When it was distributed randomly among friends and villagers, they would have become affected by the poisoned grain.

Caporeal's innovative thinking was challenged by psychologists Nicholas Spanos and Jack Gottlieb, who were quick to point out that her theory did not explain why, if food poisoning were to blame, families who ate from the same source of grain were not affected. And infants were afflicted who may not have been eating bread grains. Historically, epidemics of ergotism have appeared in areas where there was a severe vitamin A deficiency in the diet. Salem residents had plenty of milk and seafood available; they certainly did not suffer from vitamin A deficiency. Ergotism also involves extensive vomiting and diarrhea, symptoms not found in the Salem cases. A hearty appetite, almost ravenous, follows ergotism; in New England the afflicted wasted away from either an inability to eat or a lack of interest in it. The sudden onset of the Salem symptoms in late winter and early spring would be hard to trace to months of eating contaminated grain. Ergot was never seriously considered as the cause of problems at Salem, even by the colonists themselves who knew what ergotism was (it had been identified sixteen years earlier) and were trying desperately to discover the source of their problems.

An explanation that satisfies many of the unanswered questions about the events at Salem is that the symptoms reported by the afflicted New Englanders and their families in the seventeenth century were the result of an unrecognized epidemic of encephalitis. Comparisons may be made between the afflictions reported at Salem (as well as the rest of seventeenth-century New England) and the encephalitis lethargica pandemic of the early twentieth century. This partial list, created from the literature, reveals how similar the two epidemics were, in spite of the variation in medical terms of the day:

1692 SALEM	1916–1930s ENCEPHALITIS EPIDEMIC
fits	convulsions
spectral visions	hallucinations
mental "distraction"	psychoses
pinching, pricking	myoclonus of small muscle bundles on skin surface
"bites"	erythmata on skin surface, capillary hemorrhaging
eyes twisted	oculogyric crises: gaze fixed upward, downward, or to the side
inability to walk	paresis: partial paralysis
neck twisted	torticollis: spasm of neck muscles forces head to one side, spasms affect trunk and neck
repeating nonsense words	palilalia: repetition of one's own words

In both times, most of the afflicted were young women or children; the children were hit hardest, several dying in their cradles from violent fits. The afflictions appeared in late winter and early spring and receded with the heat of summer. . . . Von Economo noted that most encephalitis lethargica epidemics had historically shown the greatest number of acute cases occurring in the first quarter of the year, from midwinter to the beginning of spring. The "pricking and pinching" repeated so often in the court records at Salem can be explained by the way patients' skin surfaces exhibited twitches—quick, short, fluttering sequences of contractions of muscle bundles. Cold temperatures cause them to increase in number and spread over the body. Twitches were seldom absent in cases of hyperkinetic encephalitis lethargica during the 1920s epidemic. The skin surface also exhibited a peculiar disturbance in which red areas appeared due to dilation and congestion of the capillaries. Red marks that bleed through the skin's surface would explain the many references in court documents to suspected bites made by witches.

Examining the colonists' complaints in the trial papers uncovers many other symptom similarities: inability to walk, terrifying hallucinations, sore throat, or choking—the list goes on and on. . . .

Ultimately the witch-hunts—or at least the complaints of afflictions—ended in Salem in the autumn of 1692, and there were no more complaints the following year. An arboviral encephalitis epidemic would have receded in the fall, when the air and water grew too cold for mosquitoes' survival. By the time spring arrived, the situation had altered, and the epidemic appeared to fade. Encephalitis epidemics, like many other contagious epidemics, often recede for years—sometimes decades—between recrudescence periods. Either the agents mutate and disappear to return years later, or they run out of susceptible hosts—the only ones left are those who have an immunity to the infection.

Ticks too might have been to blame. Just as in the spread of tick-borne encephalitis throughout the northern region of Russia, ticks played a part in spreading the disease across the virgin forests of temperate North America. Peasants who worked in the forest as woodcutters were affected in Russia during the epidemic of the 1950s; in Salem, in the seventeenth century, residents also worked as woodcutters and loggers. The Putnam family, in particular, were engaged in logging and woodcutting (and in fact were involved in arguments over whether they were taking logs from property they did not own). If the Putnams brought ticks bearing disease into their homes on their bodies or clothing, other members might have been affected. Reverend Parris's household could have been infected from the large amount of firewood he negotiated to supply his family, as part of his salary. Because they were his strongest supporters, the Putnams would likely have been the ones to cut and deliver the wood to his doorstep. Firewood, in the form of large logs used in colonial fireplaces, might have harbored wood ticks that had gone into winter hibernation but came out of the bark when logs were stored beside the hearth in a warm New England house. Infestations of ticks and body lice were common in colonial homes where laundry could not be done during the winter (nowhere to dry the wet clothing) and baths were rarely taken.

Another disease that results in encephalitis is endemic to the New England area even today. Lyme disease is a contemporary problem in New England, and there is little reason to think that it would have been absent from the area in colonial times. It is an infectious disease caused by bacteria spread by deer ticks. Both people and animals can be infected with Lyme disease. It is a serious but not fatal disease today. Found throughout the United States, it is most common along the East Coast, the Great Lakes, and the Pacific Northwest. In Massachusetts, deer ticks are most often found along the coast and are common in the Connecticut River Valley. The disease most likely spreads between late May and early autumn, when ticks are active. So tiny that the larvae are no bigger than a pencil point, the ticks live for two years, during which they can infect wild and domestic animals as well as people.

Symptoms of Lyme disease include a rash where the tick was attached—which may appear anywhere between three days and a month after the innocuous bite. Some times the rash looks like a small red doughnut. Other signs include itching, hives, swollen eyelids, and flulike symptoms such as fever, headache, stiff neck, sore muscles, fatigue, sore throat, and swollen glands. The symptoms go away after a few weeks, but without medical treatment nearly half the infected people will experience the rash again in other places on their bodies. In the later stages, three major areas—the joints, the nervous system, and the heart—may be affected even months after the tick bite. People with Lyme disease can develop late-stage symptoms even if they have never had the rash. About 10 to 20 percent of the people who do not get treatment develop nervous system problems: severe headache, stiff neck, facial paralysis, or cranial nerve palsies, and weakness and/or pain in their hands, arms, feet, or legs. Symptoms may last for weeks, often shifting from mild to severe and back again.

These symptoms are found in the present form of Lyme disease; the disease could likely have mutated over the centuries, because hallucinations and paranoia, along with lethargy, are not found in today's tick-borne version of Lyme disease. Questions and problems arise when connecting Lyme disease to the situations in 1692 or 1920, but it is another factor to consider. Could ticks have been common in Salem? The colonists did not bathe regularly, and they lived close by their domestic animals. Ticks could have wintered inside the home, carried in on firewood. They would have found ample hiding places in the seams of the heavy woolen clothing commonly worn by the colonists.

What about 1920? A common nuisance of that era was the "bedbug," chinch bug, or *Cimex lectularius*. Jar lids filled with arsenic were placed under bedsteads to keep the critters from climbing into bed and feeding on people's blood. Head lice have been common throughout the ages; today's rampant epidemics in schools are nothing to ignore, though scientists reassure us that neither bedbugs nor head lice carry any type of disease. Perhaps they did at one time. Many avenues must be explored, much research must be done. Perhaps we will never know what caused encephalitis lethargica. . . .

POSTSCRIPT

Was the Salem Witchcraft Hysteria Caused by a Fear of Women?

After 1692, a few witches were tried in the British North American colonies: in Virginia (1706), North Carolina (1712), and Rhode Island (1728). The last execution for witchcraft in England occurred in 1712 and in Scotland in 1727. On the Continent, royal edicts put an end to such persecutions before the close of the seventeenth century. Documentary evidence of seventeenth-century witchcraft can be examined in George L. Burr, ed., *Narratives of the Witchcraft Cases, 1648–1706* (Charles Scribner's Sons, 1914); Paul Boyer and Stephen Nissenbaum, eds., *Salem-Village Witchcraft: A Documentary Record of Local Conflict in Colonial New England* (Northeastern University Press, 1993); David D. Hall, ed., *Witch-Hunting in Seventeenth Century New England: A Documentary History, 1638–1693*, 2d ed. (Northeastern University Press, 1999); and Frances Hall, ed., *The Salem Witch Trials Reader* (Da Capo Press, 2000).

The Salem witch trials represent one of the most thoroughly studied episodes in American history. Several scholars have concluded that the enthusiasm for learning more about the Salem witches and their accusers far outweighs the importance of the event; yet essays and books continue to roll off the presses. As suggested in the introduction to this issue, the selections by Karlsen and Carlson summarize but two of the many interpretations of the incident at Salem. Those interested in pursuing this topic further should examine Marion Starkey's *The Devil in Massachusetts: A Modern Enquiry into the Salem Witch Trials* (Knopf, 1949), which blames the episode on the lies told by the accusers. An intriguing alternative is Chadwick Hansen's *Witchcraft at Salem* (George Braziller, 1969), in which the author insists that several Salem residents did practice black magic, thereby heightening the fears of their neighbors. Paul Boyer and Stephen Nissenbaum, in *Salem Possessed: The Social Origins of Witchcraft* (Harvard University Press, 1974), emphasize the conflicts between the residents of Salem Town and Salem Village. Responses to this important monograph can be found in "Forum: Salem Repossessed," *William & Mary Quarterly* (July 2008). Mary Beth Norton has postulated that borderland threats from Native Americans and the French were conflated by Salem and Essex County residents with alleged assaults by witches to explain problems confronting seventeenth-century residents of Massachusetts Bay Colony. John Putnam Demos's *Entertaining Satan: Witchcraft and the Culture of Early New England* (Oxford University Press, 1982) applies theories and insights from the fields of psychology, sociology, and anthropology to explore the influence of witchcraft throughout New England. Also of value is Demos's earlier essay, "Underlying Themes in the Witchcraft of Seventeenth-Century New England," *American Historical Review* (June 1970). More recent studies include Larry Gragg,

The Salem Witch Crisis (Praeger, 1992), and Bernard Rosenthal, *Salem Story: Reading the Witch Trials of 1692* (Cambridge University Press, 1993). For additional discussion of the relationship between women and witchcraft, see Elizabeth Reis, *Damned Women: Sinners and Witches in Puritan New England* (Cornell University Press, 1997), and Elaine G. Breslaw, *Tituba, Reluctant Witch of Salem: Devilish Indians and Puritan Fantasies* (New York University Press, 1995).

Carol Karlsen's work reflects a growing interest in the status of colonial American women. Students in American history classes have for generations read of the founding of the colonies in British North America, their political and economic development, and the colonists' struggle for independence, without ever being confronted by a female protagonist. Only in the last three or four decades have discussions of the role of women in the development of American society made their appearance in standard textbooks. Consequently, it is useful to explore the status of women in colonial America. Surveys of American women's history that address the colonial period include June Sochen, *Herstory: A Woman's View of American History* (Alfred Publishing Company, 1974), and Nancy Woloch, *Women and the American Experience* (Alfred A. Knopf, 1984). The idea that colonial American women enjoyed a higher status than their European counterparts is supported in Richard B. Morris, *Studies in the History of American Law* (2d ed.; Octagon Books, 1964); Roger Thompson, *Women in Stuart England and America: A Comparative Study* (Routledge & Kegan, 1974); and Page Smith, *Daughters of the Promised Land: Women in American History* (Little, Brown, 1977). For a contrary view, see Lyle Koehler, *A Search for Power: The "Weaker Sex" in Seventeenth-Century New England* (University of Illinois Press, 1980). Laurel Thatcher Ulrich's *Good Wives: Image and Reality in the Lives of Women in Northern New England, 1650–1750* (Alfred A. Knopf, 1980) describes a variety of roles performed by married women.

Women in the age of the American Revolution are the focus of Linda Grant DePauw and Conover Hunt, *"Remember the Ladies": Women in America, 1750–1815* (Viking Press, 1976); Mary Beth Norton, *Liberty's Daughters: The Revolutionary Experience of American Women, 1750–1800* (Little, Brown, 1980); Linda Kerber, *Women of the Republic: Intellect and Ideology in Revolutionary America* (University of North Carolina Press, 1980); and Joy Day Buel and Richard Buel, Jr., *The Way of Duty: A Woman and Her Family in Revolutionary America* (W. W. Norton, 1984).

ISSUE 5

Was There a Great Awakening in Mid-Eighteenth Century America?

YES: **Thomas S. Kidd**, from *The Great Awakening: The Roots of Evangelical Christianity in Colonial America* (Yale University Press, 2007)

NO: **Jon Butler**, from "Enthusiasm Described and Decried: The Great Awakening as Interpretative Fiction," *Journal of American History* (September 1982)

ISSUE SUMMARY

YES: Thomas Kidd insists that preachers such as George Whitefield engineered a powerful series of revivals in the mid-eighteenth century that influenced all of the British North American colonies and gave birth to a spirit of evangelicalism that initiated a major alteration of global christian history.

NO: Jon Butler claims that to describe the religious revival activities of the eighteenth century as the "Great Awakening" is to seriously exaggerate their extent, nature, and impact on pre-revolutionary American society and politics.

Although generations of American schoolchildren have been taught that the British colonies in North America were founded by persons fleeing religious persecution in England, the truth is that many of those early settlers were motivated by other factors, some of which had little to do with theological preferences. To be sure, the Pilgrims and Puritans of New England sought to escape the proscriptions established by the Church of England. Many New Englanders, however, did not adhere to the precepts of Calvinism and therefore were viewed as outsiders. The Quakers who populated Pennsylvania were mostly fugitives from New England, where they had been victims of religious persecution. But to apply religious motivations to the earliest settlers of Virginia, South Carolina, or Georgia is to engage in a serious misreading of the historical record. Even in New England the religious mission of Massachusetts Bay Colony Governor John Winthrop's "city upon a hill" began to erode as the colonial settlements matured and stabilized.

Although religion was a central element in the lives of the seventeenth- and eighteenth-century Europeans who migrated to the New World, proliferation

90

of religious sects and denominations, emphasis upon material gain in all parts of the colonies, and the predominance of reason over emotion that is associated with the Deists of the Enlightenment period all contributed to a gradual but obvious movement of the colonists away from the church and clerical authority. William Bradford of Plymouth Colony, for example, expressed grave concern that many Plymouth residents were following a path of perfidy, and Pennsylvania founder William Penn was certain that the "holy experiment" of the Quakers had failed. Colonial clergy, fearful that a fall from grace was in progress, issued calls for a revival of religious fervor. The spirit of revivalism that spread through the colonies in the 1730s and 1740s, therefore, was an answer to these clerical prayers.

The episode known as the First Great Awakening coincided with the Pietistic movement in Europe and England and was carried forward by dynamic preachers such as Gilbert Tennant, Theodore Frelinghuysen, and George Whitefield. They promoted a religion of the heart, not of the head, in order to produce a spiritual rebirth. These revivals, most historians agree, reinvigorated American Protestantism. Many new congregations were organized as a result of irremediable schisms between "Old Lights" and "New Lights." Skepticism about the desirability of an educated clergy sparked a strong strain of anti-intellectualism. Also, the emphasis on conversion was a message to which virtually everyone could respond, regardless of age, sex, race, or social status. For some historians, the implications of the Great Awakening extended beyond the religious sphere into the realm of politics and were incorporated into the American Revolution.

In the following selections, Thomas S. Kidd writes from the traditional assumption that a powerful revivalistic force known as the "Great Awakening" occurred in the American colonies in the mid-eighteenth century. Recognizing that these revivals began before 1740 and continued well into the Revolutionary era, Kidd focuses on the activities of George Whitefield in the early 1740s. In his essay, Kidd challenges Jon Butler's contention that the influence of the Great Awakening was limited to New England and produced little change in colonial American religion. In contrast, Kidd argues that the Great Awakening produced a powerful impact in the colonies and sparked a rise in evangelical fervor that would have significant implications for global christianity.

Jon Butler claims that historians, by accepting without much question the existence of the Great Awakening, have become accomplices in Napoleon's insistence that "history is fable agreed upon." Closer scrutiny of this event, says Butler, reveals that the revivals were regional episodes that did not affect all of the colonies equally and, hence, had only a modest impact on American colonial religion. Because the mid-eighteenth-century revivals did not produce the kinds of dramatic changes—religious or political—frequently ascribed to them, Butler suggests that historians should abandon the concept of the "Great Awakening" altogether.

YES ↵

Thomas S. Kidd

The Great Awakening: The Roots of Evangelical Christianity in Colonial America

. . . Until 1982, historians took the Great Awakening as a given, but then historian Jon Butler argued that it was only an "interpretative fiction" invented by nineteenth-century Christian historians. Although Butler's argument was overextended, it helpfully provoked a revaluation of what we actually mean by "the Great Awakening." He contended that the event really amounted to just "a short-lived Calvinist revival in New England during the early 1740s." No doubt the eighteenth-century awakenings were centered in New England, but over time they came to influence parts of all the colonies, and more important, they helped birth an enormously important religious movement, evangelicalism, which shows no sign of disappearing today.

Butler also asserted that the "revivals had modest effects on colonial religion" and that they were "never radical." But if the revivals helped create evangelicalism, then not only did the awakenings make a profound change in colonial religion, but they began a major alteration of global Christian history. Moreover, . . . the revivals featured all manner of radical spiritual manifestations, unnerving antirevivalists and moderate evangelicals alike. Butler's critique does show, however, that it is not enough to evaluate evangelicalism as a homogenous whole. It had radical implications, but those implications were hotly contested by moderates, and its social potential often came to naught for women, African Americans, and Native Americans. Some evangelicals also began a great assault on the churchly establishments of colonial America, and the revolutionary move for disestablishment on the federal and state levels can largely be attributed to evangelical and deist cooperation in favor of the separation of church and state.

Butler finally claimed that, contrary to the suggestions of previous scholars, "the link between the revivals and the American Revolution is virtually nonexistent." . . . I am in substantial agreement with Butler on this point. Moreover, evangelicals' responses to the Revolution covered the whole range of opinions from enthusiastic Patriotism to staunch Loyalism. But we should also note that evangelical rhetoric and ideology helped to inspire and justify the

Patriot cause for both evangelical and nonevangelical leaders. Evangelicalism did not start the Revolution, but the Patriot side certainly benefited from the support of many evangelicals.

. . . I contend that there was, indeed, a powerful, unprecedented series of revivals from about 1740 to 1743 that touched many of the colonies and that contemporaries remembered for decades as a special visitation of the Holy Spirit. Calling this event "the" Great Awakening does present historical problems. Chief among them is that the standard framework of the "First" and "Second" Great Awakenings may obscure the fact that the evangelical movement continued to develop after 1743 and before 1800. There were important, widespread revivals that happened before the First, and between the First and Second, Great Awakenings. . . . I examine, instead, what we might call the *long* First Great Awakening and the contest to define its boundaries. Although many revivals, including the major season from 1740 to 1743, happened during this period, revivals alone did not delineate the early evangelical movement. Instead, persistent desires for revival, widespread individual conversions, and the outpouring of the Holy Spirit distinguished the new evangelicals. The long First Great Awakening started before Jonathan Edwards's 1734–35 Northampton revival and lasted roughly through the end of the American Revolution, when disestablishment, theological change, and a new round of growth started the (even more imprecise) "Second" Great Awakening. The controversial emergence of the religion of the new birth demarcated the long First Great Awakening and the first generation of American evangelical Christianity.

. . . New Englanders began to hear about George Whitefield in 1739, and many hoped that he would soon visit them. Benjamin Colman of Boston's Brattle Street Church wrote to Whitefield in December 1739 after having received a letter from him. Whitefield estimated that he might come to New England by summer 1740. Colman was deeply impressed by what he had learned about Whitefield. He had read Whitefield's *Journals,* as well as some of his sermons. Colman wrote that he had never encountered anything comparable to Whitefield's ministry, although he had witnessed "uncommon Operations of the holy Spirit . . . ; as in our Country of Hampshire of late; the Narrative of which by Mr. Edwards, I suppose you may have seen." If Whitefield would come to New England, he would find the churches' Calvinist doctrine to his liking, "how short soever we may come of your Fervours." Colman told him that the churches had been praying for him publicly, and that when he arrived he could use the commodious Brattle Street Church for meetings. In a letter to Gilbert Tennent, Whitefield wrote that he found Colman's published sermons "acute and pointed, but I think not searching enough by many degrees." If anything, Colman was too polite for Whitefield. Nevertheless, Whitefield wrote back to Colman and promised that when he came to New England "I shall endeavour to recommend an universal charity amongst all the true members of CHRIST's mystical body." Because of this universal spirit, he suggested that he might stay in the fields to preach, and out of the meetinghouses. He appreciated Colman's latitudinarianism, and they both hoped that the old division of Anglican versus dissenter would become irrelevant in light of the ministry of the new birth.

Jonathan Edwards also received word of Whitefield's revivals, and in November 1739 Whitefield wrote to him, desiring to visit Northampton to see for himself the fruit of the 1734–35 awakening. Edwards wrote back in February 1740, encouraging Whitefield to travel to Northampton but warning him not to expect much. Edwards was heartened by God's raising up Whitefield in the Church of England "to revive the mysterious, spiritual, despised, and exploded doctrines of the gospel." This might be a sign of the coming Kingdom of God, Edwards thought.

The Boston and Philadelphia newspapers began picking up stories about Whitefield's prodigious meetings in England in spring 1739, and Whitefield's fame began to spread into the hinterlands by early 1740. For instance, pastor Nicholas Gilman of Exeter, New Hampshire, on a visit to Boston, began reading Whitefield's *Journals* in mid-January 1740 and commented with admiration on Whitefield's "most Indefatigable labours to Advance the Kingdom of Christ." He borrowed more of Whitefield's sermons from Colman. In June, Gilman noted that "Mr. Whitefield [was] Now much the Subject of Conversations."

In July, Whitefield wrote to Colman to announce that he was coming soon, perhaps within a month, and to ask Colman to spread the word in friendly churches. This advance publicity worked wonderfully, and when Whitefield arrived in Newport. Rhode Island, on September 14, 1740, New England was abuzz with talk of his coming. In Newport, Whitefield was welcomed by Nathaniel Clap, a venerable Congregational minister, and the wandering Jonathan Barber of Oysterponds, Long Island. Whitefield had earlier written the disconsolate Barber, telling him that he did not presume to judge whatever dealings God had with him. As for his visionary experiences, "I rather rejoice in them, having myself been blessed with many experiences of the like nature." He told Barber to expect persecution when God dealt with him in extraordinary ways. These encouraging words led Barber to come to Newport to receive Whitefield. Upon meeting, they agreed that Barber would become part of Whitefield's entourage.

After some successes in preaching, particularly at Clap's meetinghouse, Whitefield traveled north to Boston, where he arrived on September 18. Boston was the largest town in the colonies but still only a small provincial capital with about 17,000 people. In 1740, it was in decline, and it would slowly lose population up through the American Revolution. War with Spain, and later with France, left many widows in Boston, and the city faced high taxes and inflation. The poor in Boston were many, and they responded exuberantly to Whitefield, as they would to the radical piety of James Davenport and others.

As usual, Whitefield met with Anglican authorities in Boston, most notably the Commissary Timothy Cutler, the former Congregationalist rector of Yale turned Anglican "apostate." Cutler was the most formidable proponent of Anglicanism in the colonies, and he and Whitefield did not see eye to eye about Whitefield's relationship with non-Anglicans. Cutler argued that dissenters had no legitimate ordination because they did not follow in the line of apostolic succession. Whitefield thought their ordinations were legitimate, primarily because they preached the new birth: "I saw regenerate souls among the Baptists, among the Presbyterians, among the Independents, and among the Church folks—all children of God, and yet all born again in a different way of worship," he told Cutler. Whitefield was able to leave Cutler on friendly terms, but he would receive a much warmer welcome among the Congregationalists, especially from Benjamin Colman. After visiting Cutler he preached at the Brattle Street Church to about four thousand.

Whitefield spoke from supporters' Boston pulpits as well as on Boston Common. On September 20, he preached at Joseph Sewall's Old South Church to about six thousand, and in the afternoon he addressed a crowd at the common that he estimated at eight thousand, although the papers guessed five thousand. The next day he attended Sunday morning services at the Brattle Street Church and spoke at Thomas Foxcroft's Old Brick Church in the afternoon. The crowd pressing to see him was so large that he went out to the common again and preached to an enormous assembly he totaled at fifteen thousand, close to the whole population of Boston (the newspapers guessed eight thousand). On Monday morning he sermonized at John Webb's New North Church to about six thousand. Then, in the afternoon, tragedy struck the tour. At Samuel Checkley's New South Church, the sound of a breaking board in the gallery triggered a stampede among the overflow crowd. A number of people were severely trampled, and some jumped from the balcony. Five people died. Whitefield decided to go on with the message he planned to deliver, only moving out to the common. No doubt this suggested insensitivity in Whitefield's character, but the crowd wanted him to go on, and one could hardly imagine a better moment for people to contemplate their mortality.

Whitefield visited Harvard and was not impressed with the size of the school or its spirit. He noted that "bad books," such as those by John Tillotson and Samuel Clarke, defenders of natural religion, were popular there, not the Puritan classics. Whitefield would later regret his harsh assessment of Harvard and Yale and would become a great supporter of the colleges. Whitefield also toured neighboring towns, including Roxbury and Charlestown, in his circuit. On September 27, Whitefield preached to one of his greatest crowds yet, fifteen thousand, on the common. Many were deeply affected, and Whitefield himself wrote that he felt like shouting, "This is no other than the House of God and the Gate of Heaven." Boston Common had become a portal to divine glory.

Whitefield began taking collections for the Bethesda Orphanage, and the number of pounds given was truly remarkable: perhaps £3,000 in local currency. Boston outpaced collections even in London. On September 28 alone, he collected more than £1,000 in services at the Old South and Brattle Street churches. After speaking at Brattle Street in the afternoon, Whitefield held two private meetings that showed the breadth of his appeal. The first was with the governor, Jonathan Belcher, who was an evangelical supporter of Whitefield. The second was with "a great number of negroes," who requested a private session with him. He preached to them on the conversion of the Ethiopian in Acts 8.

Whitefield visited towns up the coast from Boston from September 29 to October 6, finding some successes but also a great deal of passivity. Maine and New Hampshire had a substantial revival tradition, having seen large numbers of conversions and admissions to full communion in the 1727–28 earthquake awakening, and to a lesser extent in 1735–36 as a devastating "throat distemper" (diphtheria) raged there. He preached as far north as York, Maine, at the church of the well-respected Samuel Moody. His northern tour gave Nicholas Gilman of Exeter, who had been reading Whitefield's *Journals* and sermons for almost a year, a chance to meet him. Gilman was perhaps not as adulatory in his initial response to Whitefield as one might expect, noting that "there are Various Conjectures about Mr. Whitefield," but expressing hope that he truly was "a Man of an Excellent Spirit." Whitefield's appearance precipitated a conversion crisis for Gilman, as well, and set him on the path to becoming one of the most radical of New England's evangelicals. Whitefield won some notable converts in Maine, especially John Rogers. The pastor at Kittery, Rogers had been in the ministry for thirty years when he heard Whitefield, but he had never experienced conversion. Whitefield's ministry convinced him of his need for the new birth, and afterwards he became one of Whitefield's foremost proponents in Maine. Rogers's son Daniel, a tutor at Harvard, would soon join Whitefield's entourage and seek his own assurance of salvation. The revivals in Maine and New Hampshire would not begin in force until late 1741, however.

Returning to Boston, Whitefield continued seeing large audiences, but he also gravitated toward Tennent's confrontational style as he spoke against unconverted ministers. "I am persuaded," he wrote in his journal, "[that] the generality of preachers talk of an unknown and unfelt Christ." He felt energized by confronting the unsaved clergy: "Unspeakable freedom God gave me while treating on this head." Although some of the ministers may have grown uneasy at such talk, Whitefield drew ever-larger crowds, until he finally announced a farewell sermon on October 12, which drew a crowd estimated at twenty thousand. If reasonably accurate, this was the largest crowd ever assembled in America up to that time.

From Boston, Whitefield traveled west through New England. Delivering on his promise, Whitefield went slightly out of his way to visit Northampton. It was a poignant occasion for Edwards, who had waited five long years for revival fire to reignite in Northampton. Edwards shed tears during Whitefield's preaching. Whitefield, too, was deeply affected by his visit and impressed with Edwards's wife and children, who seemed to him models of piety and propriety. Whitefield's preaching in Northampton reached a crescendo on the Sabbath, as "Mr. Edwards wept during the whole time of exercise" in the morning. "Mr. Whitefield's sermons were suitable to the circumstances of the town," Edwards wrote later to Thomas Prince, "containing just reproofs of our back-slidings." He reported to Whitefield that the revival bore lasting fruit, including the conversion of some of the Edwardses' children. Immediately after Whitefield's departure, however, Edwards did begin a sermon series on the parable of the sower (Matthew 13), including warnings that short-lived episodes of heated preaching and crying did not make for saving religion. He subtly warned that Whitefield's brand of revivalism was ripe for religious hypocrisy. Edwards would continue to support Whitefield, but he insisted that Northampton would experience revival on his terms.

Accompanied by Edwards, Whitefield made his way south to East Windsor, the home of Edwards's parents. Along the way Whitefield kept preaching on unconverted ministers, and at one point Edwards cautioned Whitefield about not judging other ministers too harshly or trying to ascertain whether they were converted. Edwards supported Whitefield overall, but he certainly had doubts about the emotionalism and rash judgments that seemed to characterize the itinerant's ministry. In East Windsor, Whitefield preached to Timothy Edwards's congregation and then visited the elderly pastor and his wife Esther Stoddard Edwards, sharing supper and staying the night in their home.

Out of Whitefield's journey through Connecticut came two remarkable testimonies of conversion. The first was from the East Windsor saddler Samuel Belcher. Though Belcher grew up in the family of Joseph Belcher, pastor at Dedham, Massachusetts, he became "Cold and Dull" in matters of salvation, and though he experienced some concerns for his soul before 1740, they had not lasted. Whitefield's arrival signaled the beginning of a six-month-long conversion crisis. When "mr Whitefield p[re]ached here, . . . I was Greatly effected with his preaching both here and att Hartford," Belcher wrote. Belcher grew cold again, but then in April he met a man in Lebanon, Connecticut, who told of the revival there, which deeply impressed him. Then pastors Eleazar Wheelock of Lebanon and Benjamin Pomeroy of Hebron preached at East Windsor, and Belcher fell under deeper convictions than ever before. He felt the terrors of sin and the threat of damnation, "but God was pleased to enable me to Cry mightily unto him in the bitterness of my Soul for mercy in and through Jesus Christ." While he was praying, "I felt my Load Go of and my mouth was Stopt and I Could not utter one word for Some time and I felt as if my heart was Changed." When Belcher could speak again, he began praising God and he knew he had been saved. For Belcher, Whitefield's exhortations began the conversion process, but Wheelock's and Pomeroy's preaching, and his own prayers, finished the ordeal.

Whitefield's appearance also represented a beginning point for the conversion of Nathan Cole, a farmer and carpenter from Kensington, Connecticut. Cole grew up as what he called an "Arminian," likely meaning that he casually assumed that good works would save him. He began to hear reports about Whitefield's tour, and he "longed to see and hear him, and wished he would come this way." News arrived in October that Whitefield had left Boston for Northampton. Then on October 23, a messenger arrived and told him that Whitefield was coming to nearby Middletown later that morning. Cole ran in from the field to tell his wife that they were leaving immediately, fearing they would not have time to get there. As they neared the road to Middletown, he wrote that

> I saw before me a Cloud or fogg rising; I first thought it came from the great River, but as I came nearer the Road, I heard a noise something like a low rumbling thunder and presently found it was the noise of Horses feet coming down the Road and this Cloud was a Cloud of dust. . . . I could see men and horses Sliping along in the Cloud like shadows . . . every horse seemed to go with all his might to carry his rider to hear news from heaven for the saving of Souls, it made me tremble to see the Sight, how the world was in a Struggle.

When they arrived at the Middletown meeting house, Cole guessed that perhaps three or four thousand had assembled there, the countryside having emptied of its residents. Then Whitefield came to the scaffold:

> He Looked almost angelical; a young, Slim, slender, youth before some thousands of people with a bold undaunted Countenance . . . he looked as if he was Cloathed with authority from the Great God. . . . And my hearing him preach, gave me a heart wound; By Gods blessing: my old Foundation was broken up, and I saw that my righteousness would not save me; then I was convinced of the doctrine of Election: and went right to quarrelling with God about it; because that all I could do would not save me; and he had decreed from Eternity who should be saved and who not.

Cole's "quarrelling" with God lasted almost two years. Like Jonathan Edwards, he wrestled with the doctrine of predestination, thinking it abhorrent, while at the same time wondering if he himself was damned. "Hell fire was most always in my mind; and I have hundreds of times put my fingers into my pipe when I have been smoking to feel how fire felt." In the midst of his fears of hell's torments, however, God gave him a vision:

> God appeared unto me and made me Skringe: before whose face the heavens and the earth fled away; and I was Shrinked into nothing; I knew not whether I was in the body or out, I seemed to hang in open Air before God, and he seemed to Speak to me in an angry and Sovereign way what won't you trust your Soul with God; My heart answered O yes, yes, yes. . . . Now while my Soul was viewing God, my fleshly part was working imaginations and saw many things which I will omitt to tell at this time. . . . When God appeared to me every thing vanished and was gone in the twinkling of an Eye, as quick as A flash of lightning; But when God disappeared or in some measure withdrew, every thing was in its place again and I was on my Bed. My heart was broken; my burden was fallen of[f] my mind; I was set free, my distress was gone.

Cole's long conversion culminated, as it did for many early evangelicals, with a vision of God.

In New Haven, Whitefield visited with Rector Thomas Clap, who would later become one of his most bitter opponents. For now, Whitefield received a universally polite, if not entirely zealous, reception at Yale, despite his speaking to the students about "the dreadful ill consequences of an unconverted ministry." Whitefield then continued toward New York, and when he reached the border, he evaluated New England as impressive because of its godly heritage, but he feared that "Many, nay most that preach . . . do not experimentally know Christ." He loved the excitement his visit generated, though, and he thought New England was pliable enough for true revival. Pastor William Gaylord of Wilton, Connecticut, brother-in-law of James Davenport, wrote that many thought Whitefield "has a Touch of Enthusiasm" but that overheatedness could be forgiven more easily than lukewarmness. He believed

Whitefield's most profound effect might have been "stirring up" the ministers themselves, though he did have reservations about Whitefield's comments on unconverted ministers. Much of the power of Whitefield's tours lay in his ability to excite the local ministers to more fervent gospel preaching.

As Whitefield's band crossed into New York, the Harvard tutor Daniel Rogers came to the spiritual awakening he had sought during weeks of travel. After a meeting at King's Bridge (now a part of the Bronx), Rogers wrote, "It pleased God of his free Sovreign Grace to come into my poor Soul with Power and so to fill me with Peace: yea with Such Joy in the Holy Ghost as I never Experienced before—I cd not forbear Smiling nay Laughing for Joy and Gladness of Heart." Rogers shared the news with an elated Whitefield, but soon after Satan was tormenting Rogers with "Abominable Horrible Shocking Tho'ts." Assurance was not always easily gained by the new evangelicals. . . .

Whitefield continued to preach with considerable success in New York City, then moved on to Staten Island where he rendezvoused with Gilbert Tennent and John Cross. Tennent told him of his recent itineration through south Jersey, Delaware, and northern Maryland, while Cross reported that he had recently "seen great and wonderful things in his congregations." They arrived at Cross's Basking Ridge congregation on November 5, where James Davenport had been preaching in the morning. At an affecting afternoon service, Daniel Rogers recalled that a nine- or ten-year-old boy began speaking loudly, at which time Whitefield called on the crowd "to hear this Lad preaching to them." This led to a "General motion" during which many cried out, some fainted, and some fell into fits. A young man near Rogers was so moved that he had to lean on Rogers during much of the sermon until he finally fell to his knees.

The large crowd then retired to Cross's barn for the evening lecture. Tennent preached first, followed by Whitefield. Whitefield estimated that he had spoken for six minutes when one man began to shout, "He is come, He is come!" (Rogers recalled the man as crying "I have found him!") Many others began crying out "for the like favour," and Whitefield stopped to pray over them, which only heightened their fervent emotions. Rogers struggled to adequately describe the meeting, but noted that many were "weeping, Sighing, Groaning, Sobbing, screaching, crying out." The ministers finally retired, but Rogers and Davenport returned at one o'clock in the morning to resume preaching. Many in the congregation stayed up all night in the barn, praying and worshipping. "Tis a night to be remembered," Rogers wrote.

The next morning many penitents approached the departing Whitefield, including a "poor negro woman," a slave, who asked to join his entourage. Her master actually agreed to this idea (it is unlikely that he had permanent emancipation in mind), but Whitefield told her to go home and "serve her present master." Whitefield and most white evangelicals were unprepared to let the social implications of his gospel run a course to abolitionism. . . .

. . . Whitefield's tour moved on to New Brunswick, where Whitefield began telling Gilbert Tennent and Daniel Rogers to go to New England to follow up on the work there. Tennent initially refused, but after encouragement from Whitefield and an apparent vote by the entourage, Tennent agreed.

Whitefield headed south with Davenport while Rogers and Tennent began planning their new tours. In Philadelphia, Whitefield began preaching in the so-called New Building, a structure erected by supporters specifically for his visits. The one-hundred-by-seventy-foot building became Whitefield's usual pulpit in Philadelphia, and though the fervor of his earlier visit had abated, wondrous visitations continued. At one meeting, many reported experiencing the sensation of being pierced by "pointed arrows" as he preached, and a young woman fell down senseless during the meeting and had to be carried home. On another occasion Whitefield reported that he spontaneously spoke against "reasoning unbelievers," and he later found out that "a number of them were present" at his sermon. He attributed his well-timed admonition to the leading of the Holy Ghost.

Through November, Whitefield continued his tour of southern New Jersey, Pennsylvania, Delaware, and Maryland, making stops at friendly congregations in Whiteclay Creek, Fagg's Manor, Nottingham, and Bohemia Manor. Whitefield, as was often the case, fell terribly ill at Fagg's Manor, writing that "straining caused me to vomit much." But he continued preaching and praying, and "soon every person in the room seemed to be under great impressions, sighing and weeping." On December 1, Whitefield departed for South Carolina and Georgia, noting with satisfaction that he had preached perhaps one hundred seventy-five times since he arrived in Rhode Island two-and-a-half months earlier. The presence of God that attended his meetings convinced him that the British American provinces would remain his "chief scene for action." The fall 1740 tour had been a gigantic success for Whitefield. His method of theatrical field preaching rejuvenated New England's substantial revival tradition and captivated tens of thousands of listeners. His incautious remarks about unconverted ministers, however, and his friendship with such figures as Tennent, Davenport, and Cross laid the groundwork for great controversies concerning the awakenings in the years ahead.

Jon Butler ➡ **NO**

Enthusiasm Described and Decried: The Great Awakening as Interpretative Fiction

In the last half century, the Great Awakening has assumed a major role in explaining the political and social evolution of prerevolutionary American society. Historians have argued, variously, that the Awakening severed intellectual and philosophical connections between America and Europe (Perry Miller), that it was a major vehicle of early lower-class protest (John C. Miller, Rhys Isaac, and Gary B. Nash), that it was a means by which New England Puritans became Yankees (Richard L. Bushman), that it was the first "intercolonial movement" to stir "the people of several colonies on a matter of common emotional concern" (Richard Hofstadter following William Warren Sweet), or that it involved "a rebirth of the localistic impulse" (Kenneth Lockridge).

American historians also have increasingly linked the Awakening directly to the Revolution. Alan Heimert has tagged it as the source of a Calvinist political ideology that irretrievably shaped eighteenth-century American society and the Revolution it produced. Harry S. Stout has argued that the Awakening stimulated a new system of mass communications that increased the colonists' political awareness and reduced their deference to elite groups prior to the Revolution. Isaac and Nash have described the Awakening as the source of a simpler, non-Calvinist protest rhetoric that reinforced revolutionary ideology in disparate places, among them Virginia and the northern port cities. William G. McLoughlin has even claimed that the Great Awakening was nothing less than "the Key to the American Revolution."

These claims for the significance of the Great Awakening come from more than specialists in the colonial period. They are a ubiquitous feature of American history survey texts, where the increased emphasis on social history has made these claims especially useful in interpreting early American society to twentieth-century students. Virtually all texts treat the Great Awakening as a major watershed in the maturation of prerevolutionary American society. *The Great Republic* terms the Awakening "the greatest event in the history of religion in eighteenth-century America." *The National Experience* argues that the Awakening brought "religious experiences to thousands of people in every rank of society" and in every region. *The Essentials of American History* stresses how the Awakening "aroused a spirit of humanitarianism," "encouraged the notion of equal rights,"

From *Journal of American History* by Jon Butler, vol. 69, no. 2, September 1982, pp. 305–314, 316–317, 322–325. Copyright © 1982 by Organization of American Historians. Reprinted by permission.

and "stimulated feelings of democracy" even if its gains in church membership proved episodic. These texts and others describe the weakened position of the clergy produced by the Awakening as symptomatic of growing disrespect for all forms of authority in the colonies and as an important catalyst, even cause, of the American Revolution. The effect of these claims is astonishing. Buttressed by the standard lecture on the Awakening tucked into most survey courses, American undergraduates have been well trained to remember the Great Awakening because their instructors and texts have invested it with such significance.

Does the Great Awakening warrant such enthusiasm? Its puzzling historiography suggests one caution. The Awakening has received surprisingly little systematic study and lacks even one comprehensive general history. The two studies, by Heimert and Cedric B. Cowing, that might qualify as general histories actually are deeply centered in New England. They venture into the middle and southern colonies only occasionally and concentrate on intellectual themes to the exclusion of social history. The remaining studies are thoroughly regional, as in the case of books by Bushman, Edwin Scott Gaustad, Charles Hartshorn Maxson, Dietmar Rothermund, and Wesley M. Gewehr, or are local, as with the spate of articles on New England towns and Jonathan Edwards's or Isaac's articles and book on Virginia. The result is that the general character of the Great Awakening lacks sustained, comprehensive study even while it benefits from thorough local examinations. The relationship between the Revolution and the Awakening is described in an equally peculiar manner. Heimert's seminal 1966 study, despite fair and unfair criticism, has become that kind of influential work whose awesome reputation apparently discourages further pursuit of its subject. Instead, historians frequently allude to the positive relationship between the Awakening and the Revolution without probing the matter in a fresh, systematic way.

The gap between the enthusiasm of historians for the social and political significance of the Great Awakening and its slim, peculiar historiography raises two important issues. First, contemporaries never homogenized the eighteenth-century colonial religious revivals by labeling them "the Great Awakening." Although such words appear in Edwards's *Faithful Narrative of the Surprising Work of God*, Edwards used them alternately with other phrases, such as "general awakening," "great alteration," and "flourishing of religion," only to describe the Northampton revivals of 1734–1735. He never capitalized them or gave them other special emphasis and never used the phrase "the Great Awakening" to evaluate all the prerevolutionary revivals. Rather, the first person to do so was the nineteenth-century historian and antiquarian Joseph Tracy, who used Edwards's otherwise unexceptional words as the title of his famous 1842 book, *The Great Awakening*. Tellingly, however, Tracy's creation did not find immediate favor among American historians. Charles Hodge discussed the Presbyterian revivals in his *Constitutional History of the Presbyterian Church* without describing them as part of a "Great Awakening," while the influential Robert Baird refused even to treat the eighteenth-century revivals as discrete and important events, much less label them "the Great Awakening." Baird all but ignored these revivals in the chronological segments of his *Religion in America* and mentioned them elsewhere only by way of explaining the intellectual origins of the Unitarian movement, whose early leaders opposed revivals. Thus, not until the last half of the nineteenth century did "the Great Awakening" become a familiar feature of the American historical landscape.

Second, this particular label ought to be viewed with suspicion, not because a historian created it—historians legitimately make sense of the minutiae of the past by utilizing such devices—but because the label itself does serious injustice to the minutiae it orders. The label "the Great Awakening" distorts the extent, nature, and cohesion of the revivals that did exist in the eighteenth-century colonies, encourages unwarranted claims for their effects on colonial society, and exaggerates their influence on the coming and character of the American Revolution. If "the Great Awakening" is not quite an American Donation of Constantine, its appeal to historians seeking to explain the shaping and character of prerevolutionary American society gives it a political and intellectual power whose very subtlety requires a close inspection of its claims to truth.

How do historians describe "the Great Awakening"? Three points seem especially common. First, all but a few describe it as a Calvinist religious revival in which converts acknowledged their sinfulness without expecting salvation. These colonial converts thereby distinguished themselves from Englishmen caught up in contemporary Methodist revivals and from Americans involved in the so-called Second Great Awakening of the early national period, both of which imbibed Arminian principles that allowed humans to believe they might effect their own salvation in ways that John Calvin discounted. Second, historians emphasize the breadth and suddenness of the Awakening and frequently employ hurricane metaphors to reinforce the point. Thus, many of them describe how in the 1740s the Awakening "swept" across the mainland colonies, leaving only England's Caribbean colonies untouched. Third, most historians argue that this spiritual hurricane affected all facets of prerevolutionary society. Here they adopt Edwards's description of the 1736 Northampton revival as one that touched "all sorts, sober and vicious, high and low, rich and poor, wise and unwise," but apply it to all the colonies. Indeed, some historians go farther and view the Great Awakening as a veritable social and political revolution itself. Writing in the late 1960s, Bushman could only wonder at its power: "We inevitably will underestimate the effect of the Awakening on eighteenth-century society if we compare it to revivals today. The Awakening was more like the civil rights demonstrations, the campus disturbances, and the urban riots of the 1960s combined. All together these may approach, though certainly not surpass, the Awakening in their impact on national life."

No one would seriously question the existence of "the Great Awakening" if historians only described it as a short-lived Calvinist revival in New England during the early 1740s. Whether stimulated by Edwards, James Davenport, or the British itinerant George Whitefield, the New England revivals between 1740 and 1745 obviously were Calvinist ones. Their sponsors vigorously criticized the soft-core Arminianism that had reputedly overtaken New England Congregationalism, and they stimulated the ritual renewal of a century-old society by reintroducing colonists to the theology of distinguished seventeenth-century Puritan clergymen, especially Thomas Shepard and Solomon Stoddard.

Yet, Calvinism never dominated the eighteenth-century religious revivals homogenized under the label "the Great Awakening." The revivals in the middle colonies flowed from especially disparate and international sources. John B. Frantz's recent traversal of the German revivals there demonstrates that they took root in Lutheranism, German Reformed Calvinism (different from the New England variety), and Pietism (however one wants to define it). Maxson stressed the mysticism, Pietism, Rosicrucianism, and Freemasonry rampant in these colonies among both German and English settlers. In an often overlooked observation, Maxson noted that the Tennents' backing for revivals was deeply linked to a mystical experience surrounding the near death of John Tennent and that both John Tennent and William Tennent, Jr., were mystics as well as Calvinists. The revivals among English colonists in Virginia also reveal eclectic roots. Presbyterians brought Calvinism into the colony for the first time since the 1650s, but Arminianism underwrote the powerful Methodist awakening in the colony and soon crept into the ranks of the colony's Baptists as well.

"The Great Awakening" also is difficult to date. Seldom has an "event" of such magnitude had such amorphous beginnings and endings. In New England, historians agree, the revivals flourished principally between 1740 and 1743 and had largely ended by 1745, although a few scattered outbreaks of revivalism occurred there in the next decades. Establishing the beginning of the revivals has proved more difficult, however. Most historians settle for the year 1740 because it marks Whitefield's first appearance in New England. But everyone acknowledges that earlier revivals underwrote Whitefield's enthusiastic reception there and involved remarkable numbers of colonists. Edwards counted thirty-two towns caught up in revivals in 1734–1735 and noted that his own grandfather, Stoddard, had conducted no less than five "harvests" in Northampton before that, the earliest in the 1690s. Yet revivals in Virginia, the site of the most sustained such events in the southern colonies, did not emerge in significant numbers until the 1750s and did not peak until the 1760s. At the same time, they also continued into the revolutionary and early national periods in ways that make them difficult to separate from their predecessors.

Yet even if one were to argue that "the Great Awakening" persisted through most of the eighteenth century, it is obvious that revivals "swept" only some of the mainland colonies. They occurred in Massachusetts, Connecticut, Rhode Island, Pennsylvania, New Jersey, and Virginia with some frequency at least at some points between 1740 and 1770. But New Hampshire, Maryland, and Georgia witnessed few revivals in the same years, and revivals were only occasionally important in New York, Delaware, North Carolina, and South Carolina. The revivals also touched only certain segments of the population in the colonies where they occurred. The best example of the phenomenon is Pennsylvania. The revivals there had a sustained effect among English settlers only in Presbyterian churches where many of the laity and clergy also opposed them. The Baptists, who were so important to the New England revivals, paid little attention to them until the 1760s, and the colony's taciturn Quakers watched them in perplexed silence. Not even Germans imbibed them universally. At the same time that Benjamin Franklin was emptying his pockets in response to the preaching of Whitefield in Philadelphia—or at least claiming to do so—the residents of

Germantown were steadily leaving their churches, and Stephanie Grauman Wolf reports that they remained steadfast in their indifference to Christianity at least until the 1780s.

Whitefield's revivals also exchanged notoriety for substance. Colonists responded to him as a charismatic performer, and he actually fell victim to the Billy Graham syndrome of modern times: his visits, however exciting, produced few permanent changes in local religious patterns. For example, his appearances in Charleston led to his well-known confrontation with Anglican Commissary Alexander Garden and to the suicide two years later of a distraught follower named Anne LeBrasseur. Yet they produced no new congregations in Charleston and had no documented effect on the general patterns of religious adherence elsewhere in the colony. The same was true in Philadelphia and New York City despite the fact that Whitefield preached to enormous crowds in both places. Only Bostonians responded differently. Supporters organized in the late 1740s a new "awakened" congregation that reputedly met with considerable initial success, and opponents adopted a defensive posture exemplified in the writings of Charles Chauncy that profoundly affected New England intellectual life for two decades.

Historians also exaggerate the cohesion of leadership in the revivals. They have accomplished this, in part, by overstressing the importance of Whitefield and Edwards. Whitefield's early charismatic influence later faded so that his appearances in the 1750s and 1760s had less impact even among evangelicals than they had in the 1740s. In addition, Whitefield's "leadership" was ethereal, at best, even before 1750. His principal early importance was to serve as a personal model of evangelical enterprise for ministers wishing to promote their own revivals of religion. Because he did little to organize and coordinate integrated colonial revivals, he also failed to exercise significant authority over the ministers he inspired.

The case against Edwards's leadership of the revivals is even clearer. Edwards defended the New England revivals from attack. But, like Whitefield, he never organized and coordinated revivals throughout the colonies or even throughout New England. Since most of his major works were not printed in his lifetime, even his intellectual leadership in American theology occurred in the century after his death. Whitefield's lack of knowledge about Edwards on his first tour of America in 1739–1740 is especially telling on this point. Edwards's name does not appear in Whitefield's journal prior to the latter's visit to Northampton in 1740, and Whitefield did not make the visit until Edwards had invited him to do so. Whitefield certainly knew of Edwards and the 1734–1735 Northampton revival but associated the town mainly with the pastorate of Edwards's grandfather Stoddard. As Whitefield described the visit in his journal: "After a little refreshment, we crossed the ferry to Northampton, where no less than three hundred souls were saved about five years ago. Their pastor's name is Edwards, successor and grandson to the great Stoddard, whose memory will be always precious to my soul, and whose books entitled 'A Guide to Christ,' and 'Safety of Appearing in Christ's Righteousness,' I would recommend to all."

What were the effects of the prerevolutionary revivals of religion? The claims for their religious and secular impact need pruning too. One are concern involves the relationship between the revivals and the rise of the Dissenting denominations in the colonies. Denomination building was intimately linked to the revivals in New England. There, as C. C. Goen has demonstrated, the revivals of the 1740s stimulated formation of over two hundred new congregations and several new denominations. This was accomplished mainly through a negative process called "Separatism," which split existing Congregationalist and Baptist churches along prorevival and antirevival lines. But Separatism was of no special consequence in increasing the number of Dissenters farther south. Presbyterians, Baptists, and, later, Methodists gained strength from former Anglicans who left their state-supported churches, but they won far more recruits among colonists who claimed no previous congregational membership.

Still, two points are important in assessing the importance of revivals to the expansion of the Dissenting denominations in the colonies. First, revivalism never was the key to the expansion of the colonial churches. Presbyterianism expanded as rapidly in the middle colonies between 1710 and 1740 as between 1740 and 1770. Revivalism scarcely produced the remarkable growth that the Church of England experienced in the eighteenth century unless, of course, it won the favor of colonists who opposed revivals as fiercely as did its leaders. Gaustad estimates that between 1700 and 1780 Anglican congregations expanded from about one hundred to four hundred, and Bruce E. Steiner has outlined extraordinary Anglican growth in the Dissenting colony of Connecticut although most historians describe the colony as being thoroughly absorbed by the revivals and "Separatism."

Second, the expansion of the leading evangelical denominations, Presbyterians and Baptists, can be traced to many causes, not just revivalism or "the Great Awakening." The growth of the colonial population from fewer than three hundred thousand in 1700 to over two million in 1770 made the expansion of even the most modestly active denominations highly likely. This was especially true because so many new colonists did not settle in established communities but in new communities that lacked religious institutions. As Timothy L. Smith has written of seventeenth-century settlements, the new eighteenth-century settlements welcomed congregations as much for the social functions they performed as for their religious functions. Some of the denominations reaped the legacy of Old World religious ties among new colonists, and others benefited from local anti-Anglican sentiment, especially in the Virginia and Carolina backcountry. As a result, evangelical organizers formed many congregations in the middle and southern colonies without resorting to revivals at all. The first Presbyterian congregation in Hanover County, Virginia, organized by Samuel Blair and William Tennent, Jr., in 1746, rested on an indigenous lay critique of Anglican theology that had turned residents to the works of Martin Luther, and after the campaign by Blair and Tennent, the congregation allied itself with the Presbyterian denomination rather than with simple revivalism.

The revivals democratized relations between ministers and the laity only in minimal ways. A significant number of New England ministers changed their preaching styles as a result of the 1740 revivals. Heimert quotes Isaac Backus on the willingness of evangelicals to use sermons to "'insinuate themselves into the affections' of the people" and notes how opponents of the revivals like Chauncy nonetheless struggled to incorporate emotion and "sentiment" into their sermons after 1740. Yet revivalists and evangelicals continued to draw sharp distinctions between the rights of ministers and the duties of the laity. Edwards did so in a careful, sophisticated way in *Some Thoughts concerning the Present Revival of Religion in New England*. Although he noted that "disputing, jangling, and contention" surrounded "lay exhorting," he agreed that "some exhorting is a Christian duty." But he quickly moved to a strong defense of ministerial pre-rogatives, which he introduced with the proposition that "the Common people in exhorting one another ought not to clothe themselves with the like authority, with that which is proper for ministers." Gilbert Tennent was less cautious. In his 1740 sermon *The Danger of an Unconverted Ministry*, he bitterly attacked "Pharisee-shepherds" and "Pharisee-teachers" whose preaching was frequently as "unedify-ing" as their personal lives. But Gilbert Tennent never attacked the ministry itself. Rather, he argued for the necessity of a *converted* ministry precisely because he believed that only preaching brought men and women to Christ and that only ordained ministers could preach. Thus, in both 1742 and 1757, he thundered against lay preachers. They were "of dreadful consequence to the Church's peace and soundness in principle. . . . [F]or Ignorant Young Converts to take upon them authoritatively to Instruct and Exhort publickly tends to introduce the greatest Errors and the greatest anarchy and confusion."

The 1740 revival among Presbyterians in New Londonderry, Pennsylvania, demonstrates well how ministers shepherded the laity into a revival and how the laity followed rather than led. It was Blair, the congregation's minister, who first criticized "dead Formality in Religion" and brought the congregation's members under "deep convictions" of their "natural unregenerate state." Blair stimulated "soul exercises" in the laity that included crying and shaking, but he also set limits for these exercises. He exhorted them to "moderate and bound their passions" so that the revival would not be destroyed by its own methods. Above this din, Blair remained a commanding, judgmental figure who stimulated the laity's hopes for salvation but remained "very cautious of expressing to People my Judgment of the Goodness of their States, excepting where I had pretty clear Evidences from them, of their being savingly changed." . . .

Nor did the revivals change the structure of authority within the denom-inations. New England Congregationalists retained the right of individual con-gregations to fire ministers, as when Northampton dismissed Edwards in 1750. But in both the seventeenth and eighteenth centuries, these congregations sel-dom acted alone. Instead, they nearly always consulted extensively with com-mittees of ordained ministers when firing as well as when hiring ministers. In the middle colonies, however, neither the prorevival Synod of New York nor the antirevival Synod of Philadelphia tolerated such independence in congrega-tions whether in theory or in practice. In both synods, unhappy congregations had to convince special committees appointed by the synods and composed exclusively of ministers that the performance of a fellow cleric was sufficiently dismal to warrant his dismissal. Congregations that acted independently in such matters quickly found themselves censured, and they usually lost the aid of both synods in finding and installing new ministers.

Did the revivals stir lower-class discontent, increase participation in politics, and promote democracy in society generally if not in the congregations? Even in New England the answer is, at best, equivocal. Historians have laid to rest John C. Miller's powerfully stated argument of the 1930s that the revivals were, in good part, lower-class protests against dominant town elites. The revivals indeed complicated local politics because they introduced new sources of potential and real conflict into the towns. New England towns accustomed to containing tensions inside a single congregation before 1730 sometimes had to deal with tensions within and between as many as three or four congregations after 1730. Of course, not all of these religious groups were produced by the revivals, and, as Michael Zuckerman has pointed out, some towns never tolerated the new dissidents and used the "warning out" system to eject them. Still, even where it existed, tumult should not be confused with democracy. Social class, education, and wealth remained as important after 1730 in choosing town and church officers as they had been before 1730, and Edward M. Cook, Jr., notes that after 1730 most new revival congregations blended into the old order: "dissenters [took] their place in town affairs once they stopped threatening the community and symbolically became loyal members of it." . . .

What, then, ought we to say about the revivals of religion in prerevolutionary America? The most important suggestion is the most drastic. Historians should abandon the term "the Great Awakening" because it distorts the character of eighteenth-century American religious life and misinterprets its relationship to prerevolutionary American society and politics. In religion it is a deus ex machina that falsely homogenizes the heterogeneous; in politics it falsely unites the colonies in slick preparation for the Revolution. Instead, a four-part model of the eighteenth-century colonial revivals will highlight their common features, underscore important differences, and help us assess their real significance.

First, with one exception, the prerevolutionary revivals should be understood primarily as regional events that occurred in only half the colonies. Revivals occurred intermittently in New England between 1690 and 1745 but became especially common between 1735 and 1745. They were uniformly Calvinist and produced more significant local political ramifications—even if they did not democratize New England—than other colonial revivals except those in Virginia. Revivals in the middle colonies occurred primarily between 1740 and 1760. They had remarkably eclectic theological origins, bypassed large numbers of settlers, were especially weak in New York, and produced few demonstrable political and social changes. Revivals in the southern colonies did not occur in significant numbers until the 1750s, when they were limited largely to Virginia, missed Maryland almost entirely, and did not occur with any regularity in the Carolinas until well after 1760. Virginia's Baptist revivalists stimulated major political and social changes in the colony, but the secular importance of the other revivals has been exaggerated. A fourth set of revivals, and the exception to the regional pattern outlined here, accompanied the preaching tours of the Anglican itinerant Whitefield. These tours frequently intersected with the regional revivals in progress at different times in New England, the middle colonies, and some parts of the southern colonies, but even then the fit was imperfect. Whitefield's tours produced some changes in ministerial speaking styles but few permanent alterations in institutional patterns of religion, although his personal charisma supported no less than seven tours of the colonies between 1740 and his death in Newburyport, Massachusetts, in 1770.

Second, the prerevolutionary revivals occurred in the colonial backwaters of Western society where they were part of a long-term pattern of erratic movements for spiritual renewal and revival that had long characterized Western Christianity and Protestantism since its birth two centuries earlier. Thus, their theological origins were international and diverse rather than narrowly Calvinist and uniquely American. Calvinism was important in some revivals, but Arminianism and Pietism supported others. This theological heterogeneity also makes it impossible to isolate a single overwhelmingly important cause of the revivals. Instead, they appear to have arisen when three circumstances were present—internal demands for renewal in different international Christian communities, charismatic preachers, and special, often unique, local circumstances that made communities receptive to elevated religious rhetoric.

Third, the revivals had modest effects on colonial religion. This is not to say that they were "conservative" because they did not always uphold the traditional religious order. But they were never radical, whatever their critics claimed. For example, the revivals reinforced ministerial rather than lay authority even as they altered some clergymen's perceptions of their tasks and methods. They also stimulated the demand for organization, order, and authority in the evangelical denominations. Presbyterian "New Lights" repudiated the conservative Synod of Philadelphia because its discipline was too weak, not too strong, and demanded tougher standards for ordination and subsequent service. After 1760, when Presbyterians and Baptists utilized revivalism as part of their campaigns for denominational expansion, they only increased their stress on central denominational organization and authority.

Indeed, the best test of the benign character of the revivals is to take up the challenge of contemporaries who linked them to outbreaks of "enthusiasm" in Europe. In making these charges, the two leading antirevivalists in the colonies, Garden of Charleston and Chauncy of Boston, specifically compared the colonial revivals with those of the infamous "French Prophets" of London, exiled Huguenots who were active in the city between 1706 and about 1730. The French Prophets predicted the downfall of English politicians, raised followers from the dead, and used women extensively as leaders to prophesy and preach. By comparison, the American revivalists were indeed "conservative." They prophesied only about the millennium, not about local politicans, and described only the necessity, not the certainty, of salvation. What is most important is that they eschewed radical change in the position of women in the churches. True, women experienced dramatic conversions, some of the earliest being described vividly by Edwards. But, they preached only irregularly, rarely prophesied, and certainly never led congregations, denominations, or sects in a way that could remotely approach their status among the French Prophets.

Fourth, the link between the revivals and the American Revolution is virtually nonexistent. The relationship between prerevolutionary political change and the revivals is weak everywhere except in Virginia, where the Baptist revivals indeed shattered the exclusive, century-old Anglican hold on organized religious activity and politics in the colony. But, their importance to the Revolution is weakened by the fact that so many members of Virginia's Anglican aristocracy also led the Revolution. In other colonies the revivals furnished little revolutionary rhetoric, including even millennialist thought, that was not available from other sources and provided no unique organizational mechanisms for anti-British protest activity. They may have been of some importance in helping colonists make moral judgments about eighteenth-century English politics, though colonists unconnected to the revivals made these judgments as well.

In the main, then, the revivals of religion in eighteenth-century America emerge as nearly perfect mirrors of a regionalized, provincial society. They arose erratically in different times and places across a century from the 1690s down to the time of the Revolution. Calvinism underlay some of them, Pietism and Arminianism others. Their leadership was local and, at best, regional, and they helped reinforce—but were not the key to—the proliferation and expansion of still-regional Protestant denominations in the colonies. As such, they created no intercolonial religious institutions and fostered no significant experiential unity in the colonies. Their social and political effects were minimal and usually local, although they could traumatize communities in which they upset, if only temporarily, familiar patterns of worship and social behavior. But the congregations they occasionally produced usually blended into the traditional social system, and the revivals abated without shattering its structure. Thus, the revivals of religion in prerevolutionary America seldom became proto-revolutionary, and they failed to change the timing, causes, or effects of the Revolution in any significant way.

Of course, it is awkward to write about the eighteenth-century revivals of religion in America as erratic, heterogeneous, and politically benign. All of us have walked too long in the company of Tracy's "Great Awakening" to make our journey into the colonial past without it anything but frightening. But as Chauncy wrote of the Whitefield revivals, perhaps now it is time for historians "to see that Things have been carried too far, and that the Hazard is great . . . lest we should be over-run with *Enthusiasm*."

POSTSCRIPT

Was There a Great Awakening in Mid-Eighteenth Century America?

Few scholars are likely to be persuaded by Butler's insistence upon abandoning the label "Great Awakening" when referring to the colonial revivals of the mid-eighteenth century, but some do find merit in certain aspects of his interpretation. In particular, Butler's critique of efforts to link the Awakening with the American Revolution is part of a longstanding historical debate. Even if William McLoughlin's thesis that the revivals were a "key" that opened the door to the War for Independence is invalid, there is room to argue that the Revolution was not without its religious elements. In his book *Religion in America: Past and Present* (Prentice-Hall, 1961), Clifton E. Olmstead argues for a broader application of religious causes to the origins of the American Revolution. First, and consistent with McLoughlin and others, Olmstead contends that the Great Awakening did foster a sense of community among American colonists, thus providing the unity required for an organized assault on English control. Moreover, the Awakening further weakened existing ties between colonies and Mother Country by drawing adherents of the Church of England into the evangelical denominations that expanded as a result of revivalistic Protestantism. Second, tensions were generated by the demand that an Anglican bishop be established in the colonies. Many evangelicals found in this plan evidence that the British government wanted further control over the colonies. Third, the Quebec Act, enacted by Parliament in 1774, not only angered American colonists by nullifying their claims to western lands, but also heightened religious prejudice in the colonies by granting tolerance to Roman Catholics. Fourth, ministers played a significant role in encouraging their parishioners to support the independence movement. Olmstead claims that Congregationalist, Presbyterian, Dutch Reformed, and Baptist ministers overwhelmingly defended this revolutionary movement in the colonies. Finally, many of the revolutionaries, imbued with the American sense of mission, believed that God was ordaining their revolutionary activities.

Further support for these views can be found in Alan Heimert, *Religion and the American Mind from the Great Awakening to the Revolution* (Cambridge University Press, 1966); Cedric B. Cowing, *The Great Awakening and the American Revolution: Colonial Thought in the Eighteenth Century* (University of Chicago, 1971); Richard Hofstadter, *America at 1750: A Social Portrait* (Knopf, 1973); Rhys Isaac, *The Transformation of Virginia, 1740–1790* (University of North Carolina Press, 1982); Ruth H. Bloch, *Visionary Republic* (Cambridge University Press, 1985); Patricia U. Bonomi, *Under the Cope of Heaven: Religion, Society, and Politics in Colonial America* (Oxford University Press, 1986); Harry S. Stout, *The New*

England Soul: Preaching and Religious Culture in Colonial New England (Oxford University Press, 1986); and Mark A. Noll, *Christians in the American Revolution* (Regent College Publishing, 2006). Jon Butler has expanded his views on the colonial religious experience in *Awash in a Sea of Faith: Christianizing the American People* (Harvard University Press, 1990).

Students interested in further analyses of the Great Awakening should consult Edwin Scott Gaustad, *The Great Awakening in New England* (Harper & Brothers, 1957); David S. Lovejoy, *Religious Enthusiasm and the Great Awakening* (Prentice-Hall, 1969); Marilyn J. Westerkamp, *Triumph of the Laity: Scots-Irish Piety and the Great Awakening, 1625–1760* (Oxford University Press, 1987); and Frank Lambert, *Inventing the "Great Awakening"* (Princeton University Press, 1999). Richard Bushman, ed., *The Great Awakening: Documents on the Revival of Religion, 1740–1745* (University of North Carolina Press, 1989), and Thomas S. Kidd, ed., *The Great Awakening: A Brief History with Documents* (Bedford/St. Martin's, 2008), offer excellent introductions to this topic through collected sermons and first-person accounts. For biographies of two of the leading figures of eighteenth-century revivalism, see Harry S. Stout, *The Divine Dramatist: George Whitefield and the Rise of Modern Evangelicalism* (Eerdmans, 1991); Frank Lambert, *"Pedlar of Divinity": George Whitefield and the Transatlantic Revivals, 1737–1770* (Princeton University Press, 1994); Patricia Tracy, *Jonathan Edwards, Pastor: Religion and Society in Eighteenth-Century Northampton* (Hill & Wang, 1980); George M. Marsden, *Jonathan Edwards: A Life* (Yale University Press, 2003); and Philip F. Gura, *Jonathan Edwards: America's Evangelical* (Hill and Wang, 2005).

Internet References . . .

Virtual Marching Tour of the American Revolution

Sponsored by the Independence Hall Association in Philadelphia, this site is a promising work in progress. Its goal is to provide information about Revolutionary times through text and images.

http://www.ushistory.org/march/

The Constitution of the United States

Sponsored by the national Archives and Records Administration, this site presents a wealth of information on the U.S. Constitution. From here you can link to the biographies of the 55 delegates to the Constitutional Convention, take an in-depth look at the convention and the ratification process, and read a transcription of the complete text of the Constitution, including high-resolution images of each page of the document.

http://www.archives.gov/exhibits/charters/charters_of_freedom_6.html

Alexander Hamilton: The Man Who Made Modern America

Sponsored by the New York Historical Society, this site includes a virtual tour of the Hamilton traveling exhibition and links to documents and databases relating to Hamilton.

http://alexanderhamiltonexhibition.org/

Indian Removal Act

This Library of Congress Web site includes links to government documents, maps, contemporary periodicals, as well as links to external Web sites concerning this event.

http://www.loc.gov/rr/program/bib/ourdocs/Indian.html

Revolution and the New Nation

*T*he American Revolution led to independence from England and to the establishment of a new nation. As the United States matured, its people and leaders struggled to implement fully the ideals that had sparked the Revolution. What had been abstractions before the formation of the new government had to be applied and refined in day-to-day practice. The nature of post-revolutionary America, government stability, the transition of power against the backdrop of political factionalism, the extension of democracy, and the international role of the new United States had to be worked out.

- Was the American Revolution Largely a Product of Market-Driven Consumer Forces?

- Were the Founding Fathers Democratic Reformers?

- Was Alexander Hamilton an Economic Genius?

- Did Andrew Jackson's Removal Policy Benefit Native Americans?

- Did the Industrial Revolution Provide More Economic Opportunities for Women in the 1830s?

ISSUE 6

Was the American Revolution Largely a Product of Market-Driven Consumer Forces?

YES: T. H. Breen, from *The Marketplace of Revolution: How Consumer Politics Shaped America's Independence* (Oxford University Press, 2004)

NO: Carl N. Degler, from *Out of Our Past: The Forces that Shaped Modern America*, 2nd ed. (Harper Collins Publishers, 1959, 1970)

ISSUE SUMMARY

YES: Professor T. H. Breen maintains that "the colonists shared experiences as consumers provided them with the cultural resources needed to develop a bold new form of political protest"—the non-importation agreements which provided link to the break with England.

NO: Professor Carl N. Degler argues that the American Revolution was a political rebellion led by a group of reluctant revolutionaries who opposed Parliament's attempt to impose taxes without the consent of the colonists.

Was the American Revolution a true revolution? The answer may depend on how the term *revolution* is defined. *Strict constructionists*, for example, perceive revolution as producing significant and deep societal change, whereas loose constructionists define the term as "any resort to violence within a political order to change its constitution, rulers, or policies."

Early historians did not concern themselves with the social and economic aspects of the American Revolution. They instead argued over the causes of the Revolution and refought the political arguments advanced by the rebelling colonists and the British government. George Bancroft was the first historian to advance the *Whig*, or *Pro-American,* interpretation of the war. America won, he said, because God was on our side.

Bancroft's view remained unchallenged until the beginning of the twentieth century, when a group of *imperialist* historians analyzed the Revolution from the perspective of the British Empire. These historians tended to be sympathetic to the economic and political difficulties that Great Britain faced.

Both the Whig and the imperialist historians assumed that the Revolution was an external event whose primary cause was the political differences between the colonists and their British rulers. In 1909, however, historian Carl Becker paved the way for a different interpretation of the Revolution when he concluded in his study of colonial New York that an *internal* revolution had taken place. The American Revolution, said Becker, created a struggle not only for home rule but also one for who should rule at home. This *progressive*, or *conflict*, interpretation dominated most of the writings on the American Revolution from 1910 through 1945. During this time progressive historians searched for the social and economic conflicts among groups struggling for political power.

Since 1945, most professional historians have rejected what they considered to be an oversimplified conflict interpretation of the Revolution by the previous generation of progressive historians. These post-World War II historians have been called neo-Whig, neo-conservative and consensus historians because, like earlier nineteenth century historians, they consider the taxation issue between England and the colonists to be the major reason for the American Revolution. Robert E. Brown, in his studies on colonial Massachusetts and Virginia, argued that America had become a middle-class democracy before the American Revolution. Consequently, Brown maintained, there was no need for a social revolution. Most influential have been the works of Harvard University professor Bernard Bailyn, who used a neoconservative approach in analyzing the Revolution. In his *Ideological Origins of the American Revolution* (Harvard University Press, 1968), Bailyn took ideas seriously once again and saw the colonists implementing the views of radical British thinkers in their struggle for independence. The most recent statement on the American Revolution from the neoconservative perspective is *Becoming America: The Revolution Before 1776*, by Jon Butler (Howard University Press, 2000). In it, Butler argues that American colonial society—politically, socially, and economically—was dramatically transformed between 1680 and 1770.

Since the late 1960s, historians have written a great deal about blacks, women, Native Americans, and "ordinary" people. This neo-progressive interpretation of America's past has also made views on the events surrounding the Revolution more complicated. See the collection of articles edited by Alfred Young in *Beyond the American Revolution: Explorations in the History of American Radicalism* (Northern Illinois University Press, 1993); Young's own collection of essays in *Liberty Tree: Ordinary People and the American Revolution* (New York University Press, 2006); and Gary Nash's summative neo-progressive interpretation, *The Unknown American Revolution: The Unruly Birth of Democracy and the Struggle to Create America* (Viking Press, 2005).

The following readings represent two differing views on the causes of the American Revolution. Professor Carl N. Degler writes from a neo-conservative point of view. The colonists were reluctant revolutionaries who split from England because of their post 1763 taxation and regulatory policies. T. H. Breen combines political goals with economic tactics. He argues that colonists used the nonimportation agreements in order to rid themselves of the new British taxation policies.

YES ↵

T. H. Breen

The Marketplace of Revolution: How Consumer Politics Shaped American Independence

A reinterpretation of the coming of the American Revolution must deal with timing. Although it may seem obvious, we should remember that separation from Great Britain occurred at a precise historical moment. However plausible alternative dates may appear with hindsight, it did not happen during the Glorious Revolution of 1688, or at the conclusion of the Seven Years' War in 1763, which removed forever the threat of French encroachment, or, despite the spontaneous street violence associated with the Stamp Act crisis, in 1765. No one seriously advocated independence in 1768, even though Charles Townshend's Revenue Acts provoked hostility throughout the colonies. Nor, in fact, did the Tea Act of 1773 do the trick. What may seem today as irresistible momentum carrying a colonial society toward national independence could at any moment have been halted, diverted, or thwarted. British administrators need not have pursued a policy so doggedly confrontational. By the same token, Americans from different regions could have followed separate paths, concluding, for example, that those who spoke for Boston were troublesome radicals deserving whatever punishments Parliament cared to mete out. Reminding ourselves of the contingency of events is another way of drawing attention to the force of human agency—real people making choices about the politics of empire—in shaping the flow of activities that we lump together as the coming of the American Revolution.

What gave the American Revolution distinctive shape was an earlier transformation of the Anglo-American consumer marketplace. This event, which some historians have called a "consumer revolution," commenced sometime during the middle of the eighteenth century, and as modestly wealthy families acquired ever larger quantities of British manufactures—for the most part everyday goods that made life warmer, more comfortable, more sanitary, or perhaps simply more enjoyable—the face of material culture changed dramatically. Suddenly, buyers voiced concerns about color and texture, about fashion and etiquette, and about making the right choices from among an expanding number of possibilities.

From *The Marketplace of Revolution: How Consumer Politics Shaped American Independence* (Oxford University Press, 2004), pp. xiv–xvii, 298–303, 316–317 (excerpts). Copyright © 2004 by T. H. Breen. Reprinted by permission of Oxford University Press.

This was surely not a society of self-sufficient yeomen farmers. People purchased the items they most desired at local stores; they often demanded and received liberal credit. Each year the volume of imports increased, creating by 1750 a virtual "empire of goods." England experienced the same consumer revolution as did the American colonists. But there was a major difference. In a colonial marketplace in which dependency was always an issue, imported goods had the potential to become politicized, turning familiar imported items such as cloth and tea into symbols of imperial oppression. And since Americans from Savannah to Portsmouth purchased the same general range of goods, they found that they were able to communicate with each other about a common experience. Whatever their differences, they were consumers in an empire that seemed determined to compromise their rights and liberties.

[This essay] argues, therefore, that the colonists' shared experience as consumers provided them with the cultural resources needed to develop a bold new form of political protest. In this unprecedented context, private decisions were interpreted as political acts; consumer choices communicated personal loyalties. Goods became the foundation of trust, for one's willingness to sacrifice the pleasures of the market provided a remarkably visible and effective test of allegiance.

Before this moment, no massive political movement had organized itself around the denial of imported goods. In other words, although it does not receive the same acclaim from historians as does the system of checks and balances put forward in the Constitution, the consumer boycott was a brilliantly original American invention. As General Thomas Gage, a British military leader who wanted to nip rebellion in the bud, exclaimed, "I never heard of a people, who by general agreement, and without sumptuary laws to force them, that ever denied themselves what their circumstances would afford, and custom and habit prompted them to desire." But that is precisely what the colonists did. They made goods speak to power in ways that mid-century consumers and merchants had never anticipated.

The term boycott is, of course, an anachronism, since it first came into the language during the nineteenth century in recognition of the activities of an English land agent in Ireland, Charles C. Boycott. Such considerations need not deter us. We are dealing with popular political movements that were boycotts in all but name. Within the structures of voluntary associations formed to enforce non-importation of British manufactures, men and women found that they could judge for themselves whether or not other Americans were in fact fulfilling pledges of mutual support. Failure to comply exposed possible enemies who publicly demonstrated by their continued purchase of imported goods that they could not be counted on during a crisis. A strategy of political resistance centered on the marketplace quickly transformed myriad private acts of consumption into self-conscious public declarations of resistance. The non-importation agreements throughout colonial America provided an effective means for distinguishing supporters from those people who suffered humiliation as "the friends of government." In more positive terms, one's relation to everyday goods became a measure of patriotism. "What is true grandeur," asked a writer in the *New-London Gazette*, "but a noble patriotic resolution of sacrificing every other consideration to the Love of our Country. And can he be a true lover of his country . . . who would be seen strutting about the streets, clad in foreign [British] fripperies, than to be nobly independent in the russet grey?"

Commercial rituals of shared sacrifice provided a means to educate and energize a dispersed populace. These events helped participants discover the radical political implications of their own actions, even as those same rituals demonized people who inevitably held back, uncertain and afraid, victims of new solidarities they never quite understood. Indeed, the boycott movement invited colonists traditionally excluded from formal political processes—the election of representatives to colonial assemblies, for example—to voice their opinions in a raucous, open public forum, one that defined itself around sub-scription lists, voluntary associations, organized protests, destruction of goods, and incendiary newspaper exchanges. What we encounter in colony after col-ony is a radically new form of politics, a politics practiced out-of-doors, in which women and the poor experienced an exhilarating surge of empower-ment. Although during the two decades following the winning of national independence—the so-called constitutional period—well-to-do leaders had second thoughts about encouraging such groups to speak out, we should appreciate the powerfully egalitarian potential of that earlier moment. The non-importers of the 1760s and 1770s were doing more than simply obstruct-ing the flow of British-made goods. They were inviting the American people to reinvent an entire political culture. . . .

. . . How does one explain the timing of revolution? Why did the break with Great Britain not occur at an earlier moment when passions ran high and mobs roamed the streets of the major colonial ports? A glib answer would be that the colonists were not ready to mount such a united effort in 1765 or 1770. The translation of local grievance into organized rebellion required the devel-opment of ways for Americans to reach out effectively to other Americans. That process of discovery took time. The colonists drew upon their participation in a vast new consumer marketplace, an experience that persuaded them that their dependence upon British manufactures might be turned by a colonial people into a powerful political weapon. During the Stamp Act agitation they took tentative steps toward non-importation. At first, it seemed reasonable to place responsibility for the success of this strategy on the merchants. Only slowly did ordinary colonists begin to appreciate that such a plan had little chance of success. The merchants marched to different drummers. More radi-cal Americans such as Samuel Adams concluded that the protest against the Townshend duties had been a failure; after 1770 colonial consumers raced once again to the shops, buying British imports at record levels. In their dis-appointment, Adams and others undervalued changes in the political culture that were of profound significance for the character of later events. Between 1767 and 1770 Americans invented a "public" which monitored behavior in a consumer public sphere, experimented with new forms of extra-legal political participation, constituted themselves as a group with interests separate from those of the British, and forged channels of communication that promoted a sense of trust among distant strangers.

When Parliament passed the Tea Act in May 1773, the colonists were not the same people they had been in 1768. They drew upon a history of protest within the consumer marketplace, a history without precedent and entirely of their own making. Almost without fully comprehending the magnitude of their own achievement, Americans now almost instinctively moved from demands for *non-importation* to appeals for *non-consumption,* a shift of immense importance in the history of popular political protest. On this occasion they insisted that the people must take personal responsibility for their own political destiny. As one Connecticut writer observed in 1774, the former effort to make non-importation work had collapsed because "it stood on a rotten and unsolid basis. It was erected wholly on the virtue of the merchants, and rested its whole weight solely on this prop." Just as the authors of the formal political pamphlets—documents that so often structure modern accounts of the American Revolution—were struggling to comprehend a republican polity founded on the will of the people, ordinary men and women were being asked in a parallel discourse to sacrifice personal comforts for the common good. Samuel Adams understood the challenge. In a letter written in June 1774 to Richard Henry Lee about the prospects for a total American boycott, Adams observed, "It is the virtue of the yeomanry we are chiefly to depend on." In this atmosphere, the people no longer defined British imports such as tea as luxuries or as sources of debt but as poisons they had to purge in the name of liberty.

The argument is not that consumer goods caused the American Revolution. In Aristotelian terms, the claim is rather that British imports provided a necessary but not sufficient cause for the final break with Parliament. Other developments within late colonial society—the spread of evangelical Christianity, for example—helped ordinary men and women make sense of political events. And without an inspiring language of universal rights, non-importation would have been little more than a strategy in search of a proper goal. Still, imported goods invited colonists to think radical new thoughts about empire. British manufactures came to symbolize dependence and oppression. The mental link was so strong that when a small, very poor community in Massachusetts addressed the problem of the tea, it also raised questions about its place within a larger world. In response to news of the arrival of the tea ships in Boston Harbor, the inhabitants of the town of Harvard discussed the situation and found "it to be a matter of as interesting and important a nature when viewed in all its Consequences not only to this Town and Province, but to America in general, and that for ages and generations to come, as ever came under the deliberation of this Town." The intensity of the reaction of these obscure farmers helps explain why colonists from South Carolina to New Hampshire stood with Boston during the terrible days following the destruction of the tea.

During 1773 the pace of events accelerated. Following the collapse of organized resistance three years earlier, many people on both sides of the Atlantic persuaded themselves that the time of troubles had ended and Humpty Dumpty had not in fact taken a great fall. But the House of Commons, now led by Frederick Lord North, second earl of Guilford, managed once again to roil imperial waters. The new crisis resulted not from tougher American policy but rather from a much overdue attempt to bring order to the chaotic affairs of the East India Company. This grossly mismanaged enterprise possessed a monopoly to import tea from South Asia into Great Britain, but for many reasons—internal corruption being a prime candidate—the directors had run up huge operating debts, and to avoid bankruptcy they turned to the government for an emergency loan. Lord North offered to support such an arrangement, but only on condition that the Company reform its business practices. The directors argued that if they could sell their tea directly to the Americans without paying normal duties or going through wholesalers who ran up the price, they might be able to turn a profit. A concession from the government on duties would enable the Company to undersell the smugglers, who obtained their tea from the Dutch. Anxious that he not signal a retreat on the principle of parliamentary sovereignty, North refused to drop the last remaining Townshend Duty, a decision that still allowed the Company to cut prices substantially but also compelled the Americans to pay a tax which they labeled unconstitutional. When asked why he did not show greater flexibility on this point, North growled that "the temper of the people there is little deserving favour from hence." If the minister really thought the colonists would accept the Tea Act, he was in for a shock. Although some modern Americans seem to accept the notion that the federal government should bail out failing corporations, the colonists branded the legislation venal, and they vowed to teach North that their love of liberty exceeded their love of tea.

During the fall of 1773 Americans scrambled to nullify the Tea Act. Learning that Company ships would arrive in the major colonial ports sometime in November, local protest groups pressured civil authorities to prohibit the unloading of the vessels. The Sons of Liberty did their best to intimidate newly appointed tea agents, many of them prominent merchants whose personal loyalties lay with the crown. In the newspapers and in cheap broadsides, patriotic voices sounded the alarm once again, urging the colonists to resist political oppression by refusing to buy imported goods. By now the mental link between consumer sacrifice and political ideology was well established. Still, at that moment, no one could confidently predict the popular response to the Tea Act. After all, between 1770 and 1773, in addition to the smuggled Dutch tea, Americans bought some 300,000 pounds of tea annually from British merchants, knowing full well that the purchase price included the Townshend duty. Of the many entreaties broadcast during this period, few were as strongly worded as a letter in the *Pennsylvania Packet* addressed to "the Freeholders and Freemen" of Pennsylvania. "Taking for granted . . .," the writer reasoned, "that the revenue acts are opposite to the very idea and spirit of liberty, it will naturally follow, that a ship, loaded with goods which come under one of those acts is the true and literal Pandora's box, filled with poverty, oppression, slavery, and every other hated disease." Colonial consumers should be forewarned that this legislation was only the start. "Whenever the Tea is swallowed, and pretty well digested, we shall have new duties imposed on other articles of commerce." The Association of the Sons of Liberty in New York City prepared a stirring history of American non-importation from the "detestable Stamp Act" to the current campaign against tea.

What had been an imaginative although tentative strategy of consumer protest in 1765 had now evolved into the accepted mode of American resistance. If people embraced the tea, declared the Sons of Liberty, they would acquire a heavy burden of guilt. They would forever have to justify why they had failed "to defeat the pernicious Project" and thereby denied "to our Posterity, those Blessings of Freedom, which our Ancestors have handed down to us." A New York newspaper wailed that "A SHIP loaded with TEA is now on her Way to this Port, being sent out by the Ministry for the Purpose of *enslaving* and *poisoning* ALL the AMERICANS." A later issue of the same journal provided readers with a secular catechism so that they might better understand the gravity of the crisis. Compared to the formal legal and constitutional pamphlets of the day, these productions may seem simple, even childish, but they expose a level of popular mobilization that intellectual histories generally ignore. The litany not only outlined the challenge but also advised ordinary men and women what they could do to demonstrate their commitment to the common good.

> QUERIES—Respecting the TEA ACT submitted to the most serious Consideration of every person in AMERICA.
>
> Query. As there is an Act of the British Parliament in Being, that would subjugate America to *Three Pence Sterling Duty* upon every Pound Weight of Tea imported from *Britain;* and as this Duty is *voted* independent of, and without the Sanction of any of *our American* Parliaments, what ought to be done unto every one of those *traitorous Persons,* who shall aid or abet the Importation of, *or landing,* the said Tea in any part of *America,* till the Act is totally repealed, *jointly, by King, Lords, and Commons?*
>
> Answer. Such base *Traitors* to this Country, without Exception, should immediately and *resolutely* be dragged from Concealment; they should be transported, or forced from every Place in *America,* loaded with the most striking Badges of Disgrace . . .
>
> Query. What will be the most effectual Methods of Proceeding, to obtain a Repeal of the said oppressive, unconstitutional Act?
>
> Ans. TO USE NO TEA, *at least for the present,* for if any Persons should give the Sellers more than the usual Price for Tea, he ought to be held up as a mortal Enemy to *American Freedom.* And,—*brave Americans.*

In New York City, Charleston, and Philadelphia last-minute negotiations helped prevent serious violence. Either the tea ships returned to London or crown officials prudently stored the tea in safe places where it could not be sold.

In Boston events took a different turn. A crowd of five thousand men and women witnessed the arrival of the Company ships, carrying 342 chests of East India tea. Popular leaders begged the captains of these vessels to return to London, but perhaps to no one's surprise, local tea agents refused to compromise. The Hutchinson brothers, Thomas and Elisha, who represented the Company in Boston, insisted on landing the entire cargo. Samuel Adams and his friends pledged never to let that happen. The standoff pushed those who opposed the Tea Act to stake out ever more radical ground. One announcement signed by "The People" reminded "The Public, That it was solemnly voted by the Body of the People of this and the neighboring Towns . . . that the said Tea never should be landed in this Province, or pay one Farthing of Duty." Anyone who dared to assist such an attempt, declared "The People," "must betray an inhuman Thirst for Blood, and will also in great Measure accelerate Confusion and Civil War. This is to assure such public Enemies of this Country, they will be considered and treated as Wretches unworthy to live, and be made the first Victims of our just Resentment."

If crown officials and their supporters thought that such inflated rhetoric amounted to no more than bluster, they were mistaken. On December 16 Boston "Mohawks" spent much of the day throwing tea chests into the harbor, one of which, of course, found its way to Ebenezer Withington. Accounts of the Indian disguise have given this famous incident a slightly ludicrous character in American history, transforming the Tea Party into a kind of carnival event in which feathered citizens lightheartedly sparked the final confrontation with Parliament. It was nothing of the sort. As every participant understood, the destruction of the tea invited immediate and severe retaliation. They had violated private property, a provocation no British ruler could ignore. More to the point, the Tea Party represented not a break with the previous history of colonial resistance but rather an escalation of a tradition of consumer protest that had begun a decade earlier.

Boston's punishment staggered even those who expected the worst. Lord North could endure no more insolence from what seemed to him America's hotbed of radicalism. A well-placed London diarist, Matthew Brickdale, recorded the ministry's case against the community that had drowned the tea. Boston, scribbled Brickdale, "has been the ringleader of all violence and opposition to the execution of the laws of this country. New York and Philadelphia grew unruly on receiving the news of the triumph of the people of Boston. Boston had not only therefore to answer for its own violence but for having incited other places to tumults." Thinking of this sort led in the spring of 1774 to a series of statutes known collectively in the colonies as the Intolerable Acts. These bills closed Boston Harbor to all commerce until the city reimbursed the East India Company for its loss. Other acts fundamentally altered the constitution of Massachusetts Bay. Perhaps the most intrusive measure was legislation limiting town meetings throughout the colony to a single session each year, a serious blow to a people who prized the rough-and-tumble debate of local government.

One Connecticut writer who styled himself the "Conciliator" explained the larger meaning of North's punitive policy. "At length," he declared, "the Harbor of Boston is blocked up, and the Business of Importation in that Town at an End. . . . Foreign Manufactures, it seems, are considered as pernicious to the Constitution of America, and we must either disuse them, or encounter the Horrors of Slavery." The Conciliator insisted that no colonist should be surprised to discover that common consumer goods now defined the battle lines of empire. "The Language of Great-Britain in Years past, in Accents loud as Thunder, has rung this solemn Peal in our Ears—Americans! Stop your Trade."

But even in these dark hours, hope beckoned. The British "know that Economy, Frugality and Virtue will raise us above the Reach of the envenomed Arrows of Oppression. . . . Our foolish Fondness for the Toys of that Country, provokes her Resentment." The message was clear. Americans might assist Boston with food and money. If they meant to be free, however, they had to rededicate themselves to consumer sacrifice. Sounding like an Old Testament prophet who believed that virtuous consumers must atone for past market sin, the Conciliator exclaimed, "It is our Treachery to ourselves, my Countrymen, that has brought these Burdens upon us."

It did not require a miracle to persuade other Americans to pledge their support to Boston. They might, of course, have taken an easier path. After all, they might have reasoned, the Intolerable Acts did not directly affect them. Why not wait? Since Parliament had not closed their ports, they might continue to do business as usual. And yet, by and large, they stood firm when it counted most. The explanation for solidarity—a challenge informing this study from the start—was that by the summer of 1774 Americans had learned how to reach out to each other. They had begun to think continentally. The experience of mounting ever more effective consumer protests against a commercial empire had encouraged them to imagine a new, geographically inclusive identity. A decade of protest in the marketplace had forced them to define themselves as not fully British. Indeed, in defiance of parliamentary taxation they increasingly saw themselves as Americans. The North government failed to appreciate that it was no longer dealing with a loose collection of colonies which might turn on each other to gain some transient advantage.

Parliament tried to make an example of Boston and, by so doing, aroused a nation. The reaction of the planters of Queen Anne's County, Maryland, to the Boston crisis was unusual only in its eloquence. In June 1774, they declared, "Duly considering, and deeply affected with the prospect of the unhappy situation of Great Britain and British America, under any kind of disunion, this Meeting think themselves obliged, by all the ties which ever ought to preserve a firm union amongst Americans, as speedily as possible, to make known their sentiments to their distressed brethren of Boston, and therefore publish [them] to the world." The planters' first decision reflected long years of experimentation with non-importation: "[T]hey look upon the cause of Boston, in its consequences, to be the common cause of America." Resolutions of this sort poured forth from small, scattered communities. Their residents wanted to register a public commitment to a larger responsibility. . . .

In each community tea sparked a slightly different political conversation. A meeting of the inhabitants of Brookline, Massachusetts, for example, agreed with other towns that anyone who imported tea while it was still subject to a parliamentary tax should be "considered and treated by this Town as an Enemy to this Country." What struck these people as most offensive was the blatant inequity of the legislation. They were tired of being treated like second-class subjects of the crown. They had no doubt that a few well-placed individuals in England were getting richer at the expense of American rights, a kind of corporate profiteering that once had the capacity to inspire indignation. "Thus," the Brookline meeting observed, "have the Parliament discovered the most glaring Partiality in making one and the same Act to operate for the Ease and Convenience of a few of the most opulent Subjects in Britain on the one Hand, and for the Oppression of MILLIONS of Freeborn and most loyal Inhabitants of America on the other." Only a few months later, the "votable inhabitants" of Bolton staged a seminar on tea and taxation, and after considering the issue of parliamentary sovereignty from various perspectives—they termed it a "free debate"—the assembly passed without a single negative voice a number of strongly worded resolutions, the most demagogic of which declared that "in order to counteract and render abortive (according to the utmost of our power) the British act, respecting the duty on Tea to be paid *here,* we will not take of this politically forbidden fruit, if even solicited thereto by the Eves of our own bosoms, nor any other consideration whatever, whilst it remains under the circumstance of taxation." . . .

At the distance of over two centuries, public opinion can be measured only crudely through anecdotes. As colonial leaders were busy attempting to make sense of an official British policy of punishment, ordinary Americans sought as best they could to provide proof of consumer virtue. In a letter sent to Abigail during the summer of 1774, John Adams recounted a scene that warmed the heart of a weary patriotic traveler. After a hard ride of over thirty-five miles through the interior of Massachusetts, Adams finally arrived at the house where he intended to take a rest. "'Madam' said I to Mrs. Huston, 'is it lawful for a weary Traveller to refresh himself with a Dish of Tea provided it has been honestly smuggled, or paid no Duties?'" Mrs. Huston was shocked by the request. "'No sir,' said she, 'we have renounced all Tea in this Place. I cant make Tea, but I'le make you Coffee.' Accordingly I have drank Coffee every Afternoon since, and have borne it very well. Tea must be universally renounced. I must be weaned, and the sooner, the better." About Adams's contribution to the revolutionary cause, there is not the slightest doubt. It is people such as Mrs. Huston who have been undervalued. . . .

Carl Degler

→ **NO**

Out of Our Past: The Forces That Shaped Modern America

A New Kind of Revolution

On at least two scores, the American Revolution was something new under the sun. Although most of the major powers of Europe boasted overseas colonial empires, never before had a colonial people successfully rebelled against the mother country. But once it was done by the United States, the example was not ignored. Within a century after the Revolution, France, Spain, and Portugal lost portions or all of their New World empires through colonial rebellion. Nor have the echoes yet ceased. In 1945, one sour Englishman in Batavia during the rebellion of the Indonesians against the Dutch remarked, "That damned American Revolution . . . is still giving us trouble."

Despite its precedent-setting character, however, the American revolt is noteworthy because it made no serious interruption in the smooth flow of American development. Both in intention and in fact the American Revolution conserved the past rather than repudiated it. And in preserving the colonial experience, the men of the first quarter century of the Republic's history set the scenery and wrote the script for the drama of American politics for years to come.

1. Causes Were Consequences

Though the colonists had long been drifting away from their allegiance to the mother country, the chain of events which led to the Revolutionary crisis was set in motion by external factors. The shattering victory of the Anglo-American forces over the French in the Great War for the Empire (1754–63), as Lawrence Gipson has rechristened the French and Indian War, suddenly revealed how wide the gulf between colonists and mother country had become. The very fact that the feared French were once and for all expelled from the colonial backdoor meant that another cohesive, if negative, force was gone. At least one friend of Britain, looking back from the fateful days of 1776, thought that "had Canada remained in the hands of the French, the colonies would have remained dutiful subjects. Their fears for themselves in that case," he reasoned, "would have supplied the place of the pretended affection for this

From *Out of Our Past: The Forces That Shaped Modern America,* Second (Revised) edition (Harper Colophon, 1970), pp. 73–82 (refs. omitted). Copyright © 1970 by Carl N. Degler. Reprinted by permission of HarperCollins Publishers, Inc.

nation. . . ." What actual effect the removal of the French produced upon the thinking of the colonists is hard to weigh, but there can be little doubt that the Great War for the Empire opened a new era in the relations between the colonies and the mother country.

Great Britain emerged from the war as the supreme power in European affairs: her armies had swept the once-vaunted French authority from two continents; her navy now indisputably commanded the seven seas. A symbol of this new power was that Britain's ambassadors now outranked those of France and Spain in the protocol of Europe's courts. But the cost and continuing responsibilities of that victory were staggering for the little island kingdom. Before the war the annual expenditures for troops in America and the British West Indies amounted to £110,000; now three times that sum was needed to protect the western frontier, suppress Indian revolts and maintain order. Furthermore, the signing of the peace found Britain saddled with a debt of £130 million, the annual charges of which ran to another £4 million. Faced with such obligations, the British government was compelled to reassess its old ways of running an empire, particularly in regard to the raising of new revenues.

Before the war, the administration and cost of the Empire were primarily, if not completely, a British affair. Imperial defense on the high seas was in the hands of the Royal Navy, and though the colonies were called upon from time to time to assist in the war with France, the bulk of the fighting was sustained by British troops. In return, the colonies had acquiesced in the regulation of their trade through a series of so-called Navigation Acts, which were enacted and enforced by the British authority; no revenues, however, except those collected as import or export duties, were taken from the colonies by Britain.

Under the pressure of the new responsibilities, the British authorities began to cast about for a new theory and practice of imperial administration into which the colonies might be fitted as actively contributing members. Prior to the war the government had been willing to protect the West Indian sugar interests at the expense of the rest of the Empire. But now, in the interest of increased revenue, the old protective duty, which was much too high to bring any return, was cut in half, thus permitting French molasses to compete with British West Indian in the English and colonial markets. In 1766, this molasses duty, in a further effort to increase revenue, was cut to two thirds of what it had been before the war. In short, the need for imperial revenues, not private interests, was now dictating legislation. The Stamp Act of 1765 and the Townshend duties of two years later were similar efforts to spread the financial burdens of the Empire among the beneficiaries of the British triumph over the French.

It seemed only simple justice to London officialdom that the colonies should share in the costs as well as the benefits to be derived from the defeat of the ancient enemy. At no time, it should be noticed, were the colonies asked to contribute more than a portion of the price of their own frontier defense. The stamp duty, for instance, was envisioned as returning no more than a third of the total military expenditures in America; the remainder would be borne by the home government. And because the colonists had difficulty scraping together the specie with which to pay such duties, the British government agreed to spend all the revenue obtained from the stamp tax in the colonies in order to avoid depleting the scanty colonial money supply. Nor were Americans heavily taxed; it was well known that their fiscal burden was unique in its lightness. In 1775 Lord North told the House of Commons that the per capita tax payments of Britons were fifty times those of the Americans. It was not injustice or the economic incidence of the taxes which prompted the colonial protests; it was rather the novelty of the British demands.

The new imperial policies of the British government caught the Americans off guard. Reveling in the victory over the French, the colonists confidently expected a return to the lax, uninterested administration of the prewar years and especially to their old freedom from any obligation to support the imperial defenses. Therefore, when the first of the new measures, the Sugar Act of 1764, became law, the Americans protested, but on a variety of grounds and without sufficient unity to command respect. By the time of the Stamp Act in the following year, however, the colonists were ready.

The essential colonial defense, from which the colonies never deviated, was a denial that the British Parliament had any right in law or custom to lay taxes upon the colonies for revenue purposes. Such taxes, the colonials insisted, could only be levied by the colonial legislatures. Actually, this expression of the colonial constitutional position was as novel as the imperial policy. Never before had there been an occasion for such an assertion simply because England had heretofore confined her colonial legislation to the regulation of trade. It is true that the Pennsylvania Charter of 1681 specifically reserved to the British Parliament the right to tax the colony; but since Parliament had never used this power, the colonists had a case when they said the new British taxes were historically unknown and therefore unconstitutional. The details of this controversy, in which merit is by no means the exclusive possession of either side, do not concern us here. The important fact is not whether the Americans or the British were right in their respective readings of imperial constitutional history, but that the colonials believed they were right and acted accordingly. Regardless of the constitutional niceties involved, it is patent that the English had waited too long to assert their authority. Too many Americans had grown accustomed to their untrammeled political life to submit now to new English controls. In brief, the colonists suddenly realized that they were no longer wards of Britain, but a separate people, capable of forging their own destiny.

This conviction runs all through the polemics of the Revolutionary crisis. For underlying the constitutional verbiage which Englishmen and Americans exchanged were two quite different assumptions about the nature of the British Empire and the character of the American people. Whereas Englishmen saw America as a part of an Empire in which all elements were subordinate to Britain, the Americans, drawing upon their actual history, saw only a loose confederation of peoples in which there were Britons and Americans, neither one of whom could presume to dictate to the other. The colonials, in effect, now felt themselves Americans, not displaced, subordinate Englishmen. Jefferson suggested this to the King himself when he wrote in his *Summary*

View of the Rights of British America: "You are surrounded by British counsellors. . . . You have no minister for American affairs, because you have none taken from us." Furthermore, even after 1776 many a Loyalist exiled in Britain found the English annoying and strange—evidence of the fact that residence in America had worked its influence even upon those loyal to the Crown. "It piques my pride, I must confess," wrote one expatriated Loyalist, "to hear us called 'our colonies, our plantations,' in such terms and with such airs as if our property and persons were absolutely theirs, like the 'villains' in their cottages in the old feudal system."

The imperial view so confidently advanced by Grenville and others of the British administration came too late; the Americans were not interested in making a more efficient Empire to be manipulated from Whitehall. Because of this basic conflict in assumptions, American demands continued to leapfrog ahead of British concessions right up to the Carlisle Peace Mission in the midst of the Revolutionary War. Even ministerial assurances in 1769 that there would be no further imperially imposed taxes failed to divert the colonial drive toward equality with Britain. The child was truly asserting himself, and, as so often happens, the parent was reluctant to strike him down.

Measured against the age of Hitler and Stalin, the British overlords of the eighteenth century appear remarkably benign in their dealings with the colonies in the years after 1763. For it is a fact that the colonies were in revolt against a potential tyrant, not an actual one. Much more fearsome in the eyes of the politically sensitive colonials was the direction in which the British measures tended rather than the explicit content of the acts. As Bernard Bailyn has pointed out after a survey of some 400 tracts of the Revolutionary era, Americans were convinced that a conspiracy was afoot in Britain to deprive them of their liberties, though historians can find little basis for such political paranoia. But that such fear was a source of revolutionary fervor, Bailyn has no doubt. Furthermore, Englishmen could never bring themselves to enforce, with all the power at their command, what they believed was the true nature of the Empire, that is, the subordinate position of the colonies. More than once General Thomas Gage, commanding the British troops in America, reported that his forces were too scattered to preserve proper order and government in the colonies. "I am concerned to find in your Lordship's letters," he wrote from New York in 1768, "that irresolution still prevails in our Councils; it is time to come to some determination about the disposition of the troops in this Country."

Part of this irresolution was born of British confusion as to what should be the government's purpose, as the hasty repeals of the stamp and Townshend duties testify on the one hand, and the remarkably inept Tea Act reveals on the other. Part of it stemmed from the fact that within their own house, so to speak, were Americans: at times Lord Chatham himself, at all times Edmund Burke, Colonel Isaac Barré, John Wilkes, and Dr. Price, who insisted that Americans possessed the rights of Englishmen. "The seditious spirit of the colonies," George Grenville wryly complained on the floor of Commons in 1776, "owes its birth to the factions in this House."

Divided as to aims and devoid of strong leadership, the British permitted the much more united colonists, who were blessed with superb and daring leadership, to seize and hold the initiative. Not until the very end—after the destruction of the tea at Boston Harbor in 1773—did the patience of the British ministry run dry. By then, however, the years of acrimony, suspicion, and growing awareness of the differences between the two peoples had done their work, and the harsh coercive measures taken against Massachusetts only provoked counterviolence from all the colonies. Lexington and Concord, Bunker Hill and Independence Hall, were then not far behind.

By implication, the interpretation of the coming of the Revolution given here greatly subordinates the role of economic factors. Since the economic restrictions imposed upon the colonies have traditionally played a large role in most discussions of the causes of the Revolution, they deserve some comment here. Those who advance an economic explanation for the Revolution argue that the series of economic measures enacted by Britain in the century before 1750 actually operated to confine, if not stifle, the colonial economy. Therefore, it is said, the colonies revolted against Britain in an effort to break through these artificial and externally imposed limits. On the surface and from the assumptions of twentieth-century economic life, the mercantilistic system appears severe and crippling and worthy of strong colonial opposition. But before such speculative conclusions can be accepted, they deserve to be checked against the facts.

Several historians have sought to measure quantitatively the restrictive effects of English mercantilism upon the colonial economy. Their conclusions, it can be said at the outset, are generally in the negative. For example, take the three major British limitations on colonial manufactures. On the statute books the Iron Act of 1750 appears to halt the erection of additional slitting mills in the colonies, but the fact is that many were set up after that date, regardless of the act's prohibitions, and to such an extent that by 1776 there were probably more such mills in America than in England. Nor, Lawrence Harper tells us, did the Woolens Act of 1699, designed to prevent colonial competition with a major English industry, actually inhibit American endeavors in the field, since few Americans cared to engage in the industry. True, Harper concluded that the colonial beaver-hat industry suffered from the restrictions of the Hat Act of 1732, but, as he adds, that branch of economic activity could hardly be considered an important segment of the economy. And those are the three major British efforts to "stifle" American manufacturing.

Nor can the restrictions on the settlement of the West be viewed, as some historians have asserted, as a significant motive for the Revolution. For one thing, movement into the West was never absolutely halted, and as early as 1764 the Proclamation Line of the previous year was being moved westward to permit settlement beyond the mountains. Furthermore, as Thomas Abernathy has shown, the Virginia gentry—often cited as heavily involved in western land speculation and therefore concerned with restrictions on the West—were not vitally interested in the matter economically, though the religious and political implications of the later Quebec Act, for example, did arouse them. All in all, it would appear that the western land question may have been an irritating factor, but, in view of the changing and indecisive English policy, hardly a revolution-making force.

Perhaps the most that can be said quantitatively about the burden of the whole navigation or mercantilist system in which England encased the colonies is that the regulations concerning the routing of trade added between $2.6 million and $7 million to the cost of doing business in the colonies. Over against this, however, must be placed the fact that the system did not seem a burden to the colonies. Very few objections to the navigation system appear in the voluminous literature of the crisis. In fact, so acceptable did it appear to that jealous American, Benjamin Franklin, that in 1774 he suggested to Lord Chatham that all the basic Navigation Laws be re-enacted by the colonial legislatures as an earnest of colonial loyalty. Furthermore, in October of that year, the first Continental Congress publicly declared the colonies willing to "cheerfully consent to the operation of such acts of the British Parliament, as are bona fide, restrained to the regulation of our external commerce, for the purpose of securing the commercial advantages of the whole empire to the mother country, and the commercial benefits of its respective members. . . ." In short, the navigation system was acceptable. Certainly laws the repressive nature of which no one was disturbed about can hardly be accepted as the grounds for a revolution.

No better economic argument can be made for taxation as a cause for the Revolution. Despite the tradition of oppressive taxation which the myth of the Revolution has spawned, the actual tax burden of the colonies was much heavier in the seventeenth century than in the years immediately before the conflict. On a per capita basis, taxes were five times greater in 1698 than they were in 1773. The lightness of the British taxes in the pre-Revolutionary period is also shown by the fact that the duty on molasses in 1766 was only a penny a gallon, or less than the duty the federal government imposed in 1791. As Lord North pointed out in 1775, taxation of the Americans was neither excessive nor oppressive.

From the unconvincing character of the economic explanations for the coming of the Revolution, it would appear, therefore, that the underlying force impelling the break was the growing national self-consciousness of the Americans. "The Revolution was effected before the war commenced," John Adams remarked years afterward. "The Revolution was in the minds and hearts of the people. . . ." The origins of the "principles and feelings" which made the Revolution, Adams thought, "ought to be traced back . . . and sought in the history of the country from the first plantations in America." For a century and a half the Americans had been growing up and now they had finally come of age. Precisely because the Revolution was the breaking away of a young people from a parent, the substance of the Revolution was political. The argument concerned the question of parental authority, because that is the precise point at which tension appears as the child approaches maturity and seeks to assert his independence. Unfortunately for Britain, but like so many modern parents, the mother country had long before conveniently provided the best arguments in favor of freedom. And the colonists had learned the arguments well. For this reason, the rhetoric of the Revolutionary argument was in the language of the British political and constitutional tradition.

As children enjoying a long history of freedom from interference from their parent, the Americans might well have continued in their loose relationship, even in maturity, for they were conservative as well as precocious. History, however, decreed otherwise. Britain's triumph in the Great War for the Empire put a new strain on the family relationship, and so intense was the pressure that Americans could not fail to see, as the argument increased in acrimony, that they were no longer members of the English family, but rather a new people, with their own separate destiny. Some Americans saw it earlier than others; a good many saw it by 1776. John Penn, while in England in 1773, was struck by the English ignorance "with respect to *our* part of the world (for I consider myself more American than English). . . ." To South Carolinian Henry Laurens, the Boston Port Act hit at "the liberty of all Americans," not just at that of the people of Massachusetts. Once they were convinced of their essential difference as a people and that British obduracy would not melt, Americans could not accept the old familiar arrangements. Anything less than their independence as a people was unacceptable; it would take Englishmen another generation to realize that the disagreement was as deep as that.

At no time during the ten-year crisis, however, were most Americans spoiling for a rupture with England merely for the sake of a break. Indeed, no one can run through the constitutional arguments of that day without being struck with the reluctance—almost misgivings—with which Americans reached the conclusion of independence. After attending the Continental Congress in 1774, Washington, for example, was "well satisfied that" independence was not "desired by any thinking man in all North America." And, as late as July 6, 1775—over two months after the embattled farmers made their stand at the "rude bridge"—Congress denied any "designs of separation from Great Britain and establishing independent states."

This was no heedless, impetuous overthrow of an oppressor; rather it was a slowly germinating determination on the part of Americans to counter and thwart a change in their hitherto established and accepted ways of governing. Except for the long-deferred assertion of independence, the whole corpus of Revolutionary rhetoric—and nothing lends itself more to radicalism than words—was conservative, expressive of the wish to retain the old ways. The demands made upon Britain were actually pleas for a return to the old relationship: repeal the Stamp Act, the Townshend Acts, the Mutiny Acts; restore trial by jury as abrogated by the expanded admiralty courts; remove the restrictions recently placed upon western migration. One needs only to run through that famous list of grievances in the Declaration of Independence to be forcefully reminded that what these revolutionaries wanted was nothing but the *status quo ante bellum*.

"We have taken up arms," the Continental Congress carefully explained in July, 1775, two months after Lexington, "in defense of the freedom that is our birth-right, and which we ever enjoyed til the late violation of it. . . ." These men had been satisfied with their existence, they were not disgruntled agitators or frustrated politicians; they were a strange new breed—contented revolutionaries. . . .

POSTSCRIPT

Was the American Revolution Largely a Product of Market-Driven Consumer Forces?

Professor Degler summarizes the arguments of the neo-Whig or consensus school of historians writing about the Revolution from 1945 through the 1970s. The colonists were rational loyal citizens of the British Empire who accepted the trade regulations of the mercantilist system because of the benefits provided, such as guaranteed markets and the protection of the British navy against pirates.

Trouble began when the British acquired Canada from France after the Great War for Empire in 1763. No longer was France a threat to the colonists, but the British needed revenue because they were saddled with a debt of 130 million pounds plus interest. It seemed only fair that the colonists should pay their fair share of taxes. When the British enacted the Sugar Stamp and Townshend Acts, the colonists responded with the consistent argument that they were taxed without being represented in Parliament.

The disagreements over virtual and actual representation in Parliament and who had the power to tax centered around two very different assumptions about the nature of the British Empire. "Whereas Englishmen saw America as a part of an empire in which all elements were subordinate to Britain," says Degler, "the Americans, drawing upon their actual history, saw only a loose confederation of peoples in which there were Britons and Americans, neither one of whom could presume to dictate to the other."

Degler, like most consensus historians, was reacting to the earlier generation of progressives who emphasized social and economic conflicts over political motivations. He argues that the restrictions of British mercantilism upon the manufacturing hats and textiles were minor. In the case of the Iron Act of 1750, there were more slitting mills erected illegally after the act was passed.

Seventy-five years ago, Louis Hacker gave the clearest statement of the economic causes in "The First American Revolution," *Columbia University Quarterly* (1935), reprinted in Esmond Wright's edited anthology on the *Causes and Consequences of the American Revolution* (Quadrangle Books, 1966). "If in the raising of a colonial revenue lay the heart of the difficulty," he said, "how are we to account for the quick repeal of the Stamp Tax and the Townshend Acts and the lowering of the molasses duty? And, on the other hand, how are we to account for the tightening of enforcement of the Acts of Trade and Navigation at a dozen and one different points, the passage of the Currency Act, the placing of iron on the enumerated list, English seizure of control of the wine trade, and the attempt to give the East India Company a monopoly over the

134

colonial tea business? The struggle was not over high-sounding political and constitutional concepts: over the power of taxation and, in the final analysis, over natural rights: but over colonial manufacturing, wild lands and furs, sugar, wine, tea and currency, all of which meant, simply, the survival or collapse of English merchant capitalism within the imperial-colonial framework of the mercantilist system."

Professor T. H. Breen has brought back from the grave the economic interpretation of the American Revolution. He has, however, given it a new twist. The title of his book is appropriate: *The Marketplace of Revolution* demonstrates *How Consumer Politics Shaped American Independence*.

Like Degler, Breen accepts the idea that the mercantilist system benefited the colonists. He extends the argument in his book by demonstrating how both the upper- and middle-class colonists had improved their living standard in the eighteenth century by the importation of "all sorts of woolen cloth, silks, scythes, nails, glass, pewter, firearms and all sorts of cutler, the quantity we cannot ascertain," as Connecticut governor Jonathan Law explained in an inventory for the Board of Trade in the 1740s. As Professor Degler also pointed out, this mercantilist arrangement was upset when the English decided to tax the colonists directly to make up a huge governmental deficit after the Great War for Empire ended in 1763.

Breen's main thesis is that the consumer boycotts from the Stamp Act of 1765 through the Boston Tea Party of December 1773 provided the colonists with a shared experience that enabled them to develop a sense of nationhood that differentiated themselves from the British.

Breen is too good a historian to accept the consumer revolt as a mono-causal explanation for the American Revolution. There were other issues such as direct taxation, political representation, and pressure to support the Anglican Church that angered the colonists. But through his use of primary sources—letters, diaries, political resolutions, pamphlets, and, most important of all, newspapers—Breen is able to show that after the Boston Tea Party the colonists realized that a split from the British Empire was more than a distinct possibility.

Breen's interpretation has not been universally accepted. In the "Exchange: American Consumerism," *Journal of American History* (September 2006), Professor David Steigerwald complains that Breen had to resort to "abstract subjectivism as the mechanism of history" when he fashioned individuals who make distinct choices of consumer goods into groups supporting market boycotts for political freedom. Breen's response was that "within a structure of colonial dependency . . . Americans discovered that private and personal decisions could be forged into an effective weapon against a despotic authority that appeared deaf to legitimate constitutional grievances. It was within groups that the personal becomes political."

The two major interpretative articles on the subject are Jack P. Greene, "The Reappraisal of the American Revolution in Recent Historical Literature," in Greene, ed., *The Reinterpretation of the American Revolution* (Harper & Row, 1968), an anthology of essays which highlights Greene's historiographical appraisal from Bancroft to Bailyn. A second immensely detailed appraisal sympathetic to a radial interpretation of the Revolution is Alfred E. Young, "American Historians Confront the Transforming Hand of Revolution," in Ronald Hoffman and Peter Albert, eds., *The Transforming Hand of Revolution: Reconsidering the American Revolution as a Social Movement* (University of Virginia Press, 1996).

There are numerous anthologies that offer a diverse range of interpretations about the American Revolution. Two of the best-edited collections are George Athan Billias, *The American Revolution: How Revolutionary Was It?* (Holt, Rinehart & Winston, 1980), and Richard M. Fulton, *The Revolution That Wasn't: A Contemporary Assessment of 1776* (Kennikat Press, 1981), which discusses numerous theories of revolution. Among the most recent edited collections is Kirk D. Werner, ed., *The American Revolution* (Greenhaven Press, 2000). William Dudley has edited some of the most useful primary sources to a reasonable length in *The American Revolution: Opposing Viewpoints* (Greenhaven Press, 1992).

ISSUE 7

Were the Founding Fathers Democratic Reformers?

YES: John P. Roche, from "The Founding Fathers: A Reform Caucus in Action," *American Political Science Review* (December 1961)

NO: Howard Zinn, from *A People's History of the United States* (Harper Collins, 1999)

ISSUE SUMMARY

YES: Political scientist John P. Roche asserts that the Founding Fathers were not only revolutionaries but also superb democratic politicians who created a constitution that supported the needs of the nation and at the same time was acceptable to the people.

NO: According to radical historian Howard Zinn, the Founding Fathers were an elite group of northern money interests and southern slaveholders who used Shay's Rebellion in Massachusetts as a pretext to create a strong central government, which protected the property rights of the rich to the exclusion of slaves, Indians, and non-property-holding whites.

The United States possesses the oldest written constitution of any major power. The 55 men who attended the Philadelphia Convention of 1787 could scarcely have dreamed that 200 years later the nation would venerate them as the most "enlightened statesmen"of their time. James Madison, the principal architect of the document, may have argued that the Founding Fathers had created a system that might "decide forever the fate of Republican Government which we wish to last for ages," but Madison also told Thomas Jefferson in October 1787 that he did not think the document would be adopted, and if it was, it would not work.

The enlightened statesmen view of the Founding Fathers, presented by nineteenth-century historians like John Fiske, became the accepted interpretation among the general public until the Progressive Era. In 1913, Columbia University professor Charles A. Beard's *An Economic Interpretation of the Constitution of the United States* (Free Press, 1913, 1986) caused a storm of controversy because it questioned the motivations of the Founding Fathers. The Founding Fathers supported the creation of a stronger central government, argued

Beard, not for patriotic reasons but because they wanted to protect their own economic interests.

Beard's research method was fairly simple. Drawing upon a collection of old, previously unexamined treasury records in the National Archives, he discovered that a number of delegates to the Philadelphia Convention and, later, to the state ratifying conventions held substantial amounts of continental securities that would sharply increase in value if a strong national government were established. In addition to attributing economic motives to the Founding Fathers, Beard included a Marxist class conflict interpretation in his book. Those who supported the Constitution, he said, represented "personalty interests which had been adversely affected under the Articles of Confederation: money, public securities, manufactures, and trade and shipping." Those who opposed ratification of the Constitution were the small farmers and debtors.

Beard's socioeconomic conflict interpretation of the supporters and opponents of the Constitution raised another issue: How was the Constitution ratified if the majority of Americans opposed it? Beard's answer was that most Americans could not vote because they did not own property. Therefore, the entire process, from the calling of the Philadelphia Convention to the state ratifying conventions, was nonrepresentative and nondemocratic.

An economic interpretation was a product of its times. Economists, sociologists, and political scientists had been analyzing the conflicts that resulted from the Industrial Revolution, which America had been experiencing at the turn of the twentieth century. Beard joined a group of progressive historians who were interested in reforming the society in which they lived and who also shared his discontent with the old-fashioned institutional approach. The role of the new historians was to rewrite history and discover the real reason why things happened. For the progressive historians, reality consisted of uncovering the hidden social and economic conflicts within society.

In the years between the world wars, the general public held steadfastly to the enlightened statesmen view of the Founding Fathers, but Beard's thesis on the Constitution became the new orthodoxy in most college texts on American history and government. The post-World War II period witnessed the emergence of the neoconservative historians, who viewed the Beardian approach to the Constitution as overly simplistic.

In the first of the following selections, which is a good example of consensus history, John P. Roche contends that although the Founding Fathers may have been revolutionaries, they were also superb democratic politicians who framed a Constitution that supported the needs of the nation and at the same time was acceptable to the people. A good example of Beard's lasting influence can be found in the second selection in which radical historian Howard Zinn argues from the Beardian perspective. The Founding Fathers, he argues, were an elite group of northern money interests and southern slaveholders who used Shay's Rebellion in Massachusetts as a pretext to create a strong central government, which protected the property rights of the rich to the exclusion of slaves, Indians, and non-property-holding whites.

YES ⟵

John P. Roche

The Founding Fathers:
A Reform Caucus in Action

The work of the Constitutional Convention and the motives of the Founding Fathers have been analyzed under a number of different ideological auspices. To one generation of historians, the hand of God was moving in the assembly; under a later dispensation, the dialectic (at various levels of philosophical sophistication) replaced the Deity: "relationships of production" moved into the niche previously reserved for Love of Country. . . . The Framers have undergone miraculous metamorphoses: at one time acclaimed as liberals and bold social engineers, today they appear in the guise of sound Burkean conservatives, men who in our time would subscribe to *Fortune*. . . .

The "Fathers" have thus been admitted to our best circles; the revolutionary ferocity which confiscated all Tory property in reach . . . has been converted . . . into a benign dedication to "consensus" and "prescriptive rights." . . . It is not my purpose here to argue that the "Fathers" were, in fact, radical revolutionaries; that proposition has been brilliantly demonstrated. . . . My concern is with the further position that not only were they revolutionaries, but also they were democrats. Indeed, in my view, there is one fundamental truth about the Founding Fathers . . . : They were first and foremost superb democratic politicians. . . . As recent research into the nature of American politics in the 1780s confirms, they were committed (perhaps willy-nilly) to working within the democratic framework, within a universe of public approval. . . . The Philadelphia Convention was not a College of Cardinals or a council of Platonic guardians working within a manipulative, pre-democratic framework; it was a nationalist reform caucus which had to operate with great delicacy and skill in a political cosmos full of enemies to achieve the one definitive goal—popular approbation. . . .

What they did was to hammer out a pragmatic compromise which would both bolster the "national interest" and be acceptable to the people. What inspiration they got came from their collective experience as professional politicians in a democratic society. As John Dickinson put it to his fellow delegates on August 13, "Experience must be our guide. Reason may mislead us."

In this context, let us examine the problems they confronted and the solutions they evolved. The Convention has been described picturesquely as a counter-revolutionary junta and the Constitution as a coup d'état, but this has been accomplished by withdrawing the whole history of the movement

From *American Political Science Review*, vol. 55, no. 4, December 1961. Copyright © 1961 by Cambridge University Press. Reprinted by permission.

for constitutional reform from its true context. No doubt the goals of the constitutional elite were "subversive" to the existing political order, but it is overlooked that their subversion could only have succeeded if the people of the United States endorsed it by regularized procedures. . . .

I

When the Constitutionalists went forth to subvert the Confederation, they utilized the mechanisms of political legitimacy. And the roadblocks which confronted them were formidable. At the same time, they were endowed with certain potent political assets. The history of the United States from 1786 to 1790 was largely one of a masterful employment of political expertise by the Constitutionalists as against bumbling, erratic behavior by the opponents of reform. Effectively, the Constitutionalists had to induce the states, by democratic techniques of coercion, to emasculate themselves. . . . And at the risk of becoming boring, it must be reiterated that the only weapon in the Constitutionalist arsenal was an effective mobilization of public opinion.

The group which undertook this struggle was an interesting amalgam of a few dedicated nationalists with the self-interested spokesmen of various parochial bailiwicks. The Georgians, for example, wanted a strong central authority to provide military protection for their huge, underpopulated state against the Creek Confederacy; Jerseymen and Connecticuters wanted to escape from economic bondage to New York; the Virginians hoped to establish a system which would give that great state its rightful place in the councils of the republic. The dominant figures in the politics of these states therefore cooperated in the call for the Convention. In other states, the thrust towards national reform was taken up by opposition groups who added the "national interest" to their weapons system; in Pennsylvania, for instance, the group fighting to revise the Constitution of 1776 came out four-square behind the Constitutionalists, and in New York, [Alexander] Hamilton and the Schuyler [family] ambiance took the same tack against George Clinton. There was, of course, a large element of personality in the affair: there is reason to suspect that Patrick Henry's opposition to the Convention and the Constitution was founded on his conviction that Jefferson was behind both, and a close study of local politics elsewhere would surely reveal that others supported the Constitution for the simple (and politically quite sufficient) reason that the "wrong" people were against it. . . .

What distinguished the leaders of the Constitutionalist caucus from their enemies was a "Continental" approach to political, economic and military issues. To the extent that they shared an institutional base of operations, it was the Continental Congress (thirty-nine of the delegates to the Federal Convention had served in Congress), and this was hardly a locale which inspired respect for the state governments. . . . Membership in the Congress under the Articles of Confederation worked to establish a continental frame of reference, that a Congressman from Pennsylvania and one from North Carolina would share. . . . This was particularly true with respect to external affairs: the average state legislator was probably about as concerned with foreign policy than as he is today, but Congressmen were constantly forced to take the broad view of

American prestige, were compelled to listen to the reports of Secretary John Jay and to the dispatches and pleas from their frustrated envoys in Britain, France and Spain. From considerations such as these, a "Continental" ideology developed which seems to have demanded a revision of our domestic institutions primarily on the ground that only by invigorating our general government could we assume our rightful place in the international arena. . . .

Note that I am not endorsing the "Critical Period" thesis; on the contrary, Merrill Jensen seems to me quite sound in his view that for most Americans, engaged as they were in self-sustaining agriculture, the "Critical Period" was not particularly critical. In fact, the great achievement of the Constitutionalists was their ultimate success in convincing the elected representatives of a majority of the white male population that change was imperative. A small group of political leaders with a Continental vision and essentially a consciousness of the United States' international impotence, provided the matrix of the movement. To their standard other leaders rallied with their own parallel ambitions. Their great assets were (1) the presence in their caucus of the one authentic American "father figure," George Washington, whose prestige was enormous; (2) the energy and talent of their leadership (in which one must include the towering intellectuals of the time, John Adams and Thomas Jefferson, despite their absence abroad), and their communications "network," which was far superior to anything on the opposition side; (3) the preemptive skill which made "their" issue The Issue and kept the locally oriented opposition permanently on the defensive; and (4) the subjective consideration that these men were spokesmen of a new and compelling credo: American nationalism, that ill-defined but nonetheless potent sense of collective purpose that emerged from the American Revolution. . . .

The Constitutionalists got the jump on the "opposition" (a collective noun: oppositions would be more correct) at the outset with the demand for a Convention. Their opponents were caught in an old political trap: they were not being asked to approve any specific program of reform, but only to endorse a meeting to discuss and recommend needed reforms. If they took a hard line at the first stage, they were put in the position of glorifying the status quo and of denying the need for any changes. Moreover, the Constitutionalists could go to the people with a persuasive argument for "fair play"—"How can you condemn reform before you know precisely what is involved?" Since the state legislatures obviously would have the final say on any proposals that might emerge from the Convention, the Constitutionalists were merely reasonable men asking for a chance. Besides, since they did not make any concrete proposals at that stage, they were in a position to capitalize on every sort of generalized discontent with the Confederation.

Perhaps because of their poor intelligence system, perhaps because of over-confidence generated by the failure of all previous efforts to alter the Articles, the opposition awoke too late to the dangers that confronted them in 1787. Not only did the Constitutionalists manage to get every state but Rhode Island . . . to appoint delegates to Philadelphia, but when the results were in, it appeared that they dominated the delegations. Given the apathy of the opposition, this was a natural phenomenon: in an ideologically nonpolarized political atmosphere those who get appointed to a special committee are likely to be the men who supported the movement for its creation. . . . Much has been made of the fact that the delegates to Philadelphia were not elected by the people; some have adduced this fact as evidence of the "undemocratic" character of the gathering. But put in the context of the time, this argument is wholly specious: the central government under the Articles was considered a creature of the component states and in all the states but Rhode Island, Connecticut and New Hampshire, members of the national Congress were chosen by the state legislatures. This was not a consequence of elitism or fear of the mob; it was a logical extension of states'-rights doctrine to guarantee that the national institution did not end-run the state legislatures and make direct contact with the people.

II

With delegations safely named, the focus shifted to Philadelphia. While waiting for a quorum to assemble, James Madison got busy and drafted the so-called Randolph or Virginia Plan with the aid of the Virginia delegation. This was a political master-stroke. Its consequence was that once business got under way, the framework of discussion was established on Madison's terms. There was no interminable argument over agenda; instead the delegates took the Virginia Resolutions—"just for purposes of discussion"—as their point of departure. And along with Madison's proposals, many of which were buried in the course of the summer, went his major premise: a new start on a Constitution rather than piecemeal amendment. . . .

Standard treatments of the Convention divide the delegates into "nationalists" and "states'-righters" with various improvised shadings ("moderate nationalists," etc.), but these are a posteriori categories which obfuscate more than they clarify. What is striking to one who analyzes the Convention as a case-study in democratic politics is the lack of clear-cut ideological divisions in the Convention. Indeed, I submit that the evidence—Madison's Notes, the correspondence of the delegates, and debates on ratification—indicates that this was a remarkably homogeneous body on the ideological level. [Robert] Yates and [John] Lansing [of New York], who favored the New Jersey Plan] . . . left in disgust on July 10. . . . Luther Martin, Maryland's bibulous narcissist, left on September 4 in a huff when he discovered that others did not share his self-esteem; others went home for personal reasons. But the hard core of delegates accepted a grinding regimen throughout the attrition of a Philadelphia summer precisely because they shared the Constitutionalist goal.

Basic differences of opinion emerged, of course, but these were not ideological; they were structural. If the so-called "states'-rights" group had not accepted the fundamental purposes of the Convention, they could simply have pulled out and by doing so have aborted the whole enterprise. Instead of bolting, they returned day after day to argue and to compromise. An interesting symbol of this basic homogeneity was the initial agreement on secrecy: these professional politicians did not want to become prisoners of publicity; they wanted to retain that freedom of maneuver which is only possible when men are not forced to take public stands in the preliminary stages of negotiation. There was no legal means of binding the tongues of the delegates: at any stage in the game a delegate with basic principled objections to the emerging project could have taken the stump (as Luther Martin did after his exit) and denounced the convention to the skies. Yet . . . the delegates generally observed the injunction. Secrecy is certainly uncharacteristic of any assembly marked by strong ideological polarization. . . .

Commentators on the Constitution who have read *The Federalist* in lieu of reading the actual debates have credited the Fathers with the invention of a sublime concept called "Federalism." . . . Federalism, as the theory is generally defined, was an improvisation which was later promoted into a political theory. Experts on "federalism" should take to heart the advice of David Hume, who warned . . . "there is no subject in which we must proceed with more caution than in [history], lest we assign causes which never existed and reduce what is merely contingent to stable and universal principles." In any event, the final balance in the Constitution between the states and the nation must have come as a great disappointment to Madison. . . .

It is indeed astonishing how those who have glibly designated James Madison the "father" of Federalism have overlooked the solid body of fact which indicates that he shared Hamilton's quest for a unitary central government. To be specific, they have avoided examining the clear import of the Madison-Virginia Plan, and have disregarded Madison's dogged inch-by-inch retreat from the bastions of centralization. The Virginia Plan envisioned a unitary national government effectively freed from and dominant over the states. The lower house of the national legislature was to be elected directly by the people of the states with membership proportional to population. The upper house was to be selected by the lower and the two chambers would elect the executive and choose the judges. The national legislature was to be empowered to disallow the acts of state legislatures, and the central government was vested, in addition to the powers of the nation under which the Articles of Confederation, with plenary authority wherever ". . . the separate States are incompetent or in which the harmony of the United States may be interrupted by the exercise of individual legislation." Finally, just to lock the door against state intrusion, the national Congress was to be given the power to use military force on recalcitrant states. This was Madison's "model" of an ideal national government, though it later received little publicity in *The Federalist*.

The interesting thing was the reaction of the Convention to this militant program for a strong autonomous central government. Some delegates were startled, some obviously leery of so comprehensive a project of reform, but nobody set off any fireworks and nobody walked out. Moreover, in the two weeks that followed, the Virginia Plan received substantial endorsement *en principe;* the initial temper of the gathering can be deduced from the approval "without debate or dissent," on May 31, of the Sixth Resolution which granted Congress the authority to disallow state legislation ". . . contravening in its opinion the Articles of Union." Indeed, an amendment was included to bar states from contravening national treaties.

The Virginia Plan may therefore be considered, in ideological terms, as the delegates' Utopia, but as the discussions continued and became more specific, many of those present began to have second thoughts. . . . They were practical politicians in a democratic society, and no matter what their private dreams might be, they had to take home an acceptable package and defend it—and their own political futures—against predictable attack. On June 14 the breaking point between dream and reality took place. Apparently realizing that under the Virginia Plan, Massachusetts, Virginia and Pennsylvania could virtually dominate the national government—and probably appreciating that to sell this program to "the folks back home" would be impossible—the delegates from the small states dug in their heels and demanded time for a consideration of alternatives. . . .

Now the process of accommodation was put into action smoothly—and wisely, given the character and strength of the doubters. Madison had the votes, but this was one of those situations where the enforcement of mechanical majoritarianism could easily have destroyed the objectives of the majority: the Constitutionalists were in quest of a qualitative as well as a quantitative consensus; . . . it was a political imperative if they were to attain ratification.

III

According to the standard script, at this point the "states'-rights" group intervened in force behind the New Jersey Plan, which has been characteristically portrayed as a revision to the status quo under the Articles of Confederation with but minor modifications. A careful examination of the evidence indicates that only in a marginal sense is this an accurate description. It is true that the New Jersey Plan put the states back into the institutional picture, but one could argue that to do so was a recognition of political reality rather than an affirmation of states'-rights. A serious case can be made that the advocates of the New Jersey Plan, far from being ideological addicts of states'-rights, intended to substitute for the Virginia Plan a system which would both retain strong national power and have a chance of adoption in the states. The leading spokesman for the project asserted quite clearly that his views were based more on counsels of expediency than on principle. . . . In his preliminary speech on June 9, Paterson had stated ". . . to the public mind we must accommodate ourselves," and in his notes for this and his later effort as well, the emphasis is the same. The structure of government under the Articles should be retained:

> 2. Because it accords with the Sentiments of the People
>
>> [Proof:] 1. Coms. [Commissions from state legislatures defining the jurisdiction of the delegates]
>> 2. News-papers—Political Barometer. Jersey never would have sent Delegates under the first [Virginia] Plan—
>
> Not here to sport Opinions of my own. Wt. [What] can be done. A little practicable Virtue preferrable to Theory.

This was a defense of political acumen, not of states'-rights. . . .

In other words, the advocates of the New Jersey Plan concentrated their fire on what they held to be the political liabilities of the Virginia Plan—which were matters of institutional structure—rather than on the proposed scope of national authority. Indeed, the Supremacy Clause of the Constitution first saw the light of day in Paterson's Sixth Resolution; the New Jersey Plan contemplated the use of military force to secure compliance with national law; and finally Paterson made clear his view that under either the Virginia or the New Jersey systems, the general government would ". . . act on individuals and not on states." From the states'-rights viewpoint, this was heresy: the fundament of that doctrine was the proposition that any central government had as its constituents the states, not the people, and could only reach the people through the agency of the state government.

Paterson then reopened the agenda of the Convention, but he did so within a distinctly naturalist framework. Paterson's position was one of favoring a strong central government in principle, but opposing one which in fact put the big states in the saddle.

How attached would the Virginians have been to their reform principles if Virginia were to disappear as a component geographical unit (the largest) for representational purposes? Up to this point, the Virginians had been in the happy position of supporting high ideals with that inner confidence born of knowledge that the "public interest" they endorsed would nourish their private interest. Worse, they had shown little willingness to compromise. Now the delegates from the small states announced that they were unprepared to be offered up as sacrificial victims to a "national interest" which reflected Virginia's parochial ambition. Caustic Charles Pinckney was not far off when he remarked sardonically that ". . . the whole [conflict] comes to this: Give N. Jersey an equal vote, and she will dismiss her scruples, and concur in the Natil. system." What he rather unfairly did not add was that the Jersey delegates were not free agents who could adhere to their private convictions; they had to take back, sponsor and risk their reputations on the reforms approved by the Convention—and in New Jersey, not in Virginia. . . .

IV

On Tuesday morning, June 19, . . . James Madison led off with a long, carefully reasoned speech analyzing the New Jersey Plan which, while intellectually vigorous in its criticisms, was quite conciliatory in mood. "The great difficulty," he observed, "lies in the affair of Representation; and if this could be adjusted, all others would be surmountable." (As events were to demonstrate, this diagnosis was correct.) When he finished, a vote was taken on whether to continue with the Virginia Plan as the nucleus for a new constitution: seven states voted "Yes"; New York, New Jersey, and Delaware voted "No"; and Maryland, whose position often depended on which delegates happened to be on the floor, divided. Paterson, it seems, lost decisively; yet in a fundamental sense he and his allies had achieved their purpose: from that day onward, it could never be forgotten that the state governments loomed ominously in the background. . . . Moreover, nobody bolted the convention: Paterson and his colleagues took their defeat in stride and set to work to modify the Virginia Plan, particularly with respect to its provisions on representation in the national legislature. Indeed, they won an immediate rhetorical bonus; when Oliver Ellsworth of Connecticut rose to move that the word "national" be expunged from the Third Virginia Resolution ("Resolved that a national Government ought to be established consisting of a supreme Legislative, Executive and Judiciary"), Randolph agreed and the motion passed unanimously. The process of compromise had begun.

For the next two weeks, the delegates circled around the problem of legislative representation. The Connecticut delegation appears to have evolved a possible compromise quite early in the debates, but the Virginians and particularly Madison (unaware that he would later be acclaimed as the prophet of "federalism") fought obdurately against providing for equal representation of states in the second chamber. . . . On July 2, the ice began to break when through a number of fortuitous events—and one that seems deliberate—the majority against equality of representation was converted into a dead tie. The Convention had reached the stage where it was "ripe" for a solution (presumably all the therapeutic speeches had been made), and the South Carolinians proposed a committee. Madison and James Wilson wanted none of it, but with only Pennsylvania dissenting, the body voted to establish a working party on the problem of representation.

The members of this committee, one from each state, were elected by the delegates—and a very interesting committee it was. Despite the fact that the Virginia Plan had held majority support up to that date, neither Madison nor Randolph was selected (Mason was the Virginian) and Baldwin of Georgia, whose shift in position had resulted in the tie, was chosen. From the composition, it was clear that this was not to be a "fighting" committee: the emphasis in membership was on what might be described as "second-level political entrepreneurs." On the basis of the discussions up to that time, only Luther Martin of Maryland could be described as a "bitter-ender." Admittedly, some divination enters into this sort of analysis, but one does get a sense of the mood of the delegates from these choices—including the interesting selection of Benjamin Franklin, despite his age and intellectual wobbliness, over the brilliant and incisive Wilson or the sharp, polemical Gouverneur Morris, to represent Pennsylvania. His passion for conciliation was more valuable at this juncture than Wilson's logical genius, or Morris' acerbic wit. . . .

It would be tedious to continue a blow-by-blow analysis of the work of the delegates; the critical fight was over representation of the states and once the Connecticut Compromise was adopted on July 17, the Convention was over the hump. Madison, James Wilson, and Gouverneur Morris of New York (who was there representing Pennsylvania!) fought the compromise all the way in a last-ditch effort to get a unitary state with parliamentary supremacy. But their allies deserted them. . . . Moreover, once the compromise had carried (by five states to four, with one state divided), its advocates threw themselves vigorously into the job of strengthening the general government's substantive powers—as might have been predicted, indeed, from Paterson's early statements. It nourishes an increased respect for Madison's devotion to the art of politics, to realize that this dogged fighter could sit down six months later and prepare essays for *The Federalist* in contradiction to his basic convictions about the true course the Convention should have taken.

V

Two tricky issues will serve to illustrate the later process of accommodation. The first was the institutional position of the Executive. Madison argued for an executive chosen by the National Legislature and on May 29 this had been adopted with a provision that after his seven-year term was concluded, the chief magistrate should not be eligible for reelection. In late July this was reopened and for a week the matter was argued from several different points of view. . . . One group felt that the states should have a hand in the process; another small but influential circle urged direct election by the people. There were a number of proposals: election by the people, election by state governors, by electors chosen by state legislatures, by the National legislature, . . . and there was some resemblance to three-dimensional chess in the dispute because of the presence of two other variables, length of tenure and reeligibility. Finally, after opening, reopening, and re-reopening the debate, the thorny problem was consigned to a committee for resolution.

The Brearley Committee on Postponed Matters was a superb aggregation of talent and its compromise on the Executive was a masterpiece of political improvisation. (The Electoral College, its creation, however, had little in its favor as an institution—as the delegates well appreciated.) The point of departure for all discussion about the presidency in the Convention was that in immediate terms, the problem was non-existent; in other words, everybody present knew that under any system devised, George Washington would be President. Thus they were dealing in the future tense and to a body of working politicians the merits of the Brearley proposal were obvious: everybody got a piece of cake. (Or to put it more academically, each viewpoint could leave the Convention and argue to its constituents that it had really won the day.) First, the state legislatures had the right to determine the mode of selection of the electors; second, the small states received a bonus in the Electoral College in the form of a guaranteed minimum of three votes while the big states got acceptance of the principle of proportional power; third, if the state legislatures agreed (as six did in the first presidential election), the people could be involved directly in the choice of electors; and finally, if no candidate received a majority in the College, the right of decision passed to the National Legislature with each state exercising equal strength. (In the Brearley recommendation, the election went to the Senate, but a motion from the floor substituted the House; this was accepted on the ground that the Senate already had enough authority over the executive in its treaty and appointment powers.)

This compromise was almost too good to be true, and the Framers snapped it up with little debate or controversy. No one seemed to think well of the College as an institution; indeed, what evidence there is suggests that there was an assumption that once Washington had finished his tenure as President, the electors would cease to produce majorities and the chief executive would usually be chosen in the House. George Mason observed casually that the selection would be made in the House nineteen times in twenty and no one seriously disputed this point. The vital aspect of the Electoral College was that it got the Convention over the hurdle and protected everybody's interests. . . .

In short, the Framers did not in their wisdom endow the United States with a College of Cardinals—the Electoral College was neither an exercise in applied Platonism nor an experiment in indirect government based on elitist distrust of the masses. It was merely a jerry-rigged improvisation which has subsequently been endowed with a high theoretical content. . . .

The second issue on which some substantial practical bargaining took place was slavery. The morality of slavery was, by design, not at issue; but in its other concrete aspects, slavery colored the arguments over taxation, commerce, and representation. The "Three-Fifths Compromise," that three-fifths of the slaves would be counted both for representation and for purposes of direct taxation (which was drawn from the past—it was a formula of Madison's utilized by Congress in 1783 to establish the basis of state contributions to the Confederation treasury) had allayed some Northern fears about Southern over-representation. . . . The Southerners, on the other hand, were afraid that Congressional control over commerce would lead to the exclusion of slaves or to their excessive taxation as imports. Moreover, the Southerners were disturbed over "navigation acts," i.e., tariffs or special legislation providing, for example, that exports be carried only in American ships; as a section depending upon exports, they wanted protection from the potential voracity of their commercial brethren of the Eastern states. To achieve this end, Mason and others urged that the Constitution include a proviso that navigation and commercial laws should require a two-thirds vote in Congress.

These problems came to a head in late August and, as usual were handed to a committee in the hope that, in Gouverneur Morris' words, ". . . these things may form a bargain among the Northern and Southern states." The Committee reported its measures of reconciliation on August 25, and on August 29 the package was wrapped up and delivered. What occurred can best be described in George Mason's dour version (he anticipated Calhoun in his conviction that permitting navigation acts to pass by majority vote would put the South in economic bondage to the North—it was mainly on this ground that he refused to sign the Constitution):

> The Constitution as agreed to till a fortnight before the Convention rose was such a one as he would have set his hand and heart to. . . . [Until that time] The 3 New England States were constantly with us in all questions . . . so that it was these three States with the 5 Southern ones against Pennsylvania, Jersey and Delaware. With respect to the importation of slaves, [decision-making] was left to Congress. This disturbed the two Southernmost States who knew that Congress would immediately suppress the importation of slaves. Those two States therefore struck up a bargain with the three New England States. If they would join to admit slaves for some years, the two Southern-most States would join in changing the clause which required the 2/3 of the Legislature in any vote [on navigation acts]. It was done.

On the floor of the Convention there was a virtual love-feast on this happy occasion. Charles Pinckney of South Carolina attempted to overturn the committee's decision, when the compromise was reported to the Convention, by insisting that the South needed protection from the imperialism of the Northern states. But his Southern colleagues were not prepared to rock the boat and General C. C. Pinckney arose to spread oil on the suddenly ruffled waters; he admitted that:

> It was in the true interest of the S[outhern] States to have no regulation of commerce; but considering the loss brought on the commerce of the Eastern States by the Revolution, their liberal conduct towards the views of South Carolina [on the regulation of the slave trade] and the interests the weak Southn. States had in being united with the strong Eastern states, he thought it proper that no fetters should be imposed on the power of making commercial regulations; and that his constituents, though prejudiced against the Eastern States, would be reconciled to this liberality. He had himself prejudices against the Eastern States before he came here, but would acknowledge that he had found them as liberal and candid as any men whatever.

Pierce Butler took the same tack, essentially arguing that he was not too happy about the possible consequences, but that a deal was a deal. . . .

VI

Drawing on their vast collective political experience, utilizing every weapon in the politician's arsenal, looking constantly over their shoulders at their constituents, the delegates put together a Constitution. It was a makeshift affair; some sticky issues (for example, the qualification of voters) they ducked entirely; others they mastered with that ancient instrument of political sagacity, studied ambiguity (for example, citizenship), and some they just overlooked. In this last category, I suspect, fell the matter of the power of the federal courts to determine the constitutionality of acts of Congress. When the judicial article was formulated (Article III of the Constitution), deliberations were still in the stage where the legislature was endowed with broad power under the Randolph formulation, authority which by its own terms was scarcely amenable to judicial review. In essence, courts could hardly determine when ". ..the separate States are incompetent or . . . the harmony of the United States may be interrupted"; the National Legislature, as critics pointed out, was free to define its own jurisdiction. Later the definition of legislative authority was changed into the form we know, a series of stipulated powers, but the delegates never seriously reexamined the jurisdiction of the judiciary under this new limited formulation. All arguments on the intention of the Framers in this matter are thus deductive and a posteriori, though some obviously make more sense than others.

The Framers were busy and distinguished men, anxious to get back to their families, their positions, and their constituents. . . . They were trying to do an important job, and do it in such a fashion that their handiwork would be acceptable to very diverse constituencies. No one was rhapsodic about the final document, but it was a beginning, a move in the right direction, and one they had reason to believe the people would endorse. In addition, since they had modified the impossible amendment provisions of the Articles . . . to one demanding approval by only three-quarters of the states, they seemed confident that gaps in the fabric which experience would reveal could be rewoven without undue difficulty.

So with a neat phrase introduced by Benjamin Franklin (but devised by Gouverneur Morris) which made their decision sound unanimous, and an inspired benediction by the Old Doctor urging doubters to doubt their own infallibility, the Constitution was accepted and signed. Curiously, Edmund Randolph, who had played so vital a role throughout, refused to sign, as did his fellow Virginian George Mason and Elbridge Gerry of Massachusetts. Randolph's behavior was eccentric; . . . the best explanation seems to be that he was afraid that the Constitution would prove to be a liability in Virginia politics, where Patrick Henry was burning up the countryside with impassioned denunciations. Presumably, Randolph wanted to check the temper of the populace before he risked his reputation, and perhaps his job, in a fight with both Henry and Richard Henry Lee. Events lend some justification to this speculation: after much temporizing . . . Randolph endorsed ratification in Virginia and ended up getting the best of both worlds. . . .

The Constitution, then, was an apotheosis of "constitutionalism," a triumph of architectonic genius; it was a patchwork sewn together under the pressure of both time and events by a group of extremely talented democratic politicians. They refused to attempt the establishment of a strong, centralized sovereignty on the principle of legislative supremacy for the excellent reason that the people would not accept it. They risked their political fortunes by opposing the established doctrines of state sovereignty because they were convinced that the existing system was leading to national impotence and probably foreign domination. For two years, they worked to get a convention established. For over three months, in what must have seemed to the faithful participants an endless process of give-and-take, they reasoned, cajoled, threatened, and bargained amongst themselves. The result was a Constitution which the people, in fact, by democratic processes, did accept, and a new and far better national government was established. . . .

To conclude, the Constitution was neither a victory for abstract theory nor a great practical success. Well over half a million men had to die on the battlefields of the Civil War before certain constitutional principles could be defined—a baleful consideration which is somehow overlooked in our customary tributes to the farsighted genius of the Framers and to the supposed American talent for "constitutionalism." The Constitution was, however, a vivid demonstration of effective democratic political action, and of the forging of a national elite which literally persuaded its countrymen to hoist themselves by their own boot straps.

A People's History of the United States

To many Americans over the years, the Constitution drawn up in 1787 has seemed a work of genius put together by wise, humane men who created a legal framework for democracy and equality. This view is stated, a bit extravagantly, by the historian George Bancroft, writing in the early nineteenth century:

> The Constitution establishes nothing that interferes with equality and individuality. It knows nothing of differences by descent, or opinions, of favored classes, or legalized religion, or the political power of property. It leaves the individual alongside of the individual. . . . As the sea is made up of drops, American society is composed of separate, free, and constantly moving atoms, ever in reciprocal action . . . so that the institutions and laws of the country rise out of the masses of individual thought which, like the waters of the ocean, are rolling evermore.

Another view of the Constitution was put forward early in the twentieth century by the historian Charles Beard (arousing anger and indignation, including a denunciatory editorial in the *New York Times*). He wrote in his book *An Economic Interpretation of the Constitution*:

> Inasmuch as the primary object of a government, beyond the mere repression of physical violence, is the making of the rules which determine the property relations of members of society, the dominant classes whose rights are thus to be determined must perforce obtain from the government such rules as are consonant with the larger interests necessary to the continuance of their economic processes, or they must themselves control the organs of government.

In short, Beard said, the rich must, in their own interest, either control the government directly or control the laws by which government operates.

Beard applied this general idea to the Constitution, by studying the economic backgrounds and political ideas of the fifty-five men who gathered in Philadelphia in 1787 to draw up the Constitution. He found that a majority of them were lawyers by profession, that most of them were men of wealth, in land, slaves, manufacturing, or shipping, that half of them had money loaned out at interest, and that forty of the fifty-five held government bonds, according to the records of the Treasury Department.

Thus, Beard found that most of the makers of the Constitution had some direct economic interest in establishing a strong federal government: the manufacturers needed protective tariffs; the moneylenders wanted to stop the use of paper money to pay off debts; the land speculators wanted protection as they invaded Indian lands; slaveowners needed federal security against slave revolts and runaways; bondholders wanted a government able to raise money by nationwide taxation, to pay off those bonds.

Four groups, Beard noted, were not represented in the Constitutional Convention: slaves, indentured servants, women, men without property. And so the Constitution did not reflect the interests of those groups.

He wanted to make it clear that he did not think the Constitution was written merely to benefit the Founding Fathers personally, although one could not ignore the $150,000 fortune of Benjamin Franklin, the connections of Alexander Hamilton to wealthy interests through his father-in-law and brother-in-law, the great slave plantations of James Madison, the enormous landholdings of George Washington. Rather, it was to benefit the groups the Founders represented, the "economic interests they understood and felt in concrete, definite form through their own personal experience."

Not everyone at the Philadelphia Convention fitted Beard's scheme. Elbridge Gerry of Massachusetts was a holder of landed property, and yet he opposed the ratification of the Constitution. Similarly, Luther Martin of Maryland, whose ancestors had obtained large tracts of land in New Jersey, opposed ratification. But, with a few exceptions, Beard found a strong connection between wealth and support of the Constitution.

By 1787 there was not only a positive need for strong central government to protect the large economic interests, but also immediate fear of rebellion by discontented farmers. The chief event causing this fear was an uprising in the summer of 1786 in western Massachusetts, known as Shays' Rebellion.

In the western towns of Massachusetts there was resentment against the legislature in Boston. The new Constitution of 1780 had raised the property qualifications for voting. No one could hold state office without being quite wealthy. Furthermore, the legislature was refusing to issue paper money, as had been done in some other states, like Rhode Island, to make it easier for debt-ridden farmers to pay off their creditors.

Illegal conventions began to assemble in some of the western counties to organize opposition to the legislature. At one of these, a man named Plough Jogger spoke his mind:

> I have been greatly abused, have been obliged to do more than my part in the war; been loaded with class rates, town rates, province rates, Continental rates and all rates . . . been pulled and hauled by sheriffs, constables and collectors, and had my cattle sold for less than they were worth. . . .
> . . . The great men are going to get all we have and I think it is time for us to rise and put a stop to it, and have no more courts, nor sheriffs, nor collectors nor lawyers. . . .

The chairman of that meeting used his gavel to cut short the applause. He and others wanted to redress their grievances, but peacefully, by petition to the General Court (the legislature) in Boston.

However, before the scheduled meeting of the General Court, there were going to he court proceedings in Hampshire County, in the towns of Northampton and Springfield, to seize the cattle of farmers who hadn't paid their debts, to take away their land, now full of grain and ready for harvest. And so, veterans of the Continental army, also aggrieved because they had been treated poorly on discharge—given certificates for future redemption instead of immediate cash—began to organize the farmers into squads and companies. One of these veterans was Luke Day, who arrived the morning of court with a fife-and-drum corps, still angry with the memory of being locked up in debtors' prison in the heat of the previous summer.

The sheriff looked to the local militia to defend the court against these armed farmers. But most of the militia was with Luke Day. The sheriff did manage to gather five hundred men, and the judges put on their black silk robes, waiting for the sheriff to protect their trip to the courthouse. But there at the courthouse steps, Luke Day stood with a petition, asserting the people's constitutional right to protest the unconstitutional acts of the General Court, asking the judges to adjourn until the General Court could act on behalf of the farmers. Standing with Luke Day were fifteen hundred armed farmers. The judges adjourned.

Shortly after, at courthouses in Worcester and Athol, farmers with guns prevented the courts from meeting to take away their property, and the militia were too sympathetic to the farmers, or too outnumbered, to act. In Concord, a fifty-year-old veteran of two wars, Job Shattuck, led a caravan of carts, wagons, horses, and oxen onto the town green, while a message was sent to the judges:

> The voice of the People of this county is such that the court shall not enter this courthouse until such time as the People shall have redress of the grievances they labor under at the present.

A county convention then suggested the judges adjourn, which they did.

At Great Barrington, a militia of a thousand faced a square crowded with armed men and boys. But the militia was split in its opinion. When the chief justice suggested the militia divide, those in favor of the court's sitting to go on the right side of the road, and those against on the left, two hundred of the militia went to the right, eight hundred to the left, and the judges adjourned. Then the crowd went to the home of the chief justice, who agreed to sign a pledge that the court would not sit until the Massachusetts General Court met. The crowd went back to the square, broke open the county jail, and set free the debtors. The chief justice, a country doctor, said: "I have never heard anybody point out a better way to have their grievances redressed than the people have taken."

The governor and the political leaders of Massachusetts became alarmed. Samuel Adams, once looked on as a radical leader in Boston, now insisted people act within the law. He said "British emissaries" were stirring up the farmers. People in the town of Greenwich responded: You in Boston have the money, and we don't. And didn't you act illegally yourselves in the Revolution? The insurgents were now being called Regulators. Their emblem was a sprig of hemlock.

The problem went beyond Massachusetts. In Rhode Island, the debtors had taken over the legislature and were issuing paper money. In New Hampshire, several hundred men, in September of 1786, surrounded the legislature in Exeter, asking that taxes be returned and paper money issued; they dispersed only when military action was threatened.

Daniel Shays entered the scene in western Massachusetts. A poor farm hand when the revolution broke out, he joined the Continental army, fought at Lexington, Bunker Hill, and Saratoga, and was wounded in action. In 1780, not being paid, he resigned from the army, went home, and soon found himself in court for nonpayment of debts. He also saw what was happening to others: a sick woman, unable to pay, had her bed taken from under her.

What brought Shays fully into the situation was that on September 19, the Supreme Judicial Court of Massachusetts met in Worcester and indicted eleven leaders of the rebellion, including three of his friends, as "disorderly, riotous and seditious persons" who "unlawfully and by force of arms" prevented "the execution of justice and the laws of the commonwealth." The Supreme Judicial Court planned to meet again in Springfield a week later, and there was talk of Luke Day's being indicted.

Shays organized seven hundred armed farmers, most of them veterans of the war, and led them to Springfield. There they found a general with nine hundred soldiers and a cannon. Shays asked the general for permission to parade, which the general granted, so Shays and his men moved through the square, drums banging and fifes blowing. As they marched, their ranks grew. Some of the militia joined, and reinforcements began coming in from the countryside. The judges postponed hearings for a day, then adjourned the court.

Now the General Court, meeting in Boston, was told by Governor James Bowdoin to "vindicate the insulted dignity of government." The recent rebels against England, secure in office, were calling for law and order. Sam Adams helped draw up a Riot Act, and a resolution suspending habeas corpus, to allow the authorities to keep people in jail without trial. At the same time, the legislature moved to make some concessions to the angry farmers, saying certain old taxes could now be paid in goods instead of money.

This didn't help. In Worcester, 160 insurgents appeared at the courthouse. The sheriff read the Riot Act. The insurgents said they would disperse only if the judges did. The sheriff shouted something about hanging. Someone came up behind him and put a sprig of hemlock in his hat. The judges left.

Confrontations between farmers and militia now multiplied. The winter snows began to interfere with the trips of farmers to the courthouses. When Shays began marching a thousand men into Boston, a blizzard forced them back, and one of his men froze to death.

An army came into the field, led by General Benjamin Lincoln, on money raised by Boston merchants. In an artillery duel, three rebels were killed. One soldier stepped in front of his own artillery piece and lost both arms. The winter grew worse. The rebels were outnumbered and on the run. Shays took refuge in Vermont, and his followers began to surrender. There were a few more deaths in battle, and then sporadic, disorganized, desperate acts of violence against authority: the burning of barns, the slaughter of a general's horses. One government soldier was killed in an eerie night-time collision of two sleighs.

Captured rebels were put on trial in Northampton and six were sentenced to death. A note was left at the door of the high sheriff of Pittsfidd:

> I understand that there is a number of my countrymen condemned to die because they fought for justice. I pray have a care that you assist not in the execution of so horrid a crime, for by all that is above, he that condemns and he that executes shall share alike. . . . Prepare for death with speed, for your life or mine is short. When the woods are covered with leaves, I shall return and pay you a short visit.

Thirty-three more rebels were put on trial and six more condemned to death. Arguments took place over whether the hangings should go forward. General Lincoln urged mercy and a Commission of Clemency, but Samuel Adams said: "In monarchy the crime of treason may admit of being pardoned or lightly punished, but the man who dares rebel against the laws of a republic ought to suffer death." Several hangings followed; some of the condemned were pardoned. Shays, in Vermont, was pardoned in 1788 and returned to Massachusetts, where he died, poor and obscure, in 1825.

It was Thomas Jefferson, in France as ambassador at the time of Shays' Rebellion, who spoke of such uprisings as healthy for society. In a letter to a friend he wrote: "I hold it that a little rebellion now and then is a good thing. . . . It is a medicine necessary for the sound health of government. . . . God forbid that we should ever be twenty years without such a rebellion. . . . The tree of liberty must be refreshed from time to time with the blood of patriots and tyrants. It is its natural manure."

But Jefferson was far from the scene. The political and economic elite of the country were not so tolerant. They worried that the example might spread. A veteran of Washington's army, General Henry Knox, founded an organization of army veterans, "The Order of the Cincinnati," presumably (as one historian put it) "for the purpose of cherishing the heroic memories of the struggle in which they had taken part," but also, it seemed, to watch out for radicalism in the new country. Knox wrote to Washington in late 1786 about Shays' Rebellion, and in doing so expressed the thoughts of many of the wealthy and powerful leaders of the country:

> The people who are the insurgents have never paid any, or but very little taxes. But they see the weakness of government; they feel at once their own poverty, compared with the opulent, and their own force, and they are determined to make use of the latter, in order to remedy the former. Their creed is "That the property of the United States has been protected from the confiscations of Britain by the joint exertions of all, and therefore ought to he the common property of all. And he

that attempts opposition to this creed is an enemy to equity and justice and ought to be swept from off the face of the earth."

Alexander Hamilton, aide to Washington during the war, was one of the most forceful and astute leaders of the new aristocracy. He voiced his political philosophy:

> All communities divide themselves into the few and the many. The first are the rich and well-born, the other the mass of the people. The voice of the people has been said to be the voice of God; and however generally this maxim has been quoted and believed, it is not true in fact. The people are turbulent and changing; they seldom judge or determine right. Give therefore to the first class a distinct permanent share in the government. . . . Can a democratic assembly who annually revolve in the mass of the people be supposed steadily to pursue the public good? Nothing but a permanent body can check the imprudence of democracy. . . .

At the Constitutional Convention, Hamilton suggested a President and Senate chosen for life.

The Convention did not take his suggestion. But neither did it provide for popular elections, except in the case of the House of Representatives, where the qualifications were set by the state legislatures (which required property-holding for voting in almost all the states), and excluded women, Indians, slaves. The Constitution provided for Senators to be elected by the state legislators, for the President to be elected by electors chosen by the state legislators, and for the Supreme Court to be appointed by the President.

The problem of democracy in the post-Revolutionary society was not, however, the Constitutional limitations on voting. It lay deeper, beyond the Constitution, in the division of society into rich and poor. For if some people had great wealth and great influence; if they had the land, the money, the newspapers, the church, the educational system—how could voting, however broad, cut into such power? There was still another problem: wasn't it the nature of representative government, even when most broadly based, to be conservative, to prevent tumultuous change?

It came time to ratify the Constitution, to submit to a vote in state conventions, with approval of nine of the thirteen required to ratify it. In New York, where debate over ratification was intense, a series of newspaper articles appeared, anonymously, and they tell us much about the nature of the Constitution. These articles, favoring adoption of the Constitution, were written by James Madison, Alexander Hamilton, and John Jay, and came to be known as the *Federalist Papers* (opponents of the Constitution became known as anti-Federalists).

In *Federalist Paper #10,* James Madison argued that representative government was needed to maintain peace in a society ridden by factional disputes. These disputes came from "the various and unequal distribution of property. Those who hold and those who are without property have ever formed distinct interests in society." The problem, he said, was how to control the factional struggles that came from inequalities in wealth. Minority factions could be controlled, he said, by the principle that decisions would be by vote of the majority.

So the real problem, according to Madison, was a majority faction, and here the solution was offered by the Constitution, to have "an extensive republic," that is, a large nation ranging over thirteen states, for then "it will be more difficult for all who feel it to discover their own strength, and to act in unison with each other. . . . The influence of factious leaders may kindle a flame within their particular States, but will be unable to spread a general conflagration through the other States."

Madison's argument can be seen as a sensible argument for having a government which can maintain peace and avoid continuous disorder. But is it the aim of government simply to maintain order, as a referee, between two equally matched fighters? Or is it that government has some special interest in maintaining a certain kind of order, a certain distribution of power and wealth, a distribution in which government officials are not neutral referees but participants? In that case, the disorder they might worry about is the disorder of popular rebellion against those monopolizing the society's wealth. This interpretation makes sense when one looks at the economic interests, the social backgrounds, of the makers of the Constitution.

As part of his argument for a large republic to keep the peace, James Madison tells quite clearly, in *Federalist #10,* whose peace he wants to keep: "A rage for paper money, for an abolition of debts, for an equal division of property, or for any other improper or wicked project, will be less apt to pervade the whole body of the Union than a particular member of it."

When economic interest is seen behind the political clauses of the Constitution, then the document becomes not simply the work of wise men trying to establish a decent and orderly society, but the work of certain groups trying to maintain their privileges, while giving just enough rights and liberties to enough of the people to ensure popular support.

In the new government, Madison would belong to one party (the Democrat-Republicans) along with Jefferson and Monroe. Hamilton would belong to the rival party (the Federalists) along with Washington and Adams. But both agreed—one a slaveholder from Virginia, the other a merchant from New York—on the aims of this new government they were establishing. They were anticipating the long-fundamental agreement of the two political parties in the merican system. Hamilton wrote elsewhere in the *Federalist Papers* that the new Union would be able "to repress domestic faction and insurrection." He referred directly to Shays' Rebellion: "The tempestuous situation from which Massachusetts has scarcely emerged evinces that dangers of this kind are not merely speculative."

It was either Madison or Hamilton (the authorship of the individual papers is not always known) who in *Federalist Paper #63* argued the necessity of a "well-constructed Senate" as "sometimes necessary as a defense to the people against their own temporary errors and delusions" because "there are particular moments in public affairs when the people, stimulated by some irregular passion, or some illicit advantage, or misted by the artful misrepresentations of interested men, may call for measures which they themselves will afterwards be the most ready to lament and condemn." And: "In these critical moments, how salutary will be the interference of some temperate and respectable body of citizens in order to check the misguided career, and to suspend the blow meditated by the people against themselves, until reason, justice, and truth can regain their authority over the public mind?"

The Constitution was a compromise between slaveholding interests of the South and moneyed interests of the North. For the purpose of uniting the thirteen states into one great market for commerce, the northern delegates wanted laws regulating interstate commerce, and urged that such laws require only a majority of Congress to pass. The South agreed to this, in return for allowing the trade in slaves to continue for twenty years before being outlawed.

Charles Beard warned us that governments—including the government of the United States—are not neutral, that they represent the dominant economic interests, and that their constitutions are intended to serve these interests. One of his critics (Robert E. Brown, *Charles Beard and the Constitution*) raises an interesting point. Granted that the Constitution omitted the phrase "life, liberty and the pursuit of happiness," which appeared in the Declaration of Independence, and substituted "life, liberty, or property"—well, why shouldn't the Constitution protect property? As Brown says about Revolutionary America, "practically everybody was interested in the protection of property" because so many Americans owned property.

However, this is misleading. True, there were many property owners. But some people had much more than others. A few people had great amounts of property; many people had small amounts; others had none. Jackson Main found that one-third of the population in the Revolutionary period were small farmers, while only 3 percent of the population had truly large holdings and could be considered wealthy.

Still, one-third was a considerable number of people who felt they had something at stake in the stability of a new government. This was a larger base of support for government than anywhere in the world at the end of the eighteenth century. In addition, the city mechanics had an important interest in a government which would protect their work from foreign competition. As Staughton Lynd puts it: "How is it that the city workingmen all over America overwhelmingly and enthusiastically supported the United States Constitution?"

This was especially true in New York. When the ninth and tenth states had ratified the Constitution, four thousand New York City mechanics marched with floats and banners to celebrate. Bakers, blacksmiths, brewers, ship joiners and shipwrights, coopers, cartmen and tailors, all marched. What Lynd found was that these mechanics, while opposing elite rule in the colonies, were nationalist. Mechanics comprised perhaps half the New York population. Some were wealthy, some were poor, but all were better off than the ordinary laborer, the apprentice, the journeyman, and their prosperity required a government that would protect them against the British hats and shoes and other goods that were pouring into the colonies after the Revolution. As a result, the mechanics often supported wealthy conservatives at the ballot box.

The Constitution, then, illustrates the complexity of the American system: that it serves the interests of a wealthy elite, but also does enough for small property owners, for middle-income mechanics and farmers, to build a broad base of support. The slightly prosperous people who make up this base of support are buffers against the blacks, the Indians, the very poor whites. They enable the elite to keep control with a minimum of coercion, a maximum of law—all made palatable by the fanfare of patriotism and unity.

The Constitution became even more acceptable to the public at large after the first Congress, responding to criticism, passed a series of amendments known as the Bill of Rights. These amendments seemed to make the new government a guardian of people's liberties: to speak, to publish, to worship, to petition, to assemble, to be tried fairly, to be secure at home against official intrusion. It was, therefore, perfectly designed to build popular backing for the new government. What was not made clear—it was a time when the language of freedom was new and its reality untested—was the shakiness of anyone's liberty when entrusted to a government of the rich and powerful.

Indeed, the same problem existed for the other provisions of the Constitution, like the clause forbidding states to "impair the obligation of contract," or that giving Congress the power to tax the people and to appropriate money. They all sound benign and neutral until one asks: Tax who, for what? Appropriate what, for whom? To protect everyone's contracts seems like an act of fairness, of equal treatment, until one considers that contracts made between rich and poor, between employer and employee, landlord and tenant, creditor and debtor, generally favor the more powerful of the two parties. Thus, to protect these contracts is to put the great power of the government, its laws, courts, sheriffs, police, on the side of the privileged—and to do it not, as in premodern times, as an exercise of brute force against the weak but as a matter of law.

The First Amendment of the Bill of Rights shows that quality of interest hiding behind innocence. Passed in 1791 by Congress, it provided that "Congress shall make no law . . . abridging the freedom of speech, or of the press. . . ." Yet, seven years after the First Amendment became part of the Constitution, Congress passed a law very clearly abridging the freedom of speech.

This was the Sedition Act of 1798, passed under John Adams's administration, at a time when Irishmen and Frenchmen in the United States were looked on as dangerous revolutionaries because of the recent French Revolution and the Irish rebellions. The Sedition Act made it a crime to say or write anything "false, scandalous and malicious" against the government, Congress, or the President, with intent to defame them, bring them into disrepute, or excite popular hatreds against them.

This act seemed to directly violate the First Amendment. Yet, it was enforced. Ten Americans were put in prison for utterances against the government, and every member of the Supreme Court in 1798–1800, sitting as an appellate judge, held it constitutional.

There was a legal basis for this, one known to legal experts, but not to the ordinary American, who would read the First Amendment and feel confident that he or she was protected in the exercise of free speech. That basis has been explained by historian Leonard Levy. Levy points out that it was generally understood (not in the population, but in higher circles) that, despite the First Amendment, the British common law of "seditious libel" still ruled in America. This meant that while the government could not exercise "prior restraint"—that is, prevent an utterance or publication in advance—it could legally punish the speaker or writer afterward. Thus, Congress has a convenient legal basis for the laws it has enacted since that time, making certain kinds of speech a crime. And, since punishment after the fact is an excellent deterrent to the exercise of free expression, the claim of "no prior restraint" itself is destroyed. This leaves the First Amendment much less than the stone wall of protection it seems at first glance.

Are the economic provisions in the Constitution enforced just as weakly? We have an instructive example almost immediately in Washington's first administration, when Congress's power to tax and appropriate money was immediately put to use by the Secretary of the Treasury, Alexander Hamilton.

Hamilton, believing that government must ally itself with the richest elements of society to make itself strong, proposed to Congress a series of laws, which it enacted, expressing this philosophy. A Bank of the United States was set up as a partnership between the government and certain banking interests. A tariff was passed to help the manufacturers. It was agreed to pay bondholders—most of the war bonds were now concentrated in a small group of wealthy people—the full value of their bonds. Tax laws were passed to raise money for this bond redemption.

One of these tax laws was the Whiskey Tax, which especially hurt small farmers who raised grain that they converted into whiskey and then sold. In 1794 the farmers of western Pennsylvania took up arms and rebelled against the collection of this tax. Secretary of the Treasury Hamilton led the troops to put them down. We see then, in the first years of the Constitution, that some of its provisions—even those paraded most flamboyantly (like the First Amendment)—might be treated lightly. Others (like the power to tax) would be powerfully enforced.

Still, the mythology around the Founding Fathers persists. To say, as one historian (Bernard Bailyn) has done recently, that "the destruction of privilege and the creation of a political system that demanded of its leaders the responsible and humane use of power were their highest aspirations" is to ignore what really happened in the America of these Founding Fathers.

Bailyn says:

> Everyone knew the basic prescription for a wise and just government. It was so to balance the contending powers in society that no one power could overwhelm the others and, unchecked, destroy the liberties that belonged to all. The problem was how to arrange the institutions of government so that this balance could be achieved.

Were the Founding Fathers wise and just men trying to achieve a good balance? In fact, they did not want a balance, except one which kept things as they were, a balance among the dominant forces at that time. They certainly did not want an equal balance between slaves and masters, propertyless and property holders, Indians and white.

As many as half the people were not even considered by the Founding Fathers as among Bailyn's "contending powers" in society. They were not mentioned in the Declaration of Independence, they were absent in the Constitution, they were invisible in the new political democracy. They were the women of early America.

POSTSCRIPT

Were the Founding Fathers Democratic Reformers?

Roche stresses the political reasons for writing a new Constitution. In a spirited essay that reflects great admiration for the Founding Fathers as enlightened politicians, Roche describes the Constitution as "a triumph of architectonic genius; it was a patch-work sewn together under the pressure of both time and events by a group of extremely talented democratic politicians."

Roche narrates the events of the convention of 1787 with a clarity rarely seen in the writings on this period. He makes the telling point that once the dissenters left Philadelphia, the delegates were able to hammer out a new Constitution. All the Founding Fathers agreed to create a stronger national government, but differences centered around the shape the new government would take. The delegates' major concern was to create as strong a national government as possible that would be acceptable to all the states. Had the ratifying conventions rejected the new Constitution, the United States might have disintegrated into 13 separate countries.

An avowed Marxist and radical leftist, Howard Zinn is a political activist who served in a bombing squadron in the Army Air Corps in World War II, was an early member of the Student Non-Violent Coordinating Committee (SNCC), which was the most vocal civil rights group in the 1960s, and a staunch peace activist against our wars in Vietnam, Central America, and the Middle East. He believes that history should be studied and written primarily for the purpose of eliminating America's violent past and moving it in a more peaceful, equitable direction.

Zinn's *A People's History of the United States* (Harper Collins, 1999) has sold over a million copies since it was first published in 1980. His critique of the Founding Fathers draws upon the scholarship of Charles Beard's *An Economic Interpretation of the Constitution* (Free Press, 1913, 1986), which argued that the Founding Fathers were primarily interested in protecting their property rights. He believes that Shay's Rebellion, an uprising of western Massachusetts farmers who were unable to pay their taxes to the Massachusetts government, was the catalyst that inspired the men at Philadelphia in 1787 to write a new constitution. He quotes from James Madison's *Federalist Paper #10* that it will be easier to keep order in a large nation of 13 states where minority factions could be controlled by a vote of the majority. He admits that one-third of the population were small farmers, "a considerable number of people who felt that they had something at stake in the new society."

Zinn believes that there were structural difficulties with the Constitution. For example, representative government was designed to prevent tumultuous change and therefore was inherently conservative. He also argues that the major problem in American society—the division into rich and poor—transcended constitutional problems.

How does Zinn explain the support for the new government if it favored the well-to-do? "The Constitution," he says, "illustrates the complexity of the American system; that it serves the interests of a wealthy elite, but also does enough for small property owners, for middle-income mechanics and farmers, to build a broad base of support. The slightly prosperous people who make up this base of support are buffers against the blacks, the Indians, the very poor whites. They enable the elite to keep control with a minimum of coercion, a maximum of law—all made palatable by the fanfare of patriotism and unity."

The enlightened statemen's views were reasserted during the cold war in the 1950s and 1960s with the methodological critiques of Charles Beard's *An Economic Interpretation of the Constitution* (Macmillan, 1913) by Robert E. Brown, *Charles Beard and the Constitution* (Princeton University Press, 1956), and Forrest McDonald's many works, the earliest, *We the People* (University of Chicago Press, 1958), which argued that numerous interest groups in the states ratified the Constitution for a variety of political and economic reasons. The best summary of this scholarship is the widely reprinted article by Stanley Elkins and Eric McKitrick, "The Founding Fathers: Young Men of the Revolution," in Jack P. Greene, ed., *The Reinterpretation of the American Revolution 1763–1789* (Harper & Row, 1968), which argues that the Federalists were broad-minded nationalists and the less organized anti-Federalists were small-minded localists, an interpretation influenced by Cecilia Kenyon, "Men of Little Faith: the Anti-Federalists on the Nature of Representative Government," *William and Mary Quarterly* (1955).

Historian Gordon S. Wood changed the focus of the debate by trying to recapture the conflicting views of politics in the eighteenth century in *The Creation of the American Republic, 1776–1787* (University of North Carolina Press, 1969), a seminal work that has replaced Beard as the starting point for scholarship on this topic. A devastating critique of the methodological fallacies of Wood and other intellectual writers on this period can be found in Ralph Lerner's "The Constitution of the Thinking Revolutionary," in Richard Beeman et al., eds., *Beyond Confederation: Origins of the Constitution and American National Identity* (University of North Carolina Press, 1987). See other essays in *Beyond Confederation,* including Wood's response, "Interests and Disinterestedness in the Making of the Constitution." The bicentennial produced an explosion of scholarship by historians and law professors. For overviews, see Peter S. Onof, "Reflections on the Founding: Constitutional Historiography in Bicentennial Perspective," *William and Mary Quarterly,* 30 Ser., XLVI (1989), and Richard D. Bernstein, "Charting the Bicentennial," *Columbia Law Review,* LXXXVII (1987).

In recent years the anti-Federalists have received positive evaluations from both conservatives and leftists who reject the excessive accumulation of power by the national government. See conservative Herbert J. Storing, *What the Anti-Federalists Were For* (University of Chicago Press, 1981), an influential effort to analyze anti-Federalist ideas and Alfred F. Young, "The Framers of the

Constitution and the 'Genius' of the People," *Radical History Review* (vol. 42, 1988). Earlier, Jackson Turner Main revived the Beardian conflict interpretations between agrarian localists and cosmopolitan elitists in "The Anti-Federalists," *Critics of the Constitution, 1781–1788* (University of North Carolina Press, 1961), which has been superseded by Saul Cornell, *The Other Founders: Anti-Federalism and the Dissenting Tradition in America, 1788–1828* (University of North Carolina Press, 1999), a sympathetic and comprehensive analysis buttressed by research into the primary writings and secondary accounts of the anti-Federalists critically evaluated by the author.

Readers can gain a sense of the debates over ratification of the Constitution by reading some of the original texts. Two of the most convenient anthologies are Michael Kammen, ed., *The Origins of the American Constitution: A Documentary History* (New York, 1986), and Bernard Bailyn, ed., *The Debate on the Constitution,* 2 vols. (New York, 1993).

ISSUE 8

Was Alexander Hamilton an Economic Genius?

YES: John Steele Gordon, from *An Empire of Wealth: The Epic History of American Economic Power* (Harper Collins, 2004)

NO: Carey Roberts, from "Alexander Hamilton and the 1790s Economy: A Reappraisal," in Douglas Ambrose and Robert W. T. Martin, eds., *The Many Faces of Alexander Hamilton: The Life and Legacy of America's Most Elusive Founding Father* (New York University Press, 2006)

ISSUE SUMMARY

YES: Historian John Steele Gordon claims that Hamilton's policies for funding and assuming the debts of the confederation and state governments and for establishing a privately controlled Bank of the United States laid the foundation for the rich and powerful national economy we enjoy today.

NO: Professor Carey Roberts argues that in the 1790s Hamilton's financial policies undermined popular faith in the Federalist Party and diminished confidence in the federal government.

Alexander Hamilton remains the most enigmatic, elusive, and highly criticized of the group we call "the founding fathers." When contrasted with Jefferson, Hamilton comes off second best as arrogant, crude, and manipulative, an embezzler who was worst of all a "crypto-monarchist." Yet nationally syndicated conservative columnist George Will astutely observes: "There is an elegant memorial in Washington to Jefferson, but none to Hamilton. However, if you seek Hamilton's monument, look around. You are living in it. We honor Jefferson but live in Hamilton's country."

Hamilton grew up in very humble circumstances. Born out of wedlock in the West Indies in 1755, Hamilton was abandoned by his father at age 9, orphaned by the death of his mother at age 13, and left penniless. He and his older brother were assigned by the courts to live with a cousin who committed suicide less than a year after he had taken in the boys.

In spite of such a volatile childhood that limited his formal schooling, Hamilton was a voracious reader who taught himself French and became skilled in mathematics and economics. As a 16-year-old, he was employed as a clerk in the firm of Beckman and Cruger. But it was Hugh Knox, a Presbyterian minister, who recognized Hamilton's talents and changed his life forever when he collected funds to send him to the mainland for an education.

Hamilton was not only talented but also very ambitious. Washington appointed Hamilton his aide-de-camp and promoted him to the rank of lieutenant-colonel in the Continental army. He served with the general at key battles including the near disaster at Valley Forge.

Hamilton's military experiences with the financially starved Continental army, along with his service as a delegate from New York in the Confederation Congress, turned him into a staunch nationalist. He attended the Annapolis convention in 1786 to discuss the problems of interstate commerce under the Articles of Confederation, but when so few delegates showed up, he introduced a resolution for a meeting at Philadelphia the following year.

At the Constitutional Convention of 1787, Hamilton's proposal to model the new government after the British system, with lifetime appointments for the president, Supreme Court, and Senate, met with strong hostility. His two fellow New York delegates were even opposed to the government supported by the majority of the delegates. "But Hamilton was instrumental in convincing a hostile New York Convention to support the Constitution." *The Federalist Papers* were published in book form and became the bible of interpreting the Constitution.

The highpoint of Hamilton's career was his appointment as President George Washington's secretary of the treasury, where his proposals for funding the new government, assuming the debts of the states, and establishing a Bank of the United States created a political furor that is still being debated by historians today.

After his resignation from Washington's cabinet in 1795, Hamilton's advice was sought by Washington and he penned the president's famous farewell address. Though out of office, he dominated the cabinet of his opponent, President John Adams, but lost influence after his Federalist Party was thrown out of office. In the election of 1800, he supported Jefferson over Burr when a tie resulted in the electoral-college vote. When Hamilton labeled Burr "a dangerous man who ought not to be trusted with the reigns of government" and cost him the gubernatorial election in New York in 1804, Burr challenged Hamilton to a duel. Hamilton accepted and was mortally wounded on a field on July 11, 1804. He died a day later, bidding farewell to his wife and children.

Was Hamilton an economic genius or was he overrated in terms of his influence on the future American economy? In the first essay, historian John Steele Gordon believes that Hamilton's policies for funding and assuming the debts of the confederation and state governments, and for establishing a privately controlled Bank of the United States, laid the foundation for the rich and powerful national economy we enjoy today. But Professor Carey Roberts disagrees. He argues that in the context of the 1790s, Hamilton's financial policies were politically unpopular and helped undermine popular faith in the Federalist Party. Such policies also diminished confidence in the federal government because of the increasing tax burden necessary to fund the full debt and enabled some people to increase their own wealth through political influence.

YES ↵

John Steele Gordon

The Hamiltonian Creation

The importance that the Washington administration, which took office on April 30, 1789, placed on dealing with the financial situation confronting the government under the new Constitution can be judged by the numbers. While the newly created State Department had five employees, the Treasury had forty.

The tasks before the Treasury were monumental. A tax system had to be created out of whole cloth and put in place. The debt left over from the Revolution had to be rationalized and funded. The customs had to be organized to collect the duties that would be the government's main source of revenue for more than a century. The public credit had to be established so that the federal government could borrow when necessary. A monetary system had to be implemented.

The last already existed, at least in theory, established by Congress under the Articles of Confederation. In what was to be his only positive contribution to the financial system of the United States, it had been devised by Thomas Jefferson.

[B]efore the Revolution, the merchants of the various colonies had kept their books in pounds, shillings, and pence, but the money in actual circulation was almost everything *but* pounds, shillings, and pence. The question of what new unit of account to adopt was nearly as complex, because the inhabitants of the various colonies "thought" in terms of so many different, often incommensurate units.

Robert Morris, who had done so much to keep the Revolution financially afloat, tried to bridge the differences by finding the lowest common divisor of the most often encountered monetary unit of each state. He calculated this to be 1,440th of a Spanish dollar. Jefferson thought this far too infinitesimal to be practical, and Morris agreed. He proposed that his unit be multiplied by one thousand and made equal to 25/36ths of a dollar. Jefferson argued instead for just using the dollar, already familiar throughout the United States, as the new monetary unit.

The origin of the word *dollar* lies in the German word for valley, *Thal*. In the fifteenth century major silver deposits had been discovered in Bohemia, in what is now the Czech Republic. In 1519 the owner of mines near the town of Joachimsthal, the Graf zu Passaun und Weisskirchen, began minting silver coins that weighed a Saxon ounce and were called thalers, literally "from the valley." These coins, new and pure, met with great acceptance from merchants, and other rulers in the Holy Roman Empire began to imitate them with their own coinage.

From *An Empire of Wealth: The Epic History of American Economic Power* by John Steele Gordon (HarperCollins, 2004). Copyright © 2004 by John Steele Gordon. Reprinted by permission of HarperCollins Publishers.

The Holy Roman Emperor, the Hapsburg Charles V, also adopted the thaler as the standard for his own coinage in both his Austrian and Spanish lands and his new-won, silver-rich empire in the New World. The staggering amounts of gold and silver mined in Spanish America in the sixteenth and seventeenth centuries (just between 1580 and 1626, more than eleven thousand tons of gold and silver were exported to Spain from the New World) made the thaler the standard unit of international trade for centuries. *Thaler* became *dollar* in the English language, much as *Thal*, centuries earlier, had become *dale* and *dell*. It also became the most common major coin in the British North American colonies.

Jefferson, in his "Notes on the Establishment of a Money Unit, and of a Coinage for the United States," advocated not only using the dollar but making smaller units decimal fractions of the dollar. Today this seems obvious. After all, every country in the world now has a decimal monetary system, and as Jefferson himself explained, "in all cases where we are free to choose between easy and difficult modes of operation, it is most rational to choose the easy." But Thomas Jefferson was the first to advocate such a system, and the United States, in 1786, was the first country in the world to adopt one.

Spanish dollars had often been clipped into halves, quarters, and eighths, called bits, to make small change (which is why they were often called "pieces of eight"). But Jefferson advocated coinage of a half dollar, a fifth, a tenth (for which he coined the word *dime*), a twentieth, and a hundredth of a dollar (for which he borrowed the word *cent* from Robert Morris's scheme). In 1785 Congress declared that the "monetary unit of the United States of America be one dollar." But the next year Congress, while adopting the cent, five-cent, dime, and fifty-cent coins advocated by Jefferson, decided to authorize a quarter-dollar coin rather than a twenty-cent piece.

The quarter is with us yet, now the last, distant echo of the old octal monetary system of colonial days. But other echoes held on for decades. The New York Stock Exchange still gave prices in eighths of a dollar as late as 1999. And the term *shilling* long remained in common use to mean twelve and a half cents, an eighth of a dollar, although there has never been a United States coin in that denomination. The east side of Broadway, in New York, where the less fashionable stores were located, was still called the "shilling side" as late as the 1850s, while the west side of the street was called the "dollar side."

One reason the term *shilling* held on so long, of course, was that American coinage was not adequate to the ever-growing demand for it and the old hodgepodge of foreign coins thus held on as well. The first United States coin, a copper cent bearing the brisk motto "Mind Your Business," was privately minted. The Philadelphia mint was established in 1792 but minted few coins in the early years for lack of metal with which to do so.

❦

Robert Morris, bent on making money, turned down Washington's offer to name him as secretary of the treasury in the new government (it was a bad decision—he ended up in debtors' prison). The president then turned to one of his aides-de-camp during the Revolution, Alexander Hamilton, only in his early thirties.

Hamilton was the only one of the Founding Fathers not to be born in what is now the United States. He was born in Nevis, one of Britain's less important Leeward Island possessions. He was also the only one—besides Benjamin Franklin, who had made a large fortune on his own and an even larger reputation—not to be born to affluence. Indeed, he grew up in poverty after his feckless father—who had never married his mother—deserted the family when Hamilton was only a boy.

Living in St. Croix, now part of the U.S. Virgin Islands but then a possession of Denmark, Hamilton went to work at a trading house owned by the New York merchants Nicholas Cruger and David Beekman, when he was eleven years old. Extraordinarily competent and ferociously ambitious, Hamilton was managing the place by the time he was in his mid-teens, quite literally growing up in a counting house. Thus, of all the Founding Fathers, only Franklin had so urban and commercial a background. Even John Adams, a lawyer by profession, considered his family farm in Braintree (now Quincy), Massachusetts, to be home, not Boston.

Cruger, recognizing Hamilton's talents, helped him come to New York in 1772 and to attend King's College, now Columbia University. After the Revolution he studied law and began practicing in New York City, where he married Elizabeth Schuyler, from one of New York's most prominent families. After the Revolution he wrote a series of newspaper articles and pamphlets outlining his ideas of what was needed to create an effective federal government. In 1784 he founded the Bank of New York, the first bank in that city and the second in the country.

He attended the Constitutional Convention in Philadelphia and worked tirelessly to get the document ratified, writing two-thirds of *The Federalist Papers*. When Robert Morris took himself out of consideration, Hamilton, whom Morris called "damned sharp," was more than happy to take the job of secretary of the treasury.

He was also one of the very few competent to do so. While Americans had already distinguished themselves in many fields of endeavor, they "were not well acquainted with the most abstruse science in the world [public finance], which they never had any necessity to study."

Hamilton, a deep student of economics, understood public finance thoroughly, a fact that he would make dazzlingly clear in the next few years. But like so many of the Founding Fathers, he was also a deep student of human nature and knew that there was no more powerful motivator in the human universe than self-interest. He sought to establish a system that would both channel the individual pursuit of self-interest into developing the American economy and protect that economy from the follies that untrammeled self-interest always leads to.

Even before the Treasury Department was created on September 2, 1789, and Hamilton was confirmed by the Senate as its first secretary on September 11, Congress had passed a tax bill to give the new government the funds it needed to pay its bills. There was no argument that the main source of income was to be the tariff, but there was lengthy debate over what imports should be taxed and at what rate. Pennsylvania had had a high tariff under the old Articles to protect its nascent iron industry and wanted it maintained. The southern states, importers of iron products such as nails and hinges, wanted a low tariff on iron goods or none at all. New England rum distillers wanted a low tariff on its imports of molasses. Whiskey manufacturers in Pennsylvania and elsewhere wanted a high tariff on molasses, to stifle their main competition.

Congress finally passed the Tariff and Tonnage Acts (the latter imposed a duty of 6 cents a ton on American ships entering U.S. ports and 50 cents a ton on foreign vessels) in the summer of 1789. But, second only to slavery, the tariff would be the most contentious issue in Congress for the next hundred years. Pierce Butler of South Carolina even issued the first secession threat before the Tariff Act of 1789 made it through Congress.

With funding in place, Hamilton's most pressing problem was to deal with the federal debt. The Constitution commanded that the new federal government should assume the debts of the old one, but how that should be done was a fiercely debated question. Much of the debt had fallen into the hands of speculators who had bought it for as little as 10 percent of its face value.

On January 14, 1790, Hamilton submitted to Congress his first "Report on the Public Credit." It called for redeeming the old debt on generous terms and issuing new bonds to pay for it, backed by the revenue from the tariff. The report became public knowledge in New York City, the temporary capital, immediately, but news of it spread only slowly to other parts of the country, and New York speculators were able to snap up large quantities of the old debt at prices far below what Hamilton proposed redeeming it for.

Many were outraged that speculators should profit while those who had taken the debt at far higher prices during the Revolution should not see their money again. James Madison argued that only the original holders should have their paper redeemed at the full price and the speculators get only what they had paid for it. But this was hopelessly impractical. For one thing, determining who was the original holder would have often been impossible.

Even more important, such a move would have greatly impaired the credit of the government in the future. If the government could decide to whom along the chain of holders it owed past debts, people would be more reluctant to take future debt, and the price in terms of the interest rate demanded, therefore, would be higher. And Hamilton was anxious to establish a secure and well-funded national debt, modeled on that of Great Britain and for precisely the purposes that Great Britain had used its debt.

Many of those in the new government, unversed in public finance, did not grasp the power of a national debt, properly funded and serviced, to add to a nation's prosperity. But Hamilton grasped it fully. One of the greatest problems facing the American economy at the start of the 1790s was the lack of liquid capital, capital available for investment. Hamilton wanted to use the national debt to create a larger and more flexible money supply. Banks holding government bonds could issue banknotes backed by them. And government bonds could serve as collateral for bank loans, multiplying the available capital. He also knew they would attract still more capital from Europe.

Hamilton's program eventually passed Congress, although not without a great deal of rhetoric. Hamilton's father-in-law, a senator from New York in the new Congress, was a holder of $60,000 worth of government securities he hoped would be redeemed by Hamilton's program. It was said the opposition to the program made his hair stand "on end as if the Indians had fired at him."

Hamilton also wanted the federal government to assume the debts that had been incurred by the various states in fighting the Revolution. His main reason for doing so was to help cement the Union. Most of the state debt was held by wealthy citizens of those states. If they had a large part of their assets in federal bonds, instead of state bonds, they would be that much more interested in seeing that the Union as a whole prospered.

Those states, mostly northern, that still had substantial debt were, of course, all for Hamilton's proposal. Those that had paid off their debts were just as naturally against it. Jefferson and Madison—Virginia had paid off its debts—were adamantly opposed and had enough votes to defeat the measure. Hamilton offered a deal.

If enough votes were switched to pass his assumption bill, he would see that the new capital was located in the South. To assure Pennsylvania's cooperation, the capital would be moved from New York to Philadelphia for ten years while the new one was built. Jefferson and Madison agreed. Hamilton's program passed and was signed into law by President Washington, who was delighted at the prospect of the new capital being located on his beloved Potomac River.

The program was an immediate success, and the new bonds sold out within a few weeks. When it was clear that the revenue stream from the tariff was more than adequate to service the new debt, the bonds became sought after in Europe. In 1789 the United States had been a financial basket case, its obligations unsalable, it ability to borrow nil. By 1794 it had the highest credit rating in Europe, and some of its bonds were selling at 10 percent over par.

Talleyrand, the future French foreign minister, then in the United States to escape the Terror, explained why. The bonds, he said, were "safe and free from reverses. They have been funded in such a sound manner and the prosperity of this country is growing so rapidly that there can be no doubt of their solvency."

Talleyrand might have added that the willingness of the new federal government to take on the debt of the old, rather than repudiate it for short-term fiscal reasons or political advantage, also helped powerfully to gain the trust of investors. The ability of the federal government to borrow huge sums at affordable rates in times of emergency—such as during the Civil War and the Great Depression—has been an immense national asset. In large measure, we owe that ability to Alexander Hamilton's policies that were put in place at the dawn of the Republic. It is no small legacy.

To be sure, Hamilton, and the United States, had the good fortune to have a major European war break out in 1793, after Louis XVI was guillotined. This proved a bonanza for American foreign trade and for American shipping, which was protected from privateers by the country's neutrality. European demand for American foodstuffs and raw materials greatly increased, and the federal government's tariff revenues increased proportionately. In 1790 the United States exported $19,666,000 worth of goods, while imports not reexported amounted to $22,461,000. By 1807 exports were $48,700,000 and imports $78,856,000. Government revenues that year were well over five times what they had been seventeen years earlier.

***

The other major part of Hamilton's fiscal policy was the establishment of a central bank, to be called the Bank of the United States and modeled on the Bank of England.

Hamilton expected a central bank to carry out three functions. First, it would act as a depository for government funds and facilitate the transfer of them from one part of the country to another. This was a major consideration in the primitive conditions of the young United States. Second, it would be a source of loans to the federal government and to other banks. And third, it would regulate the money supply by disciplining state-chartered banks.

The money supply was a critical problem at the time. Specie—gold and silver coins—was in very short supply. In 1790 there were only three state-chartered banks empowered to issue paper money, including Hamilton's Bank of New York, but these notes had only local circulation. Hamilton reasoned that if the Bank of the United States accepted these local notes at par, other banks would too, greatly increasing the area in which they would circulate. And if the BUS refused the notes of a particular bank, because of irregularities or excess money creation, other banks would refuse them as well, helping to keep the state banks on the straight and narrow.

Hamilton had learned not to like the idea of the government itself issuing paper money, knowing that in times of need the government would be unable to resist the temptation to solve its money problems by simply printing it. Certainly the Continental Congress had shown no restraint during the Revolution, but at least it had had the excuse of no alternative. And the history of paper money since Hamilton's day has shown him to be correct. Without exception, wherever politicians have possessed the power to print money, they have abused it, at great cost to the economic health of the country in question.

Hamilton proposed a bank with a capitalization of $10 million. That was a very large sum when one considers that the three state banks in existence had a combined capitalization of only $2 million. The government would hold 20 percent of the stock of the bank and have 20 percent of the seats on the board. The secretary of the treasury would have the right to inspect its books at any time. But the rest of the bank's stock would be privately held.

"To attach full confidence to an institution of this nature," Hamilton wrote in his "Report on a National Bank," delivered to Congress on December 14, 1790, "it appears to be an essential ingredient in its structure, that it shall be under a *private* not a *public* direction—under the guidance of *individual interest,* not of *public policy;* which would be supposed to be, and, in certain emergencies, under a feeble or too sanguine administration, would really be, liable to being too much influenced by *public necessity*."

The bill passed Congress with little trouble, both houses splitting along sectional lines. Only one congressman from states north of Maryland voted against it and only three congressmen from states south of Maryland voted for it. Hamilton thought the deal was done.

But he had not counted on Thomas Jefferson, by now secretary of state, and James Madison, who then sat in the House of Representatives. Although Jefferson had personally enjoyed to the hilt the manifold pleasures of Paris while he had served as minister to Louis XVI under the old Articles of Confederation, nonetheless he had a deep political aversion to cities and to the commerce that thrives in them.

Nothing symbolized the vulgar, urban moneygrubbing he so despised as banks. "I have ever been the enemy of banks . . ." he wrote to John Adams in old age. "My zeal against those institutions was so warm and open at the establishment of the Bank of the U.S. that I was derided as a Maniac by the tribe of bank-mongers, who were seeking to filch from the public their swindling, and barren gains."

Jefferson, born one of the richest men in the American colonies—on his father's death he inherited more than five thousand acres of land and three hundred slaves—spent money all his life with a lordly disdain for whether he actually had any to spend. He died, as a result, deeply in debt, bankrupt in all but name. And regardless of his own aristocratic lifestyle, his vision of the future of America was a land of self-sufficient yeoman farmers, a rural utopia that had never really existed and would be utterly at odds with the American economy as it actually developed in the industrial age then just coming into being.

Jefferson and his allies Madison and Edmund Randolph, the attorney general, fought Hamilton's bank tooth and nail. They wrote opinions for President Washington saying that the bank was unconstitutional. Their arguments revolved around the so-called necessary and proper clause of the Constitution, giving Congress the power to pass laws "necessary and proper for carrying into Execution the foregoing Powers."

As the Constitution nowhere explicitly grants Congress the power to establish a bank, they argued, only if one were absolutely necessary could Congress do so. This "strict construction" of the Constitution has been part of the warp and woof of American politics ever since, although even Jefferson admitted that it appealed mostly to those out of power. The fact that the Constitution nowhere mentions the acquisition of land from a foreign state did not stop Jefferson, as president, from snatching the Louisiana Purchase when the opportunity presented itself.

Hamilton countered with a doctrine of "implied powers." He argued that if the federal government were to deal successfully with its enumerated duties, it must be supreme in deciding how to do so. "Little less than a prohibitory clause," he wrote to Washington, "can destroy the strong presumptions which result from the general aspect of the government. Nothing but demonstration should exclude the idea that the power exists." Further, he asserted that Congress had the right to decide what means were necessary and proper. "The national government like every other," he wrote, "must judge in the first instance of the proper exercise of its powers." Washington, his doubts quieted, signed the bill.

The sale of stock was a resounding success, as investors expected that the bank would prove very profitable, which it was. It also functioned exactly as Hamilton thought it would. The three state banks in existence in 1790 became twenty-nine by the turn of the century, and the United States enjoyed a more reliable money supply than most nations in Europe.

With the success of the Bank of the United States stock offering, the nascent securities markets in New York and Philadelphia had their first bull markets, in bank stocks. Philadelphia, the leading financial market in the country at that time, thanks to the location there of the headquarters of the Bank of the United States, established a real stock exchange in 1792. In New York a group of twenty-one individual brokers and three firms signed an agreement—called the Buttonwood Agreement because it was, at least according to tradition, signed beneath a buttonwood tree (today more commonly called a sycamore) outside 68 Wall Street. In it they pledged "ourselves to each other, that we will not buy or sell from this day for any person whatsoever any kind of Public Stock, at a less rate than one quarter per cent Commission on the specie value, and that we will give preference to each other in our negotiations."

The new group formed by the brokers was far more a combination in restraint of trade and price-fixing scheme than a formal organization, but it proved to be a precursor of what today is called the New York Stock Exchange.

A speculative bubble arose in New York, centered on the stock of the Bank of New York. Rumors abounded that it would be bought by the new Bank of the United States and converted to its New York branch. Numerous other banks were announced and their stock, or, often, rights to buy the stock when offered, was snapped up. The Tammany Bank announced a stock offering of 4,000 shares and received subscriptions for no fewer than 21,740 shares.

An unscrupulous speculator named William Duer was at the center of this frenzy in bank stocks. He had worked, briefly, for the Treasury, but had resigned rather than obey the rule Hamilton had put in place for bidding Treasury officials from speculating in Treasury securities. Hamilton was appalled by what was happening on Wall street. "'Tis time," he wrote on March 2, 1792, "there should be a line of separation between honest Men & knaves, between respectable Stockholders and dealers in the funds, and mere unprincipled Gamblers."

It didn't take long for Duer's complex schemes to fall apart, and he was clapped into debtors prison, from which he would not energe alive. Panic swept Wall street for the first time, and the next day twenty-five failures were reported in New York's still tiny financial community, including one of the mighty Livingston clan.

Jefferson was delighted with this turn of events. "At length," he wrote a friend, "our paper bubble is burst. The failure of Duer in New York soon brought on others, and these still more, like nine pins knocking down one another." Jefferson, who loved to calculate things, estimated the total losses at $5 million, which he thought was about the total value of all New York real estate at the time. Thus, Jefferson gleefully wrote, the panic was the same as though some natural calamity had destroyed the city.

In fact, the situation was not nearly that dire, especially as Hamilton moved swiftly to stabilize the market and ensure that the panic did not bring down basically sound institutions. He ordered the Treasury to buy its own securities to support the market, and he added further liquidity by allowing customs duties—ordinarily payable only in specie or Bank of the United States banknotes—to be paid with notes maturing in forty-five days.

The system Hamilton had envisioned and put in place over increasing opposition from Thomas Jefferson and his political allies worked exactly as Hamilton had intended. Several speculators were wiped out, but they had been playing the game with their eyes open and had no one to blame but themselves. The nascent financial institutions, however, survived. "No calamity truly *public* can happen," Hamilton wrote, "while these institutions remain sound." The panic soon passed and most brokers were able to get back on their feet quickly, thanks to Hamilton's swift action.

Unfortunately, Thomas Jefferson was a better politician than Hamilton, and a far better hater. The success of the Bank of the United States and its obvious institutional utility for both the economy and the smooth running of the government did not cause him to change his mind at all about banks. He loathed them all. The party forming around Thomas Jefferson would seize the reins of power in the election of 1800 and would not lose them for more than a generation. In that time, they would destroy Hamilton's financial regulatory system and would replace it with nothing.

As a result, the American economy, while it would grow at an astonishing rate, would be the most volatile in the Western world, subject to an unending cycle of boom and bust whose amplitude far exceeded the normal ups and downs of the business cycle. American monetary authorities would not—indeed could not—intervene decisively to abort a market panic before it spiraled out of control for another 195 years.

Thomas Jefferson, one of the most brilliant men who has ever lived, was psychologically unable to incorporate the need for a mechanism to regulate the emerging banking system or, indeed, banks at all, into his political philosophy. His legion of admirers, most of them far less intelligent than he, followed his philosophy for generations as the country and the world changed beyond recognition. As a direct result, economic disaster would be visited on the United States roughly every twenty years for more than a century.

Carey Roberts

→ **NO**

Alexander Hamilton and the 1790s Economy: A Reappraisal

Historians and political scientists commonly credit Alexander Hamilton's economic plans for revitalizing the American economy and providing the impetus for extended economic progress. Such arguments usually take for granted many of the criticisms levied against the policies of the states and Confederation during the 1780s. They further assume that the weakness of the American economy stemmed from the decentralized nature of its financial institutions, lack of specie, and burdensome problems of the Revolutionary debt.

There is little doubt that economic problems prevailed under the Articles of Confederation; however, it remains unclear how much Hamilton's policies corrected those problems. Hamilton's program of assumption and funding resulted in an overall increase in the nation's monetary base. The Bank of the United States (BUS) furthered the monetary expansion by following a pattern of fractional-reserve lending up until 1795. As a result, inflation continued to affect the economy during the early 1790s. Burdensome taxes were levied to pay off government debts at face value rather than at prevailing market values. And significant opposition formed against Federalist officials due to the perceived joining of monied interests to the federal government.

Without understanding the short-term consequences, our praise for the long-term results seems strained at best. If what is called "Hamiltonian" finance resulted in short-term problems, or even disasters, long-term success would be less likely. If long-term success could actually be attributed to Jeffersonian policies carried forward by Jacksonian Democrats, the place of Hamiltonian finance in our history would change drastically. Furthermore, even if it is determined that the American economy surged after 1791, attributing the rise to beneficial market conditions totally independent from federal politics could jeopardize Hamilton's place as a financial genius. Such is not the scope of this essay, nor is it a challenge to the dominant interpretation of Hamilton's character and financial vision. However, puzzling discrepancies present themselves when one compares the effects of the Federalist financial plan and its short-term consequences in the 1790s. Limitation of space prevents a full treatment of the period, but it is hoped that the following might serve as a prolegomena for further study.

From *The Many Faces of Alexander Hamilton: The Life and Legacy of America's Most Elusive Founding Father,* Douglas Ambrose and Robert W. T. Martin, eds., (New York University Press, 2006). Copyright © 2006 by New York University. Reprinted by permission.

Economic Problems of the 1790s

The first decade under the new constitution was not a period of strong economic growth, nor was it free from periods of economic distress. Data are sketchy at best, and debate still rages as to whether the economy of antebellum America was rapidly expanding or mediocre. Likewise, we may never have a complete grasp on the economic condition for the period between 1789 and 1800, a problem further complicated by the loss of records, especially those of the BUS, during the War of 1812.

While the fine details of economic growth remain elusive, much can still be said about economic conditions both before and after Hamilton and Congress implemented Hamilton's plan for the national economy. A speculative crash occurred in New York City in 1792 and spread sporadically across the eastern seaboard. Steep inflation rates existed between 1791 and 1796. And while infrastructure investments bustled throughout the East and the developing West, their creation coincided with a rapid increase in bankruptcy and insolvency. Even at this early date, the cyclical activity of the American economy appeared in short booms and busts.

Several explanations could be offered for the development of an early boom-bust cycle. One might suggest business cycles are a natural element of capitalism, and as the economy modernized, cyclical fluctuations would be expected. Sheer greed on the part of speculators could have produced more services than consumers demanded, thus causing overproduction. The financial infrastructure may have remained too immature to adequately finance the needs of investors despite Hamilton's attempt to strengthen it. State governments may have improperly managed their economic situation either by refusing to cooperate with other states or by failing to sufficiently support newly chartered companies. Investors and promoters may have been unsuccessful in getting farmers and minor merchants to see how they could benefit from a vigorous—and united—national economy.

Another explanation for a business cycle emerging early in the 1790s suggests that far from stabilizing the economy, Hamilton and the Federalist Congress destabilized financial markets causing entrepreneurs to misread the market and make incorrect business decisions.

Many important entrepreneurs in the early republic also held most of the domestic debt. As the country's public credit rose, debt holders profited from debt redemption. The Bank of the United States added to the potential for increased investment by pursuing a policy of easy money until 1796. By receiving higher profits and easier credit than market conditions allowed, entrepreneurs took much greater risks with their subsequent investments. They also mistook the dramatic deflation of the late 1780s and the inflation of the early 1790s as evidence of a strengthening economy. Prices surged after ratification of the Constitution due to perceived political actions of Congress, not due to Americans being in a position to demand more goods and services. The resulting malinvestments in transportation improvements, banking, and manufacturing far exceeded market demand and resulted in the Panic of 1792 and would add to the distress in 1796. To complicate matters further, the Treasury, following Hamilton's "Report on the Mint," fixed the exchange rate of specie so that gold slightly overvalued silver. The decision instigated a classic example of Gresham's Law, where "bad" money chases out "good" money, and in this case, the country's gold supply was steadily depleted in favor of silver.

Debt Funding, Conversion, and the Bank of the United States

There is no need to regurgitate the intricacies of the financial program proposed by Alexander Hamilton while Secretary of Treasury. Yet misunderstanding Hamilton's goals and the monetary effects of his plans creates a distorted view of Hamilton's role. Hamilton was neither a defender of an aristocracy of wealth nor was he the architect of America's economic "take-off."

Alexander Hamilton laid clear plans as to what he wished to do with the Revolutionary debt. Though not a dedicated bullionist, like most economic nationalists of his day Hamilton believed the country's economic problems grew from a lack of sufficient specie in circulation. The underlying goal required augmenting existing specie by coverting federal and state government securities into a capital pool for financiers and entrepreneurs. Financiers, traders, merchants, manufacturers, and all other businessmen would benefit by having access to cheap credit while consumers would have sufficient currency with which to purchase products. Hamilton never questioned the federal government's role in providing specie, albeit to him, that role was supervisory rather than regulatory.

Hamilton publicly reasoned that the country's credit problems weakened the federal government's ability to get more specie. Low public credit also prevented private citizens from getting loans at reasonable interest rates. The economy needed a jump-start, but not by a direct infusion of specie. Entrepreneurs, who knew how to use capital to spur on economic growth, needed the specie before average citizens. Getting specie to entrepreneurs first (or at all) proved problematic given the immature state of the country's commercial credit system. Hamilton's solution involved bringing in enough specie and then using the federal government to provide a financial network to dispense capital where it was best used. The Revolutionary War debt offered the means of accomplishing both.

Influenced by the predominant view that the economy suffered from a shortage of specie, Hamilton assumed a new credit network needed something other than a finite amount of specie. To be feasible, it must grow with the needs of the people. A rigid specie standard and a credit market where all banknotes equaled specie reserves would be too tight. The best strategy must include a combination of specie, redeemable bank notes, and government securities, where all forms of money and money substitutes traded as currency. Hamilton envisioned nothing less than a sophisticated credit market that could aid investors and supply the country with much needed currency, or as he called it, "the active capital of a country."

Hamilton believed banks could issue more credit than they held in specie reserves as long as all notes were fully redeemable in specie on demand. Like many advocates of commercial banking, Hamilton understood that a bank's depositors rarely demanded all their specie at once. At any given time, banks easily lent out more credit than they held on deposit. He did not understand, however, that the subsequent alteration in the overall purchasing power of money distorted rather than stabilized prices.

Three distinct but interrelated events came together between 1788 and 1791: funding the federal debt through the federal government, not the states; converting the old debt into new debt; and using the Bank of the United States to facilitate the acceptance of securities and bank notes as currency. Only Hamilton advocated all three from a position of high political office. Some congressmen supported him on this. But like many of the great compromises in American history, a majority probably did not exist in support of all three segments combined, only on each segment individually.

As the Philadelphia convention met and produced a new constitution, the market value of debt securities rose based on the expectation of payment. Never did the securities become worthless, but never did they actually reach par with their face value before conversion in 1790. Speculators stood to make impressive gains from buying the debt cheap in the early 1780s and selling high, as many did, in the late 1780s. Furthermore, those who kept their securities through the conversion process stood to gain even more. As late as 1789, confused debt holders did not know what to expect from Congress with regard to the debt. Their only anchor during the hectic first session of Congress was that most congressmen favored paying the debt in some manner.

Congressmen differed on whom to pay and how much. Many opponents of funding, James Madison and Thomas Jefferson excepted, knew the problem was not forsaking the initial common people and soldiers who held the debt. Rather, they saw the issue as a battle between market value on the one hand and a sizable expansion of credit, high taxation, and enlargement of the federal debt's market value, on the other. There were few if any true "repudiationists" in Congress at the time it debated funding.

Thanks to James Madison, the discrimination, or market value forces, lost. Madison, knowingly or not, sidetracked to opponents of face value funding on to questions of morality and social obligation as opposed to financial questions and taxation. By the end of the debate, discrimination meant giving original holders a portion of *face* value, illustrating how Hamilton's most vocal opponents moved toward the center. To make the opposition's position on discrimination less tenable, the difference between market value and face value shrank as the debate dragged on.

Indeed, talk of funding during the ratification process had already increased the market value of the debt and caused a wave of deflation to sweep the economy. Between 1787 and 1789 prices fell between 4 and 7 percent across the country. In Philadelphia alone, extending the dates from 1784 to 1790 shows a 20 percent deflation rate overall. By itself, deflation probably caused some market distortions, and regardless of which policy Congress followed, whether Hamilton's or an alternative, some malinvestments likely would have occurred.

Congress finally agreed to take specie from a new European loan and apply it to the national debt and the assumed value of state debts. Congress offered to exchange old securities for stock, substituting two-thirds of the principal for 6 percent stock and one-third for 6 percent deferred stock. It also paid all remaining interests and indents at 3 percent and old continental currency at 100: 1. The process of conversion both raised the market value of the debt by fully backing it with specie and turned it into usable currency. But conversion also reduced the new currency's purchasing power by infusing the economy with new specie and new notes whose value must have been slightly higher than the highest market value of old notes in the summer of 1790.

One would think conversion continued the process of deflation, but such was not the case since new notes were issued based on the face value of old notes. Because conversion exchanged notes rather than allowed the old ones to continue in circulation and because the federal government injected more notes than the total market value of the old notes, the overall supply of money increased. The resulting inflation appeared immediately as prices increased nationwide. Between 1791 and 1796, prices in Charleston increased 57 percent, Cincinnati grew by 38 percent, and Philadelphia prices rose an astonishing 98 percent. Additional foreign loans (of specie) and creating the Bank of the United States compounded the situation by further increasing the supply of specie *and* redeemable notes. Had Congress followed a policy of paying the old debt at market value, even market value over a period of months, Congress might have continued the deflation. Corresponding taxation may have softened the monetary expansion, but it was unlikely to significantly counteract its effects given the variety of products taxed and the variation of the tax burden.

It is important not to focus merely on general monetary phenomena, but to suggest monetary changes that affected individual entrepreneurs. One must be careful to keep in mind that holders of the debt purchased the bulk of it at prices far below what they were worth after 1790. Prices paid for the debt and the profits debt holders made did not reflect market demand for the debt so much as it reflected Congress's demand for its own debt. In other words, the American economy did not cause the price of securities to increase, Congress's decisions did. The subsequent rise in prices cannot be attributed to a rise in consumer spending, but to a drop in the purchasing power of government securities and BUS notes.

Far ahead of his time, Hamilton took possible inflation into account. In fact, he expected it and anticipated its effect on government securities in terms of bringing down the rate of interest. When Hamilton's proposal went to Congress, some congressmen wished to pay interest on the new stock at present rates of interest, or around 8 percent. But having more money and money substitutes available for banks to lend, the price of money dropped. Betting on interest rates to fall, Hamilton hoped to get debt holders to agree to 6 percent stock that would sell at a premium if interest rates dropped below 6 percent.

Beyond conversion and assumption, other aspects of Hamilton's plan exercised significant influence over prices. Hamilton hoped the Bank of the United States would create a commercial credit network, pool capital for investors, and strengthen the country's merchant base. But like funding and conversion, the Bank exercised an inflationary effect. It certainly increased available commercial credit to individual entrepreneurs as well as to new commercial banks chartered by various states. The bank and its branches fully redeemed its notes upon demand, but the banknotes were not fully backed by specie reserves, and notes circulated in a high proportion to specie in the vaults especially before 1796.

During the first years of the Bank's operation, it followed a course of fairly rapid credit expansion. The BUS played a substantial role in the Panic of 1792, and it may have accounted for some of the economic distress of the period up to 1796. Taking into account the Bank's proportion of notes to specie between 1792 and 1794, the Bank held about a 2:1 ratio. By January 1795, the ratio increased to 5:1 only to drop down slightly by the end of the year. The excess of fiduciary currency, or the notes issued in excess of specie reserves, likely contributed to the rise in prices from 1792 forward. New commercial banks, which pyramided their assets on top of BUS notes and stock, compounded the situation. Wisely, BUS officials changed course by late 1796, boosted their specie holdings, and the notes to specie ratio evened out to near equity by 1799–1800. Not coincidentally, 1796 marked a turning point where the Bank began loaning more capital to private investors than it did to the federal government.

Even assuming the BUS followed a conservative path, those banks whose capital came from BUS notes pursued a different course until competition from BUS branches intensified. Hamilton's consternation with state banks rested on their willingness to expand credit through fiduciary offerings at a much faster rate than the BUS. While some Federalists supported the coexistence of state banks with the Bank and its branches, Hamilton worried the inflationary tendency of the combined circulation of BUS notes and notes of state banks would wreck the fledgling commercial credit system. State banks, Hamilton thought, could not be trusted to control their credit emissions. Should the notes of state banks begin to depreciate, BUS notes might slip as well, thus jeopardizing the whole system. Hamilton must also have known other banks could curtail credit, making loans more expensive, thereby raising interest rates and detrimentally affecting the BUS.

Hamilton mistakenly saw credit as a means of stimulating investment and failed to recognize that demand for credit does not correlate to demand for the investments created with it. If credit expansion prompted investors to place that credit in things for which the economy was not strong enough to endure, then consumer demand would not be strong enough to make investments pan out. At least publicly, Hamilton insisted the opposite would occur. Investors, he claimed, would place their money in ventures sure to make a profit instead of "permanent" improvements like canals and manufacturing. Such was not the case.

A counterargument to the one given here might suggest that inflation is desirable and that deflation is to be avoided. Critics might also insist that the purpose of Hamiltonian finance, as he stated, was to raise the credit rating of the United States government and American businessmen seeking capital or credit from abroad, or to set better terms on foreign contracts. From this perspective, Hamilton was successful, thus contributing to the increase of foreign trade and the export-led expansion of the economy. If not this, then he helped lay the groundwork for institutions that used securities for a finance-led expansion of the economy.

Another way of examining Hamilton's contributions may be in order. Though many debt holders did quite well, many notable exceptions occurred that cannot be attributed to poor luck or lack of entrepreneurial wisdom. Instead, it seems that the inflationary tendencies of Hamiltonian finance produced faulty economic "signals" that misled entrepreneurs into thinking the economy was better than it actually was. Rather than analyzing what influence debt holders exerted over the formation of the new government and Hamilton's plan, a focus on how federal policies influenced their business practices reveals much about the effects of funding, conversion, and the First Bank. Such an approach would follow the one briefly outlined below concerning William Duer.

The Panic of the Early 1790s

The example of the much-maligned William Duer illustrates how economic repercussions from funding and assumption were far from positive. Duer was English by birth and, like Hamilton, spent time in the West Indies, though Duer did so only long enough to manage his father's plantation. Also like Hamilton, Duer settled in New York and married into a wealthy family. The wives of both men were even cousins. Duer briefly served in the Continental Congress but made a fortune fulfilling contracts with the Continental Army. Following the war, he speculated in real estate holdings and served on the Confederation's Treasury Board. He then became Assistant Secretary of Treasury under Hamilton in 1789 and assisted Hamilton in the creation of the Society of Useful Manufactures. Duer often used inside information to exploit the government securities market, but his misapplication—or corrupt application—of this information can account for most of his financial mistakes.

Duer lost with deflation leading up to debt conversion and with the subsequent inflation. Scholars rightly distance Hamilton from Duer with regard to their personal relationship. And Hamilton had no control over Duer's speculations. However, lack of personal involvement does not mean that repercussions from Hamilton's financial plan failed to influence Duer's decisions.

No doubt Duer's life followed that of a frontier gambler more than it did a New York aristocrat. Yet the most incredible of his speculative endeavors depended on specific actions of the federal government, either under the Articles of Confederation or under the Constitution. Two examples merit mentioning: his role in the Scioto land company and his direct influence over the Panic of 1792.

Following the Revolution, Americans started pushing the bounds of the western territory. Given the perceived shortage of specie, prospective land customers petitioned Congress in the late 1780s to accept debt certificates in the place of hard currency. Two companies led the way: the Ohio Company of Association and the Scioto Company. Duer participated in the creation of both since they were part of the same deal, though he directly influenced the Scioto Company. Land developers wished to use the companies to purchase land cheaply and sell it to needy settlers. When Congress agreed to accept specie *and* debt certificates as payment, Duer and his clients stood to make a substantial profit if the market value of the debt certificates remained low. In other words, they based their assessment of the situation on current prices in 1787 and did not expect the rapid rise in market value. In the end, the Scioto Company went broke due to mismanagement and the substantial increase of land costs as government debt values increased.

The Scioto example should not be used to discount Hamiltonian finance, which began operation after the Scioto Company became insolvent. It does, however, indicate how entrepreneurs based their decisions on the value of government securities and how changes in their value harmed some investors. Regardless of what Congress did, debt certificates would have fluctuated in value to some extent. In hindsight, Scioto investors should have known better. But how could they? There was no certainty in 1787 that Congress would even pay the national debt, and less certainty existed over whether Congress would pay the debt at face value.

Integral to Duer's association with the Scioto Company was his use of it to manage his personal speculation in government securities. In fact, the same forces that injured the land company encouraged Duer to try his hand at another form of speculation. While assistant to Hamilton, Duer counted on uncertainty about a new congressional policy: full funding of state debts. He busily purchased as much outstanding debt as possible before Congress reached a final decision in August 1790.

Afterwards, as interest rates dropped, new government debt traded at a premium. Additional stock and securities came onto the market as the Bank of the United States commenced business and supported the creation of new commercial banks. BUS shares, bank stocks, and new securities traded openly in major American cities, but no city contained as much speculative buying as New York. At the center of all this stood William Duer.

Duer participated in the selling of most forms of stocks and securities, and he worked both sides of the market. Able to control vast sums of capital, Duer bought and traded the same stock, virtually cornering the market and creating his own profits. Like other speculators in government securities, Duer commenced planning a number of important new companies ranging from banks and factories to bridges and canals. Thinking the market rise in securities knew no limit, Duer plunged everything he had into the market. He began buying on margin by taking out loans from all possible sources, including the fledgling Society for the Erection of Useful Manufacturers and wealthy New Yorkers. The activity of speculators, drawing on the extensive new credit system created by the Federalists under Alexander Hamilton, peaked in March 1792. When directors of the Bank of New York realized credit had been extended too much, their decision to stop all loans commenced a credit contraction spelling the end to William Duer's operation. By the end of March, the panic that began in New York became nationwide.

Ultimately, the federal government and Hamilton bore the greatest economic cost of the Panic of 1792. By late 1792 Hamilton and members of Congress realized projected revenue would not meet the government's demands for expenses and interest payments on the debt. The situation forced Hamilton to take out another foreign loan. The combination of economic distress and the apparent inability of the funding system and BUS to "fund" the debt without more loans elicited stern attacks from Hamilton's opponents in Congress. William B. Giles of Virginia, with the assistance of William Findley of Pennsylvania and Nathaniel Macon of North Carolina, pushed through a series of resolutions questioning Hamilton's leadership of the Treasury and accusing him of misallocation of funds.

The economy momentarily improved, but inflation rates continued to climb until 1796. At that point, the economy slipped back into a panic, albeit less severe than the one in 1792.

The question must be asked: Was William Duer representative of American entrepreneurs during the 1780s and 1790s? Certainly not, especially when considering that all American entrepreneurs did not speculate in government securities and lose all their investments in the Panic of 1792. However, Duer illustrates how expansive credit systems, like that proposed by Hamilton, cannot be sustained indefinitely and how credit booms mislead entrepreneurs and thus lay the groundwork for credit bursts. More importantly, if an insider like William Duer could not make good decisions based on the information at his disposal, how could average entrepreneurs?

Duer shows how politically generated conditions encourage speculative behavior. He based his decisions in part on the signals he received from the securities market—prices boosted by funding and assumption. And if Winifred Rothenberg is correct, debt holders were not the only people basing their decisions on market prices. Though Rothenberg's coverage covers mainly New England, it is safe to say that by the 1780s and 1790s an increasing number of Americans relied exclusively on market prices for economic decisions, prices made possible by moving away from bartering. A different policy, one that allowed for the gradual redemption of securities at market value, may have alleviated some of the extreme cases of speculation and price distortions.

Other speculators who benefited from funding and assumption followed a pattern similar to Duer's. Men like Robert Morris, Thomas Willing, James Greenleaf, Nathaniel Massie, and John Nicholson took profits made from government securities and invested them in projects the market could not sustain.

Land prices rose faster than any other investment in the inflationary climate of the early 1790s, leading numerous speculators to place investments on western expansion (or even on undeveloped land in the East). The Ohio Company, the North American Land Company, the Connecticut Land Company, and the Yazoo land claims, to name a few, began after investors wildly exaggerated the gains to be made in land development. One of the best examples fueled by inflating land prices, Washington, D.C., included several prominent debt holders like Uriah Forrest and Robert Morris, who plunged into an uncertain market and were financially ruined.

Investors thought higher land prices resulted from higher demand for property. When land prices began dropping, developers went to great lengths to get returns on their investments. William Blout, Nicholas Romayne, and John Chisholm went so far as inviting Great Britain to get Spanish holdings in North America.

The credit boom of the early 1790s also coincided with the expansion of internal improvement companies and commercial banks, whose capital was often pyramided on BUS funds, state subsidies, or mutual credit extensions. To help prospective settlers move west, or to link local eastern markets together, transportation companies quickly emerged with the assistance of state legislatures. The number of banks grew from one in 1790 to twenty in 1795. Thirty-two new navigation companies, including canals and waterways, were charted between 1790 and 1795. States granted twelve new charters in 1796, alone. Charters for bridges increased from one per year in 1791 to as many as fourteen per year in 1795, totaling forty-four between 1791 and 1796. And by 1796, there were sixteen new turnpike charters. Naturally, not all of these new companies relied on bank credit, nor did former debt holders promote them all by themselves. Some companies evolved from lucrative family holdings or from capital raised from investors. But even if some did not rely directly on credit expansion, their customers and investors often did.

New internal improvement companies faced obstacles similar to those encountered by land companies. Most investors wished to build improvements in order to expand their markets. They assumed that Federalist financial measures reinvigorated the economy and continued growth would offset the expense of linking markets together. In doing so, rural markets could be tapped to further commercial potential. Those relying exclusively on prices and available commercial credit, however, ignored the economy's weakness as well as latent hostility to their projects from farmers.

State laws required companies to have charters, which carried certain advantages such as monopoly status, state grants, and the ability to exercise eminent domain. However, charters also carried numerous restrictions that ultimately hindered profitability. And since companies often undermined the property rights of common people, rural farmers condemned the new companies for their special, political privileges. Like the land schemes, most internal improvement projects faced substantial losses. Promoters repeatedly returned to state legislatures for additional support only to be turned away by politicians weary of mounting demands and disillusioned with development schemes. In the end, national fiscal measures encouraged investment, whereas state and local policies were ignored only to the detriment of uncanny or misled investors.

Great wealth was made, as such prominent examples of John J. Astor and Stephen Girard show. But the 1790s were far from the boom time many speculators imagined. In fact, business failures, missed opportunities, and collapsed fortunes may have been the norm. Even wealth made in the decade later diminished as competition intensified and the monetary shocks wore off.

Detractors of this argument may be prepared to accept both the benefits and costs of this boom-bust cycle. The market would never have produced the transportation improvements so quickly. And in the long run, society still enjoys the fruits of the products such as better roads, canals, and a commercial banking network. All modernization efforts proceed along a bumpy path, but society ultimately benefits by laying the foundation for future stages of economic growth.

However, one must take into account that insolvent companies cannot maintain their investments. Bridges fell into disrepair, roads washed away, and canals remained unfinished. Above all, long-run benefits must take into account not only the material costs of malinvestments, but the social and political costs as well. The Federalist financial system did not solidify broad support for the federal government and Federalist Party. In fact, Hamilton's financial program failed to secure the continued support of the "monied" interests to which his opponents claimed he catered. No elite group of financiers found continued fortune at the hands of the Federalists.

Political Ramifications of Hamiltonian Finance and Federalist Policy

The political success of the Federalist Party depended upon the success of Alexander Hamilton and his financial policies. From the beginning, supporters of the Federalists counted on the new government to meet their financial interests. Three major political results proceeded from Federalist financial arrangements.

First, the economic malaise of the early 1790s undermined popular faith in the Federalist Party. As Albert Gallatin insisted in 1796, "Far from strengthening government," aspects of Hamiltonian finance "created more discontent and more uneasiness than any other measure." It is inconceivable to assume political and cultural differences alone could have instigated the first party system. It is true that issues like Jay's Treaty, for example, aggravated party feelings, as did the economic conditions of the late 1790s, for which Hamilton was not directly responsible. It is also true that the self-appointed leaders of the opposition, Madison and Jefferson, worked with Hamilton to pass key aspects of the Federalist program, including the BUS and assumption. Nevertheless, partisan attacks against Hamilton and the Federalists carried great weight as inflation intensified during the mid-1790s.

Second, confidence in the federal government shrank in light of the increasing tax burden to fund the full debt. Direct taxes, particularly that on liquor, provoked heated debate in Congress, which ultimately spilled over into the Whiskey Rebellion. However, direct taxes continued after Hamilton's departure from Philadelphia. Whether Fries's Rebellion or the Virginian assault on the carriage tax, animosities toward Federalist finance served as a conduit for even greater animosity toward the federal government.

Third, in a few cases, Hamiltonian finance enabled some people to aggrandize their wealth through political influence. John Beckley, James Monroe, and John Taylor attacked the Federalists early on for creating a privileged elite. They pointed to the large number of debt holders in Congress who passed the major elements of Hamilton's program as evidence of corruption. Examples of privilege enabled the Jeffersonians to adopt portions of the antiwealth rhetorical tradition of eighteenth-century England and extend it well into the nineteenth century.

The link between Hamiltonian finance and the business problems of the 1790s is not tenuous. Many investors profited handsomely from debt conversion and found additional resources available from new commercial banks. They had to put their new money somewhere, and, though risky, land companies and internal improvements seemed to offer the best returns. Here was the problem. Because of the new credit and steep profits from conversion, investors could afford to take advantage of pioneering companies, whereas those with limited funds were more careful with their investments. Not everyone lost, but overall, new investments in the 1790s offered disappointing results and intensified political conflict. By the late 1790s, when the Federalist leadership under John Adams began questioning financial incentives for business, or when Federalists in Congress could not pass bankruptcy protection for suffering ventures, those entrepreneurs most dependent on state aid migrated to the Republican Party.

Alexander Hamilton cannot be blamed for all of this. But the bulk of his defense of the Constitution implied that it protects and promotes the various interests of the country. Far from classical republicanism, Hamilton recognized that a government cannot deny the existence of different interest groups, nor can it seek to destroy those interests most people consider legitimate. Hoping to promote as many economic interests as possible, Hamilton constructed a financial plan from which as many people as possible got something. Entrepreneurs gained easy credit, debt holders received payment, assumption restored stability for debtor states, moral nationalists got taxes on whiskey, and politicians at least paid lip service to manufacturers and then promised farmers that grain exports would lift them to prosperity.

Entrepreneurs received mixed signals as new government securities and credit spread through the economy. The increased value of debt certificates, the lowering of interest rates, the ready availability of capital, and the expansion of banking reflected an artificial boom. The federal government was in no position to sustain the boom, and even if it were, the economy could not elevate consumer demand high enough to return investors' profits on their infrastructure improvements. At precisely the same time that Americans embraced a mature market system based on prices rather than barter, monetary shocks implemented by Alexander Hamilton and the Federalists rendered available prices insufficient to support entrepreneurial decisions.

POSTSCRIPT

Was Alexander Hamilton an Economic Genius?

Authors Gordon and Roberts are analyzing Hamilton's economic policies as secretary of the treasury from totally different perspectives. Gordon is sympathetic to the aims of Hamilton. As a staunch nationalist, Hamilton tried to establish the new nation on a firm credit basis. His funding and debt programs where the nation goes in debt to itself were designed to establish creditworthiness of the new nation in the eyes of its European trading partners. The assumption of state debts and the establishment of a Bank of the United States were also designed to increase the power of the national government over the states and to curb reckless spending. When such controls were loosened during the Jefferson and post-Jackson years when there was no strong national bank in operation, the establishment of the Federal Reserve System in 1913 was a testament to the legacy of Hamilton.

Carey Roberts is one of the few writers about Hamilton today who is critical of his economic policies. Roberts places Hamilton in the context of the political and economic environment of the 1790s. He argues, contrary to most writers, that Hamilton was concerned about the country's "lack of sufficient specie in circulation." In order to jump-start the economy, Hamilton reasoned that the specie needed to be funded to entrepreneurs and not the average citizen. The Bank of the United States was supposed to act as a check on bad investments, but in Roberts's view the Bank often encouraged reckless speculation on projects of dubious merit. Hamilton's program often favored certain business interests and did little for the agricultural sector where the vast majority was employed. The resultant hostility toward Hamilton, brought on by both his arrogant attitude and unpopular fiscal program, was partially responsible for the defeat of the Federalist Party in the congressional and presidential elections of 1800.

There is some merit in both Gordon's and Roberts's assessments of Hamilton. Roberts examines in detail some of the land deals and speculations in government securities of the reckless William Duer, a former assistant secretary of the treasury under Hamilton. Gordon downplays the negative effects of Duer and others on the economy and argues that Hamilton had gotten rid of Duer, who eventually died in debtors' prison, and moved quickly "to stabilize the market and ensure that panic did not bring down basically sound institutions." Finally, Roberts underplays the importance of Hamilton's policies in improving foreign trade, though Gordon does admit that Hamilton and the nation had the good fortune to have a major European war break out in 1793 after Louis XVI, the king of France, lost his head.

The bibliography on Alexander Hamilton is enormous. For the best journal articles published between 1925 and 1966, see Jacob E. Cooke's *Alexander*

Hamilton: A Profile (Hill and Wang, 1967). The most recent interpretations can be found in Douglas Ambrose and Robert W. T. Martin, eds., *The Many Faces of Alexander Hamilton: the Life and Legacy of America's Most Elusive Founder* (New York University Press, 2006). The most recent and comprehensive biographies are Ron Chernow's prize-winning *Alexander Hamilton* (Penguin Press, 2004) with new information on his youth; Forrest McDonald, *Alexander Hamilton: A Biography* (W. W. Norton, 1979), which contains an excellent discussion on his career as secretary of the treasury; John C. Miller, *Alexander Hamilton: Portrait in Paradox* (Harper and Brothers, 1959); and Richard Brookhiser, *Alexander Hamilton: American* (Free Press, 1999).

Most of the recent biographies are sympathetic to the Hamilton view of the economy. See John Steele Gordon's *Hamilton's Blessing: the Extraordinary Life and Times of Our National Debt* (Walker, 1997). Stephen Knott's *Alexander Hamilton and the Persistence of Myth* (University of Kansas Press, 2002) and his article "The Hamiltonian Invention of Thomas Jefferson," in Ambrose and Martin, ed., *The Many Faces of Alexander Hamilton,* trace the changing positive and negative images of Hamilton via American historians and politicians since his death.

The first party system contains a voluminous secondary literature. Most comprehensive is Stanley Elkins and Eric McKitrick, *The Age of Federalism: The Early American Republic 1788–1800* (Oxford University Press, 1994); more readable is *Joseph Ellis, Founding Brothers: the Revolutionary Generation* (Knopf, 2000); more scholarly are several essays in Ambrose and Martin, and also in Doran Ben-Atar and Barbara B. Oberg, eds., *Federalists Reconsidered* (University Press of Virginia, 1998).

Hamilton was compulsive in publishing his essays on politics and economics. Harold C. Syrett et al., have published 27 volumes of *The Papers of Alexander Hamilton* (Columbia University Press, 1961–1987). Among the many shorter versions of Hamilton's essays and letters are Michael Lind, ed., *Hamilton's Republic: Readings in the American Democratic Nationalist Tradition* (Free Press, 1997); Richard B. Morris, ed., *Alexander Hamilton and the Founding of the Nation* (The Dial Press, 1957); Jo Anne Freeman, *Alexander Hamilton: Writings* (Library of America, 2001). An attempt to make Hamilton relevant today are the quotes from *Citizen Hamilton: The Wit and Wisdom of an American Founder* (Rowman and Littlefield, 2006) by Donald R. Hickey and Connie D. Clark.

ISSUE 9

Did Andrew Jackson's Removal Policy Benefit Native Americans?

YES: Robert V. Remini, from *Andrew Jackson and His Indian Wars* (Viking Penguin, 2001)

NO: Alfred A. Cave, from "Abuse of Power: Andrew Jackson and the Indian Removal Act of 1830," *The Historian* (Winter 2003)

ISSUE SUMMARY

YES: Robert V. Remini insists that President Andrew Jackson demonstrated a genuine concern for the welfare of Native Americans by proposing a voluntary program that would remove the Five Civilized Tribes west of the Mississippi River, where they could avoid dangerous conflict with white settlers and preserve their heritage and culture.

NO: Alfred A. Cave accuses Andrew Jackson of abusing his power as president by failing to adhere to the letter of the Indian Removal Act by transforming a voluntary program into a coercive one and by ignoring the provisions in his own removal treaties that promised protection to the various southern tribes.

Andrew Jackson's election to the presidency in 1828 ushered in an era marked by a growing demand for political and economic opportunities for the "common man." As the "people's president," Jackson embodied the democratic ideal in the United States, thereby inheriting the mantle of leadership for the Jeffersonian tradition. In his role as chief executive, the hero of the Battle of New Orleans symbolized a strong philosophical attachment to the elimination of impediments to voting (at least for adult white males), the creation of opportunities for the common man to participate directly in government through office holding, and the destruction of vestiges of economic elitism that served only the rich, well-born, and able. In addition, Jackson was a nationalist who defended states' rights as long as those rights did not threaten the sanctity of the Union.

At the heart of Jackson's philosophy was a commitment to "the people"; however, his definition of "the people" was not particularly inclusive. For example, as a Tennessee slaveowner, Jackson clearly did not believe that African American slaves deserved to participate in his democratic world. Similarly, as a renowned veteran of the United States government's campaign to remove Native Americans from the path of white settlement, Jackson's attitudes toward the Indians were ambiguous, at best. Like most Democrats of his time, Andrew Jackson was no social reformer, and his brand of democracy was for whites only.

The rise of Jacksonian democracy occurred during a period of dramatic territorial growth in the years immediately following the War of 1812. A new state joined the Union each year between 1816 and 1821. As the populations of these states increased, white citizens demanded that their governments, at both the state and national levels, do something about the Native American tribes in their midst who held claims to land in these regions by virtue of previous treaties. (In fact, Andrew Jackson had negotiated several of these treaties. Some included provisions for the members of the southern tribes to remain on their lands in preparation for obtaining U.S. citizenship.) Most white settlers preferred the removal of Native Americans to western territories where, presumably, they could live unencumbered forever. The result was the "Trail of Tears," the brutal forced migration of Native Americans in the 1830s that resulted in the loss of thousands of lives.

According to historian Wilcomb Washburn, "No individual is more closely identified with . . . the policy of removal of the Indians east of the Mississippi to lands west of the river—than President Andrew Jackson." Although most historians are in agreement with the details of Jackson's Indian removal policy, there is significant debate with respect to his motivation. Did Jackson's racist antipathy to the Indians pave the way for the "Trail of Tears"? Or did he support this policy out of a humanitarian desire to protect Native Americans from the impending wrath of white settlers and their state governments who refused to negotiate with the southern tribes as sovereign nations?

Robert V. Remini, Jackson's foremost biographer, claims that the criticism of Old Hickory's Indian policy is unfair. He argues that Jackson firmly believed that removal was the only policy that would prevent the decimation of these Native Americans. Remini concludes that Jackson attempted to deal as fairly as possible with the representatives of the Choctaws, Cherokees, Chickasaws, Creeks, and Seminoles, known then as the "Five Civilized Tribes."

Albert A. Cave condemns President Jackson for abusing his presidential powers by breaking the commitments made to Native Americans under the Indian Removal Act of 1830. Privately, says Cave, Jackson favored a program of coerced removal of the Indians to lands west of the Mississippi River even while publicly announcing his support for voluntary removal. Behind the scenes, Jackson supported his representatives, who bribed corrupt tribal officials to support migration, removed from office Indian agents who opposed removal and ignored acts of harassment carried out against Native Americans who sought to remain on their traditional tribal lands.

YES ↵   Robert V. Remini

Andrew Jackson and His Indian Wars

The Indian Removal Act

From the very start of his administration, President Andrew Jackson knew exactly what he wanted to do. He said he would institute a policy of "reform retrenchment and economy." Convinced the government had become corrupt over the past decade, he promised to cleanse the "Aegean stables," inaugurate a system of rotation in distributing the patronage (his enemies called it a "spoils system"), and practice fiscal conservatism to pay off the national debt. A democrat to the core, he believed his program would "protect liberty," "restore virtue in government," and ensure "obedience to the popular will." The people are sovereign, he declared. Their will must be obeyed. "The majority is to govern."

In his inaugural address, given on a bright and sunny March 4, 1829, President Jackson stood before a cheering crowd estimated at twenty thousand and addressed these goals. He also raised the issue of the Indian. But his remarks masked his true intent. "It will be my sincere and constant desire," he declared, "to observe toward the Indian tribes within our limits a just and liberal policy, and to give that humane and considerate attention to their rights and their wants which is consistent with the habits of our Government and the feelings of our people." Anyone who knew him knew what that meant: removal of the remaining southern tribes beyond the Mississippi River.

Indeed he planned to undertake at long last the task he felt should have been completed years before, namely to involve Congress in what had been the sole action of the President to relocate the Indians in the west, where, he said, "they will always be free from the mercenary influence of White men, and undisturbed by the local authority of the states." Once the relocation was completed, the federal government could then "exercise a parental control over their interests and possibly perpetuate their race."

To ensure proper assistance in his efforts at removal, Jackson appointed his longtime friend and biographer John H. Eaton to serve as secretary of war, knowing that Eaton would execute his directions with all the loyalty and dedication with which he had performed so many other tasks for him in the past. In addition he appointed John M. Branch, a Georgian totally committed to removal, as attorney general. Such a combination of Jackson, Eaton, and Branch virtually guaranteed the speedy relocation of the southern tribes. But the President's main task involved persuading Congress to join his efforts and thereby provide additional legal and moral authority to his plan.

Jackson was anxious to start the process as soon as possible, because events were already developing that could escalate into a dangerous confrontation between the government and the state of Georgia. On December 20, 1828, approximately a month after Jackson's overwhelming election as President (and perhaps because of it), the Georgia legislature, infuriated over the Cherokee presumption in declaring its complete sovereignty after adopting a constitution modeled on the U.S. Constitution, decreed that all Indian residents within the state's boundary lines would fall under its jurisdiction after six months. Once this happened, serious trouble would surely follow. The legislature also acted because it had lost patience with the federal government for its failure to keep the promise it made in 1802 to extinguish Indian land titles within Georgia.

In view of this action and the likelihood that Alabama and Mississippi would follow suit, Jackson dispatched two Tennessee generals, John Coffee and William Carroll, to visit the Creeks and Cherokees and try to persuade them to remove voluntarily. They were instructed to inform the tribes that the President agreed with Georgia's action. Tell them, Jackson directed, that "the President is of opinion that the only mode left for the Indians to escape the effects of such enactments, and consequences more destructive . . . is, *for them to emigrate*. . . . He is sincerely anxious . . . to save these people, and relieve the States." Describe to them "the fine and fertile and abundant country" in the west where the federal government "could and *would* protect them fully in the possession of the soil, and their right of self government." There they will grow "to be our equals in privileges, civil and religious." But if they refuse to remove "they must necessarily entail destruction upon their race."

Obviously Jackson's concern over the likely extinction of Native Americans had grown stronger during the past few years. It behooved him therefore to convince the tribes to remove if they wished to "perpetuate their race." But their possible extinction never dominated his thinking. National security remained his prime concern.

It is also true that in all his dealings with Native Americans he showed genuine feelings of concern for their welfare, particularly the poor among them, and their rights as members of their particular tribes—provided their welfare and rights did not collide with those of the United States. His paternalism was appreciated by many chiefs who regarded him as their friend. They knew he had taken an Indian orphan into his home and had raised him as his son. They also knew that he anticipated Indians' becoming full-fledged citizens of the United States once they adopted the habits of white men. Given the greed of whites for Indian territory and their insatiable demands that would only accelerate in the coming years, and given the fact that the two races could not and would not "intermingle" or live side by side, Jackson felt he had no choice but to insist on removal as the only means of preventing conflict and Indian annihilation. As "hard and cruel," as the policy was, wrote one contemporary a short while later, it "is now universally felt to have been as kind as it was necessary." Indeed many historians today agree with that conclusion.

Which is not to exonerate Sharp Knife of the horrors that followed. Still, to properly understand him and why he behaved as he did, it is necessary to reemphasize that he never intended or imagined the horror that accompanied removal and that he acted out of a fierce nationalism and an overwhelming concern for the nation's security and unity. Quite frankly, Jackson was obsessed over national security, which is quite understandable considering his experiences over the years with the British and Spanish and their involvement with hostile southern tribes.

It is true that he could be a fire-breathing and ruthless opponent if crossed or contradicted. Like most Americans at the time, he was a racist (not that he had the faintest idea what that meant), and he held an assortment of wrong-headed prejudices about Native Americans. But he was not a madman intent on genocide. Nor was he intent on the wholesale punishment of Indian tribes for their alleged past "misconduct." Removal was meant to prevent annihilation, not cause it.

Carroll and Coffee followed Jackson's instructions to the letter. But they did not have his skill in a face-to-face encounter and the chiefs of both tribes absolutely refused to grant the President's request. This was their land; their fathers were buried in it; it was their home. They had no connection with the Arkansas Territory and had no desire to visit it. Not only would they refuse to emigrate, they told the commissioners, but they would counsel other tribes against emigration.

The resistance of the Indians and what had become mounting opposition by many church groups to any attempt by the government to relocate the southern tribes convinced Jackson that a major political problem was developing that could easily spin out of control. He had to take immediate executive action. So, as a first step, he ordered the army to run off all white intruders in Indian lands and if necessary destroy their cabins and fields. Next he assigned Thomas L. McKenney to undertake the task of molding public opinion in favor of removal. McKenney had served as superintendent of Indian trade and had become the head of the Bureau of Indian Affairs, beginning in 1824. He was hailed as a humanitarian who cared personally and deeply about Native Americans. And although he had supported Adams's reelection, more important, he favored removal. He also recognized that whites, from the beginning of their arrival in North America, had pushed the Indians westward and degraded their cultures until many eastern tribes had vanished. Furthermore, he appreciated the fact that Indians readily acquired the worst vices of the white race. If they were ever to make real progress toward civilization and legal equality with other Americans, they must be removed. Such was his thinking. He therefore proved to be a most effective advocate among church groups in getting them to understand that removal was best for the red people.

Jackson also cautioned key southern leaders against any action that might jeopardize the administration's new policy and generate northern opposition. Then he replaced a number of Indian agents with reliable loyalists whose commitment to removal was above question. When he took office there were twenty such agents and thirty-six subagents. Over the next two years he removed ten agents and nineteen subagents.

The urgency to bring about removal as quickly as possible increased with the discovery of gold in northeastern Georgia in the summer of 1829, bringing with it an avalanche of white squatters into Cherokee territory. And although the invasion brought boisterous demands from church groups to expel the intruders, led by Jeremiah Evarts, the administration saw it as additional proof that the whites were about to overwhelm the Indians in their eastern territory.

"Overwhelm" is hardly the word. The Cherokees were being inundated. And they cried out to their Great Father to protect them. "There are hundreds of whitemen searching and digging for gold within the limits of the nation," they wrote. ". . . The number of these intruders has been variously stated from one to two thousand . . . which we cannot but consider as depriving us of property for which the faith of the Gov't is pledged for our protection. . . . We humbly request that you will consider the subject, as soon as the pressure of business will admit, and if possible grant the wishes of our people."

Not only were Americans invading Indian territory, but the annuities owed to the tribes were frequently handed over by agents to white creditors to pay for outstanding debts. When Jackson heard that the agent for the Creeks had "paid out large sums in discharge of judgements recovered by the white citizens of Alabama," he immediately instructed the secretary of war to investigate the "impropriety" of this action and submit a report. Control of money owed the tribes, he protested, was being taken away from them without their knowledge or consent.

All of the more cordial—that is, nonviolent—relations between the two races that had been developing since the end of the Indian wars over ten years earlier now seemed close to collapsing. "Our white brothers on each side of us appear to have lost all the good feelings which formerly existed," complained several Creek chiefs. "All appear to have turned their hands to crush us." They have no regard for us or our rights as guaranteed by your treaties.

By this time, whites were more brazen and determined to take whatever Indian land was still available within settled states, and they became extremely adept at justifying their actions. A short time later, several white settlers insisted that they had moved into tribal lands with the consent of the agent and the permission of the Indians themselves. They said they had settled in the Cherokee Nation "and pitched their crops for the year." They further declared that they "will not now permit, at this season of the year, their families to be turned out of doors, and their wives and children deprived of the means of subsistence." Not "without making the manly resistance of husbands and fathers in defence of every thing sacred and dear." They had a right to settle in the Nation, they protested, and they expected the state to enforce their right.

One "old and feeble" chief wrote to his Great Father and advised him of the "dreadful consequences" if these conditions persisted. "Your white sons and daughters are moving into my country in abundance and they are spoiling my lands and taking possession of the Red peoples improvements. . . . And your soldiers have refused to prevent it." Your white children "are bringing whiskey and opening drinking houses . . . they steal our property and make false accounts against us [and then] they sue us in your state courts for what we know nothing of." And what has been the result? "My Red children . . . have been compelled to resort to there guns." When that happens "the whites have collected themselves in bodies and hunted up . . . and shot them as if. . . they had been so many wild dogs." "All I want is peace," the old chief begged. Only you my Great Father can help. "With every Respect I have the honor to be your unfortunate old brother."

This was the situation Jackson faced when he became President, and it kept getting worse over the next several years. The collision of the two peoples in the southeast had become increasingly dangerous. The worst in white culture seemed to be destroying what was left of Indian life and civilization. He had to do something. So, as his final action in inaugurating the new Indian policy, he prepared to go to Congress and request appropriate legislation to end the collision, the intrusion, the killing, and the debasement of Indian culture and "save the remaining tribes from extinction." In December 1829, when the two houses reconvened, he formally presented his proposal and provided specific details. Without doubt he fully intended to make Indian removal his administration's first piece of major legislation.

Among the Jackson papers there is a draft of his first annual message in the President's hand. In it he set down his thinking about foreign affairs, rotation, the tariff, internal improvements, the public debt, the national bank, and the Indians. The Native Americans constituted the final topic he dealt with, but the document breaks off just before he reached a conclusion. What he wrote out was a recapitulation of present conditions, particularly how the government had tried to civilize the tribes and encourage them to abandon "their wandering ways." All to no avail, he said. "It will not answer to encourage them to the idea of exclusive self government. It is impracticable." No people can form a government or social compact "until education and intelligence was first introduced." True, each tribe has a few educated and well-informed men, but the great body of southern Indians "are erratic in their habits, and wanting in those endowments, which are suited to a people who would direct themselves and under it be happy and prosperous." And while we have tried to be solicitous and caring in our treatment of them, we have told them that "it cannot be conceded to them to continue their efforts at independence within the limits of any of the states."

With these harsh words the document ends. But the draft message was subsequently turned over to advisers, including Martin Van Buren, Andrew Jackson Donelson, William B. Lewis, Amos Kendall, and James A. Hamilton, the son of Alexander Hamilton. Together they produced a final version that was delivered to Congress after it reconvened on December 7,1829, and read aloud by a clerk. It was written in a flat, somber and prosaic style, quite unlike Jackson's unique and forceful form of utterance.

It starts off by describing the current situation and what the President had recently done to correct it. These southern tribes, he said, are surrounded by whites who are destroying the resources the Indians depend on for livelihood and which will therefore doom them to "weakness and decay." Look at what happened to the Mohegans, the Narragansetts, and the Delawares, he continued. They are gone, extinct. And the same fate "is fast overtaking the Choctaw, the Cherokee, and the Creek. . . . Humanity and national honor demand that every effort should be made to avert so great a calamity." It is too late to wonder whether it was just to have included them within the territorial bounds of the United States. That step cannot be retraced. A state cannot be dismembered by Congress without its consent nor restricted in the exercise of its constitutional powers. You are now asked whether it is indeed possible to do something for the Indians that is consistent with the rights of the states and "actuated by feelings of justice and a regard for our national honor . . . to preserve their much-injured race."

As a matter of fact, something can be done. "I suggest for your consideration" the propriety of setting apart an ample area west of the Mississippi, outside the limits of any state or territory now formed, to be guaranteed to the Indian tribes, each tribe having distinct control over the portion of land assigned to it. There they can be Indians, not cultural white men; there they can enjoy their own governments subject to no interference from the United States except when necessary to preserve peace on the frontier and between the several tribes; there they can learn the "arts of civilization" so that the race will be perpetuated and serve as a reminder of the "humanity and justice of this Government."

The emigration should be voluntary, the President declared, for it would be "as cruel as unjust to compel the aborigines to abandon the graves of their fathers and seek a home in a distant land." They should be "distinctly informed" that if they choose to remain where they are within the limits of the states, then "they must be subject to their laws." But if they stay it is surely visionary to expect protection of their claims to land on which they have never dwelt nor made improvements "merely because they have seen them from the mountains or passed them in the chase." By submitting to state law if they stay and receiving protection in their persons and property like other citizens, "they will ere long become merged in the mass of our population." . . .

Actually the Indian Removal Act did not remove the Indians at all. What it did was empower the President to exchange unorganized public land in the trans-Mississippi west for land held by the Indians in the east. In addition it gave to the Indians who moved perpetual title to the new land and compensation for improvements they had made on the old. The federal government would assume all the costs involved in the removal and provide Indians with "such aid and assistance as may be necessary for their support and subsistence for the first year after their removal." Finally the act authorized an appropriation of $500,000 to carry out these provisions.

This monumental event in American history brought the entire government into the process of expelling the southern Indians from their homeland. Heretofore the early Presidents—many of whom were founding fathers of the Republic—removed Indians by executive initiative. What Jackson did was force the Congress to face up to the Indian issue and address it in the only way possible. And what it did at his direction was harsh, arrogant, racist—and inevitable. There was no way the American people would continue to allow the presence of the tribes in the fertile hills and valleys that they coveted. Sooner or later, white culture and life would engulf them.

The Indian Removal Act did not order the removal of the Indians, even though that was a foregone conclusion once the talks actually began about exchanging land. And, as far as Jackson was concerned, the Indians could refuse to remove and stay where they were; but if they stayed, they had to recognize that they were subject to state law and jurisdiction. No longer could they live under their own laws and practices. Henceforth the laws and practices would be white laws and white practices. But knowing Indians as he did, he understood that few could live under state jurisdiction. It was a hateful alternative. It therefore made sense for them to resettle in the west. That way they could preserve their Indian heritage and way of life.

Unfortunately the President's noble desire to give the Indians a free choice between staying and removing, one devoid of coercion, was disregarded by land-greedy state and federal officials, who practiced fraud and deception to enrich themselves and their friends at the expense of the native tribes. The removal process sullied virtually everyone involved in it.

Where Jackson is particularly culpable is in his insistence on speed and economy in reaching a decision with the several tribes. He wanted action immediately. He lacked patience, and by his pressure to move things along quickly he caused unspeakable cruelties to innocent people who deserved better from a nation that prided itself on its commitment to justice and equality. Removal could not be speeded up; it could not happen overnight. It would take months and years to properly transport and settle people from the country of their birth to a place they knew nothing about.

And $500,000 would not begin to cover the cost of removal. It actually took tens of millions of dollars to complete the process. Jackson wanted a quick ending to the Indian problem, and he achieved it. In his eight years in office some seventy-odd treaties were signed and ratified, adding to the public domain approximately 100 million acres of Indian land in the east at a cost of $68 million and 32 million acres of land west of the Mississippi River. But the cost in human lives and suffering was incalculable.

Eventually most Americans accepted what had happened. And even when the opposition party came to power it pursued the same savage practices against Native Americans as had the Democrats. Within a few years many thought the policy humane and enlightened. They understood the rationale behind removal and approved it. What they and Andrew Jackson failed to realize was that they had betrayed some of their most cherished ideas about American justice and decency. . . .

What Jackson did to the Indians as President was . . . end the drift and indecision of previous administrations by instituting a policy of removal that included an exchange of land. With the lessening of hostilities the tribes begged to be left alone, pleaded for protection and to be spared the necessity of contending with the power of the surrounding states whose citizens continually crowded in on them. But what they asked was impossible to provide in 1830. Perhaps it was never possible. As it turned out, the American people as a whole sided with the government and approved Jackson's policy. They did so because of their racism, their decades-old fear and mistrust of Native Americans, and their insatiable desire for the land they occupied. What resulted constitutes one of the great tragedies in the history of the United States, a tragedy for which the American people and their President must be held accountable. Like Jackson, they agreed that removal (which would make Indian land theirs) was also the only way to preserve Indian life and culture. Thus by shunting them off to the wilderness where they would no longer threaten the safety of the United States or hinder its westward and southern expansion, Americans felt they could resolve the problem of the Indian presence in a humanitarian manner that would not conflict with their Christian conscience or moral sensibility.

The distinguished scholar of Native American history Francis Paul Prucha has argued that four courses of action were available to the government in ending the everlasting white/red crisis. And four courses only. First, genocide. Exterminate the race. But no one in his right mind seriously proposed such a solution, certainly not Jackson or any other responsible official in government. Second, integrate the two societies. But Native Americans had no desire to become cultural white men. They had their own customs, laws, language, religion, government, and leaders and wanted to keep them. White man's culture was an abomination, except for those skills that could improve their standard of living. Nor did whites favor integration. As racists they feared that integration with red people would ultimately lead to integration with blacks. And that possibility horrified them. Third, protect the natives where they lived by enforcing existing treaties. Jackson knew such a policy was doomed from the start and had fifteen years of personal experience to attest to its impossibility. There was not army enough to keep squatters from invading Indian country. And future confrontations with southern states, similar to the one with Georgia, would undoubtedly follow, particularly in Alabama and Mississippi. Fourth, removal. That was the course Jackson knew would work and therefore adopted. No other alternative existed if Indians were to survive.

It needs to be remembered that removal was never just a land grab. That is too simplistic an explanation. Jackson fully expected the Indians to thrive in their new surroundings, educate their children, acquire the skills of white civilization so as to improve their living conditions, and become citizens of the United States. Removal, in his mind, would provide all these blessings.

At one point in this sad story a delegation of Chippewa, Potawatomi, and Ottawa chiefs came to Jackson in the White House and movingly described to him their suffering. "Your agent," they said, "told us at the Treaty made at Chicago in 1833 that the country assigned to us west of the Mississippi was equally good as the lands in Illinois. . . . Father—we have been deceived and we feel disappointed & dissatisfied. . . . There is scarce timber enough to build our Wigwams, and that some of our land is too poor for snakes to live upon. Our men are not accustomed to the Prairie. They have always lived in the woods."

Jackson listened to this recitation but did not hear. A long time before, he had made up his mind about what should be done with Native Americans, and nothing would change his mind, even though the eastern tribes no longer posed a danger to the country, nor was national security the issue. He believed the good of the nation and the tribes required their removal, and so thousands of men, women, and children suffered not only the loss of their property, but physical agony and even death.

To his dying day on June 8, 1845, Andrew Jackson genuinely believed that what he had accomplished rescused these people from inevitable annihilation. And although that statement sounds monstrous, and although no one in the modern world wishes to accept or believe it, that is exactly what he did. He saved the Five Civilized Nations from probable extinction.

Alfred A. Cave

NO

Abuse of Power: Andrew Jackson and the Indian Removal Act of 1830

. . . The Indian Removal Act passed by Congress in 1830 neither authorized the unilateral abrogation of treaties guaranteeing Native American land rights within the states, nor the forced relocation of the eastern Indians. Yet both occurred, on a massive scale, during Andrew Jackson's administration and were the result, not of an explicit congressional mandate, but of an abuse of presidential power. In engineering removal, Jackson not only disregarded a key section of the Indian Removal Act, but also misused the powers granted to him under the Trade and Intercourse Act of 1802. Furthermore, he failed to honor promises made in his name in order to win congressional support of the removal, and he broke a number of federal treaty commitments to Indians, including some that he had personally negotiated. While Jackson was not the only president who abused powers granted to him by the legislative branch, disregard of the extralegal character of much of his Indian policy has contributed to the over-simplistic view of Indian removal found in much of the historical literature.

In a message to the Congress of the United States dated 8 December 1829 Jackson declared of removal: "This emigration should be voluntary, for it would be as cruel as unjust to compel the aborigines to abandon the graves of their fathers, and seek a home in a distant land." The president added that "our conduct toward these people" would reflect on "our national character." This perspective on Indian affairs is particularly interesting in light of Jackson's treatment of Indians during his first year of office, which reflected his long-standing belief that Indian treaties were not really binding on the nation. The Jackson administration had refused to intervene to protect the Cherokee from the state of Georgia, which by legislative act had denied the Cherokees' right to tribal self-government and challenged their ultimate ownership of their land. Repudiating all past constitutional precedents, Andrew Jackson had declared that the federal government could not interfere with the states' management of Indian affairs within their own borders. In his 1829 message to Congress, Jackson noted that "years ago I stated to them my belief that if the states chose to extend their laws over them it would not be in the power of the federal government to prevent it." Secretary of War Eaton, speaking for the President, several months earlier had informed Cherokee leaders that the guarantees in

From *The Historian*, 65:6, Winter 2003, pp. 1333–1335, 1337–1342, 1353 (excerpts, refs. omitted). Copyright © 2003 by Phi Alpha Theta History Honor Society, University of South Florida. Reprinted by permission of Wiley-Blackwell.

treaties with the United States that they claimed protected their rights against encroachment by Georgia in fact were nothing more than temporary grants of privilege awarded by a conquering power—the United States—to a vanquished people, the Cherokee. There were, Eaton declared, no guarantees in any treaty that could be considered permanent, nor could any clause be construed as "adverse to the sovereignty of Georgia." Indeed, in the early stages of Congress's deliberations on Indian removal, the report of the House Committee on Indian Affairs, written by close associates of the president, dismissed Indian treaty-making as nothing more than an "empty gesture" to placate Indian "vanity." Such treaties were not really treaties, the committee declared, but were only a "stately form of intercourse" useful in gaining Indian acquiescence in peacemaking and land cession. Although that view was rejected in the bill finally presented to Congress, it was reflected still in the words of some pro-removal congressmen and thereby served to arouse suspicion of the administration's real intent with regard to Indian removal.

Although privately in favor of coerced removal (and as a former treaty commissioner, skilled and experienced in the coercing of Indians), President Jackson recognized that he could not obtain from Congress the aggressive removal law that many writers imagine was actually passed. Hence, Jackson did not ask that Congress authorize forced deportation, but instead sought authorization and funding to continue his predecessors' policy of granting land west of the Mississippi to tribes willing to relinquish their eastern holdings. The Indian Removal Act of 1830 made provision for the president to negotiate for land exchanges and make payments for "improvements" (i.e., houses, barns, orchards, etc.) that Indians had made on their lands. The president was also authorized to pay transportation costs to the West. An appropriation of $500,000 was provided for those purposes. Significantly, there was no provision in the bill authorizing the seizure of land that Indians declined to cede by treaty.

Members of Jackson's administration underscored the presumed voluntary nature of the president's removal program. Secretary of War John Henry Eaton assured skeptical congressmen that "nothing of a compulsory nature to effect the removal of this unfortunate race of people has ever been thought of by the President, despite assertions to the contrary." Worried by the extensive anti-removal campaign recently mounted by the Boston-based American Board of Commissioners of Foreign Missions and by some of Jackson's political opponents, Eaton in confidential correspondence twice warned the Governor of Georgia that the state must be careful to avoid "the appearance of harshness towards the Indians." Should Georgia be suspected of "injustice," it might well prove impossible to secure broad based support for Jackson's removal program. To reassure the general public, Michigan Governor and Jackson loyalist Lewis Cass, in an unsigned article in the influential *North American Review* in January 1830, declared that the administration not only understood that "no force should be used," but was determined that Indians "shall be liberally remunerated for all they may cede."

Jackson's supporters in Congress also assured doubters that the administration did not intend to force a single Indian to move against his or her will.

To cite three typical examples, Senator Robert Adams of Mississippi denied that the legislation Jackson requested would give the president any power "to drive those unfortunate people from their present abode." Indian relocation, the senator insisted, would remain "free and voluntary." Congressman James Buchanan of Pennsylvania assured the House that there was no cause for concern, as Jackson had never considered "using the power of the government to drive that unfortunate race of men across the Mississippi." Congressman Wilson Lumpkin of Georgia assured his colleagues that "no man entertains kinder feelings towards Indians than Andrew Jackson." Jackson's supporters in Congress reminded skeptics of the president's assurances that Indians belonging to tribes that had signed removal treaties, but who did not themselves wish to accompany their kinsmen on the trek westward, would receive individual land grants after tribal claims had been extinguished and would then be welcome to remain behind as citizens of the states, where they would, in Jackson's words, be "protected in their persons and property."

The Indian Removal Act passed by Congress included a clause guaranteeing that "nothing in this act contained shall be construed as authorizing or directing the violation of any existing treaty between the United States and any of the Indian tribes." Without that guarantee, and without Jackson's promise of legal protection for Indians who chose not to relocate, it is unlikely that the removal act would have passed the House of Representatives.

The Jacksonians' insistence on the voluntary nature of their removal program was a political ploy aimed at winning badly needed votes in the House of Representatives. In both houses of Congress, a substantial block of legislators stated bluntly that they did not believe that Andrew Jackson could be trusted to deal fairly with Indians, a suspicion confirmed when War Department correspondence discussing possible means of bribing and intimidating Indians reluctant to sign removal treaties fell into the hands of the opposition. As a result, Jackson's congressional critics demanded yet more explicit procedural protection of existing Indian treaty rights. In the Senate, Theodore Frelinghuysen of New Jersey offered two amendments that, by affirming explicitly that treaty rights transcended state authority, would have guaranteed continuing federal protection of "tribes and nations" that rejected removal. One amendment stipulated that in the absence of a removal treaty, the "tribes or nations . . . shall be protected in their present possessions, and in the enjoyment of all their rights of territory and government, as heretofore exercised and enjoyed, from all interruptions and encroachments." The second declared that changes in Indian status could be made only through the traditional treaty-making process, thus denying that Indian nations were subordinate to the states. In spite of significant support, however, determined opposition from southern senators meant that both amendments failed. A similar fate befell a variety of other proposed amendments, both in the Senate and the House, that would have provided more explicit federal protection of the property both of Indians who remained behind, and of those who relocated, and that would have mandated congressional inspection of the proposed Indian Territory. . . .

Indian removal as carried out by Jackson and his successor Martin Van Buren was anything but a voluntary relocation program. Numerous contemporary witnesses provide damning testimony regarding fraud, coercion, corruption, and malfeasance both in the negotiation of removal treaties and in their execution. In their zeal to secure removal treaties, agents of the Jackson administration resorted to extensive bribery of compliant and corrupt tribal officials and frequently threatened independent Indian leaders opposed to relocation. In a series of blatant violations of the specific guarantees that Andrew Jackson and his supporters had offered to Congress in 1830, federal officials, by a variety of ruses, in effect denied antiremoval majorities within Indian tribes the right to vote on the ratification of removal treaties. Furthermore, the administration systematically removed Indian agents who either opposed the removal policy or were less than zealous in coercing compliance. Moreover, Indians endeavoring to make good on Jackson's promise that they could remain within the states as individuals were subjected to all manner of harassment from state officials, speculators, and Indian-hating mobs as the federal government looked the other way.

Andrew Jackson's defenders over the years have suggested that Old Hickory ought not to be held responsible for the abuses associated with removal. Those abuses, in their view, were the work of lesser officials over whom he had little control. Jackson biographer Robert Remini, for example, has written that Old Hickory "struggled to prevent fraud and corruption" in the removal process, and sought through their relocation to protect "Indian life and culture." Furthermore, according to Remini, "as far as Jackson was concerned, the Indians could refuse to remove and stay where they were." He only asked that they acknowledge the authority of the state in which they resided. Remini recognizes that few of those who wished to remain were actually able to do so, but assures us that Andrew Jackson was not personally to blame. "Unfortunately the President's noble desire to give the Indians a free choice between staying and recovery, one devoid of coercion, was disregarded by land greedy state and federal officials, who practiced fraud and deception to enrich themselves and their friends at the expense of the native tribes."

In these assertions, Remini and other Jackson apologists are mistaken. Close examination of administrative correspondence and personal memoranda suggests that Jackson's guarantees in 1829 and early 1830 that removal would be voluntary and that those Indians who did not wish to relocate would be protected in their personal and property rights were politically expedient but fundamentally dishonest. Some rough notes in his personal papers offer some insights into the president's private thoughts about Indians as citizens of the states. In a set of points he intended to raise with his envoy to Mexico, scribbled in the summer of 1829, Jackson lists among the advantages of the possible acquisition of Texas the prospect that the "additional territory" could be used for "concentrating the Indians," thereby "relieving the states of the inconveniences which the residue within their limits at present afford." Jackson's own draft of his 1829 message to Congress contains no reference to voluntary removal. The eloquent acknowledgement that forced removal would be an act of cruelty that would reflect adversely on our national honor was added later, perhaps at the insistence of advisers hoping to reassure some northern congressmen. Jackson himself was more concerned about other political considerations. In a draft of a position paper probably written in 1831, he argued that if the states indeed had no jurisdiction over Indian lands within their boundaries and thus lacked the right to take that land when needed by white settlers, then numerous land grants, and with them countless white land titles, in the frontier states of the upper South were "void." "Such a doctrine," he wrote, "would not be well received in the west."

Jackson understood from the outset that the states would not in fact extend the full protection of the law to those Indians who remained behind. When the governor of Georgia informed Jackson that no Indian would be given a land allotment in his state, Jackson offered no objection. Instead, he warned Indians that the federal government could not protect them if they chose not to emigrate. When the Cherokee leadership indicated that they would accept a removal treaty that included the sort of allotment option earlier made available to the Choctaw, Creek, and Chickasaw, Jackson told them that they could have no land in Georgia. It is telling that in his 1830 annual message to Congress, Jackson in effect repudiated his 1829 observations about the cruelty of compelling "aborigines to abandon the graves of their fathers and seek a home in a distant land." "Doubtless," the president now declared, "it will be painful for them to leave the graves of their forefathers, but what do they do more than our ancestors did or our children are now doing?"

Jackson regarded state harassment of Indians as a useful means of encouraging removal. Georgia officials claimed that Jackson himself in 1829 told a congressman disturbed by the delays in the Cherokee removal, "Build a fire under them. When it gets hot enough, they'll move." While Jackson himself made no record of that conversation, Georgia's governor later sent a confidential letter to Jackson expressing satisfaction with "your general plans and policy in relieving the states from their remnant Indian population." The Governor was gratified that Jackson understood that "Indians cannot live in the midst of a White Population and be governed by the same laws." As for the Cherokee, who still refused to sign a removal treaty, "starvation and destruction await them if they remain much longer in their present abodes." There is no doubt that Jackson shared those sentiments. Several months after the passage of the Removal Act, he assured a correspondent concerned about delays in the forthcoming Choctaw negotiations: "Indians could not possibly live under the laws of the states." He added: "If now they refuse to accept the liberal terms offered, they only must be responsible for whatever evils and difficulties may arise." Shortly thereafter, Jackson, frustrated by the refusal of several southeastern Indian nations to heed his summons to meet with him at Franklin, Tennessee, to discuss removal, wrote his close associate William B. Lewis to predict that the activities of former Attorney General William Wirt and other antiremoval activists "will lead to the destruction of the poor ignorant Indians." "I have used all the persuasive means in my power," the president declared, "I have exonerated the national character from all imputations, and now leave the poor deluded Creeks and Cherokees to their fate, and their annihilation, which their wicked advisers has [sic] induced."

Jackson repeatedly warned that those Indians who did not agree to removal would lose their right of self-government and be subject to the laws of the states in which they resided. In so doing, he far exceeded his legal mandate under the Indian Removal Act of 1830. That law, as we have seen, explicitly upheld existing treaty rights and obligations. Rather than enforcing the laws that forbade white settlement on treaty lands, Jackson informed Indian leaders that he lacked the power to protect them from even the most extreme and oppressive actions of the state governments and of lawless whites. One chief, self-described as "old and feeble," wrote to his "Great Father" Andrew Jackson to complain that treaty provisions were no longer honored and that whites invaded Indian country to "steal our property." Making matters worse, the federal soldiers in the area refused to help the Indians, but when Indians tried to resist the squatters, they were hunted down and shot "as if . . . they had been so many wild dogs." Only the Great Father, the chief pleaded, could protect his Indian children and restore peace. We have no record of Jackson's reply. But a typical example of Jackson's response to Indian petitioners is found in his message to the Cherokee, dated 16 March 1835, wherein he declared, "you cannot remain where you now are. Circumstances that cannot be controlled, and which are beyond the reach of human laws, render it impossible that you can flourish in the midst of a civilized community. . . . Deceive yourselves no longer. . . . Shut your ears to bad counsels." While it is true that Jackson on occasion sought to curb the excesses of some of the more corrupt Indian removal contractors, and ordered some reforms in the process, a close examination of the record suggests that he was primarily concerned with dealing with those who defrauded the government or who cheated other whites, and was relatively indulgent with those who defrauded Indians.

While some writers have explained Jackson's refusal to protect the sovereignty of Indian nations against the claims of the states as an act consistent with his deep respect for states' rights, one must remember that Andrew Jackson not only refused to honor the obligations contained in treaties negotiated by his predecessors, but also ignored treaty promises made by his own administration. His newly negotiated removal treaties generally guaranteed Indians federal protection from the depredations of white squatters prior to the completion of land surveys. While the federal government clearly possessed both the right and the obligation to enforce those guarantees, Secretary of War Cass, although required by the removal treaties to direct his agents to eject intruders on Indian land, made it clear that Andrew Jackson did not want federal officers to be particularly diligent in doing so. In a letter to United States Marshal Robert L. Crawford, he wrote: "it is the President's desire" that the order "be executed with as much regard for the feelings and situations of the persons (white squatter), whose cases are embraced by it, as possible." Force, the marshal was told, should be used "only when absolutely necessary," and then only after explaining the situation at length to those who were asked to move. Soon thereafter, Jackson's administration abandoned even the pretext of removing illegal occupants of Indian land. Southern politicians had made it clear that their constituents would not tolerate any real enforcement of the protective clauses in the removal treaties. In Mississippi, Congressman Franklin Plummer declared that the settlers who had occupied Choctaw lands came from "numerous families of the first respectability" and had been encouraged by the federal agent to plant their crops on Indian land. He further warned that Mississippi would resent their eviction. Similarly, in Alabama, federal efforts to deal with an unusually violent group of squatters provoked an armed confrontation, and a period of tension between the state and the administration that ended with an agreement that the treaty provision calling for the removal of all intruders on Creek land would not be enforced.

Plummer's claim of federal collusion was well founded. Jackson's agents from the outset understood that the president expected them to be considerate of white squatters, not of the Indians the squatters had so often dispossessed. Thus they not only did not challenge state officials who encouraged whites to occupy Indian lands prior to removal, but also on occasion actively encouraged the violation of removal treaty guarantees. The removal treaties envisioned an orderly process whereby whites purchasing Indian land would take possession only after the original owners had departed. But when Congressman Plummer in the spring of 1832 expressed concern that a provision in the recent Choctaw treaty which forbade white occupation of land in Choctaw territory occupied before September 1833 might be used to disallow the rights of some Mississippians who had already bought Indian titles, Secretary of War Cass replied: "The President is happy . . . that he is not called upon to execute [those] . . . provisions of the treaty." As to the political reasons for Jackson's happiness, General Winfield Scott, in correspondence with Secretary of War Cass, noted that use of federal troops to eject white occupants of Indian land "would inflame the passions of Virginia, North Carolina, South Carolina, Georgia, and Mississippi, and thus give wider spread to the heresies of nullification and secession."

Jackson was well aware of the misdeeds of his Indian agents. After leaving office, he told Francis P. Blair that dealing with the Indian office was "the most arduous part of my duty, and I watched over it with great vigilance, and could hardly keep it under proper restraint, and free from abuse and injury to the administration." His claim that he had displayed "great vigilance" must be placed in proper context. Jackson was speaking of those who cheated the government or other whites, not those who abused Indians. One combs the record in vain for evidence that Jackson took any particular pains to protect Indians from speculators and swindlers. . . .

Antiremoval protestors frequently charged that Andrew Jackson's refusal to execute the Indian treaties and laws of the United States "constituted a gross abuse of presidential power." The charge was well-founded. Nothing in the Indian Removal Act of 1830 authorized his denial of Indian treaty rights in the removal process. While the law's affirmation that prior treaties remained in force was not as strong as Jackson's critics wished, it was nonetheless part of the law. By disregarding the obligations placed upon him by legislation providing for protection of Indian property, by denying the legitimacy of prior federal treaty commitments to Indian nations, by ignoring the promises written into his own removal treaties, and by tacitly encouraging the intimidation and dispossession of Indians, Jackson transformed the voluntary removal program authorized by Congress into a coerced removal sanctioned by the White House. The failure of subsequent Congresses dominated by Jacksonian loyalists to deal with those abuses does not alter the fact that the president was operating outside the law. It is doubtful that Jackson could have achieved his objectives in Indian removal had he either accepted the constraints contained in the enabling legislation, or honored the promises made to Congress to secure passage of that law. It is a mark of Jackson's political success that so many historians over the years have conveyed to their readers the impression that neither the constraints nor the promises existed.

POSTSCRIPT

Did Andrew Jackson's Removal Policy Benefit Native Americans?

One of the interesting sidelights of the federal government's efforts to develop a policy with regard to Native American tribes residing in individual states revolved around the questions of tribal sovereignty versus states' rights. The Cherokee, in particular, proved troublesome in this regard. Since 1791, the United States had recognized the Cherokee as a nation in a number of treaties, and in 1827 delegates of this tribe initiated action to draft a constitution that would more formally recognize this status. In doing so, Native Americans confronted a barrier in the United States Constitution that prohibited the establishment of a new state in a preexisting state without the latter's approval. In response, Georgia, where most of the Cherokee lived, opposed the plan and called for the removal of all Native Americans. At this juncture, Cherokee leaders sought an injunction to prevent the state of Georgia from enforcing its laws within Native American territory. The case reached the United States Supreme Court, which, in *Cherokee Nation v. Georgia* (1831), expressed sympathy for the Native Americans' position but denied that the Cherokee held the status of a foreign nation. The following year, in the midst of efforts to remove all Native Americans from the southeastern United States, Chief Justice John Marshall, in *Worcester v. Georgia,* ruled that the state had no right to extend sovereignty over the Cherokee within its borders. Andrew Jackson, unimpressed by Marshall's opinion, is alleged to have expressed his contempt with the retort: "Justice Marshall has made his decision, now let him enforce it."

Major studies of the Indian removal policy in Jacksonian America include Angie Debo's classic *And Still the Waters Run: The Betrayal of the Five Civilized Tribes* (University of Oklahoma Press, 1940); Allen Guttman, *States Rights and Indian Removal: The Cherokee Nation vs. the State of Georgia* (D.C. Heath, 1965); Ronald N. Satz, *American Indian Policy in the Jacksonian Era* (University of Nebraska Press, 1975); John Ehle, *Trail of Tears: The Rise and Fall of the Cherokee Nation* (Doubleday, 1988); Mary E. Young, *Redskins, Ruffleshirts, and Rednecks: Indian Allotments in Alabama and Mississippi, 1830–1860* (University of Oklahoma Press, 1961); and Arthur H. DeRosier, Jr., *The Removal of the Choctaw Indians* (University of Tennessee Press, 1970). Perhaps the best analysis of Jackson's sometimes ambiguous attitude toward Native Americans is Michael Paul Rogin's *Fathers and Children: Andrew Jackson and the Subjugation of the American Indian* (Alfred A. Knopf, 1975). The most favorable treatment of Jackson's Indian policy can be found in Francis Paul Prucha, *Indian Policy in the Formative Years: The Indian Trade and Intercourse Acts, 1780–1834* (Harvard University Press, 1962); "Andrew Jackson's Indian Policy: A Reassessment," *Journal of American History*

(December 1969), and *The Great Father: The United States Government and the American Indians* (University of Nebraska Press, 1984). A brief analysis that corresponds to Cave's conclusions is available in Anthony F. C. Wallace, *The Long, Bitter Trail: Andrew Jackson and the Indians* (Hill & Wang, 1993).

For general studies of Native American history that include discussions of Jackson's attitudes and policies with regard to Indians, see Wilcomb E. Washburn, *The Indian in America* (Harper & Row, 1975); Robert F. Berkhofer, Jr., *The White Man's Indian: Images of the American Indian from Columbus to the Present* (Alfred A. Knopf, 1978); and Francis Paul Prucha's edited collection of readings, *The Indian in American History* (Holt, Rinehart and Winston, 1971).

The historical literature on Jacksonian philosophy and policies is extensive. Remini is Jackson's definitive, generally sympathetic biographer. His three-volume study, *Andrew Jackson and the Course of American Empire, 1767–1821* (Harper and Row, 1977); *Andrew Jackson and the Course of American Freedom, 1822–1832* (Harper and Row, 1981); and *Andrew Jackson and the Course of American Democracy, 1833–1845* (Harper and Row, 1984), is the culmination of a long career of study and writing. Older though equally excellent studies include Arthur Schlesinger, Jr., *The Age of Jackson* (Little, Brown, 1946); John William Ward, *Andrew Jackson: Symbol for an Age* (Oxford University Press, 1955); and Marvin Meyers, *The Jacksonian Persuasion: Politics and Belief* (Stanford University Press, 1957). Useful primary sources on the "age of Jackson" are collected in Edward Pessen, ed., *Jacksonian Panorama* (Bobbs-Merrill, 1976). The period is also explored in Glyndon G. Van Deusen, *The Jacksonian Era, 1828–1848* (Harper and Row, 1959); Edward Pessen, *Jacksonian America: Society, Personality, and Politics* (Dorsey Press, 1969); and Henry L Watson, *Liberty and Power: The Politics of Jacksonian America* (Hill and Wang, 1990). Finally, Alexander de Tocqueville's classic *Democracy in America* (Harper-Collins, 1988) sheds a great deal of light on the still young nation of Jackson's time, from the perspective of a foreign observer.

ISSUE 10

Did the Industrial Revolution Provide More Economic Opportunities for Women in the 1830s?

YES: Nancy F. Cott, from *The Bonds of Womanhood: "Woman's Sphere" in New England, 1780–1835* (Yale University Press, 1977, 1997)

NO: Gerda Lerner, from "The Lady and the Mill Girl: Changes in the Status of Women in the Age of Jackson," *American Studies Journal* (Spring 1969)

ISSUE SUMMARY

YES: According to Nancy F. Cott, when merchant capitalism reached its mature phase in the 1830s, the roles of the middle-class family became more clearly defined, and new economic opportunities opened for women within a limited sphere outside the home.

NO: According to Gerda Lerner, while Jacksonian democracy provided political and economic opportunities for men, both the "lady" and the "mill girl" were equally disenfranchised and isolated from vital centers of economic opportunity.

Until the 1960s, the serious student of American women could store all the important historical studies of women on one shelf of a bookcase. They fell into two categories: Eleanor Flexner's *Century of Struggle* (Harvard University Press, 1959) and Andrew Sinclair's *The Better Half* (Harper and Row, 1965) were broad surveys based upon the limited sources available. This second category, for lack of a better label, I call the "we did it too" category. This area is full of biographies of pioneering women in education, health care, and the suffragists' movement. These biographies of the "female leaders" fit nicely into mainstream political history. Instead of the "presidential synthesis" we now have the "great American women's synthesis." As important as these works were, female historians were being forced to write within a framework of political history where women were basically excluded.

In order to write a real history of women, new sources and approaches would have to be found. The traditional political-military-diplomatic framework would be abandoned. A new generation of historians, sons and daughters of immigrants, African Americans, and women, influenced by the fourth wave of immigration, and the civil rights and women's liberation movements, would write about the lives of ordinary people.

One area that distinguishes the old and new history is the study of families. Though family and women's history are considered separate areas of study, the two fields often intermingle. Comparative histories of women in separate prerevolutionary colonies or with England is another approach that yields some interesting conclusions. Utilizing church, court, and census records, Lois Green Carr and Lorena S. Walsh wrote "The Planter's Wife: The Experience of White Women in Seventeenth-Century Maryland," *William and Mary Quarterly* (1977) and found that Maryland immigrant women were better off than their English counterparts because they married late, bore relatively few children, and were commonly widowed. Because they were so few in numbers, the first-generation women tended to remarry by choice and often had control over some of the property brought from their first marriages. However, there is evidence that second-generation Chesapeake women found their property and inheritance rights more constricted. Apparently, the roles of women and children in seventeenth-century New England were proscribed as in England, because the earliest Massachusetts Bay settlers migrated as family units. The witchcraft trials in Salem in 1692 tell a great deal about the status of women in New England. For example, in her study of *The Devil in the Shape of a Woman* (New York, 1982), Carol F. Karlsen noted how ministers compared female witches of New England with the evil Eve, who successfully tempted Adam to eat the forbidden fruit in the Garden of Eden.

Historians generally agree that sometime between the end of the American Revolution and the 1830s the nuclear family emerged among the middle class. Sociologists believe that family members in the traditional household have clearly defined roles. Fathers go to work in an office or a factory; children attend school; and mothers stay in the house, nurture the children, and keep order. In her study of religious literature and gift books, such as Sarah Josepha Hale's *Godey's Lady's Book,* historian Barbara Welter defined the role in "The Cult of True Womanhood 1820–1860," *American Quarterly* (Summer, 1966). According to Welter, "the attributes of True Womanhood, by which a woman judged herself and was judged by her husband, her neighbors and society, could be divided into four cardinal virtues—"piety, purity, submissiveness and domesticity. Put them all together and they spelled mother, daughter, sister, wife— woman. Without them, no matter whether there was fame, achievement, or wealth, all was ashes. With them, she was promised happiness and power."

Nancy F. Cott believes that when the modern factory system developed in the 1830s, economic opportunities opened up outside the home in industry, journalism, and within a limited sphere in business, law, and medicine. But Professor Gerda Lerner disagrees. Although Jacksonian democracy provided political and economic opportunities for men, both the lady and the "mill girl" were equally disenfranchised and isolated from vital centers of economic opportunity.

YES

Nancy F. Cott

The Bonds of Womanhood: "Woman's Sphere" in New England, 1780–1835

"Thine in the bonds of womanhood" Sarah M. Grimké signed the letters to Mary Parker which she published in Boston in 1838 as *Letters on the Equality of the Sexes and the Condition of Women*. Grimké had left behind the South Carolina plantation of her birth and become one of the first women to speak publicly against slavery. "Bonds" symbolized chattel slavery to her. She must have composed her phrase with care, endowing it intentionally with the double meaning that womanhood bound women together even as it bound them down.

It is a central purpose of mine to explain why an American feminist of the 1830s would have seen womanhood in that dual aspect. . . .

Recent historical research which has discovered shifts in family and sexual patterns in the late eighteenth century encouraged me to begin in that period. For the case of the United States—the period between 1780 and 1830 was a time of wide- and deep-ranging transformation, including the beginning of rapid intensive economic growth, especially in foreign commerce, agricultural productivity, and the fiscal and banking system; the start of sustained urbanization; demographic transition toward modern fertility patterns; marked change toward social stratification by wealth and growing inequality in the distribution of wealth; rapid pragmatic adaptation in the law; shifts from unitary to pluralistic networks in personal association; unprecedented expansion in primary education; democratization in the political process; invention of a new language of political and social thought; and—not least—with respect to family life, the appearance of "domesticity." . . .

It is fitting to begin with the decade of the 1830s in view although it is the end point of this study, for it presents a paradox in the "progress" of women's history in the United States. There surfaced publicly then an argument between two seemingly contradictory visions of women's relation to society: the ideology of domesticity, which gave women a limited and sex-specific role to play, primarily in the home; and feminism, which attempted to remove sex-specific limits on women's opportunities and capacities. Why that coincidence? Objectively, New England women in 1835 endured subordination to men in marriage and society,

From *The Bonds of Womanhood: "Women's Sphere" in New England, 1780–1835* by Nancy F. Cott (Yale University Press, 1977), pp. 1, 3, 5–9, 19, 23–27, 36–42, 43–44, 45–46, 57–59, 61–62 (excerpts, notes omitted). Copyright © 1997 by Yale University. Reprinted by permission of Yale University Press.

profound disadvantage in education and in the economy, denial of access to official power in the churches that they populated, and virtual impotence in politics. A married woman had no legal existence apart from her husband's: she could not sue, contract, or even execute a will on her own; her person, estate, and wages became her husband's when she took his name. Divorce was possible—and, in the New England states, available to wives on the same terms as husbands—but rare. Women's public life generally was so minimal that if one addressed a mixed audience she was greeted with shock and hostility. No women voted, although all were subject to the laws. Those (unmarried or widowed) who held property had to submit to taxation without representation.

This was no harsher subordination than women knew in 1770, but by 1835 it had other grievous aspects. When white manhood suffrage, stripped of property qualifications, became the rule, women's political incapacity appeared more conspicuous than it had in the colonial period. As occupations in trade, crafts, and services diversified the agricultural base of New England's economy, and wage earning encroached on family farm production, women's second-class position in the economy was thrown into relief. There was only a limited number of paid occupations generally open to women, in housework, handicrafts and industry, and schoolteaching. Their wages were one-fourth to one-half what men earned in comparable work.The legal handicaps imposed by the marriage contract prevented wives from engaging in business ventures on their own, and the professionalization of law and medicine by means of educational requirements, licensing, and professional societies severely excluded women from those avenues of distinction and earning power. Because colleges did not admit women, they could not enter any of the learned professions. For them, the Jacksonian rhetoric of opportunity had scant meaning.

The 1830s nonetheless became a turning point in women's economic participation, public activities, and social visibility. New textile factories recruited a primarily female labor force, and substantial numbers of young women left home to live and work with peers. In the mid-1830s occurred the first industrial strikes in the United States led and peopled by women. "One of the leaders mounted a pump," the Boston *Evening Transcript* reported during the first "turn-out" in Lowell, Massachusetts, to protest wage reductions, "and made a flaming Mary Woolstonecraft [sic] speech on the rights of women." Middle-class women took up their one political tool, the petition, to demand legislation enabling wives to retain rights to their property and earnings. So many women pursued the one profession open to them, primary-school teaching, that their entry began to look like a takeover, although (or, to be accurate, because) they consistently commanded much lower salaries than men. Secondary schools and academies which could prepare young women to teach multiplied. Women's growing literacy, owed in part to the employment of some as teachers of girls, swelled the audience for female journalists and fiction writers. While it had been unprecedented for Hannah Adams to support herself by her writing in the first decade of the nineteenth century, that possibility came within more women's reach. Several ladies' magazines began publication during the decade, thereby increasing the editorial and publication possibilities for women authors and causing a female audience to coalesce.

Women also entered a variety of reform movements, to pursue objects in their own self-interest as well as to improve their society. Health reformers spotlighted women's physical condition. "Moral reformers" attacked the double standard of sexual morality and the victimization of prostitutes. Mothers formed societies to consult together on the rearing of children. Even larger numbers of women joined Christian benevolent associations, to reform the world by the propagation of the faith. An insistent minority of women became active in the antislavery movement where they practiced tactics of recruitment, organization, fund raising, propagandizing, and petitioning—and initiated the women's rights movement in the United States, when some of them took to heart the principles of freedom and human rights. Although the Seneca Falls Convention of 1848 usually marks the beginning of organized feminism in this country, there were clearly feminist voices in the antislavery movement by the late 1830s.

At the same time, an emphatic sentence of domesticity was pronounced for women. Both male and female authors (the former mostly ministers) created a new popular literature, consisting of advice books, sermons, novels, essays, stories, and poems, advocating and reiterating women's certain, limited role. That was to be wives and mothers, to nurture and maintain their families, to provide religious example and inspiration, and to affect the world around by exercising private moral influence. The literature of domesticity promulgated a Janus-faced conception of women's roles: it looked back, explicitly conservative in its attachment to a traditional understanding of woman's place; while it proposed transforming, even millennial results. One might assume that this pervasive formulation was simply a reaction to—a conservative defense against—expansion of women's nondomestic pursuits. But women's educational, reform, labor force, and political activities were just beginning to enlarge in the 1830s when the concept of domesticity crystallized. Several decades' shift in the allotment of powers and functions inside and outside the household had created the constellation of ideas regarding women's roles that we call domesticity. It was hardly a *deus ex machina*. The particularization and professionalization taking place in the occupational structure between 1780 and 1835 affected women's domestic occupation as well as any other; and concomitant subtle changes in women's view of their domestic role established a substructure for their nondomestic pursuits and self-assertion. The ideology of domesticity may seem to be contradicted functionally and abstractly by feminism, but historically—as they emerged in the United States—the latter depended on the former. . . .

"A woman's work is never done," Martha Moore Ballard wrote in her journal one November midnight in 1795, having been busy preparing wool for spinning until that time, "and happy she whos[e] strength holds out to the end of the [sun's] rays." Ballard was sixty years old that year—a grandmother several times over—though she still had at home her youngest child of sixteen. Housekeeper and domestic manufacturer for a working farm where she baked and brewed, pickled and preserved, spun and sewed, made soap and dipped candles, she also was a trusted healer and midwife for the pioneer community of Augusta, Maine. During a quarter-century of practice continuing past her seventieth year, she delivered more than a thousand babies. The very processes of her work engaged her in community social life. In her medical work she became acquainted with her neighbors as she provided services for them, and domestic crafts, such as quilting and spinning, also involved her in both cooperative and remunerative social relationships. The pattern of her life was not atypical for the matron of a farm household, particularly in a frontier community, in the late eighteenth century. . . .

The basic developments hastening economic productivity and rationalizing economic organization in New England between 1780 and 1835 were extension of the size of the market, increases in agricultural efficiency, reduction in transportation costs, and consequent specialization of economic function, division of labor, and concentration of industry. In late eighteenth-century towns, subsistence farming and household production for family use prevailed, supplemented by individual craftsmen (cobblers, coopers, blacksmiths, tailors, weavers, etc.) who were established or itinerant depending on density of population in their locale, and by small industrial establishments such as sawmills, gristmills, fulling mills, ironworks, and brickyards. The Revolutionary war stimulated some forms of household production (such as "homespun"), and so did the disruption of the international market during the Napoleonic wars, but more continuous lines of change moved the New England economy from its agricultural and household-production base and gave it a commercial and then industrial emphasis by 1835.

Merchant capitalism was a primary force in this transformation. Merchant capitalists took risks, supplied capital, searched out markets, and attempted to maximize profits by producing standardized goods at the least cost, thus organizing production on a larger scale than had previously been typical. Their actions commanded a shift away from home production for family use, and from local craftsmen's production of custom or "bespoke" work for known individuals, toward more standardized production for a wider market. Mercantile capitalism flourished during the enormous expansion of New England's carrying trade and re-export business that occurred from 1793 to 1807 because of the confusion of European shipping during the Napoleonic wars. This burst of shipping energy also caused subsidiary economic activities, such as shipbuilding, and complementary businesses, such as brokerage, marine insurance, warehousing, and banking, to grow. Under the brunt of the national embargo in 1807 and the subsequent war with England this blooming of the American carrying and re-export trade faded, but since much of the capital involved was transferred to manufacturing activity overall economic productivity did not diminish greatly.

The shift to market-oriented production under merchant capitalists prepared the way for the development of manufacturing and the factory system. Under the demand of the merchant capitalist for widely distributable goods, the craftsman's shop became a larger and more specialized unit, for production only rather than (as formerly) for production and retail sale. The master craftsman became the "boss" of a larger number of journeymen and apprentices. In New England another production system, limited mainly to shoes and textiles, also preceded and overlapped with industrial manufacture. This was the "putting-out" or "given-out" system, in which a merchant or master craftsman distributed materials to individuals to work on in their homes at piece-work rates, and collected and sold the finished goods. As the given-out system developed, the individuals (often women) it employed at home performed more and more specialized and fragmentary handicrafts. Indeed, the hallmarks of economic development in this period were functional specialization and division of labor. Where there had been "jacks-of-all-trades" there came specialized laborers; where there had been eclectic merchants there came importers and exporters, wholesalers and jobbers and retailers. Farmers who had produced only for subsistence trained their eyes on, and diverted some of their energies to, the market for commercial produce. New specialists appeared in fields from insurance to banking to transportation, as incorporations of businesses multiplied and turnpikes and bridges replaced wooded paths. In order to understand shifts in women's work during these years, rapid changes of this type must be kept in mind. Whether a woman lived toward the beginning or toward the end of this half-century may have informed the character of her work as much as, or more than, her geographical location, wealth, or marital status, which were other significant factors. Comparison of the kinds of work recorded in women's diaries in the earlier and later years makes that clear.

During the late eighteenth century both unmarried and married women did their primary work in households, in families. Unmarried daughters might be called upon to help their fathers in a store or shop connected to the house: Sally Ripley, a tradesman's daughter in Greenfield, Massachusetts, more than once recorded in her diary, "This morning my Father departed for Boston, & I am again entrusted with the charge of the Store." But daughters' assistance in the housewife's realm of food preparation and preservation, dairying, gardening, cleaning, laundering, soap making, candle making, knitting, and textile and clothing manufacture was the more usual case. Mothers and daughters shared these labors. The continual and time-consuming work of spinning was the most readily delegated to the younger generation, it seems. Hannah Hickok Smith of Glastonbury, Connecticut, managed to avoid spinning, because she had five daughters at home. "The girls . . . have been very busy spinning this spring," she reported to their grandmother in 1800, "and have spun enough for about seventy yards besides almost enough for another carpet." Spinning must have taken precedence in the daughters' work, for when they had "no spinning to do of any consequence" then Mrs. Smith admitted that she "lived very easy, as the girls have done every thing." . . .

The first "manufactories" in the United States were places of business established in major cities in the 1760s to collect yarn spun and cloth woven by women in their homes by traditional hand methods. Some merchants soon put spinning wheels and looms on the premises of their manufactories, and hired women and children to work them there; but in general they employed a much larger proportion of women working in their own homes than on the manufactory premises. After Samuel Slater introduced industrial spinning machinery to New England in 1789, and other entrepreneurs established spinning mills, employing women to work the machinery, the proportions working at home and on the premises were reversed. The early mills (between 1790 and 1815) produced only yarn, which was distributed to domestic weavers like Samantha

Barrett to be made into cloth. The power loom did not appear in New England until 1814. That year the Boston Manufacturing Company introduced it at Waltham, Massachusetts, uniting under one factory roof all the operations necessary to turn raw fiber into finished cloth. Factories mass-producing cotton cloth multiplied during the 1820s.

By 1830, industrial manufacture had largely superseded home spinning and weaving in New England by producing cloth more cheaply. This changed women's work more than any other single factor, and likely had more emphatic impact on unmarried women than on mothers of families. Industrialization of textiles disrupted daughters' predictable role in the household first. Mothers' lives continued to be defined by household management and child rearing. Daughters, however, often had to earn wages to replace their contribution to family sustenance. Textile mill operatives, who were almost all between the ages of fifteen and thirty, were young women who followed their traditional occupation to a new location, the factory. New England textile factories from the start employed a vastly greater proportion of women than men.

The economic and social change of the period injected uncertainty, variety, and mobility into young women's lives—into none more dramatically than the early mill operatives'. Mary Hall began industrial employment after her academy schooling and experience in schoolteaching. In November 1830 she started folding books at a shop in Exeter, New Hampshire, not happy to be removed from her family. "Yes, I shall probably be obliged to call this, to me a land of strangers, home for the present," she wrote in her diary. "But home sweet home can never be transfer'd in the affections of Me. . . . How often this day amidst its cares and business have I been in imagination under the paternal roof seeing, hearing and conversing with its lov'd inhabitants." She was twenty-four years old. After seven months she returned home, because several family members were ill. In September 1831, she went to Lowell, Massachusetts, for employment as a cotton-mill operative. She worked in Lowell for the next five years, except for returns home to Concord for more than a year between 1832 and 1833, for the summer in 1834, for weeks in November and December 1834 (because of deaths in her family), and in November 1835 and June 1836. During her years in Lowell she worked for at least three different corporations.

Emily Chubbuck, whose family was probably poorer than Mary Hall's, had a more disjointed employment history. The fifth child in a New Hampshire family transplanted to upstate New York, she went to work in 1828, at the age of eleven, splicing rolls in a woolen factory. Her parents allowed her to keep her weekly wage of $1.25. When the factory closed in January 1829 she began attending a district school, to supplement the education she had received from an older sister. Two months later the factory reopened and she resumed work there. During the next three years, as her family moved several times in attempts to make a living, she intermittently worked for a Scottish weaver twisting thread, attended an academy, washed and ironed for her family's boarders, sewed for a mantua-maker, and attended a district school. At fourteen, despite her mother's advice to apprentice herself to a milliner, she lied about her age to obtain a schoolteaching job. Her wages were only 75 cents a week plus board. She knew that she "could earn as much with the milliner, and far more at twisting thread," but she hoped for a future in literary pursuits rather than manual employment.

There was a large class of young women who would have spun at home in early decades but whose families' incomes or priorities made factory work unlikely for them. Their work too became variable and sporadic, shifting among the options of schoolteaching, needlework, domestic work, and given-out industry. None of these was really a full-time, year-round occupation. Women tended to combine them. Rachel Stearns, under pressure of necessity, became willing to intersperse sewing in another household with her school-teaching, although earlier she had "thought it quite too degrading to go to Uncle F's and sew." Nancy Flynt, a single woman of Connecticut, wrote to her married sister around 1810, "[I am] a tugging and a toiling day and night to get a maintenance, denying myself the pleasure of calling on my nearest neighbors. . . . I would tell you how much work I have dispatched since I saw you, I have a great deal of sewing on hand now." The twenty-five-year-old daughter of the minister in Hawley, Massachusetts, decided she should learn to support herself "by the needle" and therefore began to learn the milliner's trade, but her health failed, preventing her from continuing. "Perhaps [I] flattered myself too much with the idea of being able to bear my own expenses," she reflected somewhat bitterly.

Given-out industry, which constituted a significant stage in the industrial development of New England, enabled women to earn money while staying at home. Two kinds of production organized this way drew heavily on women's labor: the stitching and binding of boots and shoes (concentrated in eastern Massachusetts) and the braiding, or plaiting, of straw bonnets. The latter was a handicraft designed before 1800 by New England women who used native rye straw for the material. By 1830 thousands carried it on in the employ of entrepreneurs who imported palm leaves from Cuba and distributed them to farmhouses to be made up into hats. Eliza Chaplin and her sister Caroline of Salem, Massachusetts, made and sold bonnets during the 1820s, the same years that they taught school. Julia Pierce taught school in the summer and had "plenty of work" to do in the winter, she said: "I have braided more than 100 hats and the other girls as many more." The working life of Amanda Elliott of Guilford, Connecticut, exemplifies the variety of this transitional period. Within six months in 1816–17 she devoted considerable time to splitting straw and braiding hats; noted five new boarders; taught school; and mentioned binding shoes, in addition to usual domestic needlework, knitting, washing, and ironing. For some fortunate young women, of course, the diminution of household manufacture for the family meant greater leisure and opportunity for education. Hannah Hickok Smith's letters after 1800 revealed that spinning gradually dwindled in importance in her daughters' occupations. "As we have had much leisure time this winter," she wrote in 1816, "the girls have employed themselves chiefly in reading writing and studying French Latin and Greek."

While economic modernization changed young unmarried women's work more conspicuously than their mothers' at first, the disruption of the integral relation between the household and the business of society was bound to redefine matrons' occupations too. Wife-and-motherhood in a rural household of the eighteenth century implied responsibility for the well-being of all the family. Upon marriage a woman took on "the Cares of the world," Elizabeth Bowen admitted as she recounted her past life, at mid-century. Fond as Esther Edwards Burr was of improving her mind, she declined an opportunity to take French lessons in the 1750s with the forceful comment, "The married woman has something else to care about besides lerning [*sic*] French!" Sarah Snell Bryant's daily diary reported in straightforward fashion her matronly duties in an educated, respectable, but impecunious farm family in western Massachusetts. During the 1790s and early 1800s she bore and nursed six children (usually returning to household cares within a few days after childbirth), and taught them all to read the Bible before sending them to school. Generally she occupied every day in making cloth and clothing— from the "hatcheling" of flax and "breaking" of wool to the sewing of shirts, gowns, and coats—knitting gloves and stockings, baking, brewing, preserving food, churning butter, gardening, nursing the sick, making candles or soap, washing, ironing, scouring, quilting with neighbors, and even entertaining visitors. During a summer when her husband was traveling, she also taught school. Contemporaries of Sarah Snell Bryant who lived in more densely populated and commercial locations might have less labor to perform, especially if their husbands' wealth allowed their families to purchase goods and services. Martha Church Challoner, who lived in Newport, a lively Rhode Island port, in the 1760s, was able to buy various fabrics, shoes, and some basic foods. She had two black women in her house as servants (or slaves, possibly), and hired others to do washing, mending, spinning, carding, sewing, and nursing. Still, she herself made candles, knit stockings, sold butter and eggs, and sewed household linens, while supervising the household. . . .

Well into the middle decades of the nineteenth century married women's work remained centered on household management and family care, although the growing ramifications of the market economy diminished the importance of household manufacture and enlarged families' reliance on money to purchase basic commodities. Greater population density, commercial expansion, technological advances in transportation and communication, specialization in agriculture, and involvement of rural residents in given-out industry all contributed to the demise of the self-contained household economy. "There is no way of living in this town without cash," Abigail Lyman reported from Boston in 1797, and smaller towns rapidly manifested the same commercial spirit and need. Hannah Hickok Smith's account book for the years 1821–24 points out the extent to which a prosperous farm matron in an "urban"-sized commercial town—Glastonbury, Connecticut—was involved in commercial transaction. She recorded the purchase of edibles and baking supplies (spices, plums, currants, raisins, sugar, molasses, salt, wine, coffee, tea); of household items (teacups, platters, chest, jug, box, coffeepot, tinware, pins) and construction materials (pine boards, nails, steel); of writing accoutrements (paper, penknife, spelling book), nursing supplies (camphor, plaister) and soap, and some luxuries (snuff, tobacco, shell combs, parasol). Furthermore, she purchased at least eleven different kinds of fabric (such as dimity, brown holland, "factory cloth"), four kinds of yarn and thread, leather, and buttons; bought silk shawls, bonnets, dresses, stockings, and kid gloves, and also paid for people's services in making clothing. The farm produced the marketable commodities of grain (oats, rye, corn) and timber, animals (calves, turkeys, fowl) and animal products (eggs, hens' feathers, quills, wool, pork), and other farm produce which required more human labor, such as butter, cider, lard, and tallow. . . .

The growing availability of goods and services for purchase might spare a married woman from considerable drudgery, if her husband's income sufficed for a comfortable living. It also heightened her role in "shoping," as Abigail Brackett Lyman spelled it (her consumer role), although that was subject to her husband's authority over financial resources. In colonial America husbands, as "providers," typically were responsible for purchasing goods—including household goods, furniture, and food staples, if they were to be bought—but in commercial towns of the late eighteenth and early nineteenth century wives more frequently became shoppers, especially for articles of dress and food. The increasing importance of monetary exchange bore hard on those who needed to replace their former economic contribution of household manufacture with income-producing employment, while meeting their domestic obligations. Taking in boarders was one alternative. Betsey Graves Johnson did that while she brought up the five children born to her between 1819 and 1830. Otherwise, married women had the same options for wage earning as single women who wished to stay at home: to take in sewing, or work in given-out industry. Schoolteaching, a slight possibility for wives, was a likelier one for widows whose children had reached school age. One widow's "cares," as described by her sister in 1841, were "enough to occupy all her time and thoughts almost. . . . [She] is teaching from 16 to 20 sholars [sic] boarding a young lady, and doing the housework, taking care of her children, &c."

These constants—"doing the housework, taking care of her children"—persisted in married women's lives. Child care required their presence at home. This responsibility revealed itself as the heart of women's domestic duties when household production declined. After four years of marriage Sarah Ripley Stearns regretfully attributed her neglect of church attendance and devotional reading not to household duties but to "the Care of my Babes, which takes up so large a portion of my time of my time [sic] attention." More than ever before in New England history, the care of children appeared to be mothers' sole work and the work of mothers alone. The expansion of nonagricultural occupations drew men and grown children away from the household, abbreviating their presence in the family and their roles in child rearing. Mothers and young children were left in the household together just when educational and religious dicta both newly emphasized the malleability of young minds. Enlightenment psychology drew tighter the connection between early influence on the child, and his or her eventual character, just as mothers' influence on young children appeared more salient. . . .

While changes in economy and society made young women's work more social, more various and mobile, the same developments reduced the social engagement, variety, and mobility in the work of wives and mothers. Housekeeping and child care continued to require married women's presence at home, while the household diminished in population, kinds of business, and range of contacts. In an intriguing development in language usage in the early nineteenth century, "home" became synonymous with "retirement" or "retreat" from the world at large. Mary Tucker quoted approvingly in 1802 an author's assertion that "a woman's noblest station is retreat." On a cousin's approaching marriage she remarked, "Sally has passed her days in the shade of *retirement* but even there many virtues and graces have ripened to perfection, she has every quality necessary for a *good wife*." Salome Lincoln's marriage to a fellow preacher in 1835 virtually ended her extradomestic pursuits; she subsequently used her preaching talents only on occasional travels with her husband. The shifting emphasis among married women's occupations emerges clearly in the comparison of Lydia Hill Almy's occupations in 1797–99 with Mary Hurlbut's in the 1830s. The former not only kept house but let rooms, collected firewood, attended to livestock, and arranged to sell tanned skins; she considered her two children "grown out of the way" and "very little troble [*sic*]" when the younger was not yet weaned. Mary Hurlbut, in contrast, appeared solely concerned with her children's lives and prospects.

Married women's work at home distinguished itself most visibly from men's work, especially as the latter began to depart from the household/farm/craftshop to separate shops, offices, and factories. The rhythms of adult men's and women's work diverged even as did their places of work. During the eighteenth century, in agricultural towns, men and women had largely shared similar work patterns; their work, tied to the land, was seasonal and discontinuous. It was conditioned by tradition, family position, and legal obligation as well as by economic incentive. E.P. Thompson has called the dominant characteristic of work in such an agricultural/artisanal economy its "task-orientation," in contrast to the "time-discipline" required under industrial capitalism. Task-orientation implies that the worker's own sense of customary need and order dictates the performance of work. Intensification or delay occurs as a response to perceived necessity: in farming, for instance, the former occurs in harvest time, or the latter during stormy weather. Irregular work patterns typically result. "Social intercourse and labour are intermingled," Thompson also has pointed out, "the working-day lengthens or contracts according to the task—and there is no great sense of conflict between labour and 'passing the time of day.'" Persons accustomed to time-discipline, however, may consider task-oriented work patterns "wasteful and lacking in urgency." Thompson's analysis derived from his study of eighteenth-century English farmers, artisans, and laborers but can be applied to their contemporaries in New England. Even eighteenth-century colonial merchants, who, as risk-taking capitalists, might be expected to initiate disciplined work habits, structured their work lives in what Thompson would denote "preindustrial" ways, intermingling their work with recreation and with the conduct of their households. "The Founding Fathers, after all, lived in a preindustrial, not simply an 'agrarian' society," as Herbert Gutman has remarked, "and the prevalence of premodern work habits among their contemporaries was natural."

The social transformation from 1780 to 1835 signalled a transition from preindustrial to modern industrial work patterns. The replacement of family production for direct use with wage earning, the institution of time-discipline and machine regularity in place of natural rhythms, the separation of work-places from the home, and the division of "work" from "life" were overlapping layers of the same phenomenon. . . .

Despite the changes in its social context adult women's work, for the most part, kept the traditional mode and location which both sexes had earlier shared. Men who had to accept time-discipline and specialized occupations may have begun to observe differences between their own work and that of their wives. Perhaps they focused on the remaining "premodern" aspects of women's household work: it was reassuringly comprehensible, because it responded to immediate needs; it represented not strictly "work" but "life," a way of being; and it also looked unsystematized, inefficient, nonurgent. Increasingly men did distinguish women's work from their own, in the early nineteenth century, by calling it women's "sphere," a "separate" sphere.

Women's sphere was "separate" not only because it was at home but also because it seemed to elude rationalization and the cash nexus, and to integrate labor with life. The home and occupations in it represented an alternative to the emerging pace and division of labor. Symbol and remnant of preindustrial work, perhaps the home commanded men's deepest loyalties, but these were loyalties that conflicted with "modern" forms of employment. To be idealized, yet rejected by men—the object of yearning, and yet of scorn—was the fate of the home-as-workplace. Women's work (indeed women's very character, viewed as essentially conditioned by the home) shared in that simultaneous glorification and devaluation.

➡ **NO**

The Lady and the Mill Girl: Changes in the Status of Women in the Age of Jackson

The period 1800–1840 is one in which decisive changes occurred in the status of American women. It has remained surprisingly unexplored. With the exception of a recent, unpublished dissertation by Keith Melder and the distinctive work of Elisabeth Dexter, there is a dearth of descriptive material and an almost total absence of interpretation. Yet the period offers essential clues to an understanding of later institutional developments, particularly the shape and nature of the woman's rights movement. This analysis will consider the economic, political, and social status of women and examine the changes in each area. It will also attempt an interpretation of the ideological shifts which occurred in American society concerning the "proper" role for women.

Periodization always offers difficulties. It seemed useful here, for purposes of comparison, to group women's status before 1800 roughly under the "colonial" heading and ignore the transitional and possibly atypical shifts which occurred during the American Revolution and the early period of nationhood. Also, regional differences were largely ignored. The South was left out of consideration entirely because its industrial development occurred later.

The status of colonial women has been well studied and described and can briefly be summarized for comparison with the later period. Throughout the colonial period there was a marked shortage of women, which varied with the regions and always was greatest in the frontier areas. This (from the point of view of women) favorable sex ratio enhanced their status and position. The Puritan world view regarded idleness as sin; life in an underdeveloped country made it absolutely necessary that each member of the community perform an economic function. Thus work for women, married or single, was not only approved, it was regarded as a civic duty. Puritan town councils expected single girls, widows, and unattached women to be self-supporting and for a long time provided needy spinsters with parcels of land. There was no social sanction against married women working; on the contrary, wives were expected to help their husbands in their trade and won social approval for doing extra work in or out of the home. Needy children, girls as well as boys, were indentured or apprenticed and were expected to work for their keep.

The vast majority of women worked within their homes, where their labor produced most articles needed for the family. The entire colonial production of cloth and clothing and in part that of shoes was in the hands of women. In addition to these occupations, women were found in many different kinds of employment. They were butchers, silversmiths, gunsmiths, upholsterers. They ran mills, plantations, tan yards, shipyards, and every kind of shop, tavern and boarding house. They were gate keepers, jail keepers, sextons, journalists, printers, "doctoresses," apothecaries, midwives, nurses, and teachers. Women acquired their skills the same way as did the men, through apprenticeship training, frequently within their own families.

Absence of a dowry, ease of marriage and remarriage, and a more lenient attitude of the law with regard to women's property rights were manifestations of the improved position of wives in the colonies. Under British common law, marriage destroyed a woman's contractual capacity; she could not sign a contract even with the consent of her husband. But colonial authorities were more lenient toward the wife's property rights by protecting her dower rights in her husband's property, granting her personal clothing, and upholding pre-nuptial contracts between husband and wife. In the absence of the husband, colonial courts granted women "femme sole" rights, which enabled them to conduct their husband's business, sign contracts, and sue. The relative social freedom of women and the esteem in which they were held was commented upon by most early foreign travelers in America.

But economic, legal, and social status tells only part of the story. Colonial society as a whole was hierarchical, and rank and standing in society depended on the position of the men. Women did not play a determining role in the ranking pattern; they took their position in society through the men of their own family or the men they married. In other words, they participated in the hierarchy only as daughters and wives, not as individuals. Similarly, their occupations were, by and large, merely auxiliary, designed to contribute to family income, enhance their husbands' business or continue it in case of widowhood. The self-supporting spinsters were certainly the exception. The underlying assumption of colonial society was that women ought to occupy an inferior and subordinate position. The settlers had brought this assumption with them from Europe; it was reflected in their legal concepts, their willingness to exclude women from political life, their discriminatory educational practices. What is remarkable is the extent to which this felt inferiority of women was constantly challenged and modified under the impact of environment, frontier conditions, and a favorable sex ratio.

By 1840 all of American society had changed. The Revolution had substituted an egalitarian ideology for the hierarchical concepts of colonial life. Privilege based on ability rather than inherited status, upward mobility for all groups of society, and unlimited opportunities for individual self-fulfillment had become ideological goals, if not always realities. For men, that is; women were, by tacit concensus, excluded from the new democracy. Indeed their actual situation had in many respects deteriorated. While, as wives, they had benefitted from increasing wealth, urbanization, and industrialization, their role as economic producers and as political members of society differed sharply from that of men. Women's work outside of the home no longer met with social approval; on the contrary, with two notable exceptions, it was condemned. Many business and professional occupations formerly open to women were now closed, many others restricted as to training and advancement. The entry of large numbers of women into low status, low pay, and low skill industrial work had fixed such work by definition as "woman's work." Women's political status, while legally unchanged, had deteriorated relative to the advances made by men. At the same time the genteel lady of fashion had become a model of American femininity, and the definition of "woman's proper sphere" seemed narrower and more confined than ever.

Within the scope of this essay only a few of these changes can be more fully explained. The professionalization of medicine and its impact on women may serve as a typical example of what occurred in all the professions.

In colonial America there were no medical schools, no medical journals, few hospitals, and few laws pertaining to the practice of the healing arts. Clergymen and governors, barbers, quacks, apprentices, and women practiced medicine. Most practitioners acquired their credentials by reading Paracelsus and Galen and serving an apprenticeship with an established practitioner. Among the semi-trained "physics," surgeons, and healers the occasional "doctoress" was fully accepted and frequently well rewarded. County records of all the colonies contain references to the work of the female physicians. There was even a female Army surgeon, a Mrs Allyn, who served during King Philip's war. Plantation records mention by name several slave women who were granted special privileges because of their useful service as midwives and "doctoresses."

The period of the professionalization of American medicine dates from 1765, when Dr. William Shippen began his lectures on midwifery in Philadelphia. The founding of medical faculties in several colleges, the standardization of training requirements, and the proliferation of medical societies intensified during the last quarter of the 18th century. The American Revolution dramatized the need for trained medical personnel, afforded first-hand battlefield experience to a number of surgeons and brought increasing numbers of semi-trained practitioners in contact with the handful of European-trained surgeons working in the military hospitals. This was an experience from which women were excluded. The resulting interest in improved medical training, the gradual appearance of graduates of medical colleges, and the efforts of medical societies led to licensing legislation. In 1801 Maryland required all medical practitioners to be licensed; in 1806 New York enacted a similar law, followed by all but three states. This trend was reversed in the 1830s and 40s when most states repealed their licensure requirements. This was due to pressure from eclectic, homeopathic practitioners, the public's dissatisfaction with the "heroic medicine" then practiced by licensed physicians, and to the distrust of state regulation, which was widespread during the Age of Jackson. Licensure as prime proof of qualification for the practice of medicine was reinstituted in the 1870s.

In the middle of the 19th century it was not so much a license or an M.D. which marked the professional physician as it was graduation from an approved medical college, admission to hospital practice and to a network of referrals through other physicians. In 1800 there were four medical schools, in 1850, forty-two. Almost all of them excluded women from admission. Not surprisingly, women turned to eclectic schools for training. Harriot Hunt, a Boston physician, was trained by apprenticeship with a husband and wife team of homeopathic physicians. After more than twenty years of practice she attempted to enter Harvard Medical School and was repeatedly rebuffed. Elizabeth Blackwell received her M.D. from Geneva (New York) Medical College, an eclectic school. Sarah Adamson found all regular medical schools closed against her and earned an M.D. in 1851 from Central College at Syracuse, an eclectic institution. Clemence Lozier graduated from the same school two years later and went on to found the New York Medical College and Hospital for women in 1863, a homeopathic institution which was later absorbed into the Flower-Fifth Avenue Hospital.

Another way in which professionalization worked to the detriment of women can be seen in the cases of Drs. Elizabeth and Emily Blackwell, Marie Zakrzewska, and Ann Preston, who despite their M.D.s and excellent training were denied access to hospitals, were refused recognition by county medical societies, and were denied customary referrals by male colleagues. Their experiences were similar to those of most of the pioneer women physicians. Such discrimination caused the formation of alternate institutions for the training of women physicians and for hospitals in which they might treat their patients. The point here is not so much that any one aspect of the process of professionalization excluded women but that the process, which took place over the span of almost a century, proceeded in such a way as to institutionalize an exclusion of women, which had earlier been accomplished irregularly, inconsistently, and mostly by means of social pressure. The end result was an *absolute* lowering of status for all women in the medical profession and a *relative* loss. As the professional status of all physicians advanced, the status differential between male and female practitioners was more obviously disadvantageous and underscored women's marginality. Their virtual exclusion from the most prestigious and lucrative branches of the profession and their concentration in specializations relating to women and children made such disadvantaging more obvious by the end of the 19th century.

This process of pre-emption of knowledge, of institutionalization of the profession, and of legitimation of its claims by law and public acceptance is standard for the professionalization of the sciences, as George Daniels has pointed out. It inevitably results in the elimination of fringe elements from the profession. It is interesting to note that women had been pushed out of the medical profession in 16th-century Europe by a similar process. Once the public had come to accept licensing and college training as guarantees of up-to-date practice, the outsider, no matter how well qualified by years of experience, stood no chance in the competition. Women were the casualties of medical professionalization.

In the field of midwifery the results were similar, but the process was more complicated. Women had held a virtual monopoly in the profession in colonial America. In 1646 a man was prosecuted in Maine for practicing as a midwife. There are many records of well-trained midwives with diplomas from European institutions working in the colonies. In most of the colonies midwives were licensed, registered, and required to pass an examination before a board. When Dr. Shippen announced his pioneering lectures on midwifery, he did it to "combat the widespread popular prejudice against the man-midwife" and because he considered most midwives ignorant and improperly trained.

Yet he invited "those women who love virtue enough, to own their Ignorance, and apply for instruction" to attend his lectures, offering as an inducement the assurance that female pupils would be taught privately. It is not known if any midwives availed themselves of the opportunity.

Technological advances, as well as scientific, worked against the interests of female midwives. In 16th-century Europe the invention and use of obstetrical forceps had for three generations been the well-kept secret of the Chamberlen family and had greatly enhanced their medical practice. Hugh Chamberlen was forced by circumstances to sell the secret to the Medical College in Amsterdam, which in turn transmitted the precious knowledge to licensed physicians only. By the time the use of the instrument became widespread it had become associated with male physicians and male midwives. Similarly in America, introduction of the obstetrical forceps was associated with the practice of male midwives and served to their advantage. By the end of the 18th century a number of male physicians advertised their practice of midwifery. Shortly thereafter female midwives also resorted to advertising, probably in an effort to meet the competition. By the early 19th century male physicians had virtually monopolized the practice of midwifery on the Eastern seaboard. True to the generally delayed economic development in the Western frontier regions, female midwives continued to work on the frontier until a much later period. It is interesting to note that the concepts of "propriety" shifted with the prevalent practice. In 17th-century Maine the attempt of a man to act as a midwife was considered outrageous and illegal; in mid-19th-century America the suggestion that women should train as midwives and physicians was considered equally outrageous and improper.

Professionalization, similar to that in medicine with the elimination of women from the upgraded profession, occurred in the field of law. Before 1750, when law suits were commonly brought to the courts by the plaintiffs themselves or by deputies without specialized legal training, women as well as men could and did act as "attorneys-in-fact." When the law became a paid profession and trained lawyers took over litigation, women disappeared from the court scene for over a century.

A similar process of shrinking opportunities for women developed in business and in the retail trades. There were fewer female storekeepers and business women in the 1830s than there had been in colonial days. There was also a noticeable shift in the kind of merchandise handled by them. Where previously women could be found running almost every kind of retail shop, after 1830 they were mostly found in businesses which served women only.

The only fields in which professionalization did not result in the elimination of women from the upgraded profession were nursing and teaching. Both were characterized by a severe shortage of labor. Nursing lies outside the field of this inquiry since it did not become an organized profession until after the Civil War. Before then it was regarded peculiarly as a woman's occupation, although some of the hospitals and the Army during wars employed male nurses. These bore the stigma of low skill, low status, and low pay. Generally, nursing was regarded as simply an extension of the unpaid services performed by the housewife—a characteristic attitude that haunts the profession to this day.

Education seems, at first glance, to offer an entirely opposite pattern from that of the other professions. In colonial days women had taught "Dame schools" and grade schools during summer sessions. Gradually, as educational opportunities for girls expanded, they advanced just a step ahead of their students. Professionalization of teaching occurred between 1820 and 1860, a period marked by a sharp increase in the number of women teachers. The spread of female seminaries, academies, and normal schools provided new opportunities for the training and employment of female teachers.

This trend, which runs counter to that found in the other professions, can be accounted for by the fact that women filled a desperate need created by the challenge of the common schools, the ever-increasing size of the student body, and the westward growth of the nation. America was committed to educating its children in public schools, but it was insistent on doing so as cheaply as possible. Women were available in great numbers, and they were willing to work cheaply. The result was another ideological adaptation: in the very period when the gospel of the home as woman's only proper sphere was preached most loudly, it was discovered that women were the natural teachers of youth, could do the job better than men, and were to be preferred for such employment. This was always provided, of course, that they would work at the proper wage differential—30 to 50 per cent of the wages paid male teachers was considered appropriate. The result was that in 1888 in the country as a whole 63 per cent of all teachers were women, while the figure for the cities only was 90.04 per cent.

It appeared in the teaching field, as it would in industry, that role expectations were adaptable provided the inferior status group filled a social need. The inconsistent and peculiar patterns of employment of black labor in the present-day market bear out the validity of this generalization.

There was another field in which the labor of women was appreciated and which they were urged to enter—industry. From Alexander Hamilton to Matthew Carey and Tench Coxe, advocates of industrialization sang the praises of the working girl and advanced arguments in favor of her employment. The social benefits of female labor particularly stressed were those bestowed upon her family, who now no longer had to support her. Working girls were "thus happily preserved from idleness and its attendant vices and crimes," and the whole community benefitted from their increased purchasing power.

American industrialization, which occurred in an underdeveloped economy with a shortage of labor, depended on the labor of women and children. Men were occupied with agricultural work and were not available or were unwilling to enter the factories. This accounts for the special features of the early development of the New England textile industry: the relatively high wages, the respectability of the job and relatively high status of the mill girls, the patriarchal character of the model factory towns, and the temporary mobility of women workers from farm to factory and back again to farm. All this was characteristic only of a limited area and of a period of about two decades. By the late 1830s the romance had worn off: immigration had supplied a strongly competitive, permanent work force willing to work for subsistence wages; early efforts at trade union organization had been shattered, and mechanization had turned semi-skilled factory labor into unskilled labor. The process led to the replacement of the New England-born farm girls by immigrants in the mills and was accompanied by a loss of status and respectability for female workers.

The lack of organized social services during periods of depression drove ever greater numbers of women into the labor market. At first, inside the factories distinctions between men's and women's jobs were blurred. Men and women were assigned to machinery on the basis of local need. But as more women entered industry the limited number of occupations open to them tended to increase competition among them, thus lowering pay standards. Generally, women regarded their work as temporary and hesitated to invest in apprenticeship training, because they expected to marry and raise families. Thus they remained untrained, casual labor and were soon, by custom, relegated to the lowest paid, least skilled jobs. Long hours, overwork, and poor working conditions would characterize women's work in industry for almost a century.

Another result of industrialization was in increasing differences in life styles between women of different classes. When female occupations, such as carding, spinning, and weaving, were transferred from home to factory, the poorer women followed their traditional work and became industrial workers. The women of the middle and upper classes could use their newly gained time for leisure pursuits: they became ladies. And a small but significant group among them chose to prepare themselves for professional careers by advanced education. This group would prove to be the most vocal and troublesome in the near future.

As class distinctions sharpened, social attitudes toward women became polarized. The image of "the lady" was elevated to the accepted ideal of femininity toward which all women would strive. In this formulation of values lower-class women were simply ignored. The actual lady was, of course, nothing new on the American scene; she had been present ever since colonial days. What was new in the 1830s was the cult of the lady, her elevation to a status symbol. The advancing prosperity of the early 19th century made it possible for middle-class women to aspire to the status formerly reserved for upper-class women. The "cult of true womanhood" of the 1830s became a vehicle for such aspirations. Mass circulation newspapers and magazines made it possible to teach every woman how to elevate the status of her family by setting "proper" standards of behavior, dress, and literary tastes. *Godey's Lady's Book* and innumerable gift books and tracts of the period all preach the same gospel of "true womanhood"—piety, purity, domesticity. Those unable to reach the goal of becoming ladies were to be satisfied with the lesser goal—acceptance of their "proper place" in the home.

It is no accident that the slogan "woman's place is in the home" took on a certain aggressiveness and shrillness precisely at the time when increasing numbers of poorer women *left* their homes to become factory workers. Working women were not a fit subject for the concern of publishers and mass media writers. Idleness, once a disgrace in the eyes of society, had become a status symbol. Thorstein Veblen, one of the earliest and sharpest commentators on the subject, observed that it had become almost the sole social function of the lady "to put in evidence her economic unit's ability to pay." She was "a means of conspicuously unproductive expenditure," devoted to displaying her husband's wealth. Just as the cult of white womanhood in the South served to preserve a labor and social system based on race distinctions, so did the cult of the lady in an egalitarian society serve as a means of preserving class distinctions. Where class distinctions were not so great, as on the frontier, the position of women was closer to what it had been in colonial days; their economic contribution was more highly valued, their opportunities were less restricted, and their positive participation in community life was taken for granted.

In the urbanized and industrialized Northeast the life experience of middle-class women was different in almost every respect from that of the lower-class women. But there was one thing the society lady and the mill girl had in common—they were equally disfranchised and isolated from the vital centers of power. Yet the political status of women had not actually deteriorated. With very few exceptions women had neither voted nor stood for office during the colonial period. Yet the spread of the franchise to ever wider groups of white males during the Jacksonian age, the removal of property restrictions, the increasing numbers of immigrants who acquired access to the franchise, made the gap between these new enfranchised voters and the disfranchised women more obvious. Quite naturally, educated and propertied women felt this deprivation more keenly. Their own career expectations had been encouraged by widening educational opportunities; their consciousness of their own abilities and of their potential for power had been enhanced by their activities in the reform movements of the 1830s; the general spirit of upward mobility and venturesome entrepreneurship that pervaded the Jacksonian era was infectious. But in the late 1840s a sense of acute frustration enveloped these educated and highly spirited women. Their rising expectations had met with frustration, their hopes had been shattered; they were bitterly conscious of a relative lowering of status and a loss of position. This sense of frustration led them to action; it was one of the main factors in the rise of the woman's rights movement.

The women, who at the first woman's rights convention at Seneca Falls, New York, in 1848 declared boldly and with considerable exaggeration that "the history of mankind is a history of repeated injuries and usurpations on the part of man toward woman, having in direct object the establishment of an absolute tyranny over her," did not speak for the truly exploited and abused working woman. As a matter of fact, they were largely ignorant of her condition and, with the notable exception of Susan B. Anthony, indifferent to her fate. But they judged from the realities of their own life experience. Like most revolutionaries, they were not the most downtrodden but rather the most status-deprived group. Their frustrations and traditional isolation from political power funneled their discontent into fairly utopian declarations and immature organizational means. They would learn better in the long, hard decades of practical struggle. Yet it is their initial emphasis on the legal and political "disabilities" of women which has provided the framework for most of the historical work on women.[1] For almost a hundred years sympathetic historians have told the story of women in America by deriving from the position of middle-class women a generalization concerning all American women. To avoid distortion, any valid generalization concerning American women after the 1830s should reflect a recognition of class stratification.

For lower-class women the changes brought by industrialization were actually advantageous, offering income and advancement opportunities, however limited, and a chance for participation in the ranks of organized labor.[2] They, by and large, tended to join men in their struggle for economic advancement and became increasingly concerned with economic gains and protective labor legislation. Middle- and upper-class women, on the other hand, reacted to actual and fancied status deprivation by increasing militancy and the formation of organizations for woman's rights, by which they meant especially legal and property rights.

The four decades preceding the Seneca Falls Convention were decisive in the history of American women. They brought an actual deterioration in the economic opportunities open to women, a relative deterioration in their political status, and a rising level of expectation and subsequent frustration in a privileged elite group of educated women. It was in these decades that the values and beliefs that clustered around the assertion "Woman's place is in the home" changed from being descriptive of an existing reality to becoming an ideology. "The cult of true womanhood" extolled woman's predominance in the domestic sphere, while it tried to justify women's exclusion from the public domain, from equal education and from participation in the political process by claims to tradition, universality, and a history dating back to antiquity, or at least to the *Mayflower*. In a century of modernization and industrialization women alone were to remain unchanging, embodying in their behavior and attitudes the longing of men and women caught in rapid social change for a mythical archaic past of agrarian family self-sufficiency. In pre-industrial America the home was indeed the workplace for both men and women, although the self-sufficiency of the American yeoman, whose economic well-being depended on a network of international trade and mercantilism, was even then more apparent than real. In the 19th and 20th centuries the home was turned into the realm of woman, while the workplace became the public domain of men. The ideology of "woman's sphere" sought to upgrade women's domestic function by elaborating the role of mother, turning the domestic drudge into a "homemaker" and charging her with elevating her family's status by her exercise of consumer functions and by her display of her own and her family's social graces. These prescribed roles never *were* a reality. In the 1950s Betty Friedan would describe this ideology and rename it "the feminine mystique," but it was no other than the myth of "woman's proper sphere" created in the 1840s and updated by consumerism and the misunderstood dicta of Freudian psychology.

The decades 1800–1840 also provide the clues to an understanding of the institutional shape of the later women's organizations. These would be led by middle-class women whose self-image, life experience, and ideology had largely been fashioned and influenced by these early, transitional years. The concerns of middle-class women—property rights, the franchise, and moral uplift—would dominate the woman's rights movement. But side by side with it, and at times cooperating with it, would grow a number of organizations serving the needs of working women.

American women were the largest disfranchised group in the nation's history, and they retained this position longer than any other group. Although they found ways of making their influence felt continuously, not only as individuals but as organized groups, power eluded them. The mill girl and the lady, both born in the age of Jackson, would not gain access to power until they learned to cooperate, each for her own separate interests. It would take almost six decades before they would find common ground. The issue around which they finally would unite and push their movement to victory was the "impractical and utopian" demand raised at Seneca Falls—the means to power in American society—female suffrage.

Notes

1. To the date of the first printing of this article (1969).
2. In 1979, I would not agree with this optimistic generalization.

POSTSCRIPT

Did the Industrial Revolution Provide More Economic Opportunities for Women in the 1830s?

Professor Gerda Lerner was a pioneer in women's history. A European refugee and playwright, she entered the New School of Social Research at the age of 40, where she also taught the earliest course on women's history in 1962. At the same time, she developed an interest in African American history when she wrote the screenplay for the film directed by her husband, *Black Like Me,* based on a best-selling memoir about a white man who dyed his skin black in order to experience what it was like to be non-white.

As a 43-old graduate student at Columbia University, she convinced her mentors that a dissertation about the Grimke sisters, who were southern abolitionists, was a viable subject. She published *The Grimke Sisters from South Carolina, Rebels Against Slavery* (Houghton Mifflin, 1967), though a number of major publishers rejected the manuscript because it lacked information about the psychological failings of the sisters.

Recognizing that women "are and always have been at least half of humankind and most of the time have been a majority," Lerner argued that women have their own history, which should not be marginalized by men nor forced to be subject to the traditional male framework of political/military/diplomatic/ economic history. Along with other pioneers, she led the search for nontraditional sources that provided information about women: demographic records; census figures; parish and birth records; property taxes; organizational files of churches, schools, police, and hospital records; and finally, diaries, family letters, and autobiographies that are more attuned to a women's point of view.

Lerner suggested that the writing of women's history could be divided into four parts: (1) "compensatory history," where historians search for women whose experiences deserve to be well-known; (2) "contribution history" of women worthy to topics and issues deemed important to the American mainstream; (3) testing familiar narratives and rewriting generalizations when they appear to be wrong; and (4) understanding gender as a social construct, and rewriting and developing new frameworks and concepts to understand women's history.

"The Lady and the Mill Girl" is a classic article that uses the conceptual framework of the "cult of motherhood" to demonstrate how the experiences of middle-class and working-class women in the Jacksonian period were different from men because women were unable to vote and were driven out of the medical, legal, and business professions, which provided upwardly mobile occupations for men. Written a decade before historians began to use the term "market revolution," Lerner's article argues that industrialization retarded women's attempts at economic advancements outside the home. The two professions dominated by women—teaching and nursing—were both poorly paid and were an extension of the family values carried outside the home.

Professor Nancy F. Cott takes a more optimistic view of the accomplishments of women in the years from 1780 to 1835. She draws upon the letters and diaries of literate New England women to trace their changing roles and attitudes. These are nontraditional sources but are essential to writing the social history of any particular group.

Through these writings, Cott documents the shifting role of women inside and outside the family. In the late eighteenth century, these women performed household chores as well as worked at home in the "putting out" system used to make textiles and shoes. (This is similar to work performed in the house today by both sexes through use of the computer.)

By the 1830s, merchant capitalism was flourishing and had created a number of factories along the various rivers in Massachusetts, Rhode Island, and Connecticut. Many single women left home temporarily and worked in these factories, which were originally intended to provide clean and safe working conditions as compared to the English mills portrayed in the novels of Charles Dickens. Cott uses the diaries of some of these workers to describe their lifestyle, but the fullest account is found in Thomas Dublin's *Women at Work: the Transformation of Work and Community in Lowell, Massachusetts, 1826–1860* (Columbia University Press, 1979). Dublin also published a primary source collection *From Farm to Factory: Women's Letters 1830–1860* (Columbia University Press, 1981, 1993). Dublin's Lowell factory workers developed a collective consciousness because they spent all their leisure hours in boarding houses and their 72-hour workweek tending the looms. Their contact with the male owners was nonexistent. The modern corporation that separated owners and management was evident at Lowell, where the Boston capitalists who started the company rarely appeared. Usually, the women tending the mills would have their only contact with their immediate male supervisors. Consequently, the women could enforce their moral standards in the boarding house and get rid of women whom they deemed promiscuous. Their collective consciousness also made it easier for the women to organize strikes when their owners cut the wages, as they did in 1834 and 1836.

Dublin points out that the strikes did not succeed. He is unclear about the reasons for their failures. The major one could be that women viewed the work at Lowell as temporary, a chance to build up a dowry that they could use to get married. The cult of motherhood was strong even for female factory workers. Marriage was still their primary goal.

The Lowell experiment was short-lived. Though the female workers supported the Ten Hour Movement, along with men working in separate organizations, the early labor movement, like the protesters in the 1880s and 1890s, failed to achieve their objectives. By the 1850s, the "Daughters of Free Men" were replaced by Irish immigrants.

Cott believes that a social transformation took place in the United States between 1780 and 1835. She accepts Professor E. P. Thompson's distinction of "task orientation of traditional artisan work patterns" in pre-industrial society with the "time, work-discipline, industrial capitalism" of the factory system. See Thompson, "Time, Work-Discipline, and Industrial Capitalism," *Past and Present* (1967).

Although Cott accepts the constraints of the women's sphere in limiting women's economic opportunities outside the home, she is much more optimistic than Lerner or Barbara Welter about the restrictions against women in professions not associated with women's sphere, such as nursing or teaching.

The bibliography on women's history is enormous. A critical analysis of "the cult of motherhood" as a framework of analysis can be found in Linda K. Kerber's "Separate Spheres, Female Worlds, Woman's Place: The Rhetoric of Women's History" *Journal of American History* (June 1988), reprinted in *Toward an Intellectual History of Women* (University of North Carolina Press, 1997).

Two excellent textbooks on women's history with extensive bibliographies are Sara M. Evans, *Born for Liberty: A History of Women in America* (The Free Press, 1989) and Nancy Woloch, *Woman and the American Experience,* 2nd ed. (McGraw Hill, 1994).

The essays in this issue deal with white middle-class women. Linda K. Kerber and Jane Sherron De Hart have pulled together a collection of essays and primary sources that focus on working-class women as well as immigrants and non-white minority groups—African Americans, Asians, Hispanics, and Native Americans—in *Women's America: Refocusing the Past,* 6th ed. (Oxford University Press, 2004). See also Vicki L. Ruiz and Ellen Carol Du Bois, eds., *Unequal Sisters: A Multicultural Reader in U.S. Women's History,* 3rd ed. (Routledge, 1990). For an example of the immigrants who succeeded the "Daughters of Freemen" at the Lowell mills, see Hasia Diner, *Erin's Daughters in America: Irish Immigrant Women in the Nineteenth Century* (Johns Hopkins University Press, 1983). Finally, Nancy Cott et al. have collected some important primary sources of women from colonial times to 1900 in *Root of Bitterness: Documents of the Social History of American Women,* 2nd ed. (Northeastern University Press, 1996).

Internet References . . .

Birth of a Nation & Antebellum America

This site, maintained by Mike Madin, provides links to a wide assortment of topics from the early national and antebellum eras.

http://www.academicinfo.net/usindnew.html

Reform and Reformers in the Antebellum Era

This page from the George Mason University website includes a summary essay by Professor Nancy Hewitt and links to six primary documents, each relating to a different reform initiative of the period.

http://chnm.gmu.edu/lostmuseum/lm/274

The Descendents of Mexican War Veterans

An excellent source for the history of the Mexican-American War (1846–1848), which includes images, primary documents, and maps.

http://www.dmwv.org/mexwar/mexwar1.htm

John Brown's Holy War

This site was developed to complement the Public Broadcasting System's program on John Brown. It includes interactive maps, information on many of Brown's abolitionist acquaintances, links to virtual tours of the farmhouse where Brown and his followers gathered prior to the Harpers Ferry raid, as well as the transcript of the video itself.

http://www.pbs.org/wgbh/amex/brown

Antebellum America

*P*ressures and trends that began building in the early years of the American nation continued to gather momentum until conflict was almost inevitable. Population growth and territorial expansion brought the country into conflict with other nations. The United States had to respond to challenges from Americans who felt alienated from or forgotten by the new nation because the ideals of human rights and democratic participation that guided the founding of the nation had been applied only to selected segments of the population.

- Was Antebellum Temperance Reform Motivated Primarily by Religious Moralism?
- Was the Mexican War an Exercise in American Imperialism?
- Was John Brown an Irrational Terrorist?

ISSUE 11

Was Antebellum Temperance Reform Motivated Primarily by Religious Moralism?

YES: Mark Edward Lender and James Kirby Martin, from *Drinking in America: A History* (The Free Press, 1982)

NO: John J. Rumbarger, from *Profits, Power, and Prohibition: Alcohol Reform and the Industrializing of America, 1800–1930* (State University of New York Press, 1989)

ISSUE SUMMARY

YES: Mark Edward Lender and James Kirby Martin argue that the impetus for the temperance movement in the first half of the nineteenth century was grounded deeply in Protestant denominations whose clergy and lay leaders supported reforms that would create a social-moral order that was best for the public welfare.

NO: John J. Rumbarger concludes that nineteenth-century temperance reform was the product of a pro-capitalist market economy whose entrepreneurial elite led the way toward abstinence and prohibition campaigns in order to guarantee the availability of a more productive work force.

In the era following the War of 1812, several dramatic changes in the United States occurred. Andrew Jackson's military triumph over the British at the Battle of New Orleans generated a wave of nationalistic sentiment in the country, even though the victory had come two weeks *after* the Treaty of Ghent officially ended the conflict with England. The republic experienced important territorial expansion with the addition of new states in each of the half-dozen years following the end of the war. A "transportation revolution" produced a turnpike, canal, and railroad network that brought Americans closer together and enhanced the opportunities for economic growth. In politics, the demise of the nation's first two-party system, following the decline of the Federalists, was succeeded by the rise to prominence of the Democratic and, later, the Whig Parties.

Although some historians have characterized this period as the "era of good feelings," it is important to remember that many Americans were aware that the nation was not without its problems. Drawing upon intellectual precepts associated with the Enlightenment, some citizens believed in the necessity of and potential for perfecting American society. Ralph Waldo Emerson captured the sense of mission felt by many nineteenth-century men and women when he wrote: "What is man for but to be a Re-former, a Re-maker of what man has made; a renouncer of lies; a restorer of truth and good, imitating that great Nature which embosoms us all, and which sleeps no moment on an old past, but every hour repairs herself, yielding to us every morning a new day, and with every pulsation a new life?" These ideas were reinforced by the encouragement for moral and spiritual perfection produced by the revival movement known as the Second Great Awakening. Significantly, revivalists like Charles G. Finney combined a desire to promote salvation through faith and spiritual conversion with an active interest in social change.

This "age of reform" was a multifaceted and often interrelated movement. Reformers, most of who were from the middle and upper classes, hoped to improve the condition of inmates in the country's prisons and asylums or to encourage temperance or even total abstinence from drinking. Some reformers emphasized the necessity of maintaining peace in the world, while others hoped to improve the educational system for the masses. Still others directed their energies into movements emphasizing clothing reform for women or dietary reform. Finally, large numbers of Americans sought to stimulate human progress through campaigns to improve the status of women and to eliminate slavery.

Thousands of Americans belonged to one or more of these antebellum reform societies, but some controversy exists as to the motivations of these reformers. Were they driven by humanitarian impulses that surfaced in the reinvigorated American republic after 1815? Or was it merely self-interest that encouraged middle- and upper-class Americans to attempt to order society in such a way as to preserve their positions of power? Who were these reformers, and what were their strategies and goals for improving the society in which Americans lived? This issue addresses these questions from the perspective of those involved in the efforts to moderate or abolish the consumption of alcohol in the United States.

In the first selection, Mark Edward Lender and James Kirby Martin examine the characteristics of temperance reformers in the first half of the nineteenth century. These reformers, they argue, drew upon the perfectionist message presented during the Second Great Awakening in an effort to create a more virtuous nation. They describe a moral elite consisting of ministers and laypeople who served as "stewards of society" by leading a mass reformation in the drinking culture of the United States that shifted over time from a focus on moral suasion to bring about more moderate consumption of "ardent spirits," to political movements for total abstinence.

In the second selection, John J. Rumbarger argues that American temperance reform was grounded in a market economy in which employers sought to impose limits on the traditional drinking habits of their employees as a means of improving the productive capacity of their work force. Temperance reform, according to Rumbarger, became a political effort to create a social order congenial to entrepreneurial capitalism.

241

YES ↵

**Mark Edward Lender and
James Kirby Martin**

Drinking in America: A History

Portland, Maine, 1851

On June 2, 1851, the governor of Maine signed into law a bill prohibiting the
sale of beverage alcohol in the state. In 1846 Maine had enacted a similar provision on a limited basis, but the earlier law had been "mild," as one temperance worker recalled, its negligible penalties "striking no terror to the hearts
of the liquor dealers." Not so the 1851 version: This statute provided for the
destruction of any liquor confiscated after the bill became law. The "Maine
Law" was America's first statewide prohibition statute, and it represented the
culmination of two generations of temperance agitation. To pass a law was one
thing; however, to enforce it was another. In 1851 the burning question was
whether the tough legislation would work. "All eyes were at once turned upon
Maine," another antiliquor crusader remembered, "to see if she would execute
her law." In reality, the immediate focus of attention was narrower than the
state: "All eyes" were actually on one city—Portland.

There was good reason. The mayor of Portland was Neal Dow, renowned
in his generation as the "Prophet of Prohibition" and, more to the point, as the
"Father of the Maine Law." While other towns moved quickly to enforce the
law—the mayor of Bangor opened Independence Day festivities by smashing
ten kegs of confiscated booze—most of the nation expected the real test to come
at the hands of Mayor Dow. He had already resolved to disappoint no one in this
regard. As soon as the governor affixed his signature, Dow issued an ultimatum:
Portland liquor dealers had sixty days to get their stocks out of town. After that,
the city would seize and destroy all liquor. People were waiting for day sixty-
one and Dow himself, who had dreamed for years of such a time, intended to
enforce prohibition to the letter, even in the face of violent opposition.

Neal Dow was a formidable man. Possessed of immense self-confidence
and burning drive, he had risen from relatively modest means to become one
of Maine's leading businessmen. He had done well in tanning, banking, and
timber. Dow was also a reformer—and a zealous one. Thoroughly committed to the rising industrial-commercial world that had nurtured him, he was
convinced that this new society was the way of the future for America. Dow's
view of the American future was an article of faith—a faith rooted deeply in
the republicanism of the Revolutionary generation. Dow also saw the good

society in holistic terms, and he linked spiritual, social, and political ideals in a single vision. Thus, the new era would be an immense benefit—it could demonstrate the abilities of a virtuous people to create a national order dedicated to justice, human dignity, and liberty. Progress and opportunity would abound within this context, sustained by citizens committed to shared values and common ideals. And if only America strove to fulfill its republican potential, Dow believed, then Providence would smile. In the thinking of the Maine crusader, God had offered the United States the chance both to provide bountifully for its own populace and to show humanity what a liberty-loving nation could accomplish in an autocratic world. In its essentials, then, Dow's world view echoed the old republicanism—drawn into the dawning industrial age of the mid-nineteenth century to be sure—but very much carved in the image of men like Benjamin Rush, who had earlier struggled to assure the survival of the republican experiment—both politically and *morally.* (We will therefore call Dow, and those of his mind, "neore-publicans.")

As a patriot and a Christian (the two were one in his mind), Dow felt called to oppose anything inimical to his vision of a virtuous United States. He was active on a number of reform fronts, but he was first and foremost a temperance man. Like Benjamin Rush, the mayor of Portland saw drunkenness as the nexus of a host of evils, none of which had a place in the good society. The list, like Rush's two generations before, was long, embracing civil disorder; immorality; the costs of courts, jails, and poorhouses; industrial accidents and inefficiency; and money wasted on liquor. Nor did he overlook the human side of the issue. Dow honestly thought that liquor was a prime disrupter of homes and a source of other domestic grief. Alcohol even damaged his own family: He once tried to dissuade a publican from selling to one of his wife's relatives; the taverner refused, the in-law went to a drunkard's grave, and Dow swore vengeance. Absolute prohibition of all beverage alcohol, he concluded, was the only cure for personal intemperance and its social ill effects. Toward that end he bent his considerable energies, sustained by the faith that he labored in a just cause. . . .

The Antiliquor Response: The Origins of the Temperance Movement

. . . There was no temperance movement at the dawn of the nineteenth century, but animosity toward drinking excesses was clearly on the rise in certain quarters. Methodists, who along with the Quakers in the 1780s had denounced the use of distilled spirits for religious reasons, spread the tenet of abstinence from hard liquor as their sect experienced an explosive growth in numbers after the Revolution. Individual ministers of other religious groups also denounced strong drink on moral grounds, and Benjamin Rush himself remained the major public champion of temperance until his death in 1813. There were even a few organized efforts to deal with specific problems. In Litchfield County, Connecticut, for instance, some two hundred of the "most respectable farmers," challenging the wisdom of the day, concluded that drinking on the job did more harm than good and, in 1789, discontinued the customary liquor rations for farm labor. In 1808, a small group in Moreau, New

York, founded the nation's first temperance society, also citing the deleterious impact of liquor on farm productivity.

Indeed, as these first temperance groups were being born, the United States was getting ready to enter an era of intense social reform activity—activity that merged temperance with goals as diverse as school reform, abolition, and women's rights. This ferment, growing out of the times, left the young republic in turmoil over a host of new social forces—forces that moved the nation steadily toward its modern character as a pluralist democracy. Thousands streamed toward the frontiers and beyond the influence of Eastern institutions; the increasingly powerful Jeffersonians (followed by the Jacksonians of the 1820s and thirties) offered citizens a democratic ideology stressing unfettered individualism as the basis of freedom, as opposed to the communal ideals of traditional republicanism; the arrival of major immigrant populations, unfamiliar with American values and having their own creeds and customs, also seemed likely to affect the character of the young nation; and around the corner loomed the industrialization process, with unknown consequences for the largely agrarian order of the postrevolutionary generation. While no one could predict where these trends would eventually lead, many Americans rejoiced at the apparent evolution of old social relationships and values and saw in the dawning age new and greater political and economic opportunities for all citizens. On the other hand, the specter of change also left a great many people, especially older native American families, perplexed and apprehensive.

Those who questioned the wisdom of these potentially radical changes were the nineteenth-century heirs of the old republicans—the neorepublicans of the stripe of Neal Dow. Like Benjamin Rush, former President John Adams, and others of the Revolutionary generation (many of whom were still alive in the early 1800s), they worshiped basic political liberty and the institutions of the republic, but only in the context of a stable social-moral order governed by men of sufficient character and virtue to appreciate what was needed for the welfare of all citizens. They were by no means against progress—many would play active roles in nineteenth-century commerce and industry—but they feared that, without proper social controls, the forces inherent in dawning American individualism and pluralism would sweep away the Revolutionary heritage. As reformers, they looked backward in seeking to provide for a stable, moral future.

For many neorepublicans, safeguarding society depended, as they frankly admitted, upon social and governmental leadership by men such as themselves—men of proven distinction, who would set high examples of personal conduct and had the courage to act vigorously in defense of accepted standards. Historians have termed this strain of thought the "stewardship tradition"; that is, a moral elite would act as stewards for the rest of the nation, guiding and correcting their behavior. The elite would also lead a mass reformation in American values, thus assuring a citizenry of sufficient virtue to sustain the republic in the face of potentially disruptive pluralist influences. Such reform ultimately stressed the elimination of all social evils, at least those that bothered the neorepublicans.

These moral stewards honestly thought that they knew best how to order the affairs of other men and women. And they were equally convinced that reform would be a vital step in fulfilling the old republican dream of establishing the United States as a beacon of promise for the rest of humanity. If they could see to it that Americans acted in a manner worthy of their destiny, Providence itself—working largely through the major Protestant denominations—would guide the fortunes of the nation. Lyman Beecher of Connecticut, a staunch Calvinist minister and a prominent neorepublican reformer, revealed much of this faith in one of his calls for national refomation. "If it had been the design of Heaven to establish a powerful nation in the full enjoyment of civil and religious liberty," he wrote in the early 1800s, "where all the energies of man might find full scope and excitement," and "to show the world by one great successful experiment of what man is capable," where else would God do it "but in this country!" From this perspective, to labor for reform and for a perfected republic was to labor for the Lord, and hundreds set to the task with determination and confidence. . . .

These neorepublican considerations were fully evident in the first major attempt to unite scattered temperance voices. That movement came into being in 1811, at the annual meeting of the general assembly of the Presbyterian church in Philadelphia. An aged Dr. Rush, then only two years from death but still a zealous guardian of the republic, sent the assembly one thousand copies of the *Inquiry* for distribution. He also urged the gathered clergymen to take a strong protem-perance stance. In his appeal, the old physician was concerned less with theological matters than with the social-moral influence of organized religious groups. The churches in general, and the Presbyterian church in particular—one of America's oldest and most prestigious sects—carried immense weight with the public, and Rush knew that any cause espoused from the pulpit would become a cause to be reckoned with.

The Presbyterian clergy did not let him down. They, too, were concerned with the social forces being let loose upon the land. As members of a denomination long identified with the fortunes of the republic, they also feared the loss of national stability and of time-honored values and social relationships. Accordingly, the assembly issued a statement denouncing the drinking habits of the day, lamenting that "we are ashamed but constrained to say that we have heard of the sin of drunkenness prevailing—prevailing to a great degree—prevailing among even some of the visible members of the household of faith." The clergy then appointed a committee to report on how to best restrain "the excessive and intemperate use of spiritous liquors." Rush was delighted, especially because these actions attracted considerable public notice.

Presbyterian leaders next rallied their state congregations. Throughout 1811 and 1812, church groups in New England and the Middle Atlantic states offered prayers, resolutions, and sermons in the nascent battle against drink. In Connecticut, the state Presbyterian association struck directly at American drinking practices. The association called not only for preaching against intemperance but also for excluding spirits from the family diet and from church gatherings; parents were urged to warn their children against liquor and "farmers, mechanics and manufacturers" to end liquor rations for their workers. Men such as Lyman Beecher also wanted temperance literature distributed and societies formed to promote public morality. After some preliminary planning, the

Society for the Promotion of Morals appeared in 1813 to combat the related vices of intemperance, Sabbath-breaking, and profanity. The same year and with similar goals in mind, some of the most prominent sons of Massachusetts founded the Massachusetts Society for the Suppression of Intemperance, the first statewide temperance organization.

Thus, the seed planted at the Presbyterian assembly of 1811 had taken root. Over the next decade, the temperance movement increased in strength and tempo. The Presbyterians, however, did not work alone. In 1816, the Methodists pledged to redouble their temperance efforts, and their ministers spread the gospel into the Midwest and South. Congregationalists, a number of Baptists, a few Anglicans, and many of the evangelical sects that flourished in the early 1800s took up the crusade as well. In fact, the chief credit for popularizing the temperance message before the mid-1820s must go to the Protestant churches, whose social influence and sheer numbers began to have a national impact.

A formal national temperance movement emerged in 1826: the American Society for the Promotion of Temperance (later known as the American Temperance Society). Leadership rested firmly in the hands of socially prominent clergy and laymen, whose proclaimed purpose was the reformation of the nation under the guidance of "holy men" who would "induce all temperate people to continue temperate" through abstinence from ardent spirits. The early temperance movement, then, was *not* a prohibitionist crusade; in adopting this moderate approach, the new society had taken a page right out of Benjamin Rush. Rush, whose memory the society revered and whose writings became movement gospel (he would eventually be known as the "Father of Temperance" and the "True Instaurator"), had counseled precisely such a course. Permitting the measured use of nondistilled beverages would prevent the drinking excesses associated with hard liquor.

Armed with this moderate doctrine, the Society for the Promotion of Temperance performed admirably. It virtually assumed the national leadership of temperance activities. The society helped organize local units, sent lecturers into the field, distributed literature (including the *Inquiry*), and served as a clearinghouse for movement information. Within three years, in large measure inspired by society proselytizing, 222 state and local antiliquor groups were at work across the land. The crusade was by no means at peak strength numerically, nor did it have any appreciable political influence at this stage; yet temperance reform now constituted a burgeoning national movement.

"Pure Water": Temperance Becomes Total Abstinence

As the temperance movement gathered momentum, additional reform motives— sometimes intertwined with neorepublican concerns for stability and national perfection—broadened the appeal. For example, the movement was a direct beneficiary of a series of religious revivals that swept the nation in the early nineteenth century. Many of the revivalists included the national perfectionist message in their calls for individual redemption and salvation, with temperance serving the cause of both. Some stressed temperance only as a means of avoiding sin and thus setting one's course toward salvation. Much to the delight of reform leaders, who saw benefits for the cause despite their elitist distaste for the revivalists, thousands of Americans swore off ardent spirits as an article of religious faith.

Fear of alcohol addiction, the enslavement to drink that Rush had described, was instrumental in bringing about a crucial change in the meaning of temperance—the shift from temperance as abstinence from distilled beverages to temperance as total abstinence. Even before the 1820s, some temperance advocates had insisted that prohibition was the only logical way to eliminate drunkenness: Alcohol was alcohol, they argued, whether in the form of beer, wine, cider, or distilled spirits; if alcohol was addictive in one beverage, why not in another? Beers and wines, from this more extreme perspective, were especially pernicious. They promised safety and health while they slowly brought about the drinker's doom. There was "no safe line of distinction between the *moderate* and the *immoderate*" use of alcohol, a Methodist report noted in 1832. That moderate use led to immoderate drinking "is almost as certain as it is insensible." The report ended by questioning "whether a man can indulge . . . at all and be considered temperate."

The most forceful statement of this position came in Lyman Beecher's *Six Sermons on Intemperance*. Beecher delivered them from the pulpit in Litchfield, Connecticut, in 1825. In 1826 he published them, and the *Six Sermons* took their place with Rush's *Inquiry* as temperance movement classics. Any drinking, he argued, was a step toward "irreclaimable" slavery to liquor; people simply could not tell when they crossed the line from moderate use to inebriety—could not tell, that is, until too late. Look out, he said, if you drank in secret, periodically felt compelled to drink, and found yourself with tremors, inflamed eyes, or a "disordered stomach." "You might as well cast loose in a frail boat before a hurricane, and expect safety," Beecher explained, and "you are gone, gone irretrievably, if you do not stop." But most could not stop; the power of alcohol was too strong. This fact, he noted, coupled with the abolition of the liquor traffic, would at least end the country's alcohol problem, as the "generation of drunkards" would "hasten out of time." Total abstinence, Beecher concluded, was the only sure means of personal salvation and societal stability. . . .

Yet most leaders in the temperance movement were leary of total abstinence. From observation, if nothing else, reformers knew all too well that Americans loved to drink—and asking them to abandon whiskey seemed radical enough. Anything more, they believed, would offend the public and weaken the temperance cause, making the movement useless as a means of perfecting the republic. In fact, the founders of the American Temperance Society, while privately favoring total abstinence, dared not make it a tenet of the new organization for fear of outraging both the public and the mass of their colleagues in reform. There was, after all, the moderation legacy of Benjamin Rush, and even some old temperance leaders remained "ardent advocates for the culture of the grape . . . as a preventive of the ravages of intemperance." Accordingly, when a motion to espouse total abstinence came before the first national temperance convention in 1833, it went down to a quick defeat—although the gathering closed by heralding "pure water" as the only truly safe substitute for ardent spirits. . . .

Yet support for prohibition in the 1830s was often haphazard. Most dry workers knew that coerced abstinence was many steps ahead of popular opinion, despite widespread sympathy for more moderate temperance ideas. To press the question too soon, they feared, could provoke an unfavorable reaction, particularly if an unwilling public saw prohibition as an invasion of civil rights. It was a dilemma for drys, but the stakes, a sober republic and all its consequent moral and civil blessings, seemed worth the gamble. They would risk offending the few to guarantee the safety of the many. Theodore Parker of New England, one of the greatest of the antebellum reformers, admitted that prohibition indeed seemed "an invasion of private rights." But he reasoned that it was "an invasion . . . for the sake of preserving the rights of all." While he believed that a drink was fine "when rightly used," Parker was convinced "that nine tenths" of the alcohol used was actually "abused." "The evil is monstrous," he concluded, "so patent, so universal, that it becomes the duty of the state to take care of its citizens; the whole of its parts."

Prohibition had minimal support outside the temperance movement itself before the 1840s, but the political potential of the idea was not lost on the more astute politicians of the day. Whether they were for or against temperance, few government officials were willing to offend dry leaders gratuitously. In fact, many highly placed national officials lent the movement a sympathetic ear. In 1832, for example, the Reverend Justin Edwards, the most active agent of the national society, prevailed upon Secretary of War Lewis Cass to end liquor rations for the army. That same year, the House of Representatives played host to a congressional temperance meeting, which solemnly denounced the manufacture of hard liquor as "incompatible with the obligations of social and moral duty, by every patriot and especially by every Christian in the country." While the legislators promised no legal action to enforce their resolutions, they did claim the right to make law on temperance issues should national well-being so require. Their statement on this count clearly revealed the continuing force of traditional republicanism: They affirmed both the right and the duty of a righteous citizenry to marshall public virtue—sacrificing personal interest for the good of the whole—in defense of communal safety. "The liberties and welfare of the nation," the assemblage recorded, "are . . . indissolubly connected with the morals and virtue of the people; and that, in the enactment of laws for the common benefit, it is" the duty of Congress to protect "the public morals from corruption." Benjamin Rush could not have stated the proposition any better.

How much of this proclamation was mere cant to satisfy dry constituents is hard to determine, although there is no reason to doubt the sincerity of many of the legislators. Some of them, such as Theodore Frelinghuysen of New Jersey and George Briggs of Massachusetts, were true believers, and in 1833 they helped organize the American Congressional Temperance Society. At the same time, politicians on all levels ended treating in their campaigns, which garnered plaudits from the dry leadership. The practice, an American Temperance Society report noted, had been unworthy of the leaders of a "great republic." And even if much of this early political support for temperance was mere expedience, it was powerful testimony to the rising influence of antiliquor forces.

Redeeming the Lost: Revivalists and Republicans

While the temperance movement mulled over the question of prohibition, events transpired that temporarily took the antiliquor initiative away from the established reform societies. A dry revival, led by men with no prior temperance connections, swept the nation in the 1840s, catching reformers almost completely by surprise. This remarkable dry explosion was the "Washingtonian movement," founded by six Baltimore topers in 1840. Sitting in Chase's Tavern one evening, or so tradition has it, these gentlemen turned to a discussion of their tippling ways, which they admitted were undermining their lives. As a consequence—and perhaps as a lark—one of the group, charged with reporting back to his companions, attended a nearby temperance lecture.The delegate emerged from the lecture a new man, not only taking the pledge himself but also persuading his friends to do the same. They decided to work for the reform of other drinkers, and calling themselves the Washington Temperance Society (in honor of the first president), they drew up a total abstinence pledge.

The group succeeded beyond its wildest expectations. Over a thousand men took the society's pledge by the end of the year, and "missionaries" then carried the Washingtonian theme to New York City, where they attracted thousands. After this, the Washingtonians came to represent a full-fledged revival. Societies patterned on the Washingtonian model sprang up everywhere; churches opened their sanctuaries for meetings; and Washingtonian lecturers, such as the spellbinding John B. Gough and John Hawkins, joined the ranks of the most sought-after speakers in the country. . . .

Yet the meteoric rise of the Washingtonians held the seeds of their eventual decline. Like all other revival phenomena, the movement lost momentum, and by 1844 its activities were on the decline. By 1847 almost all the local societies had stopped meeting (although the Boston chapter continued to gather until 1860). More important than declining momentum was the loss of church and non-Washingtonian temperance support. The established churches, which had been allies, had come to resent Washingtonian opposition to their presumed leadership of the dry struggle, and they began to close their doors to movement activities. This prompted Washingtonian attacks on the church, which in turn exacerbated bad feelings. Some clergy envied the success of the lay movement, hurt that ex-alcoholics proved better reformers than learned ministers. "As [the clergy] were neither the originators nor the leaders in the movement," wrote one temperance man, "they felt themselves ignored, [and] therefore refused to have any affiliation for, or lend any assistance to it." At the same time, and for the same reasons, the older temperance societies also began to withdraw support. The societies worried further that the Washingtonians had drained off energies that might otherwise have flowed to them and that the revivalist oriented group lacked the institutional structure and the wider reform vision necessary to preserve the republic. The neglect of legal authority in the fight against liquor was a mistake, they insisted. Even a generally sympathetic temperance observer felt compelled to note that the "triumph of moral suasion was short and doubtful." In that the emotional appeal of the Washingtonians had diverted attention from the societies working toward legal suasion, their activities were actually an "evil." It was true that the Washingtonians had neither long-range programs nor a central organization to sustain what they had won. To save drunkards and then to see thousands of them relapse because liquor was still freely available made less and less sense to the stewardship oriented socities. In their eyes, the Washingtonian experience was proof that real progress could be atained only thorugh legislation. . . .

Despite the controversies that swirled around their cause, the prohibitionists were tireless workers. Throughout the late 1840s, they incessantly lobbied their state legislatures and often allied themselves with other reform groups or political factions that sought dry votes for their own ends. In some states, prohibitionists leagued variously with antislavery Democrats, who were warring with the dominant pro-South wing of their party, and with elements of the Whigs, who were already beginning to lose their party cohesion under the stress of the sectional controversy. The societies and fraternal orders also supported these political efforts, lending votes, literature, organizational skills, and lecturers. Even commercial publishers gave a helping hand, albeit for handsome profits. They brought out an entire genre of dry novels, short stories, plays, and illustrated materials (generally known as "Temperance Tales") that glorified prohibition and warned of the dire medical, social, and moral consequences of drink. Beginning in the 1840s, the tales were best-sellers, a fact further indicating the intense popular interest in prohibition.

Enthusiasm and political pressure finally came to a head in 1851. Neal Dow's Maine Law of that year gave prohibition advocates their first great legislative breakthrough, and they moved quickly to follow up on their victory. In August 1851, another temperance convention met in Saratoga Springs and issued a battle cry for the passage of Maine Laws throughout the nation. Lobbying at the state level redoubled, and prohibition became the goal of what was now clearly one of the most comprehensive political efforts the nation had ever seen. After an enthusiastic campaign directed in part by old stalwart Lyman Beecher, Massachusetts went dry less than a year later. Maine Laws next carried the day in Vermont, Minnesota Territory, and Rhode Island (1852); Michigan (1853); Connecticut and Ohio (1854); and Indiana, New Hampshire, Delaware, Illinois, Iowa, and New York (1855). Similar measures almost won in Wisconsin (where prohibition twice cleared the legislature in 1855, only to meet a governor's veto), Pennsylvania, and New Jersey; across the border, the Canadian provinces of Nova Scotia and New Brunswick added their names to the dry column as well.

Politicized morality thus seemed well on its way to rolling back the tide of over two hundred years of American drinking habits. By the mid-1850s, many dry reformers were congratulating themselves on having destroyed the old consensus on drinking as a positive good, and they eagerly looked forward to national prohibition. Their confidence appeared fully justified. During the 1850s, enough Americans had stopped or moderated their drinking to drop national annual consumption levels well below three gallons of absolute alcohol per capita. These were the lowest rates in the nation's history, and temperance advocates everywhere nodded in agreement when the Reverend John Marsh, one of the more effective agents of the movement, proclaimed the days gone "when drinking was universal; when no table was thought . . . properly spread unless it contained a supply of intoxicating drink; when no person" was held respectable who failed to "furnish it to his guests," when no man thought of refusing liquor or of working without it, when "Ministers of the Gospel . . . were abundantly supplied by their people; when drinkers and rumsellers were unhesitatingly received as members of Christian churches." And they were equally sure that the day was almost at hand when the purified republic would no longer tolerate demon rum anywhere within its borders. . . .

John J. Rumbarger

NO

The Social and Ideological Origins of Drink Reform, 1800–1836

The Social and Ideological Origins of Drink Reform, 1800–1836

The roots of the temperance movement can be found in those social forces working to develop the expansionist tendencies of the American economy. Neither an abstract Puritan heritage nor paternalist conservatism can explain satisfactorily the dynamics that produced the movement to extirpate liquor drinking from America's culture. The earliest temperance societies, like that organized in Litchfield, Connecticut, in 1787, resulted from the efforts of wealthy farmers to curtail drinking among their laborers during harvest time. . . .

Nevertheless, these early societies defined the movement's strategic objective: the increase of productivity by the elimination of daily work breaks for alcoholic refreshment and its unpredictable consequences. These societies also illustrated a mutual desire on the part of property holders to obtain a uniform standard of labor, regardless of considerations that worked to set them in opposition to each other. These employers assumed that it was their prerogative to determine the social conditions that would lower the costs of production. In a market economy such considerations constituted sufficient reason to eliminate customary drinking, and the more so when labor scarcity deprived employers of a traditional instrument of capital accumulation, low wages.

Early concern about popular drinking was forcefully articulated by Benjamin Rush, whose writing on the subject became an ideological touchstone for the temperance movement. . . . His objective could best be obtained by employing "the force of severe manners" to curtail the social habits of drinking. . . .

Typical of the fruits of Rush's pioneering efforts was the temperance society formed by property owners in the Moreau-Northumberland region of Saratoga County, New York. At the beginning of the nineteenth century these agriculturally rich townships supported a diversified local economy of farming, lumbering, milling, and some rudimentary manufacturing. The political and social life of the area was dominated by a squirearchy, but, as elsewhere, it was difficult for them to engage in business enterprise without supplying workers with their customary alcoholic beverages. What distinguished Moreau-Northumberland's temperance pioneers was professional training among those who galvanized the squirearchy into action against liquor drinking.

Billy Clark had studied medicine; Esek Cowan had read law; Lebbius Armstrong was trained for the ministry. All three invested their surplus professional income in land and agricultural production. Clark, for example, owned several farms and had a large investment in a local paper mill. Cowan was a prosperous farm owner with a reputation for innovative husbandry. More important, however, for the purposes of temperance reform, was the common world view—quite like Rush's—the three shared. In one degree or another Moreau's temperance reformers believed society could improve with individual discipline and practical innovation, and that the criterion of improvement was business profits. William Hay, who subsequently headed the society, recalled that Clark was "convinced of the necessity of self-culture, and consequently acquired what are pertinently termed *business habits*." Hay admiringly described Clark as "pecuniarily successful as a physician and a businessman," and also wrote approvingly of Esek Cowan's various employments as a jurist, farmer, and classical scholar. For this kind of man "recreation was only change of employment," and employment was directed towards profit. . . .

These ideological conceptions nurtured temperance reform. But the reformers' stance towards other social classes was flexible: traditional rank or position was not an obstacle for association with like-minded men, provided the requisite social virtues of practical knowledge and disciplined effort could be demonstrated. Despite this apparent democratic appeal, the political ideology of a temperance "middle" class did not look to a reordering of society. Forged as it was in the crucible of business enterprise, it sought ultimately to redirect the energies and activities of capital and labor, but not to alter their social relationship. In the social context of Jeffersonian America, however, temperance ideology was radical in both theory and practice since it claimed to seek another reallocation of wealth and property according to utilitarian norms even as it sought an increase in social productivity. The assumption of the permanency of social stratification, to be dominated by a rationally selected elite, was but poorly masked by notions of individual worth taken to be demonstrated by the social virtues of innovation and discovery wedded to a discipline, including temperance, congenial to business. Because of this critical defect, temperance reformation, insofar as it envisioned a distinct "middle" class, was necessarily procapitalist.

The idea of a middle class proved especially valuable to the socialization process required by young America, which in the period 1820–50 could not compel people to alter their customary behavior sufficiently to modify the social order's value system. Indeed, the idea that personal characteristics and behavior were a form of capital may be seen as the *sine qua non* of American economic development in these years. Thus, all manner of ideologies, both secular and religious, that encouraged the development of internal modes of self-discipline as forms of "moral capital" were encouraged by the early advocates of liquor reform.

During the decades of the 1820s and 1830s temperance reform wherever it appeared became a political effort to create a social order universally congenial to entrepreneurial capitalism. It was during these years that the perceptions of men like Benjamin Rush and Billy Clark took root in business activity outside of agriculture, and attracted attention from such established institutions as the Protestant churches. But while local societies of employers who mutually agreed "that hereafter we will carry on our business without the use of distilled spirits as an article of refreshment, either for ourselves or those whom we may employ" remained on the reform scene, they proved insufficient to the task of extending temperance sentiment. To meet this need and to deal with the realities facing various enterprises, their politicization was required.

In Jeffersonian and Jacksonian America, maritime commerce ranked with agriculture in its importance to the economy. Here, too, liquor was customarily provided for laborers. . . .

In shipbuilding, workers enjoyed ceremonial provisions of strong drink in addition to their daily rations. At the completion of each major stage of construction they joined with shipowners and masters to toast their work's progress. Thus when the keel was put down, the ribs erected, the decking laid, and the masts raised and stepped there would be general celebrations fueled by large amounts of whiskey.

The earliest efforts at reform in these employment areas followed the boycott tactics that were being developed by agricultural temperance societies. In Medford, Massachusetts, for example, a local shipbuilder, Thacher Magoun, refused to permit rum or distilled spirits to be used in his shipyard. Magoun's 1817 no-rum edict was immediately interpreted by his laborers as "practically an increase in the working time, the employer thus saving the cost of time as well as the cost of the rum." Other Medford shipbuilders followed Magoun's lead, even to the point of raising wages. These boycotts could only be partially effective, however, because of the apprentice system and the grog shop, which furnished money and the means to smuggle the contraband refreshment into the yards.

By 1819, temperance advocates outside of agricultural societies had developed an analysis of the liquor problem that would eventually permit them to go beyond the limits of the boycott, and thus politicize the temperance movement. Thomas Hertell's *An Expose of the Causes of Intemperate Drinking and the Means by which It May Be Obviated* considered the entire social order to be the obstacle to temperance reform. Hertell implied that reform could only succeed if society in general were reformed with respect to drinking.

Hertell, who served for more than a dozen years on the bench of New York City's maritime court, asserted that his antiliquor convictions proceeded from the fact that "intemperate drinking is inimical to agricultural and mechanical, as well as moral improvement." He maintained that neither distillers nor the grog shop lay at the root of the problem; both were symptoms and consequences. The real cause of society's intemperate drinking was to be found in the "intemperate use of ardent liquor [which] originates in the fashions, habits, customs, and examples of what are called the upper or wealthy classes of the community." Because of the universal employment of such drinks by society's elites in both public and private, Hertell concluded that "inebriating drinks" had gained sanction as the "median universally adopted by society for manifesting friendship and good will, one to another."

Hertell believed that society's lower orders habitually emulated the upper, and so he argued that self-reformation by the wealthy must come before a general reform. Moreover, Hertell insisted that without a general temperance reform, nascent manufacturing enterprizes could not hope to succeed for "there is scarcely to be found among the laboring class, any who do not drink, and drink too much." Drinking customs were depriving manufacturers of quality manpower. "What single measure," he asked rhetorically, "would do more to further [manufacturing and agricultural development] than the destruction of the custom of giving ardent spirits to working people of every description."

Hertell's analysis of the liquor problem pulled together several strands in the developing temperance movement, and extended the focus of the reform-ers' concerns beyond agriculture and commerce to manufacturing. The reform impulse had derived from the pragmatic observation that customary drinking diminished productivity. Initially, reformers focused on the ordinary drinks—"ardent spirits"—of the working class as the principal source of abuse, and they continued to rely on the boycott as the means of curtailing and eliminat-ing drinking.

On the other hand, Hertell insisted on the need of society's elites (includ-ing the churches) to exercise rigid self-restraint. Only when this class acted to end its sanction of drinking would "useful industry . . . become fashionable," and would "the already over-run and overrated learned professions" be aban-doned for the "honorable calling" of the mechanical trades. Hertell looked to the formation of an antiliquor class consciousness that would act not only to protect its traditional base in agriculture and commerce, but also extend its concerns to American manufacturing. Of primary significance, however, is the fact that this attention to the responsibility of America's elite for the general well-being of society gave the temperance reform its peculiarly moralistic char-acter, its ambivalence about the use of the state, and its connection with the Protestant churches.

During the years leading to the politicization of the temperance move-ment, American society underwent severe stress. Between 1800 and 1820, war and depression, accompanied by the introduction of the factory system, released latent hostilities that frequently expressed themselves in inchoate public drunk-enness and disrespect towards religious and secular authority—or so it seemed to men like Lyman Beecher, the Congregationalist clergyman-reformer. Yet Beecher's consideration of social policy did not produce any effort to define the liquor problem in ways fundamentally different from those discussed. Indeed, during these years the established churches wedded themselves firmly to the emerging temperance movement in ways that sought to reinforce the move-ment's fundamental purposes. In 1812, for example, Beecher brought an ad hoc report before the General Association of Congregational and Presbyterian clergy wherein he asserted that intemperance was the mutual problem of the "Civil and Religious order," and recommended that employers cease providing liquor to their employees. Beecher also warned his colleagues that their efforts must remain within the boundaries of the "sanction of public sentiment," and thus echoed Benjamin Rush's plea for a regime of severe manners.

Ultimately the concerns of activist clergymen like Beecher were identical to those of men like Thomas Hertell and Mathew Carey, the Philadelphia publisher who helped establish the Philadelphia Society for the Promotion of National Industry. In 1820 Carey brought out Beecher's sermon, "The Means of National Prosperity," which encouraged the expansion of manufacturing, presupposing an abstemious social order, and outlined a role for the nation's churches in fostering this development. . . .

The larger vision of temperance reform articulated by Thomas Hertell and Lyman Beecher took firm root within the establishments of the Northeast during and immediately following the Napoleonic wars. Mercantile capital, the center of much early temperance concern, fueled the expansion of the nation's young manufacturing enterprises and brought to them the problems of absentee owners seeking to insure their investments in an unsure world. Made aware during these years of their own role in perpetuating the "drinking usages" of society, American capitalists organized to secure a dry working class. By 1834, Walter Channing, a pioneering member of the Massachusetts Society for the Suppression of Intemperance, recalled with some exaggerated pride that it was only when "men of great consideration . . . solemnly impressed with the ruinous progress of intemperance . . . came out as one man to make an open declaration of their convictions" that temperance reform began to progress.

The American Temperance Society (ATS), founded in January 1826 by Marcus Morton, a colleague of Channing, became the vehicle for the unified expression of class interest and coordinated action that Channing was to praise. Morton, who was "ahead of his time" in matters pertaining to labor reform, organized an umbrella society because of the deepening conviction that existing temperance societies were weak and ineffective. "Their object was," the ATS complained, "to regulate the use of ardent spirits, not to abolish it."

ATS envisioned a decentralized temperance apparatus, hierarchically organized from the local through the national level so that the smallest antiliquor organizations could "regulate their own movements and efforts according to their own views of necessity and expediency, and . . . their own wants and ability." The work of the ATS itself was to provide each and all with a common analysis of the liquor problem that corresponded to the class-conscious need for property owners to abstain totally from the use of distilled liquor, and to aid in the formation of state and local societies that adhered to this view of the problem. To oversee this work, Morton's group decided that a full-time paid secretary would be necessary and solicited contributions from "men of known and expansive benevolence, who are blessed with property," and who shared the view "that a system of general and powerful cooperation may be formed, and that a change may in a short time be effected, which will save an incalculable amount of property, and vast multitudes of valuable lives."

The man chosen to carry out the ATS reform was Justin Edwards of Andover Theological Seminary. In part Edwards's own previous skepticism about the efficacy of total abstinence from the use of distilled liquor became a major asset to the new organization. Prior to joining ATS as its secretary, Edwards had "thought [total abstinence] was going much too far . . . that the temperate use of ardent spirit was, for men who labor, in hot weather, necessary." What persuaded Edwards that the pledge of total abstinence by property owners was indeed efficacious was not theological conviction but an experiment conducted at one of the farms of a member of Morton's group in 1825. The result, Edwards testified, was that laborers "performed more labor with greater ease."

Equally and perhaps more important, in the eyes of ATS, total abstinence from hard liquor produced an apparent change in the attitude of laborers. According to Edwards the regime of enforced abstinence made the men "more respectful and uniform in their deportment . . . more contented with their living; more desirous of being present at morning and evening family devotion . . . more attentive at public worship on the Sabbath." Clearly this class-based reform effort saw a vital link between the docility of workers and their productivity on the one hand, and depriving them of liquor on the other.

The ATS, through the work of Edwards and secretaries of state societies affiliated with it, made repeated attempts to use the churches to advance the goal of abolition. Recognizing that distilleries were, for the most part, owned and operated by members of their own social class, ATS and its affiliates viewed the churches as the most appropriate vehicles available to them for the persuasion and coercion of their own. These efforts had profound and disruptive effects upon the churches and the movement itself, but what should not be lost sight of in the dogmatic hairsplitting over the extent to which abstinence was to be demanded is the intent of the reformers. "Ardent spirits" was the ordinary alcoholic beverage of workers. It had been the indifferent success of societies like the Massachusetts Society for the Suppression of Intemperance in seeking "to discontinue the too free use of ardent spirit" that had led to demands for total abolition. The ATS pledge committed affiliated societies to exclude all who "traffic" in ardent spirits and to "discountenance the use of them throughout the Community." It was thus that the churches became putative instruments of the reformers.

In their endeavor to persuade the churches to condemn both moderate drinking and the liquor traffic, ATS concentrated its efforts on the governing bodies of the various Protestant denominations. Such attempts met with indifferent success. The General Conference of the Methodist Episcopal Church, for example, condemned "the pestilential example of temperate drinking," but only inquired rhetorically if churches which tolerated manufacturers and sellers of whisky could be innocent of wrongdoing. The conference did not condemn the latter or move to excommunicate offending individuals. Thus, ATS had to rely upon the vague hopes of "some leading men" of the conference that by 1836 the church would be rid of the traffickers in drink.

The ATS also sought to bring pressure on the churches to expel liquor dealers through the efforts of such men as Wilbur Fisk, president of Wesleyan University, who castigated total abstinence church members for not insisting upon such expulsions and charged the churches with similar complicity. The

ATS executive committee joined in this criticism: "From all parts of the country . . . the greatest difficulties in the way of Temperance Reformation . . . are those members of the church, who still sell ardent spirit."

Such pressures divided the established churches even though they produced condemnations of varying strength from national and state ecclesiastical organizations. The larger ones usually confined their expressions of opinion to vague generalities and left it to specific congregations to act. The Protestant clergy was also encouraged to advance the utilitarian purposes of the reformers. Thus, a Connecticut clergyman maintained that the cause would be well served "if farmers and mechanics would agree not to drink spirits themselves, and not provide them for their workmen."

By 1834 it was clear that the established churches had not made any deep inroads against either moderate drinking or the liquor traffic. In addition, their involvement in reform entailed a necessary hindrance to it since wine was of central importance to the Christian ritual as well as the ordinary drink of the wealthy. When, in the mid-1830s, ATS pushed for total abstinence from all alcoholic beverages and demanded state action against the liquor traffic, the difficulties posed by the churches appeared to outweigh their assets. As one clerical reformer acknowledged to the 1834 New York State Temperance Convention: "I have therefore been pained to see so many inclined to connect their religion with temperance. . . . And I know many individuals, who keep themselves aloof from the temperance society on this account, who would undoubtedly join the ranks, if the cause of temperance could be kept separate from everything else."

While the American Temperance Society concentrated its efforts on arousing the consciousness of property holders through the churches, state societies continued to recruit such people to the cause of temperance by stressing the utilitarian benefits of reform. In July 1833, the *Temperance Recorder,* the official organ of the New York State Temperance Society, reported that the consolidation of the Erie Canal's several towing firms into the Albany and Buffalo Towing Company had enabled the teamsters' employers to gain "control and government" over them, with the result that their intemperate drinking habits had been effectively checked. The same issue praised the society's forwarding of a circular letter to American consuls in Europe, warning émigrés that those who drank would find it difficult to obtain employment, and urging them to affiliate with a temperance society as an aid to finding work. The New York Society, which was dominated by mercantile and landed capitalists like Edward C. Delavan of Albany and Stephen Van Rensselaer of Saratoga, urged "the proprietors of our large, as well as our small manufacturing establishments . . . to take their subject into immediate consideration," since it was clear that intemperance was more dangerous to business prosperity than even foreign competition. The New Yorkers advised that temperance societies be organized within the factories themselves, and that proprietors and owners become the officers: "Unless proprietors or agents take the lead, nothing need be expected; but by their taking the course recommended . . . all under their control will be brought speedily into this 'ark of safety.'"

But the efforts of the New York Society and ATS to use the churches to arouse a class-conscious temperance sentiment in favor of overseas economic expansion ran afoul of the churches' difficulties and weakened the desired condemnation and divided the reformers. Many reformers recognized that the association of temperance with specific political and economic issues detracted from its class appeal. If the temperance movement were to gain the class support that its adherents believed was crucial, temperance morality would have to be divorced from specific secular and religious issues, and its moral appeal would have to come from an agency not associated with the churches.

In May 1833 ATS directors convened a national convention in Philadelphia to consider these questions and to chart the future course of reform. The four hundred delegates from twenty-four states represented the country's mercantile, manufacturing, and landed capital. Indicative of the range and scope of this class of men are Gerrit Smith and Stephen Van Rensselaer. Together with John Jacob Astor, Smith's father had acquired over one million acres of land in upstate New York, some 700,000 acres of which he passed on to his son in 1819. Van Rensselaer's holdings were equally vast. Both men were outstanding proponents of internal improvements and expanded trade with the West. Smith violently opposed a governmental role in expanding these markets, but Van Rensselaer was a strong advocate of such aid.

Other representatives of mercantile wealth included Edward C. Delavan, Roberts Vaux and his son, Richard, of Philadelphia, Samuel Ward of New York whose family's wealth had been invested in the banking firm of Prime, Ward, and King, Samuel Mifflin of Philadelphia, and John Tappan of Boston. Typical of emerging manufacturing representatives were Amasa Walker of Boston, Jonas Chickering, whose piano manufacturing concern of Stewart and Chickering developed the single casting iron frame for making grand pianos, and Matthew Newkirk, whose cotton goods business provided the funds for his railroad investments. Many of them, Delavan, Newkirk, and Smith, for example, had multiple investments in land, transportation, and manufacturing.

Also attending the first national temperance convention were luminaries from the first ranks of law, politics, religion, and science, many bearing some of the oldest family names in America. Reuben Hyde Walworth, chancellor of New York State, was named the convention's president. Joseph H. Lumpkin (whose brother Wilson was a Georgia planter and governor of the state), who would himself become a member of Georgia's Supreme Court, was named convention vice president. Timothy Pitkin, the author of the first major statistical account of American commerce, was a delegate from Connecticut. John McLean, who was to become president of the College of New Jersey, was a delegate. So also was Samuel L. Southard, Democractic senator from New Jersey. Amos Twitchell, a pioneer heart surgeon, represented New Hampshire. Jonas K. Converse of Burlington, Vermont, was a delegate, as were Philadelphia philanthropists John Sargent and Joseph B. Ingersoll; businessmen-publicists such as Mathew Carey, William Goodell, Thomas Bradford, Jr., and Sylvester Graham were typical delegates.

Other men of similar stature, like chemist Benjamin Silliman of Yale, or perhaps less well known, such as George Chambers, largest landowner in Franklin County, Pennsylvania and a reformer in education and agriculture, filled out the complement of delegates to the Philadelphia meeting. Their differences in economic interest, political affiliation, and religious persuasion were transcended by a fundamental class problem: the liquor question. . . .

In the end, this effort to rely solely upon the resources of property would fail because, as Gerrit Smith had already pointed out, America was a society where the demand for labor could not be met. Would-be employers would find the pledge inadequate and the law insufficient. But from the vantage point of 1834, the antiliquor movement had achieved astounding success. It had aroused the consciousness of virtually the entire propertied class, regardless of particular economic or political interest, to the importance of extirpating the use of distilled alcohol as a precondition of capitalist development. It had created a secular temperance morality that avoided the rigidities of various theologies while, at the same time, it had been able to enlist the churches in raising the consciousness of the "employing class." And it had developed its archetypal propaganda institution, the American Temperance Society, which was controlled by entrepreneurs of all sorts, and state and local temperance societies, which were to organize local property interests for the cause. Finally, the reform was being urged in the direction of a political attack on the liquor traffic itself.

When the United States Temperance Union and its affiliates met at Saratoga Springs in 1836, there appeared to remain but two mutually compatible tasks for the reform: first, spread the new gospel that "it has been proved a thousand times, that more labor can be accomplished in a month, or a year, under the influence of simple nourishing food and unstimulating drink than through the aid of alcohol"; second, organize and launch a political assault on the liquor traffic itself. To further these ends, the USTU named Reverend John Marsh and Edward C. Delavan to its principal offices. Both were fitting choices for the work. Marsh was related by marriage to the Tappan mercantile family of Boston and New York; his cousin Samuel would head the New York and Erie railroad. Delavan, on the other hand, was an active entrepreneur whose fortune had been made, ironically, as an importer of wine, and who came to the temperance reform after Nathaniel Prime, Lynde Catlin, and he had lost three hundred thousand dollars invested in the manufacture of steam engines and other heavy iron work because, they claimed, of "the unfortunate drinking habits [of the workers], which for best of motives, we ourselves encouraged."

POSTSCRIPT

Was Antebellum Temperance Reform Motivated Primarily by Religious Moralism?

Much of the scholarly writing pertaining to the "age of reform" represents a response to the path-breaking compendium published by Alice Felt Tyler over sixty years ago. Her study, *Freedom's Ferment: Phases of American Social History from the Colonial Period to the Outbreak of the Civil War* (University of Minnesota Press, 1944), offered the thesis that antebellum reformers were motivated largely by humanitarian ideals and hoped to perfect American society. These impulses, Tyler claimed, stemmed from America's democratic spirit and the evangelical sentiment produced by the Second Great Awakening. In the following decade, other scholars began to suggest other explanations for why nineteenth-century American reformers responded as they did. For example, David Donald, in his influential essay "Toward a Reconsideration of Abolitionists," in *Lincoln Reconsidered: Essays on the Civil War Era* (Alfred A. Knopf, 1956), concluded that abolitionists were responding to a society in which power had shifted into the hands of slave owners and industrialists, thereby depriving them of leadership positions. Their crusade against slavery, then, was part of a "status revolt" designed to create for these reformers a new leadership niche and a sense of personal fulfillment.

Another significant interpretation of the antebellum reformers comes from the "social-control" school of thought. Drawing upon the works of Michel Foucault, Erving Goffman, Howard Becker, Thomas Szasz, and others, these scholars characterize American reformers as being more interested in serving their own interests than in providing assistance to mankind. As a result, middle- and upper-class reformers responding to momentous changes within their society (the same types of changes described by Donald) imposed their standards of morality and order on the lower classes and, thus, denied the latter group freedom to act as a diverse set of individuals.

Ronald G. Walters, in *American Reformers, 1815–1860* (Hill and Wang, 1978), concludes that although many nineteenth-century reformers expressed sentiments that were self-serving and bigoted, their motivations were not based entirely upon a desire to control the lower classes. Rather, reformers were convinced that improvements could and should be made to help people.

The scholarly literature on the "age of reform" is extensive. Interested students should consult Timothy L. Smith, *Revivalism and Social Reform: American Protestantism on the Eve of the Civil War* (Harper & Row, 1957); Whitney R. Cross, *The Burned-Over District: The Social and Intellectual History of Enthusiastic*

Religion in Western New York, 1800–1850 (Cornell University Press, 1950); and Clifford S. Griffin, *Their Brothers' Keepers: Moral Stewardship in the United States, 1800–1865* (Rutgers University Press, 1960). David Brion Davis, ed., *Ante-Bellum Reform* (Harper and Row, 1967) is an excellent collection of readings. The social-control thesis can be traced for various reform endeavors in Joseph R. Gusfield, *Symbolic Crusade: Status Politics and the American Temperance Movement* (University of Illinois Press, 1966); Michael B. Katz, *The Irony of Early School Reform: Education and Innovation in Mid-Nineteenth Century Massachusetts* (Beacon Press, 1968); Joseph M. Harris, *Children in Urban Society: Juvenile Delinquency in Nineteenth-Century America* (Oxford University Press, 1971); David J. Rothman, *The Discovery of the Asylum: Social Order and Disorder in the New Republic* (Little, Brown, 1971); and Gerald Grob, *Mental Institutions in America: Social Policy to 1875* (Free Press, 1973). For some of the aspects of American reform generally dismissed by Tyler as "fads," see John D. Davies, *Phrenology, Fad and Science: A Nineteenth-Century American Crusade* (Yale University Press, 1955), and Ronald L. Numbers, *Prophetess of Health: A Study of Ellen G. White* (Harper & Row, 1976). For important studies on the abolitionist movement, see citations listed in the postscript for Issue 13.

The status of women was another major concern for reformers in the ante-bellum period. Students interested in this topic should see Barbara Welter, "The Cult of True Womanhood, 1820–1860," *American Quarterly* (Summer 1966); Barbara J. Berg, *The Remembered Gate: Origins of American Feminism—The Woman and the City, 1800–1860* (Oxford University Press, 1978); Ellen C. Du Bois, *Feminism and Suffrage: The Emergence of an Independent Woman's Movement in America, 1848–1869* (Cornell University Press, 1978); Barbara Leslie Epstein, *The Politics of Domesticity: Women, Evangelism, and Temperance in Nineteenth-Century America* (Wesleyan University Press, 1981); Lori D. Ginzberg, *Women and the Work of Benevolence: Morality, Politics, and Class in the Nineteenth-Century United States* (Yale University Press, 1990); and Carolyn J. Lawes, *Women and Reform in a New England Community, 1815–1860* (University Press of Kentucky, 2000).

For students seeking an excellent narrative of the United States in the first half of the nineteenth century, see Sean Wilentz, *The Rise of American Democracy: Jefferson to Lincoln* (W. W. Norton, 2005); Daniel Walker Howe, *What Hath God Wrought: The Transformation of America, 1815–1848* (Oxford University Press, 2007); and David S. Reynolds, *Waking Giant: America in the Age of Jackson* (HarperCollins, 2008.)

ISSUE 12

Was the Mexican War an Exercise in American Imperialism?

YES: Walter Nugent, from *Habits of Empire: A History of American Expansion* (Alfred A. Knopf, 2008)

NO: Norman A. Graebner, from "The Mexican War: A Study in Causation," *Pacific Historical Review* (August 1980)

ISSUE SUMMARY

YES: Professor Walter Nugent argues that President James K. Polk was a narrow-minded, ignorant but not stupid individual with one big idea: Use the power of the Presidency to force Mexico to cede California and the current Southwest to the United States.

NO: Professor of diplomatic history Norman A. Graebner argues that President James Polk pursued an aggressive policy that he believed would force Mexico to sell New Mexico and California to the United States and to recognize the annexation of Texas without starting a war.

T he origins of the Mexican War began with the controversy over Texas, a Spanish possession for three centuries. In 1821, Texas became the northernmost province of the newly established country of Mexico. Sparsely populated with a mixture of Hispanics and Indians, the Mexican government encouraged immigration from the United States. By 1835, the Anglo population had swelled to 30,000 plus over 2,000 slaves, whereas the Mexican population was only 5,000. Fearful of losing control over Texas, the Mexican government prohibited further immigration from the United States in 1830. But it was too late. The Mexican government was divided and had changed hands several times. The centers of power were thousands of miles from Texas. In 1829, the Mexican government abolished slavery, an edict that was difficult to enforce. Finally, General Santa Anna attempted to abolish the federation and impose military rule over the entire country. Whether it was due to Mexican intransigence or the Anglos' assertiveness, the settlers rebelled in September 1835. The war was short-lived. Santa Anna was captured at the battled of San Jacinto in April 1836, and Texas was granted her independence.

For nine years, Texas remained an independent republic. Politicians were afraid that if Texas were annexed it would be carved into four or five states, thereby upsetting the balance of power between the evenly divided free states and slave states that had been created in 1819 by the Missouri Compromise. But the pro-slavery president John Tyler pushed through Congress a resolution annexing Texas in the three days of his presidency in 1845.

The Mexican government was incensed and broke diplomatic relations with the United States. President James K. Polk sent John Slidell as the American emissary to Mexico to negotiate monetary claims of American citizens in Mexico, purchase California, and settle the southwestern boundary of Texas at the Rio Grande River and not farther north at the Nueces River, which Mexico recognized as the boundary. Upon Slidell's arrival, news leaked out about his proposals. The Mexican government rejected Slidell's offer. In March 1846, President Polk stationed General Zachary Taylor in the disputed territory along the Rio Grande with an army of 4,000 troops. On May 9, Slidell returned to Washington and informed Polk that he was rebuffed. Polk met with his cabinet to consider war. By chance, that same evening Polk received a dispatch from General Taylor informing him that on April 25 the Mexican army crossed the Rio Grande and killed or wounded 16 of his men. On May 11, Polk submitted his war message claiming, "American blood was shed on American soil." Congress voted overwhelmingly for war 174 to 14 in the House and 40 to 2 in the Senate despite the vocal minority of Whig protestors and intellectuals who opposed the war.

As David M. Plecher points out in his balanced but critical discussions in *The Diplomacy of Annexation: Texas, Oregon and the Mexican War* (University of Missouri Press, 1973), the long-range effects on American foreign policy of the Mexican War were immense. Between 1845 and 1848, the United States acquired more than 1,200 square miles of territory and increased its size by over a third of its present area. This included the annexation of Texas and the subsequent states of the Southwest that stretched to the Pacific coast, incorporating California and the Oregon territory up to the 49th parallel. European efforts to gain a foothold in North America virtually ceased. By the 1850s, the British gradually abandoned their political aspirations in Central America, "content to compete for economic gains with the potent but unmilitary weapon of their factory system and their merchant marine." Meanwhile, the United States flexed her muscles at the end of the Civil War and used the Monroe Doctrine for the first time to force the French puppet ruler out of Mexico.

The following selections reflect two opposite views about the nature of the Mexican War. Walter Nugent is very critical of the United States' policy towards Mexico. He contends that President James K. Polk was a narrow-minded, bigoted but not stupid person with one big idea: Use the power of the presidency to force Mexico to cede to California and the current southwest to the United States. In the second selection, Professor Normal A. Graebner believes that President Polk pursued the aggressive policy of a stronger nation in order to force Mexico to sell New Mexico and California to the United States and to recognize America's annexation of Texas without causing a war.

YES ⤶

Walter Nugent

California and New Mexico, 1846–1848: Southward Aggression II

Generally the officers of the army were indifferent whether the annexation [of Texas] was consummated or not. . . . For myself, I was bitterly opposed to the measure, and to this day regard the war, which resulted, as one of the most unjust ever waged by a stronger against a weaker nation.

—U. S. Grant, Personal Memoirs

Our situation is truly desperate. Everything, absolutely everything, is lost, and judging by the way things are going it is doubtful whether we can save our independence, the last refuge and symbol of our honor.

—José Fernando Ramírez, 1847

The Look of Things in 1845

The Oregon acquisition was not small. It included the present states of Oregon, Washington, and Idaho, and large pieces of Montana and Wyoming. But the "Mexican Cession" of 1848, together with its postscript, the Gadsden Purchase of 1853, was twice as large. Add Texas, whose annexation by the United States started the Mexican-American conflict, and the whole area taken from Mexico was larger than the Louisiana Purchase (949,000 square miles versus 827,000). Moreover, the method was much more violent. This was the only acquisition so far that required a war. (The invasions of Canada in 1775 and 1813 were attempts at acquisition, but they failed.) The war with Mexico might well have never happened but for the determination of one man, President James K. Polk. Polk was, to use the terminology of the philosopher-historian Isaiah Berlin, a hedgehog, not a fox. Jefferson, FDR, and Bill Clinton were foxes. Jackson, Polk, and George W. Bush were hedgehogs. Whereas a fox has many ideas, in Berlin's definition, hedgehogs like Polk have one big idea. His was to acquire for the United States the territory west of Texas to the Pacific,

From *Habits of Empire: A History of American Expansion* (Alfred A. Knopf, 2008), pp. 187–189, 192–202, 206–210 (excerpts, notes omitted). Copyright 2008 © by Walter Nugent. Reprinted by permission of Random House Inc.

most importantly the harbor of San Francisco, but also, maybe, the rest of Alta (Upper) California and the province of New Mexico, which happened to be en route. He would do this by diplomacy and cash, not to mention bribery, if possible; or by military force, if necessary.

Polk was a man whose interests and intellect were blinkered and narrow. Yet his vision, though tunneled, looked far. He was almost willfully ignorant, but hardly stupid, and he never shrank from using the power of the presidency as he saw fit. Like Jackson, he was a Tennessean. He was a Jacksonian loyalist as Speaker of the U.S. House during Jackson's last two presidential years and Van Buren's first two (1835–1839). He lost a couple of elections in the early 1840s and was considered finished politically. But he captured the Democratic nomination for president in 1844 as the first true "dark horse." After favorites Van Buren and Clay both came out publicly against expansion in May 1844, Polk embraced it—both the "re-occupation" of Oregon to 54°40', and the "re-annexation" of Texas to the Rio Grande. In response, the Democratic Party and the voters rewarded him with the presidency.

In these two claims the "re" was a distortion and exaggeration. But he slipped past Clay, his more illustrious Whig opponent, by 38,367 votes out of 2.7 million, receiving 49.6 percent of the total popular vote and 50.7 percent of the Clay-Polk major-party vote. (James G. Birney of the antislavery Liberty Party got 62,000.) Polk's margin in the electoral college was 170–105. He carried neither his own Tennessee nor Clay's Kentucky. But he did win every other then-western state from Alabama to Michigan except Ohio, and he nearly won there as well. His spread-eagle platform resounded in those parts. He had to back off from the 54°40' claim, as we saw earlier; and he did not have to "re-annex" Texas because President John Tyler and Congress had already done that just before he was inaugurated. But California (and New Mexico with it) were still out there, and Texas's full statehood brought with it the threat of war with an aggrieved Mexico. That war, he could see, was both threat and opportunity.

Polk, like Jackson and Jefferson before him, maintained that Texas had been part of the Louisiana Purchase. The claim was transparently flimsy to begin with, and had been specifically repudiated in the 1819 Adams-Onís treaty. To the Polkites, however, that treaty had "faded away" under the strong light of the American overrunning of Texas. Realistically, Texas had become American, and a few voices within Mexico and among European diplomats urged Mexico to recognize the fact, even though it was political suicide. Piling insensitivity upon intransigence, the Polk policy toward Mexico could only end violently. Before and during the outbreak of war, Polk (like Madison in 1812) employed secret agents, asserted the baseness of the other side's motives and tactics, manipulated the popular mood of manifest destiny, promised more army volunteers than he could deliver, and used other unpretty devices that were not new to presidential behavior then and have become routine since. . . .

Polk's aggressiveness, California's volatility, and Texas's Rio Grande claims might have gone nowhere if conditions in Mexico had been stable. But Mexico was chaotic and had been so since Texas broke away in 1836. There was an occasional bright spot, such as New Mexico's demolition of an invasion force of Texans who attempted to annex everything east and north of the

Rio Grande in 1841. But Mexico's problems were both fundamental and superficial. It had no effective tax-collecting system. It had too many ambitious and feuding generals, preeminently the pop-up dictator, Santa Anna. Political animosities ran deep, more in the nature of competing worldviews than the relatively consensual American partisanship, which was divisive enough. Deep divisions separated clericalists, anticlericals, liberals, conservatives, monarchists, republicans, federalists, centralists—each representing not just policies but ideologies. Compromise and concerted action, even in the face of invasion, loss of territory, or loss of national existence, eluded the troubled country. Mexico was as badly positioned to defend itself and as divided as Spain was in 1808 when Napoleon invaded it. The result by 1848 was national dismemberment. It could have been national extinction.

In this context, Polk the hedgehog held the advantage. On Oregon he had "looked John Bull in the eye," at least until Aberdeen's thirty ships of the line loomed, and he still acquired everything up to the forty-ninth parallel. He could look Mexico in the eye—Santa Anna or anyone—without worrying about any ships of the line. As a result, he did as he pleased, like a true Jacksonian.

Polk's Brinkmanship

Polk's 1844 platform and March 1845 inaugural speech were thunderously clear about Oregon and Texas. But they never mentioned California. Once in office, however, Polk moved toward his cherished if not yet public project. He had told Navy Secretary George Bancroft in early 1845 that acquiring California was the most important goal of his administration. In October 1845, he told Senator Benton that by "reasserting" Monroe's "doctrine" against allowing European incursions into the hemisphere, "I had California and the fine bay of San Francisco as much in view as Oregon." California was Polk's hidden agenda. Transpacific commercial possibilities, particularly the market potential of China, likely motivated him more than visions of settlement did, but both objectives might be achieved.

President Tyler had done Polk the favor of bringing Texas all but into the Union, after the February 28 joint resolution offering annexation. The only remaining steps were ratification by the Texas Congress and, formally, by the U.S. Congress. The first came on July 4, and the second on December 29, 1845.

Texan statehood meant, of course, a casus belli with Mexico. The Mexican foreign minister had said so bluntly as early as mid-1843. The Mexican minister in Washington, Juan Nepomuceno Almonte, also made that clear. When Congress passed its joint resolution, Almonte told Secretary of State Calhoun that annexation was aggression. He demanded his passports, left Washington, and thereby broke diplomatic relations between the two countries. Any Mexican leader would have agreed that an independent Texas might be barely acceptable but the loss of it to the United States was not. Beyond that, as an issue, were the claims (some well founded, some trumped up) of U.S. citizens against Mexican taxes, customs duties, port regulations, and the like. Even in more normal times the claims issue festered. Polk's position, to the contrary, was that Mexico owed money to Americans; it had no money; it did have sparsely settled land; therefore the claims could be paid off in territory, with some cash going to Mexico as a sweetener.

Texas, from the American standpoint, was no longer on the table, but California would do very well. Polk preferred purchase via diplomatic negotiation to war, though he would go to war "if necessary." Accordingly he sent a Louisiana congressman, John Slidell, to Mexico City in the fall of 1845 to negotiate. Already, however, he prepared to "look Mexico in the eye," and in June 1845 he ordered General Zachary Taylor to proceed from Louisiana to south Texas, and Commodore David Conner to patrol the Gulf coast of Mexico, both to be ready to act if war broke out. Taylor arrived at Corpus Christi (just south of the Nueces River) by early August with eight companies of soldiers and awaited orders.

The "Disputed" Nueces Strip

When Taylor led his troops to Corpus Christi, he arrived at the banks—the southern banks—of the Nueces River. Was he still in Texas, as Texans were claiming, or was he already inside Mexico?

In south Texas, the distance along the Gulf coast from Corpus Christi, where the Nueces River flows into the Gulf, to the mouth of the Rio Grande at Port Isabel, just east of Brownsville, is about 150 miles. Padre Island guards the shore. The Nueces commences in the hills west of San Antonio and wriggles south and east roughly parallel to the Rio Grande for about three hundred miles. The Rio Grande, much longer, rises in the Rockies, flows south through Albuquerque to El Paso and then southeast to the Gulf. If it were the border, then present New Mexico and west Texas went with it. The Nueces, because it did not flow nearly as far, included none of that vast land.

When the general run of American history books discuss the Mexican-American War, they refer to the strip south of the Nueces and north of the Rio Grande as "disputed." But it had never been disputed until Texans, newly independent in 1836, started claiming it. Earlier, to be sure, Jefferson and his followers purported that, like Texas itself, the strip was part of the Louisiana Purchase. This dated back to the spurious claim that the Treaty of Utrecht of 1713 recognized French rights along the Gulf as far southwest as the Rio Grande. But Spain had been there all along, and after 1821 the region became Mexican. Here as elsewhere the Jeffersonians inflated the extent of their "noble bargain" of 1803 wherever they could. In any case the claim that Texas was part of Louisiana was specifically, and presumably permanently, abjured by the United States in the 1819 Adams-Onís treaty with Spain, which set the American-Mexican boundary at the Sabine, east and north of any conceivable historic part of Texas. The Sabine became, and is now, the border between the states of Texas and Louisiana.

Yet the claim that the Nueces strip was part of the Louisiana Purchase, and therefore part of Texas, resurfaced in the late 1820s when John Quincy Adams sent Joel Poinsett to buy Texas as far south as the Rio Grande. Following its independence in 1836, Texas claimed the Rio Grande boundary. Despite being thrown back by one of Santa Anna's armies at San Antonio in 1842, Texans maintained the claim as they traveled their bumpy road toward annexation. The United States' terms of annexation in 1845 did not explicitly accept that claim, which included not only the Gulf coast but all the land north and east of the Rio Grande to its source and then north to the forty-second parallel. In Congress's annexation resolution the border was left to be worked out over time. The time came very soon.

Clearly, the Nueces strip had never been part of Texas under either Spain or Mexico. So thinly populated was south Texas before 1821 that provincial boundaries were almost pointless, as there were virtually no people or governments there. When the San Antonio missions were founded around 1718, the Medina and San Antonio Rivers separated Texas from the province of Coahuila. By 1767 the Nueces was recognized as the boundary between Texas and Coahuila. As of 1805, Texas's southern boundary ran from the Gulf up the Nueces for over one hundred miles, then north to the Medina (near San Antonio), and then northwest another two hundred miles—none of it anywhere near the Rio Grande. The boundary stayed that way until Texas and Coahuila were made a joint state under the Mexican federal constitution of 1824. They remained a joint state, with the Texas segment consisting of the land north of the Nueces. Stephen F. Austin's empresario maps of 1829, 1833, and 1836 also showed the Nueces River, not the Rio Grande, demarcating Texas from Coahuila.

When Texans defeated Santa Anna at San Jacinto in May 1836, the captured general agreed, with his life hanging in the balance, to sign the "Treaty of Velasco." It withdrew Mexican forces to south of the Rio Grande, implying that the Nueces strip was Texan. But the Mexican Congress repudiated it. Polk, to the contrary, acted as if it were fact. In August 1845, when news came that a Mexican army was about to cross the Rio Grande, Polk asserted that the Nueces strip was "virtually" American and any Mexican crossing "must be regarded as an invasion of the United States." Thus, in his war message in May 1846, he proclaimed that "Mexico has invaded our territory and shed American blood upon the American soil." With that, the war began.

For Mexico, any American troop movement south of the Nueces was an invasion of *its* territory. The coastal strip was part of the state of Tamaulipas, and the inland area belonged to Nuevo León and Coahuila. In an 1847 book, Carlos María de Bustamante affirmed that "sending troops into Mexican territory"—Corpus Christi or anywhere else south of the Nueces—"doomed all moderation, and Mexico was left with no other recourse but to engage in battle. The territory between the Nueces and Rio Grande rivers neither by fact nor by law could have belonged to Texas. Not by fact because it was not populated by [Anglo] Texans . . . nor . . . by law because all this coast, through a territorial division recognized by all the nation and by the Texas colonists themselves, has belonged to the state of Tamaulipas." He was right. No Anglos lived there; the empresario grants did not extend south of the Nueces; and even in 1845 no Texas counties had been organized there. To the contrary, the people living on the north side of the Rio Grande were Mexican, and Mexican authorities had a duty to protect them. Quite unlike east Texas and the region of the empresario grants, there was no demographic argument for the Americans to absorb the Nueces strip. No surge of people occupied it, and the three coastal counties south of Corpus Christi to Brownsville are still the least populated of any on the coast of the Gulf.

Run-up to War

Diplomacy ensued, or started to. Word reached Polk in early November 1845 that the Mexican commander on the Rio Grande and leaders in Mexico City were ready to talk, surely a sign that strong words (Polk's preferred tactic) would push the Mexicans in his direction. With cabinet agreement, and at Buchanan's suggestion, Polk sent John Slidell to Mexico City. He was to offer to take over all outstanding claims and buy California and New Mexico. The amount was negotiable up to $25 million, depending on whether Mexico would sell both provinces. As for the claims, Mexico had agreed in 1839 to pay them, made a few payments, then had to stop. Polk was ready to have the U.S. government assume the claims and pay Mexico some cash for its northern states. Did not Mexico need money more than the land? To Polk the answer was obvious. Unfortunately for peace, no one in Mexico saw it that way.

Slidell's credentials from Polk named him "envoy extraordinary and minister plenipotentiary." But the president never asked or received the Senate's confirmation, leaving Slidell in the status of a special presidential emissary. The Mexican government accordingly refused to accept him as fully credentialed. When he arrived in Mexico City on November 29, 1845, the situation was more than usually turbulent. General Mariano Paredes y Arrillaga, commander of field forces, ousted the then unpopular Santa Anna and by early December replaced him as president with another general, José Joaquin Herrera. The foreign minister, Manuel Peña y Peña, a distinguished lawyer and jurist, was a moderate. Peña made clear to Slidell that he would be happy to receive him to discuss his purchase proposal as well as outstanding problems like the claims and borders. But if he recognized him as a new U.S. minister, he would be acquiescing in the Texas annexation, the main reason why Almonte had broken relations the previous spring. This was no quibble—John Quincy Adams would have scoffed if another country had sent someone with Slidell's faulty credentials—but Polk and Buchanan chose to be incensed at the rebuff of Slidell. The president decided that the time had come to move from "diplomacy if possible" to "force if necessary."

Herrera had taken a great risk in allowing Slidell into Mexico at all, and it cost him his job. In late December 1845, General Paredes removed Herrera (in office less than four weeks) and installed himself as president on January 2, 1846. A semicovert monarchist, Paredes followed a harder line: no truck with the United States, no recognition of Texas, certainly no boundary south of the Nueces, and no Slidell. As Polk's biographer states, "the Polk-Slidell policy of combined bullying and bribery was precisely what no Mexican regime could submit to and survive"—Paredes's least of all. Slidell dallied in Mexico City in vain hope. Meanwhile, on January 13, the Polk administration ordered General Taylor to move his forces to the Rio Grande opposite the Mexican coastal town of Matamoros, with Commodore Conner to proceed to the Texas coast for naval support. Slidell informed Polk on March 15 that he was returning empty-handed, and on March 30 he sailed home.

In cabinet meetings through February and March, Polk resisted any further action against Mexico until Slidell reported back. He did not explain why in his diary, but this was the very time when he and the cabinet were absorbing Lord Aberdeen's "thirty sail of the line" remark, and when the abrogation of the 1827 joint occupancy of Oregon was stalled in Congress. Polk paused regarding Mexico until Oregon was clarified. Nevertheless, he had still not received a response from London on the abrogation notice when he learned on May 9 that Mexican forces had crossed the Rio Grande and that several of Taylor's troops had been killed and wounded on April 25. Polk immediately wrote a message to Congress, which received it on May 11. It asked for a declaration of war, a levy of 50,000 volunteers, and $10 million.

Polk was teetering on the brink of a double war as a result of his own blunt diplomacy. He was very lucky that Aberdeen and Peel remained in power long enough to settle the Oregon question amicably, that Aberdeen's "thirty sail of the line" thus became ghosts, and that Taylor's forces were strong enough to win the first small engagements with the Mexicans. Was his stubbornness just tactical? Whatever his private thoughts, he did not admit any wavering, even to his diary. Oregon was not becoming American as a free area to balance slave-state Texas, but because the opportunity played out that way. Polk was not performing a balancing act; to the contrary, he was going to the brink of a double war. (Nor, despite suspicions that lingered for generations, was he or anyone the instrument of a "slave-power conspiracy" to annex northern Mexico to expand slavery. As events transpired, slavery never extended west of Texas. In fact, antislavery feelings strengthened because of the Mexican-American War; it was no plus for slavery.)

The war message reflects either an invincibly stubborn tunnel vision or enormous mendacity on Polk's part. In it, the president insisted and reiterated, unequivocally, that "the grievous wrongs perpetrated by Mexico upon our citizens throughout a long period of years remain unredressed. . . . We have tried every effort at reconciliation. . . . Now, after reiterated menaces, Mexico has passed the boundary of the United States, has invaded our territory and shed American blood upon the American soil." This was the first, but not the last, presidential call to arms in American history based on a string of false contentions.

On May 12 the House considered the president's requests. His friends attached to it a "preamble" blaming Mexico for invading American soil. The Democratic leadership limited House debate to two hours and much of that was consumed by the reading of supporting documents. The bill passed, 174–14. Some members objected to the preamble, because it put them on record as agreeing with Polk's claims. Yet they did not dare refuse to support the war. Garrett Davis of Kentucky, one of the few allowed to speak, objected to the preamble:

> It recites that war exists . . . and was begun by Mexico. . . . That . . . is utterly untrue. I am decidedly, strongly, in favor of the appropriation of the money. . . . For these purposes, it is sufficient for me that our country

> is at war. . . . If the bill contained any recitation upon that point in truth and justice, it should be that this war was begun by the President. The river Nueces is the true western boundary of Texas. The country between that stream and the Del Norte [the Rio Grande] is part of Mexico.

Davis nonetheless voted for the bill, as did all but fourteen diehards—all Whigs and abolitionists who abhorred slavery's extension. Forty-eight Whigs voted "yea" to avoid being branded unpatriotic.

Debate in the Senate took another day, much of it centered on who owned the Nueces strip. But the bill passed there too, 40 yea (26 Democrats and 14 Whigs) to 2 nay (both Whigs), with John C. Calhoun and two others not voting. Polk signed the bill on May 13. War was declared.

The now familiar tactic of the chief executive maneuvering Congress into a fait accompli with regard to declaring war was certainly employed by Polk in 1846. . . . Polk put Taylor's army on the Rio Grande and Conner's navy off the Mexican coast. When the inevitable skirmish happened, congressmen had no option. Either go along, declare war, or be criticized for undercutting the troops. Once American troops were "in harm's way," although Polk placed them there and thereby contrived to have Mexico fire the first shot, it was too late to object. Public opinion soon split on the Mexican War, but at the outset Congress could not buck the belligerent spirit.

As soon as the Senate passed the war bill, and before it even reached Polk for signature, he reaffirmed to Navy Secretary Bancroft that Commodore Sloat and the Pacific squadron should occupy Monterey and San Francisco. The next day Polk sent orders to Colonel (soon General) Stephen Watts Kearny at Fort Leavenworth, on the Missouri River, to head for Santa Fe and secure it. The grand strategy, set at least eleven months earlier in mid-1845, was reaching fruition: try diplomacy (Slidell and money) but position forces (Taylor and Conner). If and when diplomacy failed, send Taylor to the Rio Grande, claim the Nueces strip, provoke Mexico into armed defense of it, and then insist that American blood had been shed on American soil. Congress could not resist that strategy. Meanwhile, make a deal with Britain over Oregon, and forget about the unattainable (and baseless) claim of 54°40'. With war declared, send the army to New Mexico and the navy to the California coast. How it would all end—how much it would cost, how many would be killed, how much of Mexico would be occupied or kept—was not clear at all. But Polk's primary objective, making California American, was nearly in his grasp.

Mexico was prepared for war with the United States only in the strength of its sense of *nacionalidad,* and that existed primarily among its small elites. At the opening of the war, its land area was close to that of the United States, but its population was considerably smaller—about 7.5 or 8 million compared to the States' 17 million. As had been true since Aztec times, most lived in central Mexico. The northern states had always been underpopulated and only distantly connected to the center. The majority of the people were Indians or mestizos, divided in languages, often innocent of Spanish, practicing something close to subsistence farming and contributing little to national product or tax base. Many were Catholics, after more than three centuries of the

Spanish presence. Some, however, the *indios bárbaros* of the California interior and the Great Plains, were not only unassimilated but hostile. Comanches and Apaches raided at will many miles south of the Rio Grande, as they had ever since the Spanish pushed north of it. Mexico's preoccupation with the American invasion in 1846 provided the Comanches with further opportunities. As a result, Mexico found itself fighting on two fronts, against both the Americans and the Plains Indians.

Mexico's class structure made a unified war effort difficult. Above the Indian majority were a smaller number of largely mestizo artisans, shopkeepers, peasants, parish clergy, and others, comprising, to stretch a somewhat anachronistic term, a lower middle class. On top were people of European (usually Spanish) stock, the well landed, the upper clergy, military officers, the educated professionals. These Europeans split further into *criollos,* if they were Mexican-born, or *gachupines,* if they were the envied and often disliked Spanish-born. Ideological fissures separated the elites—clericals versus liberals, federalists versus centralists, monarchists versus republicans. Leadership, up to and including the presidency, oscillated among these groups.

Add to all that the epidemic of politically involved generals, including above all the charismatic Santa Anna, with his remarkable ability to raise armies and his ineptitude in leading them; the lack of any effective tax system and, for that matter, anything much to tax; the exemptions of the clergy and the military from the ordinary system of laws and courts; and in 1846, an army poorly paid, fed, clothed, equipped, and armed. The outcome was almost foreordained.

As nationalistic and full of their sense of destiny as the Americans of that day were, the Mexicans were equally so. No one monopolized nationalism in the nineteenth century. Though lacking the illusion that their "destiny" was "manifest," they were just as sensitive to insults to national honor and to threats to the integrity of their national territory. Americans were aggressive expansionists; Mexicans were determined to defend what they had.

The decade prior to 1846 brought Mexico's internal problems and divisions to a boil. Since the defeat at San Jacinto and de facto Texan independence in 1836, politics had never been calm. Santa Anna rode in and out of power, donning whatever cloak—centralist, federalist, liberal, conservative—would bring him back or keep him there. Only one thing was a given: no president or general could alienate any territory, even the lost territory of Texas. If he gave even a hint of that, as Herrera did by admitting Slidell in late 1845, he was ousted by someone more "patriotic." Thus war would surely come, however unready Mexico was. Defeat (and despite all of Mexico's handicaps it was not a certainty until it actually happened) was preferable to dishonor. In the two years beginning in late 1845, *during wartime,* five presidents succeeded one another; finance ministers and war ministers and commanders tumbled after one another; armies coalesced and crumbled. Mexico lost every significant battle of the war. But some were close, and most were valiantly defended. That was a wonder, in view of the country's lack of resources. . . .

Negotiations had already started. Polk had sent a negotiator, Nicholas P. Trist, with Scott, and after some initial friction Trist and Scott worked very well together. Following the capture of Mexico City, the obvious question was how to wind up the war. It could have ended in March 1847, in theory, since Polk's territorial objectives were satisfied by then. But neither side was ready to stop fighting, and the Scott campaign followed. By the fall of 1847, with the American victory seemingly complete, the question to many Americans was how much of Mexico to absorb. The United States was positioned to take more than New Mexico and California, but should it? . . .

Polk's and Mexico's Dilemmas, 1847

The Mexican dilemma was whether to round up yet more armies, fight, and probably lose more pitched battles; or to continue a war of guerrilla attrition until the Americans gave up and left; or to accept the losses of California and New Mexico, as well as Texas to the Rio Grande, sign whatever treaty they could, and stop the carnage. A strong faction, the *puros,* wanted to keep going. *Moderados* wanted a treaty. Local independence movements in Yucatán, Oaxaca, and other states threatened to spin off from the nation. How best to keep Mexico together as an independent country, and if that succeeded, should it be federal or centralized? A Mexican pamphleteer beseeched any reorganized government to "direct all its efforts to conserve the principle of *nationality* . . . at all costs." But should it agree, therefore, "to make peace, or to continue the war?"

For Polk the dilemma was whether to continue occupying Mexico, for how long, and for what. The American victories, while hardly overwhelming or even clear-cut in many cases, were trumpeted in much of the press in late 1847 as validation for putting large parts or even the whole of Mexico under American rule. The recent clamor for 54°40′ in Oregon was paralleled by cries of "all of Mexico," annexing it as far south as the Isthmus of Tehuantepec, or even extending American rule all the way to Colombia. Since the army was there, why not let it stay?

From Polk's perspective there were good reasons not to. It was expensive. He'd had to plead with Congress for the money to wage the war, and he would have to do so again to fund an occupation. He had faced an antiwar minority from the start—a tiny one in May 1846 when Congress voted to declare war, but a substantial one in 1847. The Whigs won a majority in the House of Representatives in the 1846 election and would take over in December 1847. They would write no large checks for Polk. The 1848 presidential election loomed, and both of the war-hero generals, Taylor and Scott, were Whigs. (Taylor would win the Whig nomination and the 1848 election; Scott was the 1852 Whig nominee but lost to a Democratic general, Franklin Pierce.)

In August 1846, with Congress just hours away from recessing until December, a Pennsylvania Democrat named David Wilmot added a "proviso" to an appropriations bill to the effect that slavery would not be countenanced in any territory acquired from Mexico. No sharper wedge issue existed. The Wilmot proviso did not pass then or in later forms, but it began to split the Democratic Party. Polk confided to his diary on August 10, 1846, that the bill he desired, appropriating $2 million for peace negotiations, had passed the House, but with this "mischievous & foolish amendment. . . . What connection slavery had with making peace with Mexico it is difficult to conceive." He never understood the connection, only that it further complicated ending the war, even threatening his California prize.

But "how much to take"? As early as January 1847, if not before, American occupation of the Nueces strip, New Mexico, and Upper California was an accomplished fact. The United States would not give them back. But what of the next tier of occupied states to the south: Tamaulipas, Nuevo León, Coahuila, Chihuahua, Sonora, and Baja California? What about the Gulf coast to Tampico or Veracruz? What about central Mexico itself, if the Americans conquered it—which they had by September 1847?

Opinions differed in the American public and press, but ambitions broadly surged after the capture of Mexico City in September 1847 and through that fall. The extension of slavery was directly in question, whether Polk understood it or not. It had, however, the surprising effect of moderating territorial demands. The "all of Mexico" proponents never quite answered whether Mexico or its states should become, in time, states of the American union or remain permanent territories. That question provoked argument in 1898, after the United States acquired Puerto Rico and the Philippines. It probably would have done so in 1848 had "all of Mexico" actually been annexed. Proponents resisted any idea that annexed Mexicans would become American citizens with full and equal rights, and they would do the same regarding Filipinos and Puerto Ricans later on.

Yet the temptation was as huge as Mexico was prostrate. Had not Taylor and Scott beaten the Mexicans thoroughly? Was it not the right, even duty, of Americans to spread their culture, religion, and beneficent rule over a lazy, benighted, and degenerate race? Didn't manifest destiny demand taking what could be taken? Wouldn't Providence be insulted if Americans refused this gift? A Boston pamphleteer in 1846 summed up a widespread conviction that "the Mexican republic is politically, socially and morally dissolute. . . . Anarchy is its only domestic rule; treachery its only foreign policy. . . . Her conquest would be practicable . . . her annexation would be a barrier to slavery." The author argued that if Mexico were annexed into the union as "a series of States of free laboring men," it would "stand as an impassable barrier to the extension of slavery southward." But if Mexico continued to exist, unannexed but supine, "the slavery of Texas will gradually encroach upon the northern Mexican provinces, and its course be indefinite."

From the West and Southwest came loud hyperpatriotic arguments. Eastern newspapers pointed out the need to keep a weakened Mexico from falling into European hands (as indeed happened a few years later when the Austrian archduke Maximilian was made emperor of Mexico). The lure of an Atlantic-to-Pacific canal across the Isthmus of Tehuantepec was strong, and though that did not happen, the idea persisted until the Panama Canal opened sixty-six years later. Westerners, from editors and politicians to army volunteers, coveted Mexican land. The political split on "how much to take" followed the division over the war itself, with Whigs opposed, most Democrats in favor. Abraham Lincoln, elected a Whig congressman from Illinois in 1846, served only one term in large part because he opposed the war, the all-Mexico movement, and Polk himself, whose "mind," Lincoln told the House, "taxed beyond its power, is running hither and thither, like some tortured creature on a burning surface." On December 22, 1847, Lincoln introduced eight "spot resolutions" calling on Polk to answer whether "the *spot* on which the blood of [American] citizens was shed as in his messages declared was not within the territory of Spain [and then] . . . Mexico," and related questions. Lincoln expanded the resolutions into his first major speech, which he gave on January 12, 1848. Polk never responded.

The all-Mexico debate raged in the Senate from December 15, 1847, into February 1848. Southern Democrats, John C. Calhoun most prominently, opposed "all Mexico" because absorbing it would mean expanding nonslave areas—he assumed that Mexico would never reintroduce slavery—and taking on a huge nonwhite population. In a private conversation with Polk, Calhoun "said he did not desire to extend slavery," though he would vote against a Wilmot-like antislavery provision in any peace treaty as a matter of "principle."

Many southerners, however, supported the all-Mexico movement. Among them was the powerful Treasury secretary, Robert J. Walker of Mississippi. Some military men (though not Lieutenant Ulysses S. Grant) favored large, possibly total, acquisition. The always aggressive Commodore Stockton roared in December 1847 that "if the war were to be prolonged for fifty years, and cost money enough to demand from us each half of all that we possess," he would nevertheless be confident that "the inestimable blessings of civil and religious liberty should be guaranteed to Mexico." Walt Whitman, then editor of the *Brooklyn Eagle,* called for "fifty thousand fresh troops" to "make our authority respectable," as "this talk about a peace party is all moonshine." Various generals urged permanent occupation of Mexico north of the Sierra Madre Oriental (it actually runs more north and south, but what they wanted was Tamaulipas and the coast south beyond Tampico). Others coveted the whole country.

Senator Lewis Cass of Michigan, who became the Democratic presidential nominee in 1848, agreed. When John Crittenden, a Kentucky Whig, demanded in the Senate to know why the army needed ten more regiments unless they were to occupy and perhaps annex the whole country, Cass argued that the troops had to be there to produce a "moral effect"—that is, intimidate guerrillas.

The most cogent speech against the all-Mexico idea came from Andrew Pickens Butler, a Democrat and Calhoun's South Carolina colleague. If we persist in "conquering and subjugating the Republic of Mexico," either making it part of "this Confederacy" or keeping it as a dependency, then "it would not be an extravagant proposition for the President to ask for two hundred thousand men to do it with security and safety." In other words, it would be a quagmire. American troops would not be in Mexico to fight, but "to overrun the Mexican states, to disarm the population, to confiscate the public property, to sequester the revenues, and to become . . . armed jailers." Every part of Europe, and many at home, are "a formidable opposition . . . against us."

Heated discussion continued into February, with many nuances worth noting because they reveal the twists of territorial ambition at that time. John

Bell of Tennessee opposed strengthening the army and occupying Mexico, because four of the eight million Mexicans are "degraded, vile, addicted to every vice," including "the Romish religion." Annexation would eventually mean "fifty new Representatives [and] forty new Senators, men of this mixed race." Most speakers steered clear of slavery. Southerners were not of one mind, but Calhoun's belief that large-scale annexation would weaken, not strengthen, slavery found support from Senator Jefferson Davis, among others.

As for Polk himself, his initial targets of California and New Mexico expanded after Scott's successes. In late 1847, privately and in the cabinet, he toyed with annexing everything north of the twenty-sixth parallel. His annual message to Congress of December 1847 left the door open for substantial acquisitions south of the Rio Grande. Partly as a result, the all-Mexico sentiment strengthened that winter. On January 2, 1848, he told Secretary of State Buchanan that he would be happy with Upper and Lower California, New Mexico, the Tehuantepec Isthmus, and Tampico.

But the Whig-majority House of Representatives elected in 1846 took office in December 1847 (Lincoln among them). It debated for weeks how much of Mexico to annex. Whigs were not likely to embrace the all-Mexico idea, strong though it was in the press and among the military. New England Whig papers insinuated that the real motive for large annexation was to capture the silver mines of Zacatecas and San Luis Potosí and extend slavery to all of Mexico. It was a way to provide an "outlet for our slaves," who were rapidly multiplying and threatening to overrun the South. Nor were the Whigs eager to finance the army or call for more volunteers.

The all-Mexico debate stopped abruptly when a draft peace treaty from Mexico City arrived and became known in late February 1848, because it limited the gains to New Mexico and Upper California. . . .

Norman A. Graebner   ➡ **NO**

The Mexican War: A Study in Causation

On May 11, 1846, President James K. Polk presented his war message to Congress. After reviewing the skirmish between General Zachary Taylor's dragoons and a body of Mexican soldiers along the Rio Grande, the president asserted that Mexico "has passed the boundary of the United States, has invaded our territory and shed American blood upon the American soil. . . . War exists, and, notwithstanding all our efforts to avoid it, exists by act of Mexico." No country could have had a superior case for war. Democrats in large numbers (for it was largely a partisan matter) responded with the patriotic fervor which Polk expected of them. "Our government has permitted itself to be insulted long enough," wrote one Georgian. "The blood of her citizens has been spilt on her own soil. It appeals to us for vengeance." Still, some members of Congress, recalling more accurately than the president the circumstances of the conflict, soon rendered the Mexican War the most reviled in American history—at least until the Vietnam War of the 1960s. One outraged Whig termed the war "illegal, unrighteous, and damnable," and Whigs questioned both Polk's honesty and his sense of geography. Congressman Joshua R. Giddings of Ohio accused the president of "planting the standard of the United States on foreign soil, and using the military forces of the United States to violate every principle of international law and moral justice." To vote for the war, admitted Senator John C. Calhoun, was "to plunge a dagger into his own heart, and more so." Indeed, some critics in Congress openly wished the Mexicans well.

For over a century such profound differences in perception have pervaded American writings on the Mexican War. Even in the past decade, historians have reached conclusions on the question of war guilt as disparate as those which separated Polk from his wartime conservative and abolitionist critics. . . .

In some measure the diversity of judgment on the Mexican War, as on other wars, is understandable. By basing their analyses on official rationalizations, historians often ignore the more universal causes of war which transcend individual conflicts and which can establish the bases for greater consensus. Neither the officials in Washington nor those in Mexico City ever acknowledged any alternatives to the actions which they took. But governments generally have more choices in any controversy than they are prepared to admit. Circumstances determine their extent. The more powerful a nation, the more

From *Pacific Historical Review* by Norman A. Graebner, vol. 49, no. 3, August 1980, pp. 405–426. Copyright © 1980 by University of California Press, Journals Division. Reprinted by permission.

remote its dangers, the greater its options between action and inaction. Often for the weak, unfortunately, the alternative is capitulation or war. . . . Polk and his advisers developed their Mexican policies on the dual assumption that Mexico was weak and that the acquisition of certain Mexican territories would satisfy admirably the long-range interests of the United States. Within that context, Polk's policies were direct, timely, and successful. But the president had choices. Mexico, whatever its internal condition, was no direct threat to the United States. Polk, had he so desired, could have avoided war; indeed, he could have ignored Mexico in 1845 with absolute impunity.

 ᐧᓬᐁᐧ

In explaining the Mexican War historians have dwelled on the causes of friction in American-Mexican relations. In part these lay in the disparate qualities of the two populations, in part in the vast discrepancies between the two countries in energy, efficiency, power, and national wealth. Through two decades of independence Mexico had experienced a continuous rise and fall of governments; by the 1840s survival had become the primary concern of every regime. Conscious of their weakness, the successive governments in Mexico City resented the superior power and effectiveness of the United States and feared American notions of destiny that anticipated the annexation of Mexico's northern provinces. Having failed to prevent the formation of the Texas Republic, Mexico reacted to Andrew Jackson's recognition of Texan independence in March 1837 with deep indignation. Thereafter the Mexican raids into Texas, such as the one on San Antonio in 1842, aggravated the bitterness of Texans toward Mexico, for such forays had no purpose beyond terrorizing the frontier settlements.

Such mutual animosities, extensive as they were, do not account for the Mexican War. Governments as divided and chaotic as the Mexican regimes of the 1840s usually have difficulty in maintaining positive and profitable relations with their neighbors; their behavior often produces annoyance, but seldom armed conflict. Belligerence toward other countries had flowed through U.S. history like a torrent without, in itself, setting off a war. Nations do not fight over cultural differences or verbal recriminations; they fight over perceived threats to their interests created by the ambitions or demands of others.

What increased the animosity between Mexico City and Washington was a series of specific issues over which the two countries perennially quarreled—claims, boundaries, and the future of Texas. Nations have made claims a pretext for intervention, but never a pretext for war. Every nineteenth-century effort to collect debts through force assumed the absence of effective resistance, for no debt was worth the price of war. To collect its debt from Mexico in 1838, for example, France blockaded Mexico's gulf ports and bombarded Vera Cruz. The U.S. claims against Mexico created special problems which discounted their seriousness as a rationale for war. True, the Mexican government failed to protect the possessions and the safety of Americans in Mexico from robbery, theft, and other illegal actions, but U.S. citizens were under no obligation to do business in

Mexico and should have understood the risk of transporting goods and money in that country. Minister Waddy Thompson wrote from Mexico City in 1842 that it would be "with somewhat of bad grace that we should war upon a country because it could not pay its debts when so many of our own states are in the same situation." Even as the United States after 1842 attempted futilely to collect the $2 million awarded its citizens by a claims commission, it was far more deeply in debt to Britain over speculative losses. Minister Wilson Shannon reported in the summer of 1844 that the claims issue defied settlement in Mexico City and recommended that Washington take the needed action to compel Mexico to pay. If Polk would take up the challenge and sacrifice American human and material resources in a war against Mexico, he would do so for reasons other than the enforcement of claims. The president knew well that Mexico could not pay, yet as late as May 9, 1846, he was ready to ask Congress for a declaration of war on the question of unpaid claims alone.

Congress's joint resolution for Texas annexation in February 1845 raised the specter of war among editors and politicians alike. As early as 1843 the Mexican government had warned the American minister in Mexico City that annexation would render war inevitable; Mexican officials in Washington repeated that warning. To Mexico, therefore, the move to annex Texas was an unbearable affront. Within one month after Polk's inauguration on March 4, General Juan Almonte, the Mexican minister in Washington, boarded a packet in New York and sailed for Vera Cruz to sever his country's diplomatic relations with the United States. Even before the Texas Convention could meet on July 4 to vote annexation, rumors of a possible Mexican invasion of Texas prompted Polk to advance Taylor's forces from Fort Jesup in Louisiana down the Texas coast. Polk instructed Taylor to extend his protection to the Rio Grande but to avoid any areas to the north of that river occupied by Mexican troops. Simultaneously the president reinforced the American squadron in the Gulf of Mexico. "The threatened invasion of Texas by a large Mexican army," Polk informed Andrew J. Donelson, the American charge in Texas, on June 15, "is well calculated to excite great interest here and increases our solicitude concerning the final action by the Congress and the Convention of Texas." Polk assured Donelson that he intended to defend Texas to the limit of his constitutional power. Donelson resisted the pressure of those Texans who wanted Taylor to advance to the Rio Grande; instead, he placed the general at Corpus Christi on the Nueces River. Taylor agreed that the line from the mouth of the Nueces to San Antonio covered the Texas settlements and afforded a favorable base from which to defend the frontier.

Those who took the rumors of Mexican aggressiveness seriously lauded the president's action. With Texas virtually a part of the United States, argued the *Washington Union,* "We owe it to ourselves, to the proud and elevated character which America maintains among the nations of the earth, to guard our own territory from the invasion of the ruthless Mexicans." The *New York Morning News* observed that Polk's policy would, on the whole, "command a general concurrence of the public opinion of his country." Some Democratic leaders, fearful of a Mexican attack, urged the president to strengthen Taylor's forces and order them to take the offensive should Mexican soldiers cross the Rio Grande. Others believed the reports from Mexico exaggerated, for there was no apparent relationship between the country's expressions of belligerence and its capacity to act. Secretary of War William L. Marcy admitted that his information was no better than that of other commentators. "I have at no time," he wrote in July, "felt that war with Mexico was probable—and do not now believe it is, yet it is in the range of possible occurrences. I have officially acted on the hypothesis that our peace may be temporarily disturbed without however believing it will be." Still convinced that the administration had no grounds for alarm, Marcy wrote on August 12: "The presence of a considerable force in Texas will do no hurt and possibly may be of great use." In September William S. Parrott, Polk's special agent in Mexico, assured the president that there would be neither a Mexican declaration of war nor an invasion of Texas.

Polk insisted that the administration's show of force in Texas would prevent rather than provoke war. "I do not anticipate that Mexico will be mad enough to declare war," he wrote in July, but "I think she would have done so but for the appearance of a strong naval force in the Gulf and our army moving in the direction of her frontier on land." Polk restated this judgment on July 28 in a letter to General Robert Armstrong, the U.S. consul at Liverpool: "I think there need be but little apprehension of war with Mexico. If however she shall be mad enough to make war we are prepared to meet her." The president assured Senator William H. Haywood of North Carolina that the American forces in Texas would never aggress against Mexico; however, they would prevent any Mexican forces from crossing the Rio Grande. In conversation with Senator William S. Archer of Virginia on September 1, the president added confidently that "the appearance of our land and naval forces on the borders of Mexico & in the Gulf would probably deter and prevent Mexico from either declaring war or invading Texas." Polk's continuing conviction that Mexico would not attack suggests that his deployment of U.S. land and naval forces along Mexico's periphery was designed less to protect Texas than to support an aggressive diplomacy which might extract a satisfactory treaty from Mexico without war. For Anson Jones, the last president of the Texas Republic, Polk's deployments had precisely that purpose:

> Texas never actually needed the protection of the United States after I came into office. . . . There was no necessity for it after the 'preliminary Treaty,' as we were at peace with Mexico, and knew perfectly well that that Government, though she might bluster a little, had not the slightest idea of invading Texas either by land or water; and that nothing would provoke her to (active) hostilities, but the presence of troops in the immediate neighborhood of the Rio Grande, threatening her towns and settlements on the southwest side of that river. . . . But Donelson appeared so intent upon 'encumbering us with help,' that finally, to get rid of his annoyance, he was told he might give us as much protection as he pleased. . . . The protection asked for was only *prospective* and contingent; the *protection* he had in view was *immediate and aggressive*.

For Polk the exertion of military and diplomatic pressure on a disorganized Mexico was not a prelude to war. Whig critics of annexation had predicted war; this alone compelled the administration to avoid a conflict over Texas. In his memoirs Jones recalled that in 1845 Commodore Robert F. Stockton, with either the approval or the connivance of Polk, attempted to convince him that he should place Texas "in an attitude of active hostility toward Mexico, so that, when Texas was finally brought into the Union, *she might bring war with her.*" If Stockton engaged in such an intrigue, he apparently did so on his own initiative, for no evidence exists to implicate the administration. Polk not only preferred to achieve his purposes by means other than war but also assumed that his military measures in Texas, limited as they were, would convince the Mexican government that it could not escape the necessity of coming to terms with the United States. Washington's policy toward Mexico during 1845 achieved the broad national purpose of Texas annexation. Beyond that it brought U.S. power to bear on Mexico in a manner calculated to further the processes of negotiation. Whether the burgeoning tension would lead to a negotiated boundary settlement or to war hinged on two factors: the nature of Polk's demands and Mexico's response to them. The president announced his objectives to Mexico's troubled officialdom through his instructions to John Slidell, his special emissary who departed for Mexico in November 1845 with the assurance that the government there was prepared to reestablish formal diplomatic relations with the United States and negotiate a territorial settlement. . . .

⋅⟨⊙⟩⋅

Actually, Slidell's presence in Mexico inaugurated a diplomatic crisis not unlike those which precede most wars. Fundamentally the Polk administration, in dispatching Slidell, gave the Mexicans the same two choices that the dominant power in any confrontation gives to the weaker: the acceptance of a body of concrete diplomatic demands or eventual war. Slidell's instructions described U.S. territorial objectives with considerable clarity. If Mexico knew little of Polk's growing acquisitiveness toward California during the autumn of 1845, Slidell proclaimed the president's intentions with his proposals to purchase varying portions of California for as much as $25 million. Other countries such as England and Spain had consigned important areas of the New World through peaceful negotiations, but the United States, except in its Mexican relations, had never asked any country to part with a portion of its own territory. Yet Polk could not understand why Mexico should reveal any special reluctance to part with Texas, the Rio Grande, New Mexico, or California. What made the terms of Slidell's instructions appear fair to him was Mexico's military and financial helplessness. Polk's defenders noted that California was not a sine qua non of any settlement and that the president offered to settle the immediate controversy over the acquisition of the Rio Grande boundary alone in exchange for the cancellation of claims. Unfortunately, amid the passions of December 1845, such distinctions were lost. Furthermore, a settlement of the Texas boundary would not have resolved the California question at all.

Throughout the crisis months of 1845 and 1846, spokesmen of the Polk administration repeatedly warned the Mexican government that its choices were limited. In June 1845, Polk's mouthpiece, the *Washington Union,* had observed characteristically that, if Mexico resisted Washington's demands, "a corps of properly organized volunteers . . . would invade, overrun, and occupy Mexico. They would enable us not only to take California, but to keep it." American officials, in their contempt for Mexico, spoke privately of the need to chastize that country for its annoyances and insults. Parrott wrote to Secretary of State James Buchanan in October that he wished "to see this people well flogged by Uncle Sam's boys, ere we enter upon negotiations. . . . I know [the Mexicans] better, perhaps, than any other American citizen and I am fully persuaded, they can never love or respect us, as we should be loved and respected by them, until we shall have given them a positive proof of our superiority." Mexico's pretensions would continue, wrote Slidell in late December, "until the Mexican people shall be convinced by hostile demonstrations, that our differences must be settled promptly, either by negotiation or the sword." In January 1846 the *Union* publicly threatened Mexico with war if it rejected the just demands of the United States: "The result of such a course on her part may compel us to resort to more decisive measures. . . . to obtain the settlement of our legitimate claims." As Slidell prepared to leave Mexico in March 1846, he again reminded the administration: "Depend upon it, we can never get along well with them, until we have given them a good drubbing." In Washington on May 8, Slidell advised the president "to take the redress of the wrongs and injuries which we had so long borne from Mexico into our own hands, and to act with promptness and energy."

Mexico responded to Polk's challenge with an outward display of belligerence and an inward dread of war. Mexicans feared above all that the United States intended to overrun their country and seize much of their territory. Polk and his advisers assumed that Mexico, to avoid an American invasion, would give up its provinces peacefully. Obviously Mexico faced growing diplomatic and military pressures to negotiate away its territories; it faced no moral obligation to do so. Herrera and Paredes had the sovereign right to protect their regimes by avoiding any formal recognition of Slidell and by rejecting any of the boundary proposals embodied in his instructions, provided that in the process they did not endanger any legitimate interests of the American people. At least to some Mexicans, Slidell's terms demanded nothing less than Mexico's capitulation. By what standard was $2 million a proper payment for the Rio Grande boundary, or $25 million a fair price for California? No government would have accepted such terms. Having rejected negotiation in the face of superior force, Mexico would meet the challenge with a final gesture of defiance. In either case it was destined to lose, but historically nations have preferred to fight than to give away territory under diplomatic pressure alone. Gene M. Brack, in his long study of Mexico's deep-seated fear and resentment of the United States, explained Mexico's ultimate behavior in such terms:

> President Polk knew that Mexico could offer but feeble resistance militarily, and he knew that Mexico needed money. No proper American would exchange territory and the national honor for cash, but President Polk mistakenly believed that the application of military pressure would

convince Mexicans to do so. They did not respond logically, but patriotically. Left with the choice of war or territorial concessions, the former course, however dim the prospects of success, could be the only one.

·◦◉◦·

Mexico, in its resistance, gave Polk the three choices which every nation gives another in an uncompromisable confrontation: to withdraw his demands and permit the issues to drift, unresolved; to reduce his goals in the interest of an immediate settlement; or to escalate the pressures in the hope of securing an eventual settlement on his own terms. Normally when the internal conditions of a country undermine its relations with others, a diplomatic corps simply removes itself from the hostile environment and awaits a better day. Mexico, despite its animosity, did not endanger the security interests of the United States; it had not invaded Texas and did not contemplate doing so. Mexico had refused to pay the claims, but those claims were not equal to the price of a one-week war. Whether Mexico negotiated a boundary for Texas in 1846 mattered little; the United States had lived with unsettled boundaries for decades without considering war. Settlers, in time, would have forced a decision, but in 1846 the region between the Nueces and the Rio Grande was a vast, generally unoccupied wilderness. Thus there was nothing, other than Polk's ambitions, to prevent the United States from withdrawing its diplomats from Mexico City and permitting its relations to drift. But Polk, whatever the language of his instructions, did not send Slidell to Mexico to normalize relations with that government. He expected Slidell to negotiate an immediate boundary settlement favorable to the United States, and nothing less.

Recognizing no need to reduce his demands on Mexico, Polk, without hesitation, took the third course which Mexico offered. Congress bound the president to the annexation of Texas; thereafter the Polk administration was free to formulate its own policies toward Mexico. With the Slidell mission Polk embarked upon a program of gradual coercion to achieve a settlement, preferably without war. That program led logically from his dispatching an army to Texas and his denunciation of Mexico in his annual message of December 1845 to his new instructions of January 1846, which ordered General Taylor to the Rio Grande. Colonel Atocha, spokesman for the deposed Mexican leader, Antonio López de Santa Anna, encouraged Polk to pursue his policy of escalation. The president recorded Atocha's advice:

> He said our army should be marched at once from Corpus Christi to the Del Norte, and a strong naval force assembled at Vera Cruz, that Mr. Slidell, the U.S. Minister, should withdraw from Jalappa, and go on board one of our ships of War at Vera Cruz, and in that position should demand the payment of [the] amount due our citizens; that it was well known the Mexican Government was unable to pay in money, and that when they saw a strong force ready to strike on their coasts and border, they would, he had no doubt, feel their danger and agree to the boundary suggested. He said that Paredes, Almonte, & Gen'l Santa

Anna were all willing for such an arrangement, but that they dare not make it until it was made apparent to the Archbishop of Mexico & the people generally that it was necessary to save their country from a war with the U. States.

Thereafter Polk never questioned the efficacy of coercion. He asserted at a cabinet meeting on February 17 that "it would be necessary to take strong measures towards Mexico before our difficulties with that Government could be settled." Similarly on April 18 Polk told Calhoun that "our relations with Mexico had reached a point where we could not stand still but must treat all nations whether weak or strong alike, and that I saw no alternative but strong measures towards Mexico." A week later the president again brought the Mexican question before the cabinet. "I expressed my opinion," he noted in his diary, "that we must take redress for the injuries done us into our own hands, that we had attempted to conciliate Mexico in vain, and had forborne until forbearance was no longer either a virtue or patriotic." Convinced that Paredes needed money, Polk suggested to leading senators that Congress appropriate $1 million both to encourage Paredes to negotiate and to sustain him in power until the United States could ratify the treaty. The president failed to secure Calhoun's required support.

Polk's persistence led him and the country to war. Like all escalations in the exertion of force, his decision responded less to unwanted and unanticipated resistance than to the requirements of the clearly perceived and inflexible purposes which guided the administration. What perpetuated the president's escalation to the point of war was his determination to pursue goals to the end whose achievement lay outside the possibilities of successful negotiations. Senator Thomas Hart Benton of Missouri saw this situation when he wrote: "It is impossible to conceive of an administration less warlike, or more intriguing, than that of Mr. Polk. They were *men of peace, with objects to be accomplished by means of war;* so that war was a necessity and an indispensability to their purpose."

Polk understood fully the state of Mexican opinion. In placing General Taylor on the Rio Grande he revealed again his contempt for Mexico. Under no national obligation to expose the country's armed forces, he would not have advanced Taylor in the face of a superior military force. Mexico had been undiplomatic; its denunciations of the United States were insulting and provocative. But if Mexico's behavior antagonized Polk, it did not antagonize the Whigs, the abolitionists, or even much of the Democratic party. Such groups did not regard Mexico as a threat; they warned the administration repeatedly that Taylor's presence on the Rio Grande would provoke war. But in the balance against peace was the pressure of American expansionism. Much of the Democratic and expansionist press, having accepted without restraint both the purposes of the Polk administration and its charges of Mexican perfidy, urged the president on to more vigorous action. . . .

Confronted with the prospect of further decline which they could neither accept nor prevent, [the Mexicans] lashed out with the intention of protecting their self-esteem and compelling the United States, if it was determined to have the Rio Grande, New Mexico, and California, to pay for its prizes with something other than money. On April 23, Paredes issued a proclamation declaring a defensive war against the United States. Predictably, one day later the Mexicans fired on a detachment of U.S. dragoons. Taylor's report of the attack reached Polk on Saturday evening, May 9. On Sunday the president drafted his war message and delivered it to Congress on the following day. Had Polk avoided the crisis, he might have gained the time required to permit the emigrants of 1845 and 1846 to settle the California issue without war.

What clouds the issue of the Mexican War's justification was the acquisition of New Mexico and California, for contemporaries and historians could not logically condemn the war and laud the Polk administration for its territorial achievements. Perhaps it is true that time would have permitted American pioneers to transform California into another Texas. But even then California's acquisition by the United States would have emanated from the use of force, for the elimination of Mexican sovereignty, whether through revolution or war, demanded the successful use of power. If the power employed in revolution would have been less obtrusive than that exerted in war, its role would have been no less essential. There simply was no way that the United States could acquire California peacefully. If the distraught Mexico of 1845 would not sell the distant province, no regime thereafter would have done so. Without forceful destruction of Mexico's sovereign power, California would have entered the twentieth century as an increasingly important region of another country.

Thus the Mexican War poses the dilemma of all international relations. Nations whose geographic and political status fails to coincide with their ambition and power can balance the two sets of factors in only one manner: through the employment of force. They succeed or fail according to circumstances; and for the United States, the conditions for achieving its empire in the Southwest and its desired frontage on the Pacific were so ideal that later generations could refer to the process as the mere fulfillment of destiny. "The Mexican Republic," lamented a Mexican writer in 1848, " . . . had among other misfortunes of less account, the great one of being in the vicinity of a strong and energetic people." What the Mexican War revealed in equal measure is the simple fact that only those countries which have achieved their destiny, whatever that may be, can afford to extol the virtues of peaceful change.

POSTSCRIPT

Was the Mexican War an Exercise in American Imperialism?

*H*abits of Empire (Knopf, 2008) is now the major synthesis of the political and military roots of American expansionism. Professor Nugent bluntly argues that the United States was imperialistic from its very beginnings. American expansionism has gone through three phases: The first was the *continental* expansion across North America (exclusive of Canada) from 1783 to 1853, which resulted in the displacement of the Native Americans. Empire II was *overseas* expansion from 1867 to 1917, which resulted in the acquisition and rule over non-white populations in the Pacific and Central American regions. Since the end of World War II in 1945, the United States established the third *virtual global* empire, which resulted in regime changes during the cold war years against Russia and China as well as during the current war on terrorism.

Nugent spent most of his career writing about western American history. In this book, he combines the expansion of the American people across the continent with the imperialist thrust of establishing an empire. The motivations are multicausal—"spontaneous jingoism, national security demands, and visions of overseas markets for imperial goods." If there is one key factor, it is demographics. This is especially true for empire one when the United States increased its population from 1 million in 1787 to 30 million on the eve of the Civil War. "During that period," said Stephen A. Douglas in deriding Lincoln's "House Divided" speech in a debate in 1858, "we have extended our territory from the Mississippi to the Pacific Ocean; we have acquired the Floridas and Texas, and other territory sufficient to double our geographical extent."

In his chapters on Texas and the Mexican war, part of which is included in the reader, Professor Nugent views President Polk as a narrow-minded bigot whose one big idea was to acquire California and as much of the southwest as was possible either through negotiation or force. When the Mexican government, riddled with unstable governments, corrupt politicians, and incompetent generals, refused to negotiate, Polk maneuvered the Mexican government to attack American soldiers stationed in the disputed area between the Rio Grande and Nueces Rivers.

This was not the first time, says Nugent, the chief executive maneuvered Congress into a *fait accompli* with regard to declaring war. ". . . Madison came near to doing so in 1812. George H. Bush's troop buildup before the first Gulf War and George W. Bush's before Iraq were not novelties. There may be limits on presidential power, but there are no obvious ones on a president as commander-in-chief in sending troops and ships where he wants to."

Professor Norman Graebner is one of the most popular teachers at the University of Virginia and is considered one of the most prominent members of the "realist" school of diplomatic historians. His writings were influenced by the cold war realists, political scientists, diplomats, and journalists of the 1950s who believed that American foreign policy oscillated between heedless isolationism and crusading wars without developing coherent policies that suited the national interests of the United States.

According to Graebner, President James Polk assumed that Mexico was weak and that acquiring certain Mexican territories would satisfy "the long-range interests" of the United States. But when Mexico refused Polk's attempts to purchase New Mexico and California, he was left with three options: withdraw his demands, modify and soften his proposals, or aggressively pursue his original goals. According to Graebner, the president chose the third option.

Graebner disagrees with Nugent over who started the Mexican War. He argues that Polk truly believed that President Paredes would back down and negotiate. Nugent, along with other writers such as Richard Kluger, in *Seizing Destiny: How America Grew from Sea to Shining Sea* (Knopf, 2007), maintains that Polk really wanted the war, especially after the Oregon boundary dispute with England was settled at the 49th parallel. Other historians support Graebner by putting the events into a broader focus. Walter A. McDougall, in *Promised Land, Crusader State: the American Encounter with World since 1776,* states that aside from "sheer ambition" or "the fact that Americans inhabited an undeveloped continent devoid of serious rivals . . . expansion derived from the primordial exceptional American commitment to liberty." The four barriers to expansion, continues McDougall, included Indian tribes, British lords, Mexican juntas, and "U.S. federal authorities themselves telling farmers, trappers, ranchers, merchants and missionaries: No, you can't settle here, or do business there. Go back where you came from!" (p. 78). Finally Robert Kagan, in *Dangerous Nation* (Knopf, 2006), emphasizes how the acquisition of California and the territories of New Mexico and Arizona could upset the balance of power between the equal number of free and slave states that had been created.

ISSUE 13

Was John Brown an Irrational Terrorist?

YES: James N. Gilbert, from "A Behavioral Analysis of John Brown: Martyr or Terrorist?" in Peggy A. Russo and Paul Finkelman, eds., *Terrible Swift Sword: The Legacy of John Brown* (Ohio University Press, 2005)

NO: Scott John Hammond, from "John Brown as Founder: America's Violent Confrontation with Its First Principles," in Peggy A. Russo and Paul Finkelman, eds., *Terrible Swift Sword: The Legacy of John Brown* (Ohio University Press, 2005)

ISSUE SUMMARY

YES: James N. Gilbert says that John Brown's actions conform to a modern definition of terrorist behavior in that Brown considered the United States incapable of reforming itself by abolishing slavery, believed that only violence would accomplish that goal, and justified his actions by proclaiming adherence to a "higher" power.

NO: Scott John Hammond insists that John Brown's commitment to higher moral and political goals conformed to the basic principles of human freedom and political and legal quality that formed the heart of the creed articulated by the founders of the American nation.

Opposition to slavery in the area that became the United States dates back to the seventeenth and eighteenth centuries, when Puritan leaders, such as Samuel Sewall, and Quakers, such as John Woolman and Anthony Benezet, published a number of pamphlets condemning the existence of the slave system. This religious link to antislavery sentiment is also evident in the writings of John Wesley as well as in the decision of the Society of Friends in 1688 to prohibit their members from owning bondservants. Slavery was said to be contrary to Christian principles. These attacks, however, did little to diminish the institution. Complaints that the English government had instituted a series of measures that "enslaved" the colonies in British North America raised thorny questions about the presence of *real* slavery in those colonies. How could American colonists demand their freedom from King George III, who was cast in the role of oppressive master, while denying freedom and liberty to African American slaves? Such a contradiction inspired a gradual emancipation movement in the North, which often was accompanied by compensation for the former slave owners.

In addition, antislavery societies sprang up throughout the nation to continue the crusade against bondage. Interestingly, the majority of these organizations were located in the South. Prior to the 1830s, the most prominent antislavery organization was the American Colonization Society, which offered a twofold program: (1) gradual, compensated emancipation of slaves; and (2) exportation of the newly freed to colonies outside the boundaries of the United States, mostly to Africa.

In the 1830s, antislavery activity underwent an important transformation. A new strain of antislavery sentiment expressed itself in the abolitionist movement. Drawing momentum both from the revivalism of the Second Great Awakening and the example set by England (which prohibited slavery in its imperial holdings in 1833), abolitionists called for the immediate end to slavery without compensation to masters for the loss of their property. Abolitionists viewed slavery not so much as a practical problem to be resolved, but rather as a moral offense incapable of resolution through traditional channels of political compromise. In January 1831, William Lloyd Garrison, who for many came to symbolize the abolitionist crusade, published the first issue of *The Liberator,* a newspaper dedicated to the immediate end to slavery. In his first editorial, Garrison expressed the self-righteous indignation of many in the abolitionist movement when he warned slaveholders and their supporters to "urge me not to use moderation in a cause like the present. I am in earnest—I will not equivocate—I will not excuse—I will not retreat a single inch—AND I WILL BE HEARD. . . ."

Unfortunately for Garrison, relatively few Americans were inclined to respond positively to his call. His newspaper generated little interest outside Boston, New York, Philadelphia, and other major urban centers of the North. This situation, however, changed within a matter of months. In August 1831, a slave preacher named Nat Turner led a rebellion of slaves in Southampton County, Virginia, that resulted in the death of 58 whites. Although the revolt was quickly suppressed and Turner and his supporters were executed, the incident spread fear throughout the South. Governor John B. Floyd of Virginia turned an accusatory finger toward the abolitionists when he concluded that the Turner uprising was "undoubtedly designed and matured by unrestrained fanatics in some of the neighboring states."

One such "unrestrained fanatic" was John Brown, who became a martyr in the antislavery pantheon when he was executed following his unsuccessful raid on the federal arsenal in Harpers Ferry, Virginia, in 1859. In this issue, James N. Gilbert argues that Brown's attack was comparable to recent acts of terrorism in the United States and that, despite the continuing tendency to portray his actions as those of a martyred hero, Brown clearly fits the modern definition of a domestic terrorist.

In the second selection, Scott John Hammond characterizes Brown in a more positive light. While recognizing flaws in Brown's personality and actions, Hammond nevertheless concludes that John Brown acted on the highest of principles to thwart evil by articulating an undiluted commitment with the basic principles of America's founding—individual liberty and political and legal equality.

YES ↵

A Behavioral Analysis of John Brown: Martyr or Terrorist?

The scholarly examination of the topic of terrorism has developed into a significant area of legal and criminological research. Academic and governmental studies pertaining to terrorist crimes and those who perpetrate them are now voluminous and continue to be actively pursued. Emerging as what appeared to be a new form of criminal deviance, the definition and cause of the "disease of the 70s" has challenged criminologists. While most contemporary documented incidents continue to occur outside the United States, the fear of domestic terrorism, as recent events have illustrated, remains a legitimate concern. The public and researchers alike have in the past commonly assumed that this country would continue to be spared from acts that conform to our contemporary definition of terrorist activity. Terrorism was associated with a foreign environment and viewed as exceptional in the history of American criminal violence.

But after February 26, 1993, when the New York World Trade Center was the target of a massive terrorist bombing, the attention of Americans became riveted upon the unique form of criminality that we have collectively termed terrorism. And of course this criminal act was followed by the far more deadly bombing in Oklahoma City and the attacks on the World Trade Center and the Pentagon on September 11, 2001. Although much of the media and public has treated these terrorist acts as precedent-setting domestic attacks, the history of terrorism in the United States actually dates to the founding of the nation. Of the many such violent episodes in our earlier history, John Brown's attack on Harpers Ferry in October 1859 is comparable to these more recent acts in terms of national terror and consequent social and political upheaval.

In late 1859 John Brown and twenty-one followers attempted to rally and arm large numbers of slaves by attacking and briefly holding the United States arsenal at Harpers Ferry, Virginia (presently West Virginia). Captured by federal military forces and local militia, Brown was hastily tried and executed. While the life and deeds of John Brown are immensely important for their impact on abolitionism and the American Civil War, this powerful historical figure is rarely defined as a terrorist. Instead, a vast collection of literature generally portrays Brown as either saint or madman. On one hand, there is the sympathetic traditional portrait of John Brown as an American hero of near mythical

From *Terrible Swift Sword: The Legacy of John Brown* by Peggy A. Russo and Paul Finkelman (Ohio University Press, 2005), pp. 107–113, 114–116 (notes omitted). Copyright © 2005 by Ohio University Press. Reprinted by permission.

proportions. Such an image is certainly not viewed as criminally deviant, nor does it suggest the status of criminal folk hero. But while a minority historical judgment has questioned his sanity or the radical end-justification logic he appeared to employ, few even in this camp would declare his actions truly terrorist. Civil War and military historian John Hubbell reflects this multidimensional view. Stating that while John Brown was, "in fact, a combination of humility and arrogance, submission and aggression, murder and martyrdom," his true motivation may not have been calculated terroristic cause and effect, but "an unresolved resentment of his father; his hatred of slaveholders may have been the unconscious resolution of his anger."

Thus, one can only question how and why this imagery has persisted throughout the decades. Is the terrorist label lacking due to the singular rationale of his crimes: the massive evil of slavery? Alternatively, are we correct in excluding Brown from the definition of terrorist because his actions simply fail to conform to contemporary elements that constitute such a criminal? For example, a similar definitional confusion currently exists regarding various violent attacks on abortion clinics and their personnel by those who, like Brown, rationalize their violence by moral or religious conviction. Some would define convicted murderer Paul Hill as a domestic terrorist for his premeditated attack on an abortion doctor and an escort during the summer of 1994. Yet others would fail to define his actions as terroristic due to Hill's justification of his act as a "lesser evil."

In order to define Brown precisely as a terrorist rather than as a martyr, the meaning of terrorism must be explored. As with many singular, emotion-producing labels of criminality, terrorism is easier to describe than define. The *Vice President's Task Force on Combating Terrorism* describes terrorism as a phenomenon involving "the unlawful use of threat of violence against persons or property to further political or social objectives." In a similar vein, the FBI's Terrorist Research and Analytical Center states that terroristic activity "is the unlawful use of force or violence against persons or property to intimidate or coerce a government, the civilian population, or any segment thereof, in furtherance of political or social objectives." Both definitions agree with views commonly provided by various governments. This traditional bureaucratic view stresses a triad in which both property and people are potential targets with the necessary presence of illegal actions and social or political motivations as the causative agent.

Additional attempts to conceptualize the terrorist often focus on the perpetrator's motive rather than legal definitions. To this economist Bill Anderson links the economic viewpoint, stressing that fundamental principles of economic theory are the real, often hidden, motives of such crimes. Anderson believes that after we "peel away the ideological skins and fig leaves that terrorists use to justify their violence, we come to the core reason for their actions: the terrorists' own desire for power and influence. In other words, the terrorists are seeking wealth transfers and/or power (all of which can be defined as economic or political rents) through violent means because they are not willing to pay the cost of participating in the political process."

Others prefer to explain away terrorism through an apologist approach, stressing the anger, hopelessness, and governmental violence brought against various victimized populations from which, inevitably, terrorists will be mobilized. Eqbal Ahmad, a research fellow at the Washington, D.C.–based Institute for Policy Studies, stresses this sympathetic theme when he links terrorism to government indifference to violence. He believes that individuals turn to terrorism to exercise "their need to be heard, the combination of anger and helplessness producing the impulse for retributive violence. The experience of violence by a stronger party has historically turned victims into terrorists." Thus, the apologist view firmly supports the recurring belief that terrorism is merely situational, constantly coming in and out of criminal focus according to prevailing political power or orientation. Sheikh Omar Abdel-Rahman clearly embraced the situational view when he claimed to be a victim rather than an alleged conspirator in the 1993 World Trade Center bombing. Angered over his conspiracy indictment and subsequent incarceration, he stated, "but what bothers me, and makes me feel bitter about the whole thing, is when a person who was called a freedom fighter then is now called, when the war is over, a terrorist."

A final view, particularly popular in fictional portrayals of terrorists, suggests individual psychopathology as the chief cause of terrorism. As detailed by political philosopher and professor of religion Moshe Amon, one form of terroristic crime may originate within the disturbed minds of some perpetrators, triggering myths and fantasies that can be categorized as messianic or apocalyptic. The messianic terrorist ideology streams from a conviction that one has special insight that produces an individual state of enlightenment. Terrorists are then convinced that "they are the only ones who see the real world, and the only ones who are not affected by its depravity. It is their mission, therefore, to liberate the blind people of this world from the rule of the unjust." Although this concept may be traced to early Hebrew origins, a more contemporary form is common among Latin American terrorists. Political scientist John Pottenger concludes, "The existence of social injustice and [the] individual's commitment to human liberation, demand that a radical change can turn the Christian into a revolutionary vanguard demonstrating that God not only intervenes in human history but He does so on the right side of the oppressed."

Other psychological theorists believe that the most common type of terrorist has a psychopathic or sociopathic personality. The classic traits of the psychopath—impulsiveness, lack of guilt, inability to experience emotional depth, and manipulation—are perceived as ideally suited to the commission of terrorism. The ability to kill often large numbers of strangers without compunction or to manipulate others to unwittingly further criminal ends convinces many that the psychopathic personality is a requirement for terroristic action.

With such definitions of terrorism in mind, how are we to view John Brown? After almost a century and a half, the actions of Brown have been preserved with stark clarity, yet his personality and related psychological motivations can only be surmised. John Brown was fifty-nine years old when he was executed by the state of Virginia for treason, conspiring with blacks to produce insurrection, and murder in the first degree. His criminal activities of record include embezzlement and assault with a deadly weapon against an Ohio sheriff in 1842. In 1856 a warrant was issued by a proslavery Kansas district court charging Brown with "organizing against slavery." A month later he and eight other men kidnapped and murdered five Kansans, including a constable and his two sons. The killings were particularly brutal: the victims were hacked to death by repeated sword blows. In December 1858 the state of Missouri and the federal government offered a reward for Brown's capture because he was the chief suspect in yet another criminal homicide. Finally, Brown's criminal activities culminated in the seizure of the federal armory at Harpers Ferry on October 16, 1859. A company of U.S. Marines captured him the following day, and history records his execution less than fifty days after his attack against the armory.

The question of whether John Brown was indeed a terrorist must be based on a definitional standard that defies emotional or mythical distortion. The linkage of Brown's cause to the horrors of slavery circumvents the true nature of the man and of his crimes. According to Albert Parry, author of a best-selling work on the history of terror and revolutionary violence, terrorists and those who study them offer innumerable explanations of their violence; yet their motivations can be compacted into three main concepts:

1. Society is sick and cannot be cured by half measures of reform.
2. The state is in itself violent and can be countered and overcome only by violence.
3. The truth of the terrorist cause justifies any action that supports it. While some terrorists recognize no moral law, others have their own "higher" morality.

Comparing John Brown's actions to these criteria produces an inescapable match. On many occasions Brown expressed his solid belief that society, particularly a society that would embrace slavery, was sick beyond its own cure. Brown had clearly given up on public policy reforms or legal remedies regarding slavery when he drafted his own constitution for the benefit of his followers. The document attempts to define his justifications for the upcoming attack at Harpers Ferry and utterly rejects the legal and moral foundation of the United States: "Therefore, we citizens of the United States and the Oppressed People, who by a Recent Decision of the Supreme Court are declared to have no rights which the white man is bound to respect; together with all other people regarded by the laws thereof, do for the time being, ordain and establish for ourselves the following provisional constitution and ordinances, the better to protect our persons, property, lives, and liberties: and to govern our actions."

As to the terroristic belief that violent government can only be overcome by violence, Brown's convictions were preserved for posterity by a note he handed to a jailer while being led to the gallows: "I John Brown am now quite *certain* that the crimes of this *guilty land: will* never be purged *away*; but with Blood. I had *as I now think: vainly* flattered myself that without *very much* bloodshed: it might be done."

With similar conformity, Brown's beliefs and actions demonstrated his rigid "higher" morality, which served to justify numerous crimes, including multiple homicides. As described by historian Stephen Oates, "Brown knew the Missourians would come after him . . . yet he was not afraid of the consequences for God would keep and deliver him: God alone was his judge. Now that the work was done, he believed that he had been guided by a just and wrathful God."

Brown's deeds conform to contemporary definitions of terrorism, and his psychological predispositions are consistent with the terrorist model. As observed by David Hubbard, founder of the Aberrant Behavior Center and psychiatric consultant to the Federal Bureau of Prisons, the actions and personality of the terrorist are not "merely bizarre and willfully antisocial; but a reflection of deep-seated personal and cultural pathologies." Such behavioral pathology is commonly linked to the psychopathic personality or, less frequently, to some form of paranoia. Virtually unknown to mental health authorities during Brown's lifetime, the psychopathic personality is currently considered a relatively common criminal mental abnormality among violent offenders. Although psychopathic criminals account for a small percentage of overall lawbreakers, psychologist William McCord notes that they commit a disproportionate percentage of violent crime. While psychopaths may be encountered within any violent criminal typology, they appear to be particularly well represented in various crimes of serial violence, confidence fraud, and terrorism.

The concept of psychopathy focuses on the unsocialized criminal, who is devoid of conscience and consequently in repeated conflict with society; he or she fails to learn from prior experiences. As observed by Herbert Strean, professor of social work and psychotherapy researcher at Rutgers University, the psychopath is often arrogant, callous, and lacking in empathy and tends to offer plausible rationalizations for his or her reckless behavior. While John Brown demonstrated a guilt-free conscience on many occasions, his calculating leadership in the kidnapping and murder of five people in Kansas provided beyond question his capacity to free himself of normal emotion. On the night of May 26, 1856, Brown led a small party of followers to the various cabins of his political enemies, which included Constable James Doyle and his sons. During what would later be termed the Pottawatomie Massacre, the Brown party systematically dragged the five unarmed and terrified men from their homes and murdered them in a frenzy of brutal violence. "About a hundred yards down the road Salmon and Owen [Brown's sons] fell on the Doyles with broadswords. They put up a struggle, striking out, trying to shield themselves from the slashing blades as they staggered back down the road. But in a few moments the grisly work was done. Brown, who must have watched the executions in a kind of trance, now walked over and shot Doyle in the forehead with a revolver, to make certain work of it." When later questioned about his motives during the Kansas murders, Brown offered a classic messianic psychopathic rationalization. Without a trace of remorse, he stated that the victims all deserved to die as they "had committed murder in their hearts already, according to the Big Book . . . their killing had been decreed by Almighty God, ordained from eternity."

. . . John Brown does not stand alone in the annals of American-based terrorism. Yet he obviously remains a unique, paradoxical example of a terrorist whom history has often viewed through rose-colored lenses. As opposed to alarm or disgust, the deeds of John Brown have moved some to great literary inspiration, such as Stephen Vincent Benét's epic poem *John Brown's Body*. Ralph Waldo Emerson, writing shortly before Brown's execution, referred to Brown as "the Saint, whose fate yet hangs in suspense, but whose martyrdom, if it shall be perfected, will make the gallows glorious like the Cross." Other towering figures of the arts echo the purity of Brown while conveniently ignoring his murderous past. Henry David Thoreau wrote, "No man in America has ever stood up so persistently and effectively for the dignity of human nature, knowing himself for a man, and the equal of any and all governments. . . . He could not have been tried by a jury of his peers, because his peers did not exist." Other, more contemporary sources, including scores of textbooks, continue to echo such laudatory sentiments, informing generation after generation of young Americans that John Brown was a genuine hero. Typical of many such high school and middle school American history texts, one leading book praises Brown through Emerson's words as "a new saint," while another considers him "a martyr and hero, as he walked resolutely to the scaffold."

In a pragmatic sense, it is doubtful that the heroic legend of John Brown will ever include the terrorist truth of his crimes. As observed by guerrilla warfare essayist Walter Laqueur, "terrorism has long exercised a great fascination, especially at a safe distance . . . the fascination it exerts and the difficulty of interpreting it have the same roots: its unexpected, shocking and outrageous character." While many American terrorists exert a continuing fascination, none have occupied the unique position of John Brown. By contemporary definition, he was undoubtedly a terrorist to his core, demonstrating repeatedly the various axioms from which we shape this unique crime. Brown quite purposely waged war for political and social change while simultaneously committing the most heinous crimes. As political scientist Charles Hazelip would say when defining a terrorist, he had "crossed over the blurred line of demarcation between crime and war where political terrorism begins."

Yet John Brown's obsessive target, the focus of all his energy and murderous deeds, has by its nature absolved him from the cold label of *terrorist.* History and popular opinion have quite naturally found the greater criminality of slavery to far outweigh his illegal acts. The bold tactics at Harpers Ferry, coupled with his humanistic motives to free the Virginia slaves, compels us to forgive his disturbed personality and deadly past. The attack on a key government arsenal and armory, which in a contemporary context would horrify the nation, has been judged through the passage of time to be an inevitable, gallant first strike against the soon to be formed Southern Confederacy. When taken as a whole, and to the natural dismay of our justice system, Brown's actions quite convincingly demonstrate that if the weight of moral sentiment is on one's side, terroristic violence can be absorbed into a nation's historiography in a positive sense. [Christopher] Dobson and [Ronald] Payne conclude, "the main aim of terror is to make murderers into heroes." While many will continue to debate the magnitude of John Brown's terrorism, his heroic stature has been secured by the often paradoxical judgment of history.

NO

John Brown as Founder: America's Violent Confrontation with Its First Principles

John Brown moves at an angle through our history, a transfigured personage who is deemed a force of nature, an avenging angel wielding the scourge of God, a fearsome vessel of pure fanaticism that is seductive in the abstract as well as a terrifyingly demonic power in the flesh. Some would call him a tragic hero, flawed only in his insistence on purity in thought and action coupled with a mystical detachment from the political realities of his day; and some would see in him a prototerrorist, a criminal mind living on the lunatic fringe of history, condemned by rational people in both the North and South. Lincoln, in spite of his deep opposition to slavery, saw in Brown's raid the very archetype of lawless violence and was quick to distance both himself and his party from such obviously treasonous actions. For example, directing his remarks to Southern whites in a speech at the Cooper Union Institute on February 27, 1860, Lincoln declared: "You charge that we stir up insurrections among your slaves. We deny it; and what is your proof? Harper's [sic] Ferry! John Brown! John Brown is no Republican, and you have [yet] to implicate a single Republican in his Harper's [sic] Ferry enterprise." Conversely, Emerson praised Brown and remarked that Brown would elevate the gallows to a symbol of martyrdom on the same order and import as the Cross. It was, and perhaps still is, difficult for one to be objective or neutral about Osawatomie Brown: one was either with him or against him.

What we know of Brown's life fuels all these interpretations. As a lover of freedom steeled by a devotion to strict Calvinism, Brown appears to have been a practitioner of the Christian ethic framed by the imperative of universal love and compassion for others, especially those who suffer under the yoke of oppression and injustice. For in loving and caring for "the least" of his fellow human beings, he epitomized the purity of a love of human freedom that often comes from a sense of oneness with higher moral ends. Nonetheless, this is the same John Brown who, in the course of one night, assumed the visage of the Night Rider and personally directed and participated in the murder of five defenseless men. Since these men were supporters of slavery, and some of them had previously committed violence against Free State settlers, Brown's decision to kill them is perceived by some as part of his greater mission on behalf of even

From *Terrible Swift Sword: The Legacy of John Brown* by Peggy A. Russo and Paul Finkelman (Ohio University Press, 2005), pp. 61–69, 70–71, 72–75 (excerpts; notes omitted). Copyright © 2005 by Ohio University Press. Reprinted by permission.

more defenseless slaves. Still, the manner in which Brown summarily executed these five resembles that of the vicious terrorist more than that of the righteous warrior, and the Pottawatomie Massacre chills the blood of even the most ardent foe of oppression.

These aspects of Brown's psyche reflect something about our own political soul—our "political psyche" writ large. If Brown embodies the essence of us all, then it might be conceded that Brown's more pathological qualities replicate a profound dissonance within our general political and social culture. We must consider the inevitable consequences inherent within a sociopolitical condition fractured by the collision between the ideals of democratic liberty and the appalling realities of slavery and racism. No American will impugn the principles of liberty and equality, for however they are construed or comprehended, the structuring principles of the American polity are derived from a noble vision and an aspiration for a free and dignified humanity. The presence of slavery in a country committed, at least in principle, to freedom is the worst possible incidence of ideational failure. Brown's fractured self is an embodiment of the tangled forces of light and darkness that grappled for the republic's soul; his character and actions demonstrate this, and in so doing, make him no different from the ruptured essence of our collective political self-consciousness. The Pottawatomie slaughter represents a symptom of the deeper malady, just as the abuse of any slave by an overseer represents the same type of symptomatic manifestation. In contrast to Brown's avenging violence in Kansas, the incident at Harpers Ferry was driven by a spirit imbued with the transfiguring fire of the idea of universal freedom, in the same manner as the Underground Railroad or the individual dissent of the most famous resident of Walden Pond. Both America and Brown reveal this self-negating duality.

That Brown could be so moved to action by the tragedy of his times further amplifies his character and conviction. Most citizens, absorbed in the daily process and considerations of private interest and obligation, ignore or suppress the maladies of the deeper social structure. The affairs of the state frequently demand too much concentration and emotional investment for the average citizen. Nevertheless, there will always be those among us who, like Brown, seriously regard the structuring principles of a political culture with unabashed sincerity and are thus impelled to hold our institutions and practices accountable to our own higher ideas and political ideals.

Brown judged society according to the laws of God, and he saw with a piercing clarity that neither the ruling political doctrine nor, more important, the commandments of Providence were being properly revered. Nothing could absolve us from the sin of slavery, and the distinctions between righteousness and evil were easily and sharply drawn. No ambiguity, no "gray in gray," no compromise or allowance would be tolerated; either one was with the warriors for freedom and divine righteousness or among the profane legions who served on behalf of sinful oppression. For Brown, unlike most of his fellow Americans, the only solution was an obvious one—brook no sympathy for or concession to the minions of evil, and unconditionally submit without hesitation or diffidence to the Higher Authority, never relenting until total emancipation was achieved or sublime retribution judiciously dispensed. This is what drove John

Brown to act with such intensity of conviction, which magnified every hidden idiosyncrasy. Hence, Brown is at once liberator and fanatic, messiah and monster, the very incarnation of the conflicted American political soul.

This leads us to a more direct consideration of the notion of foundations and founding. The act of founding involves at least an abstract comprehension of those first principles that constitute a political soul and the resolve to forward those principles in an undiluted form. . . .

Upon examining those individuals who are noted for participating in an act of founding, we notice something unique that separates them from the ordinary politician, activist, or statesman. This is explained with considerable clarity by Machiavelli, who typically adds the ingredient of realpolitik to his observations of founding and reformative leadership. Given the fact that all founders and reformers will inevitably encounter resistance from those enemies who "profit from the old order," and assuming that a purely good leader will "bring about his own ruin among so many who are not good," Machiavelli notes that a lawgiver or prophet must go forth armed and prepared for struggle. Machiavelli's idea of a founder is consonant with the idea of virtu, or grandeur of soul—a character of extraordinary proportions, defined in terms of "ingenuity, skill, and excellence." Machiavelli seeks a type of transcending leadership, attaching a significant martial quality to his model founders. Even Moses, a religious founder, employs the might of God against Pharaoh in order to liberate the enslaved Israelites, something that those who follow the New Testament model of the suffering Christ would unequivocally reject.

Brown's actions are like those of a prophet-warrior. However, Machiavelli's armed prophet is also a conqueror; failure is associated with those who attempt to establish founding law without the enforcing power of arms. Brown does not seem to conform easily to the prophet-warrior model, for his arms were poor, his numbers few, and his plan thwarted by overextension and local hostility. Moses was at least able to extricate the Israelite slaves from their Egyptian oppressors. Moses conquered by overcoming the power of Egypt and then *founded* both a religion and a nation through the transmission of the Law of God. It is an understatement to say that Brown's achievement falls far short of this mark.

But if one considers the substance of Brown's commitment (the emancipation of the enslaved) and the method of Brown's action (confrontation with the sinful oppressor on behalf of the oppressed), Brown's character and actions do approximate the Machiavellian hero-founder. Furthermore, although he does not conquer in the physical or political sense, he does emerge triumphant. Brown was defeated but martyred, and in the end emancipation came for his people through the violence that he had prophesied. In a sobering moment of synchronicity, Lincoln's retrospective utterance in his second inaugural address, that "until every drop of blood drawn with the lash, shall be paid by another drawn with the sword," echoes Brown's last testimony. Two years earlier, Lincoln, at Gettysburg, had referred to a "new birth of freedom," and thus implicitly defined a new act of founding in the context and terms of the emancipation. From the blood and ashes of the war against slavery, the nation would be re-formed; Brown, who did not survive to witness the nation's second birth, nonetheless prophesied the act in his words. The nation was literally made anew but in a way that reaffirmed more completely the first principles of the republic. This represents an act of founding, and Brown's strike at Harpers Ferry was the prophetic prelude. Even though John Brown is distinct from Machiavelli's legendary types in a number of ways, he certainly shares in the role of founding/reforming visionary. Indeed, Lincoln, generally regarded as the heroic and tragic, even Christlike figure of the Civil War, resembles Brown in the end, only on a larger scale and from the comparatively more acceptable authority of his office. For Lincoln used violence to preserve the Union and purge the new nation of slavery. In his second inaugural address, he finally admits what he most likely knew from the beginning, that slavery was "somehow the cause of the war," and in so doing, for a brief moment toward the end of that war, the Great Emancipator shows himself akin to the Prophet of Osawatomie.

An alternative discussion of the founder-legislator is found in Rousseau's *Social Contract*. The Rousseauian founder is less applicable to the case of John Brown than the Machiavellian model. Rousseau's founder-legislator possesses a "superior intelligence" and is capable of "beholding all the passions of human beings without experiencing them." It is unlikely that Brown possessed a superior intelligence, and Brown's personality was far from the dispassionate character that Rousseau requires of his legislator. Furthermore, Rousseau's concept of the founder is identical to the concept of the first lawgiver and by no means resembles a prophet-warrior. Martial skill is not a requisite quality of Rousseau's founder, for Rousseau is always careful to mark an acute distinction between government based on consent and authority imposed by force. . . .

At another level, however, there is a similarity between Brown and Rousseau's founder. Rousseau's founder is an individual of superhuman qualities; indeed, Rousseau's description compares the creation of human first laws to the actions of gods. Rousseau's ideal founder is not afraid to act in a way that would challenge "human nature" itself. Brown seems to act against the natural order, but he does not intend to "change" human nature so much as to salvage it and even to save us from it. As a Calvinist, Brown undoubtedly believed that our nature is fixed by original sin; hence, he departed from Rousseau in yet another way. Brown fought against our sinful nature on behalf of redemption. Again, this seems to depart from Rousseau, but one must note that Rousseau's overall view of human nature was not much different from that of Calvin. Rousseau and Calvin both argued that humanity exists in a fallen condition, and although we cannot return to our original innocence, we can recover something of it through the affirmation of freedom and morality. For Calvin and John Brown, that higher state could be achieved through the Redeemer; for Rousseau, redemption is possible through the Social Contract. Both Rousseau and Brown sought a kind of recovery and affirmation of a better state of existence, and both insisted that in order to achieve such a goal, we must struggle mightily against our corrupted natures in order to reform and ennoble our humanity.

It should also be emphasized that the element of consent is vital to Rousseau. Brown's actions cannot admit of either direct or indirect consent of the governed for a number of reasons; most obvious of these is that Brown governed no one and possessed no legal or political authority, and that Brown was wholly dissociated from normal political channels. Even so, Brown acted in a way that relates indirectly to the notion of consensual governance. Brown sought neither the approval nor the consent of the populace, for the majority of the populace ignored, permitted, supported, or participated in the possession of human beings. More importantly, the law of God is not based on consent, but like Rousseau's general will, it is always right. Additionally, a minority of the population, both the enslaved victims and the various types of free dissenters and abolitionists, had been effectively deprived of their fundamental right to consent. The only rule that the slave knew was the rule of force, and the only rule that the abolitionist experienced was ultimately deemed immoral. The case of John Brown and his small group of followers and sympathizers exemplifies the latter, and it is compatible with Rousseau's theory of consent and resistance.

Even if Brown is not a founder-legislator in the strict Rousseauian sense, there are at least two arguments in the *Social Contract* that provide theoretical and moral support for Brown's extreme actions. First, Rousseau follows Locke in affirming that the notion of consent unequivocally requires unanimity. A political culture that either legitimizes or permits slavery violates this fundamental principle of universal consent. No one consents to be a slave; the enslaved population constitutes an excluded group that indicates a government based (partially) on force that is thus (wholly) illegitimate. Lincoln saw this as well and employed a similar argument in one of his many criticisms directed at the continued allowance of slavery. Even if one counters this argument by *incorrectly* objecting that Rousseau would not have included a slave population when considering the origins of the social contract, one would still have to take into account the abolitionists who, in acting against slavery from first principles, withdrew their consent to be governed by the current instrument. The unanimity that Rousseau demanded in theory never existed in practice under a regime that allowed slavery; thus, according to these standards, the Constitution, if it did indeed support or permit slavery (an issue that is in itself open to further analysis and argument within a different context) *was therefore not legitimate*. The founding act had occurred under an initial condition that was shaped by a great error.

This directs us back to our second point. Rousseau states without ambiguity that slavery is in every instance illegitimate and immoral. Freedom cannot be surrendered or usurped, for to "renounce liberty is to renounce being a man, to surrender the rights of humanity and even its duties." Thus, slavery can never be rendered legitimate or permitted by a government or any portion of its population. Rousseau makes this clear in the cases of both voluntary and involuntary submission. Slavery can be based neither on a voluntary arrangement nor on coercion or conquest. In the case of the former, one who agrees to be a slave is "out of one's mind," for it is madness to "renounce one's very humanity." Of course, American slavery was anything but voluntary, and for Rousseau, this form of slavery is equally inhumane. . . . As Rousseau powerfully states, "So, from whatever aspect we regard the question, the right of slavery is null and void, not only as being illegitimate, but also because it is absurd and meaningless. The words *slave* and *right* contradict each other, and are mutually exclusive. It will always be equally foolish for a man to say to a man or people: 'I make with you a convention wholly at your expense, and wholly to my advantage; I shall keep it as long as I like, and you will keep it as long as I like.'" Thus, not only is a social contract left unformed if it does not include the affirmation of *every* voice that is present within the polity, it is also morally incompatible given the presence of an enslaved group regardless of how the enslavement came about. In refusing to seek the consent of the majority, Brown chose to act on behalf of those who had been excluded from the founding act of consent and against a government that under Rousseau's definition can only be interpreted as illegitimate. Surely an analysis of Brown's actions from this perspective can better illuminate the questions that revolve around the accusation of his "lawlessness."

The notion of founding entails far more than establishment of institutions or governmental charters; it also, and above all, includes critical political and social reform in the pursuit of the higher principles of a given political culture. If we are to accept, along with such martyred luminaries as Lincoln and King, the proposition that the first principles of the American founding are to be understood as the guarantee of both individual liberty *and* the advance of political and legal equality, and if we add to this Rousseau's theoretical demolition of any claim to the alleged right to own human beings as property, then we can see in Brown's holy war against slavery an act that does indeed resonate with the spirit of the founding movement. . . .

Significantly, Brown made one major attempt to assume the mantle of legislator. The provisional constitution that was drafted and signed at the anti-slavery convention in Chatham, Ontario, was intended to provide the foundations for the new society that Brown envisioned establishing in the South after his successful liberation of the slaves and, as such, emulates the type of effort associated with a founder-legislator. In the Chatham document, Brown once again shares something in common with Lincoln in the latter's reaffirmation of the first principles established within the Declaration of Independence. Brown included in the Chatham document a statement that his provisional constitution was not meant to dissolve the federal constitution, but only to reaffirm the principles of the American Revolution through amendment and modification. The banner of the Spirit of '76 was to serve as the flag of the provisional government, thus echoing Lincoln's belief that the true founding of the nation began in the struggle for liberty and equality during the Revolution. In addition to the expression of higher political ideals, Brown also provided plans for framing a new government for the freed slaves and their allies, a proposed political system that, to many, was original and revolutionary. The Brown document departed dramatically from all previous constitutional examples because of such features as a supreme court that was to be elected by the widest possible popular vote; government officials who were "to serve without pay" and be removed and punished upon misconduct; extensive public reclamation of all property that was formerly acquired at the expense of the slaves; protection of female prisoners from violation; and plans for the "moral instruction" of the new citizens. Here again, Brown comes close to Rousseau's concept of the founder: a lawgiver who attempts to make human nature anew, one who is committed through law more than through force to the moral elevation of the human spirit. This is an example of Brown designing a more democratic government aimed toward human advancement and intended to restore the principles of the original American founding. . . . Brown's actions at Chatham are also similar to the steps taken at the convention of 1776, and once his supporters had signed the document, Brown felt prepared to enter the field of battle, knowing that his deeds were formally supported by written principles and political ideals as well as by his steadfast religious faith. At Chatham, Brown exchanged arms for pen and ink and, like Jefferson and Madison, attempted to establish a new order for humanity through law. . . .

In turning back to Harpers Ferry, we must also raise the following question: Why weren't more people of conscience moved to arms, as was John Brown? This can be partially explained by the close connection between abolition and nonviolent moral suasion, as in the case of William Lloyd Garrison and the Transcendentalists, but that connection notwithstanding, it is still remarkable that, after conceding the pacifism of most free opponents of slavery, we cannot remember another case that resembles or emulates the Harpers Ferry raid. This might be the best evidence on behalf of the case for Brown as founder, for his was an act consistent both with the tenets of scripture and with the political principles of the polity within which he lived. It was committed out of the purest motivations, it was directed to the achievement of the goal of purging the pathology responsible for the republic's social and cultural ills, and it anticipated the violent methods in which slavery was finally abolished. John Brown acted from high principles against evil, and while his methods were decidedly flawed, the moral necessity of his act of resistance remains evident. Although Brown's raid on Harpers Ferry was ultimately unsuccessful, he exemplifies the true spirit of just liberty; and while he contributed neither new law to support democracy nor any new concept to develop the idea of freedom, his deeds accelerated its progress. Thomas Jefferson proclaimed the egalitarian creed when he drafted the Declaration, but he was unable to renounce his own status as master or overcome his idiosyncratic ideas about racial difference. Abraham Lincoln sincerely and eloquently reaffirmed this creed on a higher and more authentically universal level at Gettysburg, but he was unable to act immediately and abolish the pernicious institution. John Brown, however, perhaps more than any founder since Thomas Paine, fully incorporated the creed into his actions and lived the idea of equality and racial friendship with unparalleled purity and ardor. John Brown compels us to think of him as a founder—one who, unlike Jefferson and Lincoln, appears to live and act on the fringes of society, but one who, on closer examination, springs from its very center.

Measuring the character and relevance of any historical figure is a task that lends itself to a certain degree of ambiguity. Figures such as Jefferson, Lincoln, and King have all been assessed differently by their champions and critics, and interpretations of their character and descriptions of their heroism as well as their lesser acts have all undergone continual redefinition. Yet they remain, for us, heroes all the same, for in spite of any inadequacies, they reflect the perpetual quest for the affirmation of higher political principle and remain among the great movers who helped shape the conscience and the development of the republic.

John Brown differs from these men because he shaped nothing tangible, at least nothing that we can point to today as the direct creation of his actions or product of his influence. However, he is similar to them because he represents the pursuit of high ideas consistent with action. In some aspects, John Brown is more relevant than they, for in his perpetually frustrated zeal for freedom and justice, he embodies the core of the American story; we see in the growth of the nation writ large the same constant buffeting between the idea of freedom and the reality of its interminable frustration that created a similar tension in the turbulent psyche of the Osawatomie Prophet. That tension was felt by the Sage of Monticello and was manifested in the visage of the Melancholy President, but it was *incarnate* in John Brown, and through that incarnation, the hope and dread of the American soul became flesh.

If some can embrace as a great hero the figure of Robert E. Lee, the defender of a commonwealth that included slavery as an accepted institution, then is it implausible to recognize heroism in the more astonishing figure of Brown? Lee never supported secession until the deed was committed, yet he chose to renounce his commission and past loyalties after years of distinction under arms only in order to side with his state. Other distinguished Southern warriors, such as David Farragut of Tennessee and Winfield Scott, Lee's fellow Virginian, went with the North, but Lee reluctantly followed the Old Dominion into the Confederacy. Is it fair to say that whereas Lee chose his homeland, Brown chose humanity? To his credit, Lee worried over the possibility of siding against his family and friends, thus exhibiting a tenderness for his communal roots and native land that is not as evident in Brown, so is it fair to argue that Lee chose to defend the hearth while Brown chose to fight for an abstraction? Whose abstraction is more meaningful: Lee's insistence on abiding with Virginia right or wrong or Brown's devotion to a people sealed in bondage? We must bear in mind that, in spite of his protestations, Lee owned slaves, and his wife owned even more than he did. Regardless of the answer to these questions, popular history has made its judgments, and Lee is known (by most) today as a gentleman warrior, acting from duty and on principle, while Brown is considered (by many) as the guerrilla fanatic, blinded by undignified zeal and without honor. But we must ask which of the two acted on the higher principle, which violated the greater law, which one carries more blood on his hands, and who between them is a more genuinely American hero? If it is madness to conduct a private, unruly, and suicidal war against an enemy that one perceives as the very cause of sinful oppression, then what state of mind could cause a man of principle to lead thousands into death out of questionable loyalty to a political system that acknowledges oppression as a venerable institution? Who acted on the real spirit of liberty as expressed in the motto *Sic semper tyrannis?* Without intending to detract from the achievement of either man, it is still instructive to compare the actions and motivations of these past contemporaries, one widely deemed a hero, the other, quite often, a villain. At Harpers Ferry, these two men of different principles fatally met, and it is primarily on principle that their legacies stand before us today.

If we are to judge heroes on the principles that they attempt to advance, then we must develop a more comprehensive sense of the value and purity of those ideals that stir one to action. By any measure, John Brown represents the more startling manifestation of the murky dynamics that course within the continual process of the unfolding and founding of America's first principles; thus, he represents an individual of heroic, if still frightening, proportions who speaks powerfully to us today as we continue to confront our higher purposes as a political culture and democratic nation. Perhaps for this reason he is the most typical founder of all: the most consistently idealistic, the most existentially frustrated, the most American.

POSTSCRIPT

Was John Brown an Irrational Terrorist?

One of the weaknesses of most studies of abolitionism, which is reflected in both of the preceding essays, is that they generally are written from a monochromatic perspective. In other words, historians typically discuss whites within the abolitionist crusade and give little, if any, attention to the roles African Americans played in the movement. Whites are portrayed as the active agents of reform, whereas blacks are the passive recipients of humanitarian efforts to eliminate the scourge of slavery. Students should be aware that African Americans, slave and free, also rebelled against the institution of slavery both directly and indirectly, although very few rallied to the call of John Brown.

Benjamin Quarles in *Black Abolitionists* (Oxford University Press, 1969) describes a wide range of roles played by blacks in the abolitionist movement. The African American challenge to the slave system is also evident in the network known as the "underground railroad." Larry Gara, in *The Liberty Line: The Legend of the Underground Railroad* (University of Kentucky Press, 1961), concludes that the real heroes of the underground railroad were not white abolitionists but the slaves themselves, who depended primarily upon their own resources or assistance they received from other African Americans, slave and free.

Other studies treating the role of black abolitionists in the antislavery movement include James M. McPherson, *The Struggle for Equality: Abolitionists and the Negro in the Civil War and Reconstruction* (Princeton University Press, 1964); Jane H. and William H. Pease, *They Who Would Be Free: Blacks' Search for Freedom, 1830–1861* (Atheneum, 1974); R. J. M. Blackett, *Building an Antislavery Wall: Black Americans in the Atlantic Abolitionist Movement, 1830–1860* (Louisiana State University Press, 1983) and *Beating Against the Barriers: The Lives of Six Nineteenth-Century Afro-Americans* (Louisiana State University Press, 1986); Ronald K. Burke, *Samuel Ringgold Ward: Christian Abolitionist* (Garland, 1995); Nell Irvin Painter, *Sojourner Truth: A Life, A Symbol* (W. W. Norton, 1997); and Catherine Clinton, *Harriet Tubman: The Road to Freedom* (Little, Brown, 2004). Frederick Douglass's contributions are evaluated in Benjamin Quarles, *Frederick Douglass* (Atheneum, 1968; originally published 1948); Nathan Irvin Huggins, *Slave and Citizen: The Life of Frederick Douglass* (Little, Brown, 1980); Waldo E. Martin, Jr., *The Mind of Frederick Douglass* (University of North Carolina Press, 1984); and William S. McFeely, *Frederick Douglass* (W. W. Norton, 1991).

Conflicting views of the abolitionists are presented in Richard O. Curry, ed., *The Abolitionists: Reformers or Fanatics?* (Holt, Rinehart and Winston, 1965). For general discussions of the abolitionist movement, see Gerald Sorin, *Abolitionism: A New Perspective* (Praeger, 1972); Lewis Perry, *Radical Abolitionism: Anarchy and the Government of God in Antislavery Thought* (Cornell University Press, 1973); James Brewer Stewart, *Holy Warriors: The Abolitionists and American Slavery* (Hill and Wang, 1976); Lawrence J. Friedman, *Gregarious Saints: Self and Community in American Abolitionism, 1830–1870* (Cambridge University Press, 1982); Stanley Harrold, *The Abolitionists in the South, 1831–1861* (University Press of Kentucky, 1995); Richard S. Newman, *The Transformation of American Abolitionism: Fighting Slavery in the Early Republic* (University of North Carolina Press, 2002); and John Stauffer, *The Black Hearts of Men: Radical Abolitionists and the Transformation of Race* (Harvard University Press, 2002). The lives of individual participants in the abolitionist movement are discussed in Henry Mayer, *All on Fire: William Lloyd Garrison and the Abolition of Slavery* (St. Martin's, 1998); Gerda Lerner, *The Grimké Sisters from South Carolina: Pioneers for Woman's Rights and Abolition* (Schocken Books, 1967); and Irving H. Bartlett, *Wendell and Ann Phillips: The Community of Reform, 1840–1880* (Harvard University Press, 1979).

John Brown's controversial role in the movement is evaluated in W. E. B. DuBois, *John Brown* (G. W. Jacobs, 1909); Oswald Garrison Villard, *John Brown, 1800–1859: A Biography Fifty Years After* (Houghton Mifflin, 1910); Herbert Aptheker, *John Brown: American Martyr* (New Century, 1960); Stephen B. Oates, *To Purge This Land With Blood: A Biography of John Brown* (Harper and Row, 1970); Benjamin Quarles, *Allies for Freedom: Blacks and John Brown* (Oxford University Press, 1974); Paul Finkleman, ed., *His Soul Goes Marching On: Responses to John Brown and the Harper's Ferry Raid* (University of Virginia Press, 1995); Louis A. DeCaro, Jr., *"Fire From the Midst of You": A Religious Life of John Brown* (New York University Press, 2002); David S. Reynolds, *John Brown, Abolitionist: The Man Who Killed Slavery, Sparked the Civil War, and Seeded Civil Rights* (Alfred A. Knopf, 2005); and Jonathan Earle, ed., *John Brown's Raid on Harpers Ferry: A Brief History with Documents* (Bedford/St. Martin's, 2008).

Internet References . . .

AmericanCivilWar.com

The goal of this site is to provide a comprehensive source of Civil War information from the public domain or works published with the authors' permission. The sources are directed at students and Civil War buffs of all ages.

http://americancivilwar.com/index.html

The Valley of the Shadow Project

Developed under the direction of Edward Ayers and his graduate students at the University of Virginia, this site includes digital archives of thousands of primary source materials related to life in the Civil War era communities in Augusta County, Virginia, and Franklin County, Pennsylvania.

http://valley.vcdh.virginia.edu/

Abraham Lincoln Online

Dedicated to the 16th president of the United States, this site offers educational links, Lincoln's speeches and writings, information on historic places, and much more.

http://www.netins.net/showcase/creative/lincoln.html

Reconstruction Era Documents

This page includes links to various Reconstruction era documents by such authors as Frederick Douglass, Booker T. Washington, and W. E. B. DuBois.

http://www.libraries.rutgers.edu/rul/rr_gateway/research_guides/
history/civwar.shtml

Conflict and Resolution

*T*he changing nature of the United States and the demands of its own principles finally erupted into violent conflict. Perhaps it was an inevitable step in the process of building a coherent nation from a number of distinct and diverse groups. The leaders, attitudes, and resources that were available to the North and the South were to determine the course of the war itself, as well as the national healing process that followed.

- Was Slavery the Key Issue in the Sectional Conflict Leading to the Civil War?

- Is Robert E. Lee Overrated as a General?

- Was Abraham Lincoln America's Greatest President?

- Did Reconstruction Fail as a Result of Racism?

ISSUE 14

Was Slavery the Key Issue in the Sectional Conflict Leading to the Civil War?

YES: Charles B. Dew, from *Apostles of Disunion: Southern Secession Commissioners and the Causes of the Civil War* (University of Virginia Press, 2001)

NO: Marc Egnal, from "Rethinking the Secession of the Lower South: The Clash of Two Groups," *Civil War History 50* (September 2004): 261–90

ISSUE SUMMARY

YES: Charles B. Dew uses the speeches and public letters of 41 white southerners who, as commissioners in 1860 and 1861, attempted to secure support for secession by appealing to their audiences' commitment to the preservation of slavery and of white supremacy.

NO: Marc Egnal argues that the decision of Lower South states to secede from the Union was determined by an economically based struggle between residents with strong ties to the North and Upper South who embraced an entrepreneurial outlook, on one hand, and those who were largely isolated from the North and who opposed the implementation of a diversified economy, on the other hand.

In April 1861, less than a month after his inauguration, President Abraham Lincoln attempted to send provisions to Fort Sumter in South Carolina, part of the newly formed Confederate States of America. Southern troops under the command of General P. G. T. Beauregard opened fire on the fort, forcing its surrender on April 14. The American Civil War had begun.

Numerous explanations have been offered for the cause of this "war between the states." Many contemporaries and some historians saw the conflict as the product of a conspiracy housed either in the North or South, depending upon one's regional perspective. For many in the northern states, the chief culprits were the planters and their political allies who were willing to defend southern institutions at all costs. South of the Mason-Dixon line, blame was laid at the feet of the fanatical abolitionists, like John Brown (see Issue 13) and the free-soil architects of the Republican Party. Some viewed secession and war as the consequence of a constitutional struggle between states-rights advocates and defenders of the federal government, whereas others focused upon the economic rivalries or the cultural differences between North and South. Embedded in each of these interpretations, however, is the powerful influence of the institution of slavery.

In the 85 years between the start of the American Revolution and the coming of the Civil War, Americans made the necessary political compromises on the slavery issue in order not to split the nation apart. The Northwest Ordinance of 1787 forbade slavery from spreading into those designated territories under its control, and the new Constitution written in the same year held out the possibility that the Atlantic slave trade would be prohibited after 1808.

There was some hope in the early nineteenth century that slavery might die from natural causes. The Revolutionary generation was well aware of the contradiction between the values of an egalitarian society and the practices of a slaveholding aristocracy. Philosophically, slavery was viewed as a necessary evil, not a positive good. The northern states were well on their way to abolishing slavery by 1800, and the erosion of the tobacco lands in Virginia and Maryland contributed to the lessening importance of a slave labor system.

Unfortunately, two factors—territorial expansion and the market economy—made slavery the key to the South's wealth in the 35 years before the Civil War. First, new slave states were created out of a population expanding into lands ceded to the United States as a result of the Treaty of Paris of 1783 and the Louisiana Purchase of 1803. Second, slaves were sold from the upper to the lower regions of the South because the invention of the cotton gin made it possible to harvest large quantities of cotton, ship it to the textile mills in New England and the British Isles, and turn it into cloth and finished clothing as part of the new, specialized market economy.

The slavery issue came to the forefront in 1819 when some northern congressmen proposed that slavery be banned from the states being carved out of the Louisiana Purchase. A heated debate ensued, but the Missouri Compromise drew a line that preserved the balance between free and slave states and that (with the exception of Missouri) prohibited slavery north of the 36°30′ latitude.

The annexation of Texas in 1845 and the acquisition of New Mexico, Utah, and California, as a result of the Mexican-American War (see Issue 12), reopened the slavery question. Attempts at compromises in 1850 and 1854 only accelerated the conflict. The Kansas-Nebraska Act of 1854, which repealed the Missouri Compromise, allowed citizens in the new territories to decide whether they wanted slavery on the basis of the doctrine of popular sovereignty. As the second party system of Whigs and Democrats fell apart, the Republican party, who held to confine slavery to existing slave states, mounted a successful challenge against the Democrats and in 1860 elected Abraham Lincoln as president.

Charles B. Dew challenges the neo-Confederate arguments that insists that the decision to secede was driven by the federal government's abuse of states' rights. Marc Egnal, argues that the battle over secession was a product of two opposing societies in the South that espoused different approaches to economic development.

YES ↵

Charles B. Dew

Apostles of Disunion: Southern Secession Commissioners and the Causes of the Civil War

Slavery, States' Rights, and Secession Commissioners

"The Civil War was fought over what important issue?" So reads one of twenty questions on an exam administered by the Immigration and Naturalization Service to prospective American citizens. According to the INS, you are correct if you offer either one of the following answers: "Slavery or states rights."

It is reassuring to know that the INS has a flexible approach to one of the critical questions in American history, but one might ask how the single "issue" raised in the question can have an either/or answer in this instance—the only time such an option occurs on the test. Beyond that, some might want to know whether "slavery" or "states rights" is the more correct answer. But it is probably unfair to chide the test preparers at the INS for trying to fudge the issue. Their uncertainty reflects the deep division and profound ambivalence in contemporary American culture over the origins of the Civil War. One hundred and forty years after the beginning of that fratricidal conflict, neither the public nor the scholarly community has reached anything approaching a consensus as to what caused the bloodiest four years in this country's history. . . .

There is, however, a remarkably clear window into the secessionist mind that has been largely ignored by students of this era. If we want to know what role slavery may or may not have played in the coming of the Civil War, there is no better place to look than in the speeches and letters of the men who served their states as secession commissioners on the eve of the conflict.

As sectional tension mounted in late 1860 and early 1861, five states of the lower South—Mississippi, Alabama, South Carolina, Georgia, and Louisiana—appointed commissioners to other slave states and instructed them to spread the secessionist message across the entire region. These commissioners often explained in detail why their states were exiting the Union, and they did everything in their power to persuade laggard slave states to join the secessionist cause. From December 1860 to April 1861, they carried the *gospel of disunion* to the far corners of the South.

From *Apostles of Disunion: Southern Secession Commissioners and the Causes of the Civil War* by Charles B. Dew (University of Virginia Press, 2001), pp. 4, 18–21, 74–81. Copyright © 2001 by the Rectors and Visitors of the University of Virginia. Reprinted by permission of University of Virginia Press.

The overwhelming majority of the commissioners came from the four Deep South states of Mississippi, Alabama, South Carolina, and Georgia. In Mississippi and Alabama the commissioners were appointed by the governor and thus took the field first. In South Carolina, Georgia, and Louisiana, the secession conventions chose the commissioners.

The number of men sent on this vital mission varied from state to state. Mississippi and Alabama named commissioners to every one of the fourteen other slave states. South Carolina, however, only appointed commissioners to those states which had announced they were calling secession conventions, so only nine representatives eventually went out from the cradle of the secession movement to Alabama, Mississippi, Georgia, Florida, Louisiana, Texas, Arkansas, Virginia, and North Carolina. Georgia dispatched commissioners to six of these same states—Alabama, Louisiana, Texas, Arkansas, North Carolina, and Virginia—and added the border slave states of Maryland, Delaware, Kentucky, and Missouri to the list. The Louisiana Convention appointed a single commissioner, to neighboring Texas, and he did not arrive in Austin until well after the Texas Convention had passed its ordinance of secession.

In all, some fifty-two men served as secession commissioners in the critical weeks just before the Civil War. These individuals were not, by and large, the famous names of antebellum Southern politics. They were often relatively obscure figures—judges, lawyers, doctors, newspaper editors, planters, and farmers—who had had modest political careers but who possessed a reputation for oratory. Sometimes they were better known—ex-governors or state attorneys general or members of Congress. Often they had been born in the states to which they were sent; place of birth was clearly an important factor in the choice of a number of commissioners.

The commissioners appeared in a host of different venues. They addressed state legislatures, they spoke before state conventions called to consider the question of secession, they took the platform before crowds in meeting halls and in the streets, and they wrote letters to governors whose legislatures were not in session. To a man, what they had to say was, and remains, exceedingly instructive and highly illuminating.

Despite their enormous value, the commissioners' speeches and letters have been almost completely overlooked by historians and, as a consequence, by the public at large. This scholarly neglect is difficult to understand. Contemporaries in both North and South paid close attention to the commissioners' movements and what they had to say. Many of their speeches were reprinted in full in newspapers and official state publications, and several appeared in pamphlet form and apparently gained wide circulation. Accounts of the secession crisis published during and just after the war also devoted considerable space to their activities. In the late nineteenth century when editors at the War Department were assembling a documentary record of the Civil War, they included extensive coverage of the commissioners in the volume dealing with the onset of the conflict—a clear indication that they considered these men to be key players in the sequence of events leading up to the war.

Dwight Lowell Dumond highlighted the importance of the commissioners in his 1931 study of the secession movement, a book that remains the most detailed scholarly treatment of this subject. He described the commissioners' words as extraordinarily important and revealing. "From the speeches and writings of the commissioners, as nowhere else, one may realize the depth of feeling and the lack of sympathy between the two sections of the country," Dumond wrote. "Vividly denunciatory of a party pledged to the destruction of Southern institutions, almost tragic in their prophetic tone, and pleading for a unity of allied interests, they constitute one of the most interesting series of documents in American history," he went on to say.

Yet Professor Dumond's book provides little detailed coverage of what these men actually said, and that pattern has persisted in the torrent of literature on the Civil War that has appeared in subsequent decades. As Jon L. Wakelyn notes in his recent *Southern Pamphlets on Secession,* "No adequate study of the Lower South delegates sent to the Upper South exists," and that same observation could be made about the commissioners who addressed their remarks to fellow Southerners in the states of the Deep South as well. Indeed, Professor Wakelyn does not include the full text of a single commissioner's speech in his otherwise superb collection of pamphlet literature, even though, in my opinion, several of the addresses published in pamphlet form are among the most powerful and revealing expressions of the secessionist persuasion put to paper on the eve of the war.

I have managed to locate the full texts or detailed synopses of forty-one of the commissioners' speeches and public letters. It is, as Professor Dumond suggested, a truly remarkable set of documents. What is most striking about them is their amazing openness and frankness. The commissioners' words convey an unmistakable impression of candor, of white Southerners talking to fellow Southerners with no need to hold back out of deference to outside sensibilities. These men infused their speeches and letters with emotion, with passion, and with a powerful "Let's cut to the chase" analysis that reveals, better than any other sources I know, what was really driving the Deep South states toward disunion.

The explanations the commissioners offered and the arguments the commissioners made, in short, provide us with extraordinary insight into the secession of the lower South in 1860–61. And by helping us to understand the "why" of secession, these apostles of disunion have gone a long way toward answering that all-important question, "The Civil War was fought over what important issue?" . . .

John Smith Preston spent the war years in uniform. After serving in a number of different staff positions in the army, he found a home in the Confederate Bureau of Conscription. He took over that agency in 1863, was promoted to the rank of brigadier general in 1864, and headed the Conscript Bureau until the South went down to defeat. Preston lived for a time in England after the war, but in 1868 he went back to South Carolina. His reputation as an orator still intact, Preston was invited to return to his native state in 1868 to address the Washington and Jefferson Societies of the University of Virginia. On June 30 of that year, Preston spoke in Charlottesville to the young Virginians.

Much of his address was an eloquent tribute to the Founding Fathers and their principal handiwork—the Revolution, the state constitutions, and the

Constitution of the United States. Through their efforts "your fathers achieved that liberty which comes of a free government, founded on justice, order and peace," Preston said. In order to preserve the principles and the constitutional forms established by the Revolutionary generation, "you, the immediate off-spring of the founders, went forth to that death grapple which has prevailed against you," he continued. It was the North, "the victors," who rejected "the principles," destroyed "the forms," and defeated "the promised destiny of America," Preston charged. "The Constitution you fought for"—the Confederate Constitution—"embodied every principle of the Constitution of the United States, and guaranteed the free Constitution of Virginia. It did not omit one essential for liberty and the public welfare," he claimed. The Confederacy was in ashes, however, and so was true constitutional liberty. "That liberty was lost, and now the loud hosanna is shouted over land and sea—'Liberty may be dead, but the Union is preserved. Glory, glory, glory to Massachusetts and her Hessian and Milesian mercenaries,'" Preston declaimed. Yet all was not lost. Even though "cruel, bloody, remorseless tyrants may rule at Fort Sumter and at Richmond . . . they cannot crush that immortal hope, which rises from the blood soaked earth of Virginia," Preston believed. "I see the sacred image of regenerate Virginia, and cry aloud, in the hearing of a God of Right, and in the hearing of all the nations of the earth—ALL HAIL OUR MOTHER."

Passionate, unregenerate, unapologetic, unreconstructed—all these and more apply to Preston's remarks on this occasion. But so do words like "conveniently forgetful," "strongly revisionist," and "purposely misleading." Nowhere to be found are references to many of the arguments and descriptions he had used over and over again before the Virginia Convention in February 1861—things like "the subject race . . . rising and murdering their masters" or "the conflict between slavery and non-slavery is a conflict for life and death," or his insistence that "the South cannot exist without African slavery," or his portrait of the "fermenting millions" of the North as "canting, fanatics, festering in the licentiousness of abolition and amalgamation." All this was swept aside as Preston sought to paint the Civil War as a mighty struggle over differing concepts of constitutional liberty. Like Jefferson Davis and Alexander H. Stephens in their postwar writings, Preston was trying to reframe the causes of the conflict in terms that would be much more favorable to the South.

Preston was not the only former secession commissioner to launch such an effort after the war. Jabez L. M. Curry, who had served as Alabama's commissioner to Maryland in December 1860, became a leading figure in the drive to improve primary and secondary education in the postwar South. As agent for both the Peabody and Slater Funds and as supervising director of the Southern Education Board, Curry worked tirelessly to establish public schools and teacher training for both races in the states of the former Confederacy. Curry also worked diligently to justify the Lost Cause of the Confederacy. In his *Civil History of the Government of the Confederate States, with Some Personal Reminiscences,* published in Richmond in 1901, Curry offered an analysis of the coming of the war that closely paralleled the argument used by John S. Preston in 1868. "The object in quitting the Union was not to destroy, but to save the principles of the Constitution," Curry wrote. "The Southern States from the beginning of the government had striven to keep it within the orbit prescribed by the Constitution and failed." The Curry of 1901 would hardly have recognized the Curry of 1860, who told the governor of Maryland that secession meant "deliverance from Abolition domination," and who predicted that under Republican rule the South's slave-based social system would "be assaulted, humbled, dwarfed, degraded, and finally crushed out."

In 1860 and 1861 Preston, Curry, and the other commissioners had seen a horrific future facing their region within the confines of Abraham Lincoln's Union. When they used words like "submission" and "degradation," when they referred to "final subjugation" and "annihilation," they were not talking about constitutional differences or political arguments. They were talking about the dawning of an abominable new world in the South, a world created by the Republican destruction of the institution of slavery.

The secession commissioners knew what this new and hateful world would look like. Over and over again they called up three stark images that, taken together, constituted the white South's worst nightmare.

The first threat was the looming specter of racial equality. The commissioners insisted almost to a man that Republican ascendancy in Washington placed white supremacy in the South in mortal peril. Mississippi commissioner William L. Harris made this point clearly and unambiguously in his speech to the Georgia legislature in December 1860. "Our fathers made this a government for the white man," Harris told the Georgians, "rejecting the negro, as an ignorant, inferior, barbarian race, incapable of self-government, and not, therefore, entitled to be associated with the white man upon terms of civil, political, or social equality." But the Republicans intended "to overturn and strike down this great feature of our Union . . . and to substitute in its stead their new theory of the universal equality of the black and white races." Alabama's commissioners to North Carolina, Isham W. Garrott and Robert H. Smith, predicted that the white children of their state would "be compelled to flee from the land of their birth, and from the slaves their parents have toiled to acquire as an inheritance for them, or to submit to the degradation of being reduced to an equality with them, and all its attendant horrors." South Carolina's John McQueen warned the Texas Convention that Lincoln and the Republicans were bent upon "the abolition of slavery upon this continent and the elevation of our own slaves to an equality with ourselves and our children." And so it went, as commissioner after commissioner—Leonidas Spratt of South Carolina, David Clopton and Arthur F. Hopkins of Alabama, Henry L. Benning of Georgia—hammered home this same point.

The impending imposition of racial equality informed the speeches of other commissioners as well. Thomas J. Wharton, Mississippi's attorney general and that state's commissioner to Tennessee, said in Nashville on January 8, 1861, that the Republican Party would, "at no distant day, inaugurate the reign of equality of all races and colors, and the universality of the elective franchise." Commissioner Samuel L. Hall of Georgia told the North Carolina legislature on February 13, 1861, that only a people "dead to all sense of virtue and dignity" would embrace the Republican doctrine of "the social and political equality of the black and white races." Another Georgia commissioner,

Luther J. Glenn of Atlanta, made the same point to the Missouri legislature on March 2, 1861. The Republican platform, press, and principal spokesmen had made their "purposes, objects, and motives" crystal clear, Glenn insisted: "hostility to the South, the extinction of slavery, and the ultimate elevation of the negro to civil, political and social equality with the white man." These reasons and these reasons alone had prompted his state "to dissolve her connexion with the General Government," Glenn insisted.

The second element in the commissioners' prophecy was the prospect of a race war. Mississippi commissioner Alexander H. Handy raised this threat in his Baltimore speech in December 1860—Republican agents infiltrating the South "to excite the slave to cut the throat of his master." Alabamians Garrott and Smith told their Raleigh audience that Republican policies would force the South either to abandon slavery "or be doomed to a servile war." William Cooper, Alabama's commissioner to Missouri, delivered a similar message in Jefferson City. "Under the policy of the Republican party, the time would arrive when the scenes of San Domingo and Hayti, with all their attendant horrors, would be enacted in the slaveholding States," he told the Missourians. David Clopton of Alabama wrote the governor of Delaware that Republican ascendancy "endangers instead of insuring domestic tranquility by the possession of channels through which to circulate insurrectionary documents and disseminate insurrectionary sentiments among a hitherto contented servile population." Wharton of Mississippi told the Tennessee legislature that Southerners "will not, cannot surrender our institutions," and that Republican attempts to subvert slavery "will drench the country in blood, and extirpate one or other of the races." In their speeches to the Virginia Convention, Fulton Anderson, Henry L. Benning, and John S. Preston all forecast a Republican-inspired race war that would, as Benning put it, "break out everywhere like hidden fire from the earth."

The third prospect in the commissioners' doomsday vision was, in many ways, the most dire: racial amalgamation. Judge Harris of Mississippi sounded this note in Georgia in December 1860 when he spoke of Republican insistence on "equality in the rights of matrimony." Other commissioners repeated this warning in the weeks that followed. In Virginia, Henry Benning insisted that under Republican-led abolition "our women" would suffer "horrors . . . we cannot contemplate in imagination." There was not an adult present who could not imagine exactly what Benning was talking about. Leroy Pope Walker, Alabama's commissioner to Tennessee and subsequently the first Confederate secretary of war, predicted that in the absence of secession all would be lost— first, "our property," and "then our liberties," and finally the South's greatest treasure, "the sacred purity of our daughters."

No commissioner articulated the racial fears of the secessionists better, or more graphically, than Alabama's Stephen F. Hale. When he wrote of a South facing "amalgamation or extermination," when he referred to "all the horrors of a San Domingo servile insurrection," when he described every white Southerner "degraded to a position of equality with free negroes," when he foresaw the "sons and daughters" of the South "associating with free negroes upon terms of political and social equality," when he spoke of the Lincoln administration consigning the citizens of the South "to assassinations and her wives and daughters to pollution and violation to gratify the lust of half-civilized Africans," he was giving voice to the night terrors of the secessionist South. States' rights, historic political abuses, territorial questions, economic differences, constitutional arguments—all these and more paled into insignificance when placed alongside this vision of the South's future under Republican domination.

The choice was absolutely clear. The slave states could secede and establish their independence, or they could submit to "Black Republican" rule with its inevitable consequences: Armageddon or amalgamation. Whites forced to endure racial equality, race war, a staining of the blood—who could tolerate such things?

The commissioners sent out to spread the secessionist gospel in late 1860 and early 1861 clearly believed that the racial fate of their region was hanging in the balance in the wake of Lincoln's election. Only through disunion could the South be saved from the disastrous effects of Republican principles and Republican malevolence. Hesitation, submission—any course other than immediate secession—would place both slavery and white supremacy on the road to certain extinction. The commissioners were arguing that disunion, even if it meant risking war, was the only way to save the white race.

Did these men really believe these things? Did they honestly think that secession was necessary in order to stay the frenzied hand of the Republican abolitionist, preserve racial purity and racial supremacy, and save their women and children from rape and slaughter at the hands of "half-civilized Africans"? They made these statements, and used the appropriate code words, too many times in too many places with too much fervor and raw emotion to leave much room for doubt. They knew these things in the marrow of their bones, and they destroyed a political union because of what they believed and what they foresaw.

But, we might ask, could they not see the illogicality, indeed the absurdity, of their insistence that Lincoln's election meant that the white South faced the sure prospect of either massive miscegenation or a race war to the finish? They seem to have been totally untroubled by logical inconsistencies of this sort. Indeed, the capacity for compartmentalization among this generation of white Southerners appears to have been practically boundless. How else can we explain Judge William L. Harris's comments before the Mississippi State Agricultural Society in November 1858? "It has been said by an eminent statesman," Harris observed on this occasion, " 'that nothing can advance the mass of society in prosperity and happiness, nothing can uphold the substantial interest and steadily improve the general condition and character of the whole, but this one thing—compensating rewards for labor.' " It apparently never occurred to Harris that this observation might apply to the hundreds of thousands of slaves working in Mississippi in 1858 as well as to the white farmers and mechanics of his adopted state. His mind could not even comprehend the possibility that slaves, too, were human beings who, if given the opportunity, might well respond to "compensating rewards" for their labor.

In setting out to explain secession to their fellow Southerners, the commissioners have explained a very great deal to us as well. By illuminating so clearly the racial content of the secession persuasion, the commissioners would seem to have laid to rest, once and for all, any notion that slavery had nothing to do with the coming of the Civil War. To put it quite simply, slavery and race were absolutely critical elements in the coming of the war. Neo-Confederate groups may have "a problem" with this interpretation, as the leader of the Virginia Heritage Preservation Association put it. But these defenders of the Lost Cause need only read the speeches and letters of the secession commissioners to learn what was really driving the Deep South to the brink of war in 1860–61.

Marc Egnal ➡ **NO**

Rethinking the Secession of the Lower South: The Clash of Two Groups

Despite almost a century and a half of writing on secession by participants, engaged amateurs, and professional historians, there is no clear answer to the question, "Why did the Lower South secede?" In a thoughtful discussion of several books on the topic, James Moore remarked in 1986 that the picture that emerges is more a "mosaic than a monolith, a cacophony rather than a consensus." That conclusion still holds true. Some historians contend that psychology trumped rationality. Steven Channing, for example, argues that South Carolina seceded because of a "crisis of fear" fed by anxieties about abolitionists and the large slave population. Others point to more rational motives. William Barney's book on Mississippi and Alabama underscores the desperate need of the planters for fresh soils, which the newly elected Republican party now denied them. Still others emphasize ideology. Lacy K. Ford Jr. argues that South Carolinians were dedicated to republican values and preferred secession to abandoning their principles. A few scholars bring internal discord to the fore: Michael P. Johnson suggests that the tension between wealthy slaveholders and poorer whites lay at the heart of the story in Georgia. The slave lords spearheaded secession and created a "patriarchal republic" because of concerns that Republican patronage might exacerbate class conflict. Finally, and most recently, many historians have returned to the traditional wisdom that the defense of slavery drove the Confederates. James McPherson remarks that "the primacy of the slavery issue . . . has reemerged in modern historiography as the principal cause of secession."

Serious problems, however, confront any interpretation that explains secession by reference to a single ideology or mind-set, whether rational or irrational, whether focused on slavery or republicanism. Citizens in almost every state in the Deep South were seriously divided over the wisdom of secession. Explanations that trumpet a single theme might explain those who chose disunion, but they ignore the sizeable minority that rejected such rash actions. At least 40 percent of voters, and in some cases half, opposed immediate secession in Georgia, Alabama, Mississippi, Louisiana, and Florida. In Texas more than 20 percent of the electorate rejected disunion, and even South Carolina had important pockets of resistance.

From *Civil War History* by Marc Egnal vol. 50, no. 3, September 2004, pp. 261–274 (notes omitted). Copyright © 2004 by Kent State University Press. Reprinted by permission.

The nature of this division has proven elusive. Several scholars have suggested a split between unionist small farmers and secessionist slaveholders, but any generalization that seeks to link the split over secession in the Deep South to wealth or slaveholding will not stand. The ranks of ardent secessionists included many small farmers in the southern districts of South Carolina, Georgia, Alabama, and Mississippi; in peninsular Florida; and in southwestern Louisiana. To be sure, *some* nonslaveholding farmers in the Lower South were consistent, outspoken unionists; but their role should not lead us to generalize about a whole class.

Two studies that closely analyze the opposing sides in the secession debate highlight the weak connection between slaveholding and disunion in the Lower South. An analysis of the votes for the secession conventions in Alabama, Mississippi, and Louisiana concludes that "the variance in the cooperationist vote is explained by factors other than the percentage of slaveholders." The correlation computed was extremely low, with slaveholding explaining only 17 percent of the vote for secession. Another scholar reaches the same conclusion through a different method. Ralph Wooster's study of the members of the secession conventions demonstrates that comparable groups of small farmers and slaveholders stood on both sides of the issue. Wooster observes: "In the conventions of the lower South the percentage of those who held 20 slaves or more was almost the same for the secessionists and their opponents, 41.8 percent of secessionists and 41.0 percent of the cooperationists."

This essay suggests a new approach to secession and the events leading up to that crisis by contending that the battle over secession in the Lower South was the culmination of a long-standing struggle between two groups—one with strong ties to the Union and one that flourished in relative isolation from the states to the north. . . .

Two factors in particular shaped the clashing societies of the cotton states—the origins of the settlers and the patterns of the regional economy. These elements also gave rise to conflicting worldviews that guided the behavior of the two groups. The two camps, it should be emphasized, were loose coalitions. No firm geographical features defined their boundaries. Their ideological borders were permeable and shifted from issue to issue. Furthermore, the opposing sides shared many fundamental values, including a dedication to slavery and a deep-rooted racism. References to two "societies" must be taken figuratively, not literally.

Still these qualifications should not obscure the importance of these groupings. The opposing sides are not ahistorical conceptions. Contemporaries were well aware of the lines that split several states of the Deep South into northern and southern reaches and divided others along similar, geographical lines. During the crisis of 1849–52 and the secession winter of 1860–61, these warring camps shattered the Democratic party and disrupted the Whig-Opposition party. A close analysis of this division helps us understand the ardent secessionists as well as their more moderate opponents.

The first of the two forces shaping these groups was the origins of the settlers. The white people who populated the Lower South came from distinct sending areas and set the imprint of contrasting cultures on states from South

Carolina to Texas. One set of migrants came from the Upper South, although many could trace their family ties back to Northern Ireland and the continent of Europe. Typically, the ancestors of these migrants had landed in Philadelphia and resided for a time in southeastern Pennsylvania. Over the course of generations, these families had migrated south through the Appalachian highlands before spreading through large areas of the Upper and Lower South. These migrants from the Upper South arrived in South Carolina and Georgia before the Revolution and moved into the other Gulf states during the period of initial settlement. A second group of migrants came from a different "hearth": the tidewater region of South Carolina and Georgia. Many of these Lower South residents had ancestors who hailed from southern England. These two large-scale migrations divided the Deep South into distinct regions. The most important line of division separated several states into northern and southern regions. Settlers from the Upper South predominated in the northern reaches of South Carolina, Georgia, and Alabama, as well as northeastern Mississippi; Lower South residents dominated the southern districts in these states. The two groups of migrants had different outlooks, distinct family histories, and different ways of building their homes and talking to their neighbors.

John C. Calhoun described the two societies within his own state of South Carolina. "Our State was first settled on the coast by emigrants principally from England, but with no inconsiderable intermixture of Huguenots from France . . . ," he noted in 1846. "The portion of the State along the falls of the rivers and back to the mountains had a very different origin and settlement. Its settlement commenced long after, at a period, but little anterior to the war of the Revolution, and consisted principally of emigrants who followed the course of the mountains, from Pennsylvania, Maryland, Virginia & North Carolina. They had very little connection, or intercourse for a long time with the old settlement on the coast."

Migrants from the two hearths influenced politics and society in Texas and Florida, although these groups did not follow the pattern of settling along a north-south axis. In Texas, Upper South migrants dominated the northern and west central counties. Similarly, a study of Florida shows that Upper South settlers arrived in the 1830s, became wealthy cotton planters, and controlled the politics of "Middle Florida," the term for the Panhandle counties between the Suwannee and Apalachicola Rivers. These districts supported the Whigs and were moderate in sectional politics. The most striking difference between the Democratic and Whig leaders was their origins. Fully 64 percent of prominent Florida Democrats were from the Deep South, while only 37 percent of the Whigs originated from that area.

Conflicts over Southern rights often featured politicians with different origins. For example, the clash in Texas pitted John Reagan and Sam Houston, both with strong Tennessee roots, against Louis Wigfall of South Carolina. The division in Mississippi found on one side cooperationist James Alcorn, who was raised in Kentucky, and on the other side secessionist Albert Gallatin Brown of South Carolina. In Alabama moderates William King and George Smith Houston from the Upper South clashed with Georgians Dixon Hall Lewis and William Lowndes Yancey. There were exceptions to the rule. Some prominent secessionists, such as Kentuckian Jefferson Davis, were scions of the Upper South.

The distinction between these two migrations constituted the most important cultural divide in the Lower South, but it was not the only one. Several groups in the more southerly reaches of the Deep South stood apart from the migrants from South Carolina and Georgia. In Louisiana the Creoles and Acadians rejected the cotton planters' Southern nationalism. In 1842 William Elmore reported from Louisiana about Calhoun's supporters: "In the city of New Orleans he has a great many friends among the American democrats, but among the french and creole population his claims have not been canvassed." The majority of Germans in south-central Texas opposed slavery and secession; in 1854 a group of them met in San Antonio to endorse a free soil movement.The Mexicans in Texas also denounced slavery and disunion and frequently sheltered runaway slaves.

Most Northerners who settled in the Deep South decried the extremes of Southern nationalism. Such individuals composed an influential minority in the towns. For example, in Mobile, Alabama, nonresident cotton factors and representatives of Northern firms dominated commerce. "Half our real estate is owned by non residents of the same section [i.e., the North]," Joseph Lesesne reported from Mobile in 1847. "Our whole sale and retail business— every thing in short worth mentioning is in the hands of men who invest their profits at the North. The commercial privileges extended by the Constitution to these people has wholly deprived us of a mercantile class."

This discussion of migration and its impact, it should be noted, dovetails with a growing body of scholarship on antebellum mobility. These studies suggest how stable social and political structures coexisted with the "torrent of migration." In each community the small group of "persisters" held a disproportionate share of wealth and influence and provided continuity in turbulent times. Works on the antebellum North also emphasize the far-reaching impact of migration on politics. Greater New England provided a foundation for the Republican party, while settlers from the Upper South became the strongest supporters of the Democrats. Richard Steckel's precinct-level voting study illustrates this point. He concludes: "Migration was a major force—perhaps a dominant factor—shaping political conflict in the Midwest."

Economic activities constituted a second set of factors that divided the citizenry of the Lower South, reinforcing (for the most part) the divisions established by the patterns of settlement. To begin with, wheat cultivation, garden crops, and home manufactures gave the northern reaches of South Carolina, Georgia, Alabama, Mississippi, and Texas an economic unity that mirrored the settlers' shared origins. Wheat was a common note throughout much of this region. Although the quantities raised were far below the levels in the North, wheat growing was an important facet of the regional culture. The crop fostered a society of independent farmers, small milling centers, skilled craftspeople, and vigorous local exchanges. Steven Hahn's study of counties in northern Georgia indicates that seven of ten households had spinning wheels and looms, and one in ten heads of free households was an artisan. The union-leaning population of northern South Carolina, Georgia, Alabama, and

Mississippi, it must be emphasized, included large planters as well as yeomen. But nonslaveholding farmers were a particularly vigorous component.

Lines of transportation also did more to divide the Lower South than to unify it. Most of the rivers that drained these states, from the Pee Dee in South Carolina to the Pearl in Mississippi and from the Sabine to the Nueces in Texas, served the coastal region but not the counties that lay further inland. Only the Mississippi, Savannah, and Red Rivers provided navigation that went far into the interior. The Tennessee River was the route of choice for northern Alabama, but it flowed north, joining the Ohio River near Paducah, Kentucky. Beginning in the 1820s the planters of northern Alabama lobbied for improvements to this waterway, which was obstructed at Muscle Shoals. With funds from the sale of land donated by the federal government, a canal was completed in 1831. But this route soon fell into disrepair. The state legislature refused to provide the small sum needed for its upkeep, arguing the canal helped Tennessee more than Alabama.

Similarly, railroads failed to tie together the coast and northern reaches of the Lower South. Before the Civil War lines were built north from Charleston, Savannah, Mobile, and New Orleans. The impact of these railroads was mixed. The route from Charleston, which reached Atlanta by the mid-1840s, was flawed. The line did not bridge the Savannah River. While this gap inconvenienced travelers, it posed an insurmountable obstacle to the shipment of bulky goods. The Savannah line successfully spanned Georgia, entering Atlanta in 1846 and Chattanooga, Tennessee, in 1849. But in linking Georgia to the railroad terminus at Chattanooga, it strengthened the bonds between north Georgia and the Upper South. The lines that went north from Mobile and New Orleans did not reach Tennessee until the eve of the Civil War. During the 1840s and 1850s the most important railways for northern Alabama and Mississippi traveled east-west and linked these regions to the entrepots of the Upper South. In the mid-1840s capitalists in northern Alabama completed a line that paralleled the defunct canal and allowed the shipment of goods around Muscle Shoals. The Memphis & Charleston Railroad, chartered in 1850, constructed a road that began in Memphis, traversed northern Mississippi and northern Alabama, and entered Chattanooga by 1857.

The result of these links between the Upper South and the northern part of the cotton states was an overland trade that expanded markedly in the years before secession. Finished goods and foodstuffs were shipped to the Deep South; bales of cotton moved northward. Hence, commercial ties separated small farmers and planters in the northern reaches of the Deep South from small farmers and planters residing in southern parts of these states.

The decision by the Confederacy in February 1861 to levy a tariff on the import of goods provoked a discussion about the expanding trade between the Upper and Lower South. Observers also noted the correlation between this trade and divisions within the cotton states. "The inland export of cotton," B. G. Wilkins of Charleston remarked, "has assumed proportions alarming to our tradesmen, injurious to the ports, and a heavy distress upon the incomes of the tributary rail roads, besides there is a political significance that should challenge notice and command arrest. . . . Self interest will beget the opposition of the planters residing upon the confines [i.e., outskirts] of the Confederacy." William McBurney also fretted about the growth of inland trade. He remarked, "What is to hinder Wilmington and Charlotte, N.C., from becoming depots from which the upcountry of S.C. may be supplied. And so of Knoxville, Chattanooga, & Memphis, Tennessee, for the other states?" McBurney favored a light duty on goods entering the Confederacy: "A small percentage would have the advantage of giving to the Seaboard Cities the importing business and the supply of the interior merchants, whereas an entire exemption would enable to the interior merchant to do as many of them have always done—buy in northern cities—at least there would be no impediment in their way of so doing."

The separation of the Deep South into northern and southern regions was the most important division produced by economic activities, but others may be noted. The Louisiana sugar planters, who enjoyed the protection of federal tariffs, looked favorably on the Union. In the Bayou State crop preferences often became political preferences. Finally, commercial activities tied many city and townsfolk to the North and made them less willing to entertain extreme states' rights views during the secession crisis. Northern capital financed the sale of Southern staples and the import of finished goods into the South. A few traders advocated secession, but most were unionists. These city dwellers were more likely to join the Whig party, which became the party of moderation.

The division that emerged from differences in birthplaces and economic activities reflected opposing outlooks. These distinct mind-sets can best be understood in the context of the debate between historians James Oakes and Eugene Genovese. For Oakes the South was characterized by an "entrepreneurial ethos" and an "intense devotion to the capitalistic spirit of accumulation." Genovese, by contrast, emphasizes the "premodern quality of the Southern world." The slave lords, he asserted, were "precapitalist, quasi-aristocratic landowners" who "grew into the closest thing to feudal lords imaginable in a nineteenth-century bourgeois republic." Other historians and economists have chosen sides in this debate. Both sides suggest the universality of their conclusions. All planters, indeed, all white Southerners, these works contend, conformed to a single mold.

A closer look at the divisions within the Lower South suggests that we must credit the insights of both Oakes and Genovese—but in each case for only one of the two groups. The cohort with roots in the Upper South and North embodied the buoyant, entrepreneurial spirit that Oakes delineates. The bustling economic activities of the small farmers in northern counties of their states disturbed outspoken advocates of Southern rights. Daniel Hamilton of Charleston shared his concerns with radical congressman William Porcher Miles. "How long would it be after disunion," Hamilton asked in January 1860, "before we should have the same hungry manufacturing population infesting the upper part of So. Ca., Cherokee [i.e., northern] Georgia, Tennessee, North Carolina (French Broad [River] with its exhaustless water power) and even the upper portion of Alabama?" He continued: "Why not five years would elapse before they would be setting their looms to work on every stream in these locations under the impulse of occupation and the introduction of numbers, they would soon make their presence felt. . . . A few years more and you would have a strong party of our own people in favour of a protective Tariff, and advocating all those extravagant expenditures for Internal Improvements."

Wealthy planters as well as small farmers in this region shared this entrepreneurial outlook and a desire to build a more diversified economy. James Orr, the upcountry leader of the South Carolina National Democrats, pointed out the path to growth. "The first step to be taken . . . ," he explained in an 1855 speech, "to reinvigorate our decaying prosperity, and to develop our exhaustless resources, is for our planters and farmers to invest the whole of the net profits on agricultural capital in some species of manufacturing; the field is broad and inviting, and but little has yet been occupied. With prudence and energy there can be no failure in any branch." Fellow upcountry politician Benjamin Perry, who often boosted manufacturing in his newspaper, applauded these remarks: "One such speech as this of Col. Orr's will do more good in the State than all the patriotic fustian and bombast which have been delivered in South Carolina for the last twenty years." Other planters shared these views. James Alcorn, the prominent north Mississippi politician (and opponent of secession), hoped the state would support new enterprises. He observed, "The wealth of a State consists in the property and intelligence of her people; every intelligent proposition which has for its object the increase of knowledge, or the enhancement of aggregate wealth, should receive the calm judgment of the Legislature."

Merchants, traders, and other townsfolk also applauded diversification, and their views were reflected in the Whig press. The Milledgeville, Georgia, *Southern Recorder* noted in 1843 that "our climate, the face of our country, our copious and unfailing water power, the abundant supply of raw materials, and the cheap labor which we command, invite us to apply a portion of our labor and capital to manufactures." The *Mobile Advertiser* concurred, remarking in 1848 that cotton planters, "instead of investing their surplus capital in negroes and lands, [should] invest it in manufactures."

Spokesmen for the settlers who came from the South Carolina—Georgia "hearth" enunciated a different outlook, one that was more in keeping with Genovese's depiction of the Southern economy. These individuals were proud that Southerners were not like the hard-trading, entrepreneurial Yankees. In 1855 Alabama fire-eater William Lowndes Yancey expounded on the differences between the North and South: "The climate, the soil and productions of these two grand divisions of the land, have made the character of their inhabitants. Those who occupy the one are cool, calculating, enterprising, selfish and grasping; the inhabitants of the other, are ardent, brave and magnanimous, more disposed to give than to accumulate, to enjoy ease rather than to labor." Mississippi radical John F. H. Claiborne agreed. He remarked in 1860, "Sedentary and agricultural, we cherish the homesteads and laws of our ancestors, and live among the reminiscences of the past." Jefferson Davis echoed these views. During the Panic of 1857 he rejoiced in the strengths of the Southern way. "Ours was an agricultural people, and in that consisted their strength," he told an audience in Jackson, Mississippi. "Their prosperity was not at the mercy of such a commercial crisis as the one with which the country had just been visited. Our great staple was our safety."

These states' rights advocates relegated manufacturing to a minor role. Few went as far in condemning enterprise as John Forsythe, the editor of the *Columbus (Georgia) Times,* who declared in 1850, "I would to God we had fewer miles of railroad, fewer millions invested in manufactures and stocks, fewer proofs of enterprise, and thrift and money-making, and more of that chivalry of Georgia, of the olden time, which, on more than one occasion, has interposed her sovereignty to check the usurpations of the federal government." Most politicians of all persuasions favored railroads, but states' rights leaders condemned the spread of manufacturing and argued that fresh soils, not factories, were the key to continuing prosperity.

In short, the origins of the settlers and their economic activities created within the Lower South two opposing societies whose spokesmen expounded different approaches to development. One set of individuals, typically located in the towns and northern counties, favored diversification and saw advantages in links with the states to the north and, more generally, in the Union. The other group, whose strength lay in the southern reaches of the Lower South, defended an economy focused on slaves, cotton, and rice. They were more ready to separate as the threat to Southern institutions increased in the 1840s and 1850s. . . .

POSTSCRIPT

Was Slavery the Key Issue in the Sectional Conflict Leading to the Civil War?

Charles B. Dew makes a very powerful argument regarding the influence of the slavery question on the decision by 11 southern slaveholding states to secede and to join the Confederate States of America. Whose attitudes would provide a better window into the thinking of white southerners on the eve of the Civil War than those individuals commissioned to travel throughout the region to drum up support for secession? Dew, however, by no means stands alone as a proponent of the view that slavery was the main cause of the war. In *America in 1857: A Nation on the Brink* (Oxford University Press, 1990), Kenneth M. Stampp argues that conflict became inevitable after the election of James Buchanan (not Lincoln) to the presidency, the continuing firestorm in Kansas, and the Supreme Court's decision in the Dred Scott case. Eric Foner, who has written extensively on the influence of the free-soil ideology and its impact on the coming of the Civil War in such works as *Free Soil, Free Labor, Free Men: The Ideology of the Republican Party Before the Civil War* (Oxford University Press, 1970) also points out that the argument for states' rights as an explanation for the cause of the war is largely a product of the post–Civil War era and, hence, more or less an afterthought on the part of southerners who hoped to distance themselves from the institution of slavery that dominated their region in the antebellum period.

Marc Egnal's essay provides a nuanced interpretation that focuses upon economics as the main issue in determining support for secession in the Lower South. Noting that it is overly simplistic to assert that slave owners supported secession while small farmers who owned no slaves did not, Egnal goes on to assert that the debate over secession can be boiled down to a clash of two societies in the Lower South defined by the origin of the settlers and distinctive patterns of the regional economy: those in the northern parts of the states who often had ties with the North and Upper South and who favored a diversified economy that included manufacturing and industrial production; and those in the southern regions of the states who were largely isolated from the Upper South and who persisted in their commitment to cash-crop agriculture. It was this latter group, Egnal points out, which was most likely to support secession whether or not they were slave owners. Egnal's interpretation is presented in an expanded form in *Clash of Extremes: The Economic Origins of the Civil War* (Hill & Wang, 2009).

Another challenge to the belief that slavery was the sole cause of the war can be found in the works of Joel Silbey. In "The Civil War Synthesis in American Political History," *Civil War History* (June 1964); *The Partisan Imperative: The Dynamics of American Politics Before the Civil War* (Oxford University Press, 1985);

and *Party Over Section: The Rough and Ready Presidential Election of 1848* (University Press of Kansas, 2009), Silbey argues that historians, by positioning slavery as the major issue that divided the United States, have distorted "the reality of American political life between 1844 and 1861." Silbey is one of the "new political historians" who have applied the techniques of modern-day political scientists in analyzing the election returns and voting patterns of Americans' nineteenth- and early-twentieth-century predecessors. These historians use computers and regression analysis of voting patterns, favor a quantitative analysis of past behavior, and reject the traditional sources of quotes from partisan newspapers and major politicians because these sources provide anecdotal and often misleading portraits of our past. Silbey and other new political historians maintain that all politics are local. Therefore, the primary issues for voters and their politicians in the 1860 election were ethnic and cultural, and party loyalty was more important than sectional considerations.

Another approach is presented by Michael F. Holt in *The Political Crisis of the 1850s* (John Wiley & Sons, 1978). Holt also is interested in analyzing the struggles for power at the state and local levels by the major political parties, but he is critical of the ethnocultural school represented by Silbey. In Holt's view, Silbey's emphasis on voter analysis does not explain why the Whig Party disappeared nor why the Republican Party became the majority party in the northern and western states in the 1850s. Holt also rejects the more traditional view that the Civil War resulted from the "intensifying sectional disagreements over slavery." Instead, he promotes a more complicated picture of the events leading to the Civil War. Between 1845 and 1860, he maintains, three important things happened: (1) the breakdown of the Whig Party, (2) the realignment of voters, and (3) "a shift from a nationally balanced party system where both major parties competed on fairly even terms in all parts of the nation to a sectionalized polarized one with Republicans dominant in the North and Democrats in the South."

The list of books about the causes of the Civil War is extensive. Kenneth M. Stampp, ed., *The Causes of the Civil War* (Prentice-Hall, 1965) provides a collection of primary documents and historical interpretations by leading scholars. Other edited volumes of scholarly interpretations can be found in William R. Brock, ed., *The Civil War* (Harper & Row, 1969); Hans L. Trefousse, ed., *The Causes of the Civil War: Institutional Failure or Human Blunder?* (Holt, Rinehart and Watson, 1971); and Michael Perman, ed., *The Coming of the American Civil War* (3d ed.; D.C. Heath, 1993). John Niven's, *The Coming of the Civil War, 1837–1861* (Harlan Davidson, 1990) is a brief presentation, but readers seeking a compelling narrative cannot do much better than David Potter, *The Impending Crisis, 1848–1861* (Harper & Row, 1976), one of the best volumes in the prestigious New American Nation Series.

ISSUE 15

Is Robert E. Lee Overrated as a General?

YES: Alan T. Nolan, from *"Rally, Once Again!" Selected Civil War Writings of Alan T. Nolan* (Madison House, 2000)

NO: Gary W. Gallagher, from "Another Look at the Generalship of R. E. Lee," in Gary W. Gallagher, ed., *Lee the Soldier* (University of Nebraska Press, 1996)

ISSUE SUMMARY

YES: Attorney Alan T. Nolan argues that General Robert E. Lee was a flawed grand strategist whose offensive operations produced heavy casualties in an unnecessarily prolonged war that the South could not win.

NO: According to professor of American history Gary W. Gallagher, General Lee was the most revered and unifying figure in the Confederacy, and he "formulated a national strategy predicated on the probability of success in Virginia and the value of battlefield victories."

Over the past 125 years, contemporaries and historians have advanced dozens of explanations for the defeat of the Confederacy in the Civil War. Most of these can be divided into two categories: internal and external.

According to a number of historians, internal divisions doomed the Confederacy. In his book *State Rights in the Confederacy* (Peter Smith, 1961), Frank Owsley maintains that the centrifugal forces of states' rights killed the Confederacy. Owsley contends that governors in North Carolina and Georgia withheld men and equipment from the Confederate armies in order to build up their own state militias. On the Confederate tombstone, he said, should be inscribed: "Died of States' Rights."

A second version of the internal conflict argument appeared in a 1960 essay in a symposium entitled *Why the North Won the Civil War* (Louisiana State University Press, 1960). In it, the editor, Pulitzer Prize–winning historian David Donald, argued that the resistance of Southerners to conscription, taxes, and limitations on speeches that were critical of the war effort fatally crippled the Confederacy's war effort. Instead of states' rights, said Donald, the Confederate tombstone should read: "Died of Democracy."

A third variant of the internal conflict argument has recently been promoted by four Southern scholars: Richard E. Beringer, Herman Hattaway, Archer Jones, and William N. Still, Jr. Their main thesis is that the Confederacy lacked the will to win because of its inability to fashion a viable Southern nationalism, increasing religious doubts that God was on the Confederacy's side, and guilt over slavery.

Historians who emphasize external reasons for the Confederacy's failure stress two factors: the Union's overwhelming numbers and resources and the uneven quality of leadership between the two sides. The North possessed two-and-one-half times the South's population, three times its railroad capacity, and nine times its industrial production. The Unionists also appear to have had better leadership. Abraham Lincoln is ranked as America's greatest president because he united his political objectives of saving the Union and freeing the slaves with a military strategy designed to defeat the Confederacy. Lincoln's generals—Ulysses S. Grant, William T. Sherman, and Philip H. Sheridan—outsmarted the Confederate leadership. In 1864, for example, massive frontal attacks were made against the Confederates in the eastern and western theaters. At the same time, Sherman destroyed much of the agricultural base of the Southerners as he marched his troops through South Carolina and Georgia.

But what if the South had won the Civil War? Could the same external explanations that are attributed to the Union victory also be used to explain a Confederate win? Would one Confederate soldier be considered equal to four Union soldiers? Would a triumvirate of yeoman farmers, slaveholding planters, and small industrialists have proven the superiority of agrarian values over industrial ones? Would Jefferson Davis's leadership emerge as superior to Lincoln's? Would the great military leaders be Robert E. Lee, Thomas "Stonewall" Jackson, and Braxton Bragg instead of Grant, Sherman, and Sheridan?

No Civil War figure is more difficult to comprehend than General Lee. A product of the Virginia aristocracy, Lee ranked second in his class at West Point and distinguished himself as an army engineer, bridge builder, and scout during the Mexican War. While home in Virginia on an extended furlough to care for his invalid wife in October 1859, he took command of a detachment of marines to capture John Brown and his men inside the roundhouse during a raid on Harpers Ferry. Offered the command of all federal forces when the Civil War broke out, Lee made the fateful decision to resign his army commission and fight for the Confederacy.

In the first of the following selections, Alan T. Nolan challenges what he believes to be one of the biggest myths of the Civil War—the genius of Robert E. Lee. Written in the style of a lawyer's brief, Nolan portrays the "marble man" as a flawed grand strategist whose offensive operations produced heavy casualties in a war that was unnecessarily prolonged and that the South could not win.

In the second selection, Gary W. Gallagher contends that Lee was a truly revered and unifying figure in the Confederacy. According to Gallagher, most Southerners approved of Lee's offensive tactics, were appreciative of his battlefield victories, and believed that the Northern troops could not win the war unless they captured his army.

YES ⬅

Alan T. Nolan

"Rally, Once Again!"

General Lee—A Different View

I believe that Lee's generalship hurt the Confederates' chances for victory. I do not fault his tactics or operational strategy. I do fault his sense of the South's *grand strategy*. Tactics, of course, refers to *how* a battle is fought. Operational strategy concerns the plan of a campaign or battle. *Grand strategy* pertains to the use of military forces in order to win the war.

I concede that Lee was an effective and sometimes brilliant field commander, but his towering reputation results from viewing his leadership a campaign or a battle at a time and disregarding considerations of grand strategy. I argue that in grand strategic terms Lee did not understand the war, an ultimate failure that his sometimes brilliant operational strategy and tactics simply do not overcome.

In order to evaluate my thesis, one has to identify his or her own opinion as to how the South could have won: with an offensive grand strategy that risked the depletion of its inferior numbers in an effort to defeat the North militarily, or the defensive, that is, fighting the war so as to prolong it and punish the North so that it would have decided that coercion was impossible or not worth the cost. Because of its relatively limited manpower and manufacturing base, the Confederacy was never in a position to defeat the North militarily. Its only chance was to make the war so costly to the North that the North would give it up. To do this, it was essential for Lee to observe a conserving, defensive grand strategy, the counterpart of Washington's grand strategy in the Revolution. The Americans could not and did not militarily defeat the British regulars, but within a grand defensive context they kept armies in the field and harassed the enemy until it gave up the contest.

In arguing for the defensive grand strategy, I am not advocating a perimeter war, a war of position or the exclusively defensive operational strategy and tactics of General Joseph E. Johnston in the Atlanta campaign. Nor do I believe that Lee could simply have remained idle. Within a defensive context he could have maneuvered and raided, as did Washington, and still avoided the expensive battles that his offensives induced. Occasional reasoned operationally strategic offensives and tactics could have been undertaken within the framework of the grand strategic defensive. Washington's leadership is again the model.

Lee's grand strategic view was set forth in a letter of July 6, 1864, to President Davis:

> If we can defeat or drive the armies of the enemy from the field, we shall have peace. All of our efforts and energies should be devoted to that object.

This is a statement of offensive grand strategy. Lee believed that to win the war the South had to overpower the North militarily, to decimate and disperse its armies. A reference to 1862–63 is appropriate. Having taken command of the Army of Northern Virginia on June 1, 1862, for two years Lee vigorously pursued the strategic offensive in an effort to defeat the North militarily: the Peninsula, the Second Bull Run Campaign, the Maryland Campaign, Chancellorsville, and the Pennsylvania Campaign. He either attacked or, in the case of Second Bull Run and the Maryland Campaign, maneuvered offensively so as to precipitate large and costly battles. He did this although he had predicted that a siege in the Richmond defenses would be fatal to his army. In order to avoid being fixed, to avoid a siege, an army must be mobile. And mobility, the capacity to maneuver, requires numbers in some reasonable relationship to the enemy's numbers. In the course of his offensives, Lee took disproportionate, irreplaceable and unaffordable losses that undermined the viability of his army, deprived it of mobility, and ultimately committed it to a siege. A comparison of Lee's and the Federals' losses is instructive [see Table 1].

Fredericksburg, Lee's only 1862–3 genuinely defensive battle, provides a significant contrast: Burnside lost almost 11,000 killed and wounded (10.9%) as compared to Lee's 4,656 (6.4%).

Table 1

	Federals	Confederates
The Seven Days	9,796 10.7%	19,739 20.7%
Second Bull Run	10,096 13.3%	9,108 18.8%
Antietam	11,657 15.5%	11,724 22.6%
Chancellorsville	11,116 11.4%	10,746 18.7%
Gettysburg	17,684 21.2%	22,638 30.2%

Classic examples of Lee's mistaken offensive grand strategy are provided by his decisions that led to the battles at Antietam and Gettysburg. Having been victorious at Second Bull Run, Lee was in an ideal position in September 1862 to desist from a prompt offensive move. In spite of statements by some writers that he had no alternative to moving into Maryland, even Freeman concedes that after Second Bull Run he could have moved a "slight distance southward" from Manassas, "to Warrenton, for instance. . . . That would put the Army of Northern Virginia on the flank of any force advancing to Richmond, and would give it the advantage of direct rail communications with the capitaL" In spite of this alternative, Lee moved into Maryland, which forseeably drew the Federal army after him and resulted in the costly battle at Antietam. Lee knew that substantial casualties were inevitable in that battle whether he won or lost. The situation immediately after Chancellorsville is also illuminating. In that battle, Lee had demonstrated his offensive tactical brilliance—and he had taken heavy losses in the process. According to his aide, Col. Charles Marshall, and Lee's own comments, Lee then had three options: to attack Hooker across the Rappahannock, to position himself to defend against another Federal effort to attack him across the Rappahannock, and to raid into Maryland and Pennsylvania. Having wisely rejected attempting to attack Hooker across the river, Lee chose the Northern raid option. This choice ended at Gettysburg where, to quote Freeman, Lee's army was "wrecked." Surely Gettysburg, requiring a crossing and recrossing of the Potomac and with extended lines of communication, was the most risky of the options. As in the case of the 1862 move into Maryland, win, lose or draw, the Maryland-Pennsylvania move of 1863 was bound to result in substantial casualties.

Lee's offensive view of the war also appears in his dispatches after Gettysburg. On August 31, 1863, in a letter to Longstreet he said that "I can see nothing better to be done than to endeavor to bring General Meade out and use our efforts to crush his army." On October 11, 1863, he wrote the Secretary of War from near Madison Courthouse that, "Yesterday I moved the army to this position with the hope of getting an opportunity to strike a blow at the enemy." Less than a week later he informed President Davis from Bristoe Station as follows: "I have the honor to inform you that with the view of bringing on an engagement with the army of Gen. Meade . . . this army . . . arrived near Culpeper on the 11th." Later in 1863, he spoke of "preparations made to attack (Meade)," which were frustrated by Meade's retreat. In February of 1864 he wrote Davis of his desire to "drive him (the enemy) to the Potomac." Even after the Wilderness and Spotsylvania, Lee wrote Davis that "it seems to me our best policy to unite upon it (Grant's army) and endeavor to crush it." Also in 1864 he told General Jubal A. Early that "we must destroy this army of Grant's before he gets to the James River." Already reduced by his 1862–63 offensives, it was simply not possible for Lee to "crush" or "destroy" Grant's overwhelming force. He could injure or slow it down, but not destroy it. The point is that, as had been true from the beginning of his army command, even at this late date Lee thought strategically in Armageddon terms. Early's Shenandoah Valley campaign in 1864 is significant in another respect. Early was sent to the valley to draw Federal forces away from Petersburg and Richmond.

To draw Federals into the valley and *keep them there,* Early's force had only to be present in the valley. But Lee's offensive spirit caused him to tell Early to attack the Federals' valley forces. Early pursued the offensive. His outnumbered army took heavy losses and was ultimately decimated and resoundingly defeated. This permitted the Federals to be returned to Grant before Richmond. The offensive urged by Lee countered Lee's purpose in sending Early to the valley.

Lee's 1862–63 costly offensive warfare defied his own concern about relative manpower. His correspondence with Davis and the Secretary of War is replete with statements of that concern. During the 1862–63 period, he wrote regularly of the "superior numbers of the enemy," the necessity to "husband our strength," the falling off in (his army's) aggregate shows that its ranks are growing weaker and that its losses are not supplied by recruits and that the enemy can be easily reinforced, while no addition can be made to our numbers. Some may contend that Lee's grand strategy was defensive, an offensive defensive. To make this claim, they must somehow exorcise Lee's own words, his consistent advocacy of the attack, and the way he used his army for two years, until its losses deprived him of mobility and the offensive option.

Forced to the strategic defensive by 1864, Lee demonstrated the value of that posture, exacting such a price from the North that it came close to abandoning the war. I contend that had he carried out his leadership in this way during the two costly offensive years, as he did only at Fredericksburg, he would have slowed the enemy's increase in numerical superiority to the extent that it arose from Lee's heavy, disproportionate, and irreplaceable losses. He would have saved a substantial portion of the approximately 100,000 soldiers that he lost on the offensive. With these additional numbers, he could have maintained mobility and avoided a siege. Maneuvers like Early's 1864 movement in the valley could have been undertaken with sufficient numbers to be effective. The Federals, on the offensive, could have suffered for an earlier or longer period the ceaseless Federal losses that began in May of 1864. The Northern people could have politically abandoned their support of the war.

Some who disagree with me argue that the defensive would not have punished the North more than the 1862–63 offensives did. That may be so, but, as indicated by Fredericksburg, the defensive would not have wasted Lee's own force, which was the principal defect with his offensives. My detractors further contend that traditional military doctrine advocates the offensive because it permits selection of the time and place of the battle. But the endemically outnumbered Lee was not in a traditional situation that afforded him a chance of winning the war militarily. It is also said that the Southern people would not have accepted the defensive. There is no evidence that Lee or the Confederate Administration relied on this factor in pursuing the 1862–3 offensives. Further, if Lee had believed that the offensive was destructive to his chances, his obligation, and that of the Administration, was to bring the public along with them. Time, the duration of the war, was a problem for both sides, the South because of its relatively limited supply base and the North because of the risk that the public would abandon the contest as hopeless.

In short, I believe that Lee's offensive grand strategy was destructive to the South's chances. Lee's task was not to win great battles, to be spectacular, but to win the war The military historian Lt. Col. George A. Bruce states that "the art of war consists in using the forces of a nation to secure the end for which it is waged, and not in a succession of great battles that tend to defeat it." In 1862–63 Lee sought out the great battles. He went on the defensive in 1864 against his own strategic sense, only because his prior losses forced this posture. Maj. Gen. J. F. C. Fuller, the English military historian, seems to me to have fairly characterized Lee's leadership during the first two years of his command: Lee "rushed forth to find a battlefield, to challenge a contest between himself and the North." In this process, he unilaterally accomplished the attrition of his army that led to its being besieged and ultimately surrendered. His losses ultimately prevented his sustaining his army and punishing the North sufficiently to induce it to abandon the war—the only chance the South had to win. . . .

The Price of Honor: R. E. Lee and the Question of Confederate Surrender

. . . Robert E. Lee's belief in the inevitability of his final defeat, and the contrast between that belief and his combative persistence, together raise the question of his motivation. There are several worthwhile lines of inquiry regarding his motives, but before examining them it is necessary to consider briefly the question of his authority to surrender: did he have the authority to surrender his army and, if so, what circumstances permitted him to exercise that authority?

It is plain that Lee did have the right to surrender and was aware that he did. Between 7 April and 9 April 1865, as his correspondence with U. S. Grant proceeded, Lee consulted certain trusted aides and debated with himself the issue of surrender. But he insisted that, "if it is right, then I will take *all* the responsibility." On 9 April, the deed was done at Appomattox. On 12 April, Lee reported the surrender to Jefferson Davis, explaining that maintaining the battle "one day longer . . . would have been at a great sacrifice of life, and at its end I did not see how a surrender could have been avoided." In short, on 9 April 1865, believing that ultimate surrender was inevitable, he could not justify the sacrifice of life that further prolonging the combat would entail.

The situation at Appomattox was surely grim, but as has been noted, Lee had viewed the South's situation in the same grim terms for anywhere from twenty to five months prior to 9 April 1865. He had the same authority then to surrender as he had on 9 April. As the casualties and other losses—physical, financial, and emotional—mounted, what interest did Lee believe he was serving in continuing the hopeless struggle? His own statements suggest four possible answers to this question: he believed that the North was such a monstrous tyrant that defeat and death were the only moral responses; God willed his continuing to fight in spite of the inevitability of defeat; he was bound to persist because he was subject to Confederate civilian control, which did not want him to surrender; or his personal sense of duty demanded it.

The first answer suggests the philosophical proposition that there are worse fates than defeat and death. Americans in Lee's day, as well as today, were the heirs of a liberty-or-death tradition. Lee identified with this tradition. Despite his personal opposition to secession, he is quoted as having said,

"We had, I was satisfied, sacred principles to maintain and rights to defend, for which we were in duty bound to do our best, even if we perished in the endeavor." On 7 April or 8 April, sometime within two days of the surrender, General William N. Pendleton, representing a group of officers, suggested surrender to Lee. Lee rejected the idea, stating that rather than surrender "we must all determine to die at our posts." But the liberty-or-death motive does not adequately explain Lee's prolonging the war after he adopted a belief in its futility, bearing in mind that he did in fact surrender, despite his prior rhetorical flourishes. Furthermore, he flatly rejected General Edward Porter Alexander's suggestion of guerrilla warfare as an alternative means of continuing the war because of its deleterious effect on the country as a whole. His 20 April 1865 letter to President Davis also discouraged Alexander's guerrilla warfare suggestion and urged Davis to seek a general peace. And on 13 June 1865, Lee applied for amnesty and the "benefits and full restoration of all rights and privileges" as a citizen of the United States. Each of these facts contradicts the notion that Lee was motivated by the belief that ultimate resistance to the Federals was the appropriate moral position.

Untroubled by any questions concerning the correctness of Lee's conduct, his biographer Douglas Southall Freeman comes close to suggesting that Lee persisted in the war because he believed that, regardless of the odds and the inevitability of defeat, God wanted him to keep fighting. Thus, Freeman stated that "nothing of his serenity during the war or of his silent labor in defeat can be understood unless one realizes that he submitted himself in all things faithfully to the will of a Divinity which, in his simple faith, was directing wisely the fate of nations and the daily life of His children." It is certainly true that Lee had a strong personal sense of the presence of God and God's responsibility for human events. But given the general's Herculean efforts, and his reliance on God to give him victories, it seems unreasonable to suggest that he persisted in futile combat because of some sense that God intended him to do so. Had this been his conviction, he presumably would not have surrendered on 9 April 1865.

Freeman was at pains to point out that Lee accepted wholeheartedly the American constitutional premise of military subordination to the civil government: "Lee . . . applied literally and loyally his conviction that the President was the commander-in-chief." This constitutional principle was consistent with one of the general's life principles described by Freeman as "respect for constituted authority" and "his creed of obedience to constituted authority." Biographer Clifford Dowdey's description of certain events in February and March 1865 provides an interesting insight into the question of Lee's deference to authority. Referring to the period following the Hampton Roads meeting of 3 February 1865, between Confederate representatives and Abraham Lincoln and his aides, Dowdey wrote:

> Lee had held a private conversation with Virginia's Senator R. M. T. Hunter. . . . Lee urged him to offer a resolution in the Senate that would obtain better terms than, as Hunter reported Lee as saying, "were likely to be given after a surrender." Hunter claimed that Davis had already

impugned his motives for seeking peace terms, and told Lee, "if he thought the chances of success desperate, thought he ought to say so to the President." Though Lee held frequent conversations with Davis during February, it is unlikely that he ever brought himself to introduce a subject which would be so distasteful to the President.

Dowdey then recounted the views of Secretary of War James A. Seddon, his successor in that office, John C. Breckenridge, and James Longstreet, all of whom shared Lee's recognition of the fact the war was lost and peace was needed. Dowdey concluded by observing, "The crux of the matter was that men in a position to know recognized that the South was defeated, *but no one was willing to assume the responsibility of trying to convince Davis of this*"! (emphasis added). Lee had by this time become general-in-chief of the Confederate armies. Considering Dowdey's unflinching admiration for Lee, his attributing Lee's position and that of the others mentioned to an unwillingness to take responsibility is surely an unintended indictment. In any event, although it is evident that Lee accepted subordination to civilian authority, he ultimately took responsibility for the surrender and simply announced it to Davis. It cannot, therefore, be said that civilian control was the reason for Lee's persistence.

Finally, can Lee's resolve to fight on in the face of certain defeat be explained by his sense of duty and honor? Historian Gaines M. Foster has described the South as "a culture based on honor," and Bertram Wyatt-Brown has detailed the entire complex white culture of the South in terms of a code called "Honor." The authors of *Why the South Lost the Civil War* have attempted to give a short definition of the concept: "When Confederates talked of honor they did not mean pride so much as moral integrity, personal bravery, Christian graciousness, deference to and respect for others, and self-worth, recognized by their peers."

In Lee, honor and its companion, duty, were, to be sure, highly and selfconsciously developed; so too was their consequence, the self-regard that Wyatt-Brown describes. All biographies of Lee quote at length his many aphorisms about these values. He said, for example, that the Confederates were "duty bound to do our best, even if we perished." On 22 February 1865, in a letter to his wife, he stated, "I shall . . . endeavour to do my duty & fight to the last." In a March 1865 interview with General John B. Gordon, he spoke of "what duty to the army and our people required of us." Preparing to evacuate the Petersburg-Richmond line and move west toward Appomattox, "he acted," Lieutenant Colonel Walter H. Taylor noted, "as one who was conscious of having accomplished all that was possible in the line of duty, and who was undisturbed by the adverse conditions in which he found himself."

In regard to the effort to escape the pursuing Federals between Richmond and Appomattox, Freeman observed: "So long as this chance was open to him, his sense of duty did not permit him to consider any alternative" and "as long as there was a prospect of escape Lee felt it was his duty to fight on. He would not yield one hour before he must." Freeman also noted approvingly Lee's memorandum to himself: "There is a true glory and a true honor: the glory of duty done—the honor of the integrity of principle." Commenting on "the dominance of a sense of duty in [Lee's] actions," Dowdey stated that "this is not so much a sense of duty in the abstract as a duty to do the best he could. The point can clearly be seen when duty, *as a sense of the pride of a professional in his craft,* caused him to practice meticulously the techniques of command *long after any military purpose could be achieved"* (emphasis added).

Such a narrow definition of Lee's sense of honor and duty seems to be another unintended indictment by Dowdey. However defined, this sense of honor appears, after all, to have been an essentially personal emotional commitment that compelled Lee to fight on, regardless of the cost and long after he believed that it was futile to continue the contest. Referring to the Confederacy's hopeless situation during the winter of 1864–1865 and sympathetic to his personal commitment, Dowdey recognized "the moral obligation that required [Lee] to act as though defeat could be held off."

In a chapter entitled "The Sword of Robert E. Lee," Freeman set forth "an accounting of his service to the state." Having noted Lee's mobilization of Virginia, the Seven Days, the repulse of Federal offensives against Richmond, and his victories in six of ten major battles from Gaines's Mill through Spotsylvania, Freeman proceeded,

> During the twenty-four months when he had been free to employ open manoeuvre, a period that had ended with Cold Harbor, he had sustained approximately 103,000 casualties and had inflicted 145,000. Holding, as he usually had, to the offensive, his combat losses had been greater in proportion to his numbers than those of the Federals, but he had demonstrated how strategy may increase an opponent's casualties, for his losses included only 16,000 prisoners, whereas he had taken 38,000. Chained at length to the Richmond defenses, he had saved the capital from capture for ten months. All this he had done in the face of repeated defeats for the Southern troops in nearly every other part of the Confederacy. . . . These difficulties of the South would have been even worse had not the Army of Northern Virginia occupied so much of the thought and armed strength of the North. Lee is to be judged, in fact, not merely by what he accomplished with his own troops but by what he prevented the hosts of the Union from doing sooner elsewhere.

In reciting what Lee had accomplished, Freeman did not allude to the fact that for perhaps the last twenty months of these efforts, and surely for a substantial lesser period, Lee was proceeding in a cause that he personally believed was lost.

James M. McPherson has summarized the ultimate consequences of the prolonging of the war, to which Lee's accomplishments made a significant contribution:

> the South was not only invaded and conquered, it was utterly destroyed. By 1865 the Union forces had . . . destroyed two-thirds of the assessed value of Southern wealth, two-fifths of the South's livestock, and one-quarter of her white men between the ages of twenty and forty. More

than half the farm machinery was ruined, and the damage to railroads and industries was incalculable. . . . Southern wealth decreased by 60 percent (or 30 percent if the slaves are not counted as wealth). These figures provide eloquent testimony to the tragic irony of the Souths counterrevolution of 1861 to preserve its way of life.

In conjunction, the statements of Freeman and McPherson raise reasonable questions regarding Lee and history and Lee's role as an American idol. On the one hand, the Lee tradition projects a tragic hero, a man who courageously pursued a cause that he believed to be doomed. On the other hand, this heroic tradition must be balanced against the consequences of Lee's heroism. There is, of course, a nobility and poignancy, a romance, in the tragic and relentless pursuit of a hopeless cause. But in practical terms such pursuit is subject to a very different interpretation.

In reality, military leadership is not just a private or personal activity. Nor is a military leader's sense of honor and duty simply a private and personal impulse. Military leadership and the leader's sense of duty are of concern not only to the leader, but also to the followers and to the enemy, ordinary people, many of whom die, are maimed, or otherwise suffer. In short, military leadership involves responsibility for what happens to other persons. There is, therefore, no matter how sincerely a leader may believe in the justice of a cause, a difference between undertaking or continuing military leadership in a cause that the leader feels can succeed and undertaking or continuing such leadership in a cause that the leader feels is hopeless. In the latter circumstance, the leader knows that his order "once more into the breach" will kill or injure many of his soldiers as well as the enemy's and also realizes that his order and these deaths and injuries are without, in Dowdey's phrase, "any military purpose." Lacking a military purpose, they also have no political purpose. Thus they are without any rational purpose.

The absence of any rational purpose behind Lee's persistence is suggested by his sense of the meaning of the deaths of his men as revealed by his early advocate, the Reverend J. William Jones. Among the general's wartime papers that Jones found after his death were "maxims, proverbs, quotations from the Psalms, selections from standard authors, and reflections of his own." One of these, in Lee's own hand, read, "The warmest instincts of every man's soul declare the glory of the soldier's death. It is more appropriate to the Christian than to the Greek to sing: 'Glorious his fate, and envied is his lot, Who for his country fights and for it dies.'"

As suggested earlier by McPherson's description of the war's impact on the South, the conflict involved catastrophic consequences for the people of the United States both North and South. During the war as a whole more than half a million soldiers died. Untold thousands were maimed. The families of all of these men also suffered grievously. Whatever portion of the catastrophe occurred after the time when Lee had become convinced that the war was lost—whether Lee came to believe this twenty, fifteen, ten, or only five months before the end—significant harm took place, in the West as well as the East, before Lee finally called a halt to the fighting. For the plain people who suffered, Lincoln's "him who shall have borne the battle, and . . . his widow, and his orphan," the consequences of the war were dire in the extreme.

Freeman wrote bitterly about Southerners who were fearful or doubtful or who wished for peace, comparing them unfavorably to the dauntless Lee and to President Davis. But the authors of *Why the South Lost the Civil War* made a different observation: "By late 1864, very likely earlier, those Confederates who argued for an end of war, even if that meant returning to the Union, did not include only the war-weary defeatists. Many among those who took that statesman-like position may have lost their will, but they weigh more on the scales of humanity than those who would have fought to the last man."

The Lee orthodoxy insists that the Confederate officers and soldiers at Appomattox were tearful and heartbroken at their surrender—they wanted to keep fighting. But even purveyors of the orthodoxy occasionally, perhaps unwittingly, contradict the tradition. Thus, quoting Lieutenant Colonel Charles Venable, Dowdey wrote that soldiers who learned of Lee's intent to surrender were "convulsed with passionate grief." But Dowdey also reported that "Lee was aware that many of his soldiers, officers and men, were ready to end 'the long agony'. . . . He could sense the attitude." He also described enlisted men who, en route to Appomattox, "overcome by exhaustion . . . were lying stretched out flat or sitting with their heads on their knees, waiting to be gathered up by the enemy." A suggestive Federal account by an eyewitness agreed with Dowdey's report. "Billy," an enlisted man in the 1st Michigan Volunteers, wrote to his family from Appomattox on the day of the surrender. He described the pursuit to Appomattox and then added, "The best of it is the Rebs are as pleased over the surrender as we are, and when the surrender was made known to them cheer after cheer went up along their whole line." . . .

On 9 April 1865, Lee apparently felt that he had fully and finally served his personal sense of duty. He had fulfilled, at last, what Dowdey described as his personal sense of "duty to do the best he could, . . . a sense of the pride of a professional in his craft." He was prepared, at last, again quoting Dowdey, "to assume the responsibility" for introducing a subject "distasteful" to Jefferson Davis. The awful human cost of his persistence had, of course, been paid by countless other people, including his own soldiers.

Giving Lee full credit for good faith and high personal character, the historian must nonetheless—as a practitioner of a discipline regarded as one of the humanities—take into account the human and social consequences of his continuing to lead others in a war that he believed was lost. It is fair to observe that Virginia, reputedly the focus of Lee's primary interest, suffered especially devastating losses of life and property because it was the scene of almost constant warfare. The facts cast serious doubt on the traditional assumption that Lee's persistence was wholly admirable.

Gary W. Gallagher

Another Look at the Generalship of R. E. Lee

Americans have embraced Abraham Lincoln and R. E. Lee as the two great figures of the Civil War. In one of the many ironies associated with the conflict, the principal rebel chieftain overshadows Ulysses S. Grant, William Tecumseh Sherman, and all other Federal generals who helped to save the Union. Although Lee's transcendent reputation as a great captain remains firmly ensconced in the popular mind and virtually no one challenges his brilliance as a field commander, scholars increasingly have questioned his larger contribution to the Confederate war effort. Did he fail to see beyond his beloved Virginia, crippling Confederate strategic planning through a stubborn refusal to release troops badly needed elsewhere? Did his strategic and tactical choices lengthen the conflict, thereby increasing the odds that Northern civilian morale would falter? Or did his penchant for the offensive unnecessarily bleed Confederate manpower when a defensive strategy punctuated by limited counteroffensives would have conserved Southern resources? Did his celebrated victories improve the odds for Confederate nationhood, or were they nothing but gaudy sideshows that diverted attention from more significant military events elsewhere? In short, what was Lee's impact on the outcome of the war?

One of the most common criticisms of Lee alleges a lack of appreciation for the problems and importance of the trans-Appalachian Confederacy. J. F. C. Fuller frequently alluded to Lee's inability to see the war as a whole. The British author stated in one characteristic passage that Lee "was so obsessed by Virginia that he considered it the most important area of the Confederacy. . . . To him the Confederacy was but the base of Virginia." A number of subsequent historians expanded upon the idea that Lee failed to take in the entire strategic situation. Especially strident in this regard was Thomas L. Connelly, who wondered "whether Lee possessed a sufficiently broad military mind to deal with over-all Confederate matters." Connelly saw Lee as intensely parochial, blinded by a desire to protect Richmond and unwilling, or unable, to look beyond each immediate threat to his native state and its capital. When Lee did turn his attention to the West, averred Connelly, he invariably made suggestions "in the context of his strategy for Virginia." Connelly and Archer Jones reiterated many of these points in their study of Confederate command and strategy. They questioned Lee's knowledge about the geography of the West

From *Lee the Soldier* by Gary W. Gallagher (1996), pp. 275–286. Copyright © 1996 by University of Nebraska Press. Reprinted by permission.

and deplored his habit of requesting reinforcements for the Army of Northern Virginia at the expense of other Confederate armies. Even Lee's grudging deployment of two-thirds of James Longstreet's First Corps to Georgia in September 1863 had a Virginia twist—he hoped that the movement might save Knoxville and shield Virginia's western flank.

Connelly and Jones admitted that all theater commanders tended to see their own region as most important but asserted that Lee's viewing Virginia in this way proved especially harmful. He had been Jefferson Davis's military adviser in the early days of the war and remained close to the president throughout the conflict; moreover, his reputation exceeded that of any other Confederate army commander. The result was as predictable as it was pernicious for the Confederacy: "His prestige as a winner and his unusual opportunity to advise undoubtedly to some degree influenced the government to take a narrower view on strategy and to go for the short gain in Virginia where victory seemed more possible." In the opinion of Connelly and Jones, Lee's influence was such that a powerful "Western Concentration Bloc," the roster of which included Joseph E. Johnston, P. G. T. Beauregard, James Longstreet, and John C. Breckinridge, could not counter his lone voice. The consequent failure to shift forces to threatened areas west of Virginia hindered the Southern cause.

Lee's aggressive style of generalship, with its attendant high casualties, also has generated much criticism. Grady McWhiney and Perry D. Jamieson propounded the thesis that a reckless devotion to offensive tactics bled the South "nearly to death in the first three years of the war" and sealed the fate of the Confederacy. Lee fit this pattern perfectly, they observed, sustaining losses approaching 20 percent in his first half-dozen battles compared to fewer than 15 percent for the Federals. A controversial aspect of McWhiney and Jamieson's book ascribed the South's love of direct assaults to a common Celtic ancestry. Whether or not readers accept the proposition that a cultural imperative prompted Lee to order attacks, McWhiney and Jamieson succeeded in accentuating his heavy losses throughout the war. Elsewhere, McWhiney bluntly claimed that the "aggressiveness of Robert E. Lee, the greatest Yankee killer of all time, cost the Confederacy dearly."

A number of other historians agreed with McWhiney. The Army of Northern Virginia suffered more than fifty thousand casualties in the three months after Lee assumed command, claimed Thomas L. Connelly, and overall "the South's largest field army, contained in the smallest war theater, was bled to death by Lee's offensive tactics." Russell F. Weigley asserted that Lee shared Napoleon's "passion for the strategy of annihilation and the climactic, decisive battle" and "destroyed in the end not the enemy armies) but his own." J. F. C. Fuller believed that Lee's only hope for success lay in emulating "the great Fabius," who often retreated to avoid costly battles. Instead, time and again Lee "rushed forth to find a battlefield" and "by his restless audacity, he mined such strategy as his government created." Alan T. Nolan's reasoned analysis of Lee explored the question of "whether the general's actions related positively or negatively to the war objectives and national policy of his government." Nolan thought that Lee came up far short when measured against this standard. His strategy and tactics won specific contests and made headlines but traded irreplaceable manpower for only fleeting advantage. "If one covets the haunting romance of the Lost Cause," wrote Nolan, "then the inflicting of casualties on the enemy, tactical victory in great battles, and audacity are enough." But such accomplishments did not bring the Confederacy closer to independence. Lee's relentless pursuit of the offensive contravened the strategy best calculated to win Southern independence and thus "contributed to the loss of the Lost Cause."

One last piece of testimony on this point typifies a common tension between admiration for Lee's generalship and a sense that his aggressive actions might have hurt the Confederacy. In a lecture delivered at a symposium on Lee in 1984, Frank E. Vandiver commented that his subject "lost a lot of men by attacking and attacking and attacking" and "may have been too addicted to the offensive, even against outstanding firepower." Vandiver then quickly hedged his conclusion: "I think that you have to balance the fact that he lost a lot of men and stuck to the offensive against what he considered to be the strategic necessities of attack. So I would level the charge that he might have been too addicted to the offensive with some trepidation."

These historians raise serious questions about the relationship between Lee's generalship and Confederate chances for independence. A different reading of the evidence, however, suggests that Lee pursued a strategy attuned to the expectations of most Confederate citizens and calculated to exert maximum influence on those who made policy in the North and in Europe. Far from being innocent of the importance of the West and the psychological dimension of his operations, he might have seen more clearly than any of his peers the best road to Confederate independence. His victories buoyed Southern hopes when defeat lay in all other directions, dampened spirits in the North, and impressed European political leaders. They also propelled him to a position where, long before the end of the war, he stood unchallenged as a military hero and his Army of Northern Virginia had become synonymous with the Confederacy in the minds of many Southern whites. While his army remained in the field there was hope for victory; his capitulation extinguished such hope and in effect ended the war. Lee had selected a strategy that paradoxically enabled the Confederacy to resist for four years *and* guaranteed that it would not survive the surrender of his army at Appomattox.

Modern historians usually attribute Confederate military defeat to failure in the West, where vast chunks of territory and crucial cities fell to the Federals. They often add that Lee's unwillingness to send part of his own army to bolster forces beyond the Appalachians may have hastened Confederate defeat. Is this belief in the primacy of western campaigns a modern misreading of the actual situation? Certainly it was the Virginia theater that captivated foreign observers. For example, Lee's victories at the Seven Days and Second Manassas in the summer of 1862 conveyed to London and Paris a sense of impending Confederate success. Apparently unimpressed by the string of Union triumphs in the West that extended from Fort Henry through the fall of New Orleans, Prime Minister Viscount Palmerston and Emperor Napoleon III leaned toward some type of intervention by the first week in September. Northern public opinion also seemed to give greater weight to the Seven Days than to events in

Tennessee, prompting Lincoln's famous complaint to French Count Agénor-Etienne de Gasparin in early August: "Yet it seems unreasonable that a series of successes, extending through half-a-year, and clearing more than a hundred thousand square miles of country, should help us so little, while a single half-defeat should hurt us so much."

Other evidence of a Northern preoccupation with the East abounds. Albert Castel has noted that Lincoln himself, who beyond doubt believed the West to be more important, visited the Army of the Potomac several times but never favored a western army with his presence. (Jefferson Davis joined his western armies on three occasions.) Senator Charles Sumner revealed a good deal about attitudes among powerful Northern politicians when he wrote during the winter of 1865 that Secretary of War Edwin M. Stanton thought "peace can be had only when Lee's army is beaten, captured or dispersed." Sumner had "for a long time been sanguine that, when Lee's army is out of the way, the whole rebellion will disappear." So long as Lee remained active, "there is still hope for the rebels, & the unionists of the South are afraid to show themselves." Among the most telling indications of the public mood was a demand that Grant go east when he became general-in-chief of the Union armies in March 1864. He could have run the war as efficiently from Tennessee or Georgia, but the North wanted its best general to bring his talents to bear on the frustrating Virginia theater.

If anything, the South exhibited a more pronounced interest in the East. Following reverses in Tennessee and along the Mississippi River during the winter and spring of 1862, Confederates looked increasingly to Virginia for good news from the battlefield. Stonewall Jackson supplied it in the spring of 1862 with his Shenandoah Valley campaign—after that, Lee and the Army of Northern Virginia provided the only reliable counterpoint to Northern gains in other theaters and consequently earned a special position in the minds of their fellow Confederates. William M. Blackford of Lynchburg, an antislavery man who nonetheless supported the Confederacy and sent five sons into Southern service, applauded the cumulative effect of Lee's 1862 campaigns: "The defeats of the enemy in the Valley, in the Peninsular, in the Piedmont, the invasion of Maryland, the capture of Harper's Ferry and lastly the victory at Fredericksburg," he remarked, "taken all together, are achievements which do not often crown one year." Lamenting the fall of Vicksburg in late July 1863, Kate Stone, a young refugee in Texas, added that "[o]ur only hope is in Lee the Invincible." Ten months and the reverse at Gettysburg did not alter Stone's thinking about Lee. "A great battle is rumored in Virginia," she wrote in May 1864. "Grant's first fight in his 'On to Richmond.' He is opposed by the Invincible Lee and so we are satisfied we won the victory." A Louisiana officer serving in the West echoed Stone's opinion on 27 May 1864, dismissing talk of a setback in Virginia with an expression of "complete faith in General Lee, who has never been known to suffer defeat, and probably never will."

No one better illustrated the tendency to focus on Lee than Catherine Ann Devereux Edmondston of North Carolina. "What a position does he occupy," she recorded in her diary on 11 June 1864, "the idol, the point of trust, of confidence & repose of thousands! How nobly has he won the confidence, the admiration of the nation." Shifting to a comparison between Lee and officers who had failed in other theaters, Edmondston remarked: "God grant that he may long be spared to us. He nullifies Bragg, Ransom. & a host of other incapables." The *Charleston Daily Courier* implicitly contrasted Lee with Confederate generals in the West when it noted that "Grant is now opposed to a General who stands in the foremost rank of Captains, and his army is confronted with men accustomed to victory." More explicit was a Georgian who after the fall of Atlanta gazed longingly at the commander in Virginia: "Oh, for a General Lee at the head of every *corps d'armee!*"

Well before the close of the war, Lee's position in the Confederacy approximated that held by Washington during the American Revolution. "It is impossible for me to describe the emotions of my heart. . . . I felt proud that the Southern Confederacy could boast of such a man," a North Carolina lieutenant wrote after Lee had reviewed his unit in May 1863. "In fact, I was almost too proud for the occasion for I could not open my mouth to give vent to the emotions that were struggling within." The *Lynchburg Virginian* affirmed after Chancellorsville that the "central figure of this war is, beyond all question, that of Robert E. Lee." Alluding to the phenomenon of Lee's offsetting Confederate reverses in the West, the Virginian admired his "calm, broad military intellect that reduced the chaos after Donelson to form and order." "He should certainly have entire control of all military operations through-out the Confederate States," stated one of the generals artillerists in mid-1864. "In fact I should like to see him as King or Dictator. He is one of the few great men who ever lived, who could be trusted." Lee's belated elevation to general-in-chief of the Confederate armies in February 1865 prompted Edward O. Guerrant, an officer serving in southwest Virginia, to observe that "[this] has inspired our country with more hope, courage, & confidence than it has had for a year or two. . . . It puts us all in good humor, & good spirits, and for myself—I feel more confident of our final triumph than for several months past." Gen. Henry A. Wise told Lee on 6 April 1865 that there "has been no country, general, for a year or more. You are the country to these men. They have fought for you."

Testimony from soldiers lends powerful support to Wise's statements. A Georgian in the Army of Northern Virginia wrote shortly after Gettysburg that "[i]t looks like it does not do any good to whip them here in this state, and out West they are tearing everything to pieces. . . . But I am willing to fight them as long as General Lee says fight." When Lee reviewed the First Corps after its return to Virginia from East Tennessee in April 1864, a South Carolinian described an emotional scene: "[T]he men caught sight of his well known figure, [and] a wild and prolonged cheer . . . ran along the lines and rose to the heavens. Hats were thrown high, and many persons became almost frantic with emotion. . . . One heard on all sides such expressions as: 'What a splendid figure!' 'What a noble face and head!' 'Our destiny is in his hands!' 'He is the best and greatest man on this continent!'" A perceptive foreign observer picked up on this attitude when he described Lee in March 1865 as the "idol of his soldiers & the Hope of His country" and spoke of "the prestige which surrounds his person & the almost fanatical belief in his judgment & capacity wh[ich] is the one idea of an entire people."

Many Confederates tied Lee directly to the sainted Washington. During the fall of 1862, the *Columbus* (Georgia) *Times* spoke of his winning everybody's confidence and noted that he "has much of the Washingtonian dignity about him, and is much respected by all with whom he is thrown." Peter W. Alexander, perhaps the most widely read Confederate war correspondent, assessed Lee just before the battle of Fredericksburg in December 1862: "Like Washington, he is a wise man, and a good man, and possesses in an eminent degree those qualities which are indispensable in the great leader and champion upon whom the country rests its hope." Alexander added that the Confederacy "should feel grateful that Heaven has raised up one in our midst so worthy of our confidence and so capable to lead"—the "grand-son of Washington, so to speak . . . the wise and modest chief who commands the Army of Northern Virginia." In the wake of Lee's triumph at Fredericksburg in December 1862, Georgian Mary Jones expressed thanks "that in this great struggle the head of our army is a noble son of Virginia, and worthy of the intimate relation in which he stands connected with our immortal Washington. What confidence his wisdom, integrity, and valor and undoubted piety inspire!" Eliza Frances Andrews, another resident of Georgia, called Lee simply "that star of light before which even Washington's glory pales."

In line with such sentiment inside and outside his army, Lee's surrender understandably signaled the end of the war to most Confederates (as it did to most Northerners). President Davis might speak bravely of the war's simply moving into a new phase after Appomattox, but a trio of women voiced far more common sentiments. "How can I write it?" asked Catherine Edmondston. "How find words to tell what has befallen us? *Gen Lee has surrendered! . . .* We stand appalled at our disaster! . . . [That] *Lee,* Lee upon whom hung the hopes of the whole country, should be a prisoner seems almost too dreadful to be realized!" The first report of Lee's capitulation reached Eliza Andrews on 18 April 1865: "No one seems to doubt it," she wrote sadly, "and everybody feels ready to give up hope. 'It is useless to struggle longer,' seems to be the common cry, and the poor wounded men go hobbling about the streets with despair on their faces." From Florida, a young woman reacted with the "wish we were all dead. It is as if the very earth had crumbled beneath our feet." A North Carolinian in the Army of Northern Virginia spoke for many soldiers and civilians in a single succinct sentence written the day Lee agreed to Grant's terms: "The life of the 'C.S.' is gon' when Gen Lee and his army surrendered."

The foregoing testimony indicates a widespread tendency *during the war* to concentrate attention on Lee and Virginia. Lee himself discerned the centrality of his military operations to Confederate morale (after Gettysburg he commented on the "unreasonable expectations of the public" concerning the Army of Northern Virginia), as well as to perceptions in the North and Europe. A man of far more than ordinary intelligence, he read Northern and Southern newspapers assiduously, corresponded widely, and discussed the political and civilian dimensions of the conflict with a broad range of persons. He appreciated the incalculable industrial and emotional value of Richmond as well as the profound concern for Washington among Northern leaders. He knew the records and personalities of officers who led Confederate armies in the West. He watched the dreary procession of defeats from Fort Donelson and Pea Ridge through Shiloh, Perryville, Stones River, Vicksburg, and Chattanooga. Robustly aware of his own ability and the superior quality of his army, he faced successive opponents with high expectations of success. A combination of these factors likely persuaded him that victories in Virginia were both more probable and calculated to yield larger results than whatever might transpire in the West.

Within this context, it followed that the Confederacy should augment his army to the greatest degree possible. Lee's official restraint prevented his questioning overtly the competence of fellow army commanders; however, in opposing the transfer of George E. Pickett's division to the West in May 1863, he mentioned the "uncertainty of its application" under John C. Pemberton. That guarded phrase came from the pen of a man who quite simply believed he was the best the Confederacy had and thus should be given adequate resources to do his job. Braxton Bragg's sheer waste of two divisions under James Longstreet in the fall of 1863 demonstrated the soundness of Lee's reluctance to reinforce western armies at the expense of the Army of Northern Virginia. As Richard M. McMurry has suggested, the "Rebels' dilemma was that they did not have either the leadership or the manpower and materiel" to hang on to both Virginia and the West. That being the case, perhaps they should have sent available resources to Virginia: "Such a strategy would have employed their best army under their best general at the point where conditions were most favorable to them. If the Confederates could not have won their independence under such circumstances, they could not have won it anywhere under any possible circumstances." To put it another way, the Confederacy could lose the war in either the West or the East, but it could win the war only in the East.

What about Lee's supposed overreliance on the offensive? His periodic use of highly questionable and costly assaults is beyond debate. Natural audacity overcame the dictates of reason when he ordered frontal attacks at Malvern Hill, on the third day at Gettysburg, and elsewhere, and when he elected to give battle north of the Potomac after 15 September 1862. But these unfortunate decisions should not unduly influence interpretations of his larger military record. After all, Grant and Sherman also resorted to unimaginative direct attacks at various times in their careers. Many critics fail to give Lee credit for what he accomplished through aggressive generalship. At the Seven Days he blunted a Federal offensive that seemed destined to pin defending Confederates in Richmond; his counterpunch in the campaign of Second Manassas pushed the eastern military frontier back to the Potomac and confronted Lincoln with a major crisis at home and abroad. The tactical masterpiece at Chancellorsville, coming as it did on the heels of a defensive win at Fredericksburg, again sent tremors through the North. Lee failed to follow up either pair of victories with a third win at Antietam or Gettysburg; however, in September 1862 and June 1863 it was not at all clear that the Army of Northern Virginia would suffer defeat in Maryland and Pennsylvania. A victory in either circumstance might have altered the course of the conflict.

Too many critics of Lee's offensive movements neglect to place them within the context of what the Confederate people would tolerate. It is easy from a late-twentieth-century perspective to study maps, point to the defensive power of the rifle-musket, speculate about the potential of wide-scale guerrilla warfare, and reach a conclusion that Lee's aggressive strategic and tactical decisions shortened the life of the Confederacy. From the opening of the war, however, Southern civilians, newspaper editors, and political leaders clamored for decisive action on the battlefield and berated generals who shunned confrontations with the Federals.

As early as the winter of 1861–62, the Richmond Dispatch described a "public mind . . . restless and anxious to be relieved by some decisive action that shall have a positive influence in the progress of the war." In mid-June 1862, shortly after Lee assumed command of the Army of Northern Virginia, the *Richmond Enquirer* conceded the value of entrenchments but stressed the need for offensive moves. "To attack the enemy at every opportunity. To harass him, cut him up, and draw him into general engagements," insisted the *Enquirer*, "is the policy of every commander who has confidence in the strength and spirit of his army. . . . [L]et activity, aggression. Attack, stand recorded and declared as our line of policy." Three months later the Macon (Georgia) *Journal & Messenger* greeted news of Lee's raid into Maryland in typically bellicose fashion: "Having in this war exercised Christian forbearance to its utmost extent, by acting on the defensive, it will now be gratifying to all to see . . . the war carried upon the soil of those barbarians who have so long been robbing and murdering our quiet and unoffending citizens." Confederate writings, both public and private, bristle with innumerable sentiments of this type.

Although Confederates often linked Lee and George Washington, they really craved a type of generalship different from that of their Revolutionary hero. Joseph E. Johnston retreated often, fought only when absolutely necessary, and otherwise fit Washington's military mold quite closely. Such behavior created an impression in the Confederacy that he gave up too much territory far too easily. A young lieutenant in Savannah complained to his father on 12 May 1862 about the Peninsula campaign: "General Joseph Johnston, from whom we were led to expect so much, has done little else than *evacuate*, until the very mention of the word sickens one *usque ad nauseam*." Twelve days later Virginia planter William Bulware excoriated Johnston in a conversation with Edmund Ruffin. The general had avoided battle for days and given up twenty miles of ground, facts that demonstrated his "incompetency and mismanagement." Bulware predicted that Johnston would continue to withdraw, causing the "surrender of Richmond, & evacuation of all lower Virginia." Criticism intensified during Johnston's retreat toward Atlanta in 1864. "I don't think he will suit the emergency," complained Josiah Gorgas long before Johnston reached Atlanta. "He is falling back just as fast as his legs can carry him. . . . Where he will stop Heaven only knows." Long since disenchanted with Johnston's tendency to retreat (together with many other facets of his behavior), Jefferson Davis finally replaced him with John Bell Hood, an officer who understood Southern expectations and immediately went on the offensive.

Lee's style of generalship suited the temperament of his people—though many fellow Confederates initially harbored doubts about his competency to succeed Joseph Johnston in field command. Known as "Granny Lee" or the "King of Spades" early in the war, he seemed more devoted to fortifications than to smiting the enemy. Edward Porter Alexander recalled that John M. Daniel, editor of the Richmond Examiner, bitterly attacked Lee in June 1862 as one who would misuse the army: "It would only be allowed to dig, that being the West Point idea of war, & West Point now being in command; that guns & ammunition would now only be in the way, spades & shovels being the only implements Gen. Lee knew anything about, &c., &c." The correspondent for the Enquirer remarked at this same time that "you have only to go into the army, amongst the men in the ranks, to hear curses heaped upon West Point and the spade."

Questions about Lee's aggressiveness disappeared rapidly after his victory in the Seven Days. His admittedly bloody battles in 1862–63 created an aura of invincibility that offset gloomy events in the West, and that aura clung to him and his army through the defensive struggles of 1864–65. Lee's initial eighteen months as commander of the Army of Northern Virginia built credibility on which he drew for the rest of the war to sustain civilian morale. Confidence in his army as it lay pinned in the trenches at Petersburg during the summer of 1864 remained high, while Northerners experienced their darkest period of doubt. Far from hastening the demise of the Confederacy, Lee's generalship provided hope that probably carried the South beyond the point at which its citizens otherwise would have abandoned their quest for nationhood.

Nor was Lee's generalship hopelessly "old-fashioned." The simplistic notion that Grant was among the first modern generals and Lee one of the last of the old school withers under the slightest scrutiny. Lee differed in many respects from Grant and Sherman—most notably in his rejection of war against civilians—but had come to terms with many facets of a modern struggle between societies. He predicted from the beginning a long war that would demand tremendous sacrifice in the Confederacy. A member of the Virginia secession convention recounted how Lee warned the delegates shortly after Fort Sumter fell that "they were just on the threshold of a long and bloody war." He knew the Northern people well and believed "they never would yield . . . except at the conclusion of a long and desperate struggle." "The war may last 10 years," he predicted to his wife on 30 April 1861, and no part of Virginia would offer safe refuge from the armies. Clear eyed about the chances for European intervention at the time of the *Trent* affair, Lee insisted that Confederates "must make up our minds to fight our battles & win our independence alone. No one will help us." He believed in the subordination of "every other consideration . . . to the great end of the public safety," testified Colonel Charles Marshall of his staff, "and that since the whole duty of the nation would be war until independence should be secured, the whole nation should for the time be converted into an army, the producers to feed and the soldiers to fight."

Lee's actions underscored this attitude. Although wearing the uniform of a republic fond of rhetoric praising state and individual rights, he demanded that the national interest come first. He issued an order in March 1862, for example, calling for more unified control of Southern railroad traffic to better satisfy the "exigencies of the service." As early as December 1861, he urged extending the terms of service for soldiers then under arms who originally had signed on for just twelve months: "The troops, in my opinion, should be organized for the war," he wrote. "We cannot stop short of its termination, be it long or short." A staunch supporter of national conscription, Lee played a key role in the process that resulted in the Confederate conscription law of April 1862. Beyond coercing military service, Lee supported the concentration of manpower in the principal Southern field armies, the central government's right to procure needed war material through impressment, and other measures strikingly at odds with the doctrine of state rights.

Late in the war Lee publicly endorsed arming black men and granting them freedom in return for Confederate service. He thus undercut the institution of slavery (with state rights one of the twin pillars on which the Confederacy had been founded), proclaiming openly what he long had urged confidentially. Loath to disagree with his government or intrude in the political sphere during the conflict, Lee had waited to express himself officially on this question until too late to affect Confederate fortunes. He later spoke privately of telling Jefferson Davis "often and early in the war that the slaves should be emancipated, that it was the only way to remove a weakness at home and to get sympathy abroad." A presidential "proclamation of gradual emancipation and the use of the negroes as soldiers" would have furthered the Confederate cause, but Davis resisted taking this step because of the political firestorm it would ignite.

Contrary to what critics such as John Keegan say, Lee was not a man of "limited imagination" whose "essentially conventional outlook" helped undo the Confederacy. He formulated a national strategy predicated on the probability of success in Virginia and the value of battlefield victories. The ultimate failure of his strategy neither proves that it was wrongheaded nor diminishes Lee's pivotal part in keeping Confederate resistance alive through four brutally destructive years. That continued resistance held the key to potential victory— Southern armies almost certainly lacked the capacity to defeat decisively their Northern counterparts, but a protracted conflict marked by periodic Confederate successes on the battlefield more than once threatened to destroy the North's will to continue the war. Indeed, the greatest single obstacle to Northern victory after June 1862 was R. E. Lee and his Army of Northern Virginia. Without Lee and that famous field command, the Confederate experiment in rebellion almost certainly would have ended much sooner.

POSTSCRIPT

Is Robert E. Lee Overrated as a General?

Most of the biographers and military historians who write about Robert E. Lee treat him with awe and reverence. Lost-cause ex-Confederate warriors created Lee's image as a noble warrior and as a soldier of unparalleled skill. He died in 1870 while still president of Washington College in Lexington, Virginia (later renamed Washington and Lee College). After his death, monuments to the general appeared across the South, and in the twentieth century his birthday came to be celebrated as a holiday in many states below the Mason-Dixon line.

Typical were the remarks of a Virginia congressman who, in the House of Representatives on Lee's 123rd birthday, commented on the "beautiful and perfect symmetry of character" of "the matchless soldier . . . [whose] genius for war at once placed him in the front ranks of the soldier of all ages." The hagiographical treatment of Lee culminated in 1935, when Virginia newsman Douglas Southall Freeman won the Pulitzer Prize for his massively detailed and worshipful *R. E. Lee: A Biography,* 4 vols. (Scribner's, 1937–1940), a work that is still in print today and that has influenced most writings about the general.

Only a handful of books have dared to criticize this idolatrous portrait of Lee. In 1933, J. F. C. Fuller's *Grant and Lee: A Study in Personality and Generalship* (Indiana University Press, 1957) foreshadowed later criticisms of Lee's strategic vision and offensive tactics. It took almost 50 years for a second critical work to appear: Thomas L. Connelly's *The Marble Man: Robert E. Lee and His Image in American Society* (Louisiana State University Press, 1978). In it, Connelly attacked Lee's obsession with Virginia, psychoanalyzed the man probably beyond the historical evidence, and argued that the Lee image was the creation primarily of the lost-cause, post–Civil War South.

Nolan's selection is a summary of his book *Lee Considered: General Robert E. Lee and Civil War History* (University of North Carolina Press, 1991), a frank reevaluation of the traditional uncritical image of Lee. Nolan charges that Lee sustained an excessive number of casualties because his grand strategy was flawed. Although he was a brilliant tactician, says Nolan, Lee might have won the war had he resorted primarily to a defensive war and not an offensive grand strategy, which Nolan maintains caused Lee to sustain heavy casualties of irreplaceable troops to an enemy that easily outnumbered the Confederacy three to one in potential manpower.

Nolan also argues that Lee unnecessarily prolonged the war even though he knew it was lost a year before he surrendered. Nolan states that Lee's "sense of honor appears . . . to have been an essentially personal emotional commitment that compelled Lee to fight on, regardless of the cost and long after he believed that it was futile to continue the contest." Finally, Nolan denies that Lee fought on because he was subject to civilian control over the military.

Gallagher is the leader of the younger generation of historians who have been reevaluating the events of the Civil War in the 1990s. While not as worshipful as Douglas Southall Freeman about the general, Gallagher feels that critics like Nolan have gone too far. He defends Lee for his brilliance as both a tactician and a grand strategist. He defends Lee's Virginia strategy, arguing that many Western confederate generals wasted the troops that were sent them in flawed campaigns. Although he lost the war, Gallagher asserts that Lee's "style of generalship suited the temperament of his people" and that Lee was beloved during the war by both his troops and the Confederate population as a whole. Gallagher argues that Lee's only hope was to take to the offensive yet hold onto Virginia. He maintains that Lincoln, Grant, and other Northern politicians knew that if they wanted to win the war, they would have to defeat Lee's army.

The starting point for this issue is Gallagher's edited book *Lee the Soldier* (University of Nebraska Press, 1996), which contains a sample of almost every important book and article written about Lee's military career. Anything written by Gallagher is worth reading. See his collection of articles on Civil War battlefields, Ken Burns's prize-winning 11-hour PBS television series *The Civil War,* and other related topics in *Lee and His Generals in War and Memory* (Louisiana State University Press, 1998). For Gallagher's assessment of the dozen books and articles on Lee that have come out since 1995, see "An Old-Fashioned Soldier in a Modern War? Robert E. Lee as Confederate General," *Civil War History* (December 1999).

A peripheral but important question pertaining to this issue is addressed in "Why the South Lost the Civil War: Ten Experts Explain the Fall of Dixie," *American History* (October 1995). The Spring 1993 issue of the *Maryland Historical Magazine* contains a collection of articles written in the late 1980s as well as a review essay by David Osher and Peter Wallenstein, entitled *Why the Confederacy Lost,* edited by Gabor S. Boritt (Oxford University Press, 1992). These articles should be compared with those written by the historians of the previous generation who met at Gettysburg College in 1958 to discuss the reasons for the Confederate loss; these can be found in David Donald, ed., *Why the North Won the Civil War* (Louisiana State University Press, 1960). The controversial view that the South "lost its will" to win the Civil War is argued in Richard E. Beringer et al., *Why the South Lost the Civil War* (University of Georgia Press, 1986).

Two articles that reconcile the military history of the battles with the new social history are Joseph T. Glatthar, "The 'New' Civil War History: An Overview," *The Pennsylvania Magazine of History and Biography* (July 1991); and Marvin R. Cain, "A 'Face of Battle' Needed: An Assessment of Motives and Men in Civil War Historiography," *Civil War History* (March 1982). Of the many military books, start with the following three: James M. McPherson's Pulitzer Prize–winning *Battle Cry of Freedom: The Civil War Era* (Oxford University Press, 1988), which reconciles political and military events; Thomas L. Connelly and Archer Jones, *The Politics of Command: Factions and Ideas in Confederate Strategy* (Louisiana State University Press, 1973); and Russell F. Weigley's *A Great Civil War: A Military and Political History, 1861–1865* (Indiana University Press, 2000).

ISSUE 16

Was Abraham Lincoln America's Greatest President?

YES: Phillip Shaw Paludan, from *The Presidency of Abraham Lincoln* (University Press of Kansas, 1994)

NO: M. E. Bradford, from *Remembering Who We Are: Observations of a Southern Conservative* (University of Georgia Press, 1985)

ISSUE SUMMARY

YES: Phillip Shaw Paludan contends that Abraham Lincoln's greatness exceeds that of all other American presidents because Lincoln, in the face of unparalleled challenges associated with the Civil War, succeeded in preserving the Union and freeing the slaves.

NO: M. E. Bradford characterizes Lincoln as a cynical politician whose abuse of authority as president and commander-in-chief during the Civil War marked a serious departure from the republican goals of the Founding Fathers and established the prototype for the "imperial presidency" of the twentieth century.

T he American Civil War (1861–1865) produced what Arthur Schlesinger, Jr., has called "our greatest national trauma." To be sure, the War Between the States was a searing event that etched itself on the collective memory of the American people and inspired an interest that has made it the most thoroughly studied episode in American history. During the last century and a quarter, scholars have identified a variety of factors (including slavery, economic sectionalism, cultural distinctions between North and South, the doctrine of states' rights, and the irresponsibility of abolitionists and proslavery advocates) that contributed to sectional tensions and that ultimately led to war. Although often presented as "sole causes," these factors are complicated, interconnected, and controversial. Consequently, historians must consider as many of them as possible in their evaluations of the war, even if they choose to spotlight one or another as the main explanation (see Issue 15).

Most historians, however, agree that the war would not have occurred had 11 southern states not seceded from the Union to form the Confederate States of America following Abraham Lincoln's election to the presidency in 1860. Why was Lincoln viewed as a threat to the South? A southerner by birth, Lincoln's career in national politics (as a congressman representing his adopted state of Illinois) apparently had been short-circuited by his unpopular opposition to the Mexican War. His attempt to emerge from political obscurity a decade later failed when he was defeated by Stephen Douglas in a bid for a Senate seat from Illinois. This campaign, however, gained for Lincoln a reputation as a powerful orator, and in 1860 Republican Party managers passed over some of their more well-known leaders, such as William Henry Seward, and nominated the moderate Mr. Lincoln for the presidency. His victory was guaranteed by factionalism within Democratic ranks, but the election results revealed that the new president received only 39 percent of the popular vote. This fact, however, provided little solace for southerners, who mistook the new president's opposition to the extension of slavery into the territories as evidence that he supported the abolitionist wing of the Republican Party. Despite assurances during the campaign that he would not tamper with slavery where it already existed, Lincoln could not prevent the splintering of the Union.

Given such an inauspicious beginning, few observers at the time could have predicted that future generations would view Lincoln as our nation's greatest president. What factors have contributed to this assessment? The answer would appear to lie in his role as commander-in-chief during the Civil War. Is this reputation deserved? The selections that follow assess Lincoln's presidency from dramatically different perspectives.

Phillip Shaw Paludan sees unparalleled greatness in the leadership of the United States' 16th chief executive. Lincoln's greatness, Paludan concludes, derived from his ability to mobilize public opinion in the North behind his goal of saving the Union and freeing the slaves. Significantly, Paludan does not separate these accomplishments. Rather, he argues that they were inextricably connected; one could not be realized without the other.

M. E. Bradford offers a sharp critique of the conclusions reached by Paludan. By pursuing an anti-Southern strategy, Bradford argues, President Lincoln perverted the republican goals advanced by the Founding Fathers and destroyed the Democratic majority that was essential to the preservation of the Union. Furthermore, Bradford asserts, Lincoln abused his executive authority by cynically expanding the scope of presidential powers to an unhealthy extent. Finally, Bradford charges that Lincoln was uncommitted to the cause of black Americans.

YES ↵

Phillip Shaw Paludan

The Presidency of Abraham Lincoln

The oath is a simple one, made all the more austere because there is no coronation, no anointing by priest or predecessor. The office has passed from one person to another months before, first by popular election and then by a ritualistic casting of votes by presidential electors, whose names are forgotten if anyone knew them in the first place. The only requirement on the day the president takes office is an oath or affirmation: "I do solemnly swear that I will faithfully execute the Office of President of the United States, and will to the best of my ability, preserve, protect and defend the Constitution of the United States."

Each president in the history of the nation has tried to protect and defend the Constitution—some with more dedication than others. Each responded to the challenges and the opportunity that his time gave him. No president had larger challenges than Abraham Lincoln, and the testimony to his greatness rests in his keeping of that oath, which led him to be responsible for two enormous accomplishments that are part of folk legend as well as fact. He saved the Union and he freed the slaves.

He preserved the unity of the nation both in size and in structure. There were still thirty-six states at the end of his presidency; there might have been twenty-five. The population of the nation when he died was 30 million; it might have been 20 million. The constitutional instrument for changing governments was still in 1865 what it had been in 1861—win a free election and gain the majority of the electoral votes. Another option might have existed—secede from the country and make war if necessary after losing the election. A divided nation might have been more easily divided again—perhaps when angry westerners felt exploited by eastern capitalists, perhaps when urban minorities felt oppressed by powerful majorities. And there were lasting international consequences from Lincoln's achievement: Foreign oppressors of the twentieth century were not allowed to run free, disregarding the two or perhaps three or four countries that might have existed between Canada and Mexico.

Because of Lincoln, 4 million black Americans gained options beyond a life of slavery for themselves and their children. Men, women, and children were no longer bought and sold, denied their humanity—because of Lincoln, but certainly not because of Lincoln alone. Perhaps 2 million Union soldiers fought to achieve these goals. Women behind the lines and near the battlefields did jobs that men would not or could not do. Workers on farms and in factories supplied the huge army and the society that sustained it. Managers and entrepreneurs organized the resources that helped gain the victory. But Lincoln's was the voice that inspired and explained and guided soldiers and civilians to continue the fight.

Black soldiers, too, preserved the Union and freed slaves. And these black soldiers were in the army because Lincoln wanted them there, accepted the demands of black and white abolitionists and growing numbers of soldiers and sailors that they be there. Hundreds of thousands, perhaps millions, of slaves, given the chance, walked away from slavery and thus "stole" from their masters the labor needed to sustain the Confederacy and the ability of those masters to enslave them. No one would ever again sell their children, their husbands, their wives; no one would rape and murder and mutilate them, control their work and much of their leisure.

Lincoln kept his oath by leading the nation, guiding it, insisting that it keep on with the task of saving the Union and freeing the slaves.

Too often historians and the general populace (which cares very much, and may define itself in vital ways by what Lincoln did and means) have divided his two great achievements. They have made saving the Union, at least for the first half of his presidency, a different task from freeing the slaves. They have noted that Lincoln explained to Horace Greeley that he could not answer Greeley's "Prayer of Twenty Million" and simply free the slaves. His prime goal, he told Greeley, was to save the Union, and he would free none, some, or all the slaves to save that Union. But before Lincoln wrote those words he had already decided that to save the Union he would have to free the slaves.

. . . Freeing the slaves and saving the Union were linked as one goal, not two optional goals. The Union that Lincoln wanted to save was not a union where slavery was safe. He wanted to outlaw slavery in the territories and thus begin a process that would end it in the states. Slave states understood this; that is why they seceded and why the Union needed saving.

Freeing the slaves, more precisely ending slavery, was the indispensable means to saving the Union. In an immediate practical sense, those 180,000 black soldiers were an essential part of the Union army in the last two years of the war. They made up almost 12 percent of the total Union land forces by 1865, adding not only to Union numbers but subtracting from the Confederate labor force. Moreover, those black soldiers liberated even where they did not march. Their example was noted throughout the South so that slaves far from Union occupation knew that blacks could be soldiers, not just property, and they began to march toward freedom.

Ending slavery also meant saving the Union in a larger sense. Slavery had endangered the Union, hurting black people but also hurting white people, and not only by allowing them to be brutes, as Jefferson had lamented. Slavery had divided the nation, threatening the processes of government by making debate over the most crucial issue of the age intolerable in the South and, for decades, dangerous in the Congress of the United States. To protect slavery the

Confederate States of America would challenge the peaceful, lawful, orderly means of changing governments in the United States, even by resorting to war. Lincoln led the successful effort to stop them and thus simultaneously saved the Union and freed the slaves.

Why does it matter that Lincoln linked saving the Union and the emancipation of the nation from slavery? First, it is necessary to get the historical record straight. It matters also because in understanding our history Americans gain access to the kind of faith that Lincoln held that our means, our legal processes, our political-constitutional system work to achieve our best ideals. Too many people, among them the first black justice of the United States Supreme Court, Thurgood Marshall, have doubted that respect for the law and the Constitution can lead to greater equality. "The system" too often has been the villain, "institutional racism" the disease that obstructs the struggle for equality. The underlying premise of this book is that the political-constitutional system, conceived of and operated at its best, inescapably leads to equality. Lincoln operated on that premise and through his presidency tried to achieve that goal.

But how did he do that? One of his accomplishments, the one that took most of his time, was fighting and winning a war. He chose the generals, gathered the armies, set the overall strategy; he restrained the dissenters and the opponents of the war; he helped to gather the resources that would maintain the Union economy and that would enable the Union military to remain strong and unrelenting. He kept himself and his party in office, the only party that was dedicated to saving the Union and ending slavery. And he kept an eye on foreign affairs, seeing to it that Great Britain remained willing to negotiate and to watch the conflict rather than joining or trying to stop it. . . .

I am particularly interested in what Lincoln said, for the most important power of a president, as Richard Neustadt has argued, is the power to persuade. Thus it is vital for a president to inform and to inspire, to warn and to empower the polity, to bring out the "better angels of our nature"—better in the sense of allowing the nation to achieve its best aspirations. "Events have controlled me," Lincoln said, but what he did most effectively was to define those events and to shape the public opinion that, he noted, was "everything in this country." In the 1840s a Whig newspaper came close to the mark I am admiring in assessing Lincoln:

> Put the case that the same multitude were addressed by two orators, and on the same question and occasion; that the first of these orators considered in his mind that the people he addressed were to be controlled by several passions . . . the orator may be fairly said to have no faith in the people; he rather believes that they are creatures of passion, and subject to none but base and selfish impulses. But now a second orator arises, a Chatham, a Webster, a Pericles, a Clay; his generous spirit expands itself through the vast auditory, and he believes that he is addressing a company of high spirited men, citizens. . . . When he says "fellow citizens," they believe him, and at once, from a tumultuous herd they are converted into men . . . their thoughts and feeling

rise to an heroical heights, beyond that of common men or common times. The second orator "had faith in the people"; he addressed the better part of each man's nature, supposing it to be in him—and it *was* in him.

At their best American presidents recognize that their duty as the chief opinion maker is to shape a public understanding that opens options and tells the truth about what the people can be and what their problems are. Appealing to the fears we have, manipulating them to win office or pass a law or achieve another goal, does not so much *reflect* who we are as it in fact *creates* who we are. It affirms us as legitimately fearful—afraid of something that our leaders confirm to be frightening—and as being citizens whose fears properly define us.

Appealing to better angels is more complicated—it requires calling on history for original aspirations—reminding Americans for example that the basic ideal of the nation is that "all men are created equal." Equally vital, such an appeal also requires reminding Americans that they have in fact established institutions that work to that end—not only reminding them of their aspirations but also reassuring them that their history, their lived experience, reveals legitimate paths to achieving those goals. History thus acts to recall the nation's best dreams, but it also restores faith that the means to approach the dream live, abide in the institutions as well as in the values that shape the nation.

I believe that a history of the presidency of Abraham Lincoln can show how Lincoln managed to shape a public understanding, how at times he failed, but how he usually succeeded. Thus he set a standard that makes it legitimate that we, when the better angels of our nature prevail, define ourselves in important ways by who Lincoln was, by what he did, and by what he said.

***

The Lincoln presidency did not end through the operation of the political-constitutional system. There was no joyous ritual, no abiding process that had gone on for generations. It was the first assassination of a president in history. A single bullet erased the decision by the people of the Union that Abraham Lincoln should be their president. It was stunning, an awful repudiation of the system that helped define them as a people, that they had been fighting for over the last four years, that had cost them such blood and treasure.

Yet the process endured. Reacting to the murder of the president newspapers throughout the country spoke of the need to "let law and order resume their sway," as the *San Francisco Chronicle* noted. "The law must reign supreme," the *Philadelphia Evening Bulletin* declared, "or in this great crisis chaos will overwhelm us, and our own maddening feeling bring upon us national wreck and ruin which traitor arms have failed to accomplish." More specifically there was admiration and recognition for a system that could overcome even assassination. "When Andrew Johnson was sworn in as President," the Reverend Joseph Thompson told a New York audience, "the Statue of Liberty that surmounts the dome of the Capitol and was put there by Lincoln, looked down on the city and on the nation and said 'Our Government is unchanged—it has merely passed from the hands of one man into those of another.'"

The words reflected part of a larger legacy. The Union was saved, and thus the political-constitutional process endured—the nation would change governments, settle controversies, and debate alternatives at the polls, in legislative halls, and in courtrooms, not on bloody battlefields. It would be a nation whose size and diversity gave it wealth and opportunities for its citizens and huge potential influence in the world. Future autocrats would have reason to fear that influence, just as future immigrants would be drawn to it. Its power would not always be used well. Native Americans who "obstructed" national mission, foreign governments deemed "un-American" had reason to fear and to protest against invasions of their rights and the destruction of their people. But within the nation itself, because of what it stood for and fought for and preserved, there remained a conscience that could be appealed to in the name of the ideals it symbolized and had demonstrated in its greatest war. Saving the Union had meant killing slavery.

Slavery was dead. Its power to divide the Union, to erode and destroy constitutional and political debate was over. No longer was the highest court in the land able to rule that under the Constitution black people had no rights that white people had to respect and that no political party legally could say otherwise. No longer could men, women, and children be bought and sold: treated as things without ties to each other, without the capacity to fulfill their own dreams. The Thirteenth Amendment, ending slavery throughout the nation and moving through the states toward ratification, ensured that. And in the van of that amendment came protection for civil rights and suffrage. Blacks were promised that they would enter the political arena and the constitutional system—this time as participants, not as objects.

This more perfect Union was achieved chiefly through an extraordinary outreach of national authority. Certainly Lincoln extended presidential power beyond any limits seen before his time—the war demanded that; Congress agreed, the Supreme Court acquiesced, and the people sustained his power. If one compares Lincoln's use of power with executive actions before 1861, popular and even scholarly use of a word such as "dictatorship" makes limited sense. Lincoln had produced, as Edwin S. Corwin observes, "a complete transformation in the President's role as Commander in Chief." Yet war was about the expansion of power, and Congress also stepped forward, expanding national power, extending its authority. Even state governments reached further than precedent admitted, increasing expenditures, strengthening their police powers over health, morals, and safety, and establishing new regulatory agencies to shape the economy.

After the war public pressures demanded a return to peacetime boundaries. Executive authority in most areas, once the fight between Johnson and Congress was settled, rapidly contracted. A few outbursts of presidential influence showed that the White House was still occupied. Grant fought senators bitterly over the Santo Domingo Treaty and presided over an effective Treaty of Washington, which resolved claims against the British for building rebel raiders. Hayes sent federal troops to settle labor protests and worked for civil service reforms. Garfield, Arthur, and Harrison also kept busy; Cleveland's vetoes showed signs of vigor. Generally, however, the presidency declined in power. With the exception of Grant a series of one-term presidents did little to inspire demands that they stay in office. For the rest of the century no president came within miles of Lincoln's power or even close to Polk or Jackson, for that matter. By 1886 Woodrow Wilson was able to write that national government in the United States was "congressional government." M. Ostrogorsky, telling foreign audiences about America, described a lawmaking environment in which "after the [civil] war the eclipse of the executive was complete and definitive"; Lord Bryce told British and American audiences in 1894 that "the domestic authority of the President is in time of peace small." These late-nineteenth-century images may have inspired Theodore Lowi to assert in 1992 that "by 1875 you would not know there had been a war or a Lincoln."

But Lord Bryce had added a caveat about the president's domestic authority: In time of war, "especially in a civil war, it expands with portentous speed." Clearly it had been thus with Lincoln. Despite calls to retreat from the vast domains of Civil War there is a sense in which Lincoln's legacy of power in the presidency survived the retreat. Certainly presidential authority, like the national authority with which it was connected, diminished when the war was over. But national power was still available after Appomattox and for the fundamental purpose that had called it forth originally: to destroy slavery and its vestiges. The fight between Congress and Lincoln's successor has obscured the fact that congressional Republicans were acting in the same cause for which Lincoln had acted. They were not recapturing power lost to the president; they were claiming power that they had shared increasingly with Lincoln.

Before Lincoln died many of the more radical Republicans had been attacking him for moving too slowly toward emancipation and then for yielding too much to military necessity and Southern loyalists. After early statements of satisfaction with Johnson they quickly came to their senses as Johnson proved not only to be slower than Lincoln to march to their goals but also to be a bitter racist obstructionist. Thus they fought against Johnson and for goals that Lincoln had espoused and had used his power to try to achieve: civil rights, education, suffrage for the freedmen. The army, which had been the major instrument of Lincoln's expanding egalitarianism and which looked to its commander in chief for direction, shifted its allegiance to Congress. Soldiers such as Grant, whom Lincoln had charged with leading the army to save the Union, did not think it incongruous to support Congress in its battle to preserve the gains of war. And when legislators moved to weaken executive power over the army with the Tenure of Office and the Command of the Army acts, they were trying to save Lincoln's legacy by weakening Johnson.

Although President Grant retreated on other issues, he tried to protect former slaves from white Southerners' efforts to restore as much of the pre-war South as they could. Grant sent troops into Louisiana, Mississippi, North Carolina, and South Carolina to effect the Force Acts and to destroy the Ku Klux Klan. A vocal element in the Republican party continued to push for federal intervention in the South in the form of national civil rights and suffrage-enforcement laws well into the 1890s. Despite retreating from the broadest definitions of federal power when it interpreted the Civil War amendments, the Supreme Court struck down laws that kept blacks off juries, and that denied Chinese Americans equal chances to work, and it upheld federal power to protect blacks from political violence. The Justice Department prosecuted thousands of election officers under this power. Local juries usually acquitted their white neighbors, but the national prohibition remained. Because of the Lincoln presidency the constitutional system carried promises of equality, and the processes to bring those promises to life endured. One hundred years after Lincoln had been awakened by the Kansas Nebraska Act to the dangers of slavery to the constitutional system, blacks and whites would see the United States Supreme Court strike down inequality in that system (that case would, interestingly enough, also involve Kansas).

Not every element, even in that reformed constitutional system, promised equal justice. The Union that Lincoln and his forces had saved remained a Union of states. Lincoln's respect for those states, demonstrated in his commitment to reconstruct them rather than to allow Congress to govern territories and in his insistence that only a constitutional amendment, ratified by states, would secure slavery's death, strengthened later arguments that states should control the fate of their citizens, old and new. Lincoln's abiding insistence that the Constitution guided his actions meant that black equality could be hindered or denied by constitutional claims of states' rights and local self-government. Brutal racism could find shelter in such legal arguments.

Yet the triumph and the irony of his administration resided in Lincoln's commitment to the Constitution; without that there would have been no promises to keep to 4 million black Americans. Because so many Americans cherished the Union that the Constitution forged, they made war on slave masters and their friends, on a government that Alexander Stephens claimed rested "on the great truth that the negro is not the equal of the white man; that slavery . . . is his natural and normal condition."

Without the president's devotion to and mastery of the political-constitutional institutions of his time, in all probability the Union would have lacked the capacity to focus its will and its resources on defeating that Confederacy. Without Lincoln's unmatched ability to integrate egalitarian ends and constitutional means he could not have enlisted the range of supporters and soldiers necessary for victory. His great accomplishment was to energize and mobilize the nation by affirming its better angels, by showing the nation at its best: engaged in the imperative, life-preserving conversation between structure and purpose, ideal and institution, means and ends.

Melvin E. Bradford  **NO**

Remembering Who We Are: Observations of a Southern Conservative

The Lincoln Legacy: A Long View

With the time and manner of his death Abraham Lincoln, as leader of a Puritan people who had just won a great victory over "the forces of evil," was placed beyond the reach of ordinary historical inquiry and assessment. Through Booth's bullet he became the one who had "died to make men free," who had perished that his country's "new birth" might occur: a "second founder" who, in Ford's theater, had been transformed into an American version of the "dying god." Our common life, according to this construction, owes its continuation to the shedding of the sacred blood. Now after over a century of devotion to the myth of the "political messiah," it is still impossible for most Americans to see through and beyond the magical events of April 1865. However, Lincoln's daily purchase upon the ongoing business of the nation requires that we devise a way of setting aside the martyrdom to look behind it at Lincoln's place in the total context of American history and discover in him a major source of our present confusion, our distance from the republicanism of the Fathers, the models of political conduct which we profess most to admire. . . .

Of course, nothing that we can identify as part of Lincoln's legacy belongs to him alone. In some respects the Emancipator was carried along with the tides. Yet a measure of his importance is that he was at the heart of the major political events of his era. Therefore what signifies in a final evaluation of this melancholy man is that many of these changes in the country would never have come to pass had Lincoln not pushed them forward. Or at least not come so quickly, or with such dreadful violence. I will emphasize only the events that he most certainly shaped according to his relentless will, alterations in the character of our country for which he was clearly responsible. For related developments touched by Lincoln's wand, I can have only a passing word. The major charges advanced here, if proved, are sufficient to impeach the most famous and respected of public men. More would only overdo.

The first and most obvious item in my bill of particulars for indictment concerns Lincoln's dishonesty and obfuscation with respect to the nation's

From *Remembering Who We Are: Observations of a Southern Conservative* by Melvin E. Bradford (University of Georgia Press, 1985), pp. 143–155 (notes omitted). Copyright © 1985 by University of Georgia Press. Reprinted by permission.

future obligations to the Negro, slave and free. It was of course an essential ingredient of Lincoln's position that he make a success at being anti-Southern or antislavery without at the same time appearing to be significantly impious about the beginnings of the Republic (which was neither anti-Southern nor antislavery)—or significantly pro-Negro. He was the first Northern politician of any rank to combine these attitudes into a viable platform persona, the first to make his moral position on slavery in the South into a part of his national politics. It was a posture that enabled him to unite elements of the Northern electorate not ordinarily willing to cooperate in any political undertaking. And thus enabled him to destroy the old Democratic majority—a coalition necessary to preserving the union of the states. Then came the explosion. But this calculated posturing has had more durable consequences than secession and the Federal confiscation of property in slaves. . . .

In the nation as a whole what moves toward fruition is a train of events set in motion by the duplicitous rhetoric concerning the Negro that helped make Abraham Lincoln into our first "sectional" president. Central to this appeal is a claim to a kind of moral superiority that costs absolutely nothing in the way of conduct. Lincoln, in insisting that the Negro was included in the promise of the Declaration of Independence and that the Declaration bound his countrymen to fulfill a pledge hidden in that document, seemed clearly to point toward a radical transformation of American society. Carried within his rejection of Negro slavery as a continuing feature of the American regime, his assertion that the equality clause of the Declaration of Independence was "the father of all moral principle among us," were certain muted corollaries. By promising that the peculiar institution would be made to disappear if candidates for national office adopted the proper "moral attitude" on that subject, Lincoln recited as a litany the general terms of his regard for universal human rights. But at the same time he added certain modifications to this high doctrine: modifications required by those of his countrymen to whom he hoped to appeal, by the rigid racism of the Northern electorate, and by "what his own feelings would admit." The most important of these reservations was that none of his doctrine should apply significantly to the Negro in the North. Or, after freedom, to what he could expect in the South. It was a very broad, very general, and very abstract principle to which he made reference. By it he could divide the sheep from the goats, the wheat from the chaff, the patriot from the conspirator. But for the Negro it provided nothing more than a technical freedom, best to be enjoyed far away. Or the valuable opportunity to "root, hog, or die." For the sake of such vapid distinctions he urged his countrymen to wade through seas of blood.

To be sure, this position does not push the "feelings" of that moralist who was our sixteenth president too far from what was comfortable for him. And it goes without saying that a commitment to "natural rights" which will not challenge the Black Codes of Illinois, which promises something like them for the freedman in the South, or else offers him as alternative the proverbial "one-way-ticket to nowhere" is a commitment of empty words. It is only an accident of political history that the final Reconstruction settlement provided a bit more for the former slave—principally, the chance to vote Republican;

and even that "right" didn't last, once a better deal was made available to his erstwhile protectors. But the point is that Lincoln's commitment was precisely of the sort that the North was ready to make—while passing legislation to restrict the flow of Negroes into its own territories, elaborating its own system of segregation by race, and exploiting black labor through its representatives in a conquered South. Lincoln's double talk left his part of the country with a durable heritage of pious self-congratulation. . . .

The second heading in this "case against Lincoln" involves no complicated pleading. Neither will it confuse any reader who examines his record with care. For it has to do with Lincoln's political economy, his management of the commercial and business life of the part of the Republic under his authority. This material is obvious, even though it is not always connected with the presidency of Abraham Lincoln. Nevertheless, it must be developed at this point. For it leads directly into the more serious charges upon which this argument depends. It is customary to deplore the Gilded Age, the era of the Great Barbecue. It is true that many of the corruptions of the Republican Era came to a head after Lincoln lay at rest in Springfield. But it is a matter of fact that they began either under his direction or with his sponsorship. Military necessity, the "War for the Union," provided an excuse, an umbrella of sanction, under which the essential nature of the changes being made in the relation of government to commerce could be concealed. Of his total policy the Northern historian Robert Sharkey has written, "Human ingenuity would have had difficulty in contriving a more perfect engine for class and sectional exploration, creditors finally obtaining the upper hand as opposed to debtors, and the developed East holding the whip over the underdeveloped West and South." Until the South left the Union, until a High Whig sat in the White House, none of this return to the "energetic government" of Hamilton's design was possible. Indeed, even in the heyday of the Federalists it had never been so simple a matter to translate power into wealth. Now Lincoln could try again the internal improvements of the early days in Illinois. The difference was that this time the funding would not be restrained by political reversal or a failure of credit. For if anything fell short, Mr. Salmon P. Chase, "the foreman" of his "green printing office," could be instructed "to give his paper mill another turn." And the inflationary policy of rewarding the friends of the government sustained. The euphemism of our time calls this "income redistribution." But it was theft in 1864, and is theft today.

A great increase in the tariff and the formation of a national banking network were, of course, the cornerstones of this great alteration in the posture of the Federal government toward the sponsorship of business. From the beginning of the Republican Party Lincoln warned his associates not to talk about their views on these subjects. Their alliance, he knew, was a negative thing: a league against the Slave Power and its Northern friends. But in private he made it clear that the hidden agenda of the Republicans would have its turn, once the stick was in their hand. In this he promised well. Between 1861 and 1865, the tariff rose from 18.84 percent to 47.56 percent. And it stayed above 40 percent in all but two years of the period concluded with the election of Woodrow Wilson. Writes the Virginia historian Ludwell H. Johnson, it would "facilitate a massive transfer of wealth, satisfying the dreariest predictions of John C. Calhoun." The new Republican system of banking (for which we should note Lincoln was directly accountable) was part of the same large design of "refounding." The National Banking Acts of 1863 and 1864, with the earlier Legal Tender Act, flooded the country with $480 million of fiat money that was soon depreciated by about two-thirds in relation to specie. Then all notes but the greenback dollar were taxed out of existence, excepting only United States Treasury bonds that all banks were required to purchase if they were to have a share in the war boom. The support for these special bonds was thus the debt itself—Hamilton's old standby. Specie disappeared. Moreover, the bank laws controlled the money supply, credit, and the balance of power. New banks and credit for farms, small businesses, or small town operations were discouraged. And the Federalist model, after four score and seven years, finally achieved.

As chief executive, Lincoln naturally supported heavy taxes. Plus a scheme of tax graduation. The war was a legitimate explanation for these measures. Lincoln's participation in huge subsidies or bounties for railroads and in other legislation granting economic favors is not so readily linked to "saving the Union." All of his life Lincoln was a friend of the big corporations. He had no moral problem in signing a bill which gifted the Union Pacific Railway with a huge strip of land running across the West and an almost unsecured loan of $16,000 to $48,000 per mile of track. The final result of this bill was the Credit Mobilier scandal. With other laws favoring land speculation it helped to negate the seemingly noble promise of the Homestead Act of 1862—under which less than 19 percent of the open lands settled between 1860 and 1900 went to legitimate homesteaders. The Northern policy of importing immigrants with the promise of this land, only to force them into the ranks of General Grant's meat-grinder or into near slavery in the cities of the East, requires little comment. Nor need we belabor the rotten army contracts given to politically faithful crooks. Nor the massive thefts by law performed during the war in the South. More significant is Lincoln's openly disgraceful policy of allowing special cronies and favorites of his friends to trade in Southern cotton—even with "the enemy" across the line—and his calculated use of the patronage and the pork barrel. Between 1860 and 1880, the Republicans spent almost $10 million breathing life into state and local Republican organizations. Lincoln pointed them down that road. There can be no doubt of his responsibility for the depressing spectacle of greed and peculation concerning which so many loyal Northern men of the day spoke with sorrow, disappointment, and outrage. . . .

A large part of the complaint against Lincoln as a political precedent for later declensions from the example of the Fathers has to do with his expansion of the powers of the presidency and his alteration of the basis for the Federal Union. With reference to his role in changing the office of chief magistrate from what it had been under his predecessors, it is important to remember that he defined himself through the war powers that belonged to his post. In this way Lincoln could profess allegiance to the Whig ideal of the modest, self-effacing leader, the antitype of Andrew Jackson, and, in his capacity as Commander-in-Chief, do whatever he wished. That is, if he could do it in the name of preserving the Union. As Clinton Rossiter has stated, Lincoln believed there were "no limits" to his powers if he exercised them in that "holy cause." Gottfried Dietze compares Lincoln in this role to the Committee of Public Safety as it operated in the French Revolution. Except for the absence of mass executions, the results were similar. War is of course the occasion for concentration of power and the limitation of liberties within any nation. But an internal war, a war between states in a union of states, is not like a war to repel invasion or to acquire territory. For it is an extension into violence of a domestic political difference. And it is thus subject to extraordinary abuses of authority—confusions or conflations of purpose which convert the effort to win the war into an effort to effect even larger, essentially political changes in the structure of government. War, in these terms, is not only an engine for preserving the Union; it is also an instrument for transforming its nature. But without overdeveloping this structure of theory, let us shore it up with spe- cific instances of presidential misconduct by Lincoln: abuses that mark him as our first imperial president. Lincoln began his tenure as a dictator when between April 12 and July 4 of 1861, without interference from Congress, he summoned militia, spent millions, suspended law, authorized recruiting, decreed a blockade, defied the Supreme Court, and pledged the nation's credit. In the following months and years he created units of government not known to the Constitution and officers to rule over them in "conquered" sections of the South, seized property throughout both sections, arrested upwards of twenty thousand of his political enemies and confined them without trial in a Northern "Gulag," closed over three hundred newspapers critical of his policy, imported an army of foreign mercenaries (of perhaps five hundred thousand men), interrupted the assembly of duly elected legislatures and employed the Federal hosts to secure his own reelection—in a contest where about thirty- eight thousand votes, if shifted, might have produced an armistice and a nego- tiated peace under a President McClellan. To the same end he created a state in West Virginia, arguing of this blatant violation of the explicit provisions of the Constitution that it was "expedient." But the worst of this bold and ruthless dealing (and I have given but a very selective list of Lincoln's "high crimes") has to do with his role as military leader per se: as the commander and selec- tor of Northern generals, chief commissary of the Federal forces, and head of government in dealing with the leaders of an opposing power. In this role the image of Lincoln grows to be very dark—indeed, almost sinister.

The worst that we may say of Lincoln is that he led the North in war so as to put the domestic political priorities of his political machine ahead of the lives and the well-being of his soldiers in the field. The appointment of the venal Simon Cameron of Pennsylvania as his secretary of war, and of lesser hacks and rascals to direct the victualing of Federal armies, was part of this malfeasance. By breaking up their bodies, the locust hoard of contractors even found a profit in the Union dead. And better money still in the living. They made of Lincoln (who winked at their activities) an accessory to lost horses, rotten meat, and worthless guns. But all such mendacity was noth- ing in comparison to the price in blood paid for Lincoln's attempts to give the nation a genuine Republican hero. He had a problem with this project throughout the entire course of the war. That is, until Grant and Sherman "converted" to radicalism. Prior to their emergence all of Lincoln's "loyal" generals disapproved of either his politics or of his character. These, as with McClellan, he could use and discharge at will. Or demote to minor tasks. One thinks immediately of George G. Meade—who defeated Lee at Gettysburg, and yet made the mistake of defining himself as the defender of a separate Northern nation from whose soil he would drive a foreign Southern "invader." Or of Fitz John Porter, William B. Franklin, and Don Carlos Buell—all scapegoats thrown by Lincoln to the radical wolves. In place of these heterodox professionals, Lincoln assigned such champions of the "new freedom" as Nathaniel P. ("Commissary") Banks, Benjamin F. ("Beast") Butler, John C. Fremont, and John A. McClernand. Speaking in summary despair of these appointments (and adding to my list, Franz Sigel and Lew Wallace), General Henry Halleck, Lincoln's chief-of-staff, declared that they were "little better than murder." Yet in the East, with the Army of the Potomac, Lincoln make promotions even more difficult to defend, placing not special projects, divisions, and brigades but entire commands under the authority of such "right thinking" incompetents as John Pope (son of an old crony in Illinois) and "Fighting Joe" Hooker. Or with that "tame" Democrat and late favorite of the radicals, Ambrose E. Burnside. Thousands of Northern boys lost their lives in order that the Republican Party might experience rejuvenation, to serve its partisan goals. And those were "party supremacy within a Northern dominated Union." A Democratic "man-on-horseback" could not serve those ends, however faithful to "the Constitution as it is, and the Union as it was" (the motto of the Democrats) they might be. For neither of these commitments promised a Republican hegemony. To provide for his faction both security and continuity in office, Lincoln sounded out his commanders in correspondence (much of which still survives), suborned their military integrity, and employed their focus in purely political operation. Writes Johnson:

> Although extreme measures were most common in the border states, they were often used elsewhere too. By extreme measures is meant the arrest of anti-Republican candidates and voters, driving anti-Republican voters from the polls or forcing them to vote the Republican ticket, preventing opposition parties from holding meetings, removing names from ballots, and so forth. These methods were employed in national, state and local elections. Not only did the army interfere by force, it was used to supply votes. Soldiers whose states did not allow absentee voting were sent home by order of the President to swell the Republican totals. When voting in the field was used, Democratic commissioners carrying ballots to soldiers from their state were . . . unceremoniously thrown into prison, while Republican agents were offered every assistance. Votes of Democratic soldiers were sometimes discarded as defective, replaced by Republican ballots, or simply not counted.

All Lincoln asked of the ordinary Billy Yank was that he be prepared to give himself up to no real purpose—at least until Father Abraham found a general with the proper moral and political credentials to lead him on to

Richmond. How this part of Lincoln's career can be reconciled to the myth of the "suffering savior" I cannot imagine.

We might dwell for some time on what injury Lincoln did to the dignity of his office through the methods he employed in prosecuting the war. It was no small thing to disavow the ancient Christian code of "limited war," as did his minions, acting in his name. However, it is enough in this connection to remember his policy of denying medicines to the South, even for the sake of Northern prisoners held behind the lines. We can imagine what a modern "war crimes" tribunal would do with that decision. There may have been practicality in such inhumane decisions. *Practicality* indeed! As Charles Francis Adams, Lincoln's ambassador to the Court of St. James and the scion of the most notable family in the North, wrote in his diary of his leader, the "President and his chief advisers are not without the spirit of the serpent mixed in with their wisdom." And he knew whereof he spoke. For practical politics, the necessities of the campaign of 1864, had led Lincoln and Seward to a decision far more serious than unethical practices against prisoners and civilians in the South. I speak of the rejection by the Lincoln administration of peace feelers authorized by the Confederate government in Richmond: feelers that met Lincoln's announced terms for an end to the Federal invasion of the South. The emissary in this negotiation was sponsored by Charles Francis Adams. He was a Tennessean living in France, one Thomas Yeatman. After arriving in the United States, he was swiftly deported by direct order of the government before he could properly explore the possibility of an armistice on the conditions of reunion and an end to slavery. Lincoln sought these goals, but only on his terms. And in his own time. He wanted total victory. And he needed a still-resisting, impenitent Confederacy to justify his re-election. We can only speculate as to why President Davis allowed the Yeatman mission. We know that he expected little of such peace feelers. (There were many in the last stages of the conflict.) He knew his enemy too well to expect anything but subjection, however benign the rhetoric used to disguise its rigor. Adams's peace plan was perhaps impossible, even if his superiors in Washington had behaved in good faith. The point is that none of the peace moves of 1864 was given any chance of success. Over one hundred thousand Americans may have died because of the Rail-Splitter's rejection of an inexpedient peace. Yet we have still not touched upon the most serious of Lincoln's violations of the Presidential responsibility. I speak, finally, of his role in bringing on the War Between the States.

There is, we should recall, a great body of scholarly argument concerning Lincoln's intentions in 1860 and early 1861. A respectable portion of this work comes to the conclusion that the first Republican president expected a "tug," a "crisis," to follow his election. And then, once secession had occurred, also expected to put it down swiftly with a combination of persuasion, force, and Southern loyalty to the Union. The last of these, it is agreed, he completely overestimated. In a similar fashion he exaggerated the force of Southern "realism," the region's capacity to act in its own pecuniary interest. The authority on Lincoln's political economy has remarked that the Illinois lawyer-politician and old line Whig always made the mistake of explaining in simple economic terms the South's hostile reaction to anti-slavery proposals. To that blunder he added the related mistake of attempting to end the "rebellion" with the same sort of simplistic appeals to the prospect of riches. Or with fear of a servile insurrection brought on by his greatest "war measure," the emancipation of slaves behind Southern lines, beyond his control. A full-scale Southern revolution, a revolution of all classes of men against the way he and some of his supporters thought, was beyond his imagination. There was no "policy" in such extravagant behavior, no human nature as he perceived it. Therefore, on the basis of my understanding of his overall career, I am compelled to agree with Charles W. Ramsdell concerning Lincoln and his war. Though he was no sadist and no warmonger, and though he got for his pains much more of a conflict than he had in mind, Lincoln hoped for an "insurrection" of some sort—an "uprising" he could use.

The "rational" transformation of our form of government which he had first predicted in the "Springfield Lyceum Speech" required some kind of passionate disorder to justify the enforcement of a new Federalism. And needed also for the voting representatives of the South to be out of their seats in the Congress. It is out of keeping with his total performance as a public man and in contradiction of his campaigning after 1854 not to believe that Lincoln hoped for a Southern attack on Fort Sumter. As he told his old friend Senator Orville H. Browning of Illinois: "The plan succeeded. They attacked Sumter—it fell, and thus did more service than it otherwise could." And to others he wrote or spoke to the same effect. If the Confederacy's offer of money for Federal property were made known in the North and business relations of the sections remained unaffected, if the Mississippi remained open to Northern shipping, there would be no support for "restoring" the Union on a basis of force. Americans were in the habit of thinking of the unity of the nation as a reflex of their agreement in the Constitution, of law as limit on government and on the authority of temporary majorities, and of revisions in law as the product of the ordinary course of push and pull within a pluralistic society, not as a response to the extralegal authority of some admirable abstraction like equality. In other words, they thought of the country as being defined by the way in which we conducted our political business, not by where we were trying to go in a body. Though once a disciple of Henry Clay, Lincoln changed the basis of our common bond away from the doctrine of his mentor, away from the patterns of compromise and dialectic of interests and values under a limited, Federal sovereignty with which we as a people began our adventure with the Great Compromise of 1787–1788. The nature of the Union left to us by Lincoln is thus always at stake in every major election, in every refinement in our civil theology; the Constitution is still to be defined by the latest wave of big ideas, the most recent mass emotion. Writes Dietze:

> Concentrations of power in the national and executive branches of government, brought about by Lincoln in the name of the people, were processes that conceivably complemented each other to the detriment of free government. Lincoln's administration thus opened the way for the development of an omnipotent national executive who as

a spokesman for the people might consider himself entitled to do whatever he felt was good for the Nation, irrespective of the interests and rights of states, Cungress, the judiciary, and the individual. . . .

But in my opinion the capstone of this case against Lincoln . . . is what he has done to the language of American political discourse that makes it so difficult for us to reverse the ill effects of trends he set in motion with his executive fiat. When I say that Lincoln was our first Puritan president, I am chiefly referring to a distinction of style, to his habit of wrapping up his policy in the idiom of Holy Scripture, concealing within the Trojan horse of his gasconade and moral superiority an agenda that would never have been approved if presented in any other form. It is this rhetoric in particular, a rhetoric confirmed in its authority by his martyrdom, that is enshrined in the iconography of the Lincoln myth preserved against examination by monuments such as the Lincoln Memorial, where his oversized likeness is elevated above us like that of a deified Roman emperor. . . .

POSTSCRIPT

Was Abraham Lincoln America's Greatest President?

Biographer Stephen B. Oates, in *Abraham Lincoln: The Man Behind the Myths* (Harper & Row, 1984), suggests that Lincoln, at the time of his assassination, was perhaps the most hated president in history. Since Arthur Schlesinger, Jr., first polled experts on the subject in 1948, however, historians consistently have rated Lincoln the nation's best chief executive. George Washington, Thomas Jefferson, Theodore and Franklin Roosevelt, and Woodrow Wilson have done well in presidential polls conducted by Gary Maranell (1970), Steve Neal (1982), and Robert K. Murray (1983), but none so well as Abraham Lincoln. Another president, Harry Truman, himself ranked Lincoln in the category of "great" chief executives. In words that are echoed by Phillip Paludan, Truman wrote of Lincoln: "He was a strong executive who saved the government, saved the United States. He was a President who understood people, and, when it came time to make decisions, he was willing to take the responsibility and make those decisions, no matter how difficult they were. He knew how to treat people and how to make a decision stick, and that's why his is regarded as such a great Administration."

Lincoln also is the most written-about president. Interested students should consult Carl Sandburg, *Abraham Lincoln*, 6 vols. (Harcourt, Brace and World, 1926–1939), a poetic panorama that focuses upon the mythic Lincoln. Benjamin Thomas, *Abraham Lincoln: A Biography* (Knopf, 1952), and Stephen B. Oates, *With Malice Toward None: The Life of Abraham Lincoln* (Harper and Row, 1977), are both excellent one-volume biographies. David Donald followed his *Lincoln Reconsidered: Essays on the Civil War Era* (Knopf, 1956) 40 years later with *Lincoln* (Simon & Schuster, 1996), which won the Lincoln Prize. Doris Kearns Goodwin's *Team of Rivals: The Political Genius of Abraham Lincoln* (Simon & Schuster, 2005) is a beautifully written appraisal of Lincoln's approach to leadership. Richard Current, *The Lincoln Nobody Knows* (McGraw-Hill, 1958), offers incisive interpretations of many aspects of Lincoln's political career and philosophy. Psychoanalytical approaches to Lincoln are offered by George B. Forgie, *Patricide in the House Divided: A Psychological Interpretation* (Norton, 1979), and Dwight G. Anderson, *Abraham Lincoln: The Quest for Immortality* (Knopf, 1982). The events leading up to the Civil War are presented best in David M. Potter, *The Impending Crisis, 1848–1861* (Harper and Row, 1976). Lincoln's responsibility for the precipitating event of the war is explored in Richard N. Current, *Lincoln and the First Shot* (Lippincott, 1963). T. Harry Williams, *Lincoln and His Generals* (Knopf, 1952), looks at Lincoln as commander-in-chief. Peyton McCrary, *Abraham Lincoln and Reconstruction: The Louisiana Experiment* (Princeton University Press, 1978), examines Lincoln's plan for restoring the southern states to the Union. For Lincoln's role as "the Great Emancipator" and his attitudes toward race and slavery, see Benjamin Quarles, *Lincoln and the Negro* (Oxford University Press, 1962); LaWanda Cox, *Lincoln and Black Freedom: A Study in Presidential Leadership* (University of South Carolina Press, 1981); Lerone Bennett, *Forced Into Glory: Abraham Lincoln's White Dream* (Johnson Publishing, 2000); and James Oakes, *The Radical and the Republican: Frederick Douglass, Abraham Lincoln, and the Triumph of Antislavery Politics* (W. W. Norton, 2007). *The Historian's Lincoln: Pseudohistory, Psychohistory, and History*, edited by Gabor S. Boritt, (University of Illinois Press, 1988), is a valuable collection.

Several volumes on Lincoln have appeared in conjunction with the bicentennial of his birth. The best of these include Michael Burlingame's exhaustive *Abraham Lincoln: A Life* (Johns Hopkins University Press, 2008), and two more manageable volumes for general readers and specialists alike: George McGovern, *Abraham Lincoln* (Times Books, 2008), and James M. McPherson, *Abraham Lincoln* (Oxford University Press, 2009).

Modern-day disciples of Bradford who, like their mentor, do not possess academic credentials as historians, have offered shrill indictments of Lincoln and those scholars who praise his presidential leadership. For examples of the writings of this group, see Sam Dickson, "Shattering the Icon of Abraham Lincoln," *Journal for Historical Review* (Fall 1987), and two volumes by Thomas J. DiLorenzo: *The Real Lincoln: A New Look at Abraham Lincoln, His Agenda, and an Unnecessary War* (Prima Lifestyles, 2002), and *Lincoln Unmasked: What You're Not Supposed to Know about Dishonest Abe* (Crown Forum, 2006).

ISSUE 17

Did Reconstruction Fail as a Result of Racism?

YES: George M. Fredrickson, from *The Black Image in the White Mind: The Debate on Afro-American Character and Destiny, 1817–1914* (Harper & Row, 1971)

NO: Heather Cox Richardson, from *The Death of Reconstruction: Race, Labor, and Politics in the Post–Civil War North, 1865–1901* (Harvard University Press, 2001)

ISSUE SUMMARY

YES: George M. Fredrickson concludes that racism, in the form of the doctrine of white supremacy, colored the thinking not only of southern whites but of most white northerners as well and produced only half-hearted efforts by the Radical Republicans in the postwar period to sustain a commitment to black equality.

NO: Heather Cox Richardson argues that the failure of Radical Reconstruction was primarily a consequence of a national commitment to a free-labor ideology that opposed an expanding central government that legislated rights to African Americans that other citizens had acquired through hard work.

Given the complex issues of the post–Civil War years, it is not surprising that the era of Reconstruction (1865–1877) is shrouded in controversy. For the better part of a century following the war, historians typically characterized Reconstruction as a total failure that had proved detrimental to all Americans—northerners and southerners, whites and blacks. According to this traditional interpretation, a vengeful Congress, dominated by radical Republicans, imposed military rule upon the southern states. Carpetbaggers from the North, along with traitorous white scalawags and their black accomplices in the South, established coalition governments that rewrote state constitutions, raised taxes, looted state treasuries, and disenfranchised former Confederates while extending the ballot to the freedmen. This era finally ended in 1877 when courageous southern white Democrats successfully "redeemed" their region from "Negro rule" by toppling the Republican state governments.

This portrait of Reconstruction dominated the historical profession until the 1960s. One reason for this is that white historians (both northerners and southerners) who wrote about this period operated from two basic assumptions: (1) The South was capable of solving its own problems without federal government interference; and (2) the former slaves were intellectually inferior to whites and incapable of running a government (much less one in which some whites would be their subordinates). African American historians, such as W. E. B. DuBois, wrote several essays and books that challenged this negative portrayal of Reconstruction, but their works seldom were taken seriously in the academic world and rarely were read by the general public. Still, these black historians foreshadowed the acceptance of revisionist interpretations of Reconstruction, which coincided with the successes of the civil rights movement (or "Second Reconstruction") in the 1960s.

Without ignoring obvious problems and limitations connected with this period, revisionist historians identified a number of accomplishments of the Republican state governments in the South and their supporters in Washington, D.C. For example, revisionists argued that the state constitutions that were written during Reconstruction were the most democratic documents that the South had seen up to that time. Also, although taxes increased in the southern states, the revenues generated by these levies financed the rebuilding and expansion of the South's railroad network, the creation of a number of social service institutions, and the establishment of a public school system that benefited African Americans as well as whites. At the federal level, Reconstruction achieved the ratification of the Fourteenth and Fifteenth Amendments, which extended significant privileges of citizenship (including the right to vote) to African Americans, both North and South. Revisionists also placed the charges of corruption leveled by traditionalists against the Republican regimes in the South in a more appropriate context by insisting that political corruption was a *national* malady. Although the leaders of the Republican state governments in the South engaged in a number of corrupt activities, they were no more guilty than several federal officeholders in the Grant administration, or the members of New York City's notorious Tweed Ring (a Democratic urban political machine), or even the southern white Democrats (the Redeemers) who replaced the radical Republicans in positions of power in the former Confederate states. Finally, revisionist historians sharply attacked the notion that African Americans dominated the reconstructed governments of the South.

In the essays that follow, George M. Fredrickson and Heather Cox Richardson present thought-provoking analyses of the influence racism played in the failure of Reconstruction. In the first selection, Fredrickson contends that the doctrine of white supremacy that galvanized southern opposition to the political, economic, and social empowerment of African Americans after the war also dominated the thinking of white northerners, including many Radical Republicans. As a consequence, racism prevented the success of efforts to incorporate African Americans fully into American society on an equitable basis.

Heather Cox Richardson offers a post-revisionist interpretation of the failure of Reconstruction and contends that the key barrier to postwar assistance for African Americans was the nation's commitment to a free-labor ideology. Believing that social equality derived from economic success, most Americans opposed legislation, such as the Civil Rights Act of 1875, which appeared to provide special interest legislation solely for the benefit of the former slaves.

YES ↵
George M. Fredrickson

The Black Image in the White Mind: The Debate on Afro-American Character and Destiny, 1817–1914

Race and Reconstruction

Once freed, the black population of the South constituted a new element that had to be incorporated somehow into the American social and political structure, Some Radical Republicans and veterans of the antislavery crusade regarded justice and equality for the freedmen as a fulfillment of national ideals and a desirable end in itself. For a larger number of loyal Northerners the question of Negro rights was, from first to last, clearly subordinate to the more fundamental aim of ensuring national hegemony for Northern political, social, and economic institutions. But even those who lacked an ideological commitment to black equality could not avoid the necessity of shaping a new status for the Southern blacks; for there they were in large numbers, capable of being either a help or a hindrance to the North's effort to restore the Union and secure the fruits of victory.

Before 1863 and 1864, Northern leaders had been able to discuss with full seriousness the possibility of abolishing slavery while at the same time avoiding the perplexing and politically dangerous task of incorporating the freed blacks into the life of the nation. President Lincoln and other moderate or conservative Republicans, feeling the pulse of a racist public opinion, had looked to the reduction or elimination of the black population through colonization or emigration as a way of approaching the racial homogeneity which they associated with guaranteed national unity and progress. By itself the Emancipation Proclamation had not destroyed such hopes, but events soon made the colonization schemes irrelevant and inappropriate. . . .

Whatever the motivation of Radical Reconstruction and however inadequate its programs, it was a serious effort, the first in American history, to incorporate Negroes into the body politic. As such, it inevitably called forth bitter opposition from hardcore racists, who attempted to discredit radical measures by using many of the same arguments developed as part of the proslavery argument in the prewar period.

The new cause was defined as "white supremacy"—which in practice allowed Southern whites to reduce the freedmen to an inferior caste, as they had attempted to do by enacting the "Black Codes" of 1865. To further this cause in 1868, [John] Van Evrie simply reissued his book *Negroes and Negro "Slavery"* with a topical introduction and under the new title *White Supremacy and Negro Subordination.* [Josiah] Nott also entered the Reconstruction controversy. In an 1866 pamphlet he reasserted the "scientific" case for inherent black inferiority as part of an attack on the Freedmen's Bureau and other Northern efforts to deal with the Southern race question. "If the whites and blacks be left alone face to face," he wrote, "they will soon learn to understand each other, and come to proper terms under the law of necessity."

Edward A. Pollard, a Richmond journalist and prewar fire-eater, also attacked Northern Reconstruction proposals on racial grounds. His book *The Lost Cause Regained,* published in 1868, contended that "the permanent, natural inferiority of the Negro was the true and *only* defense of slavery" and lamented the fact that the South had wasted its intellectual energy on other arguments. Before the war, Pollard had advocated a revival of the slave trade because it would deflate the pretensions of uppity house servants and town Negroes by submerging them in a flood of humble primitives; he now endorsed Van Evrie's thesis that white democracy depended on absolute black subordination, and concluded his discussion of Negro racial characteristics by asserting that the established "fact" of inferiority dictated "the true *status* of the Negro." Other propagandists of white supremacy, North and South, joined the fray. A writer named Lindley Spring attacked Radical Reconstruction in 1868 with a lengthy discourse on the benighted and savage record of blacks in Africa; and a Dr. J. R. Hayes excoriated the proposed Fifteenth Amendment in 1869 with a rehash of all the biological "evidence" for Negro incapacity.

Inevitably, the pre-Adamite theory of Dr. Samuel A. Cartwright and Jefferson Davis was trotted out. In 1866 Governor Benjamin F. Perry of South Carolina made it the basis of a defense of white supremacy; and in 1867 a Nashville publisher named Buckner Payne, writing under the pseudonym "Ariel," revived a controversy among racists by expounding the doctrine at some length in a pamphlet entitled *The Negro: What Is His Ethnological Status?* Payne not only asserted that the Negro was "created before Adam and Eve" as "a *separate* and *distinct* species of the *genus homo,*" but also argued that it was because some of the sons of Adam intermarried with this inferior species, related, as it was, to the "higher orders of the monkey," that God had sent the flood as a punishment for human wrongdoing. Like almost all the racist respondents to Reconstruction, he contended that Negro equality would lead inevitably to amalgamation, and that miscegenation, in addition to resulting in the debasement of the white race, would bring on catastrophic divine intervention: "The states and people that favor this equality and amalgamation of the white and black races, *God will exterminate.* . . . A man can not commit so great an offense against his race, against his country, against his God, . . . as to give his daughter in marriage to a negro—a *beast.* . . ."

Most of the propagandists who attacked Radical measures on extreme racist grounds had a prewar record as apologists for slavery, but Hinton Rowan Helper attracted the greatest attention because of his fame or notoriety as an antebellum critic of slavery, As we have seen, Helper had never concealed his anti-Negro sentiments. A letter of 1861 summed up his philosophy: "A trio of unmitigated and demoralizing nuisances, constituting in the aggregate, a most foul and formidable obstacle to our high and mighty civilization in America are Negroes, Slavery, and Slaveholders. . . .

> Death to Slavery!
> Down with the Slaveholders!
> Away with the Negroes!"

Having done justice to the first two imperatives in *The Impending Crisis,* Helper turned after the war to the third. His *Nojoque,* published in 1867, may have been the most virulent racist diatribe ever published in the United States. It contemplated with relish the time when "the negroes, and all the other swarthy races of mankind," have been "completely fossilized." To speed up the divinely ordained process of racial extermination, Helper proposed as immediate steps the denial of all rights to Negroes and their complete separation from the whites. All this of course went in the teeth of the emerging Reconstruction policies of what had been Helper's own party, and throughout the book he excoriated "the Black Republicans" for departing from the attitudes of the prewar period, a time when Republicans had billed themselves as "the white man's party." His heroes were "White Republicans" like Secretary of State Seward and those few Republicans in the House and Senate who had remained loyal to President Johnson and joined the Democrats in efforts to prevent Federal action on behalf of Negro equality.

The active politicians—mostly Democrats—who opposed Radical Reconstruction were quite willing to resort to racist demagoguery, although they generally avoided the excesses of polemicists like Payne and Helper. President Johnson, for example, played subtly but unmistakably on racial fears in his veto messages of 1866; and later, in his third annual message to Congress, he put his views squarely on the line: ". . . it must be acknowledged that in the progress of nations negroes have shown less capacity for self-government than any other race of people. No independent government of any form has ever been successful in their hands. On the contrary whenever they have been left to their own devices they have shown an instant tendency to relapse into barbarism. . . . The great difference between the two races in physical, mental, and moral characteristics will prevent an amalgamation or fusion of them together in one homogeneous mass. . . . Of all the dangers which our nation has yet encountered, none are equal to those which must result from the success of the effort now making to Africanize the [Southern] half of our country." Equally blatant were the Northern Democratic Congressmen who made speeches against Radical measures which appealed directly to the prejudices of white workingmen. As Representative John W. Chanler of New York put it, in attacking an 1866 proposal to give the vote to Negroes in the District of Columbia: "White democracy makes war on every class, caste, and race which assails its sovereignty or would undermine the mastery of the white working man, be he ignorant or learned, strong or weak. Black democracy does not exist. The black race have never asserted and maintained their inalienable right to be a people, anywhere, or at any time."

In addition to such crude appeals to "white democracy," Democratic spokesmen in Congress provided detailed and pretentious discourses on the "ethnological" status of the Negro, drawn from writers like Nott and Van Evrie. The most notable of such efforts was the speech Representative James Brooks of New York delivered on December 18, 1867, in opposition to the First Reconstruction Act. "You have deliberately framed a bill," he accused the Radicals, "to overthrow this white man's government of our fathers and to erect an African Government in its stead. . . . The negro is not the equal of the white man, much less his master; and this I can demonstrate anatomically, physiologically and psychologically too, if necessary. Volumes of scientific authority establish the fact. . . ." Brooks then proceeded "in the fewest words possible to set forth scientific facts." He discoursed at length on "the hair or wool of the negro," on "the skull, the brain, the neck, the foot, etc.," and on the perils of miscegenation. In considering the last topic, he conceded that "the mulatto with white blood in his veins often has the intelligence and capacity of a white man," but added that he could not consent to suffrage for mulattoes because to do so would violate the divine decree "that all are to be punished who indulge in a criminal admixture of races, so that beyond the third or fourth generation there could be no further mulatto progeny." Having covered black and brown physiology, Brooks went on in standard racist fashion to portray Negro history as a great emptiness.

In general such anti-Negro arguments were simply ignored by the proponents of Radical Reconstruction, who, by and large, tried to avoid the whole question of basic racial characteristics. But Brook's speech, perhaps the most thorough presentation of the racist creed ever offered in Congress, could not go unanswered. In a brief reply, Thaddeus Stevens dismissed Brook's views as contradicting the Biblical doctrine of the unity of mankind. Resorting to sarcasm and impugning Brook's loyalty, Stevens agreed that Negroes were indeed "barbarians," because they had "with their own right hands, in defense of liberty, stricken down thousands of the friends of the gentleman who has been enlightening us today." Disregarding Brooks's point about the "intelligence and capacity of mulattoes," Stevens proposed to match Frederick Douglass against Brooks in an oratorical contest. A more serious and extended reply to Brooks was made from the Republican side of the aisle by John D. Baldwin of Massachusetts. Baldwin's speech is significant because it clearly reveals both the strengths and weaknesses of the Radical position on race as a factor in Reconstruction.

In the first place, Baldwin contended, Brooks's argument was largely a *non sequitur;* for "the question presented in these discussions is not a question concerning the equality or the inequality of human races . . . it is a question concerning human rights. It calls on us to decide whether men shall be equal before the law and have equality in their relations to the Government of their country." Races, like individuals, might indeed differ in their capacities, but this should not affect their fundamental rights. In reply to Brooks's claim that miscegenation would result from equality, Baldwin suggested that it was much more likely to result from degradation such as had occurred under slavery, a system which provided a "fatal facility" for "the mixture of races." As for

Brooks's position on political rights, it meant in effect that all Negroes should be excluded from suffrage while "even the most ignorant and brutal white man" should be allowed to vote: "If he should propose to guard the ballot by some exclusion of ignorance or baseness, made without regard to race or class, candid men would listen to him and discuss that proposition." But Brooks was propounding, according to Baldwin, a concept of white privilege and "divine right" completely incompatible with the American egalitarian philosophy. Eventually Baldwin touched gingerly on the question of inherent racial differences and conceded the point that the races were not alike, but argued that "it is quite possible that we shall find it necessary to revise our conception of what constitutes the superiority of race." The prevailing conception, he noted, had resulted from an admiration for the ability to conquer and dominate; but were such aggressive qualities "really the highest, the most admirable development of human nature?" Pointing to the recent rise of a higher regard for the gentler, more peaceable virtues, Baldwin suggested "that each race and each distinct family of mankind has some peculiar gift of its own in which it is superior to others; and that an all-wise Creator may have designed that each race and family shall bring its own peculiar contribution to the final completeness of civilization. . . ." Although he did not discuss directly how the racial character of whites and Negroes differed, he was clearly invoking the romantic racialist conceptions that had long been popular among Radicals and abolitionists.

At first glance it would appear that Baldwin's speech constituted an adequate response to the racist critique of Radical Reconstruction, despite his avoidance of Brooks's specific physiological, anatomical, and historical arguments. It was indeed "rights" that the Radicals were attempting to legislate and not the identity of the races. But if, as Baldwin conceded, the races had differing "gifts"—with the whites holding a monopoly of the kind of qualities that led to dominance and conquest—then the competitive "test" of racial capabilities that the Radicals envisioned as resulting from their program would, to follow their own logic, lead inevitably to white domination, even without the support of discriminatory laws. Furthermore, their tendency to accept the concept of innate racial differences and their apparent repulsion to intermarriage were invitations to prejudice and discrimination on the part of those whites— presumably the over-whelming majority of Americans—who were less likely to respond to romantic appeals to racial benevolence than to draw traditional white-supremacist conclusions from any Radical admissions that blacks were "different" and, in some sense, unassimilable.

❧

A few Radicals and abolitionists had early and serious doubts about the efficacy and underlying assumptions of the Reconstruction Acts of 1867 and 1868. They suspected that quick readmission of Southern states into the Union under constitutions providing for Negro suffrage and the disfranchisement of prominent ex-Confederates would not by itself give blacks a reasonable opportunity to develop their full capacities and establish a position of genuine equality. Some understanding of this problem had been reflected in the land confiscation proposals of men like Thaddeus Stevens and Wendell Phillips. But it was the Radicals who worked for extended periods among the freedmen in the South who gained the fullest awareness of what needed to be done beyond what most Congressional proponents of Radical Reconstruction thought was necessary. Charles Stearns, an abolitionist who attempted to establish a co-operative plantation in Georgia as a step toward Negro landownership, attacked the notion that legal and political rights were all that was required to give the black man a fair, competitive position. In *The Black Man of the South and the Rebels,* published in 1872, Stearns denounced Greeley's philosophy of "root hog or die," arguing that even a hog could not root without a snout. In his view, provisions for land and education, far beyond anything that was then available to the blacks, were absolutely essential. Arguing that "the black man possesses all the natural powers that we possess," he pointed out that the blacks had not yet recovered from the degrading effects of slavery and were unable, even under Radical Reconstruction, to compete successfully or maintain their rights in the face of a bitterly hostile Southern white population.

Albion W. Tourgée, an idealistic "carpetbagger" who settled in North Carolina and became a judge under its Radical regime, was an eloquent and persistent spokesman for the same point of view. Tourgée, who eventually made his experiences and perceptions the basis of a series of novels, sensed from the beginning that the Radical program, as it finally emerged from Congress, constituted a halfhearted commitment to Negro equality which was doomed to fail in the long run. In a letter to the *National Anti-Slavery Standard* in October, 1867, he announced his opposition to the "Plan of Congress" that was taking shape. "No law, no constitution, no matter how cunningly framed," he wrote, "can shield the poor man of the South from the domination of that very aristocracy from which rebellion sprang, when once states are established here. Anarchy or oligarchy are the inevitable results of reconstruction. Serfdom or bloodshed must necessarily follow. The 'Plan of Congress,' so called, if adopted, would deliver the free men of the South, bound hand and foot to their old-time, natural enemies." The Southern Republican Party, Tourgée was saying, was composed largely of impoverished blacks and lower-class whites. Even if assured of temporary political dominance by the disfranchisement of ex-Confederates, these men would soon find themselves at the mercy of the large landowners, who were in a position to apply economic pressure and undo the reforms of Reconstruction. With rare realism, Tourgée argued in effect that political power could not be maintained on the basis of suffrage alone but must be bolstered by adequate economic and social power—and this was precisely what Southern Republicans lacked.

Tourgée's predictions of course came true. As the North looked on, manifesting an increasing reluctance to interfere—a growing desire to wash its hands of the whole matter—Southern white "redeemers" toppled one Radical government after another between 1870 and 1877 and established white-supremacist regimes. Southern Radicalism, supported largely by black votes and ruling through shifting and unstable alliances of Northern "carpetbaggers," Southern white "scalawags," and emergent black spokesmen, had no chance of withstanding the economic, political, and paramilitary opposition of the white majority. In his 1879 Reconstruction novel, *A Fool's Errand*, Tourgée provided an acute assessment of what the Northern leadership had done and why it failed to achieve its original objectives:

> After having forced a proud people to yield what they had for more than two centuries considered a right,—the right to hold the African race in bondage,—they proceeded to outrage a feeling as deep and fervent as the zeal of Islam or the exclusiveness of the Hindoo caste, by giving the ignorant, the unskilled and dependent race—a race which could not have lived a week without the support or charity of the dominant one—equality of political right. Not content with this, they went farther, and by erecting the rebellious territory into self-regulating and sovereign states, they abandoned these parties to fight out the question of predominance without the possibility of national interference, they said to the colored man in the language of one of the pseudo-philosophers of that day, 'Root, hog, or die!'

The Negro never had a chance in this struggle, as the entire novel makes clear. His ignorance and poverty made him no match for the white conservative forces.

What Tourgée and a few others—notably Representative George W. Julian of Indiana—would have preferred as a plan of reconstruction was a comparatively long-term military occupation or territorial rule of the South, which would have guaranteed "Regeneration before Reconstruction." This "territorial tutelage" would have lasted for an indeterminate period, perhaps as long as twenty or thirty years—long enough to give the North a chance to prepare the freedmen for citizenship through extensive programs of education and guidance, presumably including some form of economic assistance, while at the same time working for a diminution of the racial prejudice and "disloyalty" of the whites. But such an approach was rendered impossible both by pressures which impelled Republican politicians to seek readmission of loyalist-dominated Southern states to the Union in time for the election of 1868 and by the underlying social and racial attitudes that have been described. According to the dominant "self-help" ideology, no one, regardless of his antecedents, had a claim on society for economic security or special protection, or was entitled to a social status that he had not earned through independent struggle and hard work; the just penalty for laziness, inefficiency, or vice was severe social and economic deprivation, and it was becoming an open question at this time whether society's most abysmal "failures" should even retain their full right to participate in the political process. Having been provided with Federal laws and Constitutional amendments which supposedly guaranteed his legal equality, the black man was expected to make his own way and find his "true level" with a minimum of interference and direct assistance. When the Reconstruction governments foundered, many in the North were quick to say that the blacks had had their fair chance, had demonstrated their present incapacity for self-government, and could justifiably be relegated, for the time being at least, to an inferior status.

Tourgée probably understood better than anyone how tenuous and conditional the Northern commitment to Negro equality had been. His book *An Appeal to Caesar,* published in 1884, contended that the Northern people "have always reflected the Southern idea of the negro in everything except as to his natural right to be free and to exercise the rights of the freedman. From the first [the North] seems to have been animated by the sneaking notion that after having used the negro to fight its battles, freed him as the natural result of a rebellion based on slavery, and enfranchised him to constitute a political foil to the ambition and disloyalty of his former master, it could at any time unload him upon the states where he chanced to dwell, wash its hands of all further responsibility in the matter, and leave him to live or die as chance might determine."

Heather Cox Richardson

NO

The Death of Reconstruction: Race, Labor, and Politics in the Post–Civil War North, 1865–1901

Civil Rights and the Growth of the National Government, 1870–1883

Northern Republican disillusionment with African-American attitudes toward social issues compounded the Northern association of Southern freedmen with labor radicals who advocated confiscation of wealth. Taking place during and immediately after the South Carolina tax crisis, the civil rights debates of the 1870s seemed to confirm that African-Americans were turning increasingly to legislation to afford them the privileges for which other Americans had worked individually. Civil rights agitation did more than simply flesh out an existing sketch of disaffected black workers, however; it suggested that advocates of African-American rights were actively working to expand the national government to cater to those who rejected the free labor ideal.

❧

"Civil rights," in the immediate aftermath of the war, meant something different than it gradually came to mean over the next several years. *Harper's Weekly* distinguished between "natural rights" to life, liberty, and "the fruits of . . . honest labor," and "civil rights," which were critical to a freedperson's ability to function as a free worker. Civil rights, it explained, were "such rights as to sue, to give evidence, to inherit, buy, lease, sell, convey, and hold property, and others. Few intelligent persons in this country would now deny or forbid equality of natural and civil rights," it asserted in 1867. The 1866 Civil Rights Act, written by the man who had drafted the Thirteenth Amendment, Illinois senator Lyman Trumbull, was intended to secure to African-Americans "full and equal benefit of all laws and proceedings for the security of person and property as is enjoyed by white citizens." It guaranteed only that the legal playing field would be level for all citizens; state legislatures could not enact legislation endangering a black person's right to his life or his land. By 1867, hoping to woo conservative Republican voters into the Democratic camp and to undercut the justification for black suffrage, even moderate Democrats claimed to be willing to back civil rights for African-Americans "with every token of sincerity . . . from a free and spontaneous sense of justice."

"Social" equality was a different thing—it was a result of a person's economic success rather than a condition for it. It was something to be earned by whites and blacks alike. Directly related to economic standing, a man's social standing rose as he prospered. A good social position also required that a person possess other attributes that the community valued. A place in upwardly mobile American society required religious observance and apparently moral behavior, as well as the habits of thrift and economy dictated by a plan for economic success. This gradual social elevation became a mirror of gradual economic elevation through hard work as a traditional free laborer.

Immediately after the Civil War, as Democrats insisted that black freedom would usher in social mixing between races and intermarriage, almost all Northern Republicans emphatically denied that emancipation was intended to have any effect on social issues and reiterated that African-Americans must rise in society only through the same hard effort that had brought other Americans to prominence. In 1867, a correspondent to the radical *Cincinnati Daily Gazette* from Louisiana painted a complimentary portrait of Louisiana African-Americans, then concluded that they had neither the expectation nor the desire for "social equality, that favorite bugbear." They would ridicule any attempt to break down social distinctions by legislation, knowing that the government could give them only political equality, the writer claimed, quoting his informants as saying, "Our own brains, our own conduct, is what we must depend upon for our future elevation; each one of us striving for himself and laboring to improve his mental and moral condition." Adding credence to the correspondent's representations, the Georgia Freedmen's Convention of 1866 resolved, "We do not in any respect desire social equality beyond the transactions of the ordinary business of life, inasmuch as we deem our own race, equal to all our wants of purely social enjoyment."

As the Republicans enacted legislation promoting the interests of African-Americans, however, racist Democrats insisted they were forcing social interaction to promote African-Americans artificially, at the expense of whites. When the Civil Rights Act of 1866 took effect, Democrats charged that the Republican concept of black equality before the law meant Republicans believed that blacks and whites were entirely equal. The *New York World* predicted interracial marriages; the *Columbus (Ohio) Crisis* insisted that a black orator in Richmond had told his black audience to "vote for the man who will bring you into his parlor, who will eat dinner with you, and who, if you want her, will let you marry his daughter." In 1868, *De Bow's Review* argued that negro suffrage meant that African-Americans would "next meet us at the marriage altar and in the burial vault," where they would "order the white ancestors' bones to be disinterred and removed elsewhere, and their own transferred into these hitherto held sacred white family sepulchers."

In response to Democratic attacks, in 1868 the *New York Times* reiterated that Republicans planned only for African-Americans to share the rights and opportunities of typical free laborers. It maintained that "reconstruction did not fly in the face of nature by attempting to impose social . . . equality," it simply established political and legal equality. These rights would eventually "obliterate" social prejudices as white men sought black votes. The next year the *Times* approvingly reported that abolitionist agitator Wendell Phillips had said that "the social equality of the black race will have to be worked out by their own exertion." Frederick Douglass put out the best idea, it continued later, namely: "Let the negro alone."

✦

Republican insistence that social equality would work itself out as freedpeople worked their way up to prosperity could not provide an answer for the overwhelming discrimination African-Americans faced. While many black and white Southerners accepted the established patterns of segregation, those practices meant that African-Americans' public life was inferior to that of their white counterparts. Black people could not sit on juries in most of the South, they could not be certain of transportation on railroads or accommodation at inns, their schools were poor copies of white schools. In addition to creating a climate of constant harassment for African-Americans, discrimination, especially discrimination in schooling, seemed to hamper their ability to rise economically. The Fourteenth and Fifteenth Amendments had made all Americans equal before the law, but they could not guarantee equal access to transportation, accommodations, or schools, and while many ex-slaves accepted conditions as an improvement on the past and dismissed civil rights bills as impractical, those African-Americans who had worked hard to become members of the "better classes" deeply resented their exclusion from public facilities. "Education amounts to nothing, good behavior counts for nothing, even money cannot buy for a colored man or woman decent treatment and the comforts that white people claim and can obtain," complained Mississippi Sheriff John M. Brown. Prominent African-Americans called for legislation to counter the constant discrimination they faced.

African-American proponents of a new civil rights law to enforce non-discrimination in public services had a champion in the former abolitionist Senator Charles Sumner of Massachusetts. An exceedingly prominent man, the tall, aloof Sumner was the nation's leading champion of African-American rights after the war and had advocated a civil rights measure supplementary to the Civil Rights Act of 1866 since May 1870, when he introduced to the Senate a bill (S. 916) making the federal government responsible for the enforcement of equal rights in public transportation, hotels, theaters, schools, churches, public cemeteries, and juries.

But Sumner's sponsorship of a civil rights bill immediately made more moderate congressmen wary of it; his enthusiasm for black rights frequently made him advocate measures that seemed to remove African-Americans from the free labor system and make them favored wards of a government that was expanding to serve them. Only two months after the ratification of the fifteenth Amendment had reassured moderate Republicans and Democrats alike that they had done everything possible to make all men equal in America, Sumner told the Senate that black men were not actually equal enough, but that his new bill would do the trick. When it passes, he said, "I [will] know nothing further to be done in the way of legislation for the security of equal rights in this Republic." . . .

⁓◈⁓

By 1874, most Republicans were ready to cut the freedpeople's ties to the government in order to force African-Americans to fall back on their own resources and to protect the government from the machinations of demagogues pushing special-interest legislation. When Mississippi Republicans asked President Grant in January 1874 to use the administration to shore up their state organization, the *Philadelphia Inquirer* enthusiastically reported his refusal. Grant "remove[d] his segar from his mouth and enunciate[d] a great truth with startling emphasis," according to a writer for the newspaper. The president said it was "time for the Republican party to unload." The party could not continue to carry the "dead weight" of intrastate quarrels. Grant was sick and tired of it, he told listeners. "This nursing of monstrosities has nearly exhausted the life of the party. I am done with them, and they will have to take care of themselves." The *Philadelphia Inquirer* agreed that the federal government had to cease to support the Southern Republican organizations of freedpeople and their demagogic leaders. The *New York Daily Tribune* approved Grant's similar hands-off policy in Texas, thrilled that "there [was] no longer any cause to apprehend that another State Government will be overturned by Federal bayonets."

Benjamin Butler's role as the House manager of the civil rights bill only hurt its chances, for he embodied the connection between freedpeople and a government in thrall to special interests. The symbol of the "corruption" of American government, Butler was popularly credited with strong-arming the House into recognizing the Louisiana representatives backed by the Kellogg government, which was generally believed to be an illegal creation of Louisiana's largely black Republican party, supported not by the people of the state but by federal officers. Honest men wanted to destroy "the principle which Mr. Butler and his followers represent," wrote the *New York Daily Tribune* and others. "The force in our politics of which he is the recognized exponent, and of which thousands of our politicians of less prominence are the creatures." "Butlerism" meant gaining power by promising an uneducated public patronage or legislation in their favor, and all but the stalwart Republicans and Democratic machine politicians hoped for the downfall of both Butler and what he represented.

Despite the fact that it was prosperous African-Americans who advocated the bill, it appeared to opponents that the civil rights bill was an extraordinary piece of unconstitutional legislation by which demagogues hoped to hold on to power in the South, and thus in the nation, by catering to the whims of disaffected African-Americans who were unwilling to work. The proposed law seemed to offer nothing to the nation but a trampled constitution, lazy freedpeople, and a growing government corrupted into a vehicle for catering to the undeserving.

The civil rights bill would probably never have passed the Senate had it not been for the sudden death of Charles Sumner on March 11, 1874. Before he died, Sumner charged fellow Massachusetts senator George F. Hoar to "take care of the civil-rights bill,—my bill, the civil-rights bill, don't let it fail." Even Republican enemies of the bill eulogized the "great man"; the *Chicago Tribune* reflected that "there is no man, friend or enemy, who does not pause to pay respect to the memory of Charles Sumner." African-Americans across the country mourned Sumner's death and called for the passage of his "last and grandest work," and on April 14, 1874, from the Committee on the Judiciary Senator Frederick T. Frelinghuysen reported Sumner's civil rights bill protecting African-Americans from discrimination in public facilities, schools, and juries. The committee's amendments placed firmly in the national legal apparatus responsibility for overseeing violations of the proposed law. In caucus on May 8, some Republican senators objected to "certain features" of the bill but expressed a desire to act "harmoniously" on the measure. In the next caucus, the Republicans decided to support the bill without amendments.

After an all-night session of the Senate, a handful of African-American men in the galleries applauded as the Senate passed the bill on May 23, 1874, by a vote of twenty-nine to sixteen. Rumors circulated that the president had "some doubts about signing it" if it should pass the House, and many Republicans indicated they would not mind the loss of the bill. "Respect for the dead is incumbent on us all," snarled the *New York Times*, "—but legislation should be based on a careful and wise regard for the welfare of the living, not upon 'mandates,' real or fictitious, of the dead." Referring to the apparent African-American control of Southern governments, the *Times* asked whether the freedman "stands in need of protection from the white man, or the white man stands in need of protection from him." The House Judiciary Committee could not agree on its own civil rights measure and decided to replace its bill with the Senate's. The House then tabled the bill for the rest of the session, despite the continued urging of "leading colored men" that Benjamin Butler get it taken up and passed. . . .

The civil rights bill was rescued from oblivion only by Democratic wins in the 1874 elections. Republican congressmen's desire to consolidate Reconstruction before the Democrats arrived barely outweighed party members' fears that the measure was an attempt of corrupt politicians to harness the black vote by offering African-Americans extraordinary benefits that would undermine their willingness to work. When the lame-duck Congress reconvened in December 1874, House Republican leader Benjamin Butler tried to pass a bill protecting freedmen at the polls and an army appropriations bill to shore up stalwart Republicans in the South. Democrats filibustered. Butler was unable to get a suspension of the rules to maneuver around them as fifteen Republicans joined the opposition, worried that Butler's attempt to suspend the rules was simply a means "to get through a lot of jobbing measures under cover of Civil Rights and protection of the South." With his reputation as a special-interest broker, Butler had a terrible time getting the civil rights bill off the Speaker's table. Finally Republicans agreed to let Butler take it to the floor in late January.

The galleries were full as the House discussed the bill in early February. After omitting provisions for integrated schools, churches, and cemeteries, the House passed the bill on February 5 by a vote of 162 to 100. While African-Americans in favor of a civil rights bill were horrified at the sacrifice of the school clause, all but the most radical Republicans approved the omission. "The bill . . . is worthy [of] the support of every congressman who wishes to deal equitably with the citizens of the United States, white and black," wrote even the *Boston Evening Transcript*. "This measure simply provides for the education of the blacks, and does not force their children into association with white scholars," at the same time demanding that the schools be equal. "The Republicans can stand upon such a platform as that," the *Transcript* chided unwilling party members. "The great desire and solicitude of the people are to support 'civil rights' and so execute in good faith the constitutional pledges of the nation." After initial reluctance, the Senate passed the school amendment by a vote of 38 to 62, and despite Democratic plans to talk the bill to death, the Senate repassed the civil rights bill without further amendment on February 27, 1875, with Democrats in the opposition. Grant signed the civil rights bill into law on March 1, 1875.

While some radical papers like the *Boston Evening Transcript* defended the bill—wondering "[i]f the blacks and whites cannot shave and drink together . . . how can they remain tolerably peaceful in the same community?"—its passage drew fire from conservative and moderate Northern Republicans who still read into the measure a larger political story of the corruption of a growing government by those determined to advance through government support rather than through productive labor. The *New York Times* noted that Nothern African-Americans were "quiet, inoffensive people who live for and to themselves, and have no desire to intrude where they are not welcome." In the South, however, it continued, "there are many colored men and women who delight in 'scenes' and cheap notoriety." It was these people, the "negro politician, . . . the ignorant field hand, who, by his very brutality has forced his way into, and disgraces, public positions of honor and trust—men . . . who have no feeling and no sensibility," who would "take every opportunity of inflicting petty annoyances upon their former masters." The author concluded that the law would not be enforceable, and that "it is a great mistake to seek to impose new social customs on a people by act of Congress." Noticing the immediate efforts of Southerners to circumvent the law by giving up public licenses and legislating against public disturbances, the *San Francisco Daily Alta California* agreed that the act was likely to produce more trouble than equality, and reiterated that social equality must be earned rather than enforced by law.

The true way for African-Americans to achieve equality, Republicans argued, was to work. The *New York Times* approvingly quoted an African-American minister in the South who reiterated the idea that laborers must rise socially only as they acquired wealth and standing. The *Times* recorded his warning that "character, education, and wealth will determine their position, and all the laws in the world cannot give them a high position if they are not worthy of it." Even a correspondent for the staunchly Republican *Cincinnati Daily Gazette* reflected that "Sambo . . . can go to the hotels, ride in first-class cars, and enjoy a box in the theater. To what good is all this? . . . He needs now, to be let alone, and let work out his own destiny, aided only as his wants make him an object of charity. . . .

cross

In 1883, the U.S. Supreme Court considered five civil rights cases, one each from Tennessee, New York, Kansas, Missouri, and California. On October 15, 1883, the court decided that the Civil Rights Act of 1875 was unconstitutional because federal authority could overrule only state institutional discrimination, not private actions; Justice John Marshall Harlan of Kentucky cast the only dissenting vote. With the decision, Northern Republicans stated that they had never liked the law, because it removed African-Americans from the tenets of a free labor society, using the government to give them benefits for which others had to work. The *New York Times* declared that African-Americans "should be treated on their merits as individuals precisely as other citizens are treated in like circumstances" and admitted that there was, indeed, "a good deal of unjust prejudice against" them. But the *Times* remained skeptical that legislation could resolve the problem. Even newspapers like the *Hartford Courant*, which supported the law, said it did so only because it proved that Americans were sincere in their quest for equal rights. Three days later that newspaper mused that the law had been necessary only for "the reorganization of a disordered society," and that freedpeople no longer needed its protection. The *Philadelphia Daily Evening Bulletin* agreed that public sentiment had changed so dramatically that the law was now unnecessary. Even the radical African-American *Cleveland Gazette*, which mourned the court's decision, agreed that the law was a dead letter anyway. The *New York Times* welcomed the decision, going so far as to charge the law with keeping "alive a prejudice against the negroes . . . which without it would have gradually died out."

Instead of supporting the Civil Rights Act, Republicans reiterated the idea that right-thinking African-Americans wanted to succeed on their own. The *New York Times* applauded the public address of the Louisville, Kentucky, National Convention of Colored Men that concentrated largely on the needs of Southern agricultural labor and referred not at all to civil rights. That the convention had pointedly rejected chairman Frederick Douglass's draft address, which had included support for civil rights legislation, made the *Times* conclude that most attendees were "opposed to the extreme views uttered by Mr. Douglass," and that the great African-American leader should retire, since his "role as a leader of his race is about played out."

Despite the *Times*'s conclusion, African-Americans across the country protested the decision both as individuals and in mass meetings, reflecting, "It is a mercy that Charles Sumner is not alive to mourn for his cherished Civil Rights bill." At a mass meeting in Washington, D.C., Frederick Douglass admonished that the decision "had inflicted a heavy calamity on the 7,000,000 of colored people of this country, and had left them naked and defenceless against the action of a malignant, vulgar and pitiless prejudice." When the African Methodist Episcopal (AME) Church Conference of Western States, in session in Denver, discussed the decision, delegates made "incendiary" speeches and "[a] Bishop declared that if the negroes' rights were thus trampled upon a revolution would be the result." . . .

Republicans and Democrats agreed that the only way for African-Americans to garner more rights was to work to deserve them, as all others did in America's free labor system. The *Philadelphia Daily Evening Bulletin* repeated this view:

> [F]urther advancement depends chiefly upon themselves, on their earnest pursuit of education, on their progress in morality and religion, on their thoughtful exercise of their duties as citizens, on their persistent practice of industry, on their self-reliance, and on their determination to exalt themselves, not as proscribed or despised Africans, but as American men clothed with the privileges of citizenship in the one great republic of the earth. They have it in their power to secure for themselves, by their own conduct, more really important "rights" than can be given to them by any formal legislation of Congress.

The Democratic *Hartford Weekly Times* agreed, and asserted that true black leaders, "not men like Fred. Douglass, who are 'professional' colored men, and who have been agitating something and been paid for it all of their lives," approved of the decision. "They say there is no such thing as social equality among white men, and that the colored man cannot get it by law, but by the way he conducts himself."

Republican and Democratic newspapers highlighted those African-Americans who cheerfully told their neighbors "to acquire knowledge and wealth as the surest way of obtaining our rights." From Baltimore came the news that "Mr. John F. Cook, a colored man of character, who deservedly enjoys the respect of this entire community, who has held and administered with marked ability for years the responsible office of Collector of Taxes for the District of Columbia," told a reporter that he had no fears of white reprisals after the decision, expecting whites to accord to African-Americans "what legislation could never accomplish." "These are golden words, and if all men of his race were like Mr. Cook there would never be any trouble on this subject," concluded the Republican *Philadelphia Daily Evening Bulletin*.

Even many Northern Democrats painted their own picture of an egalitarian free labor society that had no need of a civil rights law. First they restated the idea that Republican efforts for African-Americans had simply been a ploy to control the government by marshalling the black vote. Trying to make new ties to African-American voters, the Democratic *San Francisco Examiner* emphasized that Republicans had only wanted to use the black vote to create a Republican empire and that the reversal showed that Republicanism no longer offered advantages to black citizens. A reporter noted that members of the black community had said that "it was about time to shake off the Republican yoke and act in politics as American citizens, not as chattels of a party who cared but for their votes."

While the rhetoric of the *San Francisco Examiner* repeated long-standing Democratic arguments, it also reinforced the idea that some hardworking African-Americans had indeed prospered in America, and that these upwardly mobile blacks were fully accepted even in Democratic circles. In San Francisco, the paper noted, "there are . . . many intelligent and educated men and women of African descent." Using the Republican pattern of according prosperous African-Americans names, descriptions, and their own words, it interviewed the Reverend Alexander Walters, whom it described respectfully as an educated and well-traveled young man, and happily printed both his assertion that in cities across the nation and "in the West . . . race prejudice has died out," and his prediction that the court's decision would drive black voters from the Republican party. Similarly, it quoted P. A. Bell, "the veteran editor of the *Elevator*, the organ of the colored people," as saying that in California—a Democratic state—"we people are treated just as well as if there were fifty Civil Rights bills."

With the overturning of the 1875 Civil Rights Act, mainstream Republicans and Democrats, black and white, agreed that there must be no extraordinary legislation on behalf of African-Americans, who had to work their way up in society like everyone else. Stalwart Republicans who advocated additional protection for black citizens were seen as either political demagogues who wanted the black vote to maintain their power or misguided reformers duped by stories of white atrocities against freedpeople. Northern black citizens who advocated civil rights legislation, like Frederick Douglass, were either scheming politicians who, like their white counterparts, needed the votes of uneducated African-Americans, or they were disaffected workers who believed in class struggle and wanted to control the government in order to destroy capital.

Southern blacks seemed to be the worst of all these types. They appeared to want to increase the government's power solely in order to be given what others had earned, and to do so, they were corrupting government by keeping scheming Republican politicos in office.

POSTSCRIPT

Did Reconstruction Fail as a Result of Racism?

There can be little doubt that racism played some role in the failure of the Radical Republicans to realize their most ambitious goals for integrating African Americans into the mainstream of American society in the years following the Civil War. After all, white supremacy was a powerful doctrine. At the same time, we should not so cavalierly dismiss some of the more positive conclusions reached by that first generation of revisionist historians who built upon W. E. B. DuBois's characterization of Reconstruction as a "splendid failure." For example, Kenneth Stampp's *The Era of Reconstruction, 1865–1877* (Alfred A. Knopf, 1965) ends with the following statement: "The Fourteenth and Fifteenth Amendments, which could have been adopted only under the conditions of radical reconstruction, make the blunders of that era, tragic though they were, dwindle into insignificance. For if it was worth a few years of civil war to save the Union, it was worth a few years of radical reconstruction to give the American Negro the ultimate promise of equal civil and political rights." Eric Foner, too, recognizes something of a silver lining in the nation's post–Civil War reconstruction process. In *Reconstruction: America's Unfinished Revolution, 1863–1877* (Harper & Row, 1988), Foner claims that Reconstruction, though perhaps not all that radical, offered African Americans at least a temporary vision of a free society. Similarly, in *Nothing But Freedom: Emancipation and Its Legacy* (Louisiana State University Press, 1984), Foner advances his interpretation by comparing the treatment of ex-slaves in the United States with that of newly emancipated slaves in Haiti and the British West Indies. Only in the United States, he contends, were the freedmen given voting and economic rights. Although these rights had been stripped away from the majority of black southerners by 1900, Reconstruction had, nevertheless, created a legacy of freedom that inspired succeeding generations of African Americans.

On the other hand, C. Vann Woodward, in "Reconstruction: A Counterfactual Playback," an essay in his thought-provoking *The Future of the Past* (Oxford University Press, 1988), shares Fredrickson's pessimism about the outcome of Reconstruction. For all the successes listed by the revisionists, he argues that the experiment failed. He challenges Foner's conclusions by insisting that former slaves were as poorly treated in the United States as they were in other countries. He also maintains that the confiscation of former plantations and the redistribution of land to the former slaves would have failed in the same way that the Homestead Act of 1862 failed to generate equal distribution of government lands to poor white settlers.

Thomas Holt's *Black over White: Negro Political Leadership in South Carolina During Reconstruction* (University of Illinois Press, 1977) is representative of state and local studies that employ modern social science methodology to yield new perspectives. Although critical of white Republican leaders, Holt (who is African American) also blames the failure of Reconstruction in South Carolina on free-born mulatto politicians, whose background distanced them economically, socially, and culturally from the masses of freedmen. Consequently, these political leaders failed to develop a clear and unifying ideology to challenge white South Carolinians who wanted to restore white supremacy.

The study of the Reconstruction period benefits from an extensive bibliography. Traditional accounts of Reconstruction include William Archibald Dunning's *Reconstruction, Political and Economic, 1865–1877* (Harper & Brothers, 1907); Claude Bowers's *The Tragic Era: The Revolution after Lincoln* (Riverside Press, 1929); and E. Merton Coulter's, *The South During Reconstruction, 1865–1877* (Louisiana State University Press, 1947), the last major work written from the Dunning (or traditional) point of view. Some of the earliest revisionist views appeared in the scholarly works of African American historians such as W. E. B. DuBois, *Black Reconstruction in America: An Essay Toward a History of the Part Which Black Folk Played in the Attempt to Reconstruct Democracy in America, 1860–1880* (Harcourt, Brace, 1935), a Marxist analysis; John Hope Franklin, *Reconstruction: After the Civil War* (University of Chicago Press, 1961); and Kenneth M. Stampp, *The Era of Reconstruction, 1865–1877* (Alfred A. Knopf, 1965). Briefer overviews are available in Forrest G. Wood, *The Era of Reconstruction, 1863–1877* (Harlan Davidson, 1975); and Michael Perman, *Emancipation and Reconstruction, 1862–1879* (Harlan Davidson, 1987). One of the best-written studies of a specific episode during the Reconstruction years is Willie Lee Rose's *Rehearsal for Reconstruction: The Port Royal Experiment* (Bobbs-Merrill, 1964), which describes the failed effort at land reform in the sea islands of South Carolina. Richard Nelson Current's *Those Terrible Carpetbaggers: A Reinterpretation* (Oxford University Press, 1988) is a superb challenge to the traditional view of these much-maligned Reconstruction participants. Finally, for collections of interpretive essays on various aspects of the Reconstruction experience, see Staughton Lynd, ed., *Reconstruction* (Harper & Row, 1967); Seth M. Scheiner, ed., *Reconstruction: A Tragic Era?* (Holt, Rinehart and Winston, 1968); and Edwin C. Rozwenc, ed., *Reconstruction in the South,* 2d ed. (Heath, 1972).

Contributors to This Volume

EDITORS

LARRY MADARAS is professor of history emeritus at Howard Community College in Columbia, Maryland. He received a B.A. from the College of Holy Cross in 1959 and an M.A. and Ph.D. from New York University in 1961 and 1964, respectively. He has also taught at Spring Hill College, the University of South Alabama, and the University of Maryland at College Park. He has been a Fulbright Fellow and has held two fellowships from the National Endowment for the Humanities. He is the author of dozens of journal articles and book reviews.

JAMES M. SORELLE is a professor of history and former chair of the Department of History at Baylor University in Waco, Texas. He received a B.A. and M.A. from the University of Houston in 1972 and 1974, respectively, and a Ph.D. from Kent State University in 1980. In addition to introductory courses in United States and world history, he teaches advanced undergraduate classes in African American history, the American civil rights movement, and the 1960s, as well as a graduate seminar on the civil rights movement. His scholarly articles have appeared in *Houston Review*, *Southwestern Historical Quarterly*, and *Black Dixie: Essays in Afro-Texan History and Culture in Houston* (Texas A & M University Press, 1992), edited by Howard Beeth and Cary D. Wintz. He also has contributed entries to *The New Handbook of Texas*, *The Oxford Companion to Politics of the World*, *Encyclopedia of African American Culture and History*, the *Encyclopedia of the Confederacy*, and the *Encyclopedia of African American History*.

AUTHORS

MELVIN E. BRADFORD (1934–1993) was a professor of literature at the University of Dallas from 1967 until his death. His publications include *Against the Barbarians and Other Reflections on Familiar Themes* (University of Missouri Press, 1992) and *Original Intentions: On the Making and Ratification of the United States Constitution* (University of Georgia Press, 1993).

T. H. BREEN is William Smith Mason Professor of American History at Northwestern University, where he specializes in early American history. Among his many honors and awards, Breen has been a Guggenheim fellow and held distinguished professorships at both Cambridge and Oxford. Among his several award-winning monographs are *Tobacco Culture: The Mentality of the Great Tidewater Planters on the Eve of Revolution* (Princeton University Press, 1985) and Imagining the Past: East Hampton Histories (Addison-Wesley, 1989).

JON BUTLER is the Howard R. Lamar Professor of American History and Dean of the Graduate School of Arts and Sciences at Yale University. He is the author of *The Huguenots in America: A Refugee People in New World Society* (Harvard University Press, Harvard University Press, 1983); *Awash in a Sea of Faith: Christianizing the American People* (Harvard University Press, 1990); and coauthor of *Religion in American Life: A Short History* (Oxford University Press, 2002). He coedited *Religion in American History: A Reader* (Oxford University Press, 1997) and is currently writing a book on religion in modern New York City.

COLIN G. CALLOWAY is professor of history and Samson Occom Professor of Native American Studies at Dartmouth where he chairs the Native American Studies Program. He recently published *The Scratch of a Pen: 1763 and the Transformation of North America* (Oxford University Press, 2006).

LAURIE WINN CARLSON is assistant professor of history at Western Oregon University. She is the author of several scholarly historical studies, including *Cattle: An Informal Social History* (Ivan R. Dee, 2002); *Seduced by the West: Jefferson's America and the Lure of the Land Beyond the Mississippi* (Ivan R. Dee, 2003); and *William J. Spillman and the Birth Of Agricultural Economics* (University Press, 2005).

ALFRED A. CAVE is professor emeritus of history at the University of Toledo, where he served as Dean of the College of Arts and Sciences from 1973–1990. The recipient of grants from the Danforth Foundation and National Endowment for the Humanities, his books include *Jacksonian Democracy and the Historians* (University of Florida Press, 1964); *An American Conservative in the Age of Jackson: The Political and Social Thought of Calvin Colton* (Texas Christian University Press, 1969); *The Pequot War* (University of Massachusetts Press, 1996); and *Prophets of the Great Spirit: Native American Revitalization Movements in Eastern North America* (University of Nebraska Press, 2006).

NANCY F. COTT is the Jonathan Trumbull Professor of American History at Harvard University and Pforzheimer Foundation Director of the Schlesinger

Library on the History of Women in America. A specialist in nineteenth-and twentieth-century social and cultural history, her other books include *The Grounding of Modern Feminism* (Yale University Press, 1987); *A Woman Making History: Mary Ritter Beard through Her Letters* (Yale University Press, 1991); and *Public Vows: A History of Marriage and the Nation* (Harvard University Press, 2000).

CARL N. DEGLER is the Margaret Byrne Professor Emeritus of American History at Stanford University and during his distinguished academic career served as president of the American Historical Association, the Organization of American Historians, and the Southern Historical Association. His book *Neither Black Nor White: Slavery and Race Relations in Brazil and the United States* (University of Wisconsin, 1971) won the Pulitzer Prize for history. He also is the author of *In Search of Human Nature: The Decline and Revival of Darwinism in American Social Thought* (Oxford University Press, 1992) and *At Odds: Women and Family in America from the Revolution to the Present* (Oxford University Press, 1997).

MARC EGNAL is a professor of history at York University, Toronto, Canada. A specialist on the American Revolution and Civil War, he is the author of *A Mighty Empire: The Origins of the American Revolution* (Cornell University Press, 1988); *Divergent Paths: How Culture and Institutions Have Shaped North American Growth* (Oxford University Press, 1996); *New World Economies: The Growth of the Thirteen Colonies and Early Canada* (Oxford University Press, 1998); and, most recently, *Clash of Extremes: The Economic Origins of the Civil War* (Hill & Wang, 2009).

ROBERT FINLAY is a professor of history at the University of Arkansas, where he has taught since 1987. A specialist in Renaissance and world history, he is the author of *Politics in Renaissance Venice* (Rutgers University Press, 1980), which won the Howard R. Marraro Prize for the best book on Italian or Italian-American history from the American Historical Association; *The Pilgrim Art: The Culture of Porcelain in World History* (University of California Press, 2009); and numerous scholarly articles, including several on the voyages of the Ming dynasty admiral Zheng He.

CHARLES B. DEW is the Ephraim Williams Professor of American History at Williams College. Two of his books, *Apostles of Disunion* (University of Virginia Press, 2002) and *Ironmaker to the Confederacy: Joseph R. Anderson and the Tredegar Iron Works* (Yale University Press, 1966), received the Fletcher Pratt Award presented by the Civil War Round Table of New York for the best nonfiction book on the American Civil War. He is also the author of *Bond of Iron: Master and Slave at Buffalo Forge* (W. W. Norton, 1994), which received the Elliott Rudwick Prize from the Organization of American Historians.

GEORGE M. FREDRICKSON is the Edgar E. Robinson Professor of U.S. History Emeritus at Stanford University and the preeminent American scholar on the history of race. He is the author of *The Inner Civil War: Northern Intellectuals and the Crisis of the Union* (Harper & Row, 1965); *White Supremacy:*

A Comparative Study of American and South African History (Oxford University Press, 1981); and *Black Liberation: A Comparative History of Black Ideologies in the United States and South Africa* (Oxford University Press, 1995).

GARY W. GALLAGHER is the John L. Nau III Professor of History in the American Civil War at the University of Virginia. His major books include *The Confederate War* (Harvard University Press, 1997); *Lee and His Generals in War and Memory* (Louisiana State University Press, 1998); *Lee and His Army in Confederate History* (University of North Carolina Press, 2001); and *Causes Won, Lost, and Forgotten: How Hollywood and Popular Art Shape What We Know about the Civil War* (University of North Carolina Press, 2008).

JAMES N. GILBERT is a professor and former chair of the Department of Criminal Justice at the University of Nebraska–Kearney, where he has taught since 1988. Specializing in criminal investigative theory, he is the author of *Criminal Investigation* (Pearson/Prentice Hall, 2009), now in its eighth edition, as well as numerous journal articles.

JOHN STEELE GORDON is a specialist in business and financial history whose articles have appeared in numerous prominent magazines and newspapers for the past 20 years. He is a contributing editor to *American Heritage* and since 1989 has written the "Business of America" column. His other books include *Hamilton's Blessing: The Extraordinary Life and Times of Our National Debt* (Walker, 1997), *The Great Game: The Emergence of Wall Street as a World Power: 1653–2000* (1999), and *A Thread across the Ocean: the Heroic Story of the Transatlantic Cable* (Walker, 2002).

NORMAN A. GRAEBNER is the Randolph P. Compton Professor Emeritus of History at the University of Virginia in Charlottesville, Virginia. He has held a number of other academic appointments and has received distinguished teacher awards at every campus at which he has taught. He has edited and written numerous books, articles, and texts on American history, including *Foundations of American Foreign Policy: A Realist Appraisal From Franklin to McKinley* (Scholarly Resources Press, 1985) and *Empire on the Pacific: A Study in American Continental Expansion,* 2d ed. (Regina Books, 1983).

SCOTT JOHN HAMMOND is a professor of political science at James Madison University, where he specializes in political philosophy. He is the author of *Political Theory: An Encyclopedia of Contemporary and Classic Terms* (Greenwood, 2008) and coauthor of *Encyclopedia of Presidential Campaigns, Slogans, Issues, and Platforms* (Greenwood, 2008).

OSCAR HANDLIN is professor emeritus of history at Harvard University. He is the author of numerous books, including *The Uprooted: The Epic Story of the Great Migrations That Made the American People* (Little, Brown, 1951), *Boston's Immigrants, 1790–1880: A Study in Acculturation* (rev. and enl. ed., Belknap Press, 1991), and with Lilian Handlin, *Liberty in America,* 4 vols. (Harper & Row, 1986–1994).

DAVID S. JONES is an assistant professor in the History and Culture of Science and Technology at MIT. He also works as a staff psychiatrist in the Psychiatric

Emergency Center at Cambridge Hospital. He is the author of *Rationalizing Epidemics: Meanings and Uses of American Indian Mortality since 1600* (Harvard University Press, 2004).

CAROL F. KARLSEN is professor of history and women's studies at the University of Michigan. She also has published *The Salem Witchcraft Trials: A History in Documents* (Oxford University Press, 2005) and *The Journal of Esther Edwards Burr, 1754–1757* (Yale University Press, 1986).

THOMAS S. KIDD is an associate professor of history at Baylor University, where he also serves as codirector of the Program on Historical Studies of Religion for the Institute for Studies in Religion. His other books include *The Protestant Interest: New England after Puritanism* (Yale University Press, 2004) and *American Christians and Islam: Evangelical Culture and Muslims from the Colonial Period to the Age of Terrorism* (Princeton University Press, 2008).

MARK EDWARD LENDER is professor and chair of the History Department at Kean University in Union, New Jersey. He currently is serving as interim provost and previously held the position of dean of the Graduate College. His teaching and research have focused on early American military and social history. He coauthored *"A Respectable Army": The Military Origins of the Republic, 1763–1789*, rev. ed. (Harlan Davidson, 2005), with James Kirby Martin, and his most recent book is *"This Honorable Court": The United States District Court for the District of New Jersey, 1789–2000* (Rutgers University Press, 2006). Lender also is the editor of the *Dictionary of American Temperance Biography: From Temperance Reform to Alcohol Research, the 1600s to the 1980s* (Greenwood, 1984).

GERDA LERNER is Robinson-Edwards Professor of History Emerita at the University of Wisconsin at Madison. One of the foremost historians of women in America, she is the author of numerous books, including *The Grimké Sisters from South Carolina* (Houghton Mifflin, 1967) and *The Creation of Patriarchy* (Oxford University Press, 1986).

JAMES KIRBY MARTIN is Distinguished University Professor of History at the University of Houston. A specialist in early American history and the era of the American Revolution, Martin has written extensively on social, military, and political developments in this period. His most recent book is *Benedict Arnold, Revolutionary Hero: An American Warrior Reconsidered* (New York University Press, 1997), but he currently is working on American health reform and the history of smoking in America.

WILLIAM H. McNEILL is professor emeritus of history at the University of Chicago where he was the Robert A. Milliken Distinguished Service Professor prior to his retirement. He is the author of *The Rise of the West: A History of the Human Community* (University of Chicago, 1970), which received the National Book Award, *Plagues and Peoples* (Anchor Press, 1976), and *A World History* (4th ed., Oxford University Press, 1998).

GAVIN MENZIES is a retired British submarine commander and amateur historian. His most recent book is *1434: The Year a Magnificent Chinese Fleet Sailed to Italy and Ignited the Renaissance* (William Morrow, 2008).

ALAN T. NOLAN has been with the law firm of Ice Miller Donadio & Ryan in Indianapolis, Indiana, since 1948. He also has been Chairman of the Board of Trustees of the Indiana Historical Society since 1986. Nolan has written extensively on Civil War history, including the book *The Iron Brigade: A Military History*, 2d ed. (State Historical Society of Wisconsin, 1975), and he is coeditor, with Gary W. Gallagher, of *The Myth of the Lost Cause and Civil War History* (Indiana University Press, 2000).

WALTER NUGENT taught for 21 years at Indiana University before moving to Notre Dame University, where he is the Andrew V. Tackes Professor Emeritus of History. A specialist in the Gilded Age and the Progressive era, he is the author of *The Tolerant Populists: Kansas Populism and Nativism* (University of Chicago Press, 1963); *Money and American Society, 1865–1880* (Free Press, 1968); *Crossings: The Great Transatlantic Migrations, 1870–1914* (Indiana University Press, 1992); and *Into the West: The Story of Its People* (Alfred A. Knopf, 1999).

PHILIP SHAW PALUDAN (1938–2007) was a professor of history at the University of Kansas for over 30 years before accepting the Distinguished Chair in Lincoln Studies at the University of Illinois, Springfield. In addition to his study of Lincoln's presidency, which won the Lincoln Prize, he is the author of *Victims: A True Story of the Civil War* (University of Tennessee Press, 1981) and *A People's Contest: The Union and Civil War, 1861–1865* (Harper & Row, 1988).

ROBERT REMINI is professor of history emeritus and research professor of humanities emeritus at the University of Illinois at Chicago. The author of biographies of John Quincy Adams, Henry Clay, Daniel Webster, and Martin Van Buren, he is best known as one of the nation's preeminent specialists on Andrew Jackson. His three-volume biography of Jackson stands as the definitive account of "Old Hickory," and the third volume, *Andrew Jackson and the Course of American Democracy, 1833–1845* (Harper & Row, 1984), received the National Book Award.

HEATHER COX RICHARDSON is professor of history at the University of Massachusetts, Amherst. Her other books include *The Greatest Nation of the Earth: Republican Economic Policies during the Civil War* (Harvard University Press, 1997) and *West from Appomattox: The Reconstruction of America after the Civil War* (Yale University Press, 2007).

CAREY ROBERTS is assistant professor of history at Arkansas Tech University. He has presented papers and written articles on eighteenth- and nineteenth-century American history. His particular interests are northern conservatism and conflicting patterns of early nationalism.

JOHN P. ROCHE (1923–1993) was the Olin Distinguished Professor of American Civilization and Foreign Affairs at the Fletcher School of Law and Diplomacy in Medford, Massachusetts, and director of the Fletcher Media Institute. His many publications include *Shadow and Substance: Essays on the Theory and Structure of Politics* (Macmillan, 1964).

JOHN J. RUMBARGER (1938–1996) taught American political history at Rutgers University. A former editor of *Prologue*, he later served as chief historian of the Federal Emergency Management Agency.

HOWARD ZINN is professor emeritus of political science at Boston University. A political activist and prolific writer, he is the author of *SNCC: The New Abolitionists* (Beacon Press, 1964), *Postwar America: 1945–1971* (MacMillan, 1973), and *A People's History of the United States* (Harper & Row, 1980).